W9-BCW-328

Advance Praise for *Sport and the Color Line: Black Athletes and Race Relations in Twentieth-Century America*

"This brilliant collection appears at a crucial moment in history as scholars, journalists, activists, and politicians grapple with the persistence of racialized thinking in American culture. The timely essays resonate with W. E. B. Du Bois's prediction that the "color line" would be *the* defining problem of contemporary society. Miller and Wiggins have judiciously selected key interpretive analyses that collectively demonstrate how African Americans' historical involvement in sport has been neither a tragedy nor triumphant as popularly portrayed; but rather, a more complex, contradictory culmination of efforts on behalf of grassroots activists, civil rights crusaders, athletes, folk heroes, journalists, educators, politicians, and villains. This book is a *must* for all individual and institutional libraries. Anyone interested in a critical history of African American sport must buy this book."
S. W. Pope, De Montfort University, Author, *Patriotic Games: Sporting Traditions in the American Imagination.*

"Miller and Wiggins bring together a noted collection of authors. Each uses sports to document the complexities of twentieth-century race relations in the United States. The articles analyze from a range of perspectives the changing contours of the color line in sports and society at large. Anyone wishing to understand the legacy of racism in the twenty-first century should read this thoughtful and well-edited set of articles."
Jay Coakley, Sociology Department, University of Colorado

"The editors have done a masterful job of assembling the influential voices of the past with newer scholarship that addresses gender and class as well as racial issues. The selections elucidate the central role and meanings of sport in the struggle for emancipation. This is an engaging text and a welcome addition to the scholarly literature."
Gerald R. Gems, President, North American Society for Sport History

"*Sport and the Color Line* is one of the most informative, comprehensive and insightful sport history anthologies critiquing the African American sport experience at the high school, college, and professional levels. Nationally acclaimed scholars such as Dr. Harry Edwards, Rob Ruck, Donald Spivey, David Wiggins, Thomas Smith, and Susan Cahn provide an in-depth analysis of the intersection of race, gender, social class, and sport during the era of Jim Crow and post desegregation of American sports."
Dana D. Brooks is Dean and Professor of Physical Education at West Virginia University and co-editor of *Racism in College Athletics: The African American Athlete's Experience.*

SPORT AND THE COLOR LINE

SPORT AND THE COLOR LINE

Black Athletes and Race Relations in Twentieth-Century America

edited by
Patrick B. Miller and
David K. Wiggins

Routledge
New York & London

Published in 2004 by
Routledge
29 West 35th Street
New York, NY 10001
www.routledge-ny.com

Published in Great Britain by
Routledge
11 New Fetter Lane
London EC4P 4EE
www.routledge.co.uk

Routledge is an imprint of the Taylor & Francis Group.

Copyright © 2004 by Taylor and Francis Books, Inc.

Printed in the United States of America on acid-free paper.

All rights reserved. No part of this book may be reprinted or utilized in any form or by any electronic, mechanical, or other means, now known or hereafter invented, including photocopying and recording, or any other information storage or retrieval system, without permission in writing from the publisher.

10 9 8 7 6 5 4 3 2 1

Library of Congress Cataloging–in–Publication Data

Sport and the color line : black athletes and race relations in 20th century America / Patrick B. Miller & David K. Wiggins, editors.
p. cm.
Includes bibliographical references and index.
ISBN 0–415–94610–7 (hardcover : alk. paper) — ISBN 0–415–94611–5 (pbk. : alk. paper)
1. Racism in sports—United States—History—20th century. 2. African American athletes—History—20th century. 3. Discrimination in sports—United States—History—20th century. 4. United States—Race relations—History—20th century. I. Miller, Patrick B. II. Wiggins, David Kenneth, 1951–
GV706.32.S73 2003
796'.089'96073—dc21

2003014009

GARY PUBLIC LIBRARY

CONTENTS

PREFACE

ULTIMATELY, THIS BOOK is about the long and arduous struggle to relegate Jim Crow to the sidelines in American sport during the course of the twentieth century. It thus chronicles an earlier era when segregation prevailed in national pastimes and when black people, South and North, created their own athletic institutions even as they made every effort to challenge racism on the playing fields and beyond. To show how sport became a distinctive element within the larger civil rights movement would be to illuminate the complex processes of desegregation: political acumen and hard work characterized the experiences of racial reformers in sport, but their story cannot be told without reference to the terrible uncertainty that they faced at every turn. The performances of black athletes also inform this volume, although the larger project of the pieces assembled here is to discuss the *meanings* of athletic triumph and travail—to underscore the significance of sport in reinforcing black pride and reshaping the culture and consciousness of the nation. Clearly, the ways that black bodies in motion have been assessed—and reevaluated over time—is a topic that speaks to broader concerns about race relations, identity, and power in the recent American past.

It is no simple task to highlight the importance of sport in community formation, integrationist strategies, and cultural representation in the troubled history of race relations in the United States. Numerous themes and cases have been treated by scholars in a variety of fields, from history and sociology to folklore and media studies. So we needed to be selective. The contributors we chose for this volume have been expansive in their approaches to the role of sport in society, and we are grateful that many of them have revised and updated their pieces for *Sport and the Color Line*. Beyond their efforts, we are assisted in tracking down images to fit the articles by Lee Brumbaugh of the Nevada Historical Society, Wayne Wilson of the Amateur Athletic Foundation in Los Angeles, and Steve Gietshier of *The Sporting News*. Colleagues and friends, most notably Paul Spickard, provided essential background information and ideas about the framing of the issues treated here. Others, including Klaus Benesch and Kerstin Schmidt of the University of Bayreuth in Germany, provided an ideal intellectual setting for the final acts of editing this volume.

At Northeastern Illinois University, J. Matt Byerly spent considerable time creating the design for first draft of the cover of this volume. At Routledge, we were encouraged from the outset of our project by Karen Wolny and assisted time and again by Jaclyn Bergeron. Daniel Montero did stellar work as our copyeditor, and Nicole Ellis showed both patience and perseverance in moving our manuscript through the production process. Lamentably, we could not include all the scholarship that surveys the African American experience in sport, but we have been highly impressed by our readings of late. For the future, we anticipate rich new studies of the role of athletic achievement in the larger campaign for equality and opportunity in the United States and even more sophisticated interrogations of modern media images of black athletic performance.

PBM, Isla Vista, California
DKW, Fairfax, Virginia

INTRODUCTION

Athletics is the universal language. By and through it we hope to foster a better and more fraternal spirit between the races in America and so to destroy prejudices; to learn and to be taught; to facilitate a universal brotherhood.

—Howard University *Hilltop*, April 29, 1924

By applauding [Jackie] Robinson, a man did not feel that he was taking a stand on school integration, or on open housing. . . . But . . . to disregard color even for an instant, is to step away from the old prejudices, the old hatred. That is not a path on which many double back.

Roger Kahn, *The Boys of Summer* (1973)

THE YEAR 2003 marks the hundredth anniversary of the publication of W. E. B. Du Bois's *Souls of Black Folk*, a work of both lamentation and prophesy best remembered for its assertion that "the color line" would be the problem of the twentieth century. Intolerance and inequality pervaded the racial landscape at the turn of the last century, and it would be difficult to overstate the ruthlessness used to reinforce white supremacy. Du Bois was not alone in alluding to the lynching of black men and the sexual violence against African-American women as everyday acts of terrorism. Racial activists, South and North, could also map the contours of segregation—in education, housing, and employment, as well as on trains and in hotels and restaurants—as matters of custom even where they were not fortified by the laws of the land.

Yet at the same time, black Americans were enormously energetic on their own behalf. Just as they protested the incivility and barbarism that revealed the depth of racism nationwide, they also found ways to engage with mainstream institutions. Many racial reformers carefully studied the Constitution, the Congressional Record, and the history of American jurisprudence, constantly invoking the principles of equality and opportunity—whenever they appeared in official statements—to challenge Jim Crow segregation and to condemn the betrayal of the ideal of democracy in the United States. Between the era of Emancipation and what has been called the Second Reconstruction of the 1960s, moreover, African-American leaders exalted higher education not only as a mechanism of economic mobility, but also as a means of asserting their claims to *first-class* citizenship. Significantly, too, they enlisted their accomplishments as competitors in national pastimes in the larger civil rights crusade—to prove equality on the playing fields as well as in broader fields of endeavor. Nearly half a century after Du Bois's pronouncement, Jackie Robinson would display his remarkable athletic skills in "baseball's great experiment." For many Americans, black and white alike, the desegregation of major league baseball represented the most important symbolic breakthrough in race relations before the 1954 Supreme Court decision in *Brown v. Board of Education.*

The history of "muscular assimilationism" was never a simple story, however. And it certainly did not end in 1947 when Robinson first donned a Brooklyn Dodgers uniform. Today, virtually no one denies that the opening of mainstream American sport to the full participation of African Americans—as well as of other people of color and, of course, of all American women—has been a slow and often wrenching process. Since the civil rights era, historians have explored in detail the many ways African Americans deployed sporting achievement to inspire race pride and to prevail upon the dominant culture to fully abide by the doctrines of fair play and sportsmanship. More recently, scholars in a variety of fields have also addressed the African-American experience in sport with regard to the image of the black body, the intersection of race, gender, and social location in popular consciousness, and the global marketing of black sports icons. For the last two decades, the most powerful people internationally—it might be said—have been American presidents. But the most recognizable have been Muhammad Ali and Michael Jordan. To much of the rest of the world, sports have defined race relations in the United States—for better and for worse. Tellingly, an increasing number of cultural critics mark the very different life trajectories of star athletes and the mass of African-American youth in terms of the paradoxes, or other problematic dimensions, of the quest for sporting celebrity. And these observations should not only encourage us to place sport into broader contexts, but also to examine more carefully the relationship between the history of athletics and race relations during the twentieth century. Today's editorials and commentary might suggest that when we read the sports pages and consider race relations one hundred years after Du Bois's manifesto, we should also ponder substantial questions about social justice for the future of the entire nation.

The articles gathered in this book survey diverse issues and ideas with regard to the history of race relations in American sport. They include biographies of major figures and depictions of key events, yet even as they form an expansive narrative of the black athletic experience itself, these essays are devoted to the *meanings* of sport for many African Americans as well as for the larger history of desegregation and racial reform. The chronicle of athletic travail and triumph is a long one, stunning in its complications. Here it is important to note that there were forerunners to the black champions of the twentieth century as well as early attempts to link participation in sports to larger social concerns. As far back as 1810, Tom Molineaux was hailed as a black hero in the boxing ring, though the fame of this American ex-slave was gained not in his homeland but in England. In the aftermath of slavery, black Americans strove to participate in emerging national pastimes, and a number of athletes such as the jockey Isaac Murphy and baseball players like Moses Fleetwood Walker distinguished themselves at the highest levels of their sports. Yet perhaps *because* of the increasing success of African-American athletes, white hostility to their pioneering efforts grew into rigidly exclusionary practices. The process was complex and the circumstances varied from place to place, yet ultimately Jim Crow would preside over major league baseball franchises, racetracks, and most boxing venues for many years to come.

After the turn of the century, as the essays in the first section demonstrate, both the exploits of great athletes and the creation of new sporting associations helped create a sense of community among black Americans and fashion a more expansive notion of race pride. The ingenuity of both entrepreneurs and racial activists in the urban North created popular African-American baseball franchises and basketball squads as well as an increasing number of playing fields and gymnasiums in cities like Pittsburgh and Chicago, where blacks had begun to settle in increasing numbers. Meanwhile, educators at historically black colleges and universities (HBCUs), located principally in the South, encouraged the development of intercollegiate athletics, for in the words of a typical college catalog, "the best education is that which develops a strong, robust body as well as other parts of the human makeup." To turn the pages of the yearbooks published by many of those institutions in the early twentieth century, or to read the coverage in the black press of the sporting traditions at Bennett or North Carolina College, for instance, is to learn that athletics played a significant role in the African American collegiate experience—for women and men alike.

Although blacks showed an impressive vitality and sense of self-worth in creating sporting communities of their own, they continued to protest segregation and discrimination at every opportunity and made the most of the occasional exceptions to the prevailing pattern of exclusion. During the first half of the century, the black press fairly brimmed with news of athletic achievement, interpreted as a measure of racial progress. Thus African Americans could dote on the victories won and records established by "race men" in international competition such as the Olympic Games; they were aware, as well, that black baseball players more than held their own in mixed competition with white major leaguers, and for many years they told stories about the legendary Jack Johnson, heavyweight champion from 1908–1915. It would not be until the Depression decade and the war years, however, that the gathering momentum of civil rights activism reached a critical mass.

The campaign for equal opportunity in sports drew, at one level, on the status of Joe Louis and Jesse Owens as *national* heroes, especially after their symbolic victories over fascism in the late 1930s: the Berlin Olympics and the second Louis-Schmeling bout drew attention to the fact that in highly visible international arenas, America's foremost representatives were black men. African-American leaders, such as those who guided the National Association for the Advancement of Colored People (NAACP) endeavored to publicize such lessons of loyalty, especially since the Second World War was widely claimed as a defense of freedom and democracy. To a significant extent, too, the linking of racial reform to patriotism became a part of the U.S. propaganda project during the early years of the Cold War; indeed, the whole world was watching as President Truman ordered the desegregation of the military and as Branch Rickey and Jackie Robinson altered the history of major league baseball, or on a different podium, when African-American women represented both race and nation in winning gold, silver, and bronze medals during the Olympiads of the 1950s and 60s. What stands out from the essays in the second section of this volume is that the process of desegregation was halting, never sure. Racial change rarely occurred in the flash of enlightenment by university officials, the owners of professional teams, or politicians; rather, it was the result of local as well as national agitation and protest, appeals that longstanding ideals—such as fair play and sportsmanship—should finally be put into practice, then all kinds of legal leverage. Nevertheless, long after the Supreme Court declared that separate was *inherently* unequal, few commentators would have claimed that blacks and whites played on a level playing field. What is more, the process of desegregation represented not just a constitutional and political revolution; for many athletes, who confronted myriad epithets and indignities during their pioneering efforts, it was an ordeal in the most personal and poignant terms.

The relationship between the breakthroughs in sport and the larger civil rights crusade remains the subject of considerable scholarly scrutiny. Indeed, it is extremely important to know when a classroom, a locker room, or a dormitory has fully and finally become an open place. Yet, as the contributions to the final section of this book seek to show, the underlying significance of sport in the larger quest for racial justice rests on how athletic accomplishment is interpreted. Clearly, the images of black athletes have been contested within Afro-America ever since the time of Jack Johnson, but perhaps more importantly, it is the ways in which white Americans have perceived the achievements of African Americans in the sporting realm that matters most for the prospects of blacks beyond the playing fields. From the era when black sports journalists such as Edwin Bancroft Henderson promoted the ideal of "muscular assimilationism" down to the present era, many African-American commentators have elaborated success in sports as an emblem of race pride and an indicator of accomplishment that could and should be translated to every other domain of human endeavor. Such an ideological stance, however, has imposed enormous constraints on black athletes—even as it has assumed that white America will look past race to hard work and qualities of character that have long defined the athletic ideal. In fact, some of the greatest African-American performers have resisted conformity to the ideal, as the biographies of Muhammad Ali and Michael Jordan reveal: should there be a template for black athletic success when no one model exists for other notable Americans in other professions? And in fact, no matter in what forms African-American achievement has been cast, the black image in the white mind continues to be bound to stereotype and caricature, sometimes encoded in the language of pseudoscientific assertions, often exhibited in racial profiling, and from time to time still alluded to by the most prominent government officials—even one hundred years after Du Bois had made his appeal and his warning—that race relations were somehow simpler "back then." As the concluding piece in this collection suggests, in a variety of ways "back then" is also "now" for many African Americans. Ultimately, if sport stands as one of the ways to erase the color line during the twenty-first century, it cannot stand outside such traditional notions as racial pride and community solidarity, or conventionally broader paths to social mobility and social justice. Still, the next generation of scholars and students of the African-American experience will need to be innovative about the issues they confront, the problems they strive to solve. But they should not feel compelled to start from scratch. Ideally, this collection offers some historical foundations—not just lively sports stories but also an array of insights about race relations in the recent past.

I

SPORT AND COMMUNITY IN THE ERA OF JIM CROW

"AT A TIME WHEN black Americans were denied basic fairness across the board, the theory that hard work could trump racism was both noble and patently false." (Brent Staples in the *New York Times,* February 1, 2003). Indeed, before the middle of the twentieth century, when mainstream institutions—major colleges and universities, law firms, corporate offices, the U.S. military, and civil service—made their first tentative but significant efforts to include black Americans, positions of leadership and responsibility were filled principally *within* the African-American community. The walls of segregation were built thick and high during the last decades of the nineteenth century and the first years of the twentieth, and racism manifested itself not only in exclusionary practices, which pervaded the sporting world as well, but also in the myriad indignities and the outright violence regularly confronted by blacks.

No one narrative captures the ambition and despair, the frustration and striving that characterized the experience of Jim Crow for the mass of black Americans. Although there was no Mason-Dixon Line demarking the boundaries of racism in America, the Great Migration of millions of African Americans from the rural South to the urban North did suggest that greater opportunity and freedom in cities like Pittsburgh possessed substantial appeal. There, black Americans faced continued hardship, but their impressive energy in (re)creating their churches and benevolent associations, in founding business enterprises, and establishing community centers—including sporting clubs, parks, and local YMCAs—spoke to a newfound spirit and sense of hope for the future. In many ways athletic achievement, even when displayed behind the veil of segregation, informed the concept of the "New Negro"—increasingly proud and assertive.

The emerging black press captured the vitality of northern communities when discussing politics, education, the African-American social swirl of the big cities, and the mounting number of achievements in the athletic arena. Occasional opportunities for interracial competition presented themselves, and such events as Jack Johnson's victory over Jim Jeffries in 1910 were celebrated in black communities across the nation as enormously significant events. In a striking commentary on the meaning of that bout, Reverend Reverdy Ransom declared that in addition to black athletes, African-American musicians, poets, artists, and scholars would "keep the white race busy for the next few hundred years . . . in defending the interests of white supremacy. . . . What Jack Johnson seeks to do to Jeffries in the roped arena will be more the ambition of Negroes in every domain of human endeavor."

Race pride and the cultivation of institutions of uplift and assimilation also represented a central feature of the development of historically black colleges and universities (HBCUs), such as Fisk and Howard, and the poorly funded but proud state universities like Alcorn A & M and Morgan State. At these southern schools, a richly textured extracurriculum, including drama and debate, choral groups, poetry societies, AND an array of intercollegiate sports contributed to campus life for women and men, as well as strengthening the bonds between individuals and their supporting communities. Within severe economic constraints and under the surveillance of wary white southerners, black educational institutions, high schools as well as colleges, endeavored to fashion settings where success in sport prepared black youth for ever-greater possibilities.

Ultimately, Jim Crow meant that African Americans would be compelled to establish their own medical associations and bar associations because they were excluded from membership in the American Medical Association (AMA) and American Bar Association (ABA). This development paralleled the founding of Negro League baseball and other organizations meeting the needs of African-American golfers, bowlers, and tennis players. Yet such institution-building reinforced race pride and community solidarity, and set significant records of accomplishment just as they provided platforms of protest against segregation and discrimination. At mid-century the Kansas City Monarchs might claim a role in Jackie Robinson's ascent to Major League Baseball in nearly the same way that Howard University Law School launched Thurgood Marshall's career from civil rights lawyer to a place on the Supreme Court of the United States.

1

SPORT AND BLACK PITTSBURGH, 1900–1930

Rob Ruck

ONE CAN STILL FEEL a sense of neighborhood in Pittsburgh, of its ethnic pockets and groupings. Pierogies and kielbasas lend their fragrance to the Southside, and Italian remains the native tongue for many in Bloomfield and East Liberty. The Northside retains a faint Germanic ambience, and on Polish Hill a plaque marks the 1969 visit of Karol Wojtyla, now Pope John Paul II. Pittsburgh's rivers, ravines, bluffs, and hollows divide the city into dozens of smaller communities, just as they have for almost two centuries.

These formidable natural barriers were reinforced by the historic clustering of the different ethnic and racial groups that migrated to Pittsburgh in the course of the city's rise as the nation's iron and steel workshop. By the turn of the century they made Pittsburgh and its satellite mill towns into a multiethnic metropolis of over half a million people, many of whom labored to produce 40 percent of the country's steel.

Each ethnic group that came to Pittsburgh tended to settle in a particular neighborhood where nationality dictated which church one attended and where one drank. But ethnicity was not an absolute factor: one did not need an ethnic passport to move to the Hill, which loomed over the city's downtown, or to reside in Braddock, Homestead, or any of the other mill towns along the banks of the Monongahela and Allegheny rivers. These neighborhoods may have become ghettos, but they were multiethnic ones. Polish, Italian, Yiddish, and Croatian were spoken on the street and in the stores, intermingled with English and the dialect of migrants from the Black Belt.

It was in this multiethnic, industrial city that a black community began to form in the nineteenth century. Unlike the city's white immigrant neighborhoods, where the residential and occupational gains of the first generation were bequeathed to the second, black Pittsburghers found it hard to lay the foundation for community growth. White ethnic neighborhoods became increasingly stable and cohesive during the twentieth century as a result of a strong infrastructure of churches and neighborhood associations, residential persistence, and greater workplace security. Moreover, by the 1930s the steady stream of European immigrants had slowed to a trickle. The sons and daughters of the earlier migrants built on the efforts of their parents, especially at work and in becoming homeowners in tightly knit ethnic enclaves. Blacks were not so fortunate.[1]

The efforts of black Pittsburghers to achieve second-generation status were hampered by continuing waves of black immigrants and emigrants well into the 1950s. An estimated two-thirds of all blacks living in Pittsburgh in 1910 left the city by 1920, to be replaced a decade later by relative newcomers. Although blacks attained slightly greater occupational and residential stability in the 1930s, a second wave of migration during and after World War II soon recast black Pittsburgh yet again.[2]

Those blacks who came to Pittsburgh after the 1920s discovered a city that was already past its economic prime. The earlier competitive advantage held by Pittsburgh in heavy industrial production faded after World War I, resulting in long-term economic decline. Nonetheless, blacks poured into the city in unprecedented numbers between 1930 and 1960, as the black population increased from about 55,000 to over 100,000. These newcomers faced both dwindling economic opportunities and a black community that had yet to completely shed its first-generation urban status.[3]

THE MAKING OF A BLACK COMMUNITY

By 1900 there were over 20,000 blacks in Pittsburgh, the majority living on the Hill. Black Pittsburgh was a community in the making in the early twentieth century, but it was one beset by forces pulling it apart. Against a backdrop of discrimination in workplaces and neighborhoods, black Pittsburgh's already inadequate facilities were soon overwhelmed by a swelling tide of southern migrants. In the early stages of this migration, the black community appeared to divide along the lines of Pittsburgh-born versus migrant, with some parallels to the social class and occupations of the two groups. It was not until the 1920s and later that black Pittsburgh came to terms with itself and emerged with a sense of identity as both a community and a part of an emerging national black consciousness.

In the early twentieth century black Pittsburgh grew along with the city's expanding industrial base. When World War I shut off the flow of southern and eastern European immigrants to area mines and mills, blacks from the American South stepped in to fill the void. The number of blacks in the city more than doubled between 1910 and 1930, exceeding 50,000. Simultaneously, the percentage of blacks among the total city population rose from 4.8 to 8.2.[4] Drawn by the prospects of better work and improved social conditions, alternatives that the South seemed unlikely to offer, increasing numbers of blacks trekked northward to the Steel City from Virginia, Georgia, Alabama, and elsewhere. By 1930 less than a third of Pittsburgh's black population had been born in Pennsylvania.[5]

Migration affected both the demographics and the geography of black Pittsburgh. Men were more likely than women to make the trip north; hence the black community soon found a disproportionate number of black southern males on its streets and in its boardinghouses. While the migrants settled in mill towns up and down the rivers, most found their way to the district known as the Hill. A traditional gathering point for migrants of all backgrounds, the Hill had supported a black population since before the Civil War, when it was popularly known as Little Hayti.[6] About half of Pittsburgh's black population lived there in the 1930s, with the remainder clustered in smaller groups in the eastern portion of the city.[7] Over time, black enclaves developed in the Manchester and Beltzhoover sections as well. The Hill, like most of Pittsburgh and the nearby mill towns, was composed of a heavily foreign-born or second-generation population, with Irish, Italians, Jews, and Syrians living alongside blacks. While blacks and whites sometimes shared the same building and often lived side by side, there was a marked tendency toward racial and ethnic clustering within the district.[8]

There was a definite clustering, too, of migrants and old-stock blacks. Pittsburgh-born blacks were generally better off than the more recent migrants, especially those from the Deep South.[9] There was even a local black elite with middle-class aspirations, referred to as "OP's," or Old Pittsburghers. These class differences were compounded by a residential separation of most migrants from the northerners. In the nearby steel town of Homestead, across the river from Pittsburgh, skilled black workers, professionals, and shopkeepers lived in the "Hilltop" neighborhood while the migrants who labored on work gangs in the mills lived in crowded boardinghouses in the "Ward" along the river.[10] They went to different churches on Sunday and returned to different neighborhoods afterward, one a fairly pleasant residential section and the other a district with a reputation for prostitution and gambling.[11] This geographic separation held for Pittsburgh, too, as the more economically secure Pittsburgh-born blacks moved into particular parts of the Hill and into Beltzhoover and Homewood, away from the newcomers.[12]

Southern migrants and northern blacks also encountered different experiences at work. The migrants were more likely to join the industrial work force, sometimes introduced to break strikes but more often to make up for a diminishing supply of southern and eastern European labor. By contrast, Pittsburgh-born blacks could be found in domestic, clerical, or service positions. When both worked in the mills, the locals were more likely to hold the few skilled jobs allotted to black workers.[13]

This southern influx aggravated class divisions and led to two nearly separate black communities in Pittsburgh based on place of birth and occupation. The two groups lived apart, worked apart, and played apart. OP's formed their own fraternal and literary societies, while many of the migrants brought their native community organizations with them.[14] The migrants, observers noted, kept to themselves, while the older families remained aloof, believing themselves to be socially superior because of long residence in a northern city with its advantages of higher literacy rates, a broader culture, greater economic security, and a better standard of living.[15]

Another reason the black community divided was that increased numbers of newcomers taxed scanty housing and social services and heightened competition for work. The black middle classes also saw the migrants as a threat to their own public image of respectability.[16]

Black Pittsburgh's internal problems were compounded by the fact that migration was not simply a one-way exodus to the North. Many migrants, because of family ties, holidays, and the need to help out on the farm, made seasonal pilgrimages back home. With frequent returns south, these migrants were less likely to establish roots and meld with the northern-born population. The two-way flow was a common experience, at least until the early 1930s.[17] For other migrants Pittsburgh was just a temporary layover in an often frustrated quest for a better life that took them from city to city.[18]

This sense of unease over its own makeup was deepened by the material conditions facing the black community. Life was harsh for most early twentieth-century migrants, but its realities were particularly grim for blacks. The 1907 *Pittsburgh Survey* found that housing was a serious problem for black and immigrant Pittsburghers, and conditions deteriorated as the number of residents climbed. Housing accommodations were taxed well beyond their limits as families doubled and tripled up and often took on boarders as well to meet rent payments. Black homeownership remained at less than 4 percent on the Hill during the 1920s, and rental properties were scarce. Blacks moved in to virtually any space with a roof over it, crowding into abandoned boxcars, cellars, and shacks. As the black population increased, so did the tendency for blacks to live in segregated communities as whites sought to prevent them from moving to certain parts of town. Small black communities coalesced in Beltzhoover, East Liberty, and Homewood, their founders often having fled the deteriorating Hill neighborhood.[19]

The Hill, as a consequence of its population density and low per capita income, suffered from the highest incidence of disease and greatest number of public health problems in the city. Death rates in the Third and Fifth Wards were among the highest in the city, with the Third Ward having the highest death rate due to transmissible diseases in Pittsburgh. Infant mortality and deaths due to all causes were higher for blacks than whites.[20]

Nor did the world of work offer any respite. The opportunity for a better job had induced many blacks to migrate in the first place. A beachhead in industrial work was established during the relatively labor-scarce 1920s, especially in local mills, on the railroads, and in the mines.[21] Black women labored as domestics, cleaners, and laundresses, while the men were primarily engaged as porters, janitors, and laborers in the mills and on construction sites. Only a small percentage escaped low-paying, unskilled labor to practice a more skilled, rewarding occupation. However, when the Great Depression hit, black employment plummeted, and the gains of the 1920s were all but wiped out as black unemployment and underemployment in Allegheny County totaled 69 percent in 1934.[22] The upshot was that work was neither particularly steady, financially remunerative, nor likely to instill a sense of competence. Like conditions in the black community, the world of work was severely lacking.

Another factor fragmenting black Pittsburgh was its geographic dispersal. In Chicago, New York, and Philadelphia, the black community formed one contiguous area. In Pittsburgh, however, the black populace was splintered into a fairly large enclave on the Hill and smaller neighborhoods on the Southside and in East Liberty, Homewood, Manchester, Woods Run, and Beltzhoover.[23] This absence of a consolidated black community undercut black business and electoral strength. "The economic basis upon which rests the social, political and cultural life in [black] Pittsburgh is weaker and more shifting than that of any other group," social commentator J. Ernest Wright argued in 1940. "Because of such variability and the existence of several communities rather than one concentrated settlement such as Harlem or South Chicago, the group mood and outlook has not stabilized or coalesced. The group unity has remained weak."[24]

THE EVOLUTION OF A BLACK SPORTING LIFE

Black Pittsburghers took to the streets in jubilation after Jack Johnson knocked out Jim Jeffries in their racially charged 1910 championship bout, and they followed Joe Louis's career with a fascination approaching reverence. But sport also carried more subtle political meanings. Through its pantheon of sandlot and national heroes, the struggles over the desegregation of recreation and play, and its role in everyday life, sport played a central role in the coalescence of black Pittsburgh after the disruptive migrations of the World War I years. In the 1920s, 1930s, and 1940s, sport offered black Pittsburgh a cultural counterpoint to its collective lot, one that promoted internal cohesion and brought together both Pittsburgh-born residents and southern migrants in the context of a changing black consciousness. Moreover, sport helped the scattered black Pittsburgh community to gain a sense of itself as part of a national black community.

Just as experiences at work and in the community shaped black Pittsburgh's consciousness of itself, so too did its sporting life. Sport in black Pittsburgh during the early twentieth century was not solely the creation of black Pittsburghers, however. While it lent a sense of cohesion to black Pittsburgh, it did so at a time when groups and institutions external to the community sought to organize its sporting life. They ranged from local industry and city government to settlement agencies and the organized play movement. The context for their work was a black community in flux as migration reshaped it and allowed greater latitude for outside influence. While this loosely knit coalition contributed to the development of black sport, it eventually faded from the arena during the late 1920s, and in subsequent years black Pittsburgh was more fully in control of its own sporting life.

A fairly wide spectrum of sport already existed in the black community, ranging from a vibrant street life to the more restricted facilities of private clubs. In the middle, both in terms of scope and accessibility by all classes, were sandlots, neighborhood gyms, and recreation centers. But these facilities were never that abundant, and black Pittsburghers, like white immigrant and industrial workers, resorted to the streets and the materials of everyday life for their sport and recreation.[25]

STREET LIFE AND SPORT

At the beginning of the twentieth century the Hill was without a single municipal playground. Almost four decades later, a three-year study of the city and county concluded that with the exception of a few parks, "no form of recreational facility is available in proportions even approximating recognized standards. . . . If the Negro population has less access to leisure time activities than has the general population, they must be limited indeed."[26] But streets and empty lots were available, even if public and private recreational opportunities were not. Street culture has long been a part of black community life, and in Pittsburgh it took the form of endless pickup games played amid the daily interactions of neighbors and community residents on the stoop and sidewalk, in the pool hall and the barbershop. The street scene included a yearly carnival and musicians performing on street corners on the Hill, an informally organized outdoor dance hall with a phonograph and jitterbugging on Shetland Street in East Liberty, and nightly congregations along Wylie and Frankstown avenues.[27]

The street scene flourished in Pittsburgh because blacks were denied access to a wider range of recreational facilities. In some cases the streets and the rivers along which black mill-town populations lived were the only available recreational resources. In others, the facilities existed but black youths had to look elsewhere, because public recreation centers and pools were segregated on a de facto basis. Many thus gravitated to the streets and played ball there. For a brief span during the 1930s, the Works Progress Administration (WPA) pumped money and 1,500 WPA workers into Allegheny County playgrounds and recreation centers. But World War II brought an end to the program. As one columnist for Pittsburgh's black weekly, the *Pittsburgh Courier,* saw it, "There will be little else for the local children to do but return to the dusty, traffic-filled streets and alleys from which this project was intended to rescue them."[28]

BUILDING A SPORTING NETWORK FROM THE OUTSIDE

The street scene was largely spontaneous, filling in the gaps of social life without a formal organizing center. However, a wide spectrum of forces consciously began to organize black sport and recreation. Capitalizing on a growing enthusiasm for organized team sport, these forces sought to channel that energy to meet their own particular goals. Outside influences ranged from local government, social agencies, and area industry, to private social clubs and sports promoters. The general trend was toward the latter, the sports entrepreneur, who operated in conjunction with an ever stronger impulse toward self-organization by the players themselves. Increasing commercial influence also was evident as the locus of organization moved within the black community.

The making of an organized sporting life in black Pittsburgh involved both the building of an infrastructure and the sponsorship of teams, clubs, and leagues. The first required the construction of gymnasiums, pools, playing fields, and recreation centers, facilities that were scarce for black Pittsburghers before the twentieth century. The second built on a history of organized team and club sport extending back to the late nineteenth century. The efforts of a loosely knit coalition of the city, social agencies, and local industry combined with the energies of sports promoters, social clubs, and self-organized teams to build a fairly substantial black sporting network by the 1920s. The sandlot and community teams playing on local fields and in neighborhood gyms and centers were its backbone. Yet black Pittsburgh's sporting banner was already being carried by barnstorming baseball and basketball clubs and a contingent of track and field athletes representing not only their community but their country in both national and Olympic competition. As dramatic an improvement as this sporting life was, it nevertheless was inadequate and marred by racial and class discrimination.

THE CITY AND THE ORGANIZED PLAY MOVEMENT

The city government's role in the recreational and sporting life of Pittsburgh, both black and white, historically had been a limited one and was rarely supplemented by other levels of government. City Hall did add considerably to Pittsburgh's sporting facilities in the early years of the twentieth century as it acted in concert with a growing organized play movement then campaigning in urban areas across the country. This organized play movement, with its supervised playgrounds and recreation centers, was in conscious opposition to the world of street life and the sort of sport it fostered. Cary Goodman, a scholar of the movement, argues that the alternatives supported by this national play movement were intended not only to lure children away from the streets but to socialize the offspring of the immigrant population to a particular system of class-bred values and behavior.[29] The city was induced by the Pittsburgh Playground Association (PPA), the local arm of the organized play movement, to take a more activist role in promoting sport and recreation among its residents. It turned Washington Park, on the lower Hill, over to the PPA in 1903, and the group proceeded to erect a wood-frame recreational center on what had once been a dumping grounds. An athletic field and bleachers were built, and in 1908 a more modern center was constructed. The first fully equipped playground and athletic field in the city, Washington Park became a center for baseball, boxing, basketball, and football for the next forty-odd years.

By 1929 Pittsburgh's Bureau of Recreation was running seventy-eight recreational centers, eight of which were located on the Hill. There was an assortment of playgrounds, swimming pools, athletic fields, and recreation centers, with an emphasis on summer sport and recreation. Of the eight facilities on the Hill, two were year-round recreation centers—the Crawford Bath House and Washington Park—one was a swimming pool, and the others were a mix of summer playgrounds and athletic fields.

The recreation centers and the athletic fields were more of a focus for organized sport than the playgrounds, where younger children gathered. The Crawford Bath House was a combination bathhouse and club center for sport. But sport was only part of its program to help migrant blacks adjust to urban-industrial life. This program included a kindergarten and classes for adults. Lacking an athletic field, the Crawford Bath House served as a center for both girls' and boys' basketball teams and housed a boxing ring where some of Pittsburgh's finest pugilists trained, including Jackie Wilson and Charles Burley, contenders who worked out there in the 1930s and 1940s. And in 1926 the bathhouse sponsored and lent its name to a ragtag group of youths who became one of the best baseball teams in the Western Hemisphere, the Pittsburgh Crawfords.[30]

The Crawford Bath House, with an all-black staff in 1929, catered mainly to blacks. The racial mix was greater at Washington Park, where about one-third of the participants on any given day were likely to be black. The playgrounds were usually either predominantly black or predominantly white. While the city's general policy was not ostensibly segregationist, there was de facto segregation of certain centers and facilities. In some cases swimming pool hours were divided along racial lines; in others a pattern of friction and sometimes physical violence persuaded blacks not to use the pool or center.[31] But where both blacks and whites used the same facilities there seems to have been a high degree of interaction.

Most of the city-run centers catering to blacks were on the Hill, where the largest concentration of blacks in the city lived. Blacks in other parts of the city frequently went there if they wanted to use the city's recreation centers because of subtle and not-so-subtle discouragement from using centers located elsewhere. The city's services, which were criticized repeatedly for their inadequacies, were augmented by the work of various social agencies and settlement houses.

SOCIAL AGENCIES AND SETTLEMENT HOUSES

The Soho and Morgan community houses, the YMCA and YWCA, the Urban League, the Kay Club, and the black churches all directed energy into the sporting life of black Pittsburgh. The sum total of their efforts was an addition to both physical plant and the sponsorship of teams and leagues.[32]

The YMCA became the cornerstone of this social agency work in sport, but its impact in the black community was severely circumscribed by its racial and class biases. In the first place, YMCAs generally were found in communities where there was a combination of strong Protestant influence and some affluence.[33] By serving an economically favored strata, the YMCAs discouraged black participation. Moreover, certain local branches, such as the ones in McKeesport, Sewickley, and Coraopolis, simply excluded blacks. The racial compromise was to build a YMCA on the Hill, designated as the "colored" branch among the fourteen local facilities operating in 1928. This was standard operating procedure for the YMCA nationally in those years. While concentrating its energies among the most ghettoized of the black populace, the YMCA's policy of segregation left blacks in other parts of the city outside its program.[34]

Black Pittsburgh's YMCA was built at the heart of the Hill, across Centre Avenue from the building that housed the *Pittsburgh Courier*. *Courier* editor Robert L. Vann chaired the fundraising efforts for the new building, which relied heavily on the contributions of the Rosenwald Fund. Julius Rosenwald, a Chicago mail-order magnate, contributed to the

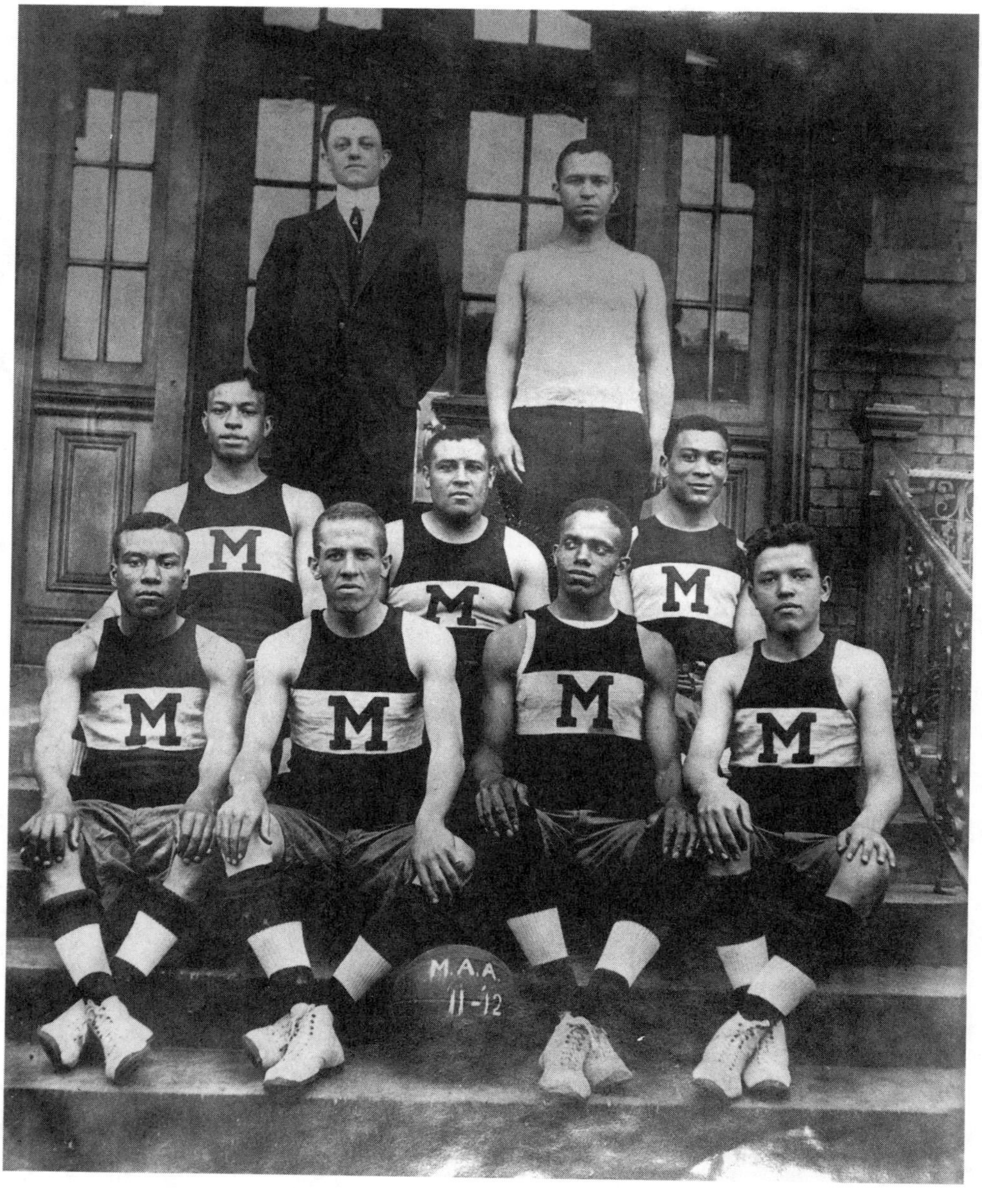

Figure 1–1
The Monticello basketball squad. Top row (from left to right): Joe Mahoney, Evan Baker; Middle row: Jim Dorsey, Seward Posey, Walter Clark; Bottom row: "Bird" Brown, Cumberland Posey, Sellers Hall, Charles Richmond. Cum Posey, a stellar player in early twentieth-century basketball and later black Pittsburgh's most successful sports entrepreneur. Courtesy of Zerbie Dorsey.

construction of more than a score of YMCAs in black communities. Completed in 1923, the Centre Avenue Y rapidly emerged as a key social and political center for black Pittsburgh. Its rooms and auditoriums were used for community meetings and served as a gathering point during political campaigns. With classrooms and club rooms, a dormitory, a pool, and a gymnasium, the YMCA had its hands in activities ranging from industrial work and health education to sport and recreation.

The YMCA provided sports facilities and sponsored teams and league activity. Blacks participated in tennis, volleyball, track and field, and swimming, as well as basketball, the most widely played sport at the YMCA. As of 1930, the YMCA had the only basketball court consistently available to blacks in the city. In the spring of 1929, eighteen different black teams played there. Although it did not sponsor baseball or football, the YMCA participated in a mushball (softball) league and helped coordinate a black industrial workers' baseball league. The black churches worked through the YMCA in establishing a church athletic league, as did the Urban League and local industry.

YMCA-sponsored teams competed within all-black leagues in addition to entering tournaments and leagues hosted by the American Athletic Union, the *Pittsburgh Press*, and regional and state YMCA bodies. Participation in the latter often meant breaching racial barriers. When the Centre Avenue Y's lightweight team won the state basketball title in 1924, it was the first black team to have played in the state YMCA tournament. Its teams also integrated volleyball and swimming meets, as well as the Keystone Softball League in 1945. In track and field, which was probably the most racially mixed amateur sport, the Centre Avenue squad won the *Pittsburgh Press*, YMCA, and Amateur Athletic Union (AAU) meets on a regular basis.

Nonetheless, the YMCA was criticized for reaching only a small part of the black community. The Urban League estimated that of over 20,000 black males between the ages of ten and fifty who lived in the city during the 1920s, the YMCA served only about 1.5 percent of them. It argued for programs that would include the "underprivileged Negro boy" and urged that additional funds and personnel be allocated to supplement the work being done. However, interviews conducted with some sixty participants in Pittsburgh's sporting past, as well as newspaper accounts of the YMCA's activities, indicate that at least its sport program reached a fairly wide cross-section of the black community. Its teams included such men as sportswriters Wendell Smith and Chester Washington from the *Pittsburgh Courier;* former collegiate athletes Everett Utterback, Max Thompson, and Woody Harris; black professional athletes Ted Page and Josh Gibson; sandlot stars Gabe Patterson and Ralph Mellix; and a host of young boys and men from working-class backgrounds.[35]

Sport in the black community was heavily biased toward males, and females were often excluded. While the YMCA was severely restricted in its activities due to a lack of suitable physical facilities, it afforded black youth a chance to play and to compete on an organized basis. In later years it also was a possible stepping-stone to a collegiate career. Some blacks made the YMCA their primary sporting outlet and spent their entire athletic lives competing for its teams and in its leagues.[36]

The settlement house movement also added to the recreational life of black Pittsburgh by sponsoring teams. Yet settlement work was for the most part a transitory phenomenon hindered by its own racial practices. Settlements were traditionally oriented toward meeting the needs of poor, frequently immigrant communities, and black Pittsburgh met both these qualifications. There were, however, but a few settlement houses that either worked within black communities or opened their facilities to blacks.[37] Moreover, these settlements were hampered by scarce funding.

Three settlements served the Hill in the migration years; two of them closed their doors by 1928. The Soho Community House, founded in 1907 in an integrated working-class neighborhood near the Hill, provided limited sporting facilities to its members, about 15 percent of whom were black. The Bryant Community Center and the Morgan Community

House were church-supported centers for blacks on the Hill. The lack of steady funding brought both to an end in the 1920s. The Morgan Community House, despite its short life span between 1919 and 1924, hosted a unique sporting aggregation.[38]

In 1919 the racially mixed but predominantly black Scholastic Club of Pittsburgh sponsored a track and field squad coached by Hunter Johnson, then trainer for the football team at the University of Pittsburgh and former head of the Century Athletic Club in New York. Johnson actively recruited blacks to come to Pittsburgh to run for the Scholastic Club. He persuaded Earl Johnson from Baltimore, Charlie West from Washington and Jefferson College, and DeHart Hubbard from his redcap stand at Pittsburgh's Union Station to move to town and train under him. The following year, 1920, Johnson became trainer and manager of the Morgan Community Athletic Club (MCAC), and Earl Johnson, Charley West, and DeHart Hubbard went with him. The MCAC sponsored baseball, basketball, and boxing in addition to track, and such players as Vic Harris and Pappy Williams developed on its squads. But the club's forte was track, and three of its members—Johnson, Hubbard, and West—represented the United States at the 1924 Olympic Games in Paris. Hubbard, a long jumper, was the first black American to win an Olympic championship. Johnson, who became a fixture in black Pittsburgh's sporting world, placed third in the 10,000-meter race behind Paavo Nurmi, the Flying Finn, and his compatriot, Willie Ritola. However, the MCAC, which had had no money to send candidates to the 1920 Olympic tryouts, soon folded due to lack of funds.[39]

There were other settlement-type centers, such as the Kay Boy's Club and the Rankin Christian Center, involved in sport and recreation, yet these centers were hampered by insufficient financing. The black churches, which provided some financial support and sponsored leagues and teams through the YMCA, and the Urban League, which acted similarly, had virtually no independent sports programs.[40] These organizations took a conscious interest in sport and recreation, however, and cooperated with the YMCA and local industry in a variety of ventures.

The churches and social agencies were undoubtedly driven by sincere concern for the plight of black Pittsburghers. But they also had a political and social agenda for the black community that reflected the realities of Pittsburgh in the 1920s. The region's growing economic base and the restriction of European immigration had created unprecedented opportunities for blacks. The YMCA, the Urban League, and many black ministers and settlement leaders wanted to make sure that blacks took advantage of the situation. Sport and recreation were inducements to boys and young men to take part in the larger programs, which, in the organizers' own words, were bent on "improving the morale, efficiency and consciousness of Negro workers."[41] They facilitated the adjustment of blacks, especially those from the South, to the routines and demands of industry. Acting as labor recruiters for industry, they also helped black laborers to make their work habits more acceptable to white society. Sport teams and recreational facilities were but a part of this larger program; the direct link was more concrete in these agencies' cooperation with local industry in the field of industrial sport and recreation.

INDUSTRIAL SPORT AND RECREATION

The capitalist world system was shaken to its very foundations in the early twentieth century. World War I, the Russian Revolution, and a labor upsurge of almost unprecedented proportions combined to pose a direct challenge to managerial authority.[42] When adverse economic conditions undercut the labor movement in the early 1920s, however, American manufacturers counterattacked and launched a broad set of changes in industrial life to ensure that the upsurge would not be repeated.

This American plan was perceived as an alternative to both Bolshevism and unionism. It stressed the open (i.e., nonunion) shop and introduced employee representation plans as a company-sanctioned forum from which workers might communicate their grievances, thus defusing shop-floor dissent. The plan revamped production as the precepts of scientific management emphasized the goals of managerial control and greater productivity. For skilled workers, management was willing to try to guarantee some semblance of employment security. Finally, the American plan made use of new plant professionals, personnel managers, who introduced a variety of workplace welfare measures including lunchrooms, company newspapers, and clean washrooms. As a *Time* magazine advertisement extolling the virtues of Scot Tissue Towels put it, "Is your washroom breeding Bolsheviks?"[43] Foremost among these schemes was a focus on athletic teams and recreation.

The immediate tasks were to solve the problem of turnover that plagued American industry and to devise a means of shaping the attitudes of the workforce. Long concerned with the supply of labor, American industry has always gone to great lengths to ensure that it would be both adequate in size and willing to work. In the early twentieth century the labor supply fluctuated dramatically with the strength of the economy and as waves of migrants flooded American cities only to retreat when war struck Europe in August 1914. When the demand for labor was high, workers commonly left one job for a better deal somewhere else. It was not unusual for a worker to accept a half-dozen or more job offers in a single day, then report only to the one offering the highest wages and best working conditions. Annual turnover rates were as high as 1,600 to 2,000 percent in a single factory during World War I.[44]

While industry was addressing its concerns over astronomical turnover and labor turbulence, it also had to consider another changing aspect of work, that of shorter workdays. The second decade of the twentieth century was the critical period in the struggle for the eight-hour workday. During that time, those who worked forty-eight hours per week or less increased from 8 to 48 percent of the work force; those working more than fifty-four hours per week dropped from almost 70 percent to less than 26 percent.[45] Even the steel industry, where the norm had been a twelve-hour day and alternate six- and seven-day workweeks with a full twenty-four-hour turnabout shift every other week, went to an eight-hour workday by the end of 1923. This decline in the number of hours worked was a vital precondition for greater participation by workers in sport and recreation. It raised questions in the minds of personnel managers as to who would direct and influence working-class leisure time.

The United States was the world's leading industrial manufacturer during the 1920s, producing a higher percentage of global manufacturing than it ever had before or would afterward. The nation's manufacturers did not reach this pinnacle by ignoring the attitudes and aspirations of their workers. On the contrary, American industry sought to take advantage of them. The writings of L. C. Gardner, the superintendent of the Homestead Works of Carnegie-Illinois Steel Company (later United States Steel), are indicative of the thinking of American industry.[46] Carnegie-Illinois sponsored a wide range of athletic teams and recreational facilities at its Monongahela River valley plants, not only for its workers but the surrounding communities.

Gardner's essay on "Community Athletic Recreation for Employees and Their Families" begins with the assumption that practical managers will "see to it that the lot of their employees is as pleasant as possible because it is good business." Gardner suggested, "The matter of recreation is one that may promise to be a cure-all. It is attractive, it looks easy to handle and a certain element of [the workforce] is outspoken for it. . . . A sane, moderate program of recreation that aims to give everybody something to do in his leisure time is one way the employer can insure his workers coming to work refreshed and alert and in a happy frame of mind."

The superintendent also urged plant managers to look beyond the confines of their factory. "Good will is not a sentiment that trickles down from above. It comes into existence at the bottom of the social structure. The place to cultivate good will is where it grows naturally—in the community, in the neighborhood, where people meet as folks." Consequently, industrial plants should foster sport in the community in addition to the plant. Gardner listed twenty-eight possible activities, ranging from sport teams to playgrounds and festivals.

Gardner justified these commitments on several grounds, beginning with the matter of labor: "The best and most logical supply of labor is in the immediate community of a plant. Every resident, man, woman, boy or girl is a potential employee." Second, he noted that community recreation "helps to make good will. And the good will of a community is a real asset." Third, the program helped workers develop "strong bodies and alert minds"; children "grow into better specimens of manhood and the adults will keep in better physical condition." Gardner also suggested that recreation instilled a certain sense of organization and ideology: "It trains leaders to work with the company and does so in non-controversial subjects, so that these leaders are likely to be anchors to windward when outside leaders attempt to gather a following." Moreover, recreation acted as a powerful force in "preaching the gospel of clean living" and allowed youngsters an outlet in games so that there would be "less desire or inclination to violate laws and destroy property." Gardner concluded, "The industrial firm that takes a long look ahead, and invests in Community Recreation can expect as a dividend, loyal, healthy, clean living and team working employees drawn from its immediate neighborhoods."

Company sport became a national phenomenon as a majority of large firms sponsored some sort of recreational program during the 1920s.[47] One automaker sponsored twenty-seven uniformed teams. Another company, with twenty-six teams, built a steel and concrete stadium with a seating capacity of 4,000. Most of the firms donated uniforms and equipment, paid the umpires and traveling costs, and provided some sort of reward or banquet for the players. Teams ranged from intramural departmental outfits, to an auto company soccer team with a national reputation, to an iron and steel company team which toured Europe each year, with all expenses being paid by the company. Some of the squads eventually turned professional: for example, the Chicago Bears, one of America's oldest professional football teams, had its beginnings as the A. E. Staley company team in Decatur, Illinois.[48]

In addition to football, basketball, and volleyball teams, many companies also provided tennis courts, baseball diamonds, and golf courses, and sponsored employee athletic associations. A midwestern company with 17,000 employees built an athletic field with a grandstand seating 10,000 complete with locker rooms, showers, six tennis courts, four baseball diamonds, horseshoe courts, a cinder running track, and a playground for workers' children. The official stance was, "Given a square-deal management, industrial amateur athletics organized on a businesslike basis will promote plant morale quicker than any other single method."[49]

Many firms worked with the local branch of the childrens' playground movement and cooperated with the YMCA, the YWCA, and the settlement houses; at times, local industries also worked with each other. Industrial athletic associations could be found in Newark, Paterson, Baltimore, Cleveland, and Johnstown, Pennsylvania.

Pittsburgh's workingmen and women were at the forefront of the labor upsurge. They confronted management at the Pressed Steel Car Company in McKees Rocks and the Westinghouse complex in East Pittsburgh, and joined the 1919 steel strike and a score of other walkouts. When the dust of battle had settled, industry responded with a variety of welfare provisions. The steel and electrical industries, which dominated Pittsburgh's river valleys, set the tone for community recreation and company sport. During the relatively prosperous Coolidge years of the 1920s, they built playgrounds, nurseries, and community centers near many of their mills. Andrew Carnegie, the titan of the American iron and steel industry, endowed combined libraries and athletic clubs in Munhall, Braddock, Duquesne, and Carnegie and contributed to the construction of Schwab Vocational High School in Homestead and Renziehausen Park in McKeesport. Westinghouse Electric and Manufacturing Company (WEMCO) and Spang-Chalfant built and maintained recreation centers in Turtle Creek and Etna. The railroads and the coal companies also sponsored teams and leagues for their workers.[50]

The Homestead Works of Carnegie-Illinois Steel conducted what was probably the most extensive sport and recreation program in the area. The Homestead Library Athletic Club (HLAC), an appendage of the Carnegie-financed Munhall Carnegie Library, could trace its athletic heritage to the late nineteenth century. In the 1890s their football team, composed of former collegians from the Ivy League, was recognized as one of the top semipro squads in the nation and its semipro baseball team, with the eminently eccentric Hall of Famer Rube Waddell on the mound, played before large and enthusiastic crowds. Throughout the early twentieth century the HLAC was a mecca for local children, who used its swimming pool, bowling alleys, and gymnasium. Concerts and plays competed for space with wrestling, water polo, swimming, and team sports. HLAC teams won national amateur championships in wrestling and in track and field and also sent members of its women's swim team to the 1928, 1932, and 1936 Olympics.

Shortly before the United States entered World War I, Carnegie-Illinois Steel expanded its community program, building two playgrounds in Munhall and two in Homestead. The company showed outdoor movies once a week and employed playground directors to supervise both young children and team sports. Older children played soccer, mushball, field hockey, basketball, or baseball, while their mothers took advantage of the well-baby clinic and brought their toddlers to the wading pool. The program was directed by the Homestead Works' employee welfare department.

This same department also sponsored baseball and basketball teams for company workers, and games were held almost every night of the week at nearby West Field. The best players from the Homestead Works often tangled with teams from other mills in exhibition and industrial league matches.[51]

Much of this company welfare was off-limits to the black community, however. What was not strictly proscribed was segregated by race. The Carnegie Library clubs in Homestead and Duquesne, with their swimming pools, gymnasiums, and books, denied membership to blacks. In the plant, blacks could play ball but only on black teams. As one historian of the black migration to Pittsburgh noted, blacks might have shopped and dined with whites in Homestead's commercial district and worked alongside them in the mill, but when it came to the company's recreational program, Jim Crow was the rule.[52]

The sum total of industry's involvement in sport in the black community was nonetheless rather impressive. Many of the larger companies employed "Negro welfare workers" during the migration, men who supervised black teams and recreation during the 1920s.[53] Earl Johnson of the Edgar Thomson Steel Works in Braddock, Cyrus T. Green of Westinghouse, Charles Deevers and J. D. Barr of Pennsylvania Railways Company, William ("Pimp") Young of Lockhart Iron and Steel, Charles Betts of Homestead Steel Works, and W. R. Johnson of the Philadelphia Company constituted a group of company welfare and community workers who aligned themselves with their counterparts at the YMCA, the Urban League, and the settlement houses. Together they promoted not only teams and athletic clubs at their respective workplaces but leagues made up of company, community, and YMCA squads.[54]

Earl Johnson, an Olympic medalist and feature writer for the *Pittsburgh Courier*'s sports pages, directed the diverse activities of the black Edgar Thomson Steel Works Club.[55] Johnson also ran for the club in national and local track and field meets. In the American Athletic Union national five-mile championship in Chicago in the fall of 1923, he defeated Willie Ritola, the Finnish marathoner who would edge him out for the silver medal the following summer at the 1924 Olympic Games in Paris.

The Edgar Thomson Works, commonly referred to as ET, fielded baseball, track and field, basketball, and boxing teams. The baseball roster included youths who would go on to play Negro League ball as well as men in the twilight of their playing careers who had previously been with the Homestead Grays or the Pittsburgh Crawfords. While the

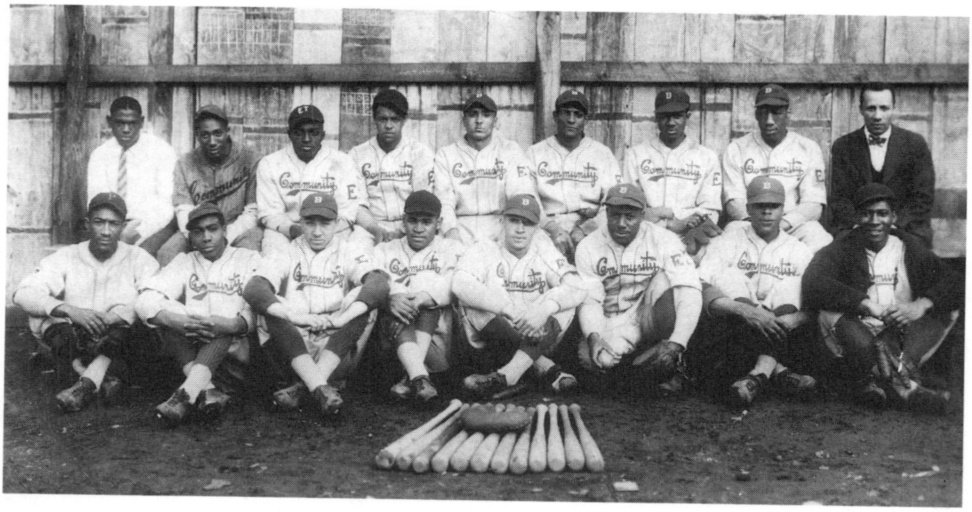

Figure 1–2
The Edgar Thomson Works team, called ET, was coached by Olympic medallist Earl Johnson. Several of the ET players jumped to the Crawfords in the late 1920s. Back row (left to right): Ted Sledge, (unidentified player), Neal Harris, Claude Johnson, Randy Hughes, (unidentified), Charlie Becotas, Watson, Earl Johnson. Front row (left to right): (unidentified player), (unidentified player), Gus Neville, Ernest Terry, Harold Tinker, (unidentified player), William Kimbo, (unidentified player). Courtesy of Harold Tinker.

ET ball club was formed to meet the recreational needs of black steelworkers, its players were frequently offered jobs and money by the company to play ball. When John Herron, financial backer and manager of the Pittsburgh Monarchs, disbanded his black sandlot team in 1926 a number of the players wound up at ET. Harold Tinker, one of the Monarchs making the switch, recalled that the ET team "wasn't doing too well, but Earl Johnson was a very progressive guy and he went out and looked for ballplayers. He took the nucleus of the Monarchs."[56] Charlie Hughes, Ormsby Roy, Neal Harris, Claude Johnson, William Kimbo, and Tinker had grown up playing ball with each other, and when the Monarchs folded they decided to stick together. An offer of employment made moving en masse to the ET squad an easy decision. Hughes recalled getting a job at the mill in order to play on the team: "It was an easy job, steady daylight and they gave you time off to play and everything."[57] His brother Walt indicated that while the team had company support and most of the players got jobs in the mills, some simply played for the team on a semiprofessional basis, receiving payment for each game played.[58] Such arrangements were fairly common on company teams. Willis Moody, a sandlot and Negro League star for a score of seasons, went to work for the Homestead plant of Carnegie Illinois Steel and wound up managing their black ball club. He was able to get men jobs so they could play on the team and also was allowed to include on the roster five players who had nothing to do with the mill. How they were remunerated was "none of my concern," he explained.[59]

The ET baseball team graced area sandlots for the better part of two decades, from 1923 through World War II. The steel company's financial support apparently tailed off in the 1930s, however, and community groups like the Oak Leaf Club and the Young Men's Business Club picked up the slack. Still headed by Earl Johnson, the ball club passed the hat at games and hosted a series of entertainment features to raise money. In the late 1930s Rufus ("Sonnyman") Jackson, co-owner of the Homestead Grays and a prominent numbers banker in Homestead, was rumored to be lending a hand. ET teams were crowned the "mythical sandlot champs" of western Pennsylvania in 1937 and 1938 after winning the honors in Pittsburgh's top sandlot circuit, the Greater Pittsburgh League.[60] Playing not only other black mill teams but white sandlot clubs as well, the ET squad often took the field for as many as sixty or seventy games a season. In 1938, for example, the team won fifty-six, lost four, and had five games end in ties. Over the years, men like Lefty Williams, Joe Strong, Bus Clarkson, Pete Watson, Fuzzy Walton, and Dodo Baden played for the team. Some made their mark in the Negro Leagues while others acquired reputations on the local sandlots. Still more played simply to take part in the game of baseball and compete on one of the area's more highly regarded squads.

Westinghouse (WEMCO), Homestead Steel, Pittsburgh Railways, Gimbel Brothers, the Philadelphia Company, Carnegie Steel, Pittsburgh Screw and Bolt, and probably another dozen or so companies sponsored teams for their black workers. Some of them, like Gimbels and the Philadelphia Company, ran entire leagues; others, like WEMCO, sponsored individual clubs. Organized in 1922, with 150 members, the WEMCO Club was open to black employees of Westinghouse and a handful of honorary white members. Pursuing "civic, social and industrial" ends with the aim of promoting good will and better relationships among the employees, the WEMCO Club sponsored basketball teams and an annual field day.[61] These field days regularly drew 1,500 to 2000 fans to Wildin Field in Wilmerding, in the Turtle Creek valley. Music, stunts, and races vied with prizes for the children, a grand drawing, and an enormous barbecue. Boxing matches and a doubleheader featuring the WEMCO team highlighted the day.[62]

Industry also helped their black company teams align themselves with neighborhood clubs and organized leagues. Beyond the pale of organized baseball and informally barred from the top local semipro and sandlot circuits during the 1920s, 1930s, and 1940s, black ball clubs for the most part played independent ball. Teams arranged games with each other on an ad hoc basis. The sports pages of the *Courier* issued periodic calls for a black baseball league comprising the better sandlot outfits, and local companies, through their employee welfare agents, backed these ventures. It was one thing to play independent ball, booking separate engagements with other teams; it was quite another proposition to organize a league, providing structure and leadership, ticket distribution, press contacts, a regular schedule, and championships. Besides the internal departmental leagues of the Philadelphia Company and Gimbel Brothers, there were at least four other workplace-based leagues in Pittsburgh during the 1920s.

The Negro Industrial Baseball League was the earliest, operating in 1922 and 1923. It stipulated that team rosters must be filled with amateurs, the majority of whom were industrial workmen connected with the same plant, but teams soon moved to import professional talent. Most of the teams were from steel mills like Fort Pitt, Carnegie, Lockhart, Woodlawn, and Coraopolis. Its first president, John T. Clark, who was also secretary of the Urban League, resigned during the 1923 season to protest the dilution of the amateur-only policy. Leadership devolved to Cyrus T. Green, league secretary and a welfare worker for Westinghouse. A second effort, the Colored Industrial and Community Basketball League, appeared a few seasons later and was the centerpiece of local amateur basketball in 1926 and 1927. Teams from Edgar Thomson, the Duquesne Steel Works, the Philadelphia Company, and the WEMCO Club represented the industrial side of the league, while the Paramount and Holy Cross athletic clubs and the North Side Scholastics and the Vandals represented the neighborhoods. The league's leadership included the tireless Earl Johnson, Max Bond, who was the physical director of the Centre Avenue branch of the YMCA and a former athlete at University of Chicago, W. R. Johnson, who was the physical activities director of the Philadelphia Company, and Cyrus T. Green. Playing their games at the ET gym and the Centre Avenue Y, the Colored Industrial and Community Basketball League attempted to bar all the "so called and recognized professional colored floor stars," an indication of encroaching commercial influence.[63]

Two other baseball leagues came together in the late 1920s and pitted industrial and community teams in regular competition. The Mon-Yough League was made up of teams from workplaces along the Monongahela and Youghiogheny rivers. Donora, Duquesne, Clairton, Wilmerding, Hays, and Christie Park were its mainstays. The Colored Industrial loop was a mix of community and mill teams, with WEMCO, Carnegie Steel, and the Philadelphia Company joining the East Liberty Greys and the Mendor, Hemlock, Bidwell, and fledgling Crawford athletic clubs.[64]

Scanning the list of team and league organizers reveals a core of activists, representing the YMCA, the Urban League, city recreation centers, settlement houses, and local industry, who were behind most league activity. Some of them went back and forth between the private and public sector but retained their commitment to recreation. Charles Betts is one such example. Betts moved to Homestead in 1911 at the age of ten and found work in his teens at Westinghouse. From 1927 to 1928 he was the assistant director of welfare there and played for the Loendi Reserves and the Homestead Athletic Association. The Great Depression cost him his job, but he was eventually hired by the WPA to turn an abandoned building into the McClure Community Center. The Carnegie Steel Works Colored Club wired the building and paid for the electricity, and the Homestead Council was petitioned to pay the rent and water bills. Betts later directed the Ammon Recreation Center on the Hill, a post he held for twenty-four years. During that time he coached the Ammon Track Club, whose ranks included Herb Douglas, an Olympic medalist in 1948. Betts also helped form the Uptown Little League in 1952. His employers changed regularly but his involvement in black sport was a constant. Leagues and organized competition were thus an arena where men like Betts cooperated in building sport and recreation in black Pittsburgh. They saw their goals as common ones.[65]

BACKING OFF: THE DECLINE OF EXTERNAL INFLUENCE

Between the efforts of social agencies and settlement houses, companies and the city, a greatly enlarged sporting network took shape in the first thirty years of the twentieth century. But this coalition dissipated with the advent of economic depression. While the need for recreational facilities and sporting opportunities was greater than ever during hard times, when enforced idleness left many with time on their hands and little else, the physical plant and sport programs sponsored by this coalition did not grow to fill the void. Indeed, company, city, and social agency commitment to sport shrunk at a rate almost proportional to the declining economy.

City and community recreational programs would have been insufficient during the 1930s even if they had been maintained at their maximum level of funding from the 1920s. But when tax revenues from depressed industries fell, social and civic programs were cut back or terminated. Police, fire, and medical care suffered throughout the Monongahela River valley, and with these essential services in trouble, it is no surprise that recreational programs received little backing.[66]

The decline of city and community support was compounded by the almost total withdrawal of industry commitment in the early 1930s. With financial retrenchment came a drive to cut expenses, and the subsidies for company sport and recreation were among the first to go. Suddenly, the tremendous sums pumped into area sport by companies whose coffers had overflowed from profits garnered during World War I and the 1920s was reduced to a trickle and then cut off completely. Recreation centers maintained by WEMCO in Turtle Creek and Spang-Chalfant in Etna were boarded up. The athletic facilities of the Carnegie Library were closed. Playground equipment bought by the companies during the early 1920s that needed upkeep and replacement simply deteriorated. Fewer teams and leagues could depend on company financing and support in terms of getting players hired and letting them off from work for practice and games.[67]

Most of the settlement houses closed of their own volition by the 1930s, and with the depression, the YMCA and other social agencies restricted their services. As their financial support declined, they had to make cuts in staff, and in some cases even close down their centers. The membership fees at some of the endowed Carnegie Libraries were reduced, but even this lower rate was often too high to keep or to attract members.[68]

The demise of this informal coalition undercut sport and recreation in black Pittsburgh, but the blow was hardly a lethal one. Nor was it the end to the role that social agencies, city and community departments, and local companies would play in sport, as all of these forces either continued to maintain some level of commitment or returned to the field when economic conditions improved.[69] Yet none of these groups were ever as much a factor in the sporting life of black Pittsburgh as they had been during the years prior to the depression.

It is difficult to assess how successful these forces were in meeting their goals because sport and recreation were usually only part of a larger program. Moreover, ascribing political aims to particular sports ventures often tortures the connections between them. Yet the settlement houses, agencies like the YMCA and the Urban League, the city, and local companies pursued these undertakings for their own reasons, which can be broken down into three sets.

The first set represented the goals of the national organized play movement and partly explained the role of the settlement houses, the social agencies, and the city in sport. Emphasizing supervised play, the movement sought to employ recreation as a means of socializing children to the values of an industrializing American society. It saw itself in opposition to the street culture of immigrant communities, both white and black.

The second set of motives overlapped with the first. The key question was how to help black migrants adjust to urban-industrial life. The YMCA and YWCA, the Urban League, and the settlement houses confronted this problem through a variety of measures, sport being one of them. A team, a league, a gymnasium, and a bathhouse were means by which these agencies reached the migrants and sought to influence them.

The third set was less ambiguous than the first two and much more ambitious. The sporting and recreational agenda of industry was perceived as a potential tonic for industrial peace, worker productivity, and a steady flow of labor from surrounding communities. The dividends of sport, to recall L. C. Gardner's advice, would be "loyal, healthy, clean-living and team working employees" who would be "anchors to windward" when the ubiquitous outside agitators appeared.[70]

How effective were the programs and efforts of these forces in meeting these ends? The values of the organized play movement certainly took root, and many of the truisms about the meaning of sport and its role in reducing juvenile delinquency and fostering clean-living youth are still potent. The organized play movement, while probably an effective means of socialization, hardly slew the enemy, street life. Nevertheless, contemporary community-based sport projects among black Pittsburghers echo the rhetoric about the role of sport for black youth.[71]

The black migration to Pittsburgh ebbed with hard times but picked up considerably when World War II refueled the economy. The efforts of the Urban League, the Y's, and the settlement houses to help migrants adjust to an urban-industrial environment and advance in terms of education and employment were partly successful, but underlying economic forces loomed large here. The role these agencies played in sport and recreation certainly enhanced their image in the black community and probably made their other programs more effective. The leaders of these agencies were often considered by the *Pittsburgh Courier* and the black community as black Pittsburgh's leadership, and their association with sport did them no harm.

The 1920s were relatively free of labor problems, and the black community proved to be a steady supplier of labor wherever industry would hire black workers. From a vantage point of fifty or more years, many of the black recipients of company largess in sport gave industry credit for their recreational activity at the same time that they acknowledged an understanding of why the companies were involved. Few seemed to think that the programs had a major impact on the thinking of black workers or suggested that it deterred anyone from later participating in the labor movement when it returned in force to Pittsburgh in the 1930s. Harold Tinker played ball for ET, but he was the first to sign a union card in his shop. Yet area firms still employ black athletes in public relations roles and hire them to advertise their products. If sport was not an antidote to labor organizing then, it at least temporarily improved the image of certain companies. By reverting to a policy of nonsupport during hard times and unionization, much of that goodwill was lost. A company or social agency could sponsor a team, but it took a sport activist or core group of players to really organize it, thus reducing the ideological impact of the sponsoring agency on the players who saw themselves or men like Earl Johnson or Sam Alexander, not Edgar Thomson Steel Works or WEMCO, as the driving force. Even in the black press, it was Earl Johnson's squad more than Edgar Thomson's, and the industrial leagues were the work of a handful of sport activists, not of industry.

The sum total of these efforts in sport was not so much to create a fair and decent set of recreational opportunities for black Pittsburgh as to foster a sense that black Pittsburgh had a shared sporting life with enough dazzle and competence to be a source of self-esteem. The legacy was that of a core of sport activists, a cadre committed to sport and recreation for black Pittsburgh with goals and values that transcended the particular funding interests employing them. It left, too, a minimal number of playgrounds and fields, gyms, and swimming pools, which, while never enough, were better than nothing. This coalition of forces pumped money into team and league sport and supported them in other ways as well. In a sense, these forces legitimized sport in the black community by involving members of the black elite.

At the same time, sport began to emerge as a source of cohesion for the community, transcending the divisions of class and place of birth. Many blacks were exposed to sport, especially sports other than baseball and basketball, because of these efforts. There was such an interest in sport that *Courier* writer Wendell Smith would claim not long afterward that he was "absolutely sure that no other section of the city is more sports conscious than this neglected, deprived civic orphan," the Hill.[72]

Another part of this legacy was a reinforcement of color lines in sport. The settlement houses, social agencies, the city, and companies all contributed in some way to the erection or maintenance of these barriers. Integrated teams and recreational opportunities existed, but they were neither guaranteed nor the norm. Ironically, the very street scene that the organized play movement wanted to eradicate was more integrated and less bothered by racial differences than the settlement houses and supervised playgrounds.[73]

This history of exclusion and the curtailment of programs sponsored by local companies, settlement houses, and social agencies left black Pittsburgh on its own in the 1930s and 1940s. Exclusion meant that black sport would have to be built by the black community, not forces external to it. The economic realities implied that black sport would require a greater degree of self-reliance. The field was increasingly left to black social clubs, sports entrepreneurs, and the players themselves. They expanded rapidly to fill whatever void was left by the disappearance of company sport and the decline of city and social agency efforts. During the 1930s and 1940s, black Pittsburgh was to sport what Harlem was to the cultural and intellectual renaissance of the 1920s. Nowhere was this more striking than on the sandlots.

NOTES

1. John Bodnar, Roger Simon, and Michael P. Weber, *Lives of Their Own: Blacks, Italians, and Poles in Pittsburgh, 1900–1960* (Urbana: University of Illinois Press, 1982), 78, 82, 131–33. The most insightful treatment of black Pittsburgh is Laurence Glasco, "Double Burden: The Black Experience in Pittsburgh," in Samuel P. Hays, *City at the Point* (Pittsburgh: University of Pittsburgh Press, 1989). Much of my interpretation has been shaped by working with Glasco, who was on my dissertation committee.

2. Bodnar et al., *Lives,* 188–96.

3. Bodnar et al., *Lives,* 187, 265.

4. Elsie Witchen, "Tuberculosis and the Negro in Pittsburgh: A Report of the Negro Health Survey" (Pittsburgh: Tuberculosis League of Pittsburgh, 1934), 2; Alonzo Moran, "Distribution of the Negro Population in Pittsburgh: 1910–30" (master's thesis, University of Pittsburgh, 1933), 10, cites Bureau of Census Press Release 3/21/32 on "State of Birth of the National Population"; U.S. Bureau of the Census, *Negroes in the United States: 1900–1932* (Washington, D.C., 1935), 6,14, 24–5. Much of this rural-to-urban migration was to southern cities, and many other migrants stopped over in southern urban areas for a few weeks or a few years before heading north. While Pittsburgh was not a major route for the migration and had a lower rate of black population growth than Chicago and Detroit, for example, the net effect was to create a sizable black community.

5. Witchen, "Tuberculosis," 2; John Nicely Rathnell, "Status of Pittsburgh Negroes in Regard to Origin, Length of Residence, and Economic Aspects of Their Lives" (master's thesis, University of Pittsburgh, 1935), 22; *Social Science Research Bulletin* 1 (no. 5, 1933): 2.

6. Andrew Buni, *Robert L. Vann of the Pittsburgh Courier: Politics and Black Journalism* (Pittsburgh: University of Pittsburgh Press, 1974), 23, cites Charles Dahlinger, *Pittsburgh and Sketch of Its Early Social Life* (New York, 1916).

7. Witchen, "Tuberculosis," 2–3; Joe T. Darden, *Afro-Americans in Pittsburgh: The Residential Segregation of a People* (Lexington, Mass.: Lexington Books, D. C. Heath and Co., 1973), 6–7.

8. Darden, *Residential Segregation,* 6–7; interviews with Bill Harris, 7/29/80, Pittsburgh; Bus Christian, 2/20/81, Pittsburgh; Wyatt Turner, 12/29/80, Pittsburgh.

9. Rathnell, "Status," 32; Bodnar et al., *Lives,* 71–2.

10. Buni, *Vann,* 32, cites Ernest Price McKinney, "These Colored United States, Pennsylvania: A Tale of Two Cities," *Messenger* (May 1932): 692.

11. Peter Gottlieb, "Making Their Own Way: Southern Blacks' Migration to Pittsburgh, 1916–30" (Ph.D. diss., University of Pittsburgh, 1977), 256. Gottlieb's dissertation was published under the same title (University of Illinois Press: Urbana, 1987).

12. Miriam Rosenbloom, "An Outline of the Negro in the Pittsburgh Area" (M.A. thesis, University of Pittsburgh, 1945), 29.

13. Gottlieb, "Making," 261; Bodnar et al., *Lives,* 60–6, cites research confirming that northern-born blacks held a higher percentage of white collar, skilled, and semiskilled jobs than southern migrants.

14. J. Ernest Wright, "Negro in Pittsburgh" (WPA Writers' Project, 1940), 13, 24. I used a typed copy of this in C. Rollo Turner's possession. A copy is now available at Hillman Library, University of Pittsburgh.

15. Wright "Negro in Pittsburgh," 11.

16. Buni, *Vann,* 32, also cites Wright, "Negro," 9–12.

17. For an excellent presentation of this argument, see Gottlieb, "Making," 109–10.

18. Bodnar et al., *Lives,* 188.

19. Buni, *Vann,* 61–2; Witchen, "Tuberculosis," 64–5; Ira DeA. Reid, "Social Conditions of the Negro in the Hill District of Pittsburgh" (General Committee on the Hill Survey, 1930), 38.

20. Witchen, "Tuberculosis," 8–9; Reid, "Social Conditions," 12. The percentage of black deaths per 1,000 population in Pittsburgh was from two to fourteen points higher than the percentage of white deaths per 1,000 every year between 1910 and 1928. In 1933, for example, the rate of deaths for blacks was 22.5 per 1,000 as compared to 12.5 per 1,000 for whites. In 1933, the black population of Pitts-

burgh (8.2 percent of the total population, according to the 1930 U.S. census) accounted for 14 percent of all deaths, 15 percent of all infant deaths, 24 percent of all deaths from pneumonia, and 35 percent of all deaths from tuberculosis.

21. Buni, *Vann*, 25, 69–71, 109.

22. Reid, "Social Conditions," 52–5; Buni, *Vann*, 24–7; William Y. Bell, "Commercial Recreation Facilities among Negroes in the Hill District" (master's thesis, University of Pittsburgh, 1938), 10. According to Wright, "Negro," 2, about one-third of black workers in Pittsburgh in 1930 were working as laborers in the steel and glass industries, the building trades, or other manufacturing and industrial activity; one-half were domestics or engaged in personal service; one-sixth were in trade or transportation; and one-fifteenth were involved in white-collar or professional work.

23. Wright, "Negro," 4.

24. Wright, "Negro," 14. An Urban League member contended, "The absence of a solidly Negro community in Pittsburgh reduces very materially the power of the Negro population to compel retail dealers to employ Negro clerks in Negro residential districts and to secure Negro political representation as in some Northern cities." A. G. Moran and F. F. Stephan, "The Negro Population and Negro Families in Pittsburgh and Allegheny County," Social Research Bulletin 1 (April 20, 1933): 4.

25. I was able to revisit the role that sport played in the making of a black Pittsburgh community in the documentary film, *Kings on the Hill: Baseball's Forgotten Men* (San Pedro Productions, 1993). See Cary Goodman, *Choosing Sides* (New York: Schocken Books, 1979), for a case study of the clash between the organized play movement and street life.

26. Philip Klein, *A Social Study of Pittsburgh* (New York: Columbia University Press, 1938), 281; Buni, *Vann*, 29; M. R. Goldman, "The Hill District As I Knew It," *Western Pennsylvania Historical Magazine* 51 (July 1, 1968): 285.

27. Bell, "Commercial Facilities," 30–1, 67–8; Ruby E. Ovid, "Recreational Facilities for the Negro in Manchester" (master's thesis, University of Pittsburgh, 1952); Hilda Kaplan and Selma Levy, "Recreational Facilities for the Negro in East Liberty District with Special Emphasis on Tracts 7G, 12D and 12E" (master's thesis, University of Pittsburgh, 1945), 14–32; Geraldine Hermalin and Ruth L. Levin, "Recreational Resources for the Negro" (master's thesis, University of Pittsburgh, 1945), 53.

28. *Pittsburgh Courier*, July 5, 1941, sec. 2, p. 3.

29. Goodman, *Choosing Sides*, 15.

30. The local black press credited the Urban League's John Clark for its existence. Reid, "Social Conditions," 711–75; *Pittsburgh American*, September 8, 1922. August Wilson, a neighbor of Charles Burley on the Hill, said that the southpaw boxer was his model for the former Negro Leaguer Troy Maxon, in his Pulitzer-prize winning play, *Fences*.

31. *Pittsburgh Courier*, April 24, 1954, 27; Reid, "Social Conditions," 72.

32. Reid, "Social Conditions," 76–78; *Pittsburgh Courier*, May 5, 1951, p. 17; February 2, 1952, p. 118; March 29, 1952, p. 28.

33. Klein, *Social Study*, 865.

34. Klein, *Social Study*, 283–4; Buni, *Vann*, 49, 338, cites YMCA, "Annual Concerted Operating Budget Canvas," Oct. 15, 1928, in the possession of Percival L. Prattis, Pittsburgh.

35. It is also safe to say that when the YMCA athletes were from the professional and middle-class ranks of the black community, they received more recognition in the black press for their play. Reid, "Social Conditions," 15–7, 75, 107; *Pittsburgh Courier*, January 27, 1934, sec. 2, p. 5; February 3, 1934, sec. 2, p. 5; February 10, 1934, sec. 2, p. 4; March 10, 1934, sec. 2, p. 5; March 17, 1934, sec. 2, p. 5; March 24, 1934, sec. 2, p. 5; January 14, 1939, p. 17; November 18, 1939, p. 16; February 11, 1954, p. 18; April 7, 1945, p. 117; December 18, 1954, p. 24.

36. Reid, "Social Conditions," 114–7, 75.

37. Klein, *Social Study*, 282.

38. Reid, "Social Conditions," 75–9.

39. *Pittsburgh Courier*, May 4, 1951, p. 17; February 2, 1952, p. 19; March 29, 1952, p. 28.

40. Reid, "Social Conditions," 95–105; *Pittsburgh Courier*, December 20, 1941, p. 17; June 9, 1945, p. 14.

41. Reid, "Social Conditions," 13.

42. David Montgomery, "The New Unionism and the Transformation of Workers' Consciousness in America: 1909–1922," *Journal of Social History* (Summer 1974): 511. This piece is an excellent analysis of the labor upsurge.

43. New American Movement reprint of 1932, *Time* magazine advertisement.

44. Montgomery, "New Unionism," 514, quoting Leon C. Marshall, "The War Labor Program and Its Administration," *Journal of Political Economy* 26 (May 1918): 429.

45. Montgomery, "New Unionism," 515; *Monthly Labor Review* 17 (Dec. 1923): 81–5.

46. L. C. Gardner, "Community Athletic Recreation for Employees and Their Families" (Carnegie Steel Co., Munhall, Pa., typeset, n.d.), found in the back room of the Munhall Carnegie Library. Gardner was superintendent of the plant in the early twentieth century. All Gardner statements are from this eight-page essay.

47. *Monthly Labor Review* 24 (May 1927): 867–82.

48. George Halas, with Gwen Morgan and Arthur Veysey, *Halas by Halas: The Autobiography of George Halas* (New York: McGraw-Hill, 1977), 54–76.

49. *Monthly Labor Review* 24 (May 1927): 874.

50. Klein, *Social Study,* 60–63; interview by the author with Russell Weiskircher, September 28, 1979, Boston, Pa.

51. Homestead Album Project, interviews with George Miller, Mel Rutter, Anna Mae and Russell Lindberg, Archives of Industrial Society, Hillman Library, University of Pittsburgh, 1976; *Homestead Daily Messenger,* December 22, 1929, October 9, 1930, September 17, 1940, April 23, 1976; *Pittsburgh Sun-Telegraph,* August 11, 1958; from typed copy, Catherine Butler to Mr. Hogan, March 10, 1943, Carnegie Munhall Library.

52. Gottlieb, "Making," 2.

53. Klein, *Social Study,* 60.

54. *Pittsburgh Courier,* February 26, 1927, sec. 2, p. 4; November 18, 1926, sec. 2., p. 6. *Pittsburgh Post,* May 28, 1922.

55. *Pittsburgh Courier,* September 8, 1923, sec. 1, p. 4; January 14, 1939, p. 16; March 25, 1939, p.17; April 1, 1939, p. 15; May 15, 1939, p. 15; June 3, 1939, p. 16; June 3, 1939, p. 15; July 26, 1941, p. 16; July 8, 1950, p. 31. These are the primary sources for the discussion of the Edgar Thomson team.

56. Interview by the author with Harold Tinker, June 19, 1980, Pittsburgh.

57. Interview by the author with Charlie Hughes, February 1, 1981, Pittsburgh.

58. Interview by the author with Walt Hughes, January 9, 1981, Pittsburgh.

59. Interview by the author with Willis Moody, January 6, 1981, Pittsburgh.

60. Robert Hughey, in *Pittsburgh Courier,* April 15, 1939, p. 15.

61. Betty Ann Weiskopf, "A Directory of Some of the Organizations to Which People in the Hill District of Pittsburgh Belong: 1943" (master's thesis, University of Pittsburgh, 1943), 43.

62. *Pittsburgh Courier,* August 8, 1925, p. 12; January 2, 1926, sec. 2, p. 2; July 17, 1926, p. 14; January 1, 1927, sec. 2, p. 6; July 21, 1928.

63. *Pittsburgh Courier,* December 18, 1926, sec. 2, p. 6.

64. For company sports, see interviews by the author with Harold Tinker, June 19, 1980, and Willis Moody, January 6, 1981; *Pittsburgh Courier,* January 1, 1927, sec. 2, p. 6; January 15, 1917. sec. 2, p. 6; February 26, 1927, sec. 2, p. 4; May 28, 1927, sec. 2, p. 5.

65. *Pittsburgh Courier,* March 1, 1941, sec. 2, p. 1; May 24, 1972.

66. Klein, *Social Study,* 62–3.

67. Klein, *Social Study,* 63; Bob Hughes, "How Many Are Playing?" *Pittsburgh Press,* April 15, 1931.

68. Klein, *Social Study,* 63.

69. George Weinstein, in *Coronet* (April 1951): 56–9. This study found over 18,000 U.S. industrial and business firms sponsoring some form of recreation or sport for their workers. The author argued that industry had learned during World War II that such programs could reduce absenteeism and increase productivity.

70. Gardner, "Community Recreation."

71. Current examples of this in Pittsburgh are the Connie Hawkins and Ozanam summer basketball leagues.

72. *Pittsburgh Courier,* March 22, 1941, p. 16.

73. Countless interviews by the author confirmed this: for example, Bill Harris, July 19, 1980; Fred Clark, December 29, 1980; Bus Christian, February 20, 1981; Wyatt Turner, December 29, 1980; Jack Parker and Joe Ware, July 15, 1980.

2

BLACK ENTREPRENEURSHIP IN THE NATIONAL PASTIME

The Rise of Semiprofessional Baseball in Black Chicago, 1890–1915

Michael E. Lomax

DURING THE 1980S AND 1990S, popular and professional historians of baseball gave increased attention to the black experience in the national pastime. They have examined the game's relationship to white society, analyzed the trials and triumphs of black ballplayers, and extolled the competency of black ballplayers as they confronted racist America. Their research has also examined the connection between black baseball and the black community, emphasizing in particular how the game served as a unifying element to communities in transition and how it helped bridge class distinctions.[1]

These efforts have dramatically expanded our knowledge, but the writings on black baseball have been somewhat narrow and limited. Most of the emphasis has been on the experience of players and the game on the field. While writers have noted the connection between black baseball and the black community, most of the research, especially in popular works, has neglected to analyze this linkage. Part and parcel of these limitations is the virtual absence of any analysis that examines the role of local businessmen, communal patterns, and the development of black baseball.

Baseball in black Chicago exemplifies the efforts of black businessmen to pursue sport as an entrepreneurial endeavor. Their attempt to establish baseball as a profitable business illustrates the efforts of black businessmen to counter discrimination and the exclusion of African Americans from places of amusement. It also illustrates how these African-American entrepreneurs responded to obstacles, such as the inability to secure credit, that adversely impacted economic development. These entrepreneurs organized a segregated enterprise within the fabric of the national economy. In other words, the segregated enterprise—black independent teams—operated within the framework of the national economy—white semiprofessional baseball. African-American baseball owners did not seek to promote their ball clubs exclusively to a black clientele. But with the expansion of the African-American community in Chicago in the 1890s, due to northern migration, black owners began catering to this growing market.[2]

Andrew "Rube" Foster was to emerge as Chicago's most prominent black baseball entrepreneur. He became the first black owner to transform a weekend enterprise into a full-time operation, and he also developed a barnstorming tour in both the West and

South in the pre-World War I years. While his Chicago American Giants was a race-based enterprise, Foster recognized the need to maintain business contacts with white baseball owners. This chapter will explore the forces that shaped black baseball in Chicago from 1890 to 1915. Four themes will serve to guide the narrative: the changing demographics of Chicago's black community, the development of Chicago's new black leadership, the origins of semiprofessional baseball, and the internal division among the enterprise's organizers leading to Rube Foster emerging as Chicago's most prominent black baseball entrepreneur.

GHETTOIZATION AND THE RISE OF SEMIPROFESSIONAL BASEBALL

The black population of Chicago expanded significantly between 1890 and 1915. During the first ten years of this period, Chicago experienced a dramatic growth in its black population, from 14,852 to 30,150, an increase of 103 percent. From 1900 to 1910, while the city's black population continued to climb steadily, its rate of increase declined; the Windy City's black population rose to 44,603, an increase of 46.3 percent. African Americans remained a minority in the Windy City, but their growing numbers made them far more conspicuous, and the large numbers of recent arrivals were pushed to reside in certain areas. In the late 1890s, most Chicago blacks lived in primarily integrated neighborhoods, with only a little more than a quarter residing in precincts in which they were a majority. By 1915, the roots of ghettoization became firmly planted as African-American enclaves emerged primarily on the south and near west sides. Few white neighborhoods had ever accepted with equanimity the purchase of homes by African-American families. As the black population increased, whites became less tolerant towards black neighbors and actively resisted black settlement in their areas.[3]

Eight or nine neighborhoods made up the core of Chicago's black community. The "black belt" extended from the downtown business district as far south as Thirty-ninth Street. It was slowly expanding to accommodate the growing population. Not only did blacks move steadily southward, but the black belt also began to widen as blacks moved into comfortable homes east of State Street. By 1910, blacks lived as far east as Cottage Grove Avenue.[4]

Simultaneous with and emerging from these demographic and residential changes was the creation of black institutions that contributed to the growing vitality and self-consciousness of the black community. The oldest and most stable African-American institution was the church. Quinn Chapel A.M.E. was the first black church in the city; it was established in 1847, fourteen years after Chicago was incorporated. By the end of the century, Chicago had more than a dozen black churches, and between 1900 and 1915 this number doubled. These institutions were attractive to African Americans who preferred to avoid white people and their prejudices. They were also important for establishing a sense of racial pride and community. Historian David Katzman states that the "push of discrimination" and the "pull of ethnocentrism combined to impel black newcomers toward the ghetto. Many migrants sought homes in areas populated by blacks, where they could find familiar people and institutions.[5]

While this dynamic of choice and constraint, which was heavily influenced by economic factors, was similar to the experiences of Chicago's European immigrants at this time, there were significant differences. For example, unfamiliarity with English made the ethnic neighborhood essential for many Europeans. Blacks, on the other hand, had no comparable imperative. White immigrants tended to live near workplaces; blacks, scat-

Figure 2–1
Rube Foster, stellar athlete and one of the most successful early entrepreneurs of black baseball. Foster was the force behind the founding of professional Negro league baseball. Courtesy of National Baseball Hall of Fame Library, Cooperstown, NY.

tered in service occupations, could not. Even when African Americans obtained industrial employment, they were excluded from neighborhoods adjoining Chicago's major industries. European immigrants lived near others of their nationality but usually in ethnically diverse neighborhoods that could hardly be described as ghettos. Whether middle or working class, black Chicagoans were less likely to share public space across ethnic boundaries. More than any other group, blacks in Chicago occupied neighborhoods defined by permanent characteristics.[6]

The sting of segregation affected more than choice of residence. Although state legislation prohibited racial discrimination in municipal services, public accommodations, and places of amusement, these laws were seldom enforced. Numerous incidents testified to a persistent pattern of discrimination in these areas. Blacks could never be certain what kind of treatment they would receive when entering a restaurant, saloon, theater, or dance hall outside of the black belt. The LaSalle Hotel, for example, turned away a luncheon meeting of one thousand clubwomen because their number included several black members. Most proprietors would accommodate an African American if they thought refusal would create a major controversy. Booker T. Washington stayed regularly at the Palmer House when he visited Chicago. But less prominent blacks were generally harassed or simply refused service in downtown establishments.[7]

It was within this context that a new black leadership began making their imprint on community development. These African American entrepreneurs, also referred to as "race men," were business leaders who deemphasized the fight for integration and dealt with discrimination by creating black institutions. The growing discrimination in Chicago and other northern cities resulted in the emergence of the physical ghetto. It prohibited African Americans from a host of social and economic institutions. Yet increased separation opened new opportunities for entrepreneurship. Between 1890 and 1915, Chicago's African Americans established a bank, a hospital, and professional baseball teams.[8]

Many of Chicago's new black leadership embraced a business concept known as cooperative business enterprises. This notion of cooperative enterprises had its roots in the black community in the late eighteenth century. Early black entrepreneurs recognized that if they were to attain any success in developing black businesses to an appreciable level in the black community, it would come only through economic cooperation. It was evident to them that no concrete help in obtaining capital and credit could be expected from white America. By the early twentieth century, cooperative business enterprises were outgrowths of the ideology of self-help and racial solidarity that developed in response to white discrimination. With blacks being excluded from many commercialized amusements, Chicago's black leaders sought to counter this discrimination by organizing their own commercial enterprises. For instance, by 1910 blacks found themselves completely shut out of the white YMCA, and as a result, the all-black Wabash Avenue YMCA was opened in 1913. Although certainly wanting to make a profit, Chicago's black leaders were genuinely motivated by a desire to provide services and facilities that were otherwise unavailable to blacks.[9]

At the same time, a development outside the African American community occurred that would significantly impact baseball in black Chicago—the rise of semiprofessional baseball. The emergence of semiprofessional baseball teams can be traced back to the 1870s. Commonly referred to as semipros, these teams could be classified into three categories: local teams or "stay-at-homes," traveling teams, and touring teams. Local teams usually played games within proximity of their home base. These teams developed a close-knit network with other semipro teams within, say, a hundred-mile radius, as a means of decreasing travel and overhead expenses. Traveling teams had no home base and would barnstorm the nation for gate receipts. Touring teams fell under both classifications and were the elite of the semipro teams. Possessing their own grounds, and the reputations as "crack" teams, these clubs could expand their travel itinerary and establish rivalries with teams in more lucrative markets, like New York City. Independent touring teams generally did not belong to a league, but they paid their players and charged admission. They commonly discharged their players in the winter, unless they toured the South. Independents often signed their players to one-year contracts, which only rarely contained a reserve clause for the following season. At the beginning of each season, players had to make new arrangements. During the season, independents either paid players a weekly salary or by a "coop" plan, a method in which a team's share of the gate receipts was divided among the players and owners.[10]

Semiprofessional teams utilized the same business practices as organized baseball did in terms of generating and distributing revenues. A home team would share a percentage of the gate receipts—normally 40 percent—or pay a guarantee, a fixed amount usually set at $250, commonly referred to as a "heavy guarantee," to the visiting team. This guarantee was essential to attract the top clubs to their home grounds.[11]

By the early 1900s, semiprofessional clubs in Chicago began forming leagues and associations. The Chicago City League featured some of the top semipro clubs of the era. Two clubs—Cap Anson's Colts and Mike Donlin's All-Stars—were formed by former major league players. The other clubs that constituted this league included the Logan Squares, the Gunthers, Donohue's Red Sox, the West Ends, the Spaldings, and Rogers Park.[12]

Essentially two factors were significant in the rise of white semipro teams in Chicago. The first was the nature of Chicago's sophisticated park system. In 1901, the Illinois legislature appropriated a $7.7 million bond for the construction of thirty-one small parks and playgrounds equipped with outdoor gymnasiums, athletic fields, swimming pools, and spacious fieldhouses, which became community centers. Parks with baseball diamonds were leased by many of the top semipro clubs, who thus established both a home base and fan constituency. These clubs were able to promote, schedule, and book their own games, thus alleviating the need for a booking agent.[13]

Finally, Chicago City League clubs, in conjunction with semipro clubs without home grounds, were members of the Park Owners Association (POA). The POA was a governing body that sanctioned league membership and scheduled games for both black and white semipro teams throughout Chicago's park system. It had twenty-two teams in the city league in 1910, eight of which had their own parks. The POA was a loose association that in the early years was not a promoter but a booking agent primarily for teams that did not possess their own grounds.[14]

The white semiprofessional clubs in Chicago established a symbiotic business relationship with black clubs. As black clubs rose to prominence and developed a winning reputation, white clubs found them to be good gate attractions. As we shall see later, two black clubs were members of the Chicago City League. This symbiotic business relationship illustrated the efforts of black entrepreneurs operating a segregated enterprise within the framework of the white semipro scene. Early black promoters did not seek to market their club exclusively to a black clientele. While black migration increased Chicago's black population in the pre-World War I era, it was not substantial enough to support professional black teams.

More important, black entrepreneurs did not seek to create a black counterculture. In other words, black businessmen were not out to isolate themselves from the larger society, selling only to blacks, nor did black fans seek to patronize black baseball games exclusively because they were black. African Americans desired to advance themselves by free competition on the open market. Black businessmen's economic philosophy was essentially a laissez faire formula for black advancement through individual commitment by individual blacks "to the gospel of work and wealth." The purpose of self-help and racial solidarity was to encourage black unity and self-assertion on a political level, while encouraging cultural and economic assimilation. This would, theoretically, result in the integration of blacks into mainstream American society. In the case of black baseball clubs, this meant white semiprofessional baseball.[15]

It was within the context of ghettoization and the rise of white semiprofessional baseball that Frank Leland emerged as black Chicago's first baseball entrepreneur. Leland was emblematic of the new black leadership that became actively involved in the ownership of black teams. He also exhibited an uncanny ability to establish contacts with local businessmen. Leland was born in 1869, graduated from Fisk University, and was on the roster of the Washington Capital City club of the National League of Colored Base Ball Clubs in 1887. This league was the only attempt to organize a black major league patterned after the white National League in the late nineteenth century. When the colored league disbanded in May 1887, Leland moved to Chicago, and along with local businessman Henry "Teenan" Jones and two ballplayers, Abe Jones and William S. Peters, formed the Union Base Ball Club. The club was renamed the Chicago Unions the following year, and by 1896, both Leland and Peters transformed it into a stay-at-home club. The Unions toured Indiana, Wisconsin, and Iowa from Thursday to Saturday and played local teams in the Windy City on Sundays. In addition to his business interests, Leland was also a member of the Republican party and was elected Cook County Commissioner.[16]

The Chicago Unions typified the early black independent clubs that began as weekend enterprises. Lucrative Sunday games were vital to the team's economic survival. One Sunday game with a total attendance of 5,000 fans, charging twenty-five cents admission, could amass a gross revenue of $1,250. After paying the visiting team their share of the gate receipts ($500), the Unions would make a profit of $750. The Unions had a significant advantage in residing in the Midwest's largest city. Moreover, according to Sol White—a top black player of the era and later chronicler of the black game—the Unions played 731 games in its existence as both amateur and professional, winning 613, losing 118, and tying 12. Clearly the Unions had established themselves as a crack team.[17]

The Unions' rise to prominence in the Midwest was instrumental in the emergence of a territorial rivalry referred to as the "World's Colored Championship." The colored championship series was a promotional tool to stimulate fan interest and generate revenue. This series of games possessed an unstructured yet logical format. Beating all the top black clubs within a particular territorial region gave a club the right to proclaim itself colored champion. The Cuban X Giants, one of the great black teams from the East and reigning colored champions, played a series of fifteen games with the Unions. But Leland's club was no match for the eastern power, and the Cubans won nine out of fourteen games.[18]

While it was not evident at the time, the Unions' loss to the Cuban X Giants marked the start of black entrepreneurs making concerted efforts to exploit Chicago's growing black market. Despite losing the series, Leland had exhibited the ability to attract a top black independent competitor. Clearly either the promise of gate receipts or another guarantee was substantial enough to make it economically feasible for the Cubans to travel to Chicago. Evidently the series caught the eye of other prospective black entrepreneurs, who recognized the market potential and sought to organize a club to challenge the Cubans.

In 1899, under the direction of John W. Patterson, a group known as the Columbia club organized the Columbia Giants. Patterson started out with the Cuban Giants in 1893 as a substitute second baseman, playing behind Sol White, but won a starting position in left field the following year. In 1896, he played for the Page Fence Giants, who went on to defeat the Cuban X Giants for the colored championship. When the Page club disbanded in 1898, Patterson and many of his teammates formed the nucleus of the Columbia Giants. Patterson also signed Chicago Unions pitcher Harry Buckner. Patterson then entered into an agreement with Chicago White Sox owner Charles Comiskey to lease his park on Thirty-ninth and Wentworth, an area within walking distance of the emerging black belt. With the Unions located a few blocks away on Thirty-seventh and Butler, both clubs now competed for the same patronage. This was an obvious conflict of interest for both clubs if they happened to schedule home games on the same Sunday afternoon. Chicago's black community was not large enough to support two teams.[19]

In 1899, while the Cuban X Giants and the Unions were playing their series, the Columbia Giants issued challenges to both clubs. The Cubans accepted, but Leland wanted to avoid the upstarts. He was apparently outraged by their territorial invasion and the loss of his top pitcher. However, Sol White asserted that out of consideration for the public the Unions agreed to a five-game series. The Unions were completely outclassed by the Columbia club, losing the series in five straight games. Patterson's Giants now turned their attention to the Cuban X Giants. A series of games was scheduled in Chicago and towns in Michigan, with the Cubans defeating the Columbia club seven games to four.[20]

After the championship series, it became evident that two clubs could not develop a lucrative operation within such close proximity of each other. By 1900, despite their success on the diamond both the Columbia Giants and the Chicago Unions were in a state of chaos, although the Unions defeated the Cuban X Giants for the first and only time. At the same time, the Columbia Giants defeated J.M. Bright's Genuine Cuban Giants of New York. But a disputed championship for local supremacy between the Columbia Giants and the Unions intensified the resentment between the clubs. The following year, financial setbacks caused the collapse of the Columbia Giants. Peters split with Leland and formed Peters' Union Giants. Leland signed several players from the disbanded Columbia club, formed the Chicago Unions Giants, and leased a park on Sixty-first and Lawrence, on the outskirts of the black belt.[21]

Leland's Union Giants continued to be a success on the field, but the club was still a financial failure. His split with Peters brought the East-West Colored Championship to a halt, and thirteen years passed before another series of this nature took place. The Union Giants were recognized as the top club in the Midwest, despite losing a local championship series to the Algona (Iowa) Brownies in 1903. Two years later, the Union Giants reportedly won 112 of 122 games. But success on the field did not necessarily result in financial rewards. By the winter of 1906, the Union Giants, renamed the Leland Giants, were a debt-ridden team. Recognizing a need for a financial fix, Leland would once again exhibit his ability to form a business coalition.[22]

THE LELAND GIANTS BASEBALL AND AMUSEMENT ASSOCIATION

In 1907, Frank Leland moved his club to Auburn Park on Seventy-ninth and Wentworth Avenue and sought a business alliance with black Chicago's emerging leadership. Leland's association with the new black leadership resulted in an effort by these "race men" to gain control of Chicago's growing black consumer market and establish a black professional league on a national scale. The creation of a commercial amusement enterprise, under the auspices of economic cooperation, became the means of achieving these goals.

Two important figures in the consolidation of Leland's ball club into a commercialized amusement and recreation enterprise were Robert R. Jackson and Beauregard Moseley. Jackson, born in 1870, was a Chicago native. He left school in the eighth grade to successfully work as a newsboy, bootblack, postal employee, and finally he established his own printing and publishing business. Moseley was active in politics at an early age. Born in Georgia, he came to Chicago just after 1890. Moseley was a lawyer and businessman and a strong advocate of cooperative business ventures. He lived in a predominantly white section of town, but his law practice drew heavily on the black community. He was also chief counsel of the Olivet Baptist Church, Chicago's largest African-American congregation.[23]

Leland, Moseley, and Jackson combined to form the Leland Giants Base Ball and Amusement Association (LGBAA). Incorporated in 1907, the LGBAA was more than just a baseball team; it was also a summer resort, skating rink, and restaurant. In 1908, the black-owned newspaper *Broad Ax* carried an advertisement offering stock options to the public. The objective of the advertisement was to raise funds for the club's new ballpark at Sixty-ninth and Halstead. The language employed typified the race rhetoric and racial solidarity that black Chicagoans advocated during the Progressive Era. It asked, "Are You In Favor Of The Race Owning and Operating This Immense And Well Paying Plant, Where More Than 1,100 Persons Will Be Employed, between May and October each year, where you can come without fear and Enjoy The Life and Freedom of a citizen unmolested or annoyed? The Answer can only be effectively given by subscribing for stock in this Corporation."[24]

These "race men" sought to establish an enterprise that would become a means of racial pride through self-help. The association also aided other institutions in the black community. It contributed annually to Provident Hospital, founded by Daniel Hale Williams, the country's best-known African-American physician and one of the outstanding surgeons of his day. On August 26, 1910, the Leland Giants played a benefit game for the hospital at Comiskey Park. The LGBAA became a venture that offered jobs to the black community, even as Moseley, Leland, and Jackson were turning a profit.[25]

At the same time, Leland made his only attempt to organize a black professional league. On November 9, 1907, the Indianapolis *Freeman* reported that a movement was put forth to form the National Colored League of Professional Ball Clubs. The effort to form this league was a clear exposition of the cooperative business philosophy. Under the direction of Leland, Elwood C. Knox, editor of the Freeman, and Ran Butler, the owner of the Indianapolis ABCs, baseball promoters encouraged race men in the leading midwestern and southern cities to form a stock company as a means of consolidation. The circuit was to be an eight team league with prospective cities to include Cincinnati, Cleveland, Louisville, Pittsburgh, Chicago, Indianapolis, Kansas City, Toledo, Detroit, Milwaukee, Memphis, Nashville, and Columbus, Ohio. In a series of meetings that took place from December 28, 1907, to January 25, 1908, the league directors elected officers and established guidelines for league entry. Leland was elected president and was the driving force behind the movement. For a club to be considered for admission it had to (1) be represented by a stock company fully organized and incorporated under state law; (2) secure a bond (the amount was not specified) determined by the league's board of directors; (3) pay $50 into the league treasury to cover expenses for league operations; and (4) secure a suitable ball park and have full support of the black press. In addition, a small percentage of the gate receipts from each city would be placed in the treasury. The season would run from May to September.[26]

Despite these organizers' efforts, the league died without throwing a pitch. Essentially, three factors led to its failure. First and foremost, there was a total lack of commitment by black baseball entrepreneurs in the aforementioned cities. According to the *Freeman,* only Chicago and Indianapolis made commitments to the enterprise. The *Freeman* also indicated that several black baseball magnates were totally against league formation, fearing it would damage their business. It appears that these black baseball entrepreneurs were reluctant to travel outside the regional format they had created for themselves. Prior to 1907, only the Cuban X Giants had ever made an extended barnstorming tour, and they were under white management. If, for example, clubs from Pittsburgh and Nashville were members of the league, it would increase the overhead expenses of the midwestern club to travel there. It would also create an unworkable format due to the majority of the prospective cities being in the Midwest.[27]

Finally, there was no clear-cut plan as to how this league would operate. In other words, there was no attempt to create a business system that would place the black game on a sound economic footing. Many of the proposals, including conditions for league entry were only suggestions. Nothing was agreed upon that indicated how the league would function. Ultimately, the failure of the league injured Frank Leland's credibility with the LGBAA's leadership. Throughout the remainder of the LGBAA's brief history, Leland would operate primarily as a figurehead within the organization. His effort to regain control of his ball club resulted in dissension within the LGBAA's organizers that would cause the association to crumble at its foundation.

INTERNAL DIVISION AND A SECOND FAILED LEAGUE

Internal division among the LGBAA organizers occurred because the multiple enterprises of the members of the association diverted their attention. This disharmony among the associations organizers was the direct result of several interacting influences: the Leland Giants emerging as the top touring team of the Midwest; Frank Leland's attempt to wrest control of the ball club away from Beauregard Moseley; and a formal ban on black traveling teams by Chicago's Park Owners Association. Although this internal dissension placed black baseball on shaky ground, it was instrumental in forming the structure of the black game in the Windy City in the Progressive Era.

The emergence of the Leland Giants as one of the country's top touring teams was due primarily to one man, Andrew "Rube" Foster. His emergence as their manager and booking agent marked the beginning of his dominance of midwestern black baseball. Foster was born in Calvert, Texas, in 1879, the son of a presiding elder of Calvert's Methodist Church. Devoutly religious, Foster neither drank nor allowed anyone to consume spirits in his household, although he was tolerant of it from others. Foster exhibited his organizational skills at a young age, operating a baseball team while in grade school. He left school in the eighth grade to pursue a career in baseball. By 1897, Poster was pitching for the Waco Yellow Jackets, a traveling team that toured Texas and the bordering states. In the spring of 1902, William S. Peters invited him to join his team, but as he sent no travel money the pitcher remained in Texas. Simultaneously, Leland had also invited Foster to join his club, initiating a stormy relationship between the two men. By mid-spring, Foster quit the Union Giants to join a white semipro team in Michigan. When its season ended, he headed east to play for the Cuban X Giants.[28]

From 1903 to 1906, Foster played for the Philadelphia Giants. Despite their success on the field, the Philadelphia Giants did not reap economic benefits for their exploits. As a result, Foster induced several of the players to jump their contracts at the end of the 1906 season. The player revolt led by Foster coincided with Leland's efforts to persuade the African-American flamethrower to manage his team. Foster accepted Leland's offer, and his first move was to release the players of the previous year despite Leland's opposition. It was evident that Foster wanted his own players, and he had just brought seven of them from the greatest team ever assembled. Next, due to Leland' failing health and his responsibilities as the newly elected Cook County Commissioner, Foster assumed the responsibilities of booking the team's games. From that time on, Foster established a business arrangement whereby gate receipts would be either divided in half or a substantial guarantee would be paid to attract the top teams.[29]

The Leland Giants' revised managerial structure was integrated into the LGBAA's corporate configuration. On January 21, 1909, the association elected the following officers: Frank Leland, president; Robert Jackson, vice president; Beauregard Moseley, secretary and treasurer; and Rube Foster, manager and captain of the team. With Leland, Moseley, and Jackson supervising the LGBAA's other businesses and Foster booking the baseball games, enough capital was generated to run an adequate operation. The LGBAA finished the year with a postseason series against the National League Chicago Cubs. Although the Cubs swept the Giants in three games, both the series and the revised organizational structure elevated the Leland Giants from the ranks of a stay-at-home to the Midwest's top touring team.[30]

From 1907 to 1910, Foster perfected the barnstorming schedule that would be his trademark for the next decade. On February 20, 1907, the Indianapolis *Freeman* reported that the Leland Giants would embark on a spring training tour. It marked the first time that a semiprofessional club that was both black owned and operated had accomplished this feat. Two years later, the *Freeman* reported that the Leland Giants had traveled 4,465 miles playing both black and white teams in Memphis, Birmingham, Fort Worth, Austin, San Antonio, Prairie View State, and Houston. The Leland Giants traveled in their own private Pullman car, as a means of upholding their reputation as an elite black independent club. In October 1910, after winning twenty straight games in the East and West, the Leland Giants made their first trip to Cuba. More important, Leland Giants' trip to the Cuban island served as a means of promoting the LGBAA. Along with the American League Detroit Tigers, the Leland Giants played the top Cuban clubs including the Havannas—an aggregate of black stars that included John Henry Lloyd and Grant "Home Run" Johnson—and the Alemendares. While the Lelands won the majority of their games, they lost a tough series to the Alemendares.[31]

By 1909, the Leland Giants' success produced a conflict of interest among the team's management. With Moseley supervising the LGBAA's other businesses and Foster managing the ball club, Leland recognized his diminished role within the organization. As a result, he attempted to regain control of the Leland Giants, but the association's investors thought it was in the corporation's best interests to retain Foster as manager. Therefore, in a hostile takeover, Moseley and Foster united to force Leland out. Foster's alliance with Moseley made the split inevitable. In 1910, Leland went to court to prevent Foster and Moseley using the name Leland Giants, but he was unsuccessful. Not only did Leland lose his team, but he lost his interests in the LGBAA's other businesses as well.[32]

In response to being forced out, Leland created in 1910 the Chicago Giants in partnership with Robert Jackson and A. H. Garrett. His goal was to make his Giants a top touring team to compete against the Leland Giants, and he also sought to have them play the top semipro clubs in the area. To accomplish this, Leland raided his old club for players, signing stars like Walter Ball and Pete Booker. Unfortunately for him the Park Owners Association thwarted his aspirations when it prohibited the scheduling of games between black traveling teams from outside the Chicago area. Its reason for this ban was that local patrons complained about the lack of contests being scheduled between some of the regional clubs. The *New York Age* speculated that the prohibition could have emerged as a result of top Cuban teams invading the area for the past two years. In addition, the Philadelphia Giants had also made a couple of barnstorming tours, playing both the top black and white semipro clubs in the Windy City. Race was assuredly an issue in the POA's decision. The POA believed that the rise of both the Leland and Chicago Giants to the status of touring teams, coupled with the arrival of Cuban clubs and the Philadelphia Giants, was a threat to its autonomy. Traveling teams touring the Windy City meant a big payday for both black and white semipro squads, but only clubs that had their own parks could enjoy this luxury. Consequently, both the POA and local teams with no parks had a vested interest in keeping the black traveling teams out.[33]

The color ban on traveling teams appears to have directly impacted the Chicago Giants. To remain in the City League, the Giants' management had to refrain from scheduling games with both black touring and black traveling teams. The conservative Leland yielded to the demand. In 1911, his Giants did not tour the South, playing only a local schedule, but the following year, it dropped out of the Chicago City League. Three factors were instrumental in the Giants' departure. First, Jackson left the club to pursue a successful career in politics. He was a significant investor in the enterprise, and his loss crippled the club. Second, the absence of this capital made it difficult for Leland to compete against the Leland Giants, and the court settlement forced him to vacate Auburn Park. Finally, Leland's failing health became a serious concern, and within two years he died at the age of forty-five. In 1913, the Chicago Giants disbanded; two years later Joe Green, the club's shortstop, reorganized the team as a weekend enterprise, passing the hat to meet expenses.[34]

Moseley had higher aspirations in mind, and neither the POA's ban nor Leland's efforts to put his former club out of business hindered them. As early as 1909, the young black lawyer advocated the need for blacks to organize their own professional league. He also recognized that the continual territorial invasion and the raiding of player rosters were destructive forces and had to be eliminated. In addition, Moseley recognized that the color line drawn by the POA would also adversely impact the LGBAA's ability to generate revenue. But the proliferation of black teams from the South and Midwest made it feasible, in Moseley's view, to form a black professional league.[35]

In 1910, Moseley called together a group of black baseball men from throughout the Midwest and the South. The proposed league was more than just a response to the color line, it was another exposition of the doctrine of self-help. In his statement of purpose, Moseley indicated that blacks "are already forced out of the game from a national standpoint" and find it increasingly difficult to play white semiprofessional teams at the local level. This "presages the day when there will be [no opportunities for black baseball players], except the Negro comes to his own rescue by organizing and patronizing the game successfully, which would of itself force recognition from white minor leagues to play us and share in the receipts." Moseley added, "let those who would serve the Race assist it in holding its back up . . . organizing an effort to secure . . . the best club of ball players possible."[36]

The prospective owners first met on December 30, 1910. Moseley was elected temporary chairman and Felix H. Payne of Kansas City temporary secretary. Eight cities were represented: Chicago, New Orleans, Mobile, Louisville, St. Louis, Columbus, Kansas City, Missouri, and Kansas City, Kansas. Moseley devised a twenty-point plan explaining how the league should operate. Utilizing the cooperative business philosophy, Moseley suggested that eight race men in each city pool their resources and form a stock company. The league projected an operating capital of $2,500 with each club paying roughly $300. Half the league's umpires would be black and paid five dollars per game. A reserve list would be developed, and players who jumped their contracts would be banned from the league. Finally, an effort would be made to limit the league to one franchise per city.[37]

The league generated a lot of enthusiasm the following year, and rumors persisted of other cities joining the loop, but it died stillborn. Like in the previous organizational effort, there was an unwillingness of investors to come forth. At its inaugural meeting, only Chicago, New Orleans, and Kansas City, Kansas, were represented by investors, the remaining five being represented by fans. Second, these entrepreneurs were not willing to follow the Leland Giants' lead in embarking on extended barnstorming tours. The majority of these clubs would not venture too far outside their established regions. Finally, migration had significantly expanded the black populations in midwestern cities, but it was still insufficient to create a market to establish both territorial regions and set population requirements for a prospective city for league entry. Even in Chicago, the black community was not large enough to support three teams—the Leland Giants, Chicago Giants, and Union Giants—not to mention becoming a viable territory in a league. It would have required maintaining the symbiotic business relationship with white semipro clubs, and the POA's ban on traveling teams made this problematic.

In 1911, Foster split with Moseley and formed the Chicago American Giants. It is not clear what led Foster to make a break with the LGBAA, but what is evident is that both the color ban and two attempts to form a league ending in failure were instrumental in his decision. The oversaturation of Chicago's black baseball market would become more of a factor when instead of having three teams vying for the Chicago black community's disposable income, now the were four: the American Giants, the Leland Giants, the Chicago Giants, and the Union Giants.

FROM PLAYER-MANAGER TO DOMINANT PROMOTER

Internal division within the LGBAA resulted in Rube Foster becoming an unpopular man in black Chicago. The actions of Leland organizing the Chicago Giants and Moseley forming a coalition of black business professionals were efforts to compete against Foster and put him out of business. The black press also took jabs at Foster, providing negative coverage and turning public opinion against him. In an effort to win over both the press and the black community, Foster made a series of moves that included: forming a partnership with John Schorling, a white tavern owner; expanding his barnstorming tour both during the winter and the local season; reviving the East-West colored championship; and fostering good press and community relations as a means of changing his public image.

Following the break with Foster, Moseley organized a booster coalition from the black community. The Leland Giant Booster Club (LGBC) was an aggregate of black middle-class businessmen and professionals. For example, the LGBC president, Jesse Boiling, was a restaurant owner who donated his Burlington Buffet as the club's official headquarters. T. W. Allen, the club's secretary, was a city inspector. Other members of the coalition included the editors of Chicago's two leading black newspapers, Robert Abbott of the *Chicago Defender* and Julius Taylor of the *Broad Ax*.[38]

The formation of the LGBC exemplified the cooperative business philosophy prevalent among the new leadership. The venture could serve as a means of promoting one another's businesses. One of the booster club's functions was to organize activities surrounding the Leland Giants' local season that had become ritualized in the prewar years. For example, at the opening of each season, the Giants had what was known as "Flag Raising Day." It was equivalent to throwing out the first ball on opening day of the major league baseball season. Another event the LGBC staged consisted of a touring car, known as the Red Devil, parading through the streets to the ballpark. But the booster club's main objective was to provide a united front against both Leland's Chicago Giants and Foster's American Giants.[39]

Despite the LGBC's enthusiasm, the venture failed as it lacked the financial and political resources to be effective. This rather conservative coalition also had no allies in the local government. Although a black political machine was being organized at this time, it did not become instrumental in black community affairs until after World War I. By 1912, the LGBC ceased to exist.[40]

Moseley had other obstacles confronting him. He was engaged in several business ventures at once besides organizing a baseball league and booking games for the Lelands, and he probably did not delegate authority to booster club members or have an adequate management team to supervise his many operations. While Moseley attempted to reach the black patrons, his facilities were located outside the black belt, where increased white hostility made venturing unpleasant for Chicago's African Americans. The African-American working class could not afford these amusements and the middle class was not large enough to sustain them. To make matters worse, Moseley had just moved into and renovated the ballpark on Sixty-ninth and Halstead, no doubt at large expense. The obstacles were more than the LGBAA could bear. By 1912, the skating rink closed for good and the Leland Giants were relegated to a local club.[41]

While the LGBAA was in a state of decline, Foster still faced opposition from the black press. Julius Taylor was disgusted by the baseball situation. In a 1912 editorial he expressed his disenchantment with the unwillingness of blacks to organize themselves as well as commit to this venture. The *Broad Ax* editor further noted that the Leland Giants' success proved to be its misfortune. Rivalry and a desire for control led to fragmentation in an effort to "compete for patronage and prowess of the Leland Giants." The issue that most upset Taylor was that the revenue baseball generated went into the coffers of white men. That same year, the *Chicago Defender* began to take jabs at Foster because it was also upset over the revenue "going over to the other race." The black newspaper insisted that this was "why so many are pulling against Rube." In addition, it was critical of the lack of support the American Giants gave black institutions in the community, primarily the *Chicago Defender*.[42]

In spite of this opposition, Foster made a series of moves that enabled his rise as dominant promoter. First was his partnership with John M. Schorling. Schorling had operated a sandlot club in Chicago for several years. He leased the grounds of the old White Sox park on Thirty-ninth and Shields after the American League team moved into their new stadium. The White Sox had torn down the old grandstand, and Schorling built a new one with a seating capacity of 9,000. He approached Foster with an offer of a partnership. Foster now had a ballpark to operate in and Schorling had the best booking agent and field manager outside of organized baseball. Over the next fifteen years they became the best management team at the semipro level.[43]

Several factors led to Foster's success. Unlike the LGBAA, whose facilities were outside the black belt, the Chicago American Giants' park was accessible to the majority of the black population. The better location facilitated gate receipts instrumental to the attraction of the top touring and traveling teams to the Midwest. More significantly, the relocation allowed Foster to accomplish what Moseley failed to achieve: corner the black market. Foster also focused his promotion solely on baseball, and he knew everything about the game. His objective was to present the finest product possible to Chicago's black community, which meant securing the best talent available and developing a winning reputation. To achieve such standards, a management team committed to baseball had to be in place. Schorling had prior baseball experience and shared Foster's objectives. This was an unpopular decision as it required that Foster go outside the black community to achieve his goals.

Even more significant, Foster's business approach became the model for future black baseball entrepreneurs to emulate. He was a businessman first and a race man second. At no time did Foster show any indications of severing any business relations with white semipros; in fact he attempted to strengthen them. Yet because these business connections increased his profits, Foster could help serve Chicago's black community by conducting several benefit games to raise funds for civic institutions. In essence, Foster had achieved the objectives spelled out in the compilation of ideologies commonly attributed to Booker T. Washington, building a segregated enterprise within the framework of a national economy. In other words, the segregated enterprise—the Chicago American Giants—through the creation of annual booking arrangements with both black and white semipros, operated successfully within the national economy of semiprofessional baseball.

From 1912 to 1915, Foster established a barnstorming tour on the West Coast during the winter months, and the Chicago American Giants became the first black semipro team to regularly play weekly games. The American Giants played in the California Winter League, a conglomerate of teams comprising former and current major and minor league players and teams from the Pacific Coast, Southern, and Northwest leagues. The American Giants won the California League Championship in its first season. On July 5, 1913, the *Chicago Defender* reported that the American Giants celebrated winning the championship with a parade, unfurling a banner and displaying their new uniforms. In addition,

Foster's alliance with Schorling enabled him to schedule games with white semipro teams during the week. Foster had now established the structure that ensured the successful operation of a black semiprofessional team.[44]

Foster's work on reviving the East-West Colored Championship was also instrumental to his success. On July 5, 1913, the *Chicago Defender* reported an upcoming championship series between the Chicago American Giants and the Lincoln Giants of New York. A series of thirteen games were scheduled in Chicago and New York. After nine games the series was tied at four victories apiece and one tie. But the Lincoln Giants won the final four games in New York earning the right to be crowned "World's Colored Champions." Although Foster's American Giants had lost the series, he had won the hearts and minds of Chicago's black community.[45]

Finally, Foster and Schorling had learned their lesson well regarding press and community relations. In the prewar years they set a precedent that became a constant throughout the war years. In addition to raising funds for civic institutions, Schorling donated the use of the ballpark for local community activities, like the Chicago Church League championship game. Foster also developed positive press relations. He began by granting an interview with the *Chicago Defender* providing readers with insights about his early career in baseball. Throughout the war years, he granted many interviews and become a local patron as well.[46]

The California Winter League championship and the East-West Colored Championship brought Foster accolades from a prominent member of Chicago's black middle class and on the sport pages of the *Chicago Defender.* Julius Avendorph, the "Ward McAllister of the South Side," was an assistant to the president of the Pullman company. He became "personally acquainted with more millionaires than any other colored man in Chicago." From 1886 up until 1910, Avendorph was considered "Chicago's undisputed social leader." Writing in the *Chicago Defender* on April 5, 1913, Avendorph extolled the American Giants for "their high class baseball playing . . . [and] for their gentlemanly conduct on the ball field." Avendorph added that the American Giants were "an example that lots of white clubs can take pattern from." When some of Chicago's black patrons berated Foster for raising his ticket prices, the *Chicago Defender* came to his defense for the first time. Chicago's black fans would "have to pay for quality and they [the fans] have certainly got their money's worth lately, referring to the colored championship." Moreover, the *Chicago Defender* reminded its readers that many of the Windy City's black fans "never knew what it was to see a game among those of their race unless forced to go to 79th Street . . . . Now it is a stone's throw from their homes."[47]

EPILOGUE

Rube Foster's American Giants operated as a segregated enterprise while maintaining a symbiotic business relationship with white semiprofessional teams. He sustained a booking pattern with the top black and white semipros on a consistent basis. In spite of the obstacles that confronted him, Foster had managed to integrate his operation within a segregated market and a national one. Because of the press coverage in Chicago and Indianapolis, Foster's American Giants had become a source of racial pride and solidarity among African Americans in the Midwest.

Despite Foster's rise as a dominant promoter, Chicago's market was still a saturated one. Joe Green continued to operate the Chicago Giants, while William S. Peters managed the

Union Giants until 1923. Robert Gilkerson, a former ballplayer, assumed control of the club and renamed it Gilkerson's Union Giants. But Green, Peters, and Gilkerson were not as ambitious as Foster, choosing to remain weekend operators and passing the hat to cover expenses. During the years of the Great Migration, Foster would absorb these clubs under his booking control, marking the beginning of his autonomy in the Midwest. In addition, Foster would make rental agreements with major league owners, like Frank Navin in Detroit, and would finance clubs like the Detroit Stars, to gain controlling interest. This midwestern alliance would form the foundation for the Negro National League in 1920. More importantly, at the community level, Foster accomplished what previous black baseball entrepreneurs sought to achieve in creating an institution that served as a source of racial pride and solidarity through self-help.[48]

NOTES

1. General histories on black baseball from the 1980s and 1990s include: Sol White, *History of Colored Base Ball, with Other Documents on the Early Black Game 1886–1936* (Lincoln: University of Nebraska Press, 1995); Richard Bak, *Turkey Stearnes and the Detroit Stars: The Negro Leagues in Detroit, 1919–1933* (Detroit: Wayne State University Press, 1994); Phil Dixon and Patrick J. Hannigan, *The Negro Baseball Leagues, 1867–1955: A Photographic History* (Mattituck, NY: Amereon House, 1992); Janet Bruce, *Kansas City Monarchs: Champions of Black Baseball* (Lawrence: University of Kansas Press, 1985); Donn Rogosin, *Invisible Men: Life in Baseball's Negro Leagues* (New York: Atheneum, 1983); Linda Zeimer, "Chicago's Negro Leagues," *Chicago History* (Winter 1994): 36–51. The most comprehensive community study examining black baseball is Rob Ruck's *Sandlot Seasons: Sport in Black Pittsburgh* (Urbana: University of Illinois Press, 1987). Neil Lanctot provides an excellent account on the business practices of early black baseball entrepreneurs, as well as the origins of white semiprofessional baseball in *Fair Dealing and Clean Playing: The Hilldale Club and the Development of Black Professional Baseball, 1910–1932* (Jefferson, NC: McFarland 1994). On the origins of white semiprofessional baseball, see also Harold Seymour, *Baseball: The People's Game* (New York: Oxford University Press, 1990). For a discussion of where the recent works on black baseball's place in the broader baseball history, see Larry R. Gerlach, "Not Quite Ready for Prime Time: Baseball History, 1983–1993," *Journal of Sport History* 21(1994): 121–9.

2. For an account on the notion of operating a segregated enterprise within the fabric of a national economy, see Vishnu V. Oak, *The Negro's Adventure in General Business* (Yellow Springs, OH, The Antioch Press, 1949).

3. *Abstract of the Eleventh Census: 1890* (Washington, D.C.: Government Printing Office, 1894), 34; *Abstract of the Twelfth Census of the United States* (Washington, D.C.: Government Printing Office 1902), 103–4; *Thirteenth Census of The United States: Taken in the Year 1910* (Washington, D.C.: Government Printing Office, 1913), 95; Allan H. Spear, *Black Chicago: The Making of a Negro Ghetto* (Chicago: University of Chicago Press, 1967), 11–27; Thomas L. Philpott, *The Slum and the Ghetto: Neighborhood Deterioration and Middle Class Reform, Chicago 1880–1930* (New York: Oxford University Press, 1978),119,147–8.

4. Spear, *Black Chicago*, 11–7.

5. David M. Katzman, *Before the Ghetto: Black Detroit in the Nineteenth Century* (Urbana: University of Illinois Press, 1973), 67–80; Spear, *Black Chicago*, 91–110; James R. Grossman, *Land of Hope: Chicago, Black Southerners, and the Great Migration* (Chicago: University of Chicago Press, 1989), 127.

6. Grossman, *Land of Hope*; Humbert S. Nelli, *Italians in Chicago 1880–1930: A Study in Ethnic Mobility* (New York: Oxford University Press, 1970), 23–5.

7. Illinois state law and treatment of African Americans outside the black belt in Spear, *Black Chicago*, 41–2.

8. The rise of the new black leadership illustrates the diverse, and often divisive, class structure at the turn of the century. Between 1865 and 1900, black leaders' primary focus was on securing equal rights for African Americans. They were absorbed in campaigns to secure the ballot, assure an integrated school system, pass and then broaden the Civil Rights Act, and finally bring suits under the act. Any attempt to organize a separate black institution was met with stiff opposition from those who regarded it as a form of self-segregation. One reason why the new black leadership was attracted

to recreation and amusement enterprises was the funds required to start such an endeavor were both short- and long-term in character. In other words, they did not require a substantial financial investment. See Abram L. Harris, *The Negro as Capitalist: Study of Banking and Business among American Negroes* (Philadelphia: The American Academy of Political and Social Service, 1936), 53–6. For accounts on black middle class formation, see E. Franklin Frazier, *Black Bourgeoisie* (Glencoe, IL: Free Press, 1957); Bart Landry, *The New Black Middle Class* (Berkeley: University of California Press, 1997). For accounts on the old black leadership in Chicago, see Spear, *Black Chicago,* 51–70; Grossman, *Land of Hope,* 123–60.

9. Earl Ofari, *The Myth of Black Capitalism* (New York: Monthly Review Press, 1970), 11–48. For the cooperative business philosophy as an outgrowth of the ideology of self-help, see Louis Harlan, *Booker T Washington: The Making of a Black Leader* (New York: Oxford University Press, 1972), 204–71. For a detailed discussion on the Wabash Avenue YMCA, see Spear, *Black Chicago,* 100–1.

10. Seymour, *Baseball,* 259–75.

11. For an account on the early business practices of professional baseball, see Gerald W. Scully, *The Business of Major League Baseball* (Chicago: University of Chicago Press, 1989), 1–12. In the 1880s, the Cuban X Giants attracted clubs from either National League or American Association with a substantial guarantee. See for example, "The Browns Strike," *Sporting Life,* September 21, 1887, p. 4.

12. Seymour, *Baseball,* 265–70.

13. For an account on Chicago's sophisticated park system, see Michael P. McCarthy, "Politics and the Parks Chicago Businessmen and the Recreation Movement," *Journal of Illinois State Historical Society* 65(1972): 158–72; see also Steven A. Riess, *City Games: The Evolution of American Urban Society and the Rise of Sports* (Urbana: University of Illinois Press, 1991), 128–39.

14. "No Color Line," *Indianapolis Freeman* September 21, 1907, p. 7; "Park Owners Association," *Chicago Defender* June 4, 1910, p. 4.

15. Wilson Jeremiah Moses, *The Golden Age of Black Nationalism 1850–1925* (Hamden, CT: Archon Books, 1978), 83–102. On the gospel of work and wealth, see Samuel R. Spencer, *Booker T Washington and the Negro's Place in America* (Boston: Little, Brown, 1955), 108–24.

16. James A. Riley, *The Biographical Encyclopedia of the Negro Baseball Leagues* (New York: Carroll & Graf Pub., 1994),474–75; Dixon and Hannigan, *Negro Baseball,* 96–7; Robert Peterson, *Only the Ball Was White: A History of Legendary Black Players and All-Black Professional Teams* (New York: Oxford University Press, 1970), 63–4; White, *History,* 29; "Frank Leland Laid to Rest," *Chicago Defender,* November 21, 1914, p. 5; "The Chicago Giants Base Ball Club," *Chicago Defender,* January 22, 1910, p. 1.

17. The estimated attendance figures for black baseball was derived from examining several newspaper accounts from both the *Chicago Broad Ax* and the *Chicago Defender* from 1907 to 1915. White, *History,* 26. See for example, "Leland Giants Making a Record," *Indianapolis Freeman* August 1, 1908, p. 7; "Lelands," *Indianapolis Freeman,* August 3, 1909, p. 4; "The Chicago Giants Show Class," *Chicago Defender,* October 29, 1910, p. 3.

18. While the notion of a colored championship could be traced back to the Philadelphia Pythians of the late 1860s, this series as a commercial endeavor coincided with the rise of black semi-professional teams in the 1880s. For a detailed account of this phenomenon, see Michael E. Lomax, "Black Baseball, Black Community, Black Entrepreneurs: The History of the Negro National and Eastern Colored Leagues, 1880–1930," (Ph.D. diss., Ohio State University, 1996), 68–77; idem, *Operating By Any Means Necessary: Black Baseball and Black Entrepreneurship in the National Pastime* (Syracuse, NY: Syracuse University Press, 2003).

19. It should be noted that in 1896 the ball players with the Cuban Giants broke with John M. Bright and signed with Edward B. Lamarant and became the Cuban X Giants. Bright continued to operate a ball club, and as a means of averting confusion, renamed it the Genuine Cuban Giants. For an account on the origins of the Page Fence Giants, see Thomas Powers, "The Page Fence Giants Play Ball," *Chronicle: The Quarterly Magazine of the Historical Society of Michigan* (Spring 1983): 14–8. For accounts regarding the origins of the Columbia Giants, see White, *History,* 28–31, 38–40; Dixon and Hannigan, *Negro Baseball,* 96–7. For Patterson's background see Riley, *Encyclopedia,* 609–10.

20. White, *History,* 28–31, 38–40. White had stated that the Unions and the Columbia Giants were at "loggerheads" with each other.

21. White, *History,* 38; Lanctot, *Fair Dealing,* 32.

22. Zeimer, "Chicago's Negro Leagues," 37; White, *History,* 39; Dixon and Hannigan, *Negro Baseball,* 97.

23. Harold F. Gosnell, *Negro Politicians: The Rise of Negro Politics in Chicago* (Chicago: University of Chicago Press, 1935), 67–8; "Major General R. R. Jackson, Assistant Supt. Armour Station Financial Secretary Appomattox Club," *Chicago Broad Ax,* December 27, 1902, p. 1; "Col. B. F. Mose-

ley," *Chicago Broad Ax,* March 30, 1901, p. 1; "Col. Beauregard F. Moseley, Lawyer, Orator, and Property Holder," *Chicago Broad Ax,* December 29, 1906, p. 1, p. 5.

24. "Opening of the Chateau de la Plaisance," *Chicago Broad Ax,* November 2, 1907, p. 1; "The Chateau de la Plaisance," *Chicago Broad Ax,* November 16, 1907, p. 1. For the advertisement offering stock options to the public, see any issue of the *Chicago Broad Ax* in 1908. For a discussion on race rhetoric and racial solidarity advocated during the Progressive Era, see Moses, *The Golden Age,* 83–102.

25. For their yearly contributions to Provident Hospital, see "Honor to Whom Honor Is Due," *Chicago Defender,* May 14, 1910, p. 4; for the benefit game for the hospital, see "Giants Take Benefit Game," *Chicago Defender,* August 27, 1910, p. 5.

26. "A National League of Professional Negro Baseball Clubs for Next Season," *Indianapolis Freeman,* November 9, 1907, p. 6; "Growing Interest Taken in Proposed League," *Indianapolis Freeman,* November 16, 1907, p. 6; "To Organize Colored League," *Indianapolis Freeman,* November 23, 1907, p. 6; "League Meeting a Successful One," *Indianapolis Freeman,* December 28, 1907, p. 6; "A Successful Meeting Is Sighted," *Indianapolis Freeman,* January 25, 1908, p. 6.

27. While the evidence is limited, one newspaper account suggests that William S. Peters attempted to block league formation by building a park "in the colored center of the population on the South Side, which would affect the Leland Giants materially." See "Make War on Leland Giants," *Indianapolis Freeman,* February 1, 1908, p. 6. For an account regarding club owners against league formation, see "League Does Not Fear Outlaws," *Indianapolis Freeman,* December 28, 1907, p. 6; "An Understanding about the League," *Indianapolis Freeman,* February 15, 1908, p. 6.

28. "A Great Historical Account of a Great Game of Ball," *Indianapolis Freeman,* September 14, 1907, p. 6; "Baseball's Greatest Figure Dead," *Chicago Defender,* December 13, 1930, 1, p. 14; John B. Holway, *Blackball Stars: Negro League Pioneers* (New York: Carroll & Graf, 1988), 9–10; Charles E. Whitehead, *A Man and His Diamonds* (New York: Vantage Press, 1980), 3, 18–19; Peterson, *Only the Ball was White,* 104–5; George E. Mason, "Rube Foster Chats about His Career," *Chicago Defender,* February 20, 1915, p. 10.

29. Mason, "Rube Foster," 10; Holway, *Blackball Stars,* 13; Whitehead, *A Man,* 22–3; Peterson, *Only the Ball Was White,* 107–8.

30. "Chateau Rink Notes," *Chicago Broad Ax,* January 30, 1909, p. 2. Cubs series in Zeimer, "Chicago's Negro Leagues," 39. In the following years Foster would issue challenges for postseason series with the Cubs; none were ever accepted. See for example, "Rube Foster Challenges the Cubs," *Chicago Defender,* October 18, 1913, p. 8.

31. "Champion Leland Giants to Go South for Spring Training," *Indianapolis Freeman,* February 20, 1907, p. 7; "Leland Giants Complete a Successful Southern Trip," *Indianapolis Freeman,* May 15, 1909, p. 7; "Chateau Rink Notes," *Chicago Broad Ax,* October 8, 1910, p. 2; "Leland Giants to Play Baseball in Cuba," *Chicago Defender,* October 8, 1910, p. 3; Lester Walton, "Baseball Flourishing in Cuba," *New York Age,* December 8, 1910, p. 6.

32. Andrew Foster, "Negro Base Ball," *Indianapolis Freeman,* December 23, 1911, p. 16; Peterson, *Only the Ball was White,* 108; "Frank C. Leland Enjoined from Using the Name Leland Giants," *Chicago Broad Ax,* April 23, 1910, p. 2.

33. In 1906, the National Association of Colored Professional Base Ball Clubs was formed. This association served as means for eastern black clubs, primarily from New York, to play Chicago City League clubs. In other words, this association formalized scheduling commitments between eastern and western black clubs, while at the same time, curbed the destructive practice of player raiding. It was through this organization that Cuban clubs from Gotham and the Philadelphia Giants played in Chicago. For a discussion of this organization see Lomax, "Black Baseball," 207–51. "The Chicago Giants Baseball Club," *Chicago Defender,* January 22, 1910, p. 1; Jack Pot, "Bars Alien Colored Clubs," *Chicago Defender,* July 23, 1910, p. 3; "Fans Object to Color Line," *Chicago Defender,* July 23, 1910, p. 1; Lester Walton, "Colored Teams Barred in Chicago," *New York Age,* July 21, 1910, p. 6; for the barnstorming tours of the Philadelphia Giants to the Midwest, see "ABC'S Easy for Giants," *Indianapolis Freeman* August 1, 1908, p. 7; Lester Walton, "Philadelphia Giants Defeat Leland Giants," *New York Age,* August 19, 1909, p. 6; idem., "Philadelphia Giants Win in Tenth," June 30, 1910, p. 6.

34. Lester Walton, "No Colored Team in Chicago League," *New York Age,* April 18, 1912, p. 6; "Frank Leland Laid to Rest," *Chicago Defender,* November 21, 1914, p. 5. For Leland vacating Auburn Park, see "The Chicago Giants in their New Home," *Chicago Defender,* June 25, 1910, p. 1.

35. For Moseley's efforts to form a black professional league, see "Attorney B. R. Moseley Favors the Formation of National Negro Baseball League,"

Chicago Broad Ax, November 26, 1910; "Call for a Conference for Persons Interested in the Formation of a National Negro Baseball League," *Chicago Broad Ax,* December 17, 1910, p. 2.

36. "Big Negro National Baseball League Formed," *Chicago Defender,* December 31, 1910, p. 1; "Big Negro National Baseball League Formed," *Chicago Broad Ax,* December 31, 1910, p. 1; "A Baseball Appeal of a Worthy Undertaking by a Worthy Men; Read and Respond," *Chicago Broad Ax,* January 21, 1911, p. 2.

37. *Ibid.*

38. For the activities and membership of the booster coalition see any issue in either the *Chicago Defender* or the Broad Ax from May to June 1911.

39. "Diamond Dust," *Chicago Defender,* May 20, 1911, p. 4; " 'Boosters' Ukase from the President." *Chicago Defender,* May 27, 1911, p. 4.

40. For a discussion of black Chicago's political situation in the prewar years, see Gosnell, *Negro Politicians,* 65–7, 81–3; see also Spear, *Black Chicago,* 118–26.

41. For the closing of the skating rink, see "The Chateau Rink," *Chicago Defender,* February 25, 1911, p. 3. The Leland Giants moved into the ballpark on Sixty-ninth and Halstead in 1910. See "Moseley's Leland Giants to Have New Park," *Chicago Defender,* March 12, 1910, p. 1.

42. "Baseball," *Chicago Broad Ax,* May 18, 1912, p. 1; "Here and There," *Chicago Defender,* July 12, 1913, p. 5; "Sporting," *Chicago Defender,* August 2, 1913, p. 3.

43. Peterson, *Only the Ball was White,* 108.

44. "Rube Foster's Review on Baseball," *Indianapolis Freeman,* December 28, 1912, p. 7; Frank Young, "Local Sports," *Chicago Defender,* March 22, 1913, p. 3; idem., "American Giants Lose," *Chicago Defender,* July 5, 1913, p. 8. As the *Chicago Defender* grew, the American Giants received better coverage.

45. "American Giants Lose," 8; "Sporting," *Chicago Defender,* August 9, 1913, p. 7; Lester Walton, "American Giants in New York," *New York Age,* July 10, 1913, p. 6; idem., "Lincoln Win Series," *New York Age,* July 24, 1913, p. 6.

46. "Benefit for the Old Folks Home," *Chicago Defender,* August 16, 1913, p. 8; Mason, "Foster Chats about his Career," 10.

47. For Julius Avendorph's background, see Spear, *Black Chicago,* 65–6; Julius Avendorph, "Rube Foster and His American Giants," *Chicago Defender,* April 5, 1913, p. 7; "Here and There," *Chicago Defender,* August 9, 1913, p. 7.

48. For an account on Rube Foster's midwestern alliance during the years of the Great Migration, see Lomax, "Black Baseball," 290–325.

3

YEAR OF THE COMET
Jack Johnson versus Jim Jeffries, July 4, 1910

Randy Roberts

"IT AMUSES ME TO hear this talk of Jeffries claiming the championship. Why, when a Mayor leaves office he's an ex-Mayor, isn't he? When a champion leaves the ring he's an ex-champion. Well, that is Jeffries; if he wants to try to get the championship back then I'm willing to take him on." Johnson was tired of hearing about Jeffries as if the former champion were still the title-holder. In fact, that was just what many white Americans believed. They believed Johnson's claim lacked legitimacy, that if Jeffries had not retired, Johnson would not be champion, which was true, since Jeffries would never have broken the color barrier. At best, Johnson was viewed as a regent, a temporary ruler who would step aside once Jeffries decided to resume his reign. And throughout 1909, as Johnson humiliated one white pretender after another, the pressure mounted for Jeffries once again to raise high his scepter.[1]

Few if any fights in history generated as much interest as the 1910 Johnson-Jeffries match. The Johnson-Burns and Johnson-Ketchel affairs were mere warm-ups; the 1910 fight was for all "the racial marbles." From the very first, it was advertised as a match of civilization and virtue against savagery and baseness. As early as April 1909 the *Chicago Tribune* realized what was at stake. It printed a picture of a cute young blond girl pointing a finger at the reader; underneath was the caption: "Please, Mr. Jeffries, are you going to fight Mr. Johnson?"[2] Her call was as clear and her point as straight as Kitchener's in his famous Great War poster. Humanity needed Jeffries. He had inherited the White Man's Burden and he could not plead retirement to cloak his weariness.

The year 1910 was the center point of Johnson's life. It was a year that a Greek dramatist would have loved, for it saw both his greatest triumph and the actions that led inexorably to his fall. During those twelve months Johnson was engulfed by restless energy. He moved about like a caged lion, seldom spending more than a night or two in any one city before traveling to another town. Always calm and pleasant in public, in his private affairs he was often violent and mean. The speed of his life was becoming increasingly difficult to control, but he did not—or could not—take his foot off the accelerator.

Johnson left California a few days after his fight with Ketchel. Belle Schreiber, his mistress, went with him, as did George Little, his manager, and a prostitute he was seeing named Lillian St. Clair, who had worked alongside Belle at the Everleigh Club. They rolled across the country in style, celebrating the entire way. Part of the way they traveled by train, sleeping and dining in the first-class cars. After Chicago they rode in Johnson's automobile, driven by his white chauffeur, Mervin Jacobowski. Parties were held in Johnson's honor in Chicago, Indianapolis, Pittsburgh, New York, and Philadelphia. It was a high time, and Johnson was the main attraction.[3]

The money, the success, the fame, the smile, the body—women now more than ever were attracted to Johnson. In New York he met Etta Terry Duryea, whom he would eventually marry. She was a sporting lady, though technically not a prostitute. Born in Hempstead, Long Island, and brought up in a fashionable section of Brooklyn, Etta had married Charles C. Duryea, an Eastern horse-racing patron. The marriage did not last long, but even after the two separated Etta continued to attend the races. One afternoon at the Coney Island track she met Johnson, and shortly thereafter the two began living together, Etta taking the unofficial title "Mrs. Jack Johnson." About her there was a certain sense of sadness. Her beauty was of a haunting sort—cold, distant, aloof. Her hair and eyes were dark, her chin pointed and dimpled. She had a beautifully shaped mouth, but one that appeared unused to smiling. In pictures her lips are always locked in a perpetual pout. But it was her eyes that registered the real sadness. They seemed to stare without seeing, as if they knew all too well that sight was not worth the effort of focus. It is difficult to look at pictures of Etta and still be surprised that she committed suicide.[4]

When Johnson left New York for Philadelphia, Etta went along. So too did Belle and Hattie. The two prostitutes were used to the arrangement, but Etta was not. There were several scenes, but nothing Johnson could not handle. The three stayed in separate hotels and waited for Johnson. That was his normal procedure when traveling with more than one woman. At any time in the day or night he might make a brief appearance for the purpose of intercourse, but he usually left after a short stay. Belle and Hattie, as prostitutes, were accustomed to such behavior. He treated Etta differently. She stayed at the hotel where he stayed. She was, it soon became clear, the number one Mrs. Jack Johnson.[5]

The changing nature of Johnson's fancy can be most easily traced through his gifts of jewelry. First the jewelry—mostly diamonds that Johnson treated like the Crown Jewels—was given to Hattie. When Johnson came to favor Belle, Hattie was forced to give the jewelry to her rival. Then came Etta, and once again the jewelry changed hands. Perhaps in an attempt to recapture Johnson's affections—and jewelry—toward the end of 1909 Belle announced that she was pregnant. This pleased Johnson. As Belle later testified, "He asked me to have this child and not to do anything to get rid of it." However, children were bad public relations in Belle's business, and the child, which she continually referred to as "it," was never born. This did not seem to weigh heavily on Johnson's mind.[6]

But by 1910 Johnson's interest was elsewhere. The Ketchel fight had dramatically enhanced his reputation and he was sought after by several vaudeville agencies. In December 1909, while in New York, he signed for a tour with Barney Gerard's "Atlantic Carnival" show. For the tour, which was due to start in early 1910, Johnson was guaranteed $1,300 per week. It was a star's salary, and initially Johnson seemed satisfied. As he left to begin the tour, a reporter for the *Chicago Tribune* noted that Johnson was "his usual happy self." He was expected only to be himself, or what whites perceived was his true nature. He was told to dance about the stage, shadow box, sing a bit, and tell a few amusing stories.[7]

He was also supposed to accept the indignities that came with being a black performer. Even the top black vaudevillians were treated shamelessly. Bert Williams, one of vaudeville's greatest stars, was doomed to be a "funny nigger" despite his desire to give the white audience "both sides of the shiftless darky—the pathos as well as the fun." The star on stage, when the curtain fell Williams was just another Jim Crow black. His cubbyhole dressing room was separated from the other, better dressing rooms reserved for white performers. He was never supposed to mix socially with the white members of the tour, and a clause in his contract specified "that at no time would he be on the stage with any of the female members of the company." As the years of isolation and frustration lengthened, Williams's smile became bitter and his humor more biting. He once observed about the fate of a black vaudevillian, "It's no disgrace to be colored, but it's so inconvenient."[8]

Johnson was also expected to live with the inconveniences. Frank Calder, a stage manager, recalled working with Johnson at the Cleveland Star Theatre and the Indianapolis Empire Theater. Even though it was bitter cold, Johnson was not allowed in the heated dressing room that the other performers used. Rather he was forced to change clothes in the cellar. Unlike Williams, Johnson rebelled against such treatment. At the Fairland Theatre in Terre Haute, he refused to perform. It was too cold, he said, to go on stage in just boxing tights and gloves. An argument with the management followed, and Johnson angrily left town.[9]

As the novelty of the stage wore off, Johnson's irritability surfaced more often. For a while he traveled alone, but this made him angry, dissatisfied, and lonesome. He sent for Etta and Belle, but this too caused problems. Finding rooms for both women during the series of one-night stands proved a logistical nightmare, and the two women violently disliked each other. During one train trip the two accidentally met and, according to Gerard, the "fur flew." Thereafter the two women were sent home, and Gerard "lent" Johnson to Frank Rose for a one-week tour in Michigan. For the use of Johnson, Rose paid Gerard $2,500. A few weeks later Johnson learned of the deal and became enraged. He felt used and told Gerard so. They argued. Johnson said Gerard owed him $2,550. Gerard said he did not, but "upon threats of violence and seeing [his] life in danger," he paid the sum. Once back safely in New York, he discontinued the tour owing to Johnson's "arbitrary habits and ego." He also initiated legal proceedings to recoup the money Johnson had scared out of him.[10]

Johnson's anger and frustration were not confined to his theatrical dealings. In New York he got into an argument with a fellow black named Norman Pinder. It was a drinking dispute. Johnson said he drank only wine; Pinder remarked that he remembered when Johnson once drank beer from a bucket like a horse. Thereupon, Pinder claimed, Johnson knocked him down, kicked him in the ribs, threw a table and chair on him, and pulled out a gun. Pinder wisely stayed on the floor, and Johnson left the saloon. When Johnson was later arrested he told the police that his only regret was that he had not hit Pinder harder. A few weeks later, when Johnson was served with a $20,000 legal suit by Pinder's attorney, he threw the paper on the ground. For lawyers, theatrical promoters, and Pinderesque citizens he had only the deepest scorn. He would do and act as he wished.[11]

Money was no longer an immediate problem. Ahead of Johnson was a rainbow, and beyond it the pot of gold. The rainbow was Jeffries, the pot of gold their proposed match. Toward the end of 1909 Jeffries succumbed to the pressures of race and dollars. Hundreds of letters were sent to Jeffries with a single theme: it was incumbent upon him as a white man to shut Johnson's smiling mouth once and for all. White Americans did not doubt that Jeffries was up to the task. They believed the Jeffries mythology—that he cured himself of pneumonia by drinking a case of whisky in two days, that with a broken leg he was still able to knock out a leading heavyweight contender, that upon inspection a physician told him that he was simply not human. Across America white bartenders told customers that if Jeffries fought Johnson, he would "probably kill the Negro." After more than a year of such stories Americans—and, more important, Jeffries—believed that he probably *would* kill Johnson.[12]

It was left to the business managers to work out the details. Sam Berger negotiated for Jeffries, George Little and Sig Hart for Johnson. They told reporters that the fight was open for bids and that the person who offered the most money could stage it. The leading promoters in America handed in their bids, which were supposed to be opened in public at the Hotel Albany in New York City. However, both boxing and the promotion of boxing matches were illegal in New York, and at the last minute the scene for the opening of the bids was shifted across the Hudson River to Meyer's Hotel in Hoboken, New Jersey. The greatest promoters of the day either were there or had sent representatives. "Tuxedo Eddie" Graney, short and "built somewhat on the spherical plan of a toy balloon," was there representing the Tuxedo Club of San Francisco. The Bay City's other leading promoter, "Sunny Jim" Coffroth, was represented by Jack Gleason. It was rumored that they already held Jeffries under contract. "Uncle Tom" McCarey, who had promoted many of Johnson's early fights, hoped to get the bout for his Pacific Club in Los Angeles. Phil King, who represented Hugh McIntosh, wanted the fight to be staged in Australia. And a relatively now promoter, George Lewis "Tex" Rickard, said he was Johnson's personal favorite.[13]

The bids were opened. They were all attractive, but Rickard's was the best. He guaranteed the fighters $101,000 and two-thirds of the movie rights. In addition, he promised a cash bonus of $10,000 for each fighter upon signing. It was money unheard of in the boxing world, but it was not just talk. Rickard was backed by Thomas F. Cole, a Minnesota millionaire who owned silver and gold mines across the United States and Alaska.

In an age when a laborer might earn only a dollar a day, the amount Jeffries and Johnson stood to make struck some observers as disgraceful. Not only would the winner get 75 percent of the $101,000 guarantee and the loser 25 percent, but additional revenues would be gained through their percentages of film rights and vaudeville contracts. Edward R. Moss, sports editor for the *New York Evening Sun,* estimated that if Jeffries won, the white fighter would make $667,750 and Johnson would earn $358,250. If Johnson was victorious, the film rights would be worth less and he would make only $360,750 to Jeffries's $158,000. Either way the amounts were staggering. "A new era is at hand in pugilism," wrote Moss. "These horny-fisted survivals of the Stone Age are . . . the real moneymakers. Primitive Nature seems to reward her followers handsomely, despite civilization's boasted triumphs."[14]

Behind the new era and manipulating the million dollar match were Tex Rickard and Jack Gleason, who was brought in on the promotion to please Jeffries. Rickard was a new sort of promoter. He did not know much about boxing, and in 1910 he had few connections in the puglistic world. He did not even look like a fight promoter, who as a species were overweight, cigar-chewing, carnival shellmen. Rickard was sleek and clean. Bob Edgren of the *New York Evening World* said Rickard was "tall, lean and sinewy as a cowboy, dark-tanned from exposure to the sun and wind, and [had] a sharp eye, thin lips, straight-nosed countenance, and [was] as alert as an eagle." And he was. If he looked like the clean-living Western movie hero William S. Hart, his past was as checkered as that of a character from a Bret Harte story. Orphaned at the age of ten, Rickard had grown up on the bloody strip of land in Missouri along the Kansas border that composed Clay County during the years when the James brothers ruled there. As a teenager he moved to Texas and worked as a horse wrangler and later a frontier marshal. In 1895 his wife and baby died and he left Texas, drifting north to Alaska. It was a time for making money and getting rich, and Rickard panned for gold, tended bar, and gambled. He managed the Northern Saloon in Nome but lost everything he earned at the poker and roulette tables. Tired of Alaska, he drifted south, this time ending up in the goldfields of South Africa.

Back in the United States, he opened the famous Northern Saloon in Goldfield, Nevada, where another gold rush was under way. There in the hot, dirty-rich town of Goldfield, Rickard tried his hand at promoting boxing matches. He did it not for the love of boxing or even the love of money, but to draw the nation's attention to Goldfield. He matched Joe Gans, the magnificent black lightweight champion from Baltimore, against the rugged Battling Nelson, and for forty-two rounds the two men butted and kicked, sweated and bled, and occasionally punched until Nelson sank a left hook in Gans's groin and lost on a foul. But the scheme worked. Overnight Goldfield became famous and Rickard became a success as both a promoter and an advertiser.[15]

No advertising genius was needed to market the Johnson-Jeffries fight. The issues in this fight were literally black and white and Rickard felt no qualms about exploiting the racism. Jeffries became the "Hope of the White Race" and Johnson the "Negroes Deliverer." Seen as a battle for racial superiority, everything about the fight was treated as having momentous importance. When San Francisco was chosen as the site for the bout, the world's attention focused on the Bay Area. An editorialist for *Current Literature* observed the fight was "casting its shadow over a palpitating world. England and France, China and Japan, Australia and Hawaii, are even now starting their delegations toward the Golden Gate." In a cartoon in the *New York Globe* entitled "Relative News Values," Jeffries and "Masta Johnson" loomed over Roosevelt and Taft and completely dwarfed men like Charles Evans Hughes, House Speaker Cannon, and William Jennings Bryan. Every public move Johnson and Jeffries made was photographed and recorded. Quite conceivably there had never been a more important athletic event in American history.[16]

The fighters retired to their training camps. Jeffries went to the tiny village of Rowardennan in the Santa Cruz Mountains along the narrow San Lorenzo River. He worked hard because he had to. He was thirty-five years old and weighed over 300 pounds, and the effort it took to prepare for a forty-five-round fight was enormous. Never a gregarious man, Jeffries became sullen and grouchy. Writers accurately compared him to a grizzly bear: "He growls and snarls and grumbles like an old grizzly when strangers come around. . . . He has a bear's aversion to being disturbed—particularly when he eats. He doesn't like to mingle much with the other animals." There was a concerted journalistic attempt to soften Jeffries' image—stories were told that he was kind to his wife and sparring partners, and that his home life was "wholesome and clean"—but it was difficult to gloss over his irritable and unfriendly disposition. Eventually reporters stopped trying to get close to him and submitted fictional pieces about how friendly Jeffries might be if he were not so unfriendly. Writers following the Jeffries camp survived on inspiration.[17]

Rumors were more common than facts. It was said that Jeffries was having difficulty losing weight and still retaining his strength. Reports close to Jeffries' camp—but usually not in it—said the boxer was having trouble sweating, a sure sign that there was something wrong with his health. Other rumors were spread that he had syphilis and was a mere hollow shell, though at 300 pounds he was admittedly a heavy hollow shell. The most persistent report, however, was that the fight had been fixed, that Johnson had agreed to lose. In a day when fixed fights were common, the report was taken seriously. Early betting, which was usually done by professional gamblers, favored Jeffries. And though the fight was not fixed, it is conceivable that during the early summer days Jeffries believed that it indeed was in the tank.[18]

Johnson trained as if he believed the fight was fixed. He arrived at the Seal Beach training quarters on April 30, but he did not begin to work out until much later. Reporters said that he was devoted to pleasure, refused to train, and spent his days relaxing on the beach. Or, even worse in Rickard's opinion, he left for daylong drives along the California roads and into the mountains. He was always good copy. One day he would entertain sportswriters by playing the bass viol and telling stories, the next day he would quarrel with Little. The relationship between Johnson and his manager was as stormy as a soap opera love affair. They would argue, tell reporters how cheap the other was, threaten lawsuits, then make up. A few days later the cycle was started anew. The only thing usual in the Johnson camp was the unusual, and through May and early June it provided the drama for the prefight buildup.[19]

That summer the old order seemed to be toppling. In Mexico an epic revolution had begun, and that May Porfirio Diaz, the very symbol of order and authority, resigned as president and left the country to the quixotic Francisco Madero. Across the Atlantic in England militant suffragettes challenged the order of the sexes. They smashed the windows at 10 Downing Street and London's shopping districts, chained themselves to the railing at Parliament Square, poured acid into mail boxes, slashed pictures in public art galleries, and when arrested went on hunger strikes. On May 7 Edward VII, king of England and uncle of Europe, died, and with him perhaps the world's best hope for peace. Since the death of his mother, Queen Victoria, Edward had guided both Europe and fashion along traditional paths; he was the English representation of the Pax Britannica and the order of the nineteenth-century world. In late May, when Halley's Comet was spotted, America and Europe seemed far less stable than they had when the comet was last seen.

Many people opposed these changes. Through reform they sought to establish the world as they believed it once existed, a world of Christian morality and puritanical virtues. Opposed to the new immigrants coming to America and to alcohol, prostitution, and other vices, this group tried to persuade other Americans to adopt their beliefs. In the late nineteenth century they looked in pity and sympathy on drinkers and prostitutes and tried to help them help themselves. However, when persuasion failed, reformers turned to more forceful techniques to remake the world in their own image. They now viewed their opponents not with sympathy but with open hostility; they hoped to win the battle not by words but through legal restrictions. To fight the battle a wide range of rural-based reform groups sprang into action. Such organizations as the Law and Order Leagues, Committees of Public Decency, and Protective Societies stood for legislated morality.[20]

In Johnson and prizefighting these reformers saw the incarnation of everything they opposed, feared, and hated. They embraced traditional, rural, puritanical values, the values that at least in popular theory had accounted for everything pure and great about America. The world of prizefighting, they argued, was as alien to those values as an illiterate Jewish immigrant from Russia. Professional boxing was viewed as an immigrant sport that attracted Irish and Polish Catholics, Russian Jews, and other undesirable sorts, which in fact it did. It was also quite correctly seen as having close ties with saloon keepers and Democratic urban machine politics. And the epitome of the evil of the prizefighting world was Jack Johnson. He drank, supported prostitutes, and threatened the very social and racial order of America. He was not the type of man rural Anglo-Saxon Protestants felt comfortable with. Instead he was a constant reminder of a powerful threat to the traditional American order.

When the site of the Johnson-Jeffries right was announced as San Francisco, reformers strapped on their swords. It was an affront to civilization, they said. In Cincinnati a million post cards were distributed among the faithful for signing and posting. They were addressed to the governor of California and contained the simple message: "STOP THE FIGHT. THIS IS THE 20TH CENTURY." Other protests were staged in California. Fifty ministers formed a prayer session on the capitol's steps in Sacramento. They prayed for Governor J. N. Gillett to see the light of civilization and reason. Finally Congressman William S. Bennett of New York, chairman of the House Committee on Foreign Relations and a good churchman, wired the president of the San Francisco Board of Trade that the "prospective fight" stood in the way of congressional efforts to secure the Panama-Pacific Exposition of 1913 for San Francisco. This message was quickly relayed to Governor Gillett.[21]

Up until then Gillett had steadfastly supported the match, claiming that it in no way conflicted with the laws of California. The potential obstruction of the Panama-Pacific Exposition, however, made him reread the statutes. After some soul-searching he concluded that the Johnson-Jeffries contest would not be a boxing exhibition, which California law permitted, but a prizefight, which state statutes forbade. In an open letter to the attorney general of California Gillett claimed, "The whole business is demoralizing to the youth of our state, corrupts public morals, is offensive to the senses of the great majority of our citizens, and should be abated, as a public nuisance, and the offenders punished."[22]

Moral outrage and economic pressure had won for the reformers. Although Mayor Pat McCarthy opposed the governor's decision, the fight was pushed out of San Francisco. Moral reformers could not contain their glee. The Reverend H. R. Jamison of Cincinnati declared, "Within the last few days there has gone to the governor of California such a deluge of letters from all parts of the country that I believe he has come to a rightful appreciation of the fight question, and that he has seen through all this betting and "fixing" business only, a way to the pocketbooks of the people. I believe he has seen the light of a good life, and that it has called to him so earnestly by day and by night that he has decided that the Jeffries-Johnson fight must not come off." This smug and confident voice underlay a grim reality. Prizefighting, like liquor and prostitution, was seen as an evil trick to rob good people of their money and their virtue, and it was up to the morally anointed to use spiritual and economic suasion to protect their weaker brethren.[23]

The man most affected by Gillett's decision was Jeffries. The ex-champion, who suffered from "constitutional peevishness," was bitter about the announcement. Walter Kelly, famous for his vaudeville character "The Virginia Judge" and the uncle of the as yet unborn Grace Kelly, was with Jeffries when they heard the news. Visiting the camp to keep his friend Jeffries from becoming too morose, Kelly and the fighter were trout fishing when a messenger boy handed Jeffries the telegram. He became pale and angry. "I should tell them all to go to hell and go back home. If it wasn't for Tex, that's just what I would do." Afterward Jeffries became increasingly gloomy, turning even more inward. "In my soul," Kelly wrote, "I believe that incident was the blow that whipped Jeff."[24]

To Rickard fell the task of finding another city to stage the fight. He had already sold $133,000 worth of tickets and had invested between $30,000 and $50,000 in the stadium, licenses, and various political payoffs. Now he had only two weeks to find another city, build a stadium, and complete the many other arrangements. He received offers from Reno, Goldfield, and Salt Lake City. He chose Reno because of its superior railroad facilities and because the mayor of the town assured him that a 20,000-seat stadium could be constructed there within the two-week deadline. Further incentives were offered by Governor Denver S. Dickerson. He told the promoter that no reform movement had any power in Nevada and no amount of protest could force him to cancel the fight. Thus guaranteed, Rickard, Jeffries, Johnson, and everyone else involved in the match boarded a train for Reno.[25]

The confused series of events had no outward effect on Johnson. Estranged from Little and asserting his independence, the champion announced, "I am my own manager and always have been." He thereupon made his own travel arrangements and left for Reno, where he arrived on June 26. He seemed totally relaxed, unlike the dyspeptic Jeffries. Reporters could not understand Johnson's calm. Though "sharp as a razor in a sort of undeveloped way," wrote one journalist, Johnson seemed oblivious to the seriousness of his task. "He fiddles away on his bull fiddle, swaps jokes with ready wit, shoots craps, plays baseball, listens dreamily to classic love songs on the phonograph," apparently unconcerned about his upcoming fight with Jeffries. San Francisco, Reno, Sydney, or London—it made no difference to Johnson.[26]

For American reformers, however, the site was important. They wanted to prevent the match from being staged anywhere in the United States. With this goal in mind, they turned their collective zeal on Reno and Governor Dickerson. On Sunday, June 26, Reverend L. H. Burwell, pastor of Reno's Methodist church, delivered a sermon on "Reno's Disgrace." He told his congregation that the fight would demoralize the community and bring "riffraff" and the "offscouring of the country" into Reno. In Cincinnati Methodist ministers passed a resolution calling on Dickerson to follow Gillett's noble example. Across the nation protest was intense, and in the end useless. Dickerson refused to budge. For many God-fearing Americans, Reno became a national disgrace. The city deserved the "reproaches of the whole country," wrote a columnist for the *Independent* magazine. "But we tell Nevada that this is its last time thus to serve the devil. . . . Just as universal condemnation and disgust compelled Mormonism to get a new revelation on polygamy, so will Nevada be plagued into decency." And the Reverend M. P. Boynton, a Chicago Baptist minister, suggested, "There should be some way by which our nation could recall the charter of a state that has become a desert and a moral menace. Nevada has no right to remain a part of our nation."[27]

This strident tone of the reformers' protests revealed their true objectives. To be sure, they opposed boxing matches in the past and would do so again. But their opposition had never been so angry and forceful. The difference between the Johnson-Jeffries match and the other prizefights they opposed was the problem of race. The Reno fight was not simply another brutal and demoralizing prizefight; it was a battle that was widely perceived as a struggle for racial supremacy. Both black and white journalists understood this. Jackson Stovall of the black *Chicago Defender,* wrote that "on the sand plains of the Sage Brush State, the white man and the Negro will settle the mooted question of supremacy." Similarly, Max Balthazar, a white writer for the *Omaha Daily News,* asserted that the crucial question to be answered in Reno was whether "the huge white man, the California grizzly, [could] beat down the wonderful black and restore to the Caucasians power of heart and lung, and withal, that cunning or keenness that denotes mental as well as physical superiority."[28]

It was this question, and not just the fight, that white reformers wished to suppress. Just to allow the fight to take place was to admit a sort of equality. It implied that blacks had an equal chance to excel in at least one arena of American life. The black journalist A. G. F. Sims realized this and criticized white reformers for attempting to prevent it: "Just because the Negro has an equal chance, that in itself, in their opinion, is enough to constitute a national disgrace." He hoped that Johnson would soundly defeat Jeffries, "just to make it a good national disgrace."[29] White reformers, therefore, considered the fight a no-win proposition. Win or lose, if the fight took place Johnson would achieve a symbolic victory for his race.

And in that victory whites saw disturbing possibilities. They were sure that if Johnson won, the result would be race war. "If the black man wins," a *New York Times* editorialist noted, "thousands and thousands of his ignorant brothers will misinterpret his victory as justifying claims to much more than mere physical equality with their white neighbors." The use of "brothers" and "neighbors" to designate blacks and whites is significant; it implies the two groups are in no way related, and that a Johnson victory would literally turn neighbor against neighbor. This prediction was echoed throughout the United States, especially in the South. Southern congressmen "talked freely of the danger of the negroes having their heads turned" by a Johnson victory. One Southern official, incensed by the very idea of the fight, remarked, "Why, some of these young negroes are now so proud that it is hard to get along with them, but if Jeffries should be beaten by Johnson they will be crowding white women off the sidewalks and there are plenty of towns where such action as that would cause deplorable troubles." Again, the words of the warning are important. Southerners believed a Johnson victory would increase the possibility of physical contact between young, proud blacks and white women. This haunting specter led naturally to thoughts of racial warfare.[30]

Whites were not alone in predicting that the fight would beget violence. Conservative blacks feared the same possibility. Black admirers of Booker T. Washington had never felt comfortable about the implications of Jack Johnson. As early as March 1909 Emmett Jay Scott, Washington's personal secretary, wrote J. Frank Wheaton, a successful black New York lawyer, about the need for Johnson to be more humble in public. Scott, and by extension Washington, hoped that Johnson would grant as few interviews as possible and would "refrain from anything resembling boastfulness." They feared that Johnson challenged an order they wished to placate and that his emancipated lifestyle eventually would cause a violent white reaction. In this vein E. L. Blackshear, principal of the State Normal and Industrial College in Prairie View, Texas, and a disciple of Washington, warned that if Johnson defeated Jeffries, "the anti-negro sentiment will quickly and dangerously collect itself ready to strike back at any undue exhibitions of rejoicing on the part of negroes." Like the white reformers with whom he had much in common, Blackshear wished that the fight could be prevented.[31]

Yet by July that was no longer a realistic hope. The fight was going to be staged, and Reno was giddy with anticipation. In the days before the fight the little mining town became famous. Visitors to Reno discovered a beautiful backdrop for an epic fight. One reporter described it as "a bright green little oasis, ten or fifteen miles across, set in a sort of dish of bare enclosing mountains—brown mountains with patches of yellow and olive-green and exquisite veils of mauve and amethyst, and at their tops, blazing white through the clear air, patches of austere snow." Situated in the Truckee Meadows, along the route that the ill-fated Donner party had followed more than a half-century before, Reno was a town of "delicious morning and evening freshness" and intense afternoon heat. The fertile valley appeared more lush because of the bare white desert that surrounded it, just as the town's wealth seemed somehow greater when juxtaposed to its muddy streets and grimy buildings. Indeed Reno was, as Harris Morton Lyon wrote, "a broad-shouldered, tancheeked, slouch-hatted, youthful town. A town that believed in red neckties and fireman's suspenders."[32]

For many Americans Reno was a moral as well as a physical desert. They assumed that most of the town's population of 15,000 was to some degree associated with vice and sin. There was the gambling—not the usual secretive gambling, conducted behind locked doors and pulled blinds, but illuminated, unabashed gambling. In Reno gambling was legal. As Lyon's New York sporting friend delightedly explained, "Gambling. Wide open. Walk right in off the street. See a swinging door and push it open. Right inside you'll find roulette and faro and—and—I never was so tickled in my life." And there was the drinking. In a four-or five-block area there were more than fifty saloons, most with bare board floors and bare wooden walls and names like Jim May's Palace, Lacey's Louvre, the Casino, the Oberon, and the Mecca. Most notoriously of all, there were the divorcees. Reno even then was the divorce capital of America. "Shoutin' the battle cry of freedom, I'm on my way to Reno," went the popular song about a suffragette trawling to Nevada to obtain a divorce. Lawyers in Reno even advertised their ability to obtain speedy settlements. Reno's indulgent attitude toward gambling, drinking, and divorce, wrote an English visitor, H. Hamilton Fyle, "tends to attract a class of visitors which cannot be said to shed any luster upon the town."[33]

According to most observers the more than 20,000 people who traveled to Reno for the fight did nothing to upgrade the town's reputation. It was a sporting crowd—boxers, ex-boxers, prostitutes, saloon owners, gamblers, pickpockets, hoboes, profligate sons of the wealthy, and high rollers of every kind. They came to drink, spin the roulette wheel, and talk about the upcoming fight. They talked and dressed loud. Bright plaid vests, thick black cigars, and large diamond rings were the order of the day. There were sporting men from England, France, Germany, Italy, Australia, and all over the United States. There were black sports as well as white sports. It was an atmosphere rife with tall tales, hard luck stories, big dreams, and grandiose plans.[34]

Perhaps at no time before had so many reporters descended upon so small a town. Upwards of 500 correspondents were present to report the town's celebrations. Every day in the week before the bout between 100,000 and 150,000 words about the fight—enough for two popular novels—were sent out from Reno. Some of the reporters were leading writers. Jack London, Rex Beach, and Alfred Henry Lewis, three of the leading writers-*cum*-Sports, detailed the activities. But far more famous were the boxers- and wrestlers-*cum*-reporters. Covering the fight for various newspapers were John L. Sullivan, James J. Corbett, Robert Fitzsimmons, Abe Attell, Battling Nelson, Tommy Burns, Frank Gotch, William Muldoon, and a host of others. Reviewing the list of correspondents, Rex Beach regretted that there were not more writers-*cum*-pugilists. "I lament at the absence of 'Walloping' Dean Howells of New England. He may not possess the literary style of a Joe Choynski or an Abe Attell,

Figure 3–1
Jack Johnson with his wife, 1910. Library of Congress.

but he has a certain following nevertheless. And 'Battling' Henry James, the Devonshire Demon. . . . His diction is stilted, perhaps, and lacking in the fluent ease and grace of 'Philadelphia Jack O'Brien's, but he is entitled to be heard."[35]

Another faction well represented in Reno was the criminal class. Thieves of all types roamed about the town's streets, and "if a hand was not dipped into your pocket sooner or later it was almost a sign of disrespect." The small police force was timid and ineffectual. Hotel rooms, trunks, Pullman cars, and safes were all robbed with alarming frequency. Nor were all the criminals there to work. Some of the more famous and prosperous had come just to watch the fight and wager a few thousand dollars. The bank robber Cincinnati Slim was there, as was Won Let, the hatchet man for the New York branch of the Hip Sing Tong. It was rumored that he had killed between twenty and thirty Chinese. Even the notorious Sundance Kid was reported to be on his way to Reno.[36]

While Reno's police force was unable to contain the crime, the rest of the town's services were similarly taxed. People slept anywhere they could find an empty space—hotel rooms, Pullman cars, cots, billiard tables, hammocks, or park benches. They slept with their hands on their money belts. Good food was as difficult to find as a good night's rest. As Lyon recalled, "Meals you got generally any way you could get them." People ate in shifts, and it was not unusual to wait three or four hours for service. It was not a time to be choosy. When you got a chance to eat you ate what was being served, and you were thankful for it.[37]

Perhaps the only visitors who were guaranteed a place to sleep and enough to eat were Johnson and Jeffries. The champion's quarters was an armed camp. Cal McVey, a friend of Johnson's, carried a shotgun, and the champion himself slept with a gun. However, if Johnson felt particularly threatened, he did not show it. His mood, at least outwardly, was light and easy. Yet even his calm temperament was interpreted by white reporters as an indication of his inferiority. Jack London remarked that the champion's "happy-go-lucky" disposition resulted from Johnson's concern for the moment and his inability to plan for the future. Alfred Lewis agreed. As "essentially African," Johnson "feels no deeper than the moment, sees no farther than his nose [and is] incapable of anticipation. . . . The same cheerful indifference to coming events [has] marked others of the race even while standing in the very shadow of the gallows. Their stolid unconcern baffled all who beheld it. They were to be hanged; they knew it. But having no fancy, no imagination—they could not anticipate.[38] Seen through white eyes, even bravery demonstrated the inferiority of blacks.

There were no displays of false cheerfulness in Jeffries' camp. At his roadhouse called Moana Springs, on the Truckee River, the atmosphere was heavy. Jeffries was even more restless and irritable than he had been in California. Every new story or rumor upset him. He was particularly angry at John L. Sullivan, the ex-champion who was perhaps the most popular fighter of all time. Sullivan, who was covering the bout for the *New York Times*, wrote (through his ghost writer) that the fight looked like a "frame-up." A few days later he went to Jeffries' quarters. He was greeted at the gate by Jim Corbett, who was helping out at the camp. It was Corbett who had taken the heavyweight title away from Sullivan, and the two men actively disliked one another. The slender Corbett asked, "What the hell do you want?" This was not the best way to say hello to Sullivan. Heated words were exchanged. John L. stared coldly at Corbett, and for a while it seemed as if the two were going to fight. Then Sullivan said, "If you're running the camp, I don't want to see him." As Walter Kelly remembered, "I had a lump in my throat as I watched John L. drive away. He was leaving the camp of a heavyweight champion without even the tribute of a handshake or a good-bye. For some reason, it just didn't seem right."[39]

It was not right. The fat, self-righteous, yet beloved Sullivan was deeply hurt by the incident. But it was typical of the mood of Jeffries's camp. He had taken all the talk about his duty to his race to heart, and the pressure showed. He prepared for the fight as if getting ready for a funeral. By the eve of the fight his friends feared that he was overwrought. He could not eat supper and retired early, but he could not sleep. William Muldoon, the famous trainer who was in Jeffries' camp, remembered that the old warhorse was heard pacing about. Mrs. Jeffries went to his door once and spoke to him, but he told her to return to her room and be quiet. Twelve hours later he came out of his room. He was ready to go to the fight.[40]

By the Fourth of July the entire nation was a bit nervous. Henry Wales of the *Chicago Tribune*, reviewing his long career as a reporter and an editor, said that no event so captured the public mind until the Lindberg flight seventeen years later. It was fitting that the fight was scheduled for the national holiday, for the celebration and the excitement were intense. Never had so illustrious a group of Sports gathered in one spot. From hoboes like Watertank Willie to bluebloods like Foxhall Keene, Payne Whitney, and Tom Shevlin, the famous Yale halfback who arrived in Reno wearing a dove-gray waistcoat and a straw hat with a club ribbon, it was the greatest holiday ever for that masculine subculture.[41]

And everyone had an opinion about who would win. The betting was ten to six or seven on Jeffries, but as Arthur Ruhl suggested, talk was overwhelmingly in favor of the white fighter: "You couldn't hurt him—Fitzsimmons had landed enough times to kill an ordinary man in the first few rounds, and Jeffries had only shaken his head like a bull and bored in. The negro might be a clever boxer, but he has never been up against a real fighter before. He has a yellow streak, there was nothing to it, and anyway, 'let's hope he kills the coon.'" Indeed most white Americans found themselves agreeing with the Chicago White Sox, who were polled on the fight. Fred Olmstead, a Southerner, hoped Jeffries would kill Johnson, and Manager Duffy as quoted by Ruhl said only, "I can't go against my race."[42]

Most boxers and intellectuals also predicted a Jeffries victory. John L. Sullivan, James J. Corbett, Robert Fitzsimmons, Tommy Bums, Abe Attell, Battling Nelson—the list is extensive. They all favored Jeffries. Even black boxers like Sam Langford and Joe Jeannette picked the white. Perhaps Jeannette, who had fought Johnson more than any other man, spoke for them all: "Why, Jeffries can lose half of his strength, have his endurance cut in two, carry a ton of extra weight and still whip Johnson. He has the 'head' and the 'heart' to do it." The head and the heart: it was also a common theme among intellectuals. A psychologist writing for the *London Lancet* remarked that Jeffries' brain should be the deciding factor, and Rex Beach predicted that Jeffries' education would be too much for Johnson. "The difference," wrote Beach, "is in both breeding and education. Jeffries realizes his responsibility all the time. When Johnson steps into the ring with him, his bubbling confidence will bubble away."[43]

Even America's churches were not immune to the excitement. In Hutchinson, Kansas, the Colored Holiness Church announced that it would hold special services during the fight to pray for Johnson. To counterbalance this plea for divine help a midwestern white minister said he would pray for Jeffries. The Reverend H. E. Trials of the First Baptist Church in Omaha told his congregation, "Every man with red blood in his veins should see

Jim Jeffries regain the heavyweight championship from Jack Johnson." Although some ministers disagreed with such statements, most did agree that there was something much greater at stake in Reno than a championship belt.[44]

On the Fourth of July the nation was ready. Every section of the country was connected electrically with Reno. At the wealthy Edgemore Club on Long Island, William Vanderbilt, Jr., Howard Gould, Lawrence Drake, and the rest of their crowd followed the action through a private bulletin service. Outside newspaper buildings in every major city crowds gathered to follow the progress of the fight. At the Tuskegee Institute Booker T. Washington, who declined to cover the bout as a reporter, set aside a special assembly room to receive telegraphic reports from Reno. If the fight was a racial Armageddon as everywhere it was advertised, then the results would be known to everyone as soon as it concluded.[45]

"The day dawned spotlessly clear, one of those still crystalline mornings which come in the thin dry air of the mountain desert country." Because of the shabbiness of the event that was to follow, reporters in Reno remembered the beauty of the morning. They recalled the order with which the drunken mob, 15,000 to 20,000 strong, moved toward the stadium on the outskirts of Reno and checked their firearms at the gate; how they poured in through the four tunnellike entrances into the huge eight-sided arena; how their voices rose strong and clear into the hot afternoon air; how a brass band climbed into the ring and played "All Coons Look Alike to Me" and other "patriotic" selections; and how the joy of anticipation seemed to affect everyone in the pinewood bleachers. It was a picture of boisterous American innocence, confident that Jeffries would triumph in the racial confrontation.[46]

Johnson was the first into the ring, wearing a gray silk robe and blue trunks with an American flag for his belt. A litany of racial slurs greeted him, but as always he seemed not to notice. Beach watched for some sign of fear, but Johnson merely "grinned and clapped his hands like a boy." Jeffries was greeted like an emperor. He looked nervous, chewing gum rapidly and glaring across the ring at Johnson. "If looks could have throttled, burned, and tore to pieces, Mr. Jack Arthur Johnson would have disappeared that instant into a few specks of inanimate dust." But Johnson did not look at Jeffries, and this was widely interpreted as a sure sign of fear. From the spectators came a wolfish hoot, "He darsen't look at him! O-o-ol! Don't let him see him! Don't let him see him!" Johnson laughed and peeked at Jeffries from behind his white trainer.[47]

Jeffries looked big but also old and tired. A few days before Jeffries had told reporters, "I realize full well just what depends on me, and I am not going to disappoint the public. That portion of the white race that has been looking to me to defend its athletic superiority may feel assured that I am fit to do my very best." Now he looked as if he were not at all sure that his very best would be good enough. William Muldoon said that the orator who experiences stage fright knew what Jeffries felt. He believed he was "the center of all human attention. The mental pressure became unbearable. . . . His Caucasian mind, sensing this vast concentration of thought, was overwhelmed."[48]

Tex Rickard, who had named himself referee, also felt the vast concentration of thought, and he feared it might erupt into violence. In order to cool the heated racial feeling, Rickard called on William Muldoon to give a speech. Muldoon, the once great wrestler, was a pompous, humorless man who genuinely believed in such notions as honor and fair play. In a forceful voice he told the spectators so. It was necessary, he said, not to judge Johnson too harshly just because he was black, and regardless who won, the verdict must be accepted in a sense of fair play. Muldoon's speech and the lemonade, which was the only beverage served in the arena, seemed to sober the crowd.[49]

During the preliminary activities not all of the tradition of the prize ring was observed. Certainly all the ex-champions were introduced by the portly, stentorian Billy Jordan, who had been imported from San Francisco to handle such matters. Although the day was exceptionally hot, Jordan and the other ring luminaries wore stiff collars, watch-chained waistcoats, suits, and hats. This formality of dress was also traditional, part of the ritual and formal rules of the sport. However, by prearranged agreement Johnson and Jeffries did not shake hands before the fight. No detail more clearly illustrated the symbolic importance of the match. Not to observe such a fundamental ritual, the very expression of sportsmanship and fair play, indicated that this was not simply another championship fight.[50]

No fight could do justice to such an extended buildup. This one did not even come close. "It was not a great battle after all, save in its setting and significance," wrote Jack London. Johnson established the tempo of the fight in the first round—slow and painful. He waited for Jeffries to lead, then threw straight right and left counters. Both fighters showed a tendency to clinch, but even there Johnson had the advantage. For all the talk of Jeffries' grizzly strength, Johnson was by far the stronger of the two men. He tossed Jeffries around with alarming ease. At the bell ending the first round Jeffries winked to his cornerman, but the gesture lacked confidence. It was the brave front of a man who knows that the game is over and he has lost.[51]

In the second round Johnson started talking to Jeffries. "Don't rush, Jim," he said as he pushed Jeffries across the ring. "I can go on like this all afternoon," he exclaimed as he hit the challenger with a solid right-hand lead. Jeffries' famous crouching, rushing, and wild-swinging style was useless against the grace and economy of Johnson's defense. Jeffries tried to respond, but before he could throw a solid punch Johnson would connect with a left or right lead. Thereupon the two would clinch. During the clinches Johnson would talk to Jeffries or to the challenger's corner.

Jeffries had several good moments, but not many. In the fourth round a Jeffries' left drew blood from Johnson's lip, and the crowd yelled, "First blood for Jeffries." But actually the cut was deceiving, Johnson's lip had been cut while training, and Jeffries had merely reopened the old wound. More often Jeffries was in pain, and he looked tired between rounds. In his corner he seldom spoke, but when he did it was to complain. Once he told his cornermen that his arms felt stiff and heavy. And he told Muldoon that his "head felt queer" and that he was having trouble judging distances. Both problems are indicative of tension. Jeffries was too tight even to fight normally.[52]

More interesting than the Johnson-Jeffries fight was what might be called the Johnson-Corbett match. Jim Corbett, who was acting as Jeffries' chief second, was the most vocal racist in Jeffries' corner. He hated all blacks, but Johnson more than the rest. And he had a theory that blacks became useless fighters when enraged. Therefore from the earliest rounds he screamed insults at Johnson. But they did not have the desired effect. Instead of making Johnson angry, the insults seemed to have a calming effect. When Corbett said something, Johnson replied politely and smiled. Arthur Ruhl, who covered the fight for *Collier's,* reported that Johnson's retorts were well-mannered, quiet, and generous; he had "the good sense or cleverness to keep the respectful ingratiating ways of the Southern

No IO. Johnson & Jeffries Contest, Reno July 4th, 1910

Figure 3–2
Jack Johnson versus Jim Jeffries, July 4, 1910, Reno, Nevada. Courtesy of Nevada Historical Society.

darkey." This infuriated Corbett, who became increasingly irrational as the fight progressed. Finally, in round twelve, Johnson called to Corbett, "I thought you said you were going to have *me* wild." The irony was lost on Corbett.[53]

Most of the reporters believed that Johnson could have ended the fight in an early round. They said he did not because he was a good businessman and a vengeful person. Financially a quick fight would have been disastrous. It would have destroyed the potential of the film as a revenue source. But beyond the money question, reporters believed Johnson enjoyed watching Jeffries suffer. By round twelve Jeffries' mouth was cut inside and out; his nose was broken and bleeding; his face and eyes were bruised and smeared with blood. Even Johnson's chest and back were covered with Jeffries' blood. There was no reason for the fight to go on. But it did.

Jeffries came out for the thirteenth still chewing gum. He tried to clinch, but Johnson delivered a left to the body and a right uppercut to the chin. Johnson followed with two more lefts to the face and another right uppercut. He then grabbed Jeffries by the shoulder and hit him with three lefts to the face and then with a stiff uppercut. Jeffries, his eyes almost closed, swung wildly but was unable to solve Johnson's defense. More punishment followed. Corbett, struck with a sudden insight, yelled for Jeffries to "cover up." The bell sounded.

The fourteenth saw more of the same. Jeffries' arms were too tired either to throw an effective punch or to block one of Johnson's—"How do you feel, Jim?" Johnson asked as he hit Jeffries with hard lefts and rights. "How do you like it?" Jeffries did not answer. He was moving like a drunk on a shifting funhouse floor. He did not even try to fight back. He just chewed his gum and accepted the brutal punishment. "Does it hurt, Jim?" Johnson asked as Jeffries walked into three consecutive rights. "They don't hurt," answered Jeffries. The round ended.

In the fifteenth Jeffries' face was bleeding and swollen, and his movements were languid. But he continued to move toward Johnson. The round-by-round report accurately, if unemotionally, reflects the horror of the scene: "He shambled after the elusive negro, sometimes crouching low . . . and sometimes standing erect. Stooping or erect, he was a mark for Johnson's accurately driven blows. Johnson simply waited for the big white man to come in and chopped his face to pieces." Finally a combination of rights and lefts forced Jeffries onto the ropes. There Johnson landed fifteen or twenty punches to Jeffries' head and face. Jeffries fell to the canvas for the first time in his career. He was dazed, and Johnson stood over him until Rickard made the champion move back. At the count of nine Jeffries struggled to his feet. Johnson charged and landed another combination of punches. Again Jeffries fell to his knees. At the count of nine he once more arose. At this stage ringsiders shouted, "Stop it, stop it. Don't let him be knocked out." But the fight continued. Jeffries was helpless. A left-right-left combination knocked Jeffries into the ropes. He sprawled over the lower rope, hanging half outside the ring. Rickard picked up the timekeeper's count. At seven one of Jeffries' handlers rushed into the ring, and Rickard stopped the fight. The "fight of the century" was over.

Silence. Insults and cheers were few. The spectators accepted the end as they might the conclusion of a horse race where the favorite broke a leg and had to be destroyed. Johnson was clearly superior, so there was nothing to argue about. Jeffries was old and tired and should never have attempted a comeback. More than talking or yelling, the sad boxing fan wanted to leave the arena as quickly as possible and find a bar that served something stronger than lemonade. Across the nation thousands of other men who crowded around newspaper offices for news of the fight experienced similar reactions. And so they went to the saloons, and when they finished drinking and brooding about the fight they expressed their displeasure in spontaneous outbursts of violence. The emotions exposed by the Johnson-Jeffries fight were quite sincere and, once uncovered, were deadly.

NOTES

1. *Los Angeles Times,* March 10, 1906, Gary Phillips Collection; John Lardner, *White Hopes and Other Tigers* (Philadelphia: Lippincott, 1951), 30.

2. *Chicago Tribune,* April 4, 1909, sec. 111, p. 4.

3. "Data Relative to the Immoral Associations of John Arthur Johnson and Belle Schreiber," Record Group 60, National Archives (hereafter RG and NA).

4. Finis Farr, *Black Champion: The Life and Times of Jack Johnson* (New York: Scribner, 1964), 73.

5. Bielaski to Garbarino, February 21, 1913, RG 60, NA: *U.S. v. Johnson,* 45–4.

6. *U.S. v. Johnson,* 82, 45–9.

7. Scully Report, March 8, 1913, RG 60, NA; Eurborshaw Report, March 10, 1913, RG 60, NA; Gerard to Horn, March 11, 1913, RG 60, NA; *Chicago Tribune,* January 1, 1910, p. 14.

8. William Stowe, Jr., "Damned Funny: The Tragedy of Bert Williams," *Journal of Popular Culture,* 10 (Summer 1976: 5–12.

9. Scully Report, March 20, 1913, RG 60, NA; *Chicago Tribune,* January 3, 1910, p. 12.

10. Gerard to Horn, March 11, 1913, RG 60, NA; Eurborshaw Report, March 10, 1913, RG 60, NA.

11. *Chicago Tribune,* January 21, 1910, p. 12; January 22, 1910, p. 10; February 2, 1910, p. 12; and February 3, 1910, p. 9.

12. Farr, *Black Champion,* 69; Charles Samuels, *The Magnificent Rube: The Life and Times of Tex Rickard* (New York: McGraw-Hill, 1957), 151–4.

13. Samuels, *Magnificent Rube,* 137–44; "The Making of the Match," *Harper's Weekly,* November 20, 1909, p. 30.

14. Samuels, *Magnificent Rube,* 143–4; Nat Fleischer, *"Fighting Furies": The Story of the Golden Era of Jack Johnson, Sam Langford and Their Contemporaries* (New York, nd), 86–91; Edward B. Moss, "In the Ring for a Million," *Harper's Weekly,* May 14, 1910, p. 13; *Current Literature,* June 1910, p. 607.

15. Samuels, *Magnificent Rube,* 1–216; Mel Heimer, *The Long Count* (New York: Atheneum, 1969), 103–12; Barton W. Currie, "Prize-Fights as Mine Boomers," *Harper's Weekly,* August 22, 1908, p. 25.

16. Moss, "In the Ring for a Million," 13; *Current Literature,* June 1910, p. 605.

17. Harry Carr, "Fighting Father Time," *Collier's,* June 11, 1910, pp. 19, 32; Homer Davenport, "The Modern Caveman," *Collier's,* June 11, 1910, 19.

18. Samuels, *Magnificent Rube,* 147–8.

19. *Chicago Tribune,* May 1, 1910, sec. 3, p. 3; May 2, 1910, p. 13; May 4, 1910, p. 13; May 6, 1910, p. 13; May 8, 1910, sec. 3, p. 3; May 11, 1910, p. 15; May 12, 1910, p. 9; June 16, 1910, p. 11; June 19, 1910, sec. 3, p. 1; and June 23, 1910, p. 11.

20. Stuart Mews, "Puritanicalism, Sport and Race: A Symbolic Crusade of 1911," in *Studies in Church History,* ed. G. J. Cuming and Derek Baker, vol. 8 (Cambridge, England: Cambridge Universith Press, 1972), 305–9.

21. *New York Times,* June 6, 1910, p. 9, and June 16, 1910, p. 2; Mews, "Puritanicalism, Sport, and Race," 307; Farr, *Black Champion,* 85–99.

22. *Chicago Tribune,* June 16, 1910, p. 11.

23.*Ibid.; New York Times,* June 16, 1910, p. 21; Mews, "Puritanicalism, Sport, and Race," 308.

24. *Chicago Tribune,* June 18, 1910, p. 13; quoted in John D. McCallum, *The World Heavyweight Boxing Championship* (Radnor, PA: Chilton Book Co., 1974), 57–9.

25. Samuels, *Magnificent Rube,* 160–6; *Chicago Tribune,* June 20, 1910, p. 11.

26. *Chicago Tribune,* June 25, 1910, p. 13, and June 27, 1910, p. 9.

27. *Ibid.;* June 27, 1910, p. 9, and June 28, 1910, p. 11; "California's Conversion," *Independent,* June 23, 1910, pp. 1404–5; quoted in Farr, *Black Champion,* 106.

28. Quoted in Al-Tony Gilmore, *Bad Nigger: The National Impact of Jack Johnson* (Port Washington, NY: Kennikat Press, 1975), 36; *Omaha Daily News,* July 3, 1910, p. 1.

29. Quoted in Gilmore, *Bad Nigger,* 34.

30. Quoted in *Current Literature,* June 1910, pp. 606–7; *Omaha Daily News,* July 2, 1910, p. 6.

31. Scott to Wheaton, Louis Harlan, ed., *Booker T. Washington Papers,* (Urbana: University of Illinois Press, 1972–1989), vol. 10, 75; *Current Literature,* June 1910, pp. 606–7.

32. Arthur Ruhl, "The Fight in the Desert," *Colliers's,* July 23, 1910, p. 22; H. Hamilton Fyle, "What the Prize-Fight Taught Me," *Outlook,* August 13, 1910, p. 827; Harris Merton Lyon, "In Reno Riotous," *Hampton's Magazine,* September 1910, p. 387.

33. Lyon, "In Reno Riotous," 386–96; Fyle, "What the Prize-Fight Taught Me," 827.

34. Lyon, "In Reno Riotous," 386–96.

35. Ruhl, "The Fight in the Desert," 12; *Chicago Tribune,* July 3, 1910, p. 1.

36. Lyon, "In Reno Riotous," 387; Farr, *Black Champion,* 97.

37. Lyon, "In Reno Riotous," 337–99.

38. *Chicago Tribune,* June 29, 1910, p. 13; quoted in Gilmore, *Bad Nigger,* 37.

39. McCallum, *The World Heavyweight Boxing Championship,* 7; *Chicago Tribune,* June 24, 1910, p. 11.

40. Edward Van Every, *Muldoon: The Solid Man of Sport* (New York: Frederick A. Stokes Co., 1929), 306.

41. Farr, *Black Champion,* 99.

42. Ruhl, "The Fight in the Desert," 22; *Chicago Tribune,* May 16, 1910, p. 12.

43. *Omaha Evening World-Herald,* July 2, 1910, p. 3; *Omaha Daily News,* June 25, 1910, p. 10; "The Psychology of the Prize Fight," *Current Literature,* July 1910, p. 57; *Chicago Tribune,* July 4, 1910, p. 1; Farr, *Black Champion,* 93.

44. *Omaha Evening World-Herald,* July 2, 1910, p. 1; *Omaha Daily News,* July 2, 1910, p. 6.

45. Gilmore, *Bad Nigger,* 41; *Booker T. Washington Papers,* vol. 10, 76.

46. Ruhl, "The Fight in the Desert," 22; *Chicago Tribune,* July 5, 1910, pp. 1, 6.

47. "Johnson Wins the Great Fight," *Harper's Weekly,* July 9, 1910, p. 8; *Chicago Tribune,* July 5, 1910, p. 6; Ruhl, "The Fight in the Desert," 22.

48. Farr, *Black Champion,* 107; *Current Literature,* August 1910, p. 129.

49. Van Every, *Muldoon,* 313–5; *Chicago Tribune,* July 5, 1910, p. 6.

50. Farr, *Black Champion,* 111; "Johnson Wins the Great Fight," 8.

51. W. C. Heinz, ed., *The Fireside Book of Boxing* (New York: Simon and Schuster, 1961), 256; *Chicago Tribune,* July 5, 1910, pp. 1, 6. (Except when otherwise noted, the description of the fight is from the various accounts in this paper.)

52. Van Every, *Muldoon,* 308–9.

53. Ruhl, "The Fight in the Desert," 13.

4

"A GENERAL UNDERSTANDING"

Organized Baseball and Black Professional Baseball, 1900–1930

Neil Lanctot

We do not believe that there exists any rule or bylaw excluding the colored man from organized baseball, but there appears to be a general understanding all along the line that Cubans, (provided they do not come too black), Chinese, Indians and every one else under the sun, be allowed his chance to measure, except the black man. . . . Perhaps, some day, a Regular American baseball man will establish a precedent—maybe.

—Black sportswriter Ira Lewis, 1920.

WHILE THE OUTLOOK FOR professional black baseball appeared increasingly negative in the spring of 1928, African Americans were momentarily encouraged by renewed discussion in several daily newspapers of the long dormant issue of organized baseball's color barrier, triggered by the appearance of Andy Cohen, a Jew, in the New York Giants starting lineup. In the nearly thirty years since the last appearance of a black player in the minor leagues, black baseball had developed dramatically, yet its sportswriters, fans, and players continued to hope for the integration of the white professional game. Even Rube Foster's formation of the Negro National League (NNL) in 1920 had been partially motivated by a desire to prepare black players for their eventual entrance into major league baseball. Although the pre-Depression era is usually considered insignificant in the fight for integration, several noteworthy developments influenced the subsequent course of the assault on baseball's color line in the 1930s and early 1940s.

Organized baseball, despite its unwritten yet unyielding ban of African Americans after 1899, hardly remained isolated from black professional baseball. Eager to supplement their modest salaries, major and minor league players arranged exhibition games against black professional clubs and strong white semipro teams during spring training, on off days, and at the end of the season. As early as 1885, the Cuban Giants booked games against the New York Metropolitans and the Philadelphia Athletics of the American Association and later faced other league clubs, including the St. Louis Browns and Cincinnati Red Stockings as well as the National League's Kansas City Cowboys, Indianapolis Hoosiers, Boston Beaneaters, and Detroit Wolverines. Bud Fowler's Page Fence Giants also competed against major leaguers, losing twice to the Cincinnati Reds in 1895.

Some major league players, however, objected to all forms of interracial competition and refused to play black teams. Cap Anson, the star first baseman and manager of the Chicago White Stockings of the National League and perhaps the most vocal advocate of the color line in baseball, threatened to cancel several games in the 1880s rather than take the field against white professional teams with black players in their lineups. In September 1887 the St. Louis Browns, with the exception of Charles Comiskey and Ed Knauff, petitioned the team's owner, Chris Von der Ahe, to protest a scheduled exhibition game in West Farms, New York, against the Cuban Giants, noting they would "cheerfully play against white people at any time." To the disappointment of a large crowd, the game was canceled, Von der Ahe offering the alibi that injuries had prevented his team's appearance.[1]

With the accelerated development and increased strength of black teams after 1900, interracial professional competition became more common as white players began to realize its lucrative possibilities. Simultaneously, African-American teams began to defeat organized baseball clubs with regularity, largely due to the ascendancy of Rube Foster, who provided black baseball with a pitcher capable of stopping any major league lineup. During his four years in the East with the Philadelphia Giants and Cuban X Giants from 1903 through 1906, Foster reportedly defeated the New York Giants, Philadelphia A's, Philadelphia Phillies, Brooklyn Dodgers, and clubs from the New England, Tri-State, and Eastern leagues. Foster continued to baffle major league opponents after jumping to the West, winning all four of the Leland Giants' victories over an outlaw team featuring major leaguers Mike Donlin and Jake Stahl in 1907.

Often heavily attended, postseason barnstorming games were invaluable in showcasing the outstanding talents of African-American players to unsuspecting white players, fans, sportswriters, and owners. After attending the Leland Giants' series against Mike Donlin's All-Stars in 1907, Chicago White Sox owner Charles Comiskey noted that he would have signed at least three Giants had they been white, a refrain often repeated by major league officials during the next forty years. The complimentary treatment and continued strong showing of black clubs against major and minor league teams during the early 1900s raised hopes that African-American players or teams might be allowed in some of the lower-ranked leagues in organized baseball. In 1907, the Boston Braves' signing of pitcher Bill Joy, supposedly a Malay from Honolulu, was enthusiastically applauded by the *Indianapolis Freeman* and viewed as a potential step toward integration. Sol White claimed that one of the "leading players and a manager in the National League" was advocating the entry of Billy Matthews, an African American who had starred on Harvard's baseball team and was currently playing in white semipro leagues in New England.

While organized baseball remained closed to blacks, the formation of the United States League in 1910 temporarily attracted national attention to the issue. Organized by G. H. Lawson, a former minor league pitcher and brother of former major leaguer Alfred Lawson, the new league hoped to equal the major leagues in scope and prestige and took the unusually progressive step of allowing unrestricted access to African-American players. Not surprisingly, the league received only lukewarm response from black players, who doubted the wisdom of joining an outlaw circuit outside organized baseball run by a promoter whose similar projects had ended in failure. The Brooklyn Royal Giants and Cuban X Giants rejected offers from Lawson, and the "Black and Tan League," as it was labeled by some cynics, never got off the ground.[2]

Despite the failure of the United States League, the question of black participation in organized baseball was continually discussed during 1910, particularly after African-

American boxer Jack Johnson's dramatic triumph over Jim Jeffries for the heavyweight championship on July 4 of that year drew increased attention to the concept of interracial competition. In August, a Milwaukee newspaper endorsed the entrance of blacks into organized baseball, citing the hypocrisy of white players who "never hesitate about playing games against the Negro clubs in the off season" yet refused to play alongside them in the major leagues. The sentiment was echoed by the prominent sportswriter Bill Phelon, who noted, "Nowhere is the color line drawn so strictly as among the big and minor leaguers, and yet the color line fades away when there is a chance to make any money by playing black teams on the outside." In addition, Phelon observed that even flagrant racists such as Georgia-born Ty Cobb had recently participated in a postseason series against a Cuban team that featured several African Americans.

Since the 1890s, organized baseball teams had traveled to Cuba in the winter to face increasingly stiff local competition. In 1908, the Cincinnati Reds, led by former manager Frank Bancroft, lost seven of eleven games to Cuban teams, incurring the wrath of team president Garry Herrmann. The Reds, however, were impressed by the brilliant pitching of José Mendez, the future manager of the Kansas City Monarchs, who won two games in the series without allowing a run in twenty-five innings. Like Foster, Mendez would prove to be a nemesis for major league teams and was the subject of generous praise from white players and journalists, who constantly bemoaned the black skin that kept him out of organized baseball.

Despite the Reds' defeat in 1908, major league teams continued to compete against Cuban clubs with only modest success. Hampered by the absence of stars Ty Cobb and Sam Crawford, the American League champion Detroit Tigers were also dealt a series loss during their trip to Cuba in 1909. A year later, the Tigers returned for a twelve-game set against the Almendares and Havana clubs, the latter supplemented by African Americans "Home Run" Johnson, Bruce Petway, Pete Hill, and John Henry Lloyd. While the Tigers took seven of the twelve games with one tie, the four black players were particularly impressive in defeat, as John Henry Lloyd (.412) and Pete Hill (.389) encountered little trouble with major league pitching. Meanwhile, catcher Bruce Petway along with future major leaguer Mike Gonzalez achieved the remarkable feat of throwing out the great Ty Cobb (second in stolen bases in 1910 with sixty-five) in each of his three stolen base attempts during the five games in which he appeared during the series. After one unsuccessful attempt, the frustrated Cobb insisted that the bases had been placed too far apart and was proven correct after measurement. While contemporary press accounts also blamed sandy basepaths for Cobb's poor base-running performance, the Tigers' George Moriarty, who stole only thirty-three bases in 1910, managed to swipe seven during the series. Unhappy with his showing, Cobb reportedly vowed never to play against blacks again.[3]

To the chagrin of American League president Ban Johnson, the world champion Philadelphia Athletics also journeyed to Cuba in 1910. Fearful of humiliating defeats at the hands of clubs outside organized baseball, Johnson particularly objected to exhibition games by World Series participants, especially since few barnstorming teams were representative of the champions at full strength. Despite Johnson's opposition, the Athletics proceeded with their tour as planned, barely managing to split the eight-game series after losing three of the first four games. Alarmed by the mediocre showing of the Athletics, the National Commission promptly enacted a new law that forbade barnstorming by league champions and required other teams to obtain both league and owner permission. As the *Sporting News* approvingly stated, "The world's championship title therefore will not be besmirched by post-season tragedies such as the series between the Athletics and the Cuban teams." While Cuban barnstorming would be largely halted after 1911, controversy over postseason tours by "unrepresentative" major league teams would continue to rage in the future.

The postseason barnstorming, however, forced organized baseball to acknowledge the high caliber of baseball played by Cuban players and paved the way for their admission to organized baseball. In 1910, four light-skinned Cuban players were signed by New Britain of the Connecticut League, and a year later, Armando Marsans and Rafael Almeidau appeared in the major leagues with the Cincinnati Reds. While others such as Mike Gonzalez and Adolfo Luque would follow, organized baseball remained closed to darker Cubans like José Mendez despite several wins over major league opponents between 1908 and 1911 and praise from Larry Doyle, Christy Mathewson, and manager John McGraw of the New York Giants. Yet Lester Walton of the *New York Age* hoped the appearance of lighter Cuban players would prepare fans and players for the future signing of "coal black" Cubans like Mendez and perhaps lead to the participation of African Americans. In the meantime, Walton suggested that some black players might "keep their mouths shut and pass for Cubans."[4]

Among major league officials, New York Giants manager John McGraw seemed the most likely candidate to acquire a black player. While managing the American League's Baltimore Orioles in 1901, McGraw signed Charlie Grant, a well-known black professional player he had discovered working during the winter as a bellhop at the Eastland Hotel in Hot Springs, Arkansas, and who he subsequently attempted to pass him off as a Native American named Charlie Tokohama. McGraws plan failed, however, as Grant's identity was inadvertently revealed by black fans who publicly congratulated him. In addition, Chicago White Sox president Charles Comiskey recognized Grant from his previous appearances in Chicago as a member of the Columbia Giants. McGraw, according to Dave

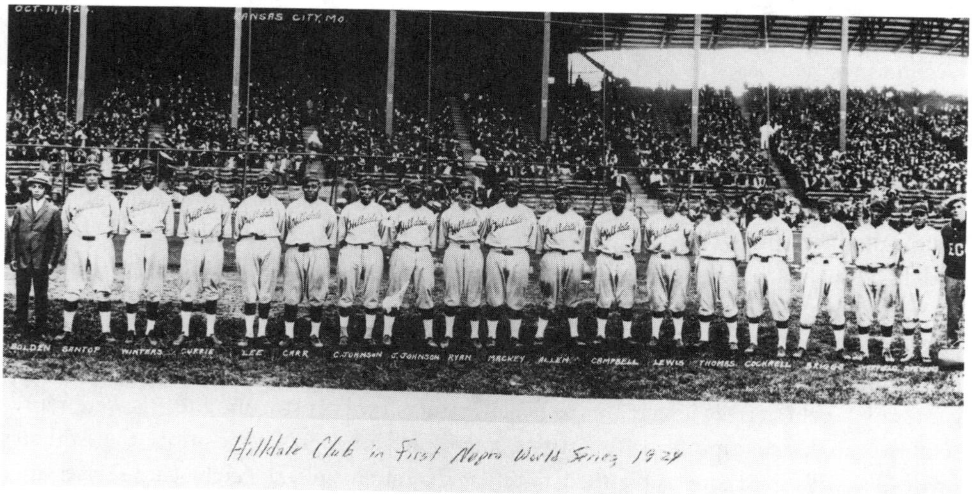

Figure 4–1
Negro league baseball players—the Hilldale Club, 1929. Courtesy of National Baseball Hall of Fame Library, Cooperstown, NY.

Wyatt of the *Indianapolis Freeman*, wept after being forced to release Grant, and the incident established McGraw's reputation as a friend of black players.

Numerous black sportswriters praised McGraw for his seemingly sympathetic attitude toward African Americans. In 1909, McGraw's donation of the receipts from a benefit game in Waco, Texas, to a local black college was noted in the African-American press, as was his later signing of Native-American catcher Chief Meyers. An admirer of the skills of black players, McGraw reportedly claimed that he would pay $30,000 for Mendez if he were white, leading observers such as the *Chicago Defender*'s William White to predict that McGraw would sign African Americans if allowed. A list of noted black baseball players that included Spottswood Poles, Dick Redding, Joe Williams, and John Henry Lloyd, discovered by McGraw's widow after his death, apparently confirmed his intentions.

While McGraw was not as "chuck full of color prejudice" as other major league officials, his reputation for racial tolerance was somewhat overrated. McGraw's autobiography contains numerous references to "darkies," and as his biographer Charles Alexander has suggested, he was no "crusader for racial justice." Except for the Charlie Grant incident, McGraw made no real attempt to challenge the color line in baseball despite his reported interest in black players. Ironically, of the six leading major league officials polled by Jimmy Powers of the *New York Daily News* at the 1933 Baseball Writers Dinner, only McGraw openly objected to the presence of blacks in organized baseball.[5]

McGraw's American League contemporary Connie Mack was also viewed as favorably inclined toward black players. Like McGraw, Mack's use of Native Americans such as Chief Bender seemed to suggest a pervasive racial tolerance that might lead to a signing of an African American. Sol White, meanwhile, cited Mack's rental of Columbia Park to the Philadelphia Giants and Cuban X Giants, his willingness to allow his Athletics to barnstorm against black professional teams, and his supposed signing of a black player while manager of Milwaukee in 1900. In 1910 the *Chicago Defender* praised Mack as a "white man with a white heart" after learning that Mack had enrolled four black children from the South in northern private schools and paid their tuition. Judy Johnson also praised Mack as a "wonderful man" and claimed that Mack once told him that the integration of major league baseball was blocked only by the vast number of blacks who would have to be allowed in. Despite his respect for black players, Mack was opposed to integration, and the Athletics showed little interest in signing black players after the color line was broken in 1946.

While hardly in favor of integration, White Sox owner Charles Comiskey had been viewed positively by African Americans since his refusal to sign a petition protesting a game against the Cuban Giants in 1887. Anxious to attract the numerous black fans who resided near his park, Comiskey hired African-American trainers and groundskeepers, donated money to charitable black causes, and leased his park on numerous occasions to black teams. Comiskey also remained friendly with Rube Foster despite his competition for patronage with the nearby American Giants. Comiskey's true racial views, however, were more accurately suggested by his comments on the supposed stinginess of black fans, particularly in Baltimore.[6]

Although harsh by modern standards, the racial views of Comiskey, McGraw, and Mack were still more enlightened than those of most white players, who, like the majority of Americans during the Progressive era, continued to believe in the inferiority of African Americans. In 1911 the *St. Louis Post-Dispatch* offered a typically racist explanation for the skills of black players:

> Less removed from the anthropoid ape, he gets down on ground balls better, springs higher for liners, has a much stronger and surer grip, and can get in and out of a base on all fours in a way that makes the higher product of evolution look like a bush leaguer.[7]

Some players' racist views translated into violence toward blacks. In 1909 George McConnell of the New York Highlanders attempted to hang a black bellboy accused of stealing from him while at spring training in Macon, Georgia. The *Indianapolis Freeman* reported that McConnell, a Tennessee native, was stopped only by the intervention of his teammates. Another southerner, Ty Cobb, made no attempt to hide his abhorrence of African Americans, One teammate recalled, "Cobb hated a colored person worse than anything." Cobb was involved in numerous racial incidents early in his career, including an altercation with a groundskeeper in Augusta, Georgia in 1907; a fight with a laborer who objected to Cobb's stepping in freshly laid concrete in Detroit in 1908; and assaults on a black watchman at a Cleveland hotel in 1909, a fan in 1910, and a butcher in 1914. Not surprisingly, Cobb's attack of an abusive white fan in 1912 that led to his famous suspension was reportedly precipitated by taunts of "coon" or "half-nigger."

Cobb, who particularly objected to blacks he perceived as "uppity," was accused of kicking Ada Morris, a black chambermaid, down a flight of stairs in a Detroit hotel in 1919 after she protested a racial insult. While the incident was suppressed by the daily papers and the Tigers, black sportswriters such as Sol White denounced Cobb, noting that his name "should never pass the lips of colored baseball fans." Yet Cobb's brilliant baseball skills continued to intrigue African Americans, and even Rollo Wilson admitted that despite a "low down opinion of the Georgia Screech as an individual . . . his ability as an athlete makes us forget that when he is in action." In 1927, John Howe of the *Philadelphia Tribune* disgustedly noted the excitement shown by some local black fans at Cobb's presence with the Philadelphia Athletics. The usually unfriendly Cobb, however, surprised black Philadelphians in August 1928 by tossing two baseballs to a group of young African-American fans after pregame practice at Shibe Park.[8]

Cobb's overt bigotry and refusal to play against blacks after 1910 perhaps represented the extreme of racial intolerance in organized baseball, yet the financial lure of postseason barnstorming led many players to set aside their prejudices, at least temporarily, and as Frank Forbes, a veteran of several professional clubs, recalled, "They didn't allow Negroes in the Majors, but hell, we were very attractive to them in October." Despite the restrictions placed on barnstorming by the National Commission in 1911, major league teams continued to schedule postseason games with black professional teams, several in the East involving the recently organized Lincoln Giants. In 1911, Lincoln was defeated by an all-star team led by Walter Johnson but bounced back a year later to beat Rube Chalmers of the Philadelphia Phillies and Louis Drucke of the New York Giants. In 1913 Lincoln took four of five postseason games against teams partially or entirely composed of white major leaguers as Joe Williams won four games, including an impressive 9–2 victory over Grover Cleveland Alexander of the Phillies (22–8, 2.79) and a 2–1 outdueling of the Athletics' Chief Bender (21–10, 2.21). A year later, Williams won another game for Lincoln, defeating the Philadelphia Phillies 10–4 at Olympic Field.

The defeats of major league barnstorming teams by black clubs elicited a variety of reactions from white fans and players. The excuse of an unrepresentative lineup was frequently employed, occasionally with some justification. In 1911 the Pittsburgh Pirates featured only one regular player in the starting lineup and were beaten by Dizzy Dismukes and the West Baden Sprudels, while other "all-star" teams featured only a few legitimate major league players. Other clubs, after initially underestimating an African-American team, subsequently rationalized their defeat by citing their opponent's atypically high caliber of play. After crushing several white minor league teams during their winter tour of California in 1913, the Chicago American Giants earned the respect of their rivals and lavish praise from the local press such as the *San Francisco Chronicle,* which gushed, "We hate to say how good this ball club really is."[9]

Realizing the strength of black professional teams and fearful of potential "disgrace" from defeat, some major league players continued to be leery of interracial competition. In 1912, the New York Giants nearly canceled a scheduled exhibition game at Paterson, New Jersey, after learning that the opponent would not be the semipro team they had expected but the Smart Sets, a black professional club. The Giants finally agreed to play, although pitcher Louis Drucke, fearful of gaining a reputation of being easily beaten by blacks refused to participate unless announced under an assumed name. With the score tied at three in the tenth inning, the Giants left the field, protesting the supposed use of an old baseball by Smart Sets pitcher Danny McClellan. While a few angry fans reportedly pelted the departing Giants with sticks and stones, the headline in the following day's *New York Times* (GIANTS PLAY NEGRO TEAM, ENDS IN RIOT) typically distorted the incident, providing a tacit condemnation of interracial competition.

With white players pressured by fans who expected easy victories and questioned defeats, a number of officials in organized baseball continued to voice increasing objections to all forms of barnstorming, particularly against black teams. In 1914, a planned series between the Lincoln Stars and an all-star team featuring five players from the world champion Boston Braves was canceled because of the opposition of Braves manager George Stallings. Meanwhile, manager Walter McCredie of the Portland Beavers of the Pacific Coast League was harshly criticized for booking his team to play Rube Foster's American Giants despite being "badly beaten" by them during the previous year. Dan Long, a former league manager, felt that no PCL team should play African-American clubs, stating that "colored players are barred in organized baseball, and I can see no reason why white players should even meet them in exhibition games, if they are barred by the baseball powers." League president Baum voiced his disapproval, and one owner proudly revealed that there were "two classes I bar from playing on my ball park—colored tossers and bloomer girls." In response, the *New York Age* asserted with some logic that opposition to interracial games stemmed more from fear of humiliation than actual color prejudice.[10]

In 1915, two controversial preseason games held in New York and Indianapolis compelled organized baseball once again to take decisive action against barnstorming. With both leagues already irate over a planned postseason western tour by two decidedly inferior "all-star teams," the Lincoln Giants' 1–0 defeat of the National League champion Philadelphia Phillies (with six regulars in the lineup) on October 17 confirmed the need to enforce stricter restrictions. Questioned by National League president John Tener, who was prepared to halt all barnstorming, Phillies owner William Baker insisted that his team had been given permission to play locally. While most observers expected the following week's scheduled game between Lincoln and Philadelphia to be canceled, the Phillies were allowed to play and won 4–2. The National Commission, however, vowed to address the barnstorming issue during the winter months.

A second disturbing incident occurred simultaneously in Indianapolis as violence erupted at an October 24 game at Washington Park between the Indianapolis ABCs and a barnstorming team led by Donie Bush of the Detroit Tigers. The arrest of Bingo DeMoss and Oscar Charleston of the ABCs for attacking an umpire prompted hundreds of fans to swarm onto the field, the disturbance eventually handled by club-brandishing police. Typically, the local white newspaper, the *Indianapolis Star,* exploited the racial angle, stating that a race riot had been "narrowly averted." Although manager C. I. Taylor and Charleston apologized for the incident, the National Association of Professional Baseball Leagues announced plans to limit future competition in Indianapolis between black professional and white all-star teams.

Hoping to halt the embarrassing defeats and avoid the controversies of the prior season, the American and National leagues restricted barnstorming privileges prior to the 1916 season. Players now required written consent from their team to participate in barnstorming or other sports such as football or basketball in the off-season. While exhibition games were played as usual during 1916, league barnstorming rules were enforced more strictly than in the past. The National Commission blocked the participation of Bill Rariden of the Giants, Ed Roush of the Reds, and Doc Crandall of the Browns, and the Indianapolis club of the American Association prevented several of its players from playing in a postseason game with the ABCs. Meanwhile, a total of fifty-one players from thirteen of the sixteen clubs were fined by the National Commission for illegal barnstorming activities during 1916.[11]

To the chagrin of organized baseball, professional black teams continued to register victories over major and minor league clubs despite the new league policy. During October 1917, organized baseball officials were forced to contend with not only Hilldale's landmark victory over the All-Americans but the Lincoln Giants' defeat of Rube Marquard (19–12, 2.55 with Brooklyn), with both games won by Joe Williams. In response, Brooklyn Dodgers owner Charles Ebbets fined Marquard a hundred dollars, the action rationalized in a subsequent press release:

> The Brooklyn team is averse to permitting its team, or any of its players, participating in games with Negroes. There are only semi-professional Negro teams, and when there is an outcome like yesterday's game, when Rube was beaten, President Ebbets believes it tends to lower the calibre of ball played by the big leagues in the eyes of the public, and at the same time make the major league team the subject of ridicule at the hands of the more caustic fans.[12]

The National Commission, meanwhile, took dramatic steps to block barnstorming by the 1917 league champions New York Giants and Chicago White Sox, holding $1,000 of each player's World Series share as bond to be disbursed only after both teams had signed an agreement not to barnstorm. During the following season, the National Commission again attempted to suppress postseason activity, disciplining several players from the world champion Boston Red Sox for barnstorming against Hilldale and white semipro clubs.

Facing diminished opportunities to compete in lucrative games against organized baseball teams, most black players reacted negatively to the new policy. Some observers, including the *Indianapolis Freeman,* felt that the recent barnstorming restriction had been enforced solely because of embarrassing defeats to black teams: "They have a very good reason for not letting their men play, and it isn't the fear of them getting hurt either." Yet veteran columnist Dave Wyatt argued that black baseball benefited little from postseason exhibitions, noting that victories by black teams could often be blamed on weak competition while white victories exposed the weaknesses in black professional baseball, As Wyatt observed, postseason games were not particularly meaningful unless a white team's lineup was intact and had been playing together over a period of time rather than assembled haphazardly, as was increasingly the case.

The regulation of postseason barnstorming reduced the already limited interaction between white major leaguers and black professional players and helped suppress discussion of the color line in baseball for several years. The successful formation of a third major league, the outlaw Federal League in 1914, led some African Americans to hope the expected depletion of major league talent would pave the way for the entrance of blacks to organized baseball. In 1914, Rube Foster told the *Seattle Post Intelligencer* that he expected blacks to be allowed in the minor leagues by 1915. While the Federal League's eventual collapse dashed hopes of integration, the league provided several parks that would later be used by black teams in Indianapolis, St. Louis, and Newark.[13]

With the color line still firmly intact, major league scouts turned their attention to several talented black players perceived as suitable candidates to pass as white, Cuban, or Native American in organized baseball. The great Cuban shortstop Pelayo Chacon was followed by scouts throughout his career but was eventually judged too dark, while fellow

Figure 4–2
Oscar Charleston, at left, longtime star of Negro league baseball. Courtesy of National Baseball Hall of Fame Library, Cooperstown, NY.

islander Christobel Torriente was rejected because of kinky hair. In the Pacific Coast League, Walter McCredie's attempt to sign a half-Hawaiian-half-Chinese player was blocked by league officials, although Jimmy Claxton of the Oakland Oaks managed to pass as white long enough to appear on a baseball card in 1916. Various schemes to sign black players would continue, and by 1929 the *Chicago Whip* claimed that twenty black players were passing for white in the major leagues.[14]

The devastating effect of World War I on organized baseball provoked renewed discussion of the issue. With numerous leagues shut down during 1918, several observers suggested that the admission of blacks might stimulate interest, and even the usually conservative *Sporting News* asked whether the "new era of World Democracy [would] change their status." An article by the nationally syndicated sportswriter Hugh Fullerton in early 1919 provided additional favorable publicity to black players. Fullerton, however, was opposed to integration of organized baseball because of potential racial conflict and suggested a black professional league with the franchises to lease major league parks when idle.

Unbeknownst to Fullerton, several black teams had already established a working relationship with organized baseball by leasing parks for important games. Prior to 1910, the Cuban X Giants and Philadelphia Giants had leased Columbia Park in Philadelphia, and New York teams had rented the Polo Grounds, Hilltop Park, and Washington Park. By the end of World War I, Rube Foster's Chicago American Giants had played at Comiskey Park in Chicago, Navin Field in Detroit, Redland Field in Cincinnati, Forbes Field in Pittsburgh, and American League Park in Washington, D.C. In 1919, Hilldale and the Bacharach Giants became the first two black teams to play at Shibe Park in Philadelphia, and a black team made its initial appearance at Ebbets Field in Brooklyn, with the first all-black game scheduled a year later. During the week of October 4–10, 1920, Hilldale made its first appearance at Phillies Park, and the New York Bacharachs and Chicago American Giants were simultaneously scheduled at Shibe Park.[15]

The continued development of black professional baseball in the postwar era resulted in expanded use of major league parks. Some teams secured grounds for an entire season. In 1921, the Cuban Stars of the NNL leased Redland Field as their home grounds, and the Washington Potomacs of the Eastern Colored League (ECL) used Griffith Stadium for local games in 1923 and 1924. In Pittsburgh the Homestead Grays began to lease Forbes Field on a regular basis during the 1920s as Cum Posey formed a profitable working relationship with Pirates owner Barney Dreyfuss. Yet the recently built Yankee Stadium, despite its proximity to New York's African-American community, remained off-limits to black teams until July 5, 1930, when the park was leased for a benefit game for the Brotherhood of Sleeping Car Porters, featuring the Lincoln Giants and Baltimore Black Sox. The game reportedly drew 14,000 fans leading to expanded access to Yankee Stadium, as the Lincoln Giants rented the park in September 1930 and the newly formed Harlem Stars in 1931. In 1931, Hilldale made its first and only appearance at Yankee Stadium and played at Griffith Stadium, Forbes Field, and Phillies Park during the same season.

Despite the superior caliber of organized baseball's parks, black teams faced considerable disadvantages as tenants. Heavy attendance was necessary to offset rental fees ranging from 25 to 33 1/3 percent on occasion, yet the more expensive major league ticket prices sometimes limited the patronage of black fans. In 1931, a second benefit game played at Yankee Stadium for the Brotherhood of Sleeping Car Porters lost money after the Yankee management received its share of the gross receipts. In addition, black teams received no profits from concessions, were forced to contend with white park personnel, and were usually forbidden to use dressing rooms and showers. By the 1940s, however, most grounds in organized baseball had been occupied by black teams, the New York Yankees and the Washington Senators maintaining especially profitable rental agreements.[16]

While park rentals helped establish relationships between white and black baseball officials, organized baseball's attitude toward integration changed little in the postwar era. In addition, the formation of the NNL in 1920 contributed to ambivalence among some fans. Already increasingly committed to building separate communities, race-conscious African-American fans feared that black players would be overshadowed in the white major leagues and felt that black professional baseball should be established on a profitable basis without the intrusion of whites.

Not surprisingly, the December 1920 founding of the ambitious fully integrated Continental League by the redoubtable G. H. Lawson was perceived as a predictable white reaction to the NNL's successful debut season. Ten years after his United States League failure, Lawson once again seemed determined to capitalize on the appeal of black players and announced that four of the new circuit's ten eastern-based franchises would be black. While Lawson's statement that at least one hundred black players were of major league caliber suggested an admiration of their skills, the new league seemingly planned to utilize African Americans as one of a number of publicity gimmicks. Unlike organized baseball, the Continental League planned no reserve clause, each team instead to be affiliated with the American Federation of Labor. In addition, hitters would be allowed two bases on a walk and were not required to circle the bases on home runs. The publicity-conscious Lawson also announced the hiring of boxer Jack Johnson as a league umpire at $1,500 per week and reportedly planned to use other black umpires.

As in 1910, Lawson secured national coverage for his project, including several articles in the *New York Times.* Despite heavy press coverage, most organized baseball officials regarded the Continental League as little more than a curiosity, and Charles Ebbets, Jr., of the Brooklyn Dodgers particularly noted the league's lack of substantial financial backing. Other observers objected to Lawson's integration policy. While offering tentative support, *Baseball Magazine* was quick to note that "through all the ages the effort to mix oil and water has failed. In this country at least all efforts to mix black and white on an [equal basis] have also failed." Meanwhile, the *Sporting News* refused to grant coverage to Lawson except to criticize the new league for reportedly planning to play games against the recently expelled members of the 1919 Chicago White Sox.

Although suspicious of Lawson's intentions, the black press was generally supportive of the Continental League, at least initially. The league's extensive involvement of African-American players, umpires, and league officials was commended as was Lawson's promise not to encroach upon NNL territory. In March 1921 the *Chicago Defender* endorsed the league, noting that "any institution that has the tendency to try and break down the color prejudice and treat all as Americans should have the patronage of all citizens." Lawson, however, alienated blacks by attempting to lure the American Giants into the league and later made an effort to seize Washington Park from the Indianapolis ABCs.

With Lawson appearing an increasing threat to the NNL, opposition to the Continental League mounted, led by veteran sportswriter Ira Lewis. To Lewis, the Continental League represented another example of white baseball men "casting an eye to the possibilities of colored baseball," coincidentally after the NNL had enjoyed a successful season and had recently expanded by luring eastern teams into the fold. In addition, Lewis questioned the advisability of black players joining an outlaw league seemingly destined to fail. As Lewis noted, "After struggling along this far, under conditions that have been worse than bitter to the pioneers, it would be the height of folly to form any kind of a deal with white baseball men that would not assure to the colored player all the advantages given any other baseball player; and particularly the chance to ride into major league baseball." Lewis's misgivings proved correct. Despite continued announcements from Lawson, the league apparently never began its season, although the existence of a black Continental League franchise in Philadelphia was noted locally.[17]

The collapse of the Continental League, however, was largely overshadowed by the recent appointment of judge Kenesaw Mountain Landis as commissioner of baseball in the aftermath of the 1919 Black Sox scandal. Black baseball fans hoped that Landis, viewed as friendly toward African Americans, might take steps to begin the integration of organized baseball. As the *Baltimore Afro-American* enthused, Landis was "eminently fair and if it was left to him, there would be colored major league baseball clubs tomorrow." Shortly after Landis took office, former Harvard black baseball star and attorney Billy Matthews wrote to the new commissioner soliciting his support for the fight against the color barrier:

> You will note that every other class of people are counted eligible to play in the big leagues. Why keep the Negro out if he can play the same grade of baseball demanded of the other groups? Are the big leagues more exclusive than the best colleges and athletic clubs in the land? Does an attitude on the part of the National Commission square with your plea of injustice to Afro-Americans? If baseball leaders would adopt the open door policy toward the Negro player, don't you think it would be another guarantee on their part that baseball in the future is to be on the level?

Despite his reputation for racial tolerance and supposed interest in black professional baseball, Landis was hardly an advocate for integration. During his lengthy tenure as commissioner, Landis avoided public discussion of the issue until the late 1930s, and then only to state that the time was still not right for black players in organized baseball. While pressure for integration would mount in the early 1940s, Landis continued to remain firmly opposed, even blocking an attempt by Bill Veeck to purchase the moribund Philadelphia Phillies and restock the team with black players. Shortly before his death in 1944, Landis finally addressed the issue of blacks in baseball: "There is no rule in organized baseball prohibiting their participation and never has been to my knowledge."[18]

Although Landis did nothing to advance the cause of integration during the 1920s, his famous 1922 suspension of Babe Ruth for violating rules prohibiting barnstorming by World Series participants would drastically affect the postseason interaction of white and black players. In response to the Ruth case, the National League and American League subsequently allowed barnstorming by World Series participants but limited barnstorming squads to no more than three players from a single team with league and commissioner permission required. Black teams, who had continued to fare well in exhibition games with major leaguers, viewed the ruling as yet another attempt to suppress interracial professional competition, which in recent years had faced increasing opposition from white officials. In 1921 several St. Louis sportswriters had severely criticized the St. Louis Cardinals for barnstorming against the NNL's St. Louis Giants. According to historian Richard Crepeau, the *Sporting News* "commented that it might be all right for the players to pick up a few extra dollars. On the other hand, in the eyes of the Cardinal fans it was 'bad stuff' to see their heroes participate in 'the grand African show.' "

Initially the new barnstorming rules had a limited effect on postseason exhibition games. In 1922, black professional teams had little difficulty securing organized baseball opponents in the off-season and achieved unparalleled success. The New York Bacharachs twice beat the world champion New York Giants, defeating Rosie Ryan (17–12, 3.01 ERA, ranked first in the National League) and Jack Scott, who had recently shut out the Yankees in the third game of the World Series. In the Midwest, the St. Louis Stars took two of three games against the Detroit Tigers (minus Ty Cobb and Harry Heilmann), and the Monarchs won five of six from the Kansas City Blues of the American Association. Other professional teams, including the Brooklyn Royal Giants, Cuban Stars, Indianapolis ABCs, and Cleveland Tate Stars, won several games against opponents from organized baseball. In 1923, black teams once again made a strong showing as Hilldale took five of six games against two barnstorming teams of Philadelphia Athletics, the Detroit Stars won two of three from the fifth-place St. Louis Browns, and the American Giants divided two games and tied a third with the Detroit Tigers.

The numerous defeats of organized baseball teams offered proof of the major league caliber of black professional teams. Noting Hilldale's victories over the barnstorming Athletics in 1923, A. Philip Randolph's *The Messenger* asked: "And now, who are really the World's Champions? Who are America's best players? Is there any reason why these Negroes should not play in the big leagues?" The *Baltimore Afro-American* hailed the postseason competition as the "real world's series" but bemoaned the limited coverage of the games in the white press. Several white sportswriters, however, did acknowledge the miserable showing of white teams in 1922 and 1923, although most chose to castigate major leaguers for their participation and gave little credit to their black opposition. In October 1922, the *North American* observed that "several teams with prominent major leaguers have been beaten in the last week by colored semipro teams and the showing made by the big league stars was said not to be first class." Commenting on the 1923 series between the St. Louis Browns and "a bunch of Negroes," a writer for the St. Louis-based *Sporting News* voiced his dismay at the "spectacle of white major league players taking the abuse of mobs of our colored brethren and liking it or seeming to because of the few dollars netted."[19]

Despite restrictions, postseason barnstorming continued throughout the decade with Hilldale, Homestead, and the Baltimore Black Sox regular participants in the East, and the American Giants in the West. After mid-decade, however, black teams competed rarely against intact major league lineups and increasingly faced "all-star" teams of varying degrees of skill. After barnstorming against a powerful team of major leaguers featuring Lefty Grove, Heinie Manush, and Jimmy Dykes in 1926, Hilldale competed against two nondescript teams with barely a recognizable name in their lineups in 1928 and 1931, winning six of eight games. With permission required, many star players were prevented from participation, such as Jack Quinn and Mickey Cochrane of the Athletics, who were forced to sit out a game with the Lincoln Giants in 1925 for failing to secure prior authorization. Black professional teams, however, continued to face strong opposition yet continued to dominate postseason competition, to the chagrin of organized baseball. In reality, the superior showing of black professional teams was hardly surprising, as Bill Foster, Rube Foster's half brother and a successful pitcher in the Negro Leagues during the 1920s and 1930s, explained:

> The major league all-stars just didn't beat those teams, those Negro teams. See, we were organized as a unit, but they just came down there with one from here, one from there. They didn't

have a whole lot of signals or anything like that. . . . An all-star, picked ball club is at a disadvantage in the technical part of baseball.[20]

Gene Benson observed that black players "played harder when we played the major leaguers because we were trying to prove something to them that we could play." Yet a number of major leaguers during the 1920s continued to show little respect for black players despite their skills and remained outwardly hostile toward all African Americans. In 1923, the Philadelphia Athletics were rocked by a controversy involving the Ku Klux Klan membership of several team members and the ineligibility of certain players because of religion or ethnicity. The later indictment (and subsequent acquittal) of Athletics pitcher Robert Hasty in the whipping of an African-American woman in Marietta, Georgia, forced the usually conservative *Sporting News* to address the subject of racism in baseball, noting that the exclusion of the "Ethiopian" had deprived baseball of some of the "greatest players the game ever has known."

Although several prominent major league players were reportedly members of the Klan, racial attitudes differed widely in organized baseball, as in American society. Baltimore-born Babe Ruth, for example, considered being called "nigger" by bench jockeys "the worst insult of all," although his biographer Robert Creamer has observed that "his personal relationship with blacks over the years was amiable." Ruth regularly barnstormed against black teams, praised the ball-playing skills of John Henry Lloyd and Dick Redding, and even met publicly with black boxer Harry Wills in 1924. Nip Winters of Hilldale noted that the Babe was "a fine man to get along with, very friendly," and Bill Drake assessed him as "a regular fellow. . . . He used to chew tobacco. I'd say, 'Ruth, give me a chew.' He'd pull out a plug, give me a bite, he'd take a bite, put it back in his pocket." Ruth, however, was less than friendly in his comments about Cuban players after his tour of the island with the New York Giants in 1920: "Them greasers are punk players. Only a few of them are any good. This guy they calls after me [Christobel Torriente of the Chicago American Giants] because he made a few homers is as black as at a ton-and-a-half of coal in a dark cellar."[21]

While hardly outspoken advocates of integration, several noted players such as Casey Stengel, Lou Gehrig, Frankie Frisch, Walter Johnson, and Honus Wagner had no qualms about barnstorming against black players and appreciated their abilities. Cool Papa Bell, meanwhile, recalled Dizzy Dean as a "good guy" and praised the racial attitudes of Paul and Lloyd Waner as well as Jimmie Foxx, who was friendly with several black players, including Gene Benson, Oscar Charleston, and Webster McDonald.

Yet like Ty Cobb, the great Rogers Hornsby, a Texas native, openly expressed his contempt for African Americans. Hornsby occasionally boycotted games against black teams and, as manager of the New York Giants in 1927, reportedly orchestrated the firing of the team's black trainer. Nearly twenty years later, Hornsby would react to the signing of Jackie Robinson: "They've been getting along all right playing together and should stay where they belong in their league."[22]

In Philadelphia, Lefty Grove and Al Simmons of the Athletics were known for their less than enlightened views of African Americans. Judy Johnson recalled his first appearance against Grove in 1926:

The best was beating Lefty Grove. He just hated us. It was nigger this and nigger that. I never wanted a hit so bad in my life as the first time I came up against him. I hit the first pitch he

> threw me right back at him. It took the cap right off his head and went right into center field for a single. Grove was pretty rattled. . . . I remember that hit more than any I ever got.

In later years, Grove denied ever playing against blacks, although there is ample evidence of postseason defeats to Hilldale in 1926 and the Baltimore Black Sox in 1928.[23]

The racial views of major and minor league officials also varied considerably during the 1920s. According to William Gibson of the *Baltimore Afro-American,* owner Jack Dunn of the Baltimore Orioles of the International League was "so full of race hate" that he would not allow his club to play the Black Sox and refused to lease his park to the team. In Chicago, the Cubs, owned by rumored Klan member William Wrigley, were hardly receptive to blacks. As Willie Powell of the American Giants noted, the Cubs were "very uppity. The White Sox didn't mind us playing in their park. But the Cubs didn't want us." In Washington, Senators owner Clark Griffith was a complex figure whose reputation for racial tolerance was primarily based on his liberal use of Cuban players during his managerial career, including Armando Marsans and Rafael Almeida in 1911 with the Cincinnati Reds, as well as Merito Acosta and Jacinto Calvo with the Washington Senators in 1913. Yet Griffith later refused to allow interracial games at Griffith Stadium during the 1920s and incurred the wrath of the local NAACP in 1925 by failing to include African-American youths in a promotion at the park.

Despite occasionally shoddy treatment from Griffith and other major league owners, many African Americans remained dedicated fans of organized baseball, a dilemma never entirely resolved by black baseball officials. With Griffith Stadium located within easy access to black Washingtonians, African Americans eagerly patronized the Senators, to the chagrin of one *Washington Tribune* columnist: "All of us are quite interested in major league baseball and rightly so, but why not develop an interest in the semi-pros and sandlotters?" After watching the Senators receive greater African-American support than the newly organized Potomacs in 1923, local sportswriter H. Scott asked, "Why then, should we continue to support, foster and fill the coffers of a national enterprise that has no place or future for men of color, although they have the ability to make the grade." Comiskey Park, also located in a black residential area, attracted numerous African-American fans, and in Philadelphia, John Howe of the *Philadelphia Tribune* criticized "colored adorers of the Athletics" who had no interest in black professional baseball. In St. Louis, blacks continued to patronize the St. Louis Cardinals and St. Louis Browns despite being forced to sit in a separate screened-in section at Sportsman's Park. In 1929, a St. Louis black newspaper chided fans who would rather "fork over six bits to see a game at Sportsman's Park . . . and get jim-crowed in the bargain" than attend games of the NNL's St. Louis Stars.[24]

As with white fans, World Series games were particularly popular with African Americans. Rube Foster regularly attended the fall classic each season, and C. I. Taylor kept a promise to take his entire team to a series game in 1917. With the Polo Grounds easily accessible to black fans, the 1921 series between the New York Giants and New York Yankees reportedly attracted over 25,000 blacks, causing the *Chicago Whip* to scold, "It is bad enough to ride on Jim Crow cars, but to go into ecstasies over a Jim Crow sport is unforgivable." In 1932, one commentator estimated that 20 percent of the 30,000 fans at Yankee Stadium for game two of the World Series were black. Even the black World Series was occasionally overshadowed by its white counterpart. During game two of the 1924 black World Series at Phillies Park, results of the white World Series game between the Senators and Giants were periodically announced, and many fans remained in the park to learn the final score.[25]

Some observers attributed the popularity of major league baseball to superior publicity available in the daily press. In Philadelphia, Otto Briggs noted that some blacks read only white newspapers and "very seldom go to see colored teams play." The *New York Amsterdam News* claimed in 1929 that there were "scores of people in Harlem that do not know there is a colored baseball club in the city." Another sportswriter agreed that the black press did not reach enough fans, remarking, "It is not uncommon to hear even youngsters calling the names of white players with ease—while it would give them a headache to name a Negro star." The *Philadelphia Tribune* noted that a group of young black children attending their first Hilldale game as guests of Bolden "had heard of the Cobb, Speaker, Hornsby, and Babe Ruth and other pale-faced stars but knew not that they had players of their own group who could hold their own with any stars of any league."[26]

Although white players attended black professional games on occasion, most had only limited contact with African Americans. In addition, the subservient position occupied by African Americans in organized baseball, as in American society, helped reinforce racial prejudices and stereotypes. As early as the 1900s, several major league teams hired African Americans as trainers, including Bill Buckner of the White Sox, Ed Mackal of the New York Giants, and Ed LaForce of the Pittsburgh Pirates—all enjoying lengthy careers. (Trainers at this time performed no medical function but mostly handled equipment, like the clubhouse attendant of the modern game.) By the 1920s, several African Americans were employed as trainers in the American Association, Pacific Coast League, and other minor leagues. Yet black trainers, like all African-American laborers, were susceptible to dismissal at the behest of whites. After the 1917 season, Bill Buckner was terminated as trainer of the White Sox, reportedly because of Eddie Collins's dislike of African Americans. While Bucker was eventually rehired, trainer Doc Jamieson of the New York Giants would be fired because of manager Rogers Hornsby's prejudices.

The continued use of blacks as mascots or good-luck charms also undermined white racial respect. As early as the 1900s, several major league teams featured African-American mascots, including the Pittsburgh Pirates, who hired Lovell Miller for thirty-five dollars a month in 1902. By the 1920s, black mascots were still a common sight. The Nashville team of the Southern Association employed a "comical" mascot named "Rubber," and some semipro teams used mascots in games against black professional clubs. In Philadelphia, Mickey Cochrane of the Athletics had an "anonymous bat boy" named "Black Cat," and Connie Mack added two black mascots as good luck for the team's pennant run in 1925. Desperate for any progress in the fight for integration, the New *York Amsterdam News* applauded Mack's decision to hire mascots as "the most radical move any major league manager has made in the annals of baseball" and hoped that the presence of blacks in the Philadelphia clubhouse might change racial attitudes.[27]

The enthusiastic reaction to a black mascot underscored the lack of progress toward integration by the end of the decade. Yet the 1920s had been noteworthy for the continued strong showing by African-American teams against opponents from organized baseball, offering convincing proof that their skills were equal if not superior to those of white players. As sportswriter and NNL official A. D. Williams noted, black players had not only defeated major league barnstorming teams but also outperformed white players in the

Cuban winter leagues. In addition, Williams cited Cuban players like Ramon Herrera, a veteran of both the Eastern Colored League's Cuban Stars and the Boston Red Sox, as proof of the caliber of black baseball. Several white journalists and officials had also attested to the high quality of professional black teams. In 1924, Mike Doolan, a former major league player and one of the umpires during the eastern games of the 1924 Hilldale-Kansas City series, classified both teams as "far better" than the International League, and Roger Pippen, a sportswriter with the *Baltimore News,* lavished praise upon several Black Sox in 1925: "Their ability astounded me. If colored players were permitted in the National, American and International Leagues, three or four of the Sox would have their names in big type in every sports page in the country."

Few white journalists, however, outwardly advocated integration during the late 1920s and would remain mostly silent on the issue until the early 1930s. One national publication, *The Nation,* briefly raised the issue in 1926, noting that while blacks participated alongside whites in college athletics, "the major leagues never admit even the most brilliant colored baseball player." Meanwhile, the short-lived journalistic discussion during the spring of 1928 typically accomplished little to change the status of black players, to their increasing frustration. As Jake Stephens noted, "You just knew you were better than the major leaguers. . . . Why, Chick Galloway of the Athletics didn't have anywhere near the range I had at shortstop. He couldn't carry my glove."

The early belief that the color line would fall if black baseball continued to develop proved a fallacy. The ECL and NNL, despite their numerous financial and administrative problems, had offered an exciting brand of baseball featuring some of the finest players in the country, yet the color line remained firmly intact. With race relations continuing to deteriorate nationally in the late 1920s, there seemed little immediate hope for relief, leaving African-American players and their fans to contend as usual with the precarious fortunes of professional black baseball.[28]

NOTES

1. *Philadelphia Tribune,* May 24, 1928; Jerry Malloy, "The Birth of the Cuban Giants: The Origins of Black Professional Baseball" (unpublished ms., courtesy of Jerry Malloy); Malloy, "Out at Home," *National Pastime: A Review of Baseball History* (Fall 1982); 26 ("cheerfully"); *Sol White's Official Base Ball Guide* (Columbia, SC: Camden House, 1984)[orig., 1907], 17–9; Phil Dixon and Patrick J. Hannigan, *Negro Baseball Leagues, 1867–1955: A Photographic History* (Mattitukh, NY: Amereon House, 1992), 72–81. Gerald Scully, for example, has noted that "with few exceptions, little of importance concerning the Negro in organized baseball seems to have occurred from 1898 to the 1930s," and Richard Crepeau has similarly asserted that the "issue was only rarely mentioned" during the 1920s; see Gerald W. Scully, "Discrimination: The Case of Baseball," in Roger Noll, ed., *Government and the Sports Business* (Washington, D.C.: Brookings Institution, 1974), 226; Richard Crepeau, *Baseball: America's Diamond Mind, 1919–1941* (Orlando: University Presses of Florida, 1980), 168.

2. White, *Base Ball Guide,* 85 ("leading players"), 127–128; *Half-Century Magazine,* March 1919, p. 8; *Indianapolis Freeman,* September 14, 21, 1907; March 19, April 16, 1910. *New York Age,* March 10, 1910; *New York Times,* March 4, 1910; *Chicago Whip,* January 22, 1920. Foster reportedly earned the nickname "Rube" after his defeat of Rube Waddell of the Athletics in the early 1900s. A newspaper account of the game has yet to be found.

3. *Indianapolis Freeman,* February 13, 1909; September 3, 1910 ("never hesitate"); February 4, 1911; February 24, 1912. *New York Age,* December 8, 1910; January 21, 1911 ("Nowhere is the"). Charles C. Alexander, *John McGraw* (New York: Oxford University Press, 1988), 17–20; John Hol-

way, *Blackball Stars: Negro League Pioneers* (Westport, CT: Mechler, 1988), 50; Michael Oleksak and Mary Adams Oleksak, *Beisbol: Latin Americans and the Grand Old Game* (Grand Rapids, MI: Masters Press, 1991), 20–21; Charles Alexander, *Ty Cobb* (New York: Oxford University Press, 1984), 98–9; Dixon and Hannigan, *Negro Baseball Leagues,* 102–103; Okeksak and Oleksak, "Cuba No Vacation for U. S. Teams in 1900s," *USA Today Baseball Weekly,* May 24–30, 1991, p. 18.

4. *Sporting News,* November 24, December 1, 15, 29, 1910; January 12, 1911 ("will not be"). Oleksak and Oleksak, "Cuba No Vacation," 18; Eugene Murdock, *Ban Johnson: Czar of Baseball* (Westport, CT: Greenwood, 1982), 66–69; Lee Allen, *Cooperstown Corner* (Cleveland, 1990), 7–9; *Indianapolis Freeman,* December 23, 1911; *New York Age,* September 28, 1911 (Walton quote).

5. *Indianapolis Freeman,* February 19, 1910; September 29, 1917. *Baltimore Afro-American,* October 27, 1928; Alexander, *John McGraw,* 75 ("crusader"); White, *Base Ball Guide,* 85; *New York Amsterdam News,* February 27, 1929; Chalk, *Pioneers of Black Sport: The Early Days of the Black Professional Athlete in Baseball, Basketball, Boxing, and Football* (New York: Dodd, Mead, 1975), 20; *New York Age,* April 1, 1909; August 24, September 28, 1911 ("chuck full"). *Chicago Defender,* May 10, 1919; Joel Zoss and John Stewart Bowman, *Diamonds in the Rough: The Untold Story of Baseball* (New York: MacMillan, 1989), 143; Dixon and Hannigan, *Negro Baseball Leagues,* 92; L. Robert Davids, ed. *Insider's Baseball: The Finer Points of the Game, as Examined by the Society for American Baseball Research* (New York: Scribners, 1983), 270.

6. *Indianapolis Freeman,* May 10, 1913; September 29, 1917. *Chicago Defender,* August 13, 1910; September 21, 1918 ("white man with a white heart"); May 10, 1919. *New York Amsterdam News,* February 27, 1929; Judy Johnson file, National Baseball Library ("wonderful man"); *Philadelphia Tribune,* November 5, 1931; Harold Seymour, *Baseball: The Golden Years* (New York: Oxford University Press, 1970), 243; Bruce Kuklick, *To Every Thing a Season: Shibe Park and Urban Philadelphia, 1909–1976* (Princeton, NJ: Princeton University Press, 1991), 145–6; John Holway, *Voices from the Great Negro Baseball Leagues* (New York: Dodd, Mead, 1975), 87. In 1928, Rollo Wilson noted that Mack was the "only owner or promoter" who refused to recognize his press standing. *Pittsburgh Courier,* May 19, 1928.

7. *New York Age,* September 28, 1911 ("less removed"); Kenneth L. Kusmer, *A Ghetto Takes Shape: Black Cleveland 1870–1930* (Champaign, IL: University of Illinois Press, 1974), 174–175.

8. *Indianapolis Freeman,* June 20, 1908; March 20, 1909. Alexander, *Ty Cobb,* 50, 67–8, 94, 98–9, 119; *New York Age,* September 16, 1909; *North American,* May 19, 1912; Zoss and Bowman, *Diamonds in the Rough,* 144–5; *Chicago Defender,* May 3, 1919; *Cleveland Advocate,* May 10, 1919 (White quote); *Pittsburgh Courier,* August 2, 1924 (Wilson quote); *Philadelphia Tribune,* February 12, 1927; August 30, 1928. Richard Bak, *Ty Cobb: His Tumultuous Life and Times* (Dallas, TX: Taylor, 1994), 178. Several other players were involved in racial violence. In 1917, Danny Shay, a former major leaguer and manager of Milwaukee of the American Association, was indicted in the murder of a black waiter but acquitted after claiming self-defense. In May 1928, in the Texas League, future major leaguer Art Shires reacted to the booing of black fans by firing a baseball into the segregated black section of the park in Waco, striking a fan who later died of his injuries; Shires was also acquitted. In 1930, Shanty Hogan of the New York Giants was stabbed by a black elevator operator after Hogan, objecting to his presence, attempted to evict him from a party. See *Baltimore Afro-American,* April 6, 1928; December 29, 1928. *New York Amsterdam News,* January 2, 1929; *Chicago Defender,* December 1, 1917; *Philadelphia Tribune,* October 16, 1930; *Philadelphia Public Ledger,* October 9, 1930.

9. Holway, *Blackball Stars,* 67 (Forbes quote), 68; *New York Age,* October 5, 19, 1911; October 31, November 7, 1912; October 2, 9, 16, 23, November 6, 1913. *Indianapolis Freeman,* September 16, 1911; April 12, December 20, 1913 ("hate to say").

10. *New York Age,* May 30, 1912; February 5 (Long, Baum quotes), October 8, 15, 22, 29, 1914; *Chicago Defender,* June 1, 1912; *New York Times,* May 27, 1912. In 1913, the *New York Times* would similarly distort an incident occurring at a game in Schenectady, New York, between the Mohawk Giants and a barnstorming team led by Walter Johnson of the Washington Senators. After the Mohawk Giants announced their refusal to participate until receiving back pay owed by the club's owner, the crowd surged onto the playing field, creating a "near riot" according to the *Times.* Order was eventually restored, and a five-inning game was played with Johnson, despite allowing only two hits and fanning eleven batters, being defeated by Frank Wickware 1–0. See *North American,* October 6, 1913; *New York Times,* October 6, 1913.

11. *New York Age,* October 7, 14, 21, 28, 1915; *New York Times,* October 14, 18, 21, 22, 23, 26, 1915; March 10, October 24, 27, December 9, 1916. *Indianapolis Freeman,* October 30 ("narrowly averted"), November 13, December 11, 1915; October 14, 1916. *Chicago Defender,* October 30, November 6, 1915; October 14, 1916.

12. *New York Age,* October 18, 1917; *Baltimore Afro-American,* October 27, 1917 ("The Brooklyn team"); *Chicago Defender,* October 27, 1917; *Philadelphia Tribune,* October 13, 1917.

13. *New York Times,* October 14, 16, 17, 1917; October 6, 1918. *Indianapolis Freeman,* May 2, 1914; October 14, 1916 ("They have"); March 24, 1917.

14. *Indianapolis Freeman,* July 10, 1915; *Chicago Defender,* January 16, 1915; July 5, 1919. *Baltimore Afro-American,* February 28, 1925; October 26, 1929. *Philadelphia Tribune,* March 21, 28, 1929; Holway, *Blackball Stars,* 126. Davids, *Insider's Baseball,* 58–62. In a strange reversal of typical practice, Chick Meade, who appeared with Hilldale in 1919 and with several other clubs during the early 1920s, reportedly passed as an African American to appear in black professional baseball after his failure to make the major leagues. See *Philadelphia Tribune,* June 25, 1931; September 22, 1932.

15. *Sporting News,* December 5, 1918 ("new era"); *Cleveland Advocate,* February 15, 1919; *Half-Century Magazine,* April 1919, p. 8; *Indianapolis Freeman,* September 14, 1907; *New York Age,* June 9, 1910; October 31, 1912; August 8, 1917. *Chicago Defender,* August 25, September 1, 1917; August 3, 31, 1918; September 20, 1919.

16. *Chicago Whip,* October 15, 1921; *Baltimore Afro-American,* March 24, 1924; *Philadelphia Tribune,* July 10, 1930; May 14, December 31, 1931. *New York Amsterdam News,* July 9, 1930; August 19, 26, 1931. *Washington Tribune,* July 28, 1923; Jules Tygiel, *Baseball's Great Experiment: Jackie Robinson and His Legacy* (New York: Oxford University Press, 1983), 22; *Pittsburgh Courier,* December 27, 1924.

17. *Indianapolis Freeman,* May 2, 1914; David Pietrusza, *Major Leagues: The Formation, Sometimes Absorption and Mostly Inevitable Demise of 18 Professional Baseball Organizations, 1871 to Present* (Jefferson, NC: McFarland, 1991), 253–6 ("Eddie Bohon"); *Chicago Defender,* March 12 ("any institution"), April 9, May 28, 1921; *Philadelphia Tribune,* April 9, 1921; Crepeau, *America's Diamond Mind,* 168 ("Through all the ages"); *Chicago Whip,* January 22, February 5, March 5, 1921; *Norfolk Journal and Guide,* February 19, April 16, 1921; *North American,* June 5, 1921; *Baltimore Afro-American,* April 29, 1921; Ira Lewis, " 'New' League Not Needed," *The Competitor,* May 1921, pp. 39, 41 (Lewis quotes). The Philadelphia representative of the Continental League was organized by George Victory, manager of the Pennsylvania Giants, and Monroe Young, a former Negro Southern League official.

18. Murdock, *Ban Johnson,* 183; *Baltimore Afro-American,* May 14, 1927 ("eminently fair"); *New York Amsterdam News,* May 11, 1927; Donn Rogosin, *Invisible Men: Life in Baseball's Negro Leagues* (New York: Athenaeum, 1987), 184, 198; Tygiel, *Baseball's Great Experiment,* 31; David Wiggins, "Wendell Smith, The *Pittsburgh Courier-Journal* and the Campaign to Include Blacks in Organized Baseball, 1933–1945," *Journal of Sports History* 10(2) (Summer 1983): 5–29; Dixon and Hannigan, *Negro Baseball Leagues,* 242–3 (Landis quote). With interracial teams rare during the 1920s, most observers predicted that the integration of organized baseball would involve the admission of entire black teams rather than individual players.

19. *New York Times,* June 10, July 29, 1922; *Philadelphia Inquirer,* July 28, August 15, October 4–13, 1922; Tygiel, *Baseball's Great Experiment,* 26; *Chicago Whip,* October 15, 22, 1921; Crepeau, *America's Diamond Mind,* 168 ("commented that," "bunch of Negroes"); *Chicago Defender,* October 14, 21, 1922; October 20, 27, 1923. Bak, *Cobb,* 99; *Baltimore Afro-American,* November 3, 1922 ("real world series"); *North American,* October 3, 21 ("Several league teams"), 1922; *The Messenger,* December 1923, 939 (quote).

20. *New York Amsterdam News,* October 14, 1925; *Baltimore Afro-American,* October 9, 1926; Holway, *Voices,* 191 (Foster quote). While John Holway has estimated that blacks won over 60 percent of nearly 450 games against barnstorming major leaguers between 1887 and 1950, no attempt was made to differentiate the levels of competition faced.

21. *Philadelphia's Baseball History,* 83 (Benson quote); *Chicago Defender,* December 29, 1923; Crepeau, *America's Diamond Mind,* 90 ("Them greasers"), 163 ("Ethiopian"); *Philadelphia Record,* November 22, 29, 1923; *Baltimore Afro-American,* February 28, 1924; *New York Amsterdam News,* October 19, 1927; Robert Creamer, *Babe: The Legend Comes to Life* (New York: Simon and Schuster, 1974), 185 ("the worst insult," "his personal"); John Holway notes (Winters quote); Holway, *Voices,* 25 (Drake quote).

22. *New York Amsterdam News,* October 28, 1925; November 10, 1926. Zoss and Bowman,

Diamonds in the Rough, 338; Holway, *Blackball Stars,* 65–6; James Bankes, "The Magnificent Pittsburgh Crawfords," in *The Ol' Ball Game: A Collection of Baseball Characters and Moments Worth Remembering* (Harrisburg, PA: Stackpole, 1990), 51, 56 ("good guy"); Bankes, *The Pittsburgh Crawfords: The Lives and Times of Black Baseball's Most Exciting Team* (Dubuque, IA: William C. Brown, 1991), 63–81; *Philadelphia Tribune,* January 26, 1928; Chalk, *Pioneers of Black Sport,* 78 (Hornsby quote); Holway, *Voices,* 30.

23. Bankes, *Pittsburgh Crawfords,* 63, 87 (Johnson quote); John Holway, *Black Diamonds: Life in the Negro Leagues from the Men Who Lived It* (New York: Stadium Books, 1991), xiii; Holway, *Voices,* 67.

24. *Baltimore Afro-American,* November 3, 1922; January 5, 1923; October 3, 1925; July 27 ("so full of race hate"), September 28, 1929. Holway, *Black Diamonds,* 41 (Powell quote); Allen, *Cooperstown Corner,* 7–9; *Chicago Defender,* May 10, 1919; June 18, 1921. *Washington Tribune,* June 10, 1922 ("All of us"); July 21, 1923; January 12, April 12, 1924 ("Why then,"); September 5, 12, 1925. *Philadelphia Tribune,* September 9, 1925; February 12, 1927 ("colored adorer"); July 25, 1929 ("fork over"). Tygiel, *Baseball's Great Experiment,* 25; *Chicago Whip,* June 23, 1928; Harold Seymour, *Baseball: The People's Game* (New York: Oxford University Press, 1990), 600.

25. *Indianapolis Freeman,* September 29, 1917; *Chicago Whip,* October 11, 1919; October 22, 1921 ("It is bad enough"). *Philadelphia Tribune,* November 22, 1924; October 6, 1932. *Philadelphia Record,* October 5, 1924. Black professional players often watched major league games to assess their own abilities. Rube Foster gave his players passes to Comiskey Park with the order "See what you can learn." While with Hilldale, Judy Johnson often attended games at Shibe Park during off days at the invitation of Connie Mack, By the 1930s, according to Johnson, black professional players were allowed free in most major league parks with the exception of St. Louis. See Holway, *Blackball Stars,* 29 (Foster quote); Bankes, *Pittsburgh Crawfords,* 88; Kevin Kerrane and Rob Beaton, "Judy Johnson: Reminiscences by the Great Baseball Player," *Delaware Today,* May 1977, p. 32.

26. *Philadelphia Tribune,* August 30 ("had heard"), December 27, 1928 (Briggs quote); June 30, 1932 ("It is not uncommon"); Art Rust, Jr., *Get That Nigger Off The Field* (New York, NY: Harcourt Brace, 1976), 5; Zoss and Bowman, *Diamonds in the Rough,* 158; *New York Amsterdam News,* May 15, 1929 ("Scores").

27. *Chicago Defender,* August 5, October 7, 1916; March 23, 1918. Lawrence S. Ritter, *The Glory of Their Times: The Story of the Early Days of Baseball Told By the Men Who Played It* (New York: MacMillan, 1966), 191; *Indianapolis Freeman,* March 8, 1913; *Philadelphia Tribune,* January 26, 1928; June 20, 1929. *Baltimore Afro-American,* July 23, 1920; April 29, 1921; August 25, 1922; February 5, 19, 1927. *New York Amsterdam News,* September 16, 1925 ("The most radical move"); June 8, 1927. *Sporting Life,* September 1922; *Chicago Whip,* February 4, June 17, 1922; *Half-Century Magazine,* April 1919, p. 8; *Philadelphia Public Ledger,* October 16, 1930; Zoss and Bowman, *Diamonds in the Rough,* 144–5; Dixon and Hannigan, *Negro Baseball Leagues,* 101.

28. *Philadelphia Tribune,* June 19, 1926; July 12, 1928. *Baltimore Afro-American,* October 10, 1924 ("far better"); May 23, 1925 (Pippen quote). *The Nation,* August 25, 1926, 161 (quote); Holway, *Voices,* xviii (Stephens quote); Kusmer, *Ghetto Takes Shape,* 187–9; *Indianapolis Freeman,* December 23, 1911. Many white sportswriters continued to regard Hilldale and other black professional teams as only semiprofessional. In response, the *Philadelphia Tribune* of October 1, 1931, noted that this identification was "really a misnomer because the Hilldale Club is not a semi-pro but a professional team and those who are in the know class realize that it is merely of cuticle pigments that keep players like Biz Mackey, Judy Johnson, Webster McDonald, Walt Cannady and a host of others from being playmates of Babe Ruth, Chuck Klein, Goose Goslin and others who have made the grade in the majors."

5

"WE WERE LADIES, WE JUST PLAYED LIKE BOYS"

African-American Womanhood and Competitive Basketball at Bennett College, 1928–1942

Rita Liberti

THROUGH THE EFFORTS OF a handful of sport history scholars, in recent years our knowledge and understanding of the collegiate athletic experiences of African-American women has grown significantly. Although in its infancy, this scholarship has moved beyond the analytic categories of race and gender to engage the complexities of class, helping to bring about an end to the mythical notion of a monolithic black female sport history. The conclusions drawn in these studies suggest that among elite black colleges and universities the tendency throughout the 1920s and 1930s was to abandon an earlier commitment to women's intercollegiate basketball.[1] School leaders at Howard, Fisk, Morgan, and Hampton believed that women's participation in competitive intercollegiate basketball ran counter to a middle-class feminine ideal grounded in refinement and respectability. Thus, support once given to intercollegiate basketball was channeled to less competitive structures, such as intramurals and play-days, with emphasis placed on activities that were deemed more suitable for female involvement including badminton, archery, and table tennis.[2]

While some African-American schools actively sought to dismantle their female basketball programs through the late 1920s and early 1930s, others were just beginning to invest institutional resources. Reflecting on this rise in involvement, in 1927, the *Chicago Defender* concluded that "women [sic] athletics are booming among dixie institutions."[3] To varying degrees, many public and private black colleges and universities across the South participated in women's basketball competition.[4] In Arkansas, for example, the Philander Smith College women's team, after having defeated all of the competition, declared themselves state champions in 1918.[5] Beginning in 1926 the Georgia-South Carolina Athletic Association, which represented seven schools in the two states, announced that the conference title and trophy was to be awarded to the women's team that played at least seven games with at least four different teams in the schedule.[6] In North Carolina several private black institutions initiated women's intercollegiate basketball teams in the 1920s, including Shaw University, Livingstone College, Barber-Scotia College, Immanuel Lutheran College, and Bennett College in Greensboro.[7] The wide range of institutional support of women's basketball by black colleges and universities reflects a spectrum of responses and attitudes concerning female participation in sport during the 1920s–1940s.

The purpose of this chapter is to examine more closely the athletic experiences of African American women in a middle-class collegiate setting, specifically Bennett College. Bennett is a fascinating exception to the pattern of elite black colleges discontinuing basketball for women during the 1930s and, as a result, provides a unique location to examine African-American women's sport history. My intent is to explore the tension between a middle-class ideology that, in part, supported traditional conceptualizations of gender relations and the support Bennett gave competitive female athletic participation in basketball. Although debate existed within the black community concerning the appropriateness of female involvement in competitive basketball, Bennett College enthusiastically supported a team, becoming one of the most successful basketball programs in the nation by the mid-1930s.[8] However, by the early years of the 1940s Bennett discontinued intercollegiate basketball, and instead focused energy and resources on intramural and play-day events. I argue that this transition not only reflected middle-class ideology, which precluded women's participation in rigorous athletic activity, but also illustrated the multiple and often contradictory and shifting roles of black middle-class women during this period.

Black women who enrolled as students and athletes in colleges and universities during this period both challenged and yielded to the boundaries of class, race, and gender arrangements in their community. This ongoing process of negotiation is one that exposes a history shaped by multiple and intersecting identities. The juxtaposition of black women's collegiate athletic experiences with those of black men and white women, for example, provide further evidence of the varied historical experiences that emerge among particular groups in our culture. Patrick Miller and Pamela Dean in their respective essays on college sport among black men and white women help to expose this notion of the myriad of histories that are constructed and shaped by specific historical and cultural contexts. As Miller notes, black male collegiate athletic achievement during the interwar years was promoted as another avenue for blacks to demonstrate the worthiness of their inclusion into the dominant culture.[9] Although women's collegiate athletic experiences were generally viewed as acceptable by the black community, their activities in sport were not put forth with the same intensity and enthusiasm. Occasional ambivalent reactions to female athleticism by members of the black community reflected adherence by some to more restrictive notions of gender and the unease surrounding women's involvement in rigorous sport. However, opposition to female participation in athletics was not universal in the black community in part because the lived experiences of women exposed them to a wider range of attitudes.

The view of female physicality in the black community, which did not necessarily preclude being a woman and an active participant in competitive sport, translated into different participation patterns for black and white women enrolled in colleges in the South. Although dissimilar with regard to the level of involvement in competitive intercollegiate athletic activities that their respective communities deemed suitable, white and black women who enrolled as students in colleges shared a common bond in their efforts to, at times, challenge existing gender ideologies. Pamela Dean's study of the athletic activities of white women at Sophie Newcomb College and North Carolina Normal and Industrial College illustrates the diversity of women's experiences generated from competing ideals of womanhood. As Dean argues, whether at Newcomb College or at the Normal College, white women constructed athletic activities within the confines and parameters of wider cultural misgivings concerning female participation in physical games.[10] In much the same way, the basketball history at Bennett College reflects the negotiation of prescriptive class and gender ideologies.[11]

The Methodist Episcopal Church founded Bennett College in 1873 as a coeducational institution for African Americans. The College's initial mission was to train men for the ministry and females as teachers to help meet the enormous need to educate newly freed blacks. In 1926, the Woman's Home Missionary Society of the Methodist Episcopal Church decided to refocus the direction of the school from a coeducational to a women's college, with the emphasis on teacher training remaining in the forefront.[12] Writing in 1928, Carol Cotter provided an early account of the philosophy of Bennett College: "If Americans of African descent are ever to step upon their rightful platform in the destiny of nations it must be at least partially through the efforts of the sisters to our men."[13] From its inception, Bennett College served as an important avenue for black women to be active participants in the struggle for racial equality and justice.

Under the leadership of college president Dr. David Jones, the enrollment of the newly reorganized Bennett quickly rose from just 10 women in 1926 to 138 by 1930.[14] The growth of basketball at Bennett seemed to parallel the general development of the college, with intercollegiate athletic contests beginning during the 1928–1929 academic year.[15] In addition to giving early support to intercollegiate basketball, Bennett also appeared committed to the general health and physical well-being of all of its students, requiring them to take two years of physical education. The 1929–1930 college catalog reassured those interested that "there is ample space for skating, tennis, basketball, hockey and all the games that delight a robust, growing girlhood."[16] By 1930, the position of physical education and intercollegiate basketball seemed fairly well established and aligned with the overall educational direction of the college.

The support that college officials at Bennett provided to its basketball program and other extracurricular activities reflected the broader aims of the college, which were to "provide its students with opportunities for the development of self-expression, leadership, and skill along individual lines of interest."[17] Bennett students from the 1930s recall the encouragement President Jones and other college faculty gave to the basketball program. Ruth Glover, star Bennett forward from 1934 to 1937, remembers that Jones was in attendance at all home games and "was right there on the sidelines rooting!" Teammate Almaleda Moore adds that for away contests Jones offered his vehicle and driver to transport the basketball squad. Across the entire Bennett College community, when describing attitudes toward basketball during the mid 1930s, Glover adds that "the spirit was on the campus."[18] Bennett student Frances Jones, daughter of President Jones, explains that basketball served as the centerpiece for campus activity, in part because African Americans had such limited access to other forms of recreation and leisure activities in the segregated South. In addition, Frances Jones fondly recalls that "we all loved our basketball" and that the popularity of the game at Bennett was due, in part, to the fact that "we beat everybody," making attendance that much more enjoyable.[19]

As Bennett president, David Jones was well aware of the obstacles that black women encountered, and he worked to create an environment at the college to prepare students to enter the world and be full participants in it. According to Jones, the "role of Negro women in the past has been a heroic one as mother, teacher, and civic leader. The responsibilities of the educated Negro woman of the future will be no less burdensome or challenging."[20] Understanding the significance of sexism and the implications that structure had upon higher education for women, Jones stated that "the struggle of women to achieve status in the American economy has been a long and sometimes discouraging and baffling effort. The idea that the woman's place is in the home is so deep-rooted, and the resistance of men to female competition so keen that the achievements of women in politics, in economics, in science have been won oft-times only because of superior qualifications and because of compensatory effort on the part of the so-called weaker sex."[21]

Under Jones's leadership the educational mission of Bennett was to train women on a number of different levels and in a wide range of settings to bring about the most effective positive change for the entire race. The 1929–1930 college catalog makes clear the broad educational goals of Bennett by stating that "attention should be given to matters relating to the refinements of family and community life . . . also that the most vigorous standards of scholarship should be maintained in all subjects of the curriculum."[22] Emphasis on academic rigor, civic responsibility, and homemaking best characterized the elements of a Bennett College education during this period. The components of this strategy were not meant as competing ideals but were viewed in totality as the best means to effect social change.

Bennett sought to uphold middle-class standards of refinement and respectability among its students in part to counter lingering stereotypes of African Americans as immoral and uncivilized. Although efforts to "uplift" the entire race rested upon middle- and upper-class African Americans, as "keepers of social standards . . . and guardians of spiritual values" black college women in particular were considered conveyers of character and culture.[23] Historian Stephanie Shaw notes many educated blacks believed that upstanding behavior by black college women reflected positively not only on the individual woman but also on the entire black community. College personnel carefully molded and monitored students' behavior, deeming actions seen as unbecoming for a "lady" inappropriate and discouraging them.[24] For students at Bennett, including Ruth Glover, being a lady meant, for one thing, dressing the part, with a clear understanding that the dress code had much more serious implications than fashion. Glover explains: "Oh, you didn't go shoppin' or uptown . . . without your hat and gloves. You had to be dressed like you were goin' to a formal affair . . . *we could get respect you see*" (emphasis added).[25]

Moreover, white assaults on the black community were often centered on the notion that African-American women contributed to the moral degradation with unkempt and uncivilized homes. As a result, emphasis on homemaking became a core element in the educational process at many black colleges and universities, including Bennett College. Beginning in 1927 the "Home-making Institute" became an annual meeting at Bennett College, with conference presentations and discussions focused on improving the home and family relations.[26] In addition, Bennett required each student to satisfactorily complete a course entitled, "The Art of Right Living," which among other goals, aimed to "help students find and solve their own problems in relation to personal hygiene, food and nutrition, clothing, family and community relationships . . ."[27] Former Bennett students with whom I have spoken recognized the practical importance of their exposure to homemaking skills and responsibilities. However, they also were clearly provided with the tools to move beyond the home and pursue leadership and professional roles in the community after graduation. Almaleta Moore notes that throughout the 1930s the basic premise of a college education for black women was "that you were training for a given profession, to go and contribute to the community where you lived."[28]

Not only did their academic preparation equip Bennett women with the skills to enhance the lives of others in the black community, but basketball also presented another way that these women could give something back to those around them. After graduating from Bennett all of the basketball players of the 1930s that I interviewed went on to careers as teachers and as basketball coaches on the elementary and high school level.[29] Graduating with a degree in French from Bennett in 1934, star center Lucille Townsend recalls that the principal at the black elementary school in Pinehurst, North Carolina, asked if she would consider teaching the fourth grade primarily because the district needed a girls' basketball coach.[30]

With an educational philosophy similar to that of many black colleges and universities throughout the late nineteenth and early twentieth centuries, Bennett College consistently underscored the notion of the relationship between college-educated blacks and the community. Writing in 1937, James T. Morton, Jr., who served on the faculty at Bennett, argued that "whether we are inclined to agree with W. E. B. Du Bois in all of his details concerning the solving value of the TALENTED TENTH, we must admit that among our group, leadership should come from the trained and aggressive."[31] Bennett administrators and faculty strove to ensure that the school was "far from being an ivory tower, or the traditional combination of finishing school and blue-stocking factory" but rather supported student initiative to take academic learning beyond the classroom to assist in the development of racial pride and justice.[32] Historian Glenda Gilmore argues that black women who were graduates of North Carolina colleges in the early twentieth century took with them "more than just a finite body of knowledge or set of skills"; rather they were "armed with a full quiver of intellectual weapons to aim at . . . discrimination."[33]

The 1937–1938 protest and boycott of the downtown movie theaters in Greensboro, led by Bennett first-year student Frances Jones, reflected an educational structure and philosophy which instilled civic duty and responsibility. When students learned that white theater owners in North and South Carolina refused to show films in which "Negro and white actors appear[ed] on an equal social basis" as opposed to stereotyped depictions of blacks, they organized a campaign by members of the black community to stop their support of the movie establishments.[34] After months of picketing their efforts were successful, leading the *Carolina Times* to conclude that "the step taken by the students in the two Negro schools in Greensboro shows more courage on the part of Negro youth than we have any record of anywhere else in the south."[35] Within the context of the Jim Crow South, the paper added that the bold actions by the college students would lead America into a "new day."[36] Frances Jones recalls that the success of the boycott was significant because it symbolized the fact that segregation was no longer considered an impenetrable "solid wall" incapable of being eradicated. Although Jones was fully aware of the potential harm that could have been perpetrated against her, she notes that there was "no room for fear." Several years after the boycott Jones learned that her father, Bennett president David Jones, was "visited by the Federal Bureau of Investigation and other government agencies" who "tried to force him to get us to stop."[37] Frances Jones remembers that the continued support that President Jones gave his students throughout the protest was an example of the fact that he demanded excellence in all of his students and encouraged their participation in various activities that fostered pride and self-respect.

Significantly, while Bennett officials created an environment that supported acts of civil disobedience in protest of racial injustice, they continually demanded that students exhibit behaviors that maintained a level of dignity. In an effort to instill ideals such as good manners, proper conduct, and self-control, college officials at Bennett and other black schools enforced strict rules and rigid codes of behavior for all students, especially women. Bennett freshmen were given the Greensboro bus and train schedules their first day on campus and told by President Jones that they would be leaving the same day via one of those routes if they broke the rules. Bennett women were rarely given the opportunity to leave campus unless on officially sanctioned business and, in such a case, a chaperone accompanied them.[38] Participation in basketball provided student-athletes with a degree of autonomy not typical of many of their peers. Travel to away basketball contests presented such a rare and special occasion to leave campus that it led some of the Bennett players to resist and ultimately bend the rules. Almaleta Moore recalls that she and her teammates risked punishment by "sneaking the team mascot out of the dormitory" so that, she too, could travel with the team.[39] Practice sessions were also considered an opportunity to escape the regulations the general student body had to follow. Basketball practice for Bennett began after study hour each evening and lasted from 9:00 P.M. to 11:00 P.M. As the other students returned to the dormitory from the library, athletes made their way to the gym. Moore acknowledges that practice sessions "were a privilege because we could get out of the dormitory that time of night."[40]

Bennett faculty and administrative staff members may have extended the higher level of personal freedom to basketball players because they were committed to the notion that physical development on the basketball court or in a physical education class reinforced their efforts to impart conduct becoming a "lady." This is suggested in college literature, which promoted the physical education program by asserting that the activities "involve total body control as they take place under conditions requiring physical exertion, intellectual accuracy and emotional control simultaneously."[41] Having the chance to travel across the roads of North Carolina was sometimes used by players as a way to mock the segregated South, turning racism on its head, if only for a brief moment. Moore remembers that "we would be riding along the highway and you'd meet some white fellas thumbing . . . and we'd hang our heads out the window and say, Jim Crow car!"[42]

The moral standards Bennett women were trained to practice and possess off the basketball court occasionally contrasted with opponents' ideas concerning respectable actions and appropriate behavior. Such was the case when Bennett, after a very successful 1934 season, competed in a three game series against the *Philadelphia Tribune* team. The contests even attracted the white press, which ordinarily gave little attention to events in the black community.[43] Press reports indicated that over one thousand spectators attended the initial game of the series, reflecting the enormous interest in women's basketball in the community.[44] The *Greensboro Daily News* prefaced the upcoming series: "After having met and defeated in rapid succession all of the college teams that would accept to play, the undefeated Bennett College team, seeking larger worlds to conquer, will risk its reputation against Otto Briggs' Tribune female team. . . . The Tribune girls, led by the indomitable, eternally famed and stellar performer, Ora Washington, national women's singles champ in tennis, comes with an enviable reputation."[45]

The Tribune team was housed on the Bennett College campus during the series, and Lucille Townsend remembers their arrival, particularly her first impression of Ora Washington. "She [Washington] looked like the worst ruffian you ever wanted to see. She looked like she'd been out pickin' cotton all day, shavin' hogs, and everything else."[46] Washington's

Figure 5–1
The Bennett College Basketball Team circa 1933. During the depression decade, Bennett stood as the epitome of black women's college basketball. Courtesy Greensboro Historical Museum, Greensboro, NC.

rugged appearance stood in opposition to the feminine ideals that Townsend and other black college-educated women were trained to regard as "earmarks of a lady," which included "always being well-groomed, appropriately dressed, scrupulously clean in body and attire with hair carefully arranged."[47]

Townsend recalls that the first game of the series was played in downtown Greensboro at the sports arena, and "ordinarily colored didn't play there. . . . It was the largest place we had ever played and I was scared."[48] She remembers that the game was replete with thrills, both on and off the court. In many ways the game did not resemble the type the Bennett players were accustomed to participating in and was thus both exciting and unsettling. Townsend explains: "They [the Tribune team] changed uniforms, they had red and white uniforms one half, and gold and purple the next half, and socks to match!" The game itself was also a departure for the Bennett team from encounters with high school and college opponents. Although Townsend had played in a number of games throughout her career that she considered physical contests, none compared to the match-up against Ora Washington and the Tribune team. She recalls, "I told the referee she's [Ora] hittin' me in the stomach every time I jump . . . he caught her when she hit me one time. . . . I doubled over and went down."[49]

Off-court actions by some members of the Tribune team provide important evidence of the diverse notions of womanhood and respectable behavior within the black community during this period. Townsend recalls the events that took place while sharing the locker room with the opposing team during half-time. "We went to the locker room and that's when them girls pulled out little half pint jars, they had corn liquor in it." She continues, "now all of them didn't have it . . . two or three of them didn't. But the rest of them would take two or three big swigs and set it down somewhere over there and go right on out and play!"[50]

The series between Bennett College and the Philadelphia Tribune team not only illustrates the popularity of women's basketball but also highlights the tensions, ambiguities, and divisions present in the black community along class and gender lines during this period. Like other black college women, Bennett students were taught to always present themselves in a refined and dignified manner. Reflecting on the actions by Ora Washington and the Tribune team, both on and off the basketball court, Lucille Townsend drew a clear line of distinction between herself and the members of the Philadelphia squad. In assessing the series and the Tribune team Townsend concludes that "they were a different class of people."[51]

Although Bennett lost the three games against the Philadelphia Tribune team, the 1934 and 1935 seasons were extremely successful for the Bennett cagers, with twenty-four victories and no defeats versus college, high school, and community teams.[52] Ruth Glover explains Bennett College's basketball dominance through the mid 1930s: "We used to practice against a group of high school boys . . . Dudley High School . . . they scrimmaged us. They would come down and teach us the tricks of the trade . . . you know how to take that ball in like that [demonstrates a one-handed shot]. That's where we learned . . . a lot of that type of getting over that floor."[53]

Beyond the basketball court, interaction between the sexes was viewed by some within the black community as unladylike and thus discouraged. In this instance, however, whatever conflict, if any, was present in the minds of Bennett personnel was surpassed by the desire to elevate the level of play of the women's basketball program by practicing against local high school boys.

By the 1934 Tribune series, basketball was an extremely popular activity at Bennett, despite the continuing and growing ambivalence within the black community over the suitability of the competitive game for girls and women. The National Association of College Women (NACW) was one group that spoke out strongly against intercollegiate competition for black women. Founded in 1910 by Mary Church Terrell as the College Alumnae Club, the NACW expanded to a national organization in 1923, and over the next three decades it did more than any other association to advance the position of black women as students and professionals within higher education.[54] Under the auspices of the NACW, a conference composed of deans and advisors to women in black colleges and universities was held at Howard University in 1929. The conference participants met to consider major problems in connection with the education of black women. The position of intercollegiate athletics for women was the central focus of one of four issues that it tackled at the 1929 meeting. The NACW *Journal* summarized the position of the women in attendance: "Inter-collegiate athletics should not be encouraged with all their undesirable physiological and sociological features. Inter-class and intra-class games serve every good purpose of the inter-collegiate games, and avoid all the harmful effects."[55]

In October of 1940, the NACW restated its position with regard to women's sport in the following recommendation: "That the Association go forward with a proposal made in 1938 to the effect that we use our efforts as an organization to eliminate from our schools intercollegiate athletics for women, urging the substitution of intramural contests and intercollegiate non-competitive play activities."[56] Similarly, Maryrose Reeves Allen, director of the physical education program for women at Howard University during this period, deemed activities such as dance, light games, archery, and badminton appropriate physical activities in which women should be encouraged to engage. While basketball is not mentioned explicitly, Allen makes a distinction by disapproving of certain activities. In 1938 she wrote that, "the heavier sports . . . have no place in a woman's life: they rob her of her feminine charms and often of her good health."[57]

The tension between femininity and athleticism is no more clearly illustrated than in the writings of Ivora (Ike) King, sport columnist for the *Baltimore Afro-American* who argued that, "the girl who is too athletic is on the wrong track to becoming a wife. Men want feminine women, not creatures who are half like themselves and the other half resembling something else. It is only natural and logical because we loathe men who act effeminate and desire a man, all man. Men want women all women . . . being too athletic and consequently too mannish, prevents her from being [so]."[58] Heterosexual appeal rested firmly on a woman's ability to remain within the confines of particular gender arrangements. For King, denying femininity to the athletic woman threatened to corrupt her gendered and sexual identities and in doing so forfeited her existence as a real woman.

To Bennett women, however, a feminine ideal of black womanhood and participation in competitive athletics remained negotiable. Bennett teammates Almaleta Moore and Ruth Glover clearly felt this way. Moore recollected that Bennett never competed against women from neighboring white schools during the mid 1930s, noting that "they were little

Figure 5–2
Bennett College Team, 1938. Courtesy Mrs. Ruth Glover Mullen.

southern ladies, that was too rough for them." But as Glover's words show, this did not mean that the Bennett women felt they compromised their respectability or womanliness by playing basketball: "We were ladies too, we just played basketball like boys."[59] Classmate Almira Henry underscores and clarifies the notion that being athletic and female was not a contradiction for Bennett women. "Being a lady does not mean being prissy, it's just an inward culture . . . always being polite and not saying things to hurt people's feelings. You could be tough as I don't know what on that basketball court, but you still have those same principles."[60] For these women, and the institution that supported their involvement in intercollegiate basketball in the 1930s, the notion that being female and athletic was dichotomous remained a falsehood. As I have briefly illustrated here, there were a wide range of responses among members of the black community to women's participation in athletics, and I argue this reflected the multiple roles and expectations of African-American women, especially those who were middle class or who aspired to middle-class status.

Thus, while some within the black community opposed all basketball competition for girls and women, others encouraged the sport but sought to place limitations on the style of play, preferring girls' rules or six player basketball rather than five member teams.[61] Throughout the 1920s and 1930s the debate among members of the black community over the suitability of five or six player basketball competition for girls and women was played out on several occasions in the black press. Proponents of games played under girls' rules argued that five player basketball was too rough for women and that "girls always look inadequate and butter-fingered under boy's [sic] rules."[62] J. H. N. Waring, Jr., principal and girls' basketball coach at Downington Industrial and Agricultural School in Pennsylvania, strongly opposed female participation in five player basketball. Like other critics, Waring argued that the five player game was too strenuous and did not bring out "the finer qualities in girls."[63] Furthermore, according to Waring, female basketball contests played under five player rules did not draw spectators because the limited physical capabilities of girls and women resulted in slow and unexciting play. He insisted too, that games were "disgusting" to athletic fans who do not enjoy seeing young school girls pulling and tugging and roughing each other like so many alley cats.[64] Waring opposed female involvement in five player basketball because he feared the physical well-being of the athletes who competed, but also because such participation disturbed his own sensibilities concerning appropriate behavior for girls and women.

Others directly opposed Waring's vision of womanhood and the resulting restrictive impact on female physicality, illustrating the wide spectrum of attitudes concerning girls' and women's participation in five player basketball. A former basketball player and current coach argued in a letter to the *Baltimore Afro-American* in 1930 that,

> Girls of today are red-blooded, virile young creatures, and are no longer content to conform to the masculine ideal of feminine inferiority and frailty. The clinging vine has given way to the freely moving, sensibly clad young Amazon of today. Such fineness of physique cannot be maintained or secured through the inadequacies of girls' rules in basketball.[65]

The correspondent's conceptualization of femininity and womanhood was in contrast to that presented by Waring, indicating that there were a divergent and wide range of opinions among members of the black community concerning the compatibility of being female and engaging in a rigorous athletic activity, such as five player basketball. These rival views on the five player basketball issue reflected the tensions and negotiations of the boundaries of black womanhood that were ongoing during the 1920s and 1930s.

Despite the wide range of opinions concerning the appropriateness of five player basketball, girls' rules began to influence college play in North Carolina, including Bennett and other colleges in the state. By 1936 North Carolina colleges and universities reconsidered their earlier devotion to five player basketball and began to compete using six player rules. The move away from five player basketball "hampered the style of quite a number of the old varsity members" on Bennett's team, but they still claimed a share of the state title with Shaw University, making it their fourth championship of the decade.[66] Following an undefeated 1937 season, one of the nation's most popular black newspapers, the *Chicago Defender* dubbed Bennett "the nation's best female cage team"; but this would be the last state championship that Bennett won.[67]

Not only were basketball rules in a state of transition at Bennett College by the latter half of the 1930s, but direction and control of the sport was also in flux. Throughout the 1920s and 1930s black physical educators and others interested in female participation in sport debated the issue of men coaching women's athletics, and some supported the notion that women should organize and direct female involvement in sport and physical activity.[68] Although female physical educators were on staff from the inception of Bennett as a women's college in 1926, male coaches directed the basketball team for many of the years between 1928 and 1938.[69] Similarly, as at other black colleges in North Carolina, female chaperones accompanied the women's basketball teams, but in most instances male faculty

Figure 5–3
The Bennett women standing on a diagonal with their names marked on the floorboards. Courtesy of Mrs. Ruth Glover Mullen.

members assumed the coaching duties.[70] By the late 1930s this pattern of male coaching dominance began to change somewhat. In 1938, female physical education instructor Mildred Burris became only the second female coach at Bennett in ten years of basketball competition.[71]

Though Bennett continued to support intercollegiate basketball through the 1941 season, by the late 1930s its athletic interests also appeared headed in another direction. In 1939 the college became the first of four black North Carolina schools to join the Women's Sports Day Association (WSDA). The WSDA was founded in 1938 by female physical education leaders at Virginia State, Hampton, as well as Maryrose Reeves Allen at Howard University. The goals of the association clearly promoted the personal philosophy of Allen, endorsing a structure that was noncompetitive and activities that "develop in women the qualities of beauty of movement, poise, femininity by affording each individual who participates an opportunity to play in an atmosphere of dignity, courtesy, and refinement."[72] The WSDA promoted a class bound ideal of womanhood grounded in female frailty and its influence was reflected in the activities pursued on the Bennett campus. In November of 1940, Bennett served as "hostess" to the handful of other colleges in the association, including: Howard University, Virginia State University, Hampton University, and North Carolina Agricultural and Technical (A&T) College, at the first of two sports days. Each school sent twenty-five women who were then divided among the other participants into teams so that "group sportsmanship among the colleges [was] emphasized."[73] This was a significant shift for Bennett, from intercollegiate basketball, which emphasized competition, travel, and winning to the intramurals and play-days of the WSDA. By 1942 the shift was complete and Bennett withdrew its support of women's intercollegiate basketball.[74]

I found no evidence to suggest who initiated the changes from intercollegiate basketball to play-day events at Bennett. However, given the promotion of play-days by the WSDA and the continued anticompetition rhetoric put forth by the NACW it is highly likely that intercollegiate basketball for women at black colleges in North Carolina, including Bennett, came under increasingly heavy scrutiny. By 1937, for example, under the auspices of the NACW, seven colleges in North Carolina, including Bennett, sent representatives to the eighth annual Conference of the Deans and Advisors to Girls and Women in Colored Schools, more than in any previous year.[75]

On the state level, Bennett was not alone in its increased focus on play-days versus intercollegiate basketball competition for women.[76] As director of physical education for women at North Carolina College during the first half of the 1940s, Vivian Merrick recalls a successful intramural and play-day structure at the college. When asked to speculate on possible reasons for the demise of women's intercollegiate basketball during the 1940s, Merrick believed that the war crisis combined with the belief, among some in the black community, that "our [women's] physical make-up" was not suited for the rigors of basketball competition.[77] Interestingly, while World War II did have enormous impact on college athletic programs, North Carolina officials worked to sustain men's basketball teams. In fact, men's basketball at several colleges in North Carolina not only continued, but flourished, with teams playing extensive schedules and traveling to compete against out-of-state opponents.[78] The same pattern cannot be seen for women enrolled as students at North Carolina black colleges and universities, as they found increasingly limited opportunities to compete in basketball through the 1940s.

Historian Cindy Himes-Gissendanner notes that nearly a decade before Bennett's reorganization away from intercollegiate play, several black colleges in the early 1930s dismantled competitive women's basketball on their campuses and promoted those activities which placed decreased emphasis on athletics. Himes-Gissendanner argues that this early 1930s movement away from competitive sport reflected ambivalence among some college officials, especially those at elite black schools, concerning the suitability of women's continued involvement in rigorous athletic activity. While I contend that Himes-Gissendanner's conclusions have merit, the Bennett basketball history through the 1930s problematizes her thesis somewhat and forces scholars to recognize the complexities of an ongoing negotiation of boundaries surrounding female physicality in the African-American community.[79]

This transition to less competitive activities during the early 1940s on the campus of Bennett College signaled the end to a brief, yet illuminating period in the history of African-American women's sport. The tensions surrounding female athleticism on the Bennett campus and in the larger black community reflected diverse responses and attitudes concerning women's involvement in sports such as competitive basketball and provide scholars with insights into the ways that class informs race and gender identity. From the late 1920s through the decade of the 1930s Bennett's administration, faculty, and student-athletes balanced and negotiated various understandings of class, race, and gender arrangements as they supported competitive women's basketball.

In a more general sense, Bennett personnel articulated a position that illustrated the societal tensions that worked to forge their identity as a black women's college. In a presentation to the NACW in 1937, Bennett faculty member Merze Tate argued that:

> The presidents of women's colleges are not endeavoring to turn out an army of masculine counterparts. Neither in the light of rapid historical progress and a sense of humor is there any longer a need to turn out an army of feminists.[80]

Tate's interest in sculpting public perception of Bennett as an institution for women that did not "masculinize" women may have been in response to fears among some in the wider African-American community that college-educated black women disrupted gender norms and might make unsuitable marriage companions to men.[81] Aware of societal gender restrictions, Bennett College officials balanced those tensions while challenging assumptions in educating black women; as Tate's further comments make clear:

> In the light of present-day thought and experiments, does the challenge of responsibility for the home involve women alone. Between the ultra-feminism of women's rights forever, and the ultra-feminists in the idea of women always to serve the men, to produce the race, and to keep the home, is the stimulating vision of women making their fullest contribution to life, whether in the home, in other service, or in both fields of activity.[82]

The particular conceptualization of womanhood that some middle-class blacks constructed, including those at Bennett, simultaneously endorsed and rejected aspects of middle-class femininity. The complexity of that continual process of cultural construction is symbolized in women's basketball, the history of which evolved and changed over the course of a decade and a half, much like the fluid notion of what it meant to be black, female, and middle class during this period. These multiple identities at times merged and blended, and in other instances were contradictory forces, exposing a history that cannot be categorized as static or fixed, but rather dynamic and shifting. Bennett College basketball from the late 1920s to the early 1940s illustrates the tensions between individual agents creating their own histories amid societal expectations and constraints.

NOTES

1. Martha H. Verbrugge, "The Institutional Politics of Women's Sports in American Colleges, 1920–1940" (paper presented at the North American Society for Sport History, Auburn, AL, May 1996); Cindy Himes-Gissendanner, "African American Women and Competitive Sport, 1920–1960," in *Women, Sport, and Culture,* ed. Susan Birrell and Cole (Champaign, IL: Human Kinetics, 1994), 81–92. Susan Cahn's discussion of ideals surrounding black womanhood concludes that "it is not clear whether wealthier African Americans approved of women's involvement in sports like basketball." Susan Cahn, *Coming On Strong: Gender and Sexuality in Twentieth-Century Women's Sport* (New York: Free Press, 1994), 312.

2. Studies, which include Verbrugge, "The Institutional Politics of Women's Sports" and Himes-Gissendanner, "African-American Women and Competitive Sport" both suggest this transition to less competitive athletic structures. For the athletic philosophy at Hampton Institute see Elizabeth Dunham, "Physical Education of Women at Hampton Institute," *Southern Workman* 53 (April 1924): 161–8. At Morgan College in Baltimore women's basketball seemed popular, frequently filling the sports pages of the *Baltimore Afro-American* newspaper from 1921 to the early 1930s. Apparently, by 1933 intercollegiate basketball for women at Morgan had ceased. See Olga H. Bowers, "Just Between Sportswomen," *Baltimore Afro-American,* February 18, 1933, p. 16. At Howard University competitive basketball was frowned upon, due at least in part, to the philosophy of physical education department chairperson, Maryrose Reeves Allen. See Maryrose Reeves Allen, "The Development of Beauty in College Women Through Health and Physical Education" (master's thesis, Boston University, 1938). Significantly, female students at Howard were permitted to compete in an exhibition badminton tournament with women from Swarthmore College, a white school located within a day's travel. The suitability of the game of badminton—a noncontact sport—as opposed to basketball is apparently the reason for this interaction. See "H.U. Badminton Team to Meet Swarthmore," *Baltimore Afro-American,* March 18, 1939, p. 23, and "HU Badminton Team Leaders Selected," *Baltimore Afro-American,* March 25, 1939, p. 21.

3. "Dixie Doings," *Chicago Defender,* February 12, 1927, p. 8.

4. This conclusion is based on an examination of the *Baltimore Afro-American, Chicago Defender, Atlanta Daily World, Pittsburgh Courier,* and *Carolina Times.*

5. "Philander Smith Wins Championship," *Chicago Defender,* April 9, 1921, p. 11.

6. "Pinson Re-Elected Head of GA.-Carolina Athletic Assn.," *Chicago Defender,* February 13, 1926, p. 11.

7. Rita Liberti, " 'We Were Ladies, We Just Played Basketball Like Boys': A Study of Women's Basketball at Historically Black Colleges and Universities in North Carolina, 1925–1945" (Ph.D. diss., The University of Iowa, 1998).

8. Newspaper accounts of women's basketball competition in the black press suggest that Bennett had one of the most successful basketball programs in the mid-1930s. See, for example, "Shaw University Girls Hand Bennett Sextette First Defeat in Three Years," *Norfolk Journal and Guide,* March 28, 1936, p. 14; "Nobody Has Licked Them For Two Years," *Baltimore Afro-American,* April 13, 1935, p. 21. Tillotson College for Women in Austin, Texas also had a very successful team during the mid-1930s. See "Tillotson Wins Texas Tournament," *Chicago Defender,* March 24, 1934, p. 16; "Tillotson Five Tops May Allen," *Chicago Defender,* March 16, 1935, p. 16.

9. Patrick B. Miller, " 'To Bring the Race along Rapidly': Sport, Student Culture, and Educational Mission at Historically Black Colleges during the Interwar Years," *History of Education Quarterly* 35 (Summer 1995): 111–33.

10. Pamela Dean, " 'Dear Sisters' and 'Hated Rivals': Athletics and Gender at Two New South Women's Colleges, 1893–1920," *Journal of Sport History* 24 (Fall 1997): 341–57.

11. I include the work of Patrick Miller and Pamela Dean because each serves as an example of the range of histories that emerge given race, class,

and gender considerations during the early to middle decades of the twentieth century. However, I argue that a detailed discussion of the collegiate athletic experiences of African-American men and white women during the first few decades of the twentieth century is beyond the scope of this paper. Moreover, I contend that a compare/contrast model serves to marginalize the experiences of African-American women by perpetuating normative standards as male and white. See, Elsa Barkley Brown, " 'What Has Happened Here': The Politics of Difference in Women's History and Feminist Politics," in *"We Specialize in the Wholly Impossible": A Reader in Black Women's History,* eds. Darlene Clark Hine, Wilma King, and Linda Reed (Brooklyn, NY: Carlson, 1995), 39–54; Patricia Hill Collins, *Black Feminist Thought: Knowledge, Consciousness, and the Politics of Empowerment* (New York: Routledge, 1990), xii–xiii.

12. Beverly Guy-Sheftall, "Black Women and Higher Education: Spelman and Bennett Colleges Revisited," *Journal of Negro Education* 51 (1982): 278–87; Barbara Solomon, *In The Company of Educated Women* (London: Yale University Press, 1985), 152–3, 168, 179; Hugh Victor Brown, *A History of The Education of Negroes in North Carolina* (Raleigh: Irving Swain Press, 1961), 73–6; Willa Player, "Improving College Education for Women at Bennett College: A Report of a Type A Project" (Ed. D. diss., Columbia Teachers College, 1948). For an early account of Bennett College before it became a women's college in 1926, see Jay S. Stowell, *Methodist Adventures in Negro Education* (New York: The Methodist Book Concern, 1922).

13. Carol Cotter, "Bennett College, An Opportunity for Negro Womanhood," *Opportunity* (May 1928): 145.

14. *Catalogue Bennett College for Women* (1929–1930), 12 in Box: "Miscellaneous Box" Bennett College Archives, Greensboro, NC. Bennett players testified to the enormous support that President David Jones gave to them as student-athletes and to the basketball program. Interviews, Edythe Robinson Tweedy, (Rocky Mount, NC), August 10, 1995; Lucille Townsend, (Richmond, VA), August 6, 1995; Clarice Gamble Herbert, (Philadelphia, PA), July 31, 1995; Almaleta Moore and Ruth Glover Mullen, (West Cape May, NJ), July 30, 1995.

15. *Baltimore Afro-American,* February 23, 1929, p. 10; *Baltimore Afro-American,* January 18, 1930, p. 14; *Baltimore Afro-American,* February 15, 1930, p. 14. By the early 1930s, several other colleges and universities in North Carolina began playing basketball, including North Carolina Agricultural and Technical College, Shaw University, Livingstone College, Fayetteville State Normal, North Carolina College, and Lutheran College. On the development of high school basketball among North Carolina black schools see Charles H. Thompson, "The History of the National Basketball Tournaments for Black High Schools" (Ph.D. diss., Louisiana State University, 1980).

16. *Catalogue Bennett College for Women* (1929–1930), "Campus," 17, in Box: "Miscellaneous Box" Bennett College Archives, Greensboro, NC.

17. Velma B. Hamilton, "An Adventure in Women's Education," *Journal of the National Association of College Women* (1935): 32.

18. Interview, Almaleta Moore and Ruth Glover Mullen.

19. Interview, Frances Jones Bonner, (Newton Centre, MA), February 1, 1998.

20. David D. Jones, "The War And the Higher Education of Negro Women," *Journal of Negro Education* 11 (July 1942): 337.

21. Jones, "The War and the Higher Education of Negro Women," 329.

22. *Catalogue Bennett College for Women* (1929–1930), p. 12 in Box: "Miscellaneous Box" Bennett College Archives, Greensboro, NC.

23. Florence M. Read, "The Place of the Women's College in the Pattern of Negro Education," *Opportunity* 15 (September 1937): 268. For further discussion of the dissemination of middle-class values among college students of this period see James D. Anderson, *The Education of Blacks in the South, 1860–1935* (Chapel Hill: The University of North Carolina Press, 1988); Raymond Wolters, *The New Negro on Campus: Black College Rebellions of the 1920s* (Princeton, NJ: The Princeton University Press, 1975); Kevin K. Gaines, *Uplifting the Race: Black Leadership, Politics, and Culture in the Twentieth Century* (Chapel Hill: The University of North Carolina Press, 1996); Linda M. Perkins, "The Impact of the 'Cult of True Womanhood' on the education of Black Women," *Journal of Social Issues* 39 (1983): 17–28; Evelyn Brooks Higginbotham, *Righteous Discontent: The Women's Movement in the Black Baptist Church, 1880–1920* (Cambridge: Harvard University Press, 1993).

24. Evelyn Brooks Higginbotham, *Righteous Discontent,* 19–46; Stephanie Shaw, *What a Woman Ought to Be and to Do: Black Professional Women Workers During the Jim Crow Era* (Chicago: University of Chicago Press, 1996), 80–90.

25. Interview, Ruth Glover Mullen.

26. Flemmie P. Kittrell, "Home Economics at Bennett College for Women," *Southern Workman* 60

(1931): 381–4; "Homemaking Institute at Bennett College March 17–25," *Carolina Times,* March 15, 1941, p. 3.

27. Constance H. Marteena, "A College For Girls," *Opportunity* 16 (October 1938): 307.

28. Interview, Almaleta Moore.

29. Interviews; Almaleta Moore, Ruth Glover Mullen, Lucille Townsend, Clarice Gamble Herbert, and Edythe Robinson Tweedy.

30. Interview, Lucille Townsend.

31. James T. Morton, Jr., "The Relationship of the College and Its Community," *Bennett College Bulletin* 12 (December 1937): 1, in Box: "Miscellaneous Box" Bennett College Archives, Greensboro, NC.

32. Lois Taylor, "Social Action at Bennett College," *Opportunity* 20 (January 1942): 8.

33. Glenda E. Gilmore, *Gender and Jim Crow: Women and the Politics of White Supremacy in North Carolina, 1896–1920* (Chapel Hill: University of North Carolina Press, 1996), 31.

34. "The Voice of Youth," *Carolina Times,* January 15, 1938, p. 4.

35. "The Voice of Youth," 4.

36. "The Voice of Youth," 4. For additional information on the boycott see, William H. Chafe, *Civilities and Civil Rights: Greensboro, North Carolina and the Black Struggle for Freedom* (New York: Oxford University Press, 1980), 26–7; "What About It Students?" *Carolina Times,* February 12, 1938, p. 4.

37. Interview, Frances Jones Bonner.

38. Interview, Almaleta Moore and Ruth Glover Mullen.

39. Interview, Almaleta Moore.

40. Interview, Almaleta Moore.

41. "The Basketball Team," *Bennett College Bulletin* 9 (May 1934): 12 in Box: "Miscellaneous Box," Bennett College Archives, Greensboro, NC.

42. Interview, Almaleta Moore.

43. "Bennett Cage Team Facing Two Games," *Greensboro Daily News,* March 9, 1934, p. 12; "Tribunes Triumph Over Bennett Team," *Greensboro Daily News,* March 13, 1934, p. 10; "Bennett Meets Eastern Squad," *Greensboro Record,* March 9, 1934, p. 10.

44. "Tribunes Dazzle Down Home Fans in Victorious Tour," *Richmond Planet,* March 24, 1934, p. 6; "Tribune Girls Defend Record On Cage Tour Through South," *Norfolk Journal and Guide,* March 31, 1934, p. 12. In the third game of the series held at the Bennett College gym the black press reported that fans traveled from over distances of one hundred miles or more to see the game. "Tribgirls Dazzle Down Home Fans in Victorious Tour," *Philadelphia Tribune,* March 22, 1934, p. 10.

45. "Bennett Cage Team Facing Two Games," *Greensboro Daily News,* March 9, 1934, p. 12.

46. Interview, Lucille Townsend.

47. Charlotte Hawkins Brown, *The Correct Thing To Do—To Say—To Wear* (Durham: The Seeman Printery, 1940), 49–50.

48. Interview, Lucille Townsend. The Sports arena was located on Commerce Plaza in downtown Greensboro. According to J. Stephen Catlett of the Greensboro Historical Museum, this facility was a multipurpose building used for athletic events and social gatherings. (Personal communication with author, March 15, 1996).

49. Interview, Lucille Townsend.

50. Interview, Lucille Townsend.

51. Interview, Lucille Townsend.

52. "Bennett Girls Win 14 Games, Claim Title," *Baltimore Afro-American,* March 31, 1934, p. 19; "They Stand Out as Real Champions," *Chicago Defender,* April 13, 1935, p. 16.

53. Interview, Ruth Glover Mullen.

54. On the National Association of College Women see: Hilda Davis and Patricia Bell-Scott, "The Association of Deans of Women and Advisors to Girls in Negro Schools, 1929–1954: A Brief Oral History," *SAGE* 6 (Summer 1989): 40–4; Linda Perkins, "The National Association of College Women: Vanguard of Black Women's Leadership and Education, 1923–1954," *Journal of Education* 172 (1990): 65–75; Mary Carter, "The Educational Activities of the National Association of College Women, 1923–1960," (master's of education thesis, Howard University, 1962).

55. "Summary of the Conference of Deans and Advisors to Women in Colored Schools," *Journal of the National Association of College Women* 6 (1929): 38.

56. E. Estelle Thomas, "The Personnel Point of View," *Quarterly Review of Higher Education Among Negroes* 8 (October 1940): 231.

57. Maryrose Reeves Allen, "The Development of Beauty in College Women Through Health and Physical Education," in the Maryrose Reeves Allen Papers, Box 160–4 (folder 4), Moorland-Spingarn Research Center, Howard University, Washington, D.C.

58. Ivora (Ike) King, "Feminine Yet Athletic," *Baltimore Afro-American,* September 19, 1931, p. 13.

59. Interview, Almaleta Moore and Ruth Glover Mullen.

60. Interview, Almira Henry Wilson, (Iowa City, IA), October 22, 1996.

61. The debate within the black community concerning the type and style of basketball to be

played by girls and women was evident throughout the 1920s, 1930s, and 1940s. "Woman Makes Season's Record," *Baltimore Afro-American,* March 5, 1927, p. 14; J. H. N. Waring, "Selects All Star Court Team From Schoolgirls," *Philadelphia Tribune,* April 16, 1931, p. 11; Ivora (Ike) King, "Women in Sports," *Baltimore Afro-American,* January 23, 1932, p. 15; C. T. Edwards, "What To Do With Athletics," *North Carolina Teachers Record* (January 1933): 18; "Clark's Undefeated Girls' Team," *Atlanta Daily World,* February 26, 1937, p. 5; Sarah L. Humphries, "Women's Sports," *Atlanta Daily World,* March 10, 1940, p. 8.

62. "Clark Co-eds Boast A Splendid Quintet," *Atlanta Daily World,* February 18, 1937, p. 11.

63. J. H. N. Waring, "Hear Me Talkin' To Ya," *Baltimore Afro-American,* March 22, 1930, 15.

64. J. H. N. Waring, "Waring Picks An All-Star Girls' Team," *Baltimore Afro-American,* April 7, 1934, p. 19.

65. "Hear Me Talkin' To Ya," *Baltimore Afro-American,* April 5, 1930, p. 14.

66. "Bennett Girls Face 6 More Games at Home," *Norfolk Journal and Guide,* February 8, 1936, p. 14.

67. "Meet The Nation's Best Female Cage Team," *Chicago Defender,* March 27, 1937, p. 14.

68. Amelia C. Roberts, "Women in Athletics," *Chicago Defender,* March 12, 1927, p. 9; Ivora King, "Women in Sports," *Baltimore Afro-American,* March 19, 1932, p. 15; "Athletic Leaders Confer At Howard," *Baltimore Afro-American,* May 24, 1930, p. 14.

69. According to the interviews I conducted with Bennett athletes the male coaches included: Dean Staley in the early 1930s, Coach Streator from 1932 to 1934, Coach Wormley in 1935, Coach Trent, Jr. in 1936 and 1937. Evidence suggests that physical education teacher Dorothy A. Barker coached the team in the late 1920s. See: "Bennett Lassies Win," *Baltimore Afro-American,* February 15, 1930, p. 14. Barker was a graduate of the Sargent School of Physical Education and joined the Bennett faculty in 1927. See *Catalogue for Bennett College 1929–1930* p. 11 in Box: "Miscellaneous Box" Bennett College Archives, Greensboro, NC.

70. Exceptions to a male coaching staff included: Barber-Scotia College and Winston-Salem Teachers' College.

71. Mildred Ann Burris joined the Bennett faculty in 1936. She completed her undergraduate degree from Temple University and graduate study at Harvard and Columbia. See: "Athletics," *Bennett College Bulletin 1939–1940* p. 85 in Box: "Miscellaneous Box" Bennett College Archives, Greensboro, NC.

72. *Handbook of the Women's Sports Day Association,* 32 (I located this handbook among miscellaneous files in the Livingstone College Archives, Salisbury, NC. The document is undated, but since Livingstone entered the WSDA in 1957 I believe that the handbook was written after that date). Bennett joined the WSDA in 1939 and was followed by North Carolina A&T in 1940, North Carolina College (Central) in 1943 and finally Livingstone in 1957. For primary source accounts of the activities of the WSDA see: "College Coeds Vie For Honors at Howard Pool," *Baltimore Afro-American,* March 1, 1941, p. 21; "Sports Day at Bennett College," *Baltimore Afro-American,* November 16, 1940, p. 21; "Beauties in Sports at Bennett College," *Carolina Times,* November 30, 1940, p. 7.

73. "Sports Day to Be Held Nov. 16," *Bennett Banner,* November 1940, p. 2.

74. "Bennett Has Intramural Basketball," *Future Outlook,* March 21, 1942. (Found in scrapbook, newspaper clippings file, Bennett College Archives, Greensboro, NC).

75. Papers of the National Association of College Women, Box 90–8 (folder 4), Moorland-Spingarn Research Center, Howard University, Washington, D.C.

76. "Women Form Athletic Association," *A.&T. Register,* October 1937, p. 5; "Intercollegiate Athletics For Women Banned," *A.&T. Register,* March 1938, p. 6; "Immanuel Lutheran's Purposes are Stated," *Norfolk Journal and Guide,* May 22, 1937, p. 15.

77. Interview, Vivian Merrick Sansom, (Durham, NC), August 10, 1996.

78. "CIAA Reaffirms Carry-On Stand for War Duration," *Baltimore Afro-American,* May 22, 1943, p. 22; Lem Graves, Jr. "Sports Are Important To Us," *Norfolk Journal and Guide,* February 20, 1943, p. 13; "A.&T. Aggies Set For Exhibition Game," *Atlanta Daily World,* March 11, 1943, p. 5; "N.C. State Championship Claimants," *Norfolk Journal and Guide,* March 11, 1944, p. 10.

79. Himes-Gissendanner, "African-American Women and Competitive Sport."

80. Merze Tate, "The Justification of a Women's College," *Bennett College Bulletin* 12 (1937) p. 15 in Box: "Miscellaneous Box" Bennett College Archives, Greensboro, NC.

81. Kevin Gaines, *Uplifting the Race,* 139–140.

82. Merze Tate, "The Justification of a Women's College," 15.

6

A SPECIAL TYPE OF DISCIPLINE
Manhood and Community in African-American Institutions, 1923–1957

Pamela Grundy

AMID THE MOUNTAINS OUTSIDE Charleston, West Virginia, in the mid-1940s, North Carolina College basketball coach John B. McLendon Jr. found himself facing an angry young white man and a potentially explosive situation. McLendon and his team had boarded the bus after a game with West Virginia State and discovered only one seat remaining open. Under the protocols of segregation, white riders had filled the front of the bus, and black riders had gone to the back. The lone empty place sat right on the dividing line, next to a young white woman with a baby in her arms. After a quick conference the team concluded that center Henry Thomas needed the most rest and should sit down. Thomas asked the woman if he could sit next to her, and she said she did not mind. The bus driver, however, had a different view. "I can see him now," McLendon recounted. "He looked up in the mirror, and he saw Henry Thomas sitting beside this girl. So he came back. And on the way back, I said to the players—they were all lined up, hanging on—I said, 'Don't forget, now, I'll do the talking.' "[1]

The bus driver ordered Thomas to get up. McLendon refused. "He's inside the law," he argued. "The law says we seat from the back, they seat from the front. It's the last seat on the bus, and he can sit in it if he wants to." The woman next to Thomas repeated that it was fine with her, which in McLendon's words "burned the bus driver up." The driver went back to the front of the bus, sat for a minute, and then returned and repeated his demand that Thomas leave the seat. As McLendon and the driver stared at each other, the other passengers became restless. "Go sit down and drive the bus," McLendon recalled them saying. "Come on bus driver, we've got to get where we're going." "Get on, and let's get out of here." "Drive the bus." As the complaints mounted, the driver turned away, went back to his seat and started the engine. But when the bus got into the mountains outside of Charleston, he pulled off the road and returned to the back. "He can't sit there," he repeated. "I'm not moving this bus till he gets up." As the passengers renewed their complaints, and as the driver's face grew red with anger, McLendon made his move. "I'll tell you what," he announced. "Since this is such a big problem to you, [and] these people have to get where they're going. . . . Ladies and gentlemen, I'll tell you what we're going to do. We're going to get off this bus."[2]

For the bus driver the team's exit may have seemed a victory, a successful reassertion of the code of white supremacy. But McLendon and his players had a different view. McLendon's strategic retreat had made his point, preserved the team's dignity, and averted violence. Most important, it had been the bus driver, rather than his African-American confronters, who had become lost in a public display of disruptive and irrational emotion. After disembarking, players joked with each other and tossed rocks into the woods, waiting for the next bus to come along. "They laughed about it," McLendon recalled. "They really thought we had won. Because you can see what kind of position you can put that kind of person in. That you're better than he is—if that's what the problem is. He's not making any points by doing that."[3]

Almost a half-century after the encounter, McLendon laid out the rationale that governed his actions, explaining the complicated contests he played with white authority and with his young players' sense of their own dignity. "One of the best ways to play the game is avoid confrontation," he explained. "The next is to make the adversary ridiculous. . . . It's a matter really of learning how to maintain a position of respect. And to do this you do try to avoid confrontation. Because if you're made to lose your dignity, stripped of your manhood in front of your players, you can't be in a position to tell them to be a man. About life, about anything. That's what you're trying to make of them, men who can handle life well. You might have to almost be ready to sacrifice your life to maintain that position in their respect."[4]

Along with coaches and educators around the country, John McLendon sought to use the discipline and strategy of competitive athletics to prepare young people for the challenges of adult life. For coaches such as McLendon, athletics performed that role in many ways, fostering individual expression, teaching players how to work with others, building self-confidence, and harnessing the exuberance of adolescence in the service of a focused set of goals. "The biggest kick you get out of it—most of these kids have turned out to be decent citizens," explained legendary Winston-Salem State coach Clarence "Bighouse" Gaines. But as the West Virginia incident made clear, black athletes and educators living in the Jim Crow South faced contests that tested character in other ways than just on the playing field and in which victory and loss were defined by a far different set of rules. In black athletic programs, standard lessons about discipline, teamwork, and determination mingled with other interests, as educators sought to gird young people against the obstacles of Jim Crow, to promote racial respect, and to transform the pageantry of school athletic events into a force that helped unite diverse and potentially divided black communities behind common goals.[5]

In the decades between the dawn of segregation and the evening when the North Carolina Eagles stepped onto the West Virginia bus, North Carolina's African Americans had worked to come to terms with a racial order that was at once oppressive and complex. Jim Crow legislation might set forth absolute racial divisions, embodied in concrete designations of "Colored" and "White." But the realities of segregated southern life encompassed myriad more ambiguous encounters and exchanges, in which African Americans took the measure of an oppressive world and looked for opportunities to assert or to maneuver, to press for advantage, or to step right to the edge of the Jim Crow line. Black schools, which sat at the crossroads of these many cultural currents, became one arena where young people learned to grapple with these many challenges, fashioning the strategies and identities with which they would confront adult life.[6]

Figure 6–1
Like other black college and high school players around the South, the North Carolina College Eagles learned lessons that went far beyond athletic strategy. A Ridgeview High School graduate is in air, with ball. Courtesy of Ernie Warlick.

On the surface, schools offered a tangible example of Jim Crow inequalities. In many communities dilapidated, drafty buildings, secondhand textbooks, and lack of bathroom facilities served as daily, painful reminders of the racial divide. "It was never the hardship which hurt so much as the contrast between what we had and what the white children had," Durham resident Pauli Murray recalled, focusing particular attention on the difference between the bare clay yard where black schoolchildren played and the facilities at a nearby white school. "Their playground, a wonderland of iron swings, sand slides, seesaws, crossbars and a basketball court, was barred from us by a strong eight-foot-high fence topped by barbed wire," she wrote. "We could only press our noses against the wire and watch them playing on the other side." Throughout the state, white officials guarded such disparities as a cornerstone of white supremacy. In 1947, when the school sanitation officer in the small town of Tryon refused to run a sewage line to the Tryon Colored School, white antilynching activist Jesse Daniel Ames offered a pointed assessment of the symbolic import she saw behind the action. "The sanitarian holds the views of some of the 'best' citizens here," Ames wrote. "Negroes get more than they deserve. They will ask for more as they get what they ask for. Soon, they will be demanding social equality, to be invited to our homes to eat and then to marry our daughters. All this as a result of our request for sewage connection for the school."[7]

Student recollections, however, make it clear that black schools were far more than the sum of their so frequently inadequate facilities. After the Civil War, many African Americans had seized on education as the most promising means for racial advancement. In the decades that followed, public schools became a major focus of community life as parents donated cash and labor to make up for state shortcomings and flocked to school plays, recitals, graduations, and sports events. Black public high schools, which North Carolina first began to build in earnest in the early 1920s, assumed particular significance. "See, it was a community thing," explained Burrell Brown, longtime teacher and coach at Hickory's Ridgeview High School. "Ridgeview was the community's activity. Wherever you lived in Hickory, and most of the people lived close to that area, they were tied up in what went on in Ridgeview." Within school walls, well-educated teachers poured their energies into their pupils, seeking not simply to educate individuals but to uplift an entire race. "There was a real sense of achievement," recalled Arthur Griffin Jr., a graduate of Charlotte's Second Ward High School. "And a sense to get a quality education. And the teachers—they'd look at you, almost as if they were wanting to *will* a good education into your head."[8]

Like their counterparts around the country, African-American educators found athletics an uncertain ally. Athletic programs at black schools suffered from many of the same problems that plagued those at white institutions. Teachers and principals regularly voiced complaints about recruiting, eligibility violations, athletic fund-raising, and the academic performance of star athletes. Disagreements over the place of sports in high schools became a regular subject at meetings of the North Carolina Negro Teachers Association, with strong opinions both in favor of and against high-level competition. At the 1939 annual meeting, for example, association members voted to eliminate both sectional and state high school tournaments. When the tournaments were restored in 1940, the decision came only after a discussion that "went on for hours with the most fiery arguments on both sides of the question."[9]

But in a world where young African Americans faced a particularly broad array of psychological challenges, the lessons that athletics had to offer could also take on heightened significance, as teachers sought to gird their students emotionally as well as intellectually for a Jim Crow world. . . . "Not only were the teachers and coaches expected to educate or train, they also became surrogate parents, advisors, and builders of character and dreams which instilled in us the belief that we could not fail if we followed their guidance," Ridgeview graduate Walter Childs recalled. "They took second-hand books, sports equipment and instruments and a building that needed improvement and accomplished the impossible. They created an atmosphere where students thirsting for knowledge were united with teachers who were willing to go the second mile to insure that they not only quenched that thirst but they also made it possible for us to achieve and experience success." His description laid particular stress on the school's athletic coaches. The men and women who ran practices, plotted strategies, celebrated victories, and consoled players after losses "instilled a special type of discipline in us that was a vital part of the sports that we played."[10]

As with their counterparts in many fields, supporters of school sports programs had to scrimp and improvise. Most schools had trouble finding funds for basic needs, with little left over for luxuries such as athletics. Rudolph Torrence, who attended West Charlotte High School in the 1940s, recalled that funding for the school's basketball team ebbed and flowed, depending on the quality of the team. "We made the state championship my senior year. And we won the state basketball championship that year," he recalled. "That year we had a pretty good team, and we did a lot more traveling than we had done in previous years, because we were winning. And our principal loved to win. And when you won, he would make sacrifices so that you could go to the next level. But by the same token, if you lost, he'd say 'I ain't spending a *dime* on you.' " Even in good times, teams and coaches

Figure 6–2
The West Charlotte Lions, 1946. Rudolph Torrence is at center. Courtesy of Mrs. Gloria P. Munoz-Martin and the late coach T. M. "Jack" Martin.

found themselves responsible for raising money to provide uniforms, equipment, and transportation. As Burrell Brown succinctly put it, "Everything was just about from your pocket. There was no money any kind of way, really."[11]

Black school athletics in fact became a major lesson in doing much with little, and the ability to succeed with limited means became a point of pride. At Charlotte's Second Ward High School, student editors filled their school newspaper with descriptions of economic disadvantage overcome. "Basketball prospects around Second Ward High School appear very encouraging thus far," students reported in 1934. "Although the team has many obstacles confronting them, they will do the best they can. The players proved this when they agreed to bring enough money to purchase a ball so that they might begin practice early." Two years later a call for female players emphasized the importance of determination over both wealth and appearance. "The Second Ward Girls' Basketball Team has just been organized," the article ran. "We are planning to do something no other Second Ward team has ever done—win every game that we play. We want students from all classes. We want fat ones, skinny ones, short ones, tall ones. . . . The only requirements are tennis shoes, shorts, and the will to win. If you don't have the first named two, come anyway, if you have the third, because you can wear soft leather or rubber soled shoes and any kind of a short skirt. Come on girls and help us make our wish come true."[12]

Although neither state funds nor private donations provided much support for coaches or athletic facilities, African-American educators at all levels developed their own programs and their own governing organizations. By the late 1920s, teams of both boys and girls were traveling the considerable distances between the state's new high schools to defend the honor of their institutions and communities. By the 1930s, a statewide organization that eventually became known as the North Carolina High School Athletic Council governed school competition and had begun sponsoring state championships. The Colored (later Central) Intercollegiate Athletic Association (CIAA), which regulated competition for most of the state's black colleges, saw steady expansions in funding and in public notice, particularly as its member schools emerged from the hardships of the depression and began to find more funding for athletic activities.[13]

This developing athletic system held particular significance for young black men. African-American communities warmly encouraged young women's athletic endeavors—"The same crowd who came to see the guys was there to see us play," Mary Alyce Clemmons recalled—and young women reveled in the joys of physical exertion and athletic rivalry. But while female athletes often viewed their sporting endeavors as one element in a multifaceted sense of womanhood, athletics formed a cornerstone of black male identity, immersing its participants in a multigenerational male world that linked grade-school boys with college players, and high school athletes with fathers and grandfathers. In arenas set well apart from the repressions and restrictions of a Jim Crow world, young men throughout the state fashioned athletic games into powerful sites of self-discovery and individual expression.[14]

Rudolph Torrence recalled that he was on the football field from the time that he could "walk, talk, whatever." On the playground, where pickup games were ruled by "instinct and gut" aspiring athletes started out as "peewees," playing only minor roles: "What would happen, the larger boys would organize. They would take X number of peewees to balance it off. So actually I was just a balancing act at the beginning. . . . The big guys they'd say, 'Well, I'll take this peewee, and that peewee, or whatever.' And that was the way that we did it." The peewees' contributions consisted largely of hiking the football or "piling on" the other players after tackles had been made, but they were proud to be included in the masculine endeavor. "You wanted to participate, and whatever you could contribute in whatever way, then you did," Torrence said. "Mostly, you would be the person who would center the ball—a non-eventful kind of position. But it gave you an opportunity to participate in the sport."[15]

As young men grew, their developing size and strength became a source of considerable pride. Les Hunter explained that in his early teenage years, "I can remember really being misused, elbowed. I was very timid." But as he kept playing, his confidence began to build. "I got over being timid," he continued. "I was starting to get big, was able to bluff somebody. I learned how to fight back. Guys were getting a little scared. That gave me a little confidence. From then on, I think I was alright." Such physical confidence was frequently paired with the pleasures of self-expression, particularly as basketball began to gain new status. Growing up in Charlotte in the 1940s and 1950s, future West Charlotte star Paul Grier spent much of his spare time in the company of fellow basketball devotees, devising dramatic feats in the alley behind his house. "I just put up a goal," Grier explained. "Now it wasn't a goal, it was a tire rim. I started with a tennis ball. Then I found a volleyball in the creek, and pumped it up some kind of way, patched it up, and started to shoot. And then when I got a basketball—good God that was it then. We put the rim about high enough where we could dunk it, and we'd just try everything on it. And then we'd raise it a little bit from time to time." On city streets and playgrounds such play became a colorful and competitive assertion of self. "When you're playing street ball," Charlotte resident Titus Ivory noted, "it's you against the other guy, which makes it: 'Hey, I've got to do my thing, because if I don't, I'll get had. If I do, I'll have somebody else.' "[16]

In black communities around the state, athletic contests became both glue and challenge, weaving sports events, both formal and informal, into a rich verbal culture of rivalry and exchange. "Bragging rights," Titus Ivory recalled, were one of the sweetest parts of victory. "It was so good to be on top," he explained, "especially when we started out in junior high school. Most of the junior high schools were in a pretty close perimeter. And in that perimeter it was like bragging rights. If you beat Irwin, you had the bragging rights for this side of town. If you beat J.T. then you had the bragging rights for the whole city, because you beat the two top teams that existed at that time. . . . We'd have parties and at the parties the guys who would be on the winning side would usually come in with their chests all hung out, you know. It was like you were on top of the world at that time, because you had beat your opponent."[17]

High school coaches tapped into these sporting networks, keeping their eyes on promising young men and encouraging them from an early age. Titus Ivory recalled the pride he felt in being noticed by legendary West Charlotte football coach Thomas "Jack" Martin when Ivory was still in grade school: "I think the first time I ever saw him was when my grandmother was in the hospital, and he came to visit my grandmother," Ivory recalled. "And he looked at me and said, 'Gee, you are getting big.' Said, 'I'm going to make you a football player.' And the next year I went out, and I played a lot, because he saw that I was going to be a large guy." Such ambitions were also encouraged by players themselves, who took pride in grooming their successors. "It just so happened that in Hickory we had quite a nice little gathering of athletes," Burrell Brown explained. "And, well, we worked with them. We worked with the boys who played with us, and the boys who played with us worked with the other little fellows. They taught our system to the other little fellows. The little fellows would come and tell us, 'When we're old enough, we're going to play for you.' We'd smile. But they were telling the truth."[18]

At times this athletic interest could stray from the broader goals that most black educators held. Just as some educators were more concerned with community power and prestige than with the quality of their schools, in some athletic programs the local status that came with athletic victories took precedence over long-term goals. Athletes themselves could also reject the discipline and self-restraint promoted by coaches such as Brown, Martin, or McLendon, drawing instead on the values of a developing urban street culture, within which masculinity was frequently defined through defiant physical courage and dramatic self-assertion.[19]

More often, however, coaches imposed a far more rigorous discipline, seeking to add new layers of significance to the lessons of the playground. As players moved into high school, games that had once been ruled by "instinct and gut" gave way to more systematic strategy, as coaches worked to blend the exuberant energy of playground ball into disciplined team effort. Such efforts stressed a different side of manhood; coaches tempered young athletes' outer confidence with an emphasis on inner discipline, focusing on restrained dignity, rigorous rationality, and rapid, calculating thought. Charles McCullough, who took over basketball coaching responsibilities at West Charlotte in the 1950s, became one of many coaches renowned for his discipline. "He had that kind of respect where ain't nobody going to do nothing wrong in front of him," recalled former player Willie "Scoopie" Joplin. "Because they know he ain't going to deal with that. He'll tell you, 'Son, you can't play for me.' And that's that. And when he said that—you might be the best player in the school. But he would do that, he wouldn't let you play."[20]

Coaches taught their lessons through even the smallest details of the game. Second Ward High player Kenneth Diamond Jr. recalled the way his coach's insistence on the rationality of substance over style manifested itself on the free throw line. While Diamond and his teammates favored the overhand free throws that were coming into vogue, their coach held fast to the older method of underhand shooting, a technique that could look clumsily old-fashioned but gave most players a better angle at the basket. Players had to stick to these rules, Diamond recalled, unless they could prove the coach's calculations wrong. "They used to make us shoot the underhand free throw," he explained. "You don't see that any more—in fact, some people refer to it now as a granny shot. . . . My coach made all of us shoot that way, unless you could make nine out of ten the way you wanted to shoot. If you could make nine out of ten with your style, he would let you shoot it your way. If not, everybody had to shoot the granny shot."[21]

This kind of discipline, which laid out a set of principles but also gave players room to prove themselves, was a common coaching technique, aimed at teaching students self-reliance rather than strict obedience. "I didn't have a lot of rules," Bighouse Gaines explained. "But I respected them, they respected me." When faced with a talented but flamboyant playground athlete, John McLendon did not bar the player's signature moves but set clear limits on their use. "He was kind of a hot dog, let's put it like that," McLendon explained. "I told him, 'The first time you make a bad pass going behind your back I'm going to pull you out.' "[22]

Titus Ivory recalled the ways that Thomas Martin sought to conceal his authority and build up his players. "Coach Martin used to take us aside and he used to talk to us individually," Ivory explained. "I ended up being the captain on my senior team. Which meant that I had to share in the leadership role. But he would always take me aside and tell me to transfer information from him to the players. . . . I knew that he would do that to me sort of to build my confidence, and to make it seem as if the instructions were coming from a fellow player, instead of coming from him." Ridgeview coach Burrell Brown built player involvement into a system that he described in a contribution to a national coaches' magazine. "You can't induce the average American boy to do your bidding willingly without showing him your need for cooperation," he wrote. "That is why, during the playing season, we have many squad meetings and encourage participation in strategy planning and schedule discussions. Even though player suggestions might not be used, there is created a feeling of being an integral part of an interesting project, rather than that of being a pawn selected to follow a master's inflexible instructions."[23]

An interest in flexibility and self-reliance also extended beyond the playing field. In 1938, George W. Cox, an energetic and many-talented director at North Carolina's most conspicuously successful black-owned business enterprise, the North Carolina Mutual Insurance Company, addressed a banquet celebrating Hillside High School's state football championship. In his remarks Cox laid particular stress on flexibility—lauding, in the words of a *Carolina Times* reporter, "the mind of the Negro boy as being versatile, that is being able to change from one thing to another with the greatest of ease." Burrell Brown also hinted at this broader view when he talked about the discipline Ridgeview coaches sought to instill. "You've got to learn discipline," he said. "You've got to learn to think quickly. You learn to know when to get out of the way of trouble. There's just so many ways you can give it to them, and that's the way we taught it."[24]

As McLendon's encounter on the West Virginia bus made clear, thinking quickly and avoiding trouble were particularly important skills for young black men. Black athletes and spectators could appreciate strategic thought both for its sheer mental pleasure and for the larger role it played in their everyday existence, where tasks ranging from securing a bank loan to walking unmolested down the street were often accomplished only through planning, foresight, and diplomacy. *Carolina Times* editor Louis Austin caught the spirit of this outlook in a 1938 editorial, when he described every African American's "necessity of being alert and using his mentality to carry him through many difficult situations that would destroy the average human.' " At the same time, the discipline of self-restraint related to the realities of a world where even slight breaches of racial etiquette could spark a violent response. Athletic discipline thus became part of a broader cultural array of warnings and strategies that ranged from the tales of tricksters who devised inventive schemes to avert direct confrontations, to the fast-paced exchange of insults in the verbal dozens, which encouraged participants to develop both verbal eloquence and cool self-control.[25]

Athletics also touched on a final facet of the mental discipline that was crucial to black educators' efforts: the ability to maintain self-assurance in the face of mental as well as physical challenge. George Cox's address to the Hillside High School banquet praised not only mental versatility but also emotional resilience. "In the game of sport is found the best example of how one conducts himself, so much that he can be or may be the supporting character in his community," Cox asserted, going on to quote Rudyard Kipling's "If," whose series of conditional clauses had become an icon of U.S. sporting culture: "If you can lose and start again at your beginnings and never breathe a word about your loss. . . . If you can meet with triumphs and disasters and treat those two impostors just the same." The writer who reported on the evening summed up the racial spin that Cox gave to the verse as he overturned conventional interpretations of Kipling's popular poetry as the highest expression of a specifically white manhood and invoked visions of sport as a proving ground for African-American ability. "His point was don't be afraid of resistance that the color of the skin makes no difference. In connection with this he spoke of Joe Louis and Jesse Owens, Negro athletes of today."[26]

Viewed from this perspective, Kipling's "If" in fact seemed especially suitable advice for young black men, who confronted a world in which they were frequently portrayed through demeaning stereotypes, where whites regularly projected their own fears and anxieties onto African Americans, and where every facet of public life, from the Bibles used in courtrooms to the bathrooms in railroad stations, embodied the assumption that some groups of human beings were more deserving than others:

If you can keep your head when all about you
  Are losing theirs and blaming it on you,
If you can trust yourself when all men doubt you,
  But make allowance for their doubting too;
If you can wait and not be tired by waiting,
  Or being lied about, don't deal in lies,
Or being hated don't give way to hating,
  And yet don't look too good, nor talk too wise. . . .[27]

Such lines spoke to a number of the conditions with which young African Americans contended as they moved from their own communities into a wider world. Specifically, the verse advocated distancing oneself from irrational emotions and ideas and cleaving to an inner, rigorously rational core. As such, it was as much a discipline of thought as action. John McLendon waxed eloquent on the importance of such self-awareness and its application both on the court and in the world. "What it meant: you have to maintain yourself, all you are capable of, at all times," he explained. "You can't lower yourself to be a marginal playing team, dirty tactics. If you are in the right, well, you're going to prevail. Even though the system appears to be against you, it's really not you being any less, it's because somebody's worried about you already being much more than they want you to be. You play the game of life the way you play this situation," Herman Cunningham, a graduate of Monroe's Winchester Avenue High School, offered a similar assessment when he recalled his coach's strategy for dealing with the small size of one year's football team. "The coach, you see, he taught us discipline," Cunningham explained. "He said, 'Weight don't mean anything. Use your head.' "[28]

Their prestigious community positions, their connections to the outside world, and their close work with their players made athletic coaches, like many of their teaching colleagues, into powerful role models for young men, particularly in communities where high rates of mortality and difficult economic circumstances often played havoc with family dynamics. "Most of the kids that I grew up with were single parent kids," Rudolph Torrence explained as he talked about his high school coach's influence in his life. In his case the combination of his mother's early death and his father's work as a plasterer, which kept him on the road, had profound effects on family relationships. Although the elder Torrence always provided for his children, he remained a distant figure in their lives. As coach Thomas Martin spurred Torrence on to greater efforts and offered a wide range of advice about both sports and life, "he was filling the slack for the father role, for me and for most of the other guys."[29]

The deep-seated poverty that beset most black communities further expanded coaches' responsibilities, which frequently extended to providing necessities as basic as clothes and food. "We had a training schedule that we wanted followed," Burrell Brown explained. "Which included—even though your parents can't get you steak—we used to go and get pills that were supposed to have all this in it. Now it may not have, I don't know, but some of those kids didn't have a meal. And we'd say: 'All right, take some of these pills'. . . . Some of these kids just didn't have a meal." Bighouse Gaines recalled one strategy he used to give some of his more impoverished players extra food without threatening their sense of dignity. "You make it convenient to have him come home, help you pick up two leaves out of the driveway or something, and meanwhile say, 'Clara's got a ham in here. . . .' "[30]

Even as high school coaches worked to keep their players fed and to prepare them for life after graduation, they also sought to expand their opportunities by helping them win college scholarships. In many ways black athletes with the talent to gain scholarships played for higher stakes than their white counterparts. White athletes who indulged their athletic inclinations at the expense of study or career preparation could turn to manufacturing work, public utility employment, or sales jobs that offered relatively secure livings—often trading on local acclaim or on their potential contributions to company athletic teams to win coveted positions. African Americans faced far more restricted possibilities and far greater competition for those jobs that were available to them. As a result, as Burrell Brown put it, "In that day and time, if you went to college your chances for getting the better jobs, whatever were open, it was better for you."[31]

High school athletes did not always see such an array of opportunities and perils, focusing more on the immediate pleasures of their sport and on the acclaim it won in their communities, as well as among young women. "The boys wanted to go to college just to play some more ball, and if possible maybe get a job, maybe get a wife, whatever," Brown explained. Still, their coaches stayed focused on the larger view. "Even though I talked around to them that way—'yeah, you might get you a wife'—I wasn't thinking about a wife," Brown continued. "I want you to have a future."[32]

In pursuing their ends, coaches also worked closely with the communities around them. At Ridgeview, for example, coaches Burrell Brown, J. C. Johnson, and Samuel Davis tapped into the male networks that fostered athletic interest, as well as into the cherished tradition of bragging rights. Ridgeview teams were inspired "to perform to the maximum," Walter Childs recalled, through techniques that included "comparing one team to last year's team, bringing back former members to practice and assist the team, and always having the practice open for parents, usually fathers, to watch. All of these things as well as the 'bragging rights' system used by former players to motivate the team to match or beat their record created the need for the team to be the best."[33]

In close-knit communities such as Hickory, discipline was both highly personal and woven into community consciousness. Like many black coaches around the state, Ridgeview coaches laid down curfews, which they personally enforced. "Back in those days, we worked on the floor, and when we were off the floor, we were all in the same area," Brown explained. "So we might happen in on them. So they had to be kind of looking out.' The coaches were aided in their job by watchful community members, particularly when the stakes were high. If an athlete failed to come home on time, or if someone in the community spotted a star out on the town the night before a big game, the phone would often ring for Brown, Johnson, or Davis, who would then head out to locate the offenders and send them home. In the relatively compact black community of Hickory, they usually had little trouble. "You know, kids didn't have cars like they have now," Brown explained. "So they'd be somewhere in the area. Might be having a little party or something, hanging out. In the area. You'd find them. If we could beat the person to them that was going to tell them so they could run."[34]

Athletes had such trouble dodging curfews in large part because athletic prowess had become a major source of pride in communities around the state, focusing the energies and interests of a wide spectrum of individuals. The spectators that crammed into Second Ward High School's gymnasium, James Ross recalled, represented the full spectrum of Charlotte's African-American society, from school principal A. G. Grigsby, with his meticulous conduct and attire, to the less-than-respectable young men who sat in a back corner and "had cheers that cheerleaders couldn't do." At Second Ward, as at schools around the state, this multifaceted participation could help turn games into pageants of both community cohesion and racial pride, as coaches, players, cheerleaders, and members of the audience all contributed to the event.[35]

When Second Ward and crosstown rival West Charlotte met in the Second Ward gymnasium enthusiasm filled the space. "Everybody would show," explained Second Ward player James Truesdell. "The barbers, or whoever. People would close their business to come see us play." Fellow Second Ward player Walter Holtzclaw echoed Truesdell's words. "It was standing room only," Holtzclaw noted. "We had to have policemen here to keep people back off the court. So you were really playing around this black line here. It was just like that. They packed as many as they could in. And it was just a high that you can't explain. You really have to be there."[36]

When a wide spectrum of community members demonstrated a collective interest in the fortunes of school teams, the ties such actions created could play particularly significant roles within black communities. As elsewhere in North Carolina, a growing emphasis on formal schooling, with its corresponding promotion of middle-class ambitions and ideals, created its own tensions, as educators' efforts to "uplift" their fellow African Americans at times grated against local values, identities, and forms of expression. Officials at black colleges had looked to sports to build race pride and solidarity in part over the frustrations they developed when they realized that many African Americans showed little inclination to follow their cultural lead, turning instead to activities that took different forms and served different ends. Even as black teachers sought to inspire their students with Shakespeare, symphonies, and related forms of "elevated" culture, other African Americans congregated in juke joints, at evangelical church services, or in other alternate spaces, voicing dreams, joys, and sorrows through sounds and gestures influenced more by folk tradition or by the latest styles of an expanding commercial culture than by educators' cultural aspirations.[37]

The capacity of school sports to bring together sometimes-conflicting interests thus had particular meanings within African-American communities. Sports events brought the drama and collective spirit of vernacular black culture into educational institutions, incorporating local style into a structure that emphasized the disciplined organization that middle-class educators prized so highly. Such cultural amalgamations, along with similar balances struck in pursuits such as school bands or dramatic productions, could help acknowledge and strengthen racial ties even as the artistic power they so frequently displayed

Figure 6–3
Second Ward High School team, 1949. Courtesy of the Robinson-Spangler Carolina Room, Public Library of Charlotte and Mecklenburg County.

sparked pride in what many considered a distinctive and dynamic black cultural style. For black intellectuals who spent much of the first part of the twentieth century publicly wrestling with their cultural past, an institution that combined creativity rooted in vernacular culture with education-linked activities offered a solution to a troubling dilemma, making it possible to claim allegiance both to middle-class ideals that cut across racial boundaries and to a specifically black heritage. At the same time athletic contests gave community cultural endeavors a place within the symbolically potent sphere of educational pursuits. If ongoing attempts to build black institutions depended on creating spaces where black citizens could both agree and argue, where they could work to at once fashion and critique understandings of their racial heritage and their existing circumstances, school athletics became one such arena.[38]

Charlotte's Queen City Classic, the fall football game that matched West Charlotte and Second Ward, served as a clear example. A large portion of the city's black community turned out for the game, with wealthier citizens driving newly polished automobiles to the city's Memorial Stadium and others walking up the streets, dressed in their Sunday best, for an event that would dramatize both rivalry and connection. The heated rivalry between the schools made for a volatile atmosphere. "There would be fights—there were always fights," James Ross recalled. "All kinds of things were settled at the Classic." Yet when young Arthur Griffin looked around him, he also saw a kind of unity. "You could just walk up Seventh Street . . . all the way up to the Park Center," he explained. "And right behind Park

Center was Memorial Stadium [, and it] was this huge event for little kids to even think about looking at something as great as the Queen City Classic. Your two black high schools, West Charlotte versus Second Ward. It would fill up Memorial Stadium. And so for us growing up, that was the event. All these black people just filling up a big, huge arena was just—it was just unheard of."[39]

Such connections had the potential to contribute to a push for changes in North Carolina's racial order. The role that school athletics could play in building community bonds, as well as the uses to which such connections could be put, was suggested in one of the ways that supporters of Greensboro's Dudley High School reacted to the Supreme Court's landmark *Brown* decision. Dudley was considered one of North Carolina's top academic high schools, with a strong student body and a highly trained corps of teachers. But when black Greensboro organizations began to use the threat of *Brown* as leverage for improvements at African-American schools, a vocal and united front of Dudley parents and administrators focused their initial efforts on demands for a new school gymnasium.[40]

On an individual level the mix of discipline, community support, and intergenerational connections that athletics fostered could make the experience particularly powerful, encouraging precisely the kind of confidence and deep-seated self-awareness that young African Americans needed to make their way in a challenging and often hostile world. Herman Cunningham attempted to explain this often ineffable sensation while describing his experience playing football for Winchester High. "The guy who lived right behind me, he played . . . and one up the street there, he played," he said. "It was a number of them played, and were good athletes at that time, and motivated us. It was a carryover all the way, step by step. From down in the lower echelon grades up. The guys that were coming up the channels of the school when we were playing, they were inspired to come in after we got out. And it just passed it on, just cycled all the way down." He concluded with an assessment of the broader meaning of such connections, which suggested the significance that sports could hold in that kind of community context. "By doing this, it made a good motivation for them to enjoy themselves playing, because they had the whole person into the game. Not just there for publicity or something like that. It was for real."[41]

By the late 1940s, even as black high school athletics helped build up communities and individuals, sports were beginning to take on broader ramifications in North Carolina colleges. Nowhere did these efforts show more dearly than in CIAA basketball, where a new group of talented coaches and players was taking the game to new heights of skill and recognition, reaching toward regional and national renown. The CIAA climb began in 1939, when Durham's North Carolina College hired John McLendon as its basketball coach. McLendon hailed from Kansas, where a new, fast-paced style of basketball had become all the rage. For McLendon, the stylistic shift meant abandoning complexly patterned half-court strategies in favor of a hard-driving, attacking style that dominated the entire court—an approach that would eventually become known as the fast break. McLendon could trace his athletic heritage back to James Naismith himself—Naismith had been his advisor at the University of Kansas—and he drew much of his inspiration from Naismith's own interest in athletic spontaneity. In explaining the origins of his approach, McLendon once described an afternoon when he and Naismith happened on a group of Kansas players. "He asked them for the ball. 'Whenever on the court you had it, that's there where your offense begins. And whenever the other team has the ball that's where your defense begins,' he said. I took that to mean that you played basketball on the entire court. Your offense started off the boards or whenever you got possession, that's when your offense begins. You don't come down the court, stop, and decide 'O.K., now I'm going to run and play this and that.' The same on defense, if you get the ball anywhere on the court, you don't retreat, you attack."[42]

McLendon absorbed the lesson and took it a step further. Naismith had not believed in coaching, preferring a free-flowing form of play. McLendon developed conditioning drills, complex plays, and a wide-ranging strategic philosophy. "Contrary to its reputation," he later wrote, "the fast break is not an 'aimless,' 'helter-skelter,' 'run and shoot,' 'fire horse' game except in the appearance of its rapid, often demoralizing, action. It is a planned attack with multiple applications; it is a designed offense which can be utilized in one or more of its several phases each time a team gains possession of the ball." In McLendon's estimation the style also influenced its practitioners in ways that raised versatility to an art. While fast-break basketball was "a winner at the turnstiles," he wrote, "more importantly, it is a game of increased challenge to the young contestant. . . . The challenge lies in the player's learning to make the most of the many choices confronting him. The high-speed game requires quick sound reactions, lightning-quick decisions, and corresponding physical and mechanical adjustments to meet the ever-changing situations."[43]

The fast break carried the North Carolina Eagles on unprecedented scoring sprees. In February 1943, Rudolph "Rocky" Robinson scored fifty-eight points against Shaw University to break the nation's single-game scoring record. A year later, in another game with Shaw, the Eagles racked up sixty-seven points during the second half, another national record. The team began to draw enormous crowds. In the fall of 1952 North Carolina College proudly unveiled a 4,300-seat gymnasium with a million-dollar price tag. Barely two months later college officials announced that the press of spectators wanting to see the school's games was so great that they would begin radio broadcasts for the fans unable to secure seats. The accomplishments of the Eagles also set other teams scrambling to keep up. "I know we got to the finals in a tournament with McLendon's team—'49 I guess it was," recalled Bighouse Gaines, who would go on to win 828 games with Winston-Salem State and join McLendon in the Basketball Hall of Fame. "We thought we'd done a heck of a job coaching and got beat 119 to 65. . . . We looked at each other and said 'Let's go get some basketball players.' "[44]

CIAA coaches were not, however, content with local fame. Rather, they avidly sought ways to showcase their talented squads before a wider public. At the close of World War II a group of coaches and administrators revived a prewar plan for an end-of-season basketball tournament, as "a grand way of celebrating the play of the season by bringing the best teams together." Such an event, supporters argued, would serve many purposes, making possible "a time for fellowship with those from other member institutions, a great social occasion, a time for some Presidents to show off their best athletes and coaches . . . a time for some students and alumni to brag over their team, a time to crown the best tournament team, a time for the big pro scouts to see most top athletes together, a time to make the necessary money to operate the association and finally the time for the news media to extol the merits of the occasion and let the fans in other parts of the country know what the Association has achieved."[45]

In 1946, with a five hundred dollar budget, the inaugural contest opened in the Turner Arena in Washington, D.C. It did not disappoint. A week of stellar play was capped by a championship game that went into triple overtime as the underdog North Carolina Eagles battled the powerful Virginia Union Panthers. The game saw fourteen lead changes and was tied ten times as the small but speedy Eagles contested the methodical Panther play. In the second overtime the Panthers led by four points with less than a minute left. But the Eagles rallied to a tie, and the third overtime was all theirs. "In the final five minutes of overtime play, the 'whiz kids' romped and cavorted just like it was the first half of the tournament game reported *Norfolk Journal and Guide* sports editor Lem Graves Jr., who called the game his "all time sports 'thrill-of-a-lifetime' " despite the loss by his home state team. "Passing with lightning precision, and cutting into the basket in magnificent form, they dropped in four baskets in succession and then put on an 'ice' show to run the time out." The Eagles triumphed 64–56. North Carolina assistant coach Leroy Walker, who would go on to worldwide renown as a coach of track and field and an ambassador of sports, later explained, "I remember thinking that a better script . . . couldn't have been written by Hollywood."[46]

As it grew into a major event, the CIAA tournament became a celebration not simply of the players on the court but also of the thousands of students and graduates who packed the stands. Legendary player and coach Al Attles, a 1960 graduate of North Carolina A&T, recalled the impact of his first CIAA tournament by describing the exhilarating effects of "the unbelievable spirit," the "fashions exhibited," and the "outstanding parade of great players." He also laid special stress on the racial accomplishment the tournament represented: "The most important aspect, I feel, was the pride of this small segment of the educational world showing what Black people can do with their own energies and determination." The mix of pride and excitement, as well as the opportunity to meet up with old friends and acquaintances, made the CIAA one of the most beloved events in North Carolina, with thousands of devoted fans returning every year. In 1970, more than two decades after the inaugural event, one such fan expressed this loyalty in no uncertain terms, declaring, I would rather chew nails without teeth, testify against the Mafia, and vote for Lester Maddox than miss a C.I.A.A. basketball tournament."[47]

The growing prominence of the CIAA tournament became part of a broad-based postwar shift in African Americans' visions of their place in U.S. society—a shift that had also influenced the growing interest in high school play. The years that followed World War II brought a new energy to black communities around the country as African Americans took advantage of expanding national prosperity and a shifting racial climate to launch new efforts for recognition and equality. CIAA president George Singleton made such determination clear at the association's annual meeting in 1945, the year the league approved the tournament plans. After listing the CIAA athletes who had been killed in military service, he urged his audience to carry such efforts forward. "These young men and thousands of others have died in this gigantic struggle to bring about conditions of lasting peace," he told the gathered members. "They have died that all men everywhere might have the right to walk the world with dignity, to worship and speak with freedom, to enjoy freedom from want and fear, to enjoy equality of opportunity for gainful employment and preparation therefore, and to a decent and respectable standard of living. They have died in order that the philosophy of the master race shall forever be eliminated from the thinking and actions of the people of the earth."[48]

Singleton continued his address with a forceful reassertion of the belief that athletic talent could be used to further African-American efforts to implement at home the principles of democracy they had fought for abroad. "The important part which athletics can play in breaking down the barriers of discrimination has already been demonstrated conclusively," he argued. "Negro heroes of the nation's gridirons, courts and tracks have undoubtedly served as ambassadors of inter-racial good will in the past. You must prepare them for an even greater future role in this regard. In every phase of American life, economic, social, political, religious, and educational, we must see to it that the principles for which these young men have died shall be translated into practical application here at home. We must see to it that they shall not have died in vain. That is our responsibility to them."[49]

Singleton's forceful celebrations of athletic strife joined an array of postwar pronouncements that brought talk of competition to new heights within black educational rhetoric. Despite a long-standing interest in the potential of sports to shape individual character and promote racial understanding, throughout the first half of the twentieth century many black educators remained skeptical about the broader value of school athletics. In places like North Carolina the competitive rhetoric that was so tightly tied to athletic endeavors also held an uncertain position in many circles of African-American society. While African Americans throughout North Carolina enjoyed the clash and drama of competitive sports and had rejoiced in the triumphs of black athletes such as Jesse Owens and Joe Louis, in other areas of life economic and racial hardship had fostered a deep commitment to mutual endeavor.[50]

After World War II, however, the rhetoric of competition began to assume new prominence at black institutions. When Morgan State University's Martin Jenkins addressed the 1950 meeting of the North Carolina Negro Teachers Association, for example, he began his talk with an optimistic description of growing opportunities in colleges, the armed forces, and athletics. "In light of this trend we must now, everywhere, educate Negro children for full participation in American life," he told his audience. "This means that the children in your school, your children, must come out prepared to compete on equal terms with all other citizens; to ask no quarter; and to exercise fully their rights and responsibilities as American citizens." A few years later *North Carolina Teachers Record* editor W. L. Greene continued to press competitive themes, invoking the "greater freedom of the individual to participate in the opportunities offered by a dynamic society" and criticizing older modes of education in which " 'cooperation' was often stressed as a way to success." Educators, he wrote, "must meet the challenge of adapting our operations to the growing needs of society and we must also train youth to enter into society without fear and with the will to meet the competition of their contemporaries in all areas of employment."[51]

The postwar period brought a corresponding growth of athletic programs, sparked both by increases in school funding and by the new attitudes of players and coaches. This new restlessness appeared in details as small as team uniforms, as many high school coaches began to challenge the tradition of playing in uniforms passed down from white schools. When Burrell Brown arrived at Ridgeview High in 1947, shortly after finishing a stint of military service, he immediately joined with fellow coach J. C. Johnson to improve the school's teams, starting with their uniforms. "We were in bad shape for uniforms," Brown recalled. "We were using castoffs from Hickory High School for football, and they had I don't know what for basketball. We came in here, the Ridgeview colors were orange and blue, and they were playing in blue and gold. . . . So Johnson and I got together immediately. And we started getting them uniforms. . . . We knew it was important. It'd make the young players feel better. Make them feel like somebody, if they went out there in brand new uniforms occasionally instead of somebody else's castoffs." When Brown explained his new interest in this outward mark of status, he pointed directly to the changing times. "They had had people who didn't mind," he concluded. "We were a little younger at that time, and we minded."[52]

As Ridgeview partisans sold ice cream and conducted raffles to raise money for orange uniforms, other coaches planned even bolder actions, working to schedule integrated matches and beginning to press for equal participation in national athletic organizations. While even the most daring coaches did not openly flout restrictions on integrated competition within North Carolina, they laid plans to advance the issue elsewhere. By the early 1940s, following a celebrated set of games between the Panthers of Virginia Union and the renowned Blackbirds of majority white Long Island University, black college coaches eagerly sought contests with white teams. At North Carolina College, for example, John McLendon arranged matches that included Brooklyn College, the marines of North Carolina's Camp LeJeune, and even a team representing the Duke Medical College, which made an undercover trip to the Eagles gym in 1944.[53]

At first, McLendon recalled, his main goal was to build his players' confidence both in themselves and in the methods that he was using. "Because of the exclusion of blacks in sports, if you were practicing the games that other people were playing, you really had no way to decide whether you were really playing it well," he explained. "Because [the white teams] were the ones you read about in the newspapers. You read about some of our teams once a week in the weeklies. . . . I was kind of a hard taskmaster, tried to do it tough-love style, that's what they call it these days. And get my fellows to achieve. But they weren't sure that they were coming up to the standard that I had set. . . . It's almost like, you're in another world and you don't know whether you're really doing what you're supposed to do or not. So the only way to prove that is to play them." When the Eagles emerged triumphant from their first integrated game, a 1942 match with Brooklyn College, McLendon saw immediate results. "When we played that game, and our guys won the game, they felt like, 'Well, we're really playing basketball. Coach is a real coach here. He's not just coaching a game that only we play, but he's coaching a game that they play, and all these pictures we see on Sunday—we're better than they are.' "[54]

By the 1950s, black institutions around the country were actively pursuing bids for national recognition, sending applications to national athletic associations and pressing to be included in national tournaments. Such efforts met with initial resistance, particularly from the NCAA, whose rules gave black schools little chance to prove themselves worthy of inclusion in the organization's national tournament. While the NCAA rated schools according to their performance against major opponents within their own districts, CIAA teams fell into the all-southern District Three, where ongoing prohibitions against integrated sport made full intradistrict competition impossible. In 1950, John McLendon blasted this policy in an uncharacteristically emotional column that reflected both his frustration at the NCAA's recalcitrance and his confidence in his team's abilities.

"A few teams in the East will play CIAA opponents," McLendon wrote. "However, there is not a single team in District Three which has the nerve, spine, backbone, or guts to play a CIAA opponent. Not a single institution in District Three will play a CIAA opponent on any terms since every one of them is bound by the chains of negative inter-racial practice. Some which are not so steeped in this phenomenal stupidity are afraid of the loss of athletic prestige which would naturally result after CIAA prowess on the court enacted its inevitable toll." He concluded with a final statement: "The NCAA may mean NATIONAL COLLEGIATE ATHLETIC ASSOCIATION to some people, but to us it means NO COLORED ATHLETES ALLOWED."[55]

A year later, after the NCAA thwarted black coaches' opportunity to make their case by holding its 1951 annual meeting at a segregated hotel in Dallas, Texas, McLendon and his colleagues turned their efforts to the more sympathetic National Association of Intercollegiate Athletics (NAIA). After two years of discussion, NAIA leaders voted to consider eligible black colleges for tournament berths and to allow the winner of a new black college tournament to participate in its national championship contest. In 1953, the Tigers from Tennessee A&I State University became the first black college team to take part in an integrated national tournament. In 1957, after John McLendon had taken over coaching duties at Tennessee State, the Tigers took the NAIA crown, the first integrated national title won by a historically black school. The same year North Carolina A&T became the first historically black institution to play in an NCAA tournament, taking part in the inaugural "college division" event, which would eventually become the Division II tournament. A decade later Winston-Salem State, coached by Bighouse Gaines and starring the peerless Earl "The Pearl" Monroe, would bring the first NCAA basketball title ever won by a historically black school back to North Carolina.[56]

With their direct challenges of national athletic organizations, North Carolina's black institutions began to realize decades of hopeful talk about using college athletic teams to foster racial respect. Throughout the 1950s, efforts at athletic integration within the state and in the South at large would proceed at a snail's pace. But confidence in the institutions and the athletes that black schools had developed would prove an ongoing spur to action. Such an approach showed clearly in the spring of 1952, when the NCAA informed A&T coach Cal Irvin and athletic director William "Bill" Bell that their membership application had been approved, making A&T one of the first African-American schools accepted by the organization. Students and administrators rejoiced at the news, seeing the recognition as "another step in the emancipation of colored athletes." School sports columnist Richard Moore joyously summed up A&T's achievements, concluding with a prediction which suggested that the "best citizens" of Tryon, North Carolina, had indeed calculated accurately when they denied the Tryon Colored School its sewer hookup, reasoning that, in the words of Jesse Daniel Ames, "They will ask for more as they get what they ask for." "These are only a few of the advancements made over a number of years," Moore wrote. "So you see, we are grateful indeed for our own accomplishments. Realizing that the fight is not nearly over, we are more determined to continue."[57]

NOTES

1. John McLendon interview by the author, Winston-Salem, NC, February 26, 1998, tape 1, side A. Southern Historical Collection, Wilson Library, University of North Carolina, Chapel Hill (hereafter SHC)

2. *Ibid.*

3. *Ibid.*

4. *Ibid.*

5. Clarence "Bighouse" Gaines interview by the author, Winston-Salem, NC, March 8, 2000, tape 1, side B. In author's possession. The literature on black schools in North Carolina, and the South has grown enormously in recent years. Particularly useful works include William H. Chafe, *Civilities*

and Civil Rights: Greensboro, North Carolina and the Black Struggle for Freedom (New York: Oxford University Press, 1980); James D. Anderson, *Education of Blacks in the South: 1860–1935* (Chapel Hill: University of North Carolina Press, 1988); Glenda Gilmore, *Gender and Jim Crow: Women and the Politics of White Supremacy, 1896–1920* (Chapel Hill: University of North Carolina Press, 1996); James L. Leloudis, *Schooling the New South: Pedagogy, Self, and Society in North Carolina, 1880–1920* (Chapel Hill: University of North Carolina Press, 1996); David S. Cecelski, *Along Freedom Road: Hyde County, North Carolina and the Fate of Black Schools in the South* (Chapel Hill: University of North Carolina Press, 1994); and Vanessa Siddle Walker, *Their Highest Potential: An African American School Community in the Segregated South* (Chapel Hill: University of North Carolina Press, 1996).

6. For a thoughtful account of the complexities, dilemmas, and opportunities found in the day-to-day operation of Jim Crow segregation, see Grace Elizabeth Hale, *Making Whiteness: The Culture of Segregation in the South, 1890–1940* (New York: Pantheon, 1998), 121–97. For a discussion of strategies of resistance pursued within the segregated space of city buses, see Robin D. G. Kelley, *Race Rebels: Culture, Politics, and the Black Working Class* (New York: Free Press, 1996), 55–75.

7. Pauli Murray, *Proud Shoes: The Story of an African American Family* (New York: Harper and Row, 1978), 269; Jesse Daniel Ames to N. C. Newbold, January 30, 1947, folder A, section July 1946–June 1947, box 15, General Correspondence of Director, Division of Negro Education Records, Department of Public Instruction, North Carolina State Archives, Raleigh. The building and funding of black schools is covered in Anderson, *Education of Blacks in the South,* 202–4, Frederick A. Rodgers, *The Black High School and Its Community* (Lexington, MA: D.C. Heath, 1975), 112; and Thomas W. Hanchett, "The Rosenwald Schools and Black Education in North Carolina" *North Carolina Historical Review* 65 (October 1988): 387–444.

8. Burrell Brown interview by the author, Hickory, NC, March 31, 1993, 4. Museum of the New South, Charlotte, NC; Arthur Griffin, Jr. interview by the author, Charlotte, N.C., May 7, 1999, tape 1, side A (SHC). For accounts of the roles black teachers played in their students' lives, see Chafe, *Civilities and Civil Rights,* 20–4; Cecelski, *Along Freedom Road,* 57–68; and Walker, *Their Highest Potential.*

9. *Carolina Times,* March 30, 1940, p. 2. A detailed treatment of debates over athletics at black colleges can be found in Patrick B. Miller, "To 'Bring the Race along Rapidly': Sport, Student Culture, and Educational Mission at Historically Black Colleges During the Interwar Years," *History of Education Quarterly* 35 (Summer 1995): 111–133.

10. *1986 Panther,* 16, a commemorative edition of the Ridgeview High School annual, Hickory, NC, produced for the 1986 alumni reunion. Copy in the North Carolina Collection, University of North Carolina, Chapel Hill.

11. Rudolph Torrence interview by the author, Charlotte, NC, May 27, 1998 tape 1, side B (SHC); Brown interview, 4.

12. *Charlotte Second Ward Herald,* January 1934, p. 4, and January 1936. A description of similar pride in resourcefulness at black colleges can be found in Miller, "To 'Bring the Race along Rapidly,' " 118–9.

13. Rodgers, *Black High School,* 54; *North Carolina Teachers Record,* January 1933, p. 18. For a description of black high school organizations around the South, see Nelson George, *Elevating the Game: The History and Aesthetics of Black Men in Basketball* (New York: Simon and Schuster, 1992), 26–30.

14. David Ramsey, prod. *Enduring Rivalry.* Charlotte, NC: Museum of the New South.

15. Torrence interview, tape 1, side A.

16. Bill Finger, "Just Another Ball Game," *Southern Exposure* 7 (Fall 1979): 75; Paul Grier, Sr. interview by Peter Felkner, Charlotte, NC, July, 1993, tape 1, side A. Museum of the New South; Titus Ivory interview by the author, Charlotte, NC, March 24, 1993, 4. Museum of the New South. George, *Elevating the Game,* offers an extended analysis of the development of a distinctive African-American street basketball style. Another description can be found in Dan Rose, *Black American Street Life: South Philadelphia, 1969–1971* (Philadelphia: University of Pennsylvania Press, 1987), 1–3.

17. Ivory interview, 3.

18. Ivory interview, 11; Pamela Grundy, The *Most Democratic Sport: Basketball and Culture in the Central Piedmont, 1893–1994.* (Charlotte, NC: Museum of the New South), 1994, 40–1.

19. For a brief description of the urban "hipster" side of masculine identity, seen in the context of conflicts with authority on Birmingham city buses, see Kelley, *Race Rebels,* 65–7.

20. Willie L. "Scoopie" Joplin interview by the author, Charlotte, NC, April 2, 1999, tape 1, side A (SHC).

21. Vermelle Ely and Kenneth Diamond, Jr. interview by the author, Charlotte, NC, March 10, 1993, tape 1, side A. In author's possession.

22. Gaines interview, tape 1, side A; George, *Elevating the Game,* 90.

23. Ivory interview, 11; *Coaching Clinic,* August 1963, 22.

24. *Carolina Times,* January 22, 1938, p. 4; Grundy, *Most Democratic Sport,* 40–1.

25. *Carolina Times,* June 11, 1938, p. 4. Austin made this comment while discussing the achievements of nationally known black athletes. For a description of the dozens and related forms of black folk culture, see Lawrence Levine, *Black Culture and Black Consciousness: Afro-American Folk Thought from Slavery to Freedom* (New York: Oxford University Press, 1977), 344–68.

26. *Carolina Times,* January 22, 1938, p. 7. A thoughtful discussion of Kipling's significance for white North Carolinians during the period can be found in Gilmore, *Gender and Jim Crow,* 61–4.

27. Rudyard Kipling, *Rudyard Kipling's Verse, Inclusive Edition, 1885–1926* (Garden City, NY: Doubleday, Doran, 1941), 648.

28. McLendon interview, tape 1, side A; Herman Cunningham interview by the author, Monroe, NC, September 7, 1993, 3. Museum of the New South.

29. Torrence interview, tape 1, side A.

30. Brown interview, 9; Gaines interview, tape 1, side B.

31. Grundy, *Most Democratic Sport,* 41.

32. *Ibid.*

33. *1986 Panther,* 42.

34. Brown interview, 7, 3. For a broader discussion of the parental nature of relationships between black teachers and their students during this period, see Walker, *Their Highest Potential,* 65–139.

35. James Ross interview by the author and Thomas Hanchett, Charlotte, NC, February 10, 2000, tape 1, side B (SHC).

36. Both Holtzclaw and Truesdell appear in Ramsey, *Enduring Rivalry.*

37. For a description of some of these social and cultural rifts within black communities, see Kelley, " 'We Are Not What We Seem:' Rethinking Black Working-Class Opposition in the Jim Crow South," *Journal of American History* 80 (June 1993): 75–112.

38. For issues relating to the constructions of such communities, see Kelley, *Race Rebels,* 51–3. For the dilemmas of black intellectuals, see Raymond Wolters, *The New Negro on Campus: Black College Rebellions of the 1920s* (Princeton, NJ: Princeton University Press, 1975), 341–43.

39. Ross interview, tape 1, side B; Griffin interview, tape 1, side A.

40. Chafe, *Civilities and Civil Rights,* 18, 62.

41. Cunningham interview, 2.

42. George, *Elevating the Game,* 87.

43. John B. McLendon, Jr., *Fast Break Basketball: Fundamentals and Fine Points* (West Nyack, NY: Parker Pub. Co., 1965), ix, 11.

44. *Carolina Times,* January 28, 1950, p. 4; December 20, 1952, p. 2; January 3, 1953, 5; February 28, 1953, p. 2; Gaines interview, tape 1, side B. By 1954, scoring at black schools was so high that Winston-Salem State was averaging ninety-four points a game. See *Carolina Times,* January 6, 1954, p. 5.

45. John B. McLendon Jr., ed., *The First CIAA Championship Basketball Tournament,* (Westmont, IL: Scotpress, 1988), 27; copy in the North Carolina Collection, University of North Carolina, Chapel Hill.

46. *Ibid.,* 38–39, 46.

47. McLendon, *First CIAA Championship,* 24, 13.

48. *The 1945 Bulletin of the CIAA* (Norfolk, VA: Guide Quality Press, 1945), 13, folder 1, box 9, Clarence "Bighouse" Gaines Papers, Winston-Salem State University Archives, Winston-Salem, N.C.

49. *Ibid.*

50. Brown interview, 7–8. *The North Carolina Teachers Record* is replete with discussions of the importance of cooperative endeavor. See, for example, January 1932, p. 8; October 1932, pp. 74–75; and May 1934, p. 43.

51. *North Carolina Teachers Record,* May 1950, p. 14, and October 1957, p. 8.

52. Brown interview, 4–5. Although Brown and Johnson were from other states, many native North Carolinians also intensified their demands for better treatment in this period. For a description of postwar shifts in attitude toward state funding in one North Carolina community, see Walker, *Their Highest Potential,* 57–9. See also Chafe, *Civilities and Civil Rights,* 24–8. J. C. Johnson later became coach of LeMoyne-Owen College in Memphis, Tennessee, where his accomplishments included winning an NCAA championship in 1975 and being named national coach of the year. See *1986 Panther,* 6.

53. McLendon interview, tape 1, side B. Informal integrated games were in fact relatively commonplace within the state, but most such matches were carefully concealed from public attention.

54. *Ibid.*

55. *Carolina Times,* March 18, 1950, p. 8.

56. Milton S. Katz and John B. McLendon Jr., *Breaking Through: The NAIA and the Integration of Intercollegiate Athletics in Post World War II America* (privately printed, 1988) copy in North Carolina Collection, University of North Carolina, Chapel Hill), 7, 37. When black coaches first presented their petition, the NAIA was known as the National Association of Intercollegiate Basketball (NAIB), but the organization changed its name soon afterward. The NCAA justified its exclusion of black colleges in part by relegating them to small-college status at a time when the organization did not sponsor a small-college tournament. See *ibid.,* 13. For an account of Earl Monroe's Winston-Salem State career, see George, *Elevating the Game,* 165–71.

57. *Tryon, NC Register,* March 1952.

II

THE ORDEAL OF DESEGREGATION

WRITING IN OCTOBER, 1936, Roy Wilkins—activist and editor of the *Crisis*—took the occasion of a football game between the University of North Carolina and NYU to comment in expansive terms about race relations in America. The contest occurred in a northern venue during that fateful autumn, and significantly, it matched a team from the once-Confederate South against a contingent that included an African-American athlete. This was, in fact, one of the first *intersectional,* interracial match-ups in the history of intercollegiate competition.

Wilkins had discussed the game only briefly in his own journal—the organ of the National Association for the Advancement of Colored People—but his vigorous account appearing in the pages of the *New York Amsterdam News* gave full voice to the integrationist ideals of the mass of black Americans of his era: This was a crossing of the color line that deserved to be headline news as well as a model for the future. He had heard "no boos" from Carolina fans, Wilkins reported, and "none of the familiar cries of 'Kill the Negro.' So far the University of North Carolina is still standing and none of the young men representing it on the gridiron appears to be any worse off for having spent an afternoon competing against a Negro player. It is a fairly safe prediction," Wilkins continued, "that no white North Carolinian's daughter will marry a Negro as a result of Saturday's play, much to the chagrin of the peddlers of the bugaboo of social equality."

Wilkins then cast his praise for the actions of UNC in a broader context, condemning those institutions that refused to advance even one small step on the issue of race. The theory behind the "shenanigans" generally called "Gentlemen's Agreements" was "that the prestige of a Southern school suffers in some way if its sons compete in games with Negroes," he asserted. "Not only that, but the South and the white race generally were supposed to suffer something or other. Sociology, anthropology, and political science were dragged into the argument, the whole thing topped off by a rehash of the war of 1860–1865." When "the North Carolinians merely said they would not object and would not protest" if a black man competed, racial reformers knew they had accomplished something very simple and at the same time quite profound, breaking the tradition of southern schools forcing their hometown rules on northern institutions. Carolina's decision to play NYU, with its African-American star, suggested to Wilkins "that a younger generation of white Southerners want to approach the difficult business of race relations on a different basis than that used by their fathers and grandfathers." Ultimately, he hoped such an action would "set an example for other Southern schools," and he anticipated upcoming contests that might have the same admirable outcome. (Roy Wilkins, "Watchtower," *New York Amsterdam News,* October 24, 1936).

Clearly, the desegregation of sports at mid-century offers some of the most dramatic moments of the civil rights crusade. Sadly, though, Wilkins' comments on the 1936 football contest were overly optimistic. In fact, for many years thereafter, the racial breakthroughs in the athletic realm had to be lined up against numerous setbacks. It is important to emphasize that there was nothing certain, no clear pattern of racial progress on the playing fields. Thus black leaders like Wilkins, along with a legion of African-American sportswriters, continued to extol victories won and records established, even as they applauded every act of enlightenment and denounced every instance of discrimination they discovered. Within the subtly crafted racial calculus of "muscular assimilationism," the successes of African-American athletes in a widely popular realm of endeavor lent themselves to the larger prize: persuading white America that blacks should be allowed to participate fully in the social, political, and economic life of the nation.

The ideal of equality and opportunity in sport—fair play in all its particulars—represented a substantial portion of the larger argument for racial justice. African Americans drew inspiration from champions such as Jesse Owens and Joe Louis, not merely as folk heroes, but also in the aftermath of the 1936 Summer Olympics and the second Louis-Schmeling bout, as *national* heroes. If someone like Wilkins could have created a narrative of racial reform from the 1936 football competition between UNC and NYU, then perhaps from the career of Joe Louis to the early exploits of Jackie Robinson in major league baseball, the path to integration would have been swift and sure. What the essays in this section reveal, however, is that massive resistance to the claims by blacks for full citizenship rights would play out on diamond and gridiron as well as at lunch counters and bus stops and high schools. During the 1950s and 1960s, at the very same moment in history that a battle flag of the Confederacy was first set within the state flags of Georgia and Mississippi, for instance, those states—and others—enacted new legislation prohibiting interracial athletic competition.

Racial reform in the sporting realm was fitful, at best, following no formula. It required that some athletes, like Jackie Robinson, make huge sacrifices in their personal lives so as to embody the hopes of myriad like-minded race men and women; it depended upon local activists, such as the NYU students who protested discrimination on their campus when a black athlete, a classmate, was banned from intersectional competition. The dynamic between the forces for civil rights on the playing fields and those in opposition was also embedded in deeper contexts: Cold War politics, for instance, and what desegregation and the civil rights movement in the United States meant to the emerging postcolonial nations of Africa and Asia. From different perspectives, the essays in this section also examine the politics of pursuing a national championship in basketball or a prestigious bowl appearance in football, the cultural dynamics in a city such as Indianapolis, Indiana, where the best basketball team happened to be from an all-black high school, and the ways and means of the nation's capital, where the Kennedy White House finally wielded the clout sufficient to eradicate lily-whitism from the Washington franchise of the National Football League.

Ultimately, in the midst of so much that was, indeed, a political dimension of civil rights activism, the personal also needs to be addressed. How many athletes, and their families and friends, endured incivility and threats of violence as they simply stepped forward to compete in a new place? How do we measure the cost of the individual sacrifices made in behalf of the larger crusade? Is there a remedy for bitterness and alienation, stemming from so many injustices in the past, other than honest plans for something more affirmative for the future?

7

JOE LOUIS
American Folk Hero

William H. Wiggins, Jr.

> *Hail the king! Make way for the king . . . And everybody does. Along Route 2 which leads to Pompton Lakes you see thousands of people scattered, peering through brush and over harvester machines all straining for one purpose—to see Joe Louis . . . as it (Joe Louis' car) passes . . . you hear screams and yells by the townfolks . . . Soon you begin to think this Joe Louis must be a hero.*
>
> —*Chicago Defender,* February 15, 1936

WHO WAS JOSEPH LOUIS BARROW? What were the physical, personal, and spiritual qualities that he possessed that made him a genuine American folk hero? What were some of his heroic words and deeds at the time of the Great Depression and during World War II, which are still cited today by many Americans of all races, creeds, and colors? This chapter will attempt to answer these questions by looking at the first twenty-eight years of Joe Louis's life. The period covered begins on May 13, 1914, when he was born, the seventh child of poor sharecroppers Lillian and Monroe "Mun" Barrow, on a farm near Lafayette, Alabama, and ends on March 10, 1942 in Madison Square Garden, where Joe Louis gave a memorable patriotic speech at a big World War II rally. In less than half of his life (he died of a massive, heart attack on April 12, 1981, a month shy of his sixty-seventh birthday) Joe Louis had risen from his humble birth as just another unknown brown baby to international celebrity status as the one and only "Brown Bomber."

Joe Louis's fistic comet flashed across a dark and foreboding America. It was the time of the Great Depression and World War II, two periods that left a deep and lasting impression on American culture. Both eras unleashed a sense of fear and uncertainty among Americans, the consequences of which are still evident in some aspects of contemporary life and thought. The economic devastation of the Great Depression seriously eroded the confidence that most Americans had in the free enterprise system and in the American Dream of success through hard work and thrift. Some of the unemployed who were forced to stand in soup lines for their daily sustenance began to doubt the reality of that dream. Their precious hopes for a better life lay dashed amid the rubble of the 1929 stock market crash. During the 1930s, a significant number of American parents went to bed each night fearful that they and their children would be doomed to a bleak, poor existence unless the economy turned around soon. They would always be one of the have-nots and never one of the haves.

World War II was their second cultural nightmare. With each successive conquest, Nazi Germany, with its impressive military might and political ideology of Aryan supremacy, loomed ever larger as a nation that just might be able to topple America from its prominence as a world power and replace its democratic government, in which all citizens are free to express their opinions and elect their leaders, with Nazi fascism, a political system that would deny all of these constitutionally guaranteed rights. It was this national climate of fear and uncertainty that prompted President Franklin Delano Roosevelt to attempt to reassure his fellow citizens by saying during one of his radio fireside chats: "We have nothing to fear, but fear itself."

The first eight years of his boxing career (1934–1942) cut a swath of boxing brilliance across these two watershed eras in American history. Also during this time, Joe Louis came to be perceived by a significant number of Americans as a folk hero, one they could entrust to defend their threatened cultural values. During the Great Depression, Joe Louis came to symbolize the cultural values of the work ethic, honesty, and fair play for a large segment of black Americans. Walter White, executive secretary of the NAACP and other black leaders of the time proudly cited the Brown Bomber's rigorous training habits as a refutation of the popular racial stereotype held by some whites, especially southern whites, that all blacks are lazy. During World War II, Joe Louis symbolized the cherished American values of patriotism, freedom, and democracy for a significant segment of white Americans. Eleanor Roosevelt, the nation's First Lady, although not an avid boxing fan, was nonetheless greatly impressed with Joe Louis's unparalleled patriotic acts of donating his entire purses from matches with Buddy Baer and Abe Simon in 1942 to the United States Navy and Army Relief Funds, respectively.

I have organized this chapter into four parts. "Joe Louis Becomes a Man" examines his life from his birth in 1914 to the end of his amateur boxing career in 1934. "Joe Louis Becomes a Great Depression Hero" chronicles his Horatio Alger climb from earning just fifty dollars for his first professional fight with Jack Kracken (1934) to the end of the 1930s when he was earning close to two million dollars from fights with such heavyweight boxers as Primo Carnera and Max Baer (1935), Max Schmeling (1936), Jim Braddock (1937), Max Schmeling (1938), and "Two Ton" Tony Galento (1939). "Joe Louis Becomes a World War II Hero" discusses the emergence of the Brown Bomber as America's patriotic hero, with special attention to such fights as the rematch with Max Schmeling in 1938 as well as successful title defenses against Billy Conn (1941) and Buddy Baer and Abe Simon (1942). "The Champ Is Dead, Long Live the Champ" explores the significant impact that Joe Louis continues to have on American life and thought, long after he lost the heavyweight title to Rocky Marciano on October 26, 1951.

JOE LOUIS BECOMES A MAN

> *As the years go by, I often reflect on the things that influenced me. Sometimes I look and think, "How come me? How come I'm a world champion? How come I've got all the responsibilities it carries, when I only looked forward to a simple, poor country life?" I guess it has something to do with having a strong mother, a good stepfather, and a special God-given talent.*
>
> —Joe Louis in *Joe Louis: My Life,* (1978)

Joseph Louis Barrow, like many black children born during the first two decades of this century, came from the South and was reared in very humble circumstances. His parents, Munrow "Mun" Barrow and Lillian Reese Barrow, were hardworking, God-fearing Alabama sharecroppers who struggled to eke out a living for themselves and their eight children from the sale of cotton and vegetables they grew on the 120-acre red-clay farm they rented from a wealthy, white, absentee landowner. The emotional strain, however, proved too much for Mun Barrow. In 1916, when Joe Louis was only two years old, Mun Barrow was placed in the epileptic ward of Searcy Hospital for the Negro Insane in Mt. Vernon, Alabama. But his mother refused to break under the burden of rearing eight children by herself. At the age of sixty-four, when recalling his childhood and his seven brothers and sisters (Susie, Lonnie, Eulalia, Emmarell, De Leon, Alvanius, and Vunice), Joe Louis paid tribute to his mother's iron will and unwavering work ethic with these words: "My momma was Lily Reese before she got married . . . and she was, for those days, a big woman—five foot six and 170 pounds. . . . She could plow a good straight furrow, plant and pick with the best of them—cut cord wood like a lumberjack then leave the fields for an hour earlier than anyone else and fix a meal to serve her family. God! I loved that woman."[1]

In the intervening years, Lillian Barrow married Patrick Brooks, a widowed sharecropper with eight children of his own. Joe Louis paid his stepfather this glowing tribute: "Patrick Brooks was all the father I really knew. He was a good stepfather who worked hard and did the best he could. He was always fair and treated all those sixteen children as equally as a man could. His kids and my brothers and sisters fit in like one big family."[2]

Soon after he remarried, Mr. Brooks was visited by some of his relatives who had moved north to Detroit, Michigan. After seeing their poor living conditions in Alabama, they encouraged Lillian and Patrick to move with their sixteen children to Detroit where they could enjoy a higher standard of living. But before the family did finally migrate to Detroit in 1926, Joe Louis enjoyed an active childhood in the Camp Hill community, tucked away deep in Alabama's Buckalew Mountains. Young Joe Louis attended the community's one-room school, which enrolled all of the Camp Hill children from ages seven to seventeen. Joe Louis, by his own admission, didn't like school. Looking back on those days, Louis offered this explanation for his playing hooky: "Well, for sure, I didn't like school. Maybe because I stayed so much by myself and maybe because everybody was so busy working, no one had the time to teach me to talk properly. I stammered and stuttered, and I guess I was so plain nervous that the other kids laughed at me. So when Eulalia walked back home to get us younger kids, Vunice would go into school, but I didn't. Why should I stay in school and be made fun of, when there were snakes to catch or a cool spot under a shady tree where I could watch clouds change shapes?"[3]

Young Joe Louis and his older sisters and brothers played hooky throughout the school term, which lasted from October until April, the planting and harvesting seasons in the community. But summer was the time for mischief and fun for young Joe Louis. As a boy he remembers getting drunk after drinking half a bottle of moonshine whiskey he found in the house. On another occasion, he remembers eating some of the fried chicken lunch that his mother had entrusted to him to deliver to his older brothers and sisters who were in the cotton field chopping cotton in the hot Alabama sun. When he delivered this somewhat diminished lunch basket to his tired and hungry older brothers and sisters, Joe "got one hell of a whipping."

"Skin the Tree" and "Knocking" were two games that Joe Louis and his boyhood friends liked to play. To play Skin the Tree, the children would hide in tree branches. The trick was to select a young sapling to hide in, one that would bend over and almost touch the ground, thus allowing the child who was hiding to jump down easily when discovered and to run and touch home base before the child who was "it" could beat them to home base.

Knocking was a game that proved to be Joe Louis's earliest introduction to his life's profession. Joe Louis describes Knocking in this manner: "There was another fighting game we played, called 'knocking.' I was only about eight years old, but I'd put a chip on my shoulder and dare bigger guys than me to knock it off. If they did, we would fight. Most times it was more noise and running and throwing a few stones than anything else."[4]

Joe Louis left many of these childhood experiences behind when he migrated north to Detroit in 1926, but there were some experiences that he carried with him to his new home, particularly his strong dislike of school. It didn't matter that his new Duffield Elementary School had many classrooms instead of the old one-room he used to attend in Alabama. Louis still hated school. Because of this deeply ingrained dislike of school, as well as some serious learning disabilities, he advanced only from the third to the sixth grade at his new school. There was one school activity, however, that Louis did like: "Only time I shined was when they had assembly—I carried the flag. That was supposed to be some kind of honor job. No way I could mess that up. I was tall, strong, and they tell me I was a nice-looking kid. Those assembly days, Momma made sure I had a clean, starched shirt and a blue tie. That's the only thing about school I liked."[5]

Fortunately, Miss Vada Schwader, one of Joe Louis's favorite teachers at Duffield, suggested that he transfer to the Bronson Industrial Institution, an all-boys vocational school in Detroit. The transfer proved good for him. Under the expert tutelage of Mr. Hayes, his manual training teacher, Joe Louis learned to make tables, cabinets, and other items of furniture, which he brought home and gave to his mother. Under the encouraging instruction of Mr. Smith, his gym teacher, young Joe Louis's interest in sports, especially baseball, began to develop. In an early biography, Louis recalled the success that he had playing baseball on the Bronson school team. "I always wanted to be a baseball player. I started out as a catcher on the Bronson softball team. Our teacher offered 25 cents for any home run we socked out against the other teams. The offer was withdrawn after I knocked ten homers over the fence. My greatest ambition then was to be a ball player. I might have become a good one, I don't know."[6]

Champion Joe Louis did not forget the kindness and guidance of these two teachers. When he returned to Detroit in 1939 to defend his title against Bob Pastor, he gave them choice tickets to the fight. After school and on weekends, Joe Louis teamed up with his best childhood friend, Freddie Guinyard, to hustle odd jobs moving heavy crates of fruits and vegetables at the Eastern Market near their Black Bottom neighborhood. They were an odd couple: Freddie with his slight build and slick tongue and Joe with his muscular build and tied tongue. Louis recalled how they combined their respective talents to earn extra money carrying ice: "Everybody in the family was trying as hard as they could to get food to put in our stomachs. Me and Freddie, when we were about fifteen or sixteen, got a job together on an ice wagon. I guess you have to go back some to remember that there were no refrigerators or freezers in those days, at least not for the poor people. Everybody was dependent on the iceman to keep food from spoiling. We didn't travel around in some truck that needed gas and fixing up. We used a wagon with an old horse pulling it. We'd put thick wraps of brown burlap over the ice to keep it from melting too fast. Anyway, when it came time to deliver, Freddie stayed downstairs watching the horse while I carried fifty or sixty pounds of ice up a couple of flights. Freddie thought he was tricking me into doing all the heavy work, but I knew he was too small and skinny to carry the weight, anyhow. I didn't mind, though. Hard work never bothered me, and it built me up for my profession."[7]

Joe also worked for a while at the River Rouge plant of the Ford Motor Company, where he earned twenty-five dollars a week pushing heavy truck bodies onto a conveyor belt. While working on this assembly line, Joe Louis recalls making a decision that radically changed the course of his life. "Eventually, I couldn't stand it anymore. I figured, if I'm going to hurt that much for twenty-five dollars a week, I might as well go back and try fighting again. I covered myself, though. I asked my boss for a six-month leave of absence. I could come back to the factory if things went bad in the ring. I left Ford in January, 1933, and I never returned."[8]

Thurston McKinney, another boyhood friend of Joe Louis, had introduced him to boxing a few years earlier. Thurston, who was the Golden Glove Welterweight Champion of Detroit, succeeded, after much pleading, in getting his pal to stop taking the violin lessons that his mother had arranged and to begin taking boxing lessons at Brewster's East Side Gymnasium under the instruction of Atler Ellis, the athletic director, and Holman Williams, a young middleweight fighter, who saw great boxing potential in Joe Louis.

Louis's amateur boxing career began with a loss to Johnny Miler in 1932 and ended with a knockout win over Joe Bauer in 1934. It was during this two-year apprenticeship that young Joe Louis not only learned the "thrill of victory and the agony of defeat," but he also began to display for the first time the discipline and determination that would later make him one of the greatest heavyweight boxers of all time.

It was in his first amateur fight in 1932 that Joe Louis dropped his family name of Barrow. There are two stories about why he decided to drop his family name when he became a fighter. One story goes that the young fighter didn't want his mother to know that he was fighting. The other story contends that Louis instructed the ring announcer to introduce him as Joe Louis because his full name was too long. Whatever the reason, this fight with Johnny Miler marked the initial utterance of what was to become one of the most famous and revered names in the history of American sports: Joe Louis.

After his initial amateur loss to Johnny Miler, Joe Louis rebounded to win his next fourteen bouts by early-round knockouts. Each of these victories carried the added bonus of a twenty-five dollar merchandise check that Joe Louis gave to his mother to help feed the family. Before his amateur career was over, Joe Louis would go on to win the National Light-Heavyweight Golden Gloves Championship; however, he lost the 1933 National AAU title to Max Merk in Boston. After scoring an impressive first-round knockout over Joe Bauer on June 12, 1934, Louis set out for Chicago to seek his fame and fortune as a professional prizefighter.

JOE LOUIS BECOMES A GREAT DEPRESSION HERO

> *Horatio Alger never wrote a more inspiring "rags to riches" tale than the true life of Joseph Louis Barrow. . . . Less than seven years ago he was working as a laborer for $5 a day in the Ford automobile plant in Detroit.*
>
> —*Pittsburgh Courier,* July 13, 1940

Joe Louis's move to Chicago was financed by John Roxborough and Julian Black, two wealthy businessmen who made their money from the illegal numbers games that they ran in their respective hometowns of Detroit and Chicago. Joe Louis recalled how his former manager was revered in his old Black Bottom neighborhood: "Mr. Roxborough . . . had a reputation for helping a lot of people, he even sent some through college. Roxborough had a

Figure 7–1
Joe Louis. Courtesy University of Notre Dame.

real estate office, but that was just a front. He was a big-time numbers man. Now, you have to think back some. In those days it was hard living if you were black, and it was harder still because the Depression was on. If you were smart enough to have your own numbers operation and you were kind and giving in the black neighborhoods, you got as much respect as a doctor or lawyer."[9] And Louis also explained how Julian Black became his comanager. "Seems like a few years earlier Mr. Roxborough was in financial trouble with his numbers business and Julian Black had bailed him out with a lot of money. Now that Mr. Roxborough was doing well again, as he never forgot a favor, he wanted to return one."[10]

Roxborough and Black entrusted the development of their young boxer to Jack Blackburn, a wiry old trainer who had held his own in a boxing match with Jack Johnson, who in 1908 was the first black American to win the World Heavyweight Boxing Championship. Blackburn taught Louis how to maintain his balance when delivering a punch. This deliberate shuffling of the feet gave rise to the popular dance, "The Joe Louis Shuffle." But, more importantly, the shuffle became one of the strategies for a string of early-round knockouts by the Brown Bomber. Louis's work with Blackburn proved to be more than a trainer-fighter relationship. Both men began to refer to each other affectionately as "Chappie"; and Joe, a lonely boy away from home, began to look on Chappie Blackburn as a surrogate father. One example of the deep and abiding respect that Louis had for Blackburn was naming his daughter Jacqueline in his old trainer's honor.

Under John Roxborough and Julian Black's shrewd matchmaking and Jack Blackburn's wise training, Joe Louis began to earn a lot of money. In his first twenty-six fights, beginning with Jack Kracken and ending with Max Baer, Joe Louis earned $371,645. For his first professional fight with Jack Kracken on July 4, 1934 he earned only fifty dollars. But the purses began to slowly mount during that year. For example, he earned $250 for knocking out Buck Everett (August 27, 1934), $1,000 for knocking out Charley Massera (November 30, 1934), and $2,750 for knocking out Lee Ramage (December 14, 1934). In 1935, the size of his fight purses dramatically increased. On January 4 he returned to his hometown of Detroit and earned $4,200 for beating Patsi Perroni in a 10-round decision. On March 29 he returned again to Detroit and earned $6,000 for a 10-round decision win over Natie Brown. He continued the year with two big $100,000-plus fights with Primo Carnera on June 25 in New York and Kingfish Levinsky on August 7 in Chicago, and climaxed the year with a $215,375 purse for his fight with Max Baer on September 24 in New York.

Louis shared his ring earnings with his family, especially his mother. After the Charley Massera fight he went to the Detroit Welfare Office and repaid all of the money that his parents had to accept when they were on relief. And on Easter Sunday of 1935, he surprised his mother with the gift of a completely furnished new dream house, for which he paid $13,500 in cash. Later, during the Great Depression, he bought his mother a small chicken farm on the outskirts of Detroit.

The Louis family was not alone in its appreciation of his huge ring earnings. Many of his fellow black Americans began to praise his athletic feats in poems that they sent to the *Chicago Defender, Pittsburgh Courier,* and other regional black weekly newspapers. The following excerpt, which praised Joe Louis for his last two big wins appeared in a poem published in the *Chicago Defender.*

Joe started at scratch and he's climbing and how,
Let's back him and cheer him
He'll never lose now.
He's made enough hist'ry to cover a page.
His vict'ries will ring out way down thro' the age.
The 'King Fish' [Levinsky] he fought Joe
They thought he would win
But they were mistaken for Joe found his chin.
Carnera was monstrous and knew a few tricks
But—Joe took him easy. He lasted but six.[11]

Yet another verse captures the jubilation that erupted in black communities across America after a Joe Louis victory:

Traffic jammed streets
Throughout suburban towns
Echoed with yells,
While tin pans, tin cans,
Radios, and ringing bells
Could be heard for miles around.
And tiny tots a little over five
Could be heard in heated arguments.
"I told you Joe Louis would win.
Hey! Johnny Brown!
Where's my two cents?"[12]

Somewhere along the way of recording his impressive string of victories, Joe Louis became a major racial hero. For example, a study of the front pages of the *Chicago Defender* during the five-year period of 1933 to 1938 revealed that Joe Louis received more front-page coverage than any other black American leader. During this period, Joe Louis appeared on the *Defender*'s front page eighty times; Haile Selassie, the Emperor of Ethiopia, was featured on the front page twenty-four times; and Oscar De Priest, the first black elected Congressman since 1901, merited only twenty front-page stories in his hometown newspaper. On the children's pages of these newspapers, doting parents from Michigan to Mississippi published pictures of the newborn sons that they had named Joe Louis in honor of the Brown Bomber. A black newspaper editor expressed the sentiments of many black Americans when he wrote: "The life of Joe Louis would be a good textbook to teach Negro children everywhere."[13]

There were several reasons why Joe Louis became a role model for America's youth, especially young black Americans. First, he lived a clean life. In an advertisement for a popular children's laxative, Joe Louis is reported as saying: "I thank God every day that she brought me up right. . . . I don't smoke or drink and I go to bed early because that's the way my mother taught me to live."[14] During the 1930s, he gave a portion of his ring earnings to New York City's Free Milk Fund to ensure that poor children received proper nourishment. On the eve of his fight with "Two Ton" Tony Galento, the Brown Bomber told a group of his young fans gathered at New York City's Metropolitan Opera House to hear a benefit performance of "Rigoletto," "If you want to grow up big and knock out tough eggs [like Galento] drink plenty of 'cowchowder [milk].' "[15] And Lou Gehrig, the legendary New York Yankee's first baseman, told reporters after listening to Louis's bout with Galento: "I rooted for Louis . . . He hasn't made a move that has not been dignified in his whole career. He's been ever a gentleman and an example for the kids of this nation. He isn't photographed surrounded by beer bottles and with his shirttail sticking out."[16]

Louis was also a popular role model because of his moral living. On more than one occasion he was photographed quietly reading the Bible. And whenever he visited his mother in Detroit, he usually attended Sunday services at the same local Calvary Baptist Church that his family attended. One of his fans wrote a poem that read in part:

> The world admires a manly man
> And God admires him too,
> Although it seems that in His plan
> He only made a few.
> Joe Louis loves the Sunday School
> and proudly goes to church.
> While ambling on sedately cool
> For lofty things in search.[17]

Ironically, the Brown Bomber was also a role model for America's children because he stressed the value of acquiring a good education. Black newspapers carried numerous stories and photographs of Joe Louis taking the time to study his English grammar, American history, world geography, math, and current event lessons after finishing his daily boxing training. Russell Cowans, a black reporter and college graduate, was one of several tutors hired by John Roxborough and Julian Black to educate Joe Louis. Interestingly, when Joe Louis was asked to name the most satisfying experience he had as heavyweight boxing champion of the world, he said it was attending, with his mother and older sister Eulalia, the graduation of his baby sister Vunice from Howard University. Louis also made it a practice to attend numerous public gatherings of children in order to encourage them to stay in school and get a good education.

In August Joe Louis would often attend Chicago's annual Bud Billiken Day Parade. This annual event, still observed in the Windy City, was named after a popular newspaper educator much like today's television personalities Captain Kangaroo and Mister Rogers. And at least during one Christmas he returned to his hometown of Detroit and played Santa Claus to more than 15,000 school children by personally supervising the distribution of boxes of candy, toys, and autographed pictures of himself at several east-side elementary schools, including Garfield, Trowbridge, Lincoln, Russell, Bishop, Leland, Barstrow, Capron, and yes, Duffield, his old neighborhood school. Frank Cody, superintendent of Detroit's public school system, called Miss Vada Schwader's former flag bearer an inspiration to the 265,000 pupils in the city's public school system.

It took Louis's loss to Max Schmeling, on June 19, 1936, to bring out the heroic qualities of courage and determination that were to permanently bond the Brown Bomber to his hoards of black American fans. For a people whose very day-to-day existence was an endless cycle of bitter defeats and an occasional small victory in their struggle for human dignity, the Brown Bomber's impressive string of victories in 1934 and 1935 imbued them with a new unshakable confidence that no fighter could defeat their champion. It was inevitable, they thought, that Louis would become the second black man to win the heavyweight boxing championship title. It was, as this poet fan put it, just a matter of time.

> Now, Joe Louis, even if thou art a youth,
> And thy opponents, men-of-war;
> If thou keep the faith, Joe Louis,
> The title from them thou will debar.[18]

Another fan captured the confident attitude that pervaded black Americans when their beloved Brown Bomber signed to fight the German heavyweight Max Schmeling. This poet expressed the growing euphoria within the black community when he wrote: "So bring on your Schmeling! Your very best man/Joe Louis will take him! We all know he can!"[19]

But their beloved Brown Bomber did lose. He was knocked down for the first time in his illustrious career and knocked out in the twelfth round. The picture of their fallen hero stretched out unconscious on the ring's canvas was splashed on the front pages of many white daily newspapers and all black weekly newspapers. Rumors abounded. Some of his supporters believed that he had been doped; others reasoned that their hero was the victim of overconfidence. A small number argued that Max Schmeling was the better fighter that night. Although divided on the cause of their folk hero's defeat, a majority of black Americans, especially the children, were united in expressing their support for his comeback. Little Miss Essex Mae Moore of Perry, Florida, expressed her continued loyalty for her fallen hero in this letter to Bud Billiken: "I am reading about Joe Louis, it seems that some of the writers think his friends are against him because he was defeated. We, the Billikens of Perry, want Joe to know that 'win or lose,' we are with him."[20]

Jimmie R. R.Waldon, a thirteen-year-old ninth-grader from Camden, Arkansas, expressed similar sentiments in a poem that he wrote and sent to Bud Billiken:

Joe, if at first you don't succeed,
Try, try once more.
Victory is ahead of you,
Put aside the answer, No!

Don't give up the battle yet,
Put the defeat behind.
Try working for the goal;
Just keep it in your mind.

You've got to do it, for the Race—
You've started, it's nearly done.
Keep pressing for the goal,
Until the victory is won.[21]

And Hortense Courtney, another Bud Billiken Club member from Lawrence, New York, expressed her confidence in Louis's ability to win the heavyweight championship even though he had lost to Max Schmeling. She begins her poem with these words of consolation:

You were fighting smoothly, Joe
Until Schmeling came along.
So boldly hold your nerve, Joe
Don't let your courage slip
Stand bravely to your career, Joe
And don't give up the ship.

And she ends with this vision of future triumph:

If only in your next fight, Joe,
You will do your level best.
There awaits for all a crown, Joe
So take a manly grip.

There awaits for you the championship.
If you don't give up your grip.[22]

Undoubtedly, Joe Louis took heart from these words of encouragement from his loyal fans. His new string of knockout victories during the remainder of 1936 spawned a renewed sense of confidence and anticipation in himself and his followers by the beginning of 1937. The bitter defeat by Schmeling in 1936 had been brushed aside by then. One of Louis's fans expressed this renewed sense of confidence shared by Joe and his American public with these lines:

The sensational 'Bomber' met his Waterloo,
But seemingly the beating didn't stick;
He started his short knockout victories anew,
And came back to the top with a kick.[23]

Many black Americans expressed joy and renewed confidence where on June 22, 1937, Joe Louis made his comeback by scoring an eighth round knockout over heavyweight champion Jim Braddock to become the second black American to win the World's Heavyweight Boxing Championship. An unknown fan penned the following poem, which describes Joe Louis's knockout of Braddock in a tone of admiration and confidence commonly expressed by many of the Brown Bomber's followers before his bitter upset loss to Max Schmeling. He describes this historic knockout from the vantage point of Jim Braddock's surprised fans:

When the awful eighth approached them,
And they saw big Jim go down,
Like a giant of the forest,
By a dark tornado blown,
For Joe had spied his opening,
And cut loose that mighty right
It landed 'thud' and poor old Jim
Went out just like a light.
Perhaps with me you won't agree
But next time if you're around
Be careful with your money when the Bomber comes to town.[24]

An editorial in a black newspaper clearly expressed the great sense of joy and hope that victories such as this instilled in many poor black Americans caught in the grip of the Great Depression: "Part of the secret of the almost miraculous success of Joe Louis lies in his temperance, determination, and persistent training. . . . Everybody can't be the world's greatest heavyweight or entertainer, but the world is full of opportunities for people who are willing to do what it takes to become really good in any line that the world wants done."[25]

In sum, the sensational transformation of Joseph Louis Barrow from awkward novice to polished Heavyweight Champion of the World kept similar dreams of Horatio Alger success alive in the hearts and minds of many downtrodden black and white Americans during the Great Depression of the 1930s.

JOE LOUIS BECOMES A WORLD WAR II HERO

> *Joe Louis was an American hero, especially during the war years. But while white America loved him and cheered for him, he was still a black. . . . They cheered him when he went into the Army, but he went into a segregated Army. He fought to make the world safe for democracy, but in a segregated situation. . . . There were many contradictions at that time.*
>
> —Vernon E. Jordan, Jr., *Joe Louis: 50 Years an American Hero* (1988)

During the last two years of the decade of the 1930s, Louis's image changed from a Horatio Alger-type figure who achieved great financial success through thrift and hard work to his new role as an American patriotic hero. This transformation began in New York City's Yankee Stadium on the night of June 22, 1938, when he scored a sensational first-round knockout against Max Schmeling, and climaxed four years later on 10 March 1942 in New York City's Madison Square Garden, when he delivered a memorable patriotic speech at a World War II rally hosted by the United States Navy Relief Society.

Sandwiched between these two events was a series of championship fights and patriotic acts, which marked the emergence of Joe Louis as a major living symbol of American democracy. In 1940, Louis expressed deep personal patriotic sentiments, which were to become the creed that he and many of his black fans lived by during World War II:

> This is the best country I know of . . . and I'd gladly fight to defend it. Every colored man I've ever known has been 100 percent American and I'll always be loyal to my country and my race. I'd never let either down. . . .
>
> I'd never be a traitor to my country. Look what this country did for me. It gave me a chance to win the heavyweight title. . . . And I've tried to prove myself worthy of it. Uncle Sam can certainly depend upon me to do my part for my country if any foreign army tries to invade it.[26]

It all began with Louis's 1938 rematch with Max Schmeling. The political mood of the country had changed dramatically in the brief two-year span between their first meeting in 1936, when Max Schmeling scored a stunning twelfth-round knockout upset win over the previously undefeated Louis. With the increasing militaristic tension of the times, both fighters became living symbols of their respective countries' fundamental beliefs. Joe Louis was summoned to the White House by President Roosevelt on the eve of the bout for words of encouragement; and Adolf Hitler invited Max Schmeling's wife to hear the fight broadcast at his home. Hence, Schmeling was cast as the champion of Nazi Germany's ideology of Aryan supremacy and Louis, who just two years earlier had been viewed by many white Americans as just another Negro fighter, was now embraced by most of the white American public as the appointed defender of their American democracy. A *Chicago Defender* article expressed these sentiments: "Many white Americans who ordinarily find no reason to celebrate a race victory let go a few whoops for Joe—because the Bomber, even if black, is an American, and his victory was not one for his race alone, but for millions of Americans anxious to see the title remain in this country."[27]

This fight, like all the patriotic speeches that Louis was to deliver during his reign as America's World War II hero, was extremely brief and highly effective. It was all over in only two minutes an four seconds of the first round. Jubilant Brown Bomber fans mailed a flood of victory poems to the editors of black weekly newspapers. A little girl from Pittsburgh began her poem with these lines:

> Joe Louis won the fight,
> Hit him left and right.
> Schmeling lost the crown
> Right in the very first round.[28]

At the same time, a Chicago teenager lamented missing the brief fight broadcast in these poetic lines:

> Well the clock hands drug the hour,
> And we kids were glad you bet
> 'Gran' then turned her set much higher
> One by one we all got set.
> Not quite all—I beg your pardon,

'Gran,' you see, must get so near
She kept tuggin' and kept pullin'
Trying to fix her comfy chair
Til we kids all got so flustered
Changing places, oh so fast
That we never heard a single lick
That Joseph Louis passed.
Folks next door let out a holler
Then we all run out, ya know
Just to find out what had happened
T'was a technical K.O.
Well we didn't know the big word,
But it finally got around.
And we understood the champion
Simply knocked poor 'Maxie' down.[29]

The Brown Bomber's quick knockout also inspired two of his fans to use the tunes of popular songs to compose song parodies that praised Louis's punching prowess. A Chicago teenager used the tune of the hymn "Amazing Grace" to praise his hero:

Amazing grace and sweet of sound
Joe Louis knocked Max Schmeling down
Schmeling arose and wiped his chin
Joe Louis knocked him down again.

He had no time to weave and bob,
Joe's left hand made a finished job,
The fight was not out in the sun,
But it was copped by Louis in one.[30]

In Washington, D.C., playgrounds were filled with little girls chanting the following jump rope rhyme to the tune of the patriotic song "America."

My country t'is of thee
I live in Germany
My name is France
Hot dogs and sauerkraut
Joe Louis knocked Schmeling out
So what is there to cry about
Let freedom ring[31]

Both white and black newspapers carried numerous articles emphasizing again and again the political symbolism of the Brown Bomber's win. A Portland, Oregon newspaper published a postfight editorial that captured the serious political implications of the fight:

It was indeed a day of dolor for the Hitlerized version of the proud Aryan race when Schmeling was smacked down by Louis, They say that in his Bavarian mountain retreat the dictator himself kept vigil to receive the radio account, confident that racial superiority and the good German will must triumph.

Not only did the black man win, however, but he attained the conquest in greater time than a burgomaster would require to bury his whiskers in a brimming stein. Alas, the Aryan tradition!

What national socialism needs now in Germany is a wailing wall, such as the one where Israel laments its fall, but, the suggestion being obviously impracticable, it can weep in its beer. The bickering at Yankee Stadium was the first in which a prize fighter delivered left hooks and right-hand smashes for democracy, the equality of peoples, and the brotherhood of man, while supposing he was merely fighting for his cut.[32]

The *Chicago Defender,* one of America's largest black weeklies, aptly summarized the symbolic political significance of the Brown Bomber's win for his loyal black fans.

Then came the end, with Donovan stopping the one-man massacre. Shouts of joy rang to the stars. From thousands of homes and taverns poured Dusky Americans, their faces flushed. It was as if each had been in the ring himself, as if every man, woman and child of them had dealt destruction with fists upon the Nordic face of Schmeling and of the whole Nazi system he symbolized. It was more than the victory of one athlete over another, it was the triumph of a repressed people against the evil forces of racial oppression and discrimination condensed—by chance—into the shape of Max Schmeling.

It was a time for celebration, and for a night Aframerica drank the heady wine of glorious success. Chicago's southside became a living ocean of smiling faces as crowds flowed out upon the streets. Tin-can bands formed, automobiles paraded dragging old tubs and strings of tin cans behind them.[33]

It was only fitting that for the next three summers Joe Louis would ride down these same Chicago Southside streets as the parade marshal of the annual Bud Billiken Day Parade. A 1940 *Chicago Defender* article reminded its readers: "It is quite befitting that Joe Louis participate in this Americanism Day parade. You will remember that Louis as champion has not drawn the line on the men of various nationalities he has been called upon to fight. He has defended the United States in the prize ring and as a true American."[34]

A 1941 article in the same newspaper made clear references to Joe Louis's smashing defeat of Max Schmeling in 1938, which stamped him forever as a true patriotic hero:

This year's fete will be a patriotic one and has been titled an Americanism Day celebration. Because Joe Louis has defended the U.S. against foreign invasion in the pugilistic ring, the Billikens of Chicagoland believe he should be singled out as the No. I American and to that end, the patriotic festivities are to center around him. . . .

So if you feel that Joe Louis is the No. 1 American and if you are proud of the record that he has made in the ring, for goodness sakes be on South Parkway Saturday morning, August 2 at 11 o'clock and cheer him as he rides by. ALL the noise you can make will be gladly appreciated by the champ.[35]

After successfully defending his title with a sixth-round knockout of Lou Nova, Louis performed two noteworthy patriotic acts. First, in October of 1941 he began a three-month boxing exhibition tour of American Army posts to bolster the morale of the troops. A *Life* article attested to the great success that these tours had in lifting the morale of the troops and promoting racial brotherhood: "There is no doubt that Joe Louis's trip has proven a success from its inception. And in it many find not only educational and morale-building values, but also a quiet parable in racial good will, for hardworking Joe makes a good impression and hundreds of white soldiers, officers and men, are proud to shake his hand."[36]

After the tour Louis performed a second patriotic act that helped to boost the morale of the American civilian population, whose confidence had been badly shaken by the Japanese surprise attack on Pearl Harbor. He joined the Army. This magnanimous patriotic act, which meant he would forfeit making big money in his boxing career, stirred deep emotions of gratitude and admiration by many Americans of all races, classes, and creeds. Louis was a master of the one-liner and drew a chuckle from many of his countrymen when he downplayed the importance of Japan's recent bombing of Pearl Harbor by saying that America would beat Japan because its soldiers are "all lightweights. They don't have any heavyweights."[37]

On January 9, 1942, one day before he was inducted into the United States Army, Joe Louis fought the first of two benefit bouts to raise funds for the Navy Relief Fund and the Army Relief Fund. Buddy Baer was his opponent in the first benefit bout for the Navy and Abe Simon was his opponent in his second benefit bout for the Army held on March 27, 1942. Louis contributed his entire purse of $47,000 to the Navy Relief Fund for his fight with Baer and his entire purse of $35,000 for the second bout with Simon to the Army Relief Fund. These two acts of patriotism are unparalleled in the annals of American sports.

Louis's altruistic acts take on even greater significance when placed in the socio-historical context of the times. Both the Army and Navy practiced racial segregation at that time, and in many ways were a reflection of America's restrictive Jim Crow laws and customs. At the time Louis made these two large financial contributions, blacks in the South were forced to attend underfunded segregated schools, drink from segregated public water fountains, walk through doors marked "For Colored Only," and sit in dingy segregated waiting rooms at the train station. Blacks who tried to flee these oppressive conditions by migrating North found themselves, like Louis's family, restricted to living in certain targeted areas by unscrupulous white realtors and denied the hope of economic advancement by trade unions that would not allow them membership and by paternalistic or racist employers who set their pay lower than what they paid to white workers performing the same job.

At the time of these two benefit bouts, the *Pittsburgh Courier*, under the aggressive editorship of Robert Vann, and the *Chicago Defender*, under the crusading editorship of Robert Abbott, were both waging intense campaigns to have the Navy reverse its policy of not promoting black sailors beyond the rank of messman consigned to such menial tasks as washing dishes, shining shoes, cooking, and waiting tables. In support of Louis's decision, Vann wrote:

> Joe Louis, heavyweight champion of the world, has agreed to place his title at stake in a bout against Buddy Baer at Madison Square Garden January 9 for the benefit of the Navy Relief Fund.
>
> Press reports state that Louis will receive no pay for the bout in which he will risk his most prized possession against a formidable opponent.
>
> The United States Navy maintains a policy of rigid and exasperating discrimination against Negroes. Negroes who seek to serve their country in the Navy are restricted to mops, dust cloths, shoe brushes, and cuspidors for the glory, comfort and conveniences of naval officers. They are barred altogether from the Marine Corps.

In spite of all this, Joe Louis, who has established himself as the greatest sportsman of our times, keeps his promise made several months ago to give everything he had for his country's cause.

In this one grand dramatic gesture, Joe focuses the white light of justice on the forces of racial hate and prejudice in our Navy, exposing them in all their meanness.[38]

Despite a barrage of letters from his irate black fans to the *Courier, Defender,* and other smaller regional black weeklies Louis refused to change his mind. To those fans who questioned the rationale of his turning over his entire purse to the government, he replied: "I am doing this for my country and for the Navy. I don't think it would be right to demand anything after the fight. It would be like giving a fellow a Christmas present one day and then asking him for a big favor the next. I'm going to do this for the Navy and then we'll wait and see if the Navy does anything for my people."[39] Cynical reporters covering the fight and looking for an angle or their stories the next day found it in Louis's brief remark, "Ain't fightin' for nothin', I'm fightin' for my country." And to those black fans who felt he should reject the Navy's request, just as the Navy had rejected their requests for first-class citizenship, the Brown Bomber said:

I have no apology to offer for what I am doing for the United States Navy. . . . I know very well what I am doing. I know there's discrimination against my people in the Navy, but I believe this is the most effective method to fight it. . . . Already the boys in the Navy on the west coast are beginning to get favorable reaction from their superior officers. . . . They told me that ever since it was learned that the Navy Relief Society was to reap the cash receipts of my fight, the whole attitude towards the Negro sailor has changed.[40]

Joe Louis was lionized at two awards banquets held at the time of these two benefit bouts, On January 21, 1942 following his knockout of Buddy Baer, the Boxing Writers' Association of New York hosted a special dinner at Ruppert's Brewery in Manhattan to honor the Brown Bomber. J. Edgar Hoover, the then-young director of the Federal Bureau of Investigation, praised Louis's sportsmanship with these words:

For years I have been following Joe Louis around to watch him fight. I am happy to be here to pay my humble tribute to you, Joe.

"To me, Joe symbolized fair play. He is the champ because he never hit below the belt. He has always been a good sport. He played a square, clean, fair game at all times.

"Joe has been a great hero to the youth of this country. I am paying tribute to a great American."[41]

New York City Mayor James J. "Jimmy" Walker also made reference to Louis's recent benefit bout with Buddy Baer in his tribute: "Joe, all the Negroes in the world are proud of you because you have given them reason to be proud. You never forgot your own people. When you fought Buddy Baer and gave your purse to the Navy Relief Society, you took your title and your future and bet it all on patriotism and love of country. Joe Louis, that night you laid a rose on the grave of Abraham Lincoln."[42]

On March 10, 1942, the Navy Relief Society held a patriotic awards dinner in Madison Square Garden. Joe Louis, who attended the affair as the guest of Wendell Willkie, was asked to make some remarks. Dressed in his soldier's uniform, Louis walked confidently to the microphone and said in his deep, resolute voice: "I'm really happy that I'm able enough to do what I'm doing, what I have done and what I'm going to do. I'm only doing what any red-blooded American would do. We're all going to do our part, and we will win because we are on God's side."[43]

Carl Byoir, one of the 20,000 Americans in attendance that night, was inspired to write the poem "Joe Louis Named the War," which was later published in the *Saturday Evening Post*. Joe Louis's patriotic words and deeds combined to make him an important American hero during World War II. A reporter for his hometown *Detroit Evening News* expressed the genuine sentiments of white and black Americans when he wrote this apt description of Louis: "If there is a more real American in this land, a more sincerely patriotic young man, if there is anyone who is more truly a gentleman in the finest sense of that loosely used word, we don't know him."[44] During World War II when America desperately needed a hero, there was Joe Louis, a supreme American patriotic hero.

THE CHAMP IS DEAD, LONG LIVE THE CHAMP

> *Joe Louis, we love your name. To the host of witnesses gathered here, you tell the story. Let them run extra editions of the newspaper as they once did. Tell the people that Joe is still in the center of the ring without a challenger or a peer.*
>
> —Jesse Jackson's eulogy of Joe Louis in *Straight From the Heart*, 1987

Time erodes memory. This has been proven true more often than not in American culture, where the focus is on the present and the future. Often in our society, heroes of the past, even the recent past, are relegated to where-are-they-now columns in newspapers and magazines or to what-ever-happened-to-so-and-so questions at class reunions, weddings, funerals, and other social events that periodically bind us together. This loss of fame is doubly true for American sports heroes. First, their fans often forget them once their careers are over. And second, we rarely incorporate any of their words and deeds into our collective cultural consciousness after they die. Notable exceptions are Babe Ruth, Lou Gehrig, Jesse Owens—and Joe Louis.

Although Joe Louis was soundly defeated and humiliated in his last professional fight in 1951 by Rocky Marciano (who knocked the aging champion out of the ring before scoring an eighth-round knockout), he continued to be accorded respect and admiration by many Americans from all races, creeds, and colors. In 1973, for example, twenty-two years after suffering his defeat by Marciano, Louis's sixtieth birthday was the subject of feature articles in *Ebony* and *Esquire* magazines. In *Ebony* these two glowing tributes were published about the Brown Bomber:

> Louis . . . was something more than a great fighter. Destroying opponent after opponent in the late Thirties and Forties, he became a symbol, a living legend, the first authentic black folk hero. White Americans could take their choice of idols: Franklin Delano Roosevelt, Babe Ruth, Buck Jones, Clark Gable. For black Americans, who held no high office in government, were barred from big league baseball and worked only as comics in the movies, Joe Louis was the consummate hero.
>
> Joe Louis, now in his 60th year, remains an American idol. Children not yet in their teens, men old enough to remember the great ones of half a century ago and women of all ages, shapes and colors seek him out to touch him, to praise him, to hear the rich Alabama accent delivered with New York speed.[45]

During his retirement years, Louis's fans demonstrated their deep affection in more tangible ways as well. Barry Gordy, the founder and president of Motown Records, organized a major benefit featuring such famous entertainers as Bill Cosby and Red Foxx to raise money to pay off Joe's outstanding federal tax bill. And Frank Sinatra hosted a gala birthday party for the Brown Bomber in Las Vegas, which featured a surprise visit by Joe's old opponent, Max Schmeling.

The American media also sustained a fascination with Joe Louis after his retirement from the boxing ring. Television, which was still in its infancy in the 1950s, courted his appearances. For example, Louis and Leonard Reed, his longtime friend and show business partner, performed their comedy act before the nation on the *Ed Sullivan Show.* He and Rose Morgan, his second wife, were contestants on the TV game show, *High Finance,* in a vain effort to win a sizeable cache to help reduce his tax debt. Martha Jefferson, his third wife, along with a host of family and friends that included daughter Jacqueline, son Joe, Jr., brothers and sisters, former managers Julian Black and John Roxborough, childhood friend Sugar Ray Robinson, and former opponent Ezzard Charles, appeared on the popular TV biography show, *This Is Your Life,* which was devoted to Louis's life.

Joe Louis also appeared in several feature-length Hollywood films after he retired from the ring in 1951. Two years after his last fight, *The Joe Louis Story* was produced, starring Coley Wallace. Also during the decade of the 1950s, Louis appeared as himself in the film, *The Fight Never Ends,* featuring an all-black cast and starring Ruby Dee. This film addressed the growing problem of juvenile delinquency. Joe Louis, once again, was cast as a positive role model for America's black youth.

Ten years after his death there is a growing interest in collecting Joe Louis memorabilia. Joe Louis fight posters, clocks, coin banks, bubble gum cards, photographs, and films are still in great demand by private collectors and public museums. His hometown of Detroit is the site of two Joe Louis sculptures. Pat Graham was commissioned by *Sports Illustrated* to design and cast "Monument to Joe Louis," a massive bronze sculpture of an arm and fist measuring twenty-four feet by twenty-four feet by six feet. This sculpture, a subject of considerable controversy in the community, is mounted at a busy intersection in downtown Detroit. A second and more conventional Joe Louis sculpture by Ed Hamilton was commissioned by Detroit Mayor Coleman Young, who grew up in the Champ's old Black Bottom neighborhood. This piece, a twelve foot bronze statue of the Brown Bomber dressed in his boxing attire and posed in his familiar shuffling boxing stance, is mounted in the galleria of Cobo Hall, one of the city's major sports arenas and convention centers.

The name Joe Louis dots the American architectural landscape. The Detroit Red Wings play their hockey games in the Joe Louis Arena. America's sports mecca, New York City's Madison Square Garden, is bound on one side by Joe Louis Plaza. Many other American cities and towns have named streets in honor of Joe Louis. The name and image of Joe Louis is preserved on the bronze plaque that marks his burial plot in Arlington National Cemetery. His gravesite is one of the more popular stops for the thousands of Americans who annually visit this final resting place of many of our nation's heroes.

References to Joe Louis also can be found in contemporary American films. Eddie Murphy has produced two films with Joe Louis references. *Coming to America* features a barbershop scene in which Murphy plays an old barber arguing with one of his white customers that Joe Louis was a greater boxer than Rocky Marciano. In *Harlem Nights,* which is set in the 1930s, Murphy has included a black heavyweight boxing champion whose characterization is clearly based on Louis. The Public Broadcasting System has presented a TV film adaptation of Kurt Vonnegut's short story, "D.P.," about a World War II orphan whose father was a black GI and mother was a German girl. The boy, whom the village elders call "Joe Louis" because of his brown skin, runs away in search of his identity, hoping to find the man he thinks is his real father, Joe Louis, the American Brown Bomber. And the Arts and Entertainment Network System has televised *Joe Louis: Champion for All Times,* a two-hour film biography by Budd Schulberg. Filmmaker Spike Lee includes film footage of Joe Louis's knockout of Jim Braddock in *Born to Fight,* an MTV video that he produced for Tracy Chapman's song of the same title.

The Louis legacy continues on the pages of today's daily newspapers. A reporter covering Nelson Mandela's triumphant tour of America in 1990 makes this telling comparison: "Not since the days when Joe Louis was the heavyweight boxing champion of the world have black Americans offered a hero's crown to any living black as enthusiastically as they handed it to Nelson Mandela during his U.S. tour."[46] Ultimately, there is still evidence that some of today's youth do have a glimmer of understanding of the heroic role that Joe Louis played during the 1930s and 1940s. Brian Singleton, the janitor at Detroit's Wheeler Recreation Center in the Brewster housing project where Joe Louis began his legendary boxing career in 1932, made this poignant comment regarding the framed painting of Joe Louis that hangs on one of the lobby walls: "You know, just about everything else around here has been tore up or painted over with graffiti, at one time or another. . . . But no one has ever touched that picture. Not Joe Louis. Not the Champ."[47]

NOTES

1. Joe Louis, with Edna Rust and Art Rust, Jr., *Joe Louis: My Life* (New York: Harcourt Brace Jovanovich, 1978), 2–3.
2. *Ibid.,* 6.
3. *Ibid., 5.*
4. *Ibid.,* 6.
5. *Ibid., 13.*
6. Gene Kessler, *Joe Louis: The Brown Bomber* (Racine, WI: Whitman, 1936), 17.
7. Louis, *My Life,* 14–5.
8. *Ibid., 24.*
9. *Ibid.,* 26.
10. *Ibid., 28–9.*
11. James Thomas Jordan, "To a Fighting Man." *Chicago Defender,* June 20, 1936.
12. Ruth Olga Mae Davis, "To Joe Louis." *Chicago Defender,* January 25, 1936.
13. J. Alston Atkins, "Joe Wins Again." *Houston Informer,* December 21, 1935.
14. "Joe Louis Gives His Mother Plenty Credit," *Chicago Defender,* August 31, 1935.
15. "Joe Takes Time Out to Gulp with Kiddies." *Pittsburgh Courier,* March 16, 1940.
16. "Gehrig Praises Louis," *Pittsburgh Courier,* July 15, 1939.
17. William Henry Huff, "Joe Louis." *Chicago Defender,* August 10, 1935.
18. *Chicago Defender,* September 14, 1935.
19. *Chicago Defender,* June 20, 1936.
20. Essex Mae Moore, "She's Striving to Get More Readers," *Chicago Defender,* September 19, 1936.
21. Johnnie R. R. Waldon, "Success, Joe," *Chicago Defender,* December 19, 1936.
22. Hortense Courtney, "Little Girl Gets Poetic: 'Don't Give Up, Joe,' " *Chicago Defender,* July 18, 1936.
23. Harold E. Grady, "1936 Is Now History," *Chicago Defender,* January 9, 1937.
24. H. H. H., "Jim Went Down." *Chicago Defender,* July 17, 1937.
25. *Houston Informer,* August 17, 1935.
26. Joe Louis, as told to Ches Washington. " 'I'll Be Ready When My Country Calls'—Louis." *Pittsburgh Courier,* August 24, 1940.
27. "Joy, Tragedy in Wake of Joe's Victory." *Chicago Defender,* July 2, 1938.
28. M. H. Howard, "To Joe Louis." *Chicago Defender,* July 9, 1938.
29. Marnie L. McWinnie, "The Fight." *Chicago Defender,* July 9, 1938.
30. *Chicago Defender,* July 9, 1938
31. James Borchert, *Alley Life in Washington: Family, Community, Religion, and Folklife in the*

City, 1850–1970 (Urbana, IL: University of Illinois Press, 1980).

32. "Other Papers Say—Joe and the Aryan Issue." *The Oregonian,* reprinted in *Chicago Defender,* July 23, 1938.

33. *Chicago Defender,* July 2, 1938.

34. "Invite Joe Louis to Bud's Picnic. Expect the 'Bomber' to Frolic with Us," *Chicago Defender,* July 13, 1940.

35. "Joe Louis All Set for Bud's Picnic. All Chicagoland Will Cheer 'Bomber' in Big Parade." *Chicago Defender,* July 26, 1941.

36. "Louis on Tour: Sergeant Joe Starts 100-Day Boxing Swing Around Nation's Army Posts." *Life,* September 13, 1943, 34–5.

37. "Fighter Joe Louis Signs Up to Fight for the U.S. for Purse $21 a Month" *Life,* January 26, 1942, p. 24.

38. "Mr. Knox, It's Your Move!" *Pittsburgh Courier,* editorial. November 22, 1941.

39. *Pittsburgh Courier,* January 3, 1942.

40. David W Kellum, " 'No Apology to Make'—Joe Louis Considers Act Blow At Discrimination." *Chicago Defender,* December 6, 1941.

41. James Edmund Boyack, "Louis Hailed at Writers' Banquet." *Pittsburgh Courier,* January 31, 1942.

42. Chris Mead, *Champion: Joe Louis, Black Hero in White America* (New York: Penguin, 1986), 216.

43. " 'God Is on Our Side'—Joe Louis Reminds 20,000 at Navy Show," *Pittsburgh Courier,* March 21, 1942.

44. Bob Murphy, "Bob Tales: Great as a Fighter, Joe Is Tops as an American." *Detroit Evening Times,* May 26, 1942.

45. Louis Robinson, "Joe Louis at Sixty." *Ebony* (October 1973): 64–72.

46. *Louisville Courier Journal,* July 1, 1990.

47. William E. Schmidt, "Detroit Journal: In Joe Louis' Shadow, The Discipline to Win." *New York Times,* September 19, 1989.

8

"END JIM CROW IN SPORTS"

The Leonard Bates Controversy and Protest at New York University, 1940–1941

Donald Spivey

STUDENTS AT NEW YORK University made a significant contribution to the civil rights movement when, during 1940 and 1941, they took a stand against racial discrimination in collegiate athletics. An historical examination of the event, the issues involved, the era itself, and the internal and external impact of the protest can tell us much about the nature of social activism, establishment reaction, the educational and social environment of the period, the development of big-time intercollegiate athletics, and the importance of sport and the black athlete to the history of American race relations.

Jim Crow has been an ever-present factor in American society, and it was alive and well during the years just prior to the entrance of the United States into World War II. Despite the nation's fervently professed ideals of democracy and equality, and the denunciation of Hitlerism, racism and discrimination pervaded every segment of American society even as the country prepared to enter yet another war to make the world safe for democracy and freedom.

Blacks were discriminated against, segregated, and despised as they sought to participate in the war effort. The economic and employment opportunities that the burgeoning war economy made possible were for blacks severely circumscribed. In Chicago, for example, thirty-five industries had been awarded National Defense contracts in excess of $160,000,000 by 1940. The Chicago chapter of the Urban League reported that blacks received none of the newly created jobs nor practically any benefits to them or their communities from the new defense contracts.[1]

To be treated unfairly in the employment realm was one problem. To be treated as subhuman was more pernicious. Local draft boards often took it upon themselves to act as a bulwark against integrating the military, declaring blacks as physically unfit for military service without specificity. The popular view in the South likened the Negro to the monkey, possessing a tail and, in general, a subspecies. Some southern draft boards rejected all black draftees and volunteers in their districts as physically or otherwise unfit for military duty. Northern boards were also tainted with the brush of Jim Crow. William Pickens, field secretary of the NAACP, complained to Clarence Dykstra, national director of the Selective Service, that Negro draftees and volunteers were being discriminated against. Pickens wrote directly to Colonel Arthur McDermott, director of Selective Service for the New

York area, and to Governor Lehman, that the NAACP objected to the draft board's policy in New York to send all of the colored men for examinations to Harlem Hospital and all of the white men to Lutheran Hospital, the official examination center. Evidently, too, some white physicians felt that it was beneath them to have to give physical examinations to blacks.[2]

Once in the military the problems did not subside. The black serviceman was usually relegated to grunt duty in the most literal sense of the word. They served as porters, drivers, latrine and gravediggers. There were, of course, blacks who would be used in combat. The average black military man would, however, serve in a more traditional capacity. The United States Navy encouraged blacks to enlist because there was a shortage of galley servants, The Navy advertised in the *San Francisco Chronicle* prior to the war, calling upon Negroes, ages seventeen to twenty-eight, to enlist as mess attendants in the naval reserve at twenty-one dollars a month with uniforms and subsistence. An editorial in the black press blasted the Navy for being arrogant and chided them for substantiating the complaint of Negro seamen that despite any talent or efficiency they may show, they could not rise above the menial job of officers' mess attendant where they were at the mercy of the whims and petty spite of white naval officers, many of whom came from southern states.[3]

So bad was the relationship between blacks and the military industrial complex in the period before the war that race leaders organized a conference to address the issue. At the two-day national conference held in Hampton, Virginia, November 25 and 26, 1940, the two hundred delegates, headed by historian Rayford W. Logan, passed a formal resolution condemning racial discrimination and prejudice in industries holding defense contracts and within the various branches of the armed forces of the nation.[4] That the nation, moving closer to war, could continence the continued existence of discrimination and segregation in its military and the defense industry was indicative of just how completely ingrained the color line was in American institutional life and just how thoroughly inconsistent and hypocritical the nation was in its professed democratic, economic, social, and moral ideals.

There was one institution in which the inconsistency and incompatibility of Jim Crowism with American democratic principles was more glaring and flagrant than in the arena of national defense—sports. The sanctum of sport is premised on unofficial doctrines of equality of opportunity, sportsmanship, and fair play. It is thus a perfect arena for the exposure of the dual nature of American society, with its paradoxical blending of democracy and inequality. In the prewar years there were many positive strides toward racial integration in sports. Three black athletes, Jesse Owens, Joe Louis, and Henry Armstrong, became the darlings of the American public, both black and white. Owens's four gold medals in the 1936 Olympic Games were a triumph for American democracy over Nazism. The same was said of Louis's defeat of Max Schmeling in their second fight in 1938. Armstrong won the resounding respect of pugilism's fans everywhere, holding world championships in three weight divisions. But these men confronted numerous barriers and unpleasant incidents owing to their race. Armstrong withdrew from several important bouts because they were scheduled to be held in segregated arenas. Other black professional athletes, such as Josh Gibson and Satchel Paige of the Negro Baseball League, failed in their lifetimes to receive the recognition and monetary reward they deserved.[5]

In collegiate sports the paradox was at its zenith. The collegian was seen as an amateur, a purist who played for the love of the game and not, like the professional, for the almighty dollar. Hence college athletics, with the possible exception of the church, best embodied

American virtues and values in a working, social context. The athletic field was a proving ground to verify and glorify the rightness of hard work, preparedness, self-sacrifice, teamwork, individual merit, stick-to-itiveness, valor, and fair play. In the game, the player had the opportunity to prove his mettle, demonstrate his physical prowess (if not his mental acuteness), champion a cause, defend the honor of his school, "win the big one," and earn the accolades of his peers. The spectators, too, held a similarly lauded view of the game and the role of their knights, the athletes.[6]

Intercollegiate sports in reality during the prewar years was far less generous to black collegiate athletes who suffered racial abuses and discrimination at the hands of opponents, teammates, coaches, spectators, sports journalists, and postseason selection committees. Ozzie Simmons, for example, quit the University of Iowa football team because he was unable to further endure the racial bigotry on and off the playing field. Kenny Washington of UCLA, despite being the leading ground gainer in collegiate football in 1939 with over 1,000 yards, was not selected to the All-American team nor invited to play in the College All-Star Game because of his color. That same year, the Cotton Bowl committee denied Lou Montgomery, the black star running back for Boston College, the right to play in the bowl game in Dallas against Clemson. Boston College, Clemson University, and the Cotton Bowl committee honored the Jim Crow tradition in collegiate sports against having an interracial game if one of the parties involved objected. In this case, the Cotton Bowl committee and Clemson University raised said objection. Boston College consented, leaving Montgomery at home when the team ventured to Dallas. This so-called gentlemen's agreement was a common practice in intercollegiate athletics, along with a host of other discriminatory traditions that were tacitly accepted.[7]

Students at New York University, however, raised a loud clamor that took the form of a mass movement against the gentlemen's agreement at their school. Their protest was profound, having a substantive sociopolitical impact, and educational, cultural, philosophical, and historical value. The student action began at NYU in October of 1940 when it was learned that Leonard Bates, who was black and the starting fullback on the Violets football team, would not be allowed to accompany his teammates to Columbia, Missouri, and play in the slated game against the University of Missouri Tigers on November 2. Missouri, like most teams in the South, objected to playing against a Negro. What appalled the NYU students was that their university acquiesced to Missouri's request that Bates be excluded from the game. "Bates Must Play" became the rallying cry of some two thousand students and sympathizers as they took to the streets on October 18, picketing the NYU administration building. The huge placards that the picketers bore made the demands clear: "Bates Must Play" "Don't Ban Bates" "Ban Gentlemen's Agreement" "End Jim Crow in Sports" "End Jim Crowism at NYU" "No Nazi Games" and "No Missouri Compromise."[8]

Immediately after the demonstration, the students formed the All-University Committee on "Bates Must Play," headed by Argyle A. Stoute. Meeting on October 21 the committee passed four resolutions: that Len Bates be released from his gentleman's agreement and be allowed to make his own decision as to whether he would or would not play, that New York University never again enter upon any contract with Jim Crow schools, that the University administration make a statement clarifying its views on this issue, and that if the administration failed to comply with the aforementioned resolutions, there should be a boycott of all the home games for the remainder of the season. Following the meeting, the committee distributed hundreds of buttons bearing in violet the slogan: "Bates Must Play." Over the next ten days they and their supporters orchestrated daily rallies, distributed sev-

Figure 8–1
Leonard Bates in uniform for the New York University football squad. Courtesy New York University Archives.

eral thousand flyers, and circulated petitions demanding that either Bates be allowed to play against Missouri or that the university cancel the game.[9]

The press's coverage of the protest at NYU raises serious questions about fairness and sensitivity in American journalism during that era. Why did the white press differ markedly from the black press in its coverage of the protest and the issues and individuals involved? It is true that this was a "black story," but it was also an American one that encompassed concerns and questions regarding social justice, education, race relations, law, and more. White newspapers, including those in the northeast, gave either no or at best limited attention to the story. The *New York Times,* with the incident occurring literally within its backyard, evidently considered what was happening at NYU a news item unfit to print. The *Times* devoted no major coverage to the protest or its aftermath. In its general coverage of NYU football, the paper continued to speak of coach Mal Stevens in highly favorable terms. In the opinion of the *Times*, he was "a man of great truth." On the one occasion when the newspaper devoted four sentences to what was taking place on the campus, it predicted that the protest would quickly abate.[10]

In the black press, the NYU story did receive major attention. Black papers with national circulations, such as the *Baltimore Afro-American, Chicago Defender,* and others, gave it either front or second page coverage, and then continued to follow the situation at NYU with routine updates. Content analysis of the commentaries in the black press indicates that they rendered a decidedly negative assessment of NYU administration's position and handling of the Missouri matter. In the black newspapers, Coach Stevens, for example, was described as a man of poor character and "wishwashy." While there was great empathy in black papers for Leonard Bates's plight, several of them also criticized him. One paper characterized him as a plantation Negro for "not turn[ing] in his uniform rather than suffer[ing] humiliation" and for remaining silent while his fellow students actively denounced the Jim Crow policy. "Perhaps Bates wants a job down in the rural section of some southern county where he has to 'mister' the dog catcher," a black editor remarked. "Folk don't want him up North if he hasn't any manhood and most colored folk down South don't want him there."[11]

The NYU student body was mixed in its opinion of what should be done about the "Missouri Crisis," if anything. A substantial number of students advocated moderation. The Student Council went on record in opposition to Jim Crowism and the gentlemen's agreement but criticized the actions of the All-University Committee on "Bates Must Play." Why these differences of opinion within the student body? For the most part, an examination of the "Bates Must Play" movement suggests the importance of social stratification and class as determinants of an individual's or a group's social philosophy and political and policy formulations.

A physical and social dichotomy existed within the student body at NYU. The institution was essentially comprised of two campuses and two student bodies at the time of the Bates issue: its original site at Washington Square, which opened in 1832, in the heart of the city; and its University Heights campus, established in 1894, located in the Bronx. Washington Square housed several colleges and the administrative offices. The campus attracted an ethnically and culturally diverse student body and was wedded to its cosmopolitan environment and the problems associated with city life. The University Heights campus, on the other hand, was established on the principle of providing a more idyllic educational setting. The Heights sought a bucolic existence, an intellectual setting free from the distractions of urban America. It remained "an elite oasis of calm and splendid isolation" from the city's diverse people until 1973 when it moved back to Washington Square and merged with the University's other colleges.[12]

The All-University Committee on "Bates Must Play" was the product of Washington Square students and the movement was concentrated on that campus. Heights students were considerably more circumspect on the Bates issue than their counterparts at Washington Square. In their official student newspaper, the *Heights Daily News,* they recommended a conservative approach to resolving the problem. "Unmoved by the confused and impractical attempts of the Washington Square colleges," the paper asserted, "the students at the Heights have taken a firm and undeniable lead towards remedying the situation" confronting the school. Their solution was to have the athletic department "refrain" from scheduling contests "in the future" with "teams that find members of our eleven unsuitable." For the present, they asked "not for cancellation of this year's Missouri game nor for Bates' playing in it." The editorial, moreover, warned against moral posturing and "bringing up again issues which have been in existence since before the Civil War. Neither is this an effort on the part of anyone to change the ethics of another school whose ideas on fairness differ so radically from ours. We disagree with Missouri, but we are hardly in a position to condemn them for holding the same principles as does the greater part of the South."[13] The Student Council championed the Heights point of view. Alan Brooks, sports editor for the *Heights Daily News* and a member of the council, publicly criticized the "Bates Must Play" campaign. He lambasted the All-University Committee, calling their effort "a perfect example of bungling."

Brooks criticized them for "constant refusal to heed the facts of the case" and "their vociferous howling of 'Bates Must Play,' " which, in his opinion, had "carried the affair to ridiculous heights." He further accused the committee and its supporters of having "transfigured a serious affair into a cheap burlesque act." The only "practical solution," according to Brooks, was that which the Student Council recommended at its meeting of October 22.[14]

At that meeting the council was predictably cautious in its recommendations. After all, the Student Council was headquartered on the Heights campus and Heights students and faculty dominated it. At the beginning of the meeting, however, the group briefly contemplated taking a firm stand on the Bates matter. It was moved and seconded that they go on record as

> opposing the conditions and provisions which will keep Leonard Bates out of the Missouri game of November 2, 1940, and that we, as duly elected representatives of New York University strongly suggest that the Athletic Association of New York University cancel and refuse to schedule in the future any and all athletic relations with said Missouri University.[15]

The architect of the motion surprisingly was Alan Brooks. Professor Bronstein, the faculty representative on the council, evidently found Brooks's motion intemperate and objected to it. His objection was seconded and the motion defeated by a vote of five to three. Bronstein then offered an amendment to Brooks's original motion, "striking out all but the enacting clause." One of the students, a Mr. Antin, moved to repeal Bronstein's amendment. His motion against the Bronstein amendment was ruled out of order. The final, amended motion passed seven to nothing. Indicative of the conservatism at the Heights, the council passed a tame resolution:

> BE IT RESOLVED that the Student Council go on record as opposing the type of conditions under which we are to play the Missouri game of November 2, 1940 and that we desire the Athletic Board of the University to refrain from scheduling schools which entertain similar discriminations.[16]

At Washington Square or the Heights, "Bates Must Play" was the leading topic of ethical and political debate. Was Jim Crow right? Most students answered emphatically—no. In a democratic and free society it was simply wrong to discriminate against another human being. Do we at NYU have a right to tell Missouri or any other school what beliefs or policy it must embrace with respect to the race question? Some answered yes. Others answered no. They wrestled with the moral imperative of collegiate athletics. Is competition in and of itself good? Does sport build character? Does sport foster democratic principles or is it too militaristic? The students explored the concept of individualism versus teamwork. They intellectualized about the meaning of fair play in a capitalist society. Was sport a microcosm of society? They addressed questions of race, religion, and gender in their discussion of Jim Crowism and how the gentlemen's agreement had been used against Jews, blacks, and women. Do private citizens have a right to discriminate in social clubs, private establishments, or personal relations? Discussion was heated, lively, and possibly enlightening. Into the wee hours of the morning, small groups of students could be found on both campuses grappling with the many questions surrounding "Bates Must Play."

Inevitably the seeking of truth led to faultfinding and to placing the ultimate blame. The accusatory finger pointed to the NYU administration. Why schedule games with institutions that discriminate? In the *Education Sun,* the publication of the College of Education, which was located on the Washington Square campus, students debated why the protest arose when it did. "Perhaps it is the appearance of a Negro on a team which has aroused this action," the *Sun* suggested. "But it seems to us that since this wave of feeling concerns the whole question of racial prejudice, the furor [sic] should have been raised when the schedule was first announced. Whether there was a Negro on the team or not, Missouri was known to be guilty of race prejudice and should not have been accepted as an opponent." The *Washington Square Bulletin,* the official student newspaper of the Washington Square campus, seconded the opinion of the *Sun* in insisting that "all relations with Missouri and other Jim Crow schools be broken. No football team is worth the sacrifice of the ideals of liberty and freedom. The game should be canceled."[17]

The *Bulletin,* in arriving at the conclusion that the game with Missouri should be scratched, considered a factor that had been overlooked in much of the debate and activism: What about the safety of Len Bates if the game were held and he be allowed to play in it? Jim Herbert, a black and former world-class NYU track athlete, agreed with the paper's position. He refused to sign the petition of the All-University Committee on "Bates Must Play." In his opinion, Bates stood an excellent chance of being critically injured if he competed against a racially hostile team such as Missouri. "If he plays it will be the first instance of legalized lynching," the *Bulletin* argued. "For this reason we disagree with the petition circulated by the All-University Committee on Bates must Play. The Committee is acting with a purely idealistic viewpoint."[18]

Based on the long history of incidents in interracial football contests, the question of whether it would be safe for Bates to play was a legitimate one. Football, after all was only a sport, but when you added the ingredients of personal pride, valor, ethnicity, religion, sectionalism, or race, the game moved to a higher level of significance. Athletes performed with great determination and intensity when individual honor and that of the alma mater were at stake. When any two teams played one another, hometown identity and possibly social or class vindication could be on the line. The player's parents, sweetheart, relatives, friends, and fellow students witnessed the competition and shared vicariously in the glory of victory or the agony of defeat. Fans, like players, became deeply immersed in the game, excited, emotional. Derogatory remarks were routinely shouted at opposing team members. If you were Jewish, such as NYU's Irv Hyman, you were often called a dirty Jew,

Figure 8–2
Protesters at NYU during a petition drive: "Bates Must Play" was the banner appeal. Courtesy of New York University Archives.

hymie, or kike. The Villanova spectators spouted so many nasty epithets at Hyman that the NYU student body demanded an apology after the game. If you were black, such as Len Bates, you could expect someone to call you a nigger every time you ran with the ball, caught a pass, threw a block, or made a tackle. White players seemed to reach down a little bit deeper inside to play with greater ferocity when they were up against a black. Even when two interracial teams squared off on the field, the racial dimension was still prevalent as was the determination by players to "get that nigger off the field."[19]

Injury to the black player frequently occurred as white opponents redoubled their efforts against him. In 1923, black footballer Jack Trice of Iowa State University paid the ultimate price. On that October afternoon Iowa State took on the University of Minnesota in one of the hardest hitting games in the history of collegiate football. Race played no part in the Minnesota match according to Robert Fisher, one of the white players on the Iowa State team. Other eyewitnesses believed that race was a factor in the game and in what happened to Trice afterwards. Trice himself thought that race was always an issue when you are black. Since the game against Minnesota was to be his first gridiron contest (three other teams had refused to play Iowa State with a black on the team), he felt the weight of his race on his shoulders. The evening prior to the competition, Trice wrote a note and placed it in his pocket. It read: "The honor of my race, family, and self is at stake. Everyone is expecting me to do big things. *I will*! My whole body and soul are to be thrown recklessly about on the field tomorrow. Every time the ball is snapped, *I will* be trying to do more than my part. On all defensive plays I must break through the opponents line and stop the play in their territory."[20]

And he did. By all accounts, Jack Trice played a stupendous game against Minnesota. It was an unforgettable contest. You knew that this would be an event long remembered when on the opening kickoff the hitting was so ferocious that three players left the field dazed and limping. The first play from scrimmage had the audience in awe, not so much from the efforts of the ball carrier but from the thunderous sounds of the blocking and utter viciousness of the tackling. The intensity of the game swelled on each snap of the ball. The blows were so violent that one spectator was heard to remark that he thought it was getting ready to rain. The teams went after each other, play after play, hit after hit. Sounds and stench filled the air. Athletes yelled, growled, moaned, and farted. They went at one another with all that they had.[21]

By the end of the first half, both sides were battered, bruised, cut, and bleeding. This was Knute Rockne rock'em sock'em style ball played at its primordial best. Every yard was earned with blood, sweat, and tears. Players gave no quarter and took no prisoners. This was a football game. It was a match for the strong of heart and stout of character. Through it all, Trice played above everyone else on the field. Time and again the opposition ran power sweeps directly at him, and he stopped them cold. He played like a man possessed, giving a superhuman effort on every down, On one eventful sweep just before the end of the third quarter, Trice threw himself in the path of three blockers and stopped Minnesota for no gain. But he was hurt. He had to be carried off the field on a stretcher and was unable to continue for the remainder of the contest, which Iowa State lost. It is questionable whether Minnesota fans were expressing sympathy or disdain when they chanted repeatedly *"we're sorry"* as the injured brown-skinned warrior was carried from the field.[22]

Trice was taken to a nearby hospital. It is unclear whether he received attention at the medical facility or was refused service there because of his color. At any rate, he was deemed fit to travel with the team back to Iowa. He made the return trip lying on a bed of straw in the rear of a Pullman car. On occasions he coughed and gasped for air. By arrival in Ames, Iowa, Trice's condition had deteriorated. He was taken to a local hospital where he died later that night of a punctured lung and other internal injuries received in the Minnesota match.[23]

You could count on a spirited contest when any two football teams of quality met on the gridiron. When a team from the North met a team from the South, the contest took on heightened athletic importance and intensity along with political, psychological, and cultural dimensions. Add the specter of race, and it was the Civil War revisited. The game in which Trice met his death was between two northern schools. Minnesota, moreover, had been one of the first universities in the Big Ten Conference to have a black on its team when it signed Bob Marshall, who played from 1901 to 1904.

The football matches between southern and interracial northern squads were often brutal beyond belief, especially for the participating black athlete. Edwin B. Henderson, in his work, *The Negro in Sports,* is essentially correct in his statement that many southern teams, when they played in the North, were willing to temporarily suspend the gentlemen's agreement and compete against Negroes. He tells us that the University of North Carolina, for example, in 1936 "willingly played New York University's team on which was [Ed] Williams." Williams was the standout performer on an otherwise fair NYU squad, a legitimate star running back, one of the very best on the East Coast, including those of the powerful Fordham and Columbia teams. He and his Violet cohorts, however, were no match for the Tarheels of North Carolina. Henderson fails to mention what happened to the black star in the North Carolina contest. Williams took a merciless beating at the hands of the Tarheels. An NYU alumnus, who had been a spectator at the affair, recounted how Williams was "carried off the field unconscious and was ruined as a football player."[24]

The possibility of harm coming to Leonard Bates if he competed in the meeting with the Tigers of Missouri was real, but the NYU administration was disingenuous when it intimated that his well-being was an important factor in their decision to keep him out of the game. They attempted to skirt the major issue, the moral imperative demanded of the students that the university speak out and let the world know that it opposed discrimination on and off the playing field. The students wanted to know how could NYU, an institution that "believes in liberal traditions" and "democratic principles" remain mute in the face of such an ugly violation of basic human and constitutional rights. They continued to question why a game with the Missouri Tigers had been scheduled in the first place. Several other institutions had branded Missouri a "Jim Crow School." In April of 1939, the University of Wisconsin, Notre Dame University, and the University of Missouri scheduled a triangular track meet. Missouri asked Wisconsin to withdraw its Negro athletes from the meet. When Notre Dame heard of Missouri's request, it joined with Wisconsin in severing relations with the University of Missouri. The NYU Athletic Association's justification for continuing its association with Missouri was that the game had been arranged before the track incident occurred. That explanation failed to persuade NYU students who were pushing the issue, trying to find conceptual clarity and the university's true position on race. Students queried the ethics and political wisdom of having athletic competition with a school like Missouri and risking the prestige of NYU. It simply made no sense to them to engage in sport with an institution that symbolized "all the repulsive and filthy [sic] evils that we fought against in the Civil War some eighty years ago?" Student activists reasoned that the ultimate showdown with the Tigers had to take place off the gridiron and in the hearts and souls of the leadership of the university. The Bates incident, as they saw it, afforded their institution "the opportunity to take the first step which would let the academic world and the world at large know exactly how we at New York U. feel on the matter of race prejudice and intolerance."[25]

The recalcitrance of the school's leadership angered and unified the student body. Washington Square students were furious with the administration and contemplated a massive boycott to shut down the entire university. The inaction of the university's leaders confused students at the Heights and they felt betrayed. Heights students labeled the administration "obnoxious" and "as intolerant as Missouri when you accepted these terms and completely ignored the feelings of a man who was good enough to play in our other contests yet not worthy of playing against the Tiger eleven." Student organizations from Washington Square and the Heights jointly chided the administration, reminding them that they were "supposed to be opposed to the theory of race supremacy."[26] The administration defended itself and used Leonard Bates to support its position. Professor Philip O. Badger, head of the New York University Board of Athletic Control, said that Bates understood the situation and was uninterested in playing in the game at Columbia, Missouri. George Sheiebler, NYU's director of publicity for the athletic department, at a press conference on October 30, 1940, produced a letter that Bates wrote. The letter was addressed to the president of the Negro Cultural Society of which Bates was a member. Sheiebler had somehow acquired the letter which, according to Bates, had never been intended for release to the public as his statement on the Missouri question, the gentlemen's agreement, or Jim Crow in sports. The letter read:

> In view of the situation which had been precipitated by the question of whether I would play in the football game between New York University and the University of Missouri at Columbia, Missouri, on November 2nd, I feel it necessary to clarify my position in the matter.
>
> When I entered New York University, it was explained to me in a perfectly friendly manner by the University Board of Athletic Control that a series of games had already been arranged

> between New York University and Missouri in which I would be unable to participate in so far as those games played in Missouri were concerned. At that time, I stated I did not wish to play in the game scheduled to be played at Columbia, Mo. My major concern has been to gain a college education. Football is a secondary matter.[27]

The administration used Bates's own words to justify its compliance with the gentlemen's agreement. The letter was genuine although used out of context and for an audience for which it was not intended. The way that the athletic department presented his words suggested that Leonard Bates wanted to stay out of the Missouri game. This was untrue. "By playing up one part of this letter," Bates retorted the following day after the publicity office released his letter, "the press succeeded in creating the impression that I do not wish to play. This, however, is false. I would like to play." He had been informed of the gentlemen's agreement when he entered NYU and said at that time that he was agreeable to being omitted from games against teams that opposed playing a Negro, but that the decision was not his. He was an athlete and wanted to perform. Regarding the matter of the campus protest that he be allowed to participate in the Missouri contest, Bates had vacillated at first but then came out in support of the movement. Nearly fifty years later, Leonard Bates reiterated in emphatic terms that "I wanted to play. I remember the bogus way the athletic department tried to put my letter. They made it sound like I did not want to play. I very much wanted to play Missouri. I wanted to play!"[28]

Bates was not the first black at NYU to be a victim of the gentlemen's agreement in sports. The school had a long tradition of playing southern teams and accepting the color line covenant. In 1929, the case of Violets halfback Dave Myers gained national attention. NYU was scheduled to play at home against the University of Georgia on November 9 of that year. When it was learned that the Violets had acquiesced to Jim Crow and would leave Myers out of the lineup, a public outcry ensued, demanding that either he be permitted to play or that the meeting with the Bulldogs of Georgia be canceled. When NYU announced that it intended to go forward with the game under Georgia's stipulation, this proved for many that the university was "no better than their Southern brethren in the matter of racial prejudice."[29]

NYU's decision was thoroughly condemned. Friends of Meyers urged him to "turn in his football togs rather than sit on the bench because of a color prejudice." Others challenged the university, demanding that it change its way and institute positive reforms. "If a New York city university allows the Mason-Dixon line to be erected in the center of its playing field," Bob Gibson, sports columnist for the *Baltimore Afro-American* wrote, "then that New York city university should disband its football team for all time." The NAACP prodded NYU to take a firm stand in opposition to the Jim Crowing of Myers, serving notice on the school that it was prepared to file a lawsuit against both institutions if Myers was denied his right to play.[30]

The university responded with a variety of answers to the problem. Chick Meehan, who was then the head football coach of the Violets, at first defended the gentlemen's agreement as binding. He also attempted to downgrade Myers's importance to the team, claiming that the black lad was an undistinguished performer and could either sit on the bench for the Georgia game or watch the match from the stands. The coach added that it would be dangerous for Myers to compete because Georgia would try to hurt him. He cited Myers's mother, who had expressed worry that the southern team would intentionally try to cripple her son. Dave Myers, in an interview, dampened the swell of protest on his behalf when he announced that he thought that his coach knew best and that he supported Meehan's decision. The coach and the administration, however, began to change their statements as pressure mounted from the press, students, and the NAACP. Professor Giles L. Courtney, who headed the NYU Board of Athletic Control during the incident, began to suggest in public statements that there was still a high likelihood that the game with Georgia would be canceled if the Bulldogs refused to withdraw the color line. When the time came for the actual game, the University administration issued a joint statement that Dave Myers was injured and would be unable to play against Georgia. They claimed that a corps of eminent surgeons examined Myers and that the "acromio-clavicular ligaments of his left shoulder had been injured in the previous game and that if he played this coming week he would be in danger of permanent injury."[31] Outside sources never confirmed the alleged injury. Myers was absent when the Violets took on the Bulldogs, and the gentlemen's agreement was thus honored.

The treatment that Len Bates received on the team mirrored the daily struggle of blacks in the society at large. Blacks were treated as social outcasts or, at best, second-class citizens who were segregated and humiliated. Hotels and restaurants routinely refused to serve them. Paul Robeson, famous actor, singer, political activist, and former Rutgers All-American, sued Vanessi's restaurant in San Francisco in November of 1940 for discriminating against him and eight others in his dinner party. A. Philip Randolph and Milton P. Webster of the Brotherhood of Sleeping Car Porters condemned the Central Labor Committee of the American Federation of Labor for attempting to segregate black delegates at the annual convention meeting scheduled to be held in New Orleans at the end of the year. In this same period, Harlem residents demanded and received assurances that the charge that the Red Cross segregated the blood of donors according to race was untrue."[32]

These were the times of which Leonard Bates was a part. He was black and had experienced similar and other adversity firsthand. Bates had been a high school dropout for five years before returning to earn his diploma. A friend at NYU knew of his great football ability and convinced coach Mal Stevens to recruit Bates with a full athletic scholarship. He entered the University in 1939 and was married that same year. Bates was a New Yorker and liked the city. The campus experience was difficult but survivable. Instructors were generally fair-minded although aloof. The athletic department was nonprogressive and in disarray. Philip O. Badger, a professor of marketing and head of the NYU Board of Athletic Control, was, in Bates's words, "a disaster. I would not care to comment further about him." On the team, he found head coach Stevens "difficult" and no champion of civil rights. Stevens was an elitist who tolerated blacks in a limited capacity. Trained as a physician, he had coached at Yale before coming to NYU. He had been given credit for finding a way to play Chuck "Indian" Jones, an NYU black athlete, without the objection of their southern opponent in 1938. Stevens had simply listed Jones on the roster as an Indian since he was nicknamed that and light in complexion. Thus Jones made an end around the gentlemen's agreement. Leonard Bates, however, was unmistakably black and had no desire to deny his race. Bates felt that the coach and the athletic department should have refused to play Jim Crow schools. He was also disappointed that his teammates remained silent when he was Jim Crowed. "They could have spoken out or refused to play if I didn't play. I got along very well with them [the players]," Bates reflected. "They were supportive until that Missouri thing."[33]

Beyond the issue of playing in the Missouri game, there were other incidents of discrimination against him. Southern teams would, on occasion, forgo the gentlemen's agreement when they played in the North. Bates played in the games against Texas A&M, Tulane, and Georgetown as these contests were held at Yankee Stadium or at Ohio Field on the Heights campus. If the northern team traveled southward, the gentlemen's agreement was strictly enforced. Mississippi, for example, passed a law in 1949 prohibiting interracial sporting events of any kind within its borders. Opposition to interracial sports also existed in the North. When NYU traveled to West Point, New York, to scrimmage the Cadets of Army, Bates was excluded from that contest. " 'You have the flu for this one' is what coach Stevens told me," Bates recalled. "They didn't want you to play at West Point because some of the students were southerners." On the trip to play Penn State University, he also learned that it was forbidden for a black to room with a white. When the pairing off for room assignments began at the hotel, one white player, Tommy Pace, chose Bates for his roommate. The coach vetoed that selection. "Lenny, I got you covered," coach Stevens said. Bates was the only black on the team and the only player assigned to a single room. Another humiliating experience for Bates came while he was at the famous Penn Relays, the annual track meet held at the University of Pennsylvania in Philadelphia. Bates was a discus thrower on the Violets track team. After competing in the meet that afternoon, he and a fellow member of the team decided to have a beer at a nearby pub. Bates reminisced about what ensued: "I remember how the white bartender acted. He didn't want to serve me. After I finished my beer, he took my glass and broke it. Threw it away. My friend from the team said, 'Let's smash up the place.' I said, 'No. Let's be civilized even though he [the bartender] isn't.' "[34]

One of the two prerequisites of Jim Crowism is a lack of civilization. The other is a misunderstanding of or disregard for one's own best interest. NYU's athletic program exhibited at least one of the prerequisites. The football team contributed to its own detriment when it bowed to the gentlemen's agreement. To have your most talented athlete sit on the bench when he is desperately needed in the game is an insult to the sport, the fans, and the players. It is also a poignant indicator of the depth of institutional racism.

NYU sports had a long history of complying with the gentlemen's agreement and suffering the negative results. In the 1929 game against Georgia, coach Meehan benched Dave Myers though he was their best athlete. Myers had gained fame the previous year as a javelin thrower and as a football player. One year later he had become a genuine star. On the gridiron he was a standout in every game he played. In the contest against the mighty Penn State team, the week prior to the scheduled clash with the Georgia Bulldogs, Myers was shifted from his regular position at guard to quarterback. He ran, passed, and played defense in the game. Time and again he brought the 30,000 spectators to their feet with spectacular plays. One sportswriter referred to him as a "human catapult, who flung himself recklessly at the white-shirted Penn State line, and who reaped all the NYU glory." His brilliant play and field generalship enabled NYU to upset Penn State, 7–0. An ecstatic Violets fan gave Myers all the credit for the win, calling him a virtual one-man team. A more conservative witness of the game and estimator of Myers's importance to NYU's football fortunes said that the young colored lad "is half of the NYU team." He was by any estimate essential if the Violets were to have a chance at victory. Nevertheless, because of his color Myers was omitted from the match with Georgia, and his team lost.[35]

Likewise, Len Bates was a vital but expendable commodity in deference to the color line. By the second game of the 1940 season, students were referring to him as the heart and soul of the team. The press dubbed him "the brilliant Negro back." The big sophomore fullback was a pillar of strength and dependability for the injury-riddled Violets. Coach

Stevens called him "unharnessed power." He was that. At 205 pounds, strong, and fast, Bates awed opponents and teammates alike. He was a crashing runner who could be counted on for yards when nothing else worked. Coach Stevens, however, had only used Bates as a substitute during the first three games of the 1940 season. But after the Syracuse drubbing, in which the Violets were beaten and bruised by a score of forty-seven to thirteen, it was announced that Bates would start for the first time in the upcoming game against Holy Cross.[36]

The Violets were a three touchdown underdog as they took on the Holy Cross Crusaders. The superb play of Bates sparked the team to give one of its best performances of the year. NYU held Holy Cross on the first series of downs, forcing them to punt. Len Bates was back to receive. He brought the fans to their feet as he returned the ball twenty yards to midfield. Bates sparked the ensuing drive, banging out five and six tough yards at a crack. After a successful pass, the Violets were on the Crusaders six-yard line. Bates got the call and blasted for five yards, running over two or three Crusaders, before he was gang-tackled and finally brought down only one foot from the goal line. This was fullback territory, as Mal Stevens had coached. On the following play, however, another back, Woodrow Whittekind, ran the ball in for the score. The Violets led Holy Cross seven to six at the half. They would go on to lose to the Crusaders 13–7 in what was, nevertheless, one of their best performances that year against a quality opponent.[37] Bates figured prominently in any plans for success that his team entertained for the remainder of the season. To face Missouri without his services substantially diminished the Violets' chances. Proven ability to help the team took a backseat to Jim Crow tradition.

Despite the efforts of the "Bates Must Play" movement and Bates's proven contribution to the team, the NYU squad kept to the agreement and left him behind when it traveled southward to take on Missouri. It was chilly and overcast on October 31, 1940, as the Violets headed for the train station to depart New York. Waiting at the station to see them off was a small group of student ill-wishers bearing the familiar sign: "Bates Must Play." The team ignored them and entrained. Arriving in St. Louis the following day, the squad worked out at Washington University in preparation for the big game.[38]

Halfway across the state at the University of Missouri campus at Columbia, where the game would be played that Saturday, there was no talk of the gentlemen's agreement or any discussion of racial discrimination. Jim Crowism was the norm in the state of Missouri. The *St. Louis Post-Dispatch* did mention Bates's absence, reporting matter-of-factly: "The New Yorkers are nothing to cheer a coach's heart this season and without Len Bates in their backfield, they're strictly 'suckers' for a passing team. And, since the contract with Missouri stipulated that the Negro ball carrier would not play, Bates is not being taken on the trip."[39]

His absence from the game was sorely apparent as the Tigers toyed with the Violets and humiliated them. NYU was unable to move the ball against the Missouri defense. An observer for the Associated Press reported that "New York, playing without Negro halfback Leonard Bates, couldn't get its offense clicking effectively until the fourth period.[40] By then it was much too late. Perhaps the protesters back in New York City felt a sense of divine retribution as their team fell to Missouri 33–0.

That the team lost the Missouri match did nothing to placate the protesters. They believed that the game should have been canceled because of the race issue. Rather than subsiding, the protest on the NYU campus escalated. On November 4, 1940, two days after the "Missouri Massacre," students at Washington Square and the Heights held public forums to address the question of Jim Crow in collegiate sports and the role of their university. The All-University Committee on "Bates Must Play" found new life and new members. They challenged the university's commitment to democratic ideals and criticized its administrative leadership, especially Harry Woodburn Chase, chancellor of the university, and Professor Badger.

They charged the institution with giving "tacit approval to bigotry by playing Jim Crow teams" and criticized it for the hypocrisy of its "vaunted democratic idealism." They demanded that the institution denounce Jim Crowism as morally wrong and that it make policy changes in the sports programs of the university. "We either show the whole world that we are unalterably opposed to blind, ignorant, lynch philosophy," a *Bulletin* editorial asserted, "or we stop referring to ourselves as a school that prepares young people for a full share in a rational democratic society." Failing that, it was suggested that students boycott the sports program of the University and refrain from attending any athletic events.[41]

The protest was evolving into a second phase, which would be a familiar process in the activism of the 1960s, that of direct confrontation. A new and more broad-based student organization emerged at NYU, The Council for Student Equality. The council was formed as a permanent watchdog to fight discrimination on campus and to challenge the inaction of the university administration on the race issue. They organized rallies, public forums, workshops, distributed thousands of informational flyers, and continuously berated the administration for its position on the issue. The council took the administration to task when it found that gentlemen's agreements also existed in NYU's two other major team sports on which blacks participated: basketball and track.

Specifically, the council uncovered in early December of 1940 that Jim Coward, a star player on the basketball team, had been deemed ineligible for the Georgetown and North Carolina games in January because of his race. Massive demonstrations with several thousand participants were held in front of the administration building. The picketers carried placards denouncing the University administration and yelled such chants as "Coward Must Play" and "Don't Jim Crow Jim Coward."[42]

The same color line restrictions were occurring on the much heralded track team. The council's investigation during February 1941, disclosed that the team had agreed to participate in a track meet that Catholic University sponsored. The meet was scheduled to be held in Washington, D.C. in late March, and blacks were excluded. George Hagans, David Lawyer, and Fabian Francis would have to be left at home. The action doubly outraged students in that George Hagans was co-captain of the team. He and Lawyer were the standout performers on NYU's crack mile relay squad. Francis was one of the team's top sprinters. More demonstrations were held and the mood of the protesters was turning decisively ugly. Several students, purportedly representing a cross section of various campus organizations, were ejected from the office of Professor Badger when they sought to meet with him to voice their concern over Jim Crow in the athletic program. They condemned the athletic department and the university for agreeing to send an "all-white team to the Washington contest."[43]

Lester Rodney, sports editor of the *Daily Worker*, the official newspaper of the Communist Party of America, may have captured the unbridled sentiment of the disgruntled students when he lambasted the NYU administration for having "capped its infamous record of discrimination against Negro athletes with the most brazen and contemptuous piece of Jim Crow ever pulled on an American student body. This time it is track." He criticized the leadership of the University for "having overridden the loudly expressed will of 90 percent of the NYU student body in the case of football player Bates and basketball player Coward" and pointedly accused the athletic department "headed by Philip O. Badger and blessed by Chancellor Chase" of having injected its "putrid brand of Hitlerism into the sport of track, the sport to which Negro stars have traditionally made their most magnificent contribution."[44]

NYU's administration reacted to the growing tide of rebelliousness. It took strong exception to the accusations that the institution was racist and that the school or the administration countenanced discrimination against black athletes. Dean McConn, speaking on behalf of the administration, characterized the university as a friend of the Negro and nondiscriminatory. Athletic director Badger explained that colored players were excluded when the team traveled south because "he did not want to insult NYU Negroes by taking them in Jim Crow railroad coaches." The gentlemen's agreement was acceptable to the administration because the South was then inhospitable to Blacks.[45]

These explanations failed to satisfy student protesters and the battle was joined. On Monday, March 3, 1941, The Council for Student Equality began circulating a petition calling upon the NYU Board of Athletic Control to halt its policy of Negro discrimination. The administration moved to stop the petition. When the council failed to heed the administration's warnings to desist, its leadership was charged with violating university rules and regulations and brought before Dean McConn on Thursday afternoon of March 6. After a brief discussion, the dean suspended Naomi Bloom, Jean Bornstein, Mervyn Jones, Robert Schoenfeld, Argyle Stoute, Anita Kreiger, and Evelyn Maisel. McConn said that the students were suspended for circulating a petition without permission and for spreading false information about the university.[46]

The suspension of the "student seven" galvanized the protest movement. Students at Washington Square, with some support from the Heights, urged the university administration to reinstate the suspended students. Student representatives from both campuses and various organizations such as the Philosophical Society, Debating Team, Math Club, League of Women, the Jewish Students' Organization, fraternities, sororities, and others, requested that Dean McConn reverse his decision on the student seven. A petition with more than two thousand signatures was sent to the administration in support of reinstatement. The administration received telegrams and letters from all over the nation supporting the student seven. Paul Robeson wired that all American athletes deplore the gentlemen's agreement. The NAACP and the Urban League praised the dissidents. The Council on African Affairs and the Communist Party denounced the NYU administration. Football star Kenny Washington called for an end to gentlemen's agreements everywhere. Professor Walter Rautenstrauch of Columbia University lectured on the evils of Jim Crow in education. Student organizations and athletes of the City College of New York endorsed the protesters, as did groups at Holy Cross, St. Mary's in Texas, and Rutgers. Harvard students launched a demonstration challenging their institution's color line policies in sports. They then organized a nationwide conference on the Cambridge campus to discuss the issues. Four hundred delegates from sixty-five colleges attended. The Harvard administration reacted quickly, banning games with any team that invoked the gentlemen's agreement. Boston University ushered in reforms in its sports program as did the University of Maryland. William Brooks, one of the NYU black students involved in the demonstrations, captured the essence of what was happening when he commented that he felt "students are acting right in protesting this discrimination" and that what was occurring could have "national significance" and be a "step forward in the field of education."[47] The student action at NYU was making a difference throughout the country.

Finally, Violet students launched their boldest effort. Civil rights scholars continue to see the founding of the Congress of Racial Equality (CORE) in 1942 as the birth of the "ins," in particular the use of the sit-in as a protest technique—a strategy widely utilized in the 1950s and 1960s. Actually, the sit-in had been employed before CORE: residents of Harlem used it against area public utilities companies in the 1930s, striking automobile workers used it in 1936–1937, and student protesters at NYU used it on the afternoon of March 10, 1941. Waiting to greet the Faculty Disciplinary Committee when it reached the fifth floor of the Washington Square main administration building for its meeting to review the suspension of the student seven were nearly 150 peaceful sit-in demonstrators who were there to lend their support in favor of reinstatement. The student press contended that the entire student population of NYU, which numbered above three thousand, thought that the punishment given the student seven was too severe and should be reversed.[48]

The Faculty Disciplinary Committee disagreed with the students. The NYU faculty was on most issues quite conservative, including the question of Jim Crow in the sports program. When asked for their opinion about the gentlemen's agreement and the fate of the student seven, the typical faculty response was: "I don't know enough about the situation." "I am in no position to express a judgment." "I believe I am entitled to hold my own opinion." "I don't think the matter warrants discussion." "What suspension, I haven't heard much about it." and "It is not for the faculty to decide." This abdication of authority on the part of the faculty was upsetting to the *Bulletin,* which conducted a survey of the professors and concluded that they were either afraid or ignorant of the facts. The disciplinary committee had what it considered to be the facts and was not hesitant to render an opinion. The committee suggested that the protest movement was the result of misinformation and the influence of instigators from outside the university community. Specifically, the committee found that the student seven had, despite a warning from the dean's office that they desist, willfully dispersed untruths about the athletic program when it said that the Negro members of the two-mile relay team were banned from the Washington meet. The committee pointed out that the three colored athletes in question were not members of the two-mile relay team and that a statement from the head track coach, Emil Von Elling, supported this fact. Two of the athletes were members of the one-mile relay team and the other was a sprinter. The committee was technically correct but avoided the more pertinent issue that, in fact, the three athletes were barred from the track meet because they were black. Mervyn Jones, one of the student seven, spoke before the committee and remarked how it was hardly fortuitous that the suspended students were members of organizations that had consistently fought Jim Crowism at NYU. According to Dean Baltzy, chairman of the disciplinary committee, however, "There has been no racial discrimination at New York University. The reverse is true. Yet individuals and organizations persistently raise the cry of racial discrimination and raise it in leaflets of the most sensational character, designed not to calm passions but to stir them." Chairman Baltzy further added that it was his belief that the protest movement on campus was the result of outside agitators. "It is a well known part of the policy of Communist organizations," he concluded, "and it is very clear further that those organizations are acting under instructions of an authority which is in itself in alliance with that government which above all others is hostile to racial equality."[49] The suspension of the seven was upheld.

The position of the administration with respect to the university's sports programs went unchanged for the time being and the school's athletic teams continued to honor the gentlemen's agreement. In the 1941 football season, the Violets once again battled Missouri. Ironically, Len Bates would have been allowed to play against the Tigers this time since they were the visiting team and the game was being held in Yankee Stadium, but he had suffered a severe shoulder injury earlier in the season and was unable to play for the remainder of the year. At any rate, football was curtailed at NYU after the 1941 season for the duration of the Second World War.[50]

The war impacted on public consciousness and on the commitment to reform. The modern civil rights movement emerged in the postwar years and flowered in the 1950s and 1960s, bringing profound changes to American race relations, even within athletics. The students' protest at New York University during 1940–1941 had been a harbinger of that movement.

POSTSCRIPT

On May 4, 2001, at an annual campus dinner for student athletes, New York University formally honored the Bates Seven—those students it had suspended sixty years earlier for their protest activities. Most of those former students—Evelyn Maisel Witkin, Anita Krieger Appleby, Jean Borstein Azulay, Mervyn Jones, Naomi Bloom Rothschild, Robert Schoenfeld, and Argyle Stoute—eventually graduated, going on to become novelists, scientists, and teachers. The tribute occurred as a response to a letter-writing campaign initiated by Ms. Witkin, Donald Spivey, and NYU history professor, Jeffrey T. Sammons. "This brings attention to a most important but seemingly under-represented, little-known chapter in collegiate athletics," Sammons stated. "Sometimes, sport can, instead of challenging what is discriminatory, contribute to it and make it stronger, at the expense of fair play." Leonard Bates, last interviewed in 1988 by Professor Spivey, was listed as deceased in the university's alumni database. We know, though, that he graduated from NYU's school of education in 1943, served in the military, and after returning to New York worked for many years as a guidance counselor in the public school system.[51] [PBM]

NOTES

1. "Race Workers Ignored by Local Defense Industries," *Chicago Defender,* December 14, 1940, p. 4.

2. "Hastie Says Our Uncle Toms Hinder Fight on Segregation in U.S. Army," *Chicago Defender,* November 30, 1940, p. 1; "Uncover Bias in Inspection of Draftees," *Chicago Defender,* December 14, 1940, p. 4.

3. "Navy Wants Race Seamen, But Only for Chambermaid, Galley Service," *Chicago Defender,* December 7, 1940, p. 5; *San Francisco Chronicle,* December 1–4, 1940.

4. "Hit Discrimination in National Defense Work," *Chicago Defender,* December 7, 1940, p. 1; George Q. Flynn, "Selective Service and American Blacks During World War II," *Journal of Negro History* 49 (Winter 1984): 14–25.

5. Frederic C. Jaher, "White America Views Jack Johnson, Joe Louis, and Muhammad Ali," in *Sport in America: New Historical Perspectives,* ed., Donald Spivey, (Westport, CT: Greenwood Press, 1985), 145–192; Anthony Edmonds, "The Second Louis-Schmeling Fight: Sport, Symbol, and Culture," *Journal of Popular Culture* 7 (Summer 1973): 42–50; Jeffrey T. Sammons, *Beyond the Ring: The Role of Boxing in American Society* (Urbana, IL: University of Illinois Press, 1988); William Brashler, *Josh Gibson: A Life in the Negro Leagues* (New York, NY: Harper Row, 1978); Robert Peterson, *Only the Ball Was White* (Englewood Cliffs, NJ: Prentice-Hall, 1970); Donald Spivey, "The Black Athlete in Big-Time Intercollegiate Sports, 1941–1968," *Phylon* 44 (June 1983): 116–125; *Chicago Defender,* December 7, 1940, p. 9; December 28, 1940, p. 22.

6. Allen Guttmann, *Sports Spectators* (New York, NY: Columbia University Press, 1986); Benjamin Rader, *American Sports* (Englewood Cliffs, NJ: Prentice-Hall, 1983); Harry Edwards, *Sociology of Sport* (Homewood, IL: Dorsey Press, 1973);

Steven A. Riess, "Sport and the American Dream," *Journal of Social History* 14 (1980): 295–301; Peter Levine and Peter Vinten-Johansen, "Sports Violence and Social Crisis," in Spivey, *Sport in America,* 219–238.

7. Spivey, "The Black Athlete in Big-Time Intercollegiate Sports," 117–120; Donald Spivey and Thomas A. Jones, "Intercollegiate Athletic Servitude: A Case Study of the Black Illini Student-Athletes, 1931–1967," *Social Science Quarterly* 55 (March 1975): 939–47; Edwin B. Henderson, *The Negro in Sports* (Washington, D.C.: Associated Publishers, 1949); Harry Edwards, *Revolt of the Black Athlete* (New York, NY: Free Press, 1969).

8. "Bates Must Play Group Adopts Four Resolutions," *Education Sun,* October 23, 1940, p. 1; *Heights Daily News,* October 23, 1940, p. 1, New York University Archives.

9. See *Washington Square Bulletin,* New York University Archives; *Heights Daily News,* and *Education Sun,* October 23, 1940; November 3, 1940.

10. *New York Times,* October 23, 1940, p. 29; October 26, 1940, p. 21; October 29, 1940, p. 35; October 30, 1940, p. 31.

11. "Ban on Grid Star Stirs NYU," *Baltimore Afro-American,* October 26, 1940, pp. 1–2, 20; November 26, 1940, p. 20; "Race Issue Stirs New York University Campus," *Chicago Defender,* October 26, 1940, pp. 1, 23; *Pittsburgh Courier,* October 26, 1940, p. 16; November 2, 1940, p. 17; November 9, 1940, pp. 1, 17; "NYU Students Protest Ban on Bates," *Philadelphia Afro-American,* October 26, 1940, pp. 1, 21.

12. William H. Exum, *Paradoxes of Protest: Black Student Activism in a White University* (Philadelphia, PA: Temple University Press, 1985), 10–3; *Education Sun,* October 23, 1940, p. 2; *Heights Daily News,* October 24, 1940, pp. 1, 3.

13. *Heights Daily News,* October 24, 1940, pp. 1, 3, 9.

14. Alan Brooks, "Violets Should Drop Missouri From Future Court Schedules," *Heights Daily News,* October 24, 1940, p. 3.

15. "Minutes of the Student Council Meeting," October 22, 1940, New York University Archives, Student Affairs, Box 12, Folder 12. Washington Square students established their own student council, but I am unable to verify if it was officially recognized by the university. The group evidently did not have the ear of the administration at any rate.

16. *Ibid.*

17. "Bates Is Not The Issue," *Education Sun,* October 23, 1941, pp. 2–3; "Break Sports Relations With Intolerant Jim Crow Colleges," *Washington Square Bulletin,* October 22, 1940, p. 1.

18. *Washington Square Bulletin,* October 22, 1940, p. 1.

19. Art Rust, Jr., *Get That Nigger Off The Field* (New York, NY: Harcourt Brace, 1976), 1–64; Harry Edwards, *Sociology of Sport,* 175–236; Spivey, "Intercollegiate Athletic Servitude," 943–7.

20. Robert Fisher, George Trice, Nelson Trice, interview by the author, May 7, 1988; see accounts of the game in *Chicago Defender, Baltimore Afro-American,* and *Pittsburgh Courier;* Lou Ransom, "White University Rights 65-Year Wrong Done to Black Athlete," *Jet Magazine,* May 1988, pp. 48–52.

21. *Ibid.*

22. *Ibid.*

23. *Ibid.*

24. "Local Stars for NYU," *Daily Worker,* November 17, 1936, p. 8; Henderson, *The Negro in Sports,* 121; *Washington Square Bulletin,* October 22, 1940, p. 1.

25. *Washington Square Bulletin,* October 21, 1940, p. 1; "Statement From AA Board Would Speed Conclusion of Bates Issue," *Heights Daily News,* October 29, 1940, p. 9; *Education Sun,* October 23, 1940, p. 3; *Washington Square Bulletin,* October 22, 1940, p. 1; *Heights Daily News,* October 22, 1940, pp. 2–3; October 24, 1940, pp. 2–3.

26. *Ibid.*

27. *Heights Daily News,* October 31, 1940, p. 3; *Washington Square Bulletin,* October 29, 1940; Leonard Bates, interview, New York City, June 2, 1988.

28. Leonard Bates, interview, June 2, 1988.

29. "New York University Called Upon to Cancel Georgia Game," *Baltimore Afro-American,* October 26, 1929, p. 1.

30. Rollo Wilson, "Downed By His Own Team," *Pittsburgh Courier,* November 2, 1929, p. 6; November 16, 1929, p. 6; *Baltimore Afro-American,* November 2, 1929, p. 14; Exum, *Paradoxes of Protest,* 12.

31. *Pittsburgh Courier,* November 16, 1929, p. 6; *Baltimore Afro-American,* November 9, 1929, p. 15; November 16, 1929, p. 15.

32. "Sue in Jim-Crow Row," "Brotherhood Snubs A.F.L. Jim Crow Fete Plan," *Chicago Defender,* November 30, 1940, p. 2; "Black Blood, White Blood, All Same Says Red Cross," *Chicago Defender,* December 7, 1940, p. 1.

33. Leonard Bates, interview, June 2, 1988.

34. *Ibid.* Also note *Violets Yearbook* (1941). Bates was omitted from photograph of football team.

35. *Baltimore Afro-American,* October 26, 1929, p. 1; November 2, 1929, p. 14; November 9, 1929, p. 15; November 16, 1929, p. 15; *Pittsburgh*

Courier, November 2, 1929, p. 6; November 16, 1929, p. 6; Henderson, *Negro in Sports,* 84, 108.

36. *Heights Daily News,* October 11, 1940, p. 12; "Coach Stevens to Start Bates at Fullback Slot," *Heights Daily News,* October 19, 1940, pp. 1, 3. The *New York Times* considered Bates a superb running back and gave him substantial coverage through the Holy Cross game, but very little attention to the forthcoming Missouri match and the issue of Jim Crow. See, for example, *New York Times,* October 11, 1940, p. 27; October 18, 1940, p. 27; October 19, 1940, p. 12; October 16, 1940, p. 31; October 22, 1940, p. 29; October 25, 1940, p. 26; October 31, 1940, p. 33.

37. *New York Times,* October 20, 1940, sec. 5, p. 1; *Violets Yearbook* (1941), 126–7.

38. "Bates Left Behind as NYU Entrains," *New York Times,* November 1, 1940, p. 34. The *Times,* in one of its rare mentions of the Jim Crow issue, devoted four lines in a small column to Bates's absence.

39. "Violets in Poor Shape for Tigers," *St. Louis Post-Dispatch,* October 31, 1940, p. 3B; November 2, 1940, p. 4B; *Kansas City Times,* November 2, 1940, p. 20; *Atlanta Constitution,* November 3, 1940, p. 6B; *New York Times,* November 21, 1940, p. 21; *Kansas City Times,* October 22, 1940, p. 11; *Kansas City Star,* October 31, 1940, pp. 14, 18; *Kansas City Star,* October 18, 1940, p. 22; November 3, 1940, p. IB; *Kansas City Times,* October 19, 1940, p. 12.

40. *Hartford Courant,* November 3, 1940, part 4, p. 1; "Missouri Crushes New York U., 33 To 0," *St. Louis Post Dispatch,* November 3, 1940, part 2, p. 1; *Violets Yearbook* (1941), 125, 128.

41. "Smash Racial Bigotry," *Washington Square Bulletin,* November 4, 1940, pp. 1–2.

42. *Washington Square Bulletin,* March 6, 1941, p. 1; "NYU Should Define Policy on Scheduling," *Heights Daily News,* October 15, 1941, p. 3; "NYU Students Have Put Schools Jim Crow Policy on Run With Great Fight," *Daily Worker,* January 18, 1941, p. S1.

43. "NYU Will Send All White Team to Washington Contest," *Washington Square Bulletin,* March 6, 1941, p. 1.

44. Lester Rodney, "NYU Heads Bar Negro Track Stars From Meet," *Daily Worker,* March 4, 1941, p. S1.

45. "McConn Suspends Seven Students for Violating Administrative Ruling on Circulation of Council for Student Equality Petition; Protest Organized," *Washington Square Bulletin,* March 10, 1941, pp. 1–2; "NYU Students in 'Sitdown' for Suspended 7," *Daily Worker,* March 11, 1941, p. 8; "Discipline Committee Suspends Seven Students For Semester; Faculty Upholds Action by 66–6 Vote; Independent Group Formed for Reinstatement," *Washington Square Bulletin,* March 13, 1941, pp. 1–4; *Daily Worker,* October 19, 1940, p. 8; November 4, 1940, p. 8; February 12, 1941, p. 8; April 24, 1941, p. 8.

46. *Washington Square Bulletin,* March 10, 1941, pp. 1–2.

47. "NYU Students in 'Sitdown' for Suspended 7," *Daily Worker,* March 11, 1941, p. 8; "Discipline Committee Suspends Seven Students For Semester; Faculty Upholds Action by 66–6 Vote; Independent Group Formed for Reinstatement," *Washington Square Bulletin,* March 13, 1941, pp. 1–4; *Daily Worker,* October 19, 1940, p. 9; November 4, 1940, p. 8; February 12, 1941, p. 8; April 24, 1941, p. 8; Spivey, "The Black Athlete in Big Time Intercollegiate Sports," 119–20.

48. *Ibid.*

49. See Dean Baltzy's statement, "The Discipline Committee Says," in *Washington Square Bulletin,* March 13, 1941, pp. 1–2.

50. Leonard Bates, interview, June 2, 1988; *Violets Yearbook* (1942), 124–32; "NYU is Crushed by Missouri," *New York Times,* November 9, 1941, sec. 5, p. 3.

51. See Edward Wong, "N.Y.U. Embraces 7 Students It Once Barred," *New York Times,* May 4, 2001.

9

JACKIE ROBINSON

"A Lone Negro" in Major League Baseball

Jules Tygiel

A lone Negro in the game will face caustic comments. He will be made the target of cruel, filthy epithets. Of course, I know the time will come when the ice will have to be broken. Both by the organized game and by the colored player who is willing to volunteer and thus become a sort of martyr to the cause.

—Washington Senators owner Clark Griffith, 1938

WHEN JACKIE ROBINSON ARRIVED in Brooklyn in 1947, gasoline-powered buses were replacing the electric trolleys that had given the team its name. These two developments—the appearance of a black baseball player and the invasion of the internal combustion engine—symbolized the forces transforming Brooklyn. Wartime migrations had sprinkled the borough's predominantly white, middle-class population with blacks from the South and Latinos from Puerto Rico. At the same time, the greater availability of the automobile and the rapid construction of highways facilitated the exodus of the expanding white middle class to the suburbs and points farther west. The Robinsons journeyed from California to New York; many more people traveled in the other direction. At the dawning of the age of Jackie Robinson, Brooklyn had entered its twilight era, a victim of the postwar transition affecting America's venerable industrial regions. Within a decade these changes would realign the borough's ethnic and racial composition, undermine its local economy, and, to emphasize the decline, banish its baseball club to the land of freeways. What meaning hath the term "Dodgers" in a city with no trolleys?

Robinson joined a Dodger squad that had set a new Brooklyn attendance record as it tied for first place in 1946. A playoff loss to the Cardinals kept Brooklyn out of the World Series. Few people, however, predicted that the team would reemerge as a contender. "Brooklyn is the one club which appears to lack peace of mind," wrote Tom Spink in the *Sporting News,* picking the club for fifth place.[1] For Jackie Robinson, relative tranquility characterized the initial week of the 1947 season. In the first two contests, facing the Boston Braves, the rookie first baseman eked out one bunt single, "He seemed frantic with eagerness, restless as a can of worms," observed a Boston correspondent.[2] On April 18, the Dodgers crossed the East River to play the New York Giants. Over 37,000 people flocked to the Polo Grounds to witness Robinson's first appearance outside of Brooklyn. Robinson responded with his first major league home run. The following day the largest Saturday afternoon crowd in National League history, more than 52,000 spectators, jammed into the Giants ballpark. Robinson stroked three hits in four at-bats in a losing cause. Rain postponed a two-game set in Boston, and on April 22 Robinson and the Dodgers returned to Brooklyn, where a swirl of events abruptly shattered the brief honeymoon. The next three weeks thrust Robinson, his family, his teammates, and baseball into a period of unrelenting crises and tension.

The Dodgers first opponents of the homestand were the Philadelphia Phillies, managed by Alabaman Ben Chapman. While playing for the Yankees in the 1930s Chapman had gained a measure of notoriety for his anti-Semitic shouting jousts with spectators. Now he ordered his players to challenge Robinson with a stream of verbal racial taunts "to see if he can take it." From the moment the two clubs took the field for their first contest, the Phillies, led by Chapman, unleashed a torrent of insults at the black athlete. "At no time in my life have I heard racial venom and dugout abuse to match the abuse that Ben sprayed on Robinson that night," writes Harold Parrott. "Chapman mentioned everything from thick lips to the supposedly extra-thick Negro skull . . . [and] the repulsive sores and diseases he said Robinson's teammates would become infected with if they touched the towels or the combs he used."[3] The onslaught continued throughout the series.

The Phillies' verbal assault on Robinson in 1947 exceeded even baseball's broadly defined sense of propriety. Fans seated near the Phillies dugout wrote letters of protest to Commissioner Chandler, and newsman Walter Winchell attacked Chapman on his national Sunday night radio broadcast. Chandler notified Philadelphia owner Robert Carpenter that the harassment of Robinson must cease or he would be forced to invoke punitive measures. Chapman, while accepting Chandler's edict, defended his actions. "We will treat Robinson the same as we do Hank Greenberg of the Pirates, Clint Hartung of the Giants, Joe Garagiola of the Cardinals, Connie Ryan of the Braves, or any other man who is likely to step to the plate and beat us," said Chapman, listing some regular targets of ethnic insults. "There is not a man who has come to the big leagues since baseball has been played who has not been ridden." During his own playing career, alleged Chapman, "I received a verbal barrage from the benches that would curl your hair. . . . They wanted to see if I would lose my temper and forget to play ball." Robinson, argued Chapman, "did not want to be patronized" and had received the same test administered to all rookies.[4]

Chapman's defense drew support from many fans and sportswriters. According to the *Sporting News*, the Phillies received "an avalanche of letters and telephone calls . . . commending Chapman for his fair stand toward Robinson." Several sportswriters also accepted Chapman's explanation. J. Roy Stockton concluded, "If the dugouts treat Jackie just as they treat any other enemy player, especially the good ones, they'll give him a riding eventually. That's baseball." Even Sam Lacy indirectly approved Chapman's stance. Lacy turned his column over to a "friend," who argued that Chapman "seems to have a pretty good explanation to me." The friend condemned Lacy and other writers who "keep on crying that you want Jackie treated like every other ballplayer. . . . The Phillies and Chapman took you at your word."[5]

The general consensus, however, judged the Phillie behavior unacceptable. Robinson's Dodger teammates led the protest. By the second day of the series they lashed back at Chapman demanding that he cease baiting Robinson. Chapman's fellow Alabamans marched in the forefront of Robinson's defenders. Eddie Stanky called him a "coward" and challenged him to "pick on somebody who can fight back." Even Dixie Walker reprimanded Chapman, a close personal friend. Dodger president Branch Rickey later claimed that this incident, more than any other, cemented Dodger support for Robinson. "When [Chapman] poured out that string of unconscionable abuse he solidified and unified thirty men, not one of whom was willing to sit by and see someone kick around a man who had his hands tied behind his back," asserted Rickey.[6]

Robinson publicly downplayed the incident. In his "Jackie Robinson Says" column which appeared in the *Pittsburgh Courier,* the Dodger first baseman wrote, "Some of the Phillies' bench jockeys tried to get me upset last week, but it didn't really bother me." The following week he added, "I don't think [Chapman] was really shouting at me the first time we played Philadelphia." Several writers praised Robinson for his restraint. In later years he revealed his true emotions as he withstood the barrage of insults. "I have to admit that this day of all the unpleasant days of my life brought me nearer to cracking up than I have ever been," he wrote in 1972. "For one wild and rage-crazed minute I thought, 'To hell with Mr. Rickey's 'noble experiment.' " The ordeal tempted Robinson to "stride over to that Phillies dugout, grab one of those white sons of bitches and smash his teeth with my despised black fist."[7]

Hitting slumps are an integral part of baseball, but Robinson's early season problems came at an inopportune moment. His batting skein stemmed not only from the adjustment to major league pitching and the harassment by opponents but from the outside pressures that gathered about him. "He's not a ballplayer," complained Rickey, "He's a sideshow attraction." Even before the season had started, Rickey reported, Robinson had received 5,000 invitations to appear "at all sorts of events." "There are too many well-wishers and too many seeking to exploit him," said the Dodger president. In addition, Robinson and his wife felt obligated to answer all of the encouraging mail, making further demands on his time. "The boy is on the road to complete prostration," worried Rickey.[8]

The daily flood of mail included not only congratulatory messages, but threats of violence. In early May, the Dodgers turned several of these notes over to the police. The letters, according to Robinson, advised "that 'somebody' was going to get hurt if I didn't get out of baseball," and "promised to kill any n-s who interfered with me." In the aftermath of the threats and in light of the burden that answering the mail placed on the Robinsons, Rickey requested that they allow the Dodgers to open and answer all correspondence.[9] In addition, Robinson agreed to refuse all invitations to speak or be honored as well as opportunities for commercial endorsements.

The Dodgers released details of the threatening letters to the press on May 9. On that same day Robinson faced other unpublicized challenges in Philadelphia, the initial stop on the club's first extended road trip. Rickey had been forewarned that Robinson would not get a warm reception in Philadelphia. Herb Pennock, the former major league pitcher who served as the Phillies general manager, had called Rickey demanding that Robinson remain in Brooklyn. "[You] just can't bring that nigger here with the rest of your team, Branch. We're just not ready for that sort of thing yet," exhorted Pennock, according to Parrott who listened on the line. Pennock threatened that the Phillies would boycott the game. Rickey called Pennock's bluff and calmly responded that the Dodgers would accept a forfeit victory. The Phillie executive retreated.[10]

When the Dodgers arrived in Philadelphia on May 9, the Benjamin Franklin Hotel, where the club bad lodged for several years, refused to accept Robinson. Team officials had anticipated problems in St. Louis and Cincinnati, but not in the City of Brotherly Love. The pre-

Figure 9–1
Jackie Robinson, publicity photo for the Brooklyn Dodgers. Courtesy of National Baseball Hall of Fame Library, Cooperstown, NY.

ceding year, a local judge had cited the Benjamin Franklin for discrimination and the owners had signed a pledge disavowing this behavior. Before their arrival, the Dodgers had included Robinson's name on the reservation list and hotel officials raised no objections. Nonetheless, when the Brooklyn club appeared, the hotel denied Robinson entry. Rather than force a confrontation, Robinson arranged for alternative quarters. On subsequent trips, the Dodgers transferred their Philadelphia headquarters to the more expensive Warwick hotel.[11]

At Shibe Park, Robinson endured another distasteful chore. The negative publicity inspired by the Phillies' treatment of him in Brooklyn had led both team owners to request a conciliatory photograph of Robinson and Chapman shaking bands. Chapman, pressured by the Phillies' ownership, went so far as to say that be would "be glad to have a colored player" on his team, though be continued to maintain that be had treated Robinson fairly. For Robinson the journey to the Philadelphia dugout to pose with Chapman entailed a painful necessity. "I can think of no occasion where I had more difficulty in swallowing my pride and doing what seemed best for baseball and the cause of the Negro in baseball than in agreeing to pose for a photograph with a man for whom I had only the very lowest regard," he later confessed.[12]

Chapman's public moderation notwithstanding, the Phillies resumed their earlier harassment. Although Commissioner Chandler had limited their racial repertoire, Phillie bench jockeys replaced it with an act inspired by the recent death threats. "Some of these grown men sat in the dugout and pointed bats at me and made machine gun-like noises," Robinson later recounted.[13]

A third, more ominous development, which also surfaced on May 9, overshadowed these incidents. *New York Herald Tribune* sports editor Stanley Woodward unveiled an alleged plot by National League players, led by the St. Louis Cardinals, to strike against Robinson. Woodward charged that the Cardinals, at the urgings of a Dodger player, had planned a strike during the first Dodger-Cardinal confrontation three days earlier. Only the stalwart actions of National League President Ford Frick and Cardinal owner Sam Breadon had averted the walkout, wrote Woodward. The two executives had confronted the players and Frick had delivered, "in effect," the following ultimatum:

> If you do this you will be suspended from the league. You will find that the friends you think you have in the press box will not support you, that you will be outcasts. I do not care if half the league strikes. Those who do it will encounter quick retribution. They will be suspended, and I don't care if it wrecks the National League for five years. This is the United States of America, and one citizen has as much right to play as another.
>
> The National League will go down the line with Robinson whatever the consequence. You will find that if you go through with your intention that you have been guilty of madness.[14]

Cardinal officials immediately denied the report. Breadon called the story "ridiculous" and Manager Eddie Dyer dismissed it as "absurd." St. Louis players also refuted Woodward's charges and to this day, most team members steadfastly reject stories of a conspiracy against Robinson. "I know that there was a lot of things being written that we objected to playing against the Dodgers being Jackie Robinson was there," recalls Red Schoendienst. "But it wasn't true at all. I can't remember anybody talking about Jackie Robinson or the Dodgers for bringing up Robinson." Marty Marion, Stan Musial, and Enos Slaughter also deny contemplating a strike. "I've read stories that a strike was imminent, but I don't remember that at all," Marion told interviewer Bill Marshall.[15]

Reconstructed thirty-five years later, the strike saga amounts to somewhat more than the denials of the players would indicate, but quite a bit less than Woodward's allegations implied. Robinson's promotion undeniably aroused considerable discontent among the Cardinals and other teams. The idea of organizing a strike probably surfaced. Cardinal captain Terry Moore admitted as much the day the story broke. He told St. Louis sportswriter Bob Broeg that he did not doubt that there had been "high-sounding strike talk that meant nothing." How far this talk actually proceeded is difficult to discern. Dick Sisler, a rookie on the Cardinals in 1947, recalls, "Very definitely there was something going on at the time whereby they said they weren't going to play." The planning, says Sisler, was done "by a lot of the older players. I don't think the younger fellows had anything at all to say."[16]

The Cardinal club seemed a logical fulcrum for the strike movement. Most of the Cardinal regulars came from the South, including Moore, Marion, and Slaughter, usually identified as the ringleaders of the conspiracy. The animosity between the Dodgers and Cardinals, who had tied for first place in 1946 and expected to contend for the pennant again, was well known. Branch Rickey bad assembled both teams and both bore his aggressive, hard-nosed trademark. "The Brooklyn Dodgers and Cardinals were kind of enemies," recalls Marion. "I don't think we had any personal love for anybody on the club and I don't think they had any for us."[17] In addition, the Cardinals had started poorly, losing eleven of their first thirteen games, prompting many observers, including owner Breadon, to surmise that something other than baseball had disrupted the team.

Rumors of the impending mutiny reached Breadon in St. Louis and on May 1 he flew to New York where the Cardinals were playing the Giants. Breadon informed National League President Frick of the strike rumors. Frick, in less eloquent terms than attributed to him by Woodward, advised Breadon to warn the Cardinals that the National League would defend Robinson's right to play and that a refusal to take the field would lead to their suspensions. Breadon conferred with player representatives Moore and Marion, both of whom denied the rumors. According to Frick, Breadon reported back, "It was just a tempest in a teapot. A few of the players were upset and popping off a bit. They didn't really mean it."[18] If an uprising indeed bad been brewing, it ended with these discussions. On May 6, the Cardinals appeared as scheduled at Ebbets Field and lost to Robinson and the Dodgers.

Both Frick and Breadon assumed that this closed the matter. Meanwhile, Woodward had learned of the strike rumors and received confirmation from Frick of the warnings issued to the Cardinals. On May 9, the day after the completion of the St. Louis series, Woodward broke the story.

Woodward often receives credit for averting a player rebellion. This was not the case. As Wendell Smith wrote, the incident was "greatly exaggerated and it made a better newspaper story than anything else."[19] If the discontent in the Cardinal locker room had reached the point of conspiratorial action, and no firm evidence exists to support this, the actions of Frick and Breadon, and not the belated revelations of the sportswriter, effectively crushed the revolt.

Nonetheless, Woodward's allegations, exaggerated or not, marked a significant turning point. The account of Frick's steadfast renunciation of all efforts to displace the black athlete, following so closely after Chandler's warning to Chapman, placed the baseball hierarchy openly in support of Robinson. In addition, the uproar created by the Woodward story dashed any lingering hopes among dissident players that public opinion, at least as reflected in the press, endorsed their opinions.

The prospect of a player strike, unlike the Chapman episode, inspired an almost totally negative response. While some writers like Stockton argued that "undue importance has been placed in some quarters on inconsequential happenings," most condemned the very idea of an effort to bar Robinson. "There is a great lynch mob among us and they go unhooded and work without the rope," wrote Jimmy Cannon denouncing this "venomous conspiracy." John Lardner labelled the accused ringleaders as "athletes of great playing ability with mental batting averages of .030." The *Sporting News* alone voiced an opposite view. It reprinted its 1942 editorial arguing that blacks and whites alike favored segregation. This view, claimed the journal, which it still adhered to, "takes on a new interest in light of the stir caused by recent events."[20]

But even the *Sporting News* conceded that "the presence of Negroes in the major leagues is an accomplished fact." Sportswriters generally agreed that the legitimacy of baseball integration could no longer be questioned. "The universal opinion is that it is up to his admirers as well as Robinson himself whether he remains in the big leagues," wrote Edgar Brands. "What player feeling there is may be well repressed."[21]

May 9, 1947 marked perhaps the worst day of Jackie Robinson's baseball career. Threats on his life, torment from opposing players, discrimination at the team hotel, and rumors of a player strike simultaneously engulfed the black athlete. The following day, Jimmy Cannon, describing Robinson's relations with his teammates, reported, "He is the loneliest man I have ever seen in sports." And, if as the *Sporting News* argued, "It remains only to judge Robinson on his ability as a player,"[22] he appeared to many jurors to present a weak case. Although he had ended his zero for twenty slump, his batting average still languished near the .250 mark. After one month of regular season play the fate of the great experiment still seemed uncertain.

Amidst the swirl of controversy that followed the Dodgers on their first major road trip, the national interest in Jackie Robinson grew apparent. On Sunday, May 11, the Dodgers faced the Phillies in a doubleheader before the largest crowd in Philadelphia baseball history. Scalpers sold two dollar tickets for six, "just like the World Series." Two days later in Cincinnati 27,164 fans turned out despite an all-day rain "to size up Jackie Robinson."[23] Bad weather diminished the crowds for two games in Pittsburgh, but when the skies cleared, 34,814 fans appeared at Forbes Field for the May 18 series finale. The following day the Dodgers met the Cubs in Chicago. Two hours before game time Wrigley Field had almost filled. A total of 46,572 fans crammed into the ballpark, the largest attendance in stadium history. The tour concluded in St. Louis where the Dodgers and Cardinals played before the biggest weekday crowd of the National League season.

"Jackie's nimble/Jackie's quick/Jackie's making the turnstiles click," crowed Wendell Smith. Jimmy Cannon hailed him as "the most lucrative draw since Babe Ruth." By May 23 when the Dodgers returned to Brooklyn, Robinson had emerged as a national phenomenon.[24]

Robinson had also erased all doubts about his playing abilities. At the start of the road trip many still questioned whether Robinson belonged in the big leagues. On May 13, the day of his first appearance in Cincinnati, a writer in that city commented, "But for the fact that he is the first acknowledged Negro in major league history and so much attention has been focused on him, he would have been benched a week ago." The reaction to these remarks by Brooklyn sportswriters, however, surprised the midwesterner. The next day he reported that despite Robinson's unimpressive statistics, eastern writers agreed that Robinson was "quite a ballplayer and a cinch to stick with the Dodgers."[25] Dodger officials felt so confident of

Robinson's abilities that during the past week they had eliminated his two primary first base competitors, sending Ed Stevens to Montreal and selling Howard Schultz to the Phillies.

In city after city Robinson showed skeptical sportswriters and fans that the Dodgers had not erred. He batted safely in the first ten games of the May excursion, hitting .395 over that span. By June, Robinson had convinced even the most hardened opponents of integration of his exceptional talents. "He is a major leaguer in every respect," allowed Ben Chapman. Starting on June 14, Robinson hit safely in twenty-one consecutive games. At the end of June, he was batting .315, leading the league in stolen bases, and ranked second in runs scored. "Aside from getting up early in the morning, the thing a baseball writer dislikes most is to write about the same player day after day," complained Bill Roeder, "but there is no getting away from the fact that Jackie Robinson has been the headline man."[26]

Robinson's impressive statistics revealed only a portion of the tale. "Never have records meant so little in discussing a player's value as they do in the case of Jackie Robinson," wrote Tom Meany. "His presence alone was enough to light a fire under his own team and unsettle his opponents." Sportswriter John Crosby asserts, "He was the greatest opportunist on any kind of playing field, seeing openings before they opened, pulling off plays lesser players can't even imagine." Robinson's intense competitiveness provided the crucial ingredient. A seasoned athlete, even in his rookie year, Robinson seemed to thrive on challenges and flourished before large audiences. At Montreal the preceding year, Dink Carroll had observed, "Robinson seems to have that same sense of the dramatic that characterized such great athletes as Babe Ruth, Red Grange, Jack Dempsey, Bobby Jones, and others of that stamp. The bigger the occasion, the more they rose to it."[27] Robinson's drive not only inspired his own dramatic performances but intimidated and demoralized enemy players. Robinson "stirred up the situation both ways," recalls St. Louis sportswriter Bill Toomey. "He stirred up the Dodgers and Dodger fans in anticipation of victory and he stirred up the resentment of fans and players on other teams. To some degree because he was black, but most of all because he beat 'em." "This guy didn't just come to play," asserts Leo Durocher, "He came to beat ya. He came to stuff the goddamn bat right up your ass."[28]

At the plate and in the field, Robinson radiated dynamic intensity, but his true genius materialized on the base paths. Sportswriters struggled to capture the striking image of Robinson in motion. They called him "the black meteor," or an "Ebony Ty Cobb," and "the Bojangles of the Basepaths." "He looks awkward, but he isn't," recorded *Time.* "He steps and starts as though turned off and on with a toggle switch. . . . Once in motion he wobbles along, elbows flying, hips swaying, shoulders rocking creating the illusion that he will fly to pieces with every stride."[29]

"He brought a new dimension into baseball," says Al Campanis. "He brought stealing back to the days of the twenties whereas up until that time baseball had become a long-ball hitting game." But the phenomenon went beyond base stealing. Robinson's twenty-nine steals in 1947 were actually less than the league leader of the preceding year. The style of play and the design of his baserunning antics better measure the magnitude of Robinson's achievement. He revolutionized major league baseball by injecting an element of "tricky baseball," so common in the Negro Leagues. In an age in which managers bemoaned the lost art of bunting, Robinson, in forty-six bunt attempts, registered fourteen hits and twenty-eight sacrifices, a phenomenal .913 success rate. His tactics often went against the timeworn conventional wisdom of baseball. He stole and advanced extra bases when traditional logic dictated against it. Tom Meany told the tale of a Dodger-Giant game in 1947 when Robinson doubled with one out in a tie game and then tagged up on a routine fly ball to center field. A Giant executive sitting next to Meany angrily denounced Robinson as a "showboat." "That's bush stuff," exclaimed the baseball man. "With two out he's just as valuable on second as he is on third. What's he going to do now—steal home I suppose?" On the next pitch, Robinson did just that, putting the Dodgers in the lead.[30]

Nor did Robinson's effectiveness require the stolen base. "He dances and prances off base keeping the enemy infield upset and off balance, and worrying the pitcher," reported *Time.* In Donald Honig's *Baseball: Between the Lines,* pitchers Gene Conley and Vic Raschi, both relate incidents not of Robinson batting or stealing, but of his talents of distraction. "Robinson had broken my concentration," recalls Raschi of a game in the 1949 World Series. "I was pitching more to Robinson [on first base] than I was to [Gil] Hodges and as a result I threw one up into Gil's power and be got the base hit that beat me." Conley tells an almost identical tale with Carl Furillo getting the game-winning blow. "Carl Furillo got all the headlines," says Conley, "but I knew it was Robinson who had distracted me just enough to hang that curve."[31]

These attributes were much in evidence in 1947, though Branch Rickey warned, "You haven't seen Robinson yet. Maybe you won't really see him until next year. You'll see something when he gets to bunting and running as freely as he should."[32] Rickey did not exaggerate. Robinson did not reach his peak as a ballplayer for another two seasons.

Figure 9–2
Jackie Robinson turning a double play against the New York Giants. Courtesy of National Baseball Hall of Fame Library, Cooperstown, NY.

Many National League players attributed Robinson's 1947 success to an unwillingness of opponents to challenge him. "Some of the fellows may be riding Jackie, but an even greater number are going out of their way to avoid him," commented one unidentified athlete. "They just don't want to get involved in a close play where Jackie might be accidentally spiked or knocked around." Several pitchers complained privately that they feared throwing tight to Robinson to move him away from the plate, giving him an advantage in the batter's box.[33]

There is ample evidence, however, that the majority did not adhere to this view. "Jackie Robinson can usually count on the first pitch being right under his nostrils," reported the *Cincinnati Enquirer* in July. " 'They're giving him the smell of leather,' as the boys say." By the time the season was half over, pitchers had hit Robinson seven times, more than any National Leaguer in the entire preceding season. Tom Meany later wrote, "Often his great reflexes kept him from being hit more often than be was. He boasted early in his career that though he might be hit often, he would never be beaned. He never was." Robinson himself often joked with reporters about his league leading hit-by-pitch statistics. After being struck twice during his early season slump be cracked, "Since I can't buy a hit these days, they're doing me a favor." Later in the season he suggested, "Guess I just haven't learned to duck major league pitching." But neither Robinson nor most other observers doubted that the black athlete reigned as the most popular target among the league's pitchers.[34]

Opponents also tested Robinson at his first base position. Playing second at Montreal, Robinson had offered an open target for runners barreling into second base trying to break up a double play. At first base fewer opportunities for physical contact existed, but the stretch required to tag the bag exposed Robinson's leg to the runner's spikes on close plays. A novice at the position, Robinson could not always protect himself. Several sympathetic players warned Robinson that he would "have to watch his tagging foot," a flaw he readily acknowledged. But some opponents deliberately attempted to spike him, making, according one account, "a pincushion out of Robinson."[35]

Only a scattering of overt racial incidents marred Robinson's first season. On June 22, after Eddie Stanky had shattered Cincinnati pitcher Ewell Blackwell's bid for a second consecutive no-hit game, Blackwell unleashed a stream of racial epithets at Robinson, the next batter. In May, against the Cubs, who proved one of the most troublesome clubs for Robinson, shortstop Len Merullo landed on top of Robinson on a pick-off play at second base. As they untangled from the pile, Merullo deliberately kicked the black man. Robinson started to swing at the shortstop but suddenly held back. "Plenty of times I wanted to haul off when somebody insulted me for the color of my skin," Robinson told a reporter. "But I had to hold to myself. I knew I was kind of an experiment. . . . The whole thing was bigger than me."[36]

In spring training Rickey had advised Robinson, "I want you to win the friendship of people everywhere. You must be personable, you must smile, and even if they are worrying you to death, make the public think you don't mind being bothered." Robinson created precisely this image. He publicly thanked opposing players, like Hank Greenberg and Frank Gustine, who welcomed him into the league. In his "Jackie Robinson Says" column, Robinson also diplomatically praised the St. Louis Cardinals. Robinson's obvious intelligence, self-deprecating wit, and public willingness to forgive and understand his tormentors, made him an American hero. "Throughout it all," wrote Pittsburgh sportswriter Vince Johnson, "he has remained a gentleman and a credit to the game, as well as to his race."[37]

Robinson's exemplary demeanor won over his teammates as well. In early May when Jimmy Cannon described Robinson as the "loneliest man I have ever seen in sports," his comments were not inaccurate. But they came at a time when Robinson's isolation on the Dodger squad was receding. When Robinson had joined the Dodgers reporters had described the locker room scene as one of "cool aloofness" amidst a tense atmosphere. In dealing with his teammates Robinson continued the policy that he had pursued at Montreal. "Jackie wouldn't sit with any white player that first year unless he was asked to," recalls Bobby Bragan. In part, this was a facet of Robinson's personality. "I sort of keep to myself by habit," he explained. "Even in the colored leagues I was that way."[38] But, this behavior also reflected a decision to avoid forcing himself on those who objected to his presence.

Among northern teammates, playing alongside Robinson posed few problems. For southerners, on the other hand, it often required a significant adjustment. Several players feared repercussions at home for their involuntary role in baseball integration. "I didn't know if they would spit on me or not," recalled Dixie Walker of his Alabama neighbors. "It was no secret that I was worried about my business. I had a hardware and sporting goods store back home." Pee Wee Reese later said that in family discussions, "The subject always gets around to the fact that I'm a little southern boy playing shortstop next to a Negro second baseman and in danger of being contaminated." Both Walker and Kirby Higbe, before the Dodgers traded him, received insulting letters. "I got more than a thousand letters from people down South calling me 'nigger-lover,' " writes Higbe, "telling me I ought to quit playing baseball and come home rather than play with a nigger."[39]

The press carefully scrutinized the interplay between Dixie Walker and Robinson. On opening day, recalls then acting manager Clyde Sukeforth, photographers urged him to arrange a picture of Robinson and Walker together. Sukeforth refused, citing Walker's business concerns. Throughout the season, if Robinson happened to be on base when Walker hit a home run, he would refrain from the customary home plate handshake, not wishing to embarrass either Walker or himself. Walker, despite his distaste for integration, never went out of his way to be unpleasant to Robinson, who later described him as a man of "innate fairness." On one occasion, the southerner approached his black teammate in the locker room and offered several batting tips. This incident prompted sportswriter Vincent X. Flaherty to report, "[Robinson's] best friend and chief advisor among the Dodgers is Dixie Walker." This represented more than a mild exaggeration. (In Robinson's personal scrapbooks this item is accompanied by the handwritten comment, "Some sportswriters fall for anything.")[40] Nonetheless, Robinson and Walker maintained good relations throughout the season.

Rickey, recognizing the strain created by this unnatural pairing, persisted in his efforts to trade the Alabama outfielder. On June 4, he arranged a deal with the Pirates. That evening, however, Pete Reiser resumed his acquaintance with the Ebbets Field wall and Rickey, suddenly short an outfielder, cancelled the deal. After the season Walker rejected an offer from the Dodger president to manage one of Brooklyn's top farm clubs and Rickey traded him to Pittsburgh, bringing the awkward Walker-Robinson relationship to a close.[41]

During the course of the 1947 season and subsequent campaigns, Robinson developed his closest friendship with Pee Wee Reese, the shortstop from Kentucky. The alliance emerged out of mutual respect and Reese's unaffected acceptance of Robinson as a teammate. Two incidents typified the Robinson-Reese rapport. In June, the Dodgers stopped in Danville, Illinois, to play an exhibition game with one of their farm teams. Reese joined a golf foursome with pitcher Rex Barney, Harold Parrott, and reporter Roscoe McGowan. Robinson and Wendell Smith played behind them. At the fourth hole, Reese halted the game and invited the two blacks to merge with his foursome. As the three teammates joked and kidded each other, wrote one observer, "Reese and Barney showed, without knowing it, during the golf game that they like Robinson and he is one of them." Early in the following season in Boston, Brave bench jockeys rode Reese mercilessly for playing alongside a black man. Reese strode over to Robinson, placed his arm around his teammate's shoulder, and prepared to discuss the upcoming game. The gesture silenced the Boston bench.[42]

Reese has frequently protested that people have exaggerated his role in the Robinson drama. "You know I didn't go out of my way to be nice to you," be once told Robinson. Jackie replied, "Pee Wee, maybe that's what I appreciated most."[43]

Dan Dodson, the sociologist who assisted Rickey in his preparations for the "noble experiment," drew two prescriptions from the Dodger experience. "Don't worry about the attitudes of people who are asked to accept new members," be advised. "When relationships are predicated on the basis of goals other than integration—in the Dodger case, winning the pennant—the people involved would adjust appropriately." But equally important, according to Dodson, was an absence of coercion in interpersonal contacts. "Don't meddle with relationships between members once integration starts," he admonished. "Let members work out their relationships. Forcing relationships makes for trouble."[44]

The Dodger clubhouse in 1947 aptly demonstrated the validity of these principles. With little outside interference from club management, the Brooklyn players gradually rallied to Robinson's side. Eddie Stanky, the second baseman from Alabama, became Robinson's leading defender against the taunts, brushbacks, and spikes of opposing players. Walker, explaining his unsolicited batting tips to Robinson, related, "I saw things in this light. When you're on a team, you got to pull together to win."[45]

Robinson's acceptance by the Dodger players occurred with surprising rapidity, even more so than at Montreal. Within six weeks, says Bragan, the barriers had fallen. Eating, talking, and playing cards with Robinson seemed natural. Reporters traveling with the Dodgers agreed. By the end of May, Smith could report "There is more warmth toward him these days in both the dugout and the clubhouse." Toward the end of the season, wrote white sportswriter Gordon Cobbledick, the Dodgers viewed Robinson with "Something approaching genuine warmth and affection."[46]

The evolution of Dodger attitudes toward Robinson reflected a process occurring throughout the nation. Robinson's aggressive play, his innate sense of dignity, and his outward composure under extreme duress captivated the American people. Only Joe Louis, among black celebrities, had aroused the public imagination as Robinson did in the summer of 1947. Robinson's charismatic personality inspired not merely sympathy and acceptance, but sincere adulation from both whites and blacks alike.

To black America, Jackie Robinson appeared as a savior, a Moses leading his people out of the wilderness. "When times got really hard, really tough, He always send you somebody," said Ernest J. Gaines's fictional heroine Miss Jane Pittman. "In the Depression it was tough on everybody, but twice as hard on the colored, and He sent us Joe [Louis] . . . after the war, He sent us Jackie."[47]

Thousands of blacks thronged to the ballparks wherever he appeared. At games in the National League's southernmost cities blacks swelled attendance. Many traveled hundreds of miles to see their hero in action. The *Philadelphia Afro-American* reported that orders by blacks for tickets for the first Dodger-Phillies series had "poured in" from Baltimore, Washington, and other cities along the eastern seaboard. For games in Cincinnati, a "Jackie Robinson special" train ran from Norfolk, Virginia, stopping en route to pick up black fans.[48]

Throughout the season black newspapers continued to campaign for proper crowd behavior, and the deportment of the African-American spectators drew widespread praise. Blacks nonetheless found it difficult to restrain their enthusiasm. Robinson himself wrote that while the sight of so many blacks pleased him, their indiscriminate cheering sometimes proved embarrassing. "The colored fans applauded Jackie every time he wiggled his ears," complained one black sportswriter after a game in Cincinnati.[49]

As a boy, white columnist Mike Royko attended Robinson's first game at Wrigley Field in Chicago. Twenty-five years later be described the event:

> In 1947, few blacks were seen in downtown Chicago, much less upon the white North side at a Cub game.
>
> That day they came by the thousands, pouring off the northbound ELs and out of their cars. They didn't wear baseball-game clothes. They had on church clothes and funeral clothes—suits, white shirts, ties, gleaming shoes, and straw hats. I've never seen so many straw hats. . . . The whites tried to look as if nothing unusual was happening, while the blacks tried to look casual and dignified. So everybody looked ill at ease. For the most part it was probably the first time they bad been so close to each other in such large numbers.

When Robinson batted, recalls Royko, "They applauded, long, rolling applause. A tall middle-aged black man stood next to me, a smile of almost painful joy on his face, beating his palms together so hard they must have hurt." When Robinson struck out, "the low moan was genuine."[50]

The scenes at the ballparks represented only the surface level of black adulation of Robinson, "No matter what the nature of the gathering, a horse race, a church meeting, a ball game," explained Sam Lacy, "the universal question is: 'How'd Jackie make out today?' " In many cities pages of advertisements in the black press heralded Robinson's appearances as black businesses sought to identify themselves with the new hero. Clothing stores advised blacks to "Dress Sporty for the Jackie Robinson Game"; bars and nightclubs suggested they "Drop in after the game." Robinson's visit, reported the *Philadelphia Afro-American,* "will give the city something of a holiday setting and night spot owners were twirling their thumbs in happy anticipation of a boom in business."[51]

The idolatry even reached into regions where major league baseball remained an exercise in imagination. Bernice Franklin, a woman from Tyronza, Arkansas, an all-black town, wrote to Robinson: "I own and operate a rural general store and right now the farmers are gathering for your game this afternoon. . . . There is no greater thrill than a broadcast of a Dodgers' ball game. . . . We are so proud of you."[52] Black Americans affixed their loyalty not only to Robinson, but to the Brooklyn Dodgers as well. For many years, blacks throughout the nation would be Dodger fans, in honor of the team that had broken the color barrier.

Robinson's popularity was not confined to blacks; white fans also stormed baseball arenas to view the new sensation. At the start of the season the St. Louis edition of the *Pittsburgh Courier* warned its readers that tickets for the Dodger games were "going like hot cakes and it isn't the Sepia fans that are buying the bulk of them." In Brooklyn, the fans rallied behind Robinson "350 percent," recalls Joe Bostic. "They were with him, not just Jackie, they were with the idea. He became a state of mind in a community that was already baseball-oriented." After the games at Ebbets Field, fans waited for more than an hour for Jackie to appear. "Many wanted autographs and others simply wanted to touch him," reported Sam Lacy. "It was just as though [he] had suddenly been transformed into some kind of matinee idol."[53]

Awards flooded in from a wide variety of sources ranging from the Freedom Awards from the United Negro and Allied Veterans of America to the "Negro Father of the Year Award" presented by the National Father's Day Committee. Local writers composed poems in his honor. *Time* magazine published a lengthy story on the Dodger rookie sensation, highlighting his ebony face in a sea of white baseballs on the cover.[54]

The volume of letters that Robinson received also reflected his popularity. From the day of his promotion to the Dodgers through the end of the World Series, each day brought "piles of mail." The Dodgers hired a special secretary to handle his correspondence and Arthur Mann composed answers to all letters, both the inspirational and the insulting. Robinson reviewed, sometimes revised, and signed each response.

The Robinsons and the Dodgers disposed of most letters containing threats and insults, but a sample of the vitriolic language and personal attacks survive in letters to Branch Rickey. W. J. "Buck" Blankenship of Jackson, California, wrote criticizing the [Leo] Durocher suspension, but added, "The blow that the commissioner dealt was not as severe as the one that the Brooklyn club handed itself when it signed Jackie Robinson." A Philadelphia writer told Rickey, "You should be ashamed of yourself. . . . If you want to do something for the negro, why not give some educated negro your job," and added, "The next time you take a shower get a negro to take one with you or does that just apply to some other man's son?" After asking Rickey if he would want his children to marry a Negro, the disgruntled critic concluded, "Well Good-Nite Dictator and Happy Dreams." Drew Linard Smith, an attorney from New Orleans, voiced similar sentiments:

> Your decision to break a big league tradition by playing a Negro on the Brooklyn team is indeed deplorable, In fact, it is inconceivable that any white man would force a Negro on other white men as you have done. . . . I tell you Rickey anything the Negro touches he ruins and your club will be no exception. . . . The first time Robinson steps out of line you will see what I mean. He will inevitably do this too because he will be egged on by a militant and aggressive Negro press forever propagandizing for the amalgamation of the races.[55]

The opprobrium heaped upon the central actors in the integration drama reflects the stereotypes and the deep-seated prejudice of the era. But the torrent of sympathy and acclaim that Robinson inspired drowned out these negative sentiments. The surviving sampling of letters to Robinson reveals the thoughts of people from all sections of the country and in many walks of life: a deputy sheriff from Detroit, a black teenager from Johnson City, Tennessee, an accountant from Ontario, Canada, and a dry cleaner from Bellevue, Ohio. Robinson heard from doctors, ministers, lawyers, and college professors; from black and white students at every educational level; from a magazine editor in Rockford, Illinois and the president of a life insurance company in Durham, North Carolina. Twenty-four patients at the Oak Knoll Tuberculosis Sanitarium in Mackinaw, Illinois, wrote in support. Most letters, particularly after the early weeks of the season, contained words of advice and encouragement and reflected the impact of Robinson's ordeal upon the American public.

The letters often displayed a touching warmth, as people confessed, "This is the first fan letter I've written" or identified not only their names, but small facts about their lives. "I'm no autograph hunter, only an old doctor," wrote one man. "I am white, 76, played college football, but never baseball. I am a Methodist, ex-school teacher, ex-prison warden," revealed another. . . . Several correspondents described their own experiences when inserted into situations as the sole representative of their race. "I know what you are going through because I went through the same thing in a much smaller way," wrote G. Gilbert Smith of Jersey City. "I was the first Negro machinist in a big shop during the war. They did all the little dirty underhanded things to me that they must be doing to you." Matt Kirwan of Bellevue, Ohio, related his experiences as the only white employee at a dry-cleaning plant in Fort Lauderdale. "At first the colored boys didn't speak to me. I didn't know what was wrong," wrote Kirwan. "When we got acquainted and they found out I was from the north, I didn't have any better friends in Florida."

Robinson's early season difficulties brought numerous letters denouncing the Philadelphia players and the accused St. Louis strikers. "I happen to be a white Southerner," wrote a man from Richmond on May 19, "but I just want you to know that not all us Southerners are SOB's." A letter from Corpus Christi, Texas, dated May 11 advised him to "Stay in there and fight, Jackie. For there will be others to follow you in the Big Leagues if you are successful." A midshipman at Annapolis wrote of Robinson's tormentors, "Personally, I'd like to paste them on the jaw. I think it's a shame that we have such people existing in *our* country."

Correspondents repeatedly reminded the black pioneer of his responsibilities to his race and to the United States. "Whether colored men are athletes, preachers, educators, or scientists," advised a city councilman from Grove, Kansas, "if they are leaders in their line they have moral responsibilities to their race." Harold MacDowell of Newark informed Robinson that "there are thousands of American youngsters of your complexion and my different complexion who are going to learn their first lesson in sociology from your experience. . . . Remember you are on a stage all the time. Your mistakes will be attributed to all Negroes."

Robinson's correspondence reflected the changes in racial attitudes that he inspired. His dynamic presence instilled a sense of pride in black Americans and led many whites to reassess their own feelings. The affection for Robinson grew so widespread that at the year's end voters in an annual public opinion poll named him the second most popular man in America. Only Bing Crosby registered more votes.[56]

Toward the close of the 1947 season, the *Philadelphia Tribune*, a black newspaper, ran a playful story headlined, PAPERS PROVE, JACKIE ROBINSON ISN'T WHITE. Sportswriters, noted the *Tribune*, repeatedly referred to Robinson as the "nimble Negro" or the "Negro flash" or myriad variations on that theme. John Drebinger of the *New York Times* referred to Robinson in this manner five times in one story. "It was so dark in the ninth inning," offered a Cleveland writer, "Jackie Robinson was only a blur."[57]

The *Tribune* story spotlighted a significant truth about Robinson's rookie season. Despite his growing acceptance, Robinson remained an oddity in organized baseball. Throughout the season, even after he had established himself as a bona fide major league player, Robinson confronted difficulties and challenges unknown to other athletes. The burdens of racial pioneering and the restrictions imposed on his behavior still rested heavily on his shoulders.

On the road, hotel accommodations remained problematical. Throughout the Jim Crow era the issue of housing black players had loomed as a major obstacle to integration. Even in many northern cities, the better hotels did not allow blacks. In border cities like St. Louis and Cincinnati segregation remained the rule. Rickey and his advisers had determined that the Dodgers would not challenge local customs. "The position was taken that the Brooklyn club could not assume the responsibility for discrimination in these places," explained Dodson.[58] Where objections to Robinson's presence were raised, other arrangements would be made. If another hotel would accept the entire team, the Dodgers would alter their future plans.

In Boston, Pittsburgh, and Chicago, Robinson had no problems. In Philadelphia and St. Louis, officials barred him and he stayed at Negro hotels. The Dodgers anticipated that Robinson would not be allowed to stay with the team in Cincinnati, but the Netherlands-Plaza Hotel accepted him under the provision that he eat his meals in his room so as not to offend other guests.

The Dodgers dared not tamper with one taboo—the prohibition on interracial roommates. One of the most common taunts that Brooklyn players heard from rival bench jockeys and fans was the charge that they were "sleeping with Robinson." In 1947, Robinson usually roomed with Wendell Smith, who traveled with the team as both a reporter and a Dodger employee.

While Jackie toured National League cities, Rachel Robinson unobtrusively learned the life of a baseball wife. She spent most of her days housecleaning, toting the considerable amount of laundry generated by Jackie, Jr., to the laundromat, and rushing off to the ball games, which she never missed. "We were trying to make it as a family and that was as important and problematic as dealing with the baseball scene which was much more structured by other people," recalls Rachel. The threatening mail and crank letters unsettled them, she says, "But it wasn't in a period of kidnappings or things like that so we never worried about the baby being hurt, or our being accosted too much except by some crazy or irrational person who might shoot from the stands."[59]

Rachel's relationship with the Dodger wives paralleled Jackie's experience. For the first month of the season, she did not know any of them, as the players' wives did not sit in a single location. "One day a young girl asked if I was Mrs. Robinson," Rachel told a reporter. "When I said I was, she introduced herself as Mrs. Clyde King. After the game she took me down under the stands, showed me where the wives usually wait for their husbands and introduced me to the other girls." By early July, Rachel recounted, "When they gossip I join right in and gossip with them." The response of the Dodger fans also encouraged Rachel. "The fans don't realize I'm his wife," she explained, "so I hear what they really think. It's wonderful the way they're pulling for Jackie to make good."[60]

Throughout the first half of the season, the Robinsons lived on a tight budget. Despite his magnificent performance and ticket-selling feats, Robinson received only $5,000, the major league minimum. Baseball rules forbade any midseason bonuses or salary increases. In addition, Rickey's protective prohibition on endorsements forced Robinson to turn down many lucrative offers. For the first month of the season, the family continued to live in the cramped confines of the McAlpin Hotel. In May they moved to Brooklyn where they shared a tenement apartment with a "widow courting." The tenement was filled with cockroaches and the widow and her suitor "occupied the living room all the time so Jack and I were stuck back in this little bedroom the whole season."[61]

While their living conditions remained poor, the Robinsons' financial position improved. Rickey lifted the ban on advertisements in midseason and Robinson's smiling face began to appear in New York and national black newspapers promoting Bond Bread, Turfee Hats, and although he did not smoke, Old Gold cigarettes. On September 23, Rickey allowed the athlete's admirers to stage a Jackie Robinson Day at Ebbets Field. The chairman of the event vowed that the gifts would add up to "as much or more than any player has received on a similar occasion." Well-wishers bestowed an estimated ten thousand dollars worth of goods on Jackie and Rachel, including a Cadillac, a television set, and a chest of silver. Contributions came from Harlem and other black communities throughout the nation.[62]

Robinson also received numerous money-making propositions for the winter and fall. He signed up for a theatrical tour of New York, Washington, and Chicago, traveling with three vaudeville acts. For each of his appearances Robinson would receive a minimum of $2,500. The articulate athlete became a popular radio guest and signed contracts to coauthor an autobiography and to star in a Hollywood movie. Sources estimated that despite his low salary, Robinson's income for 1947 exceeded that of all major leaguers with the exception of Bob Feller and Hank Greenberg.[63]

On the field, meanwhile, Robinson had emerged as one of the crucial figures in the Dodger pennant drive. The Dodgers moved into first place in July, but in mid-August the Cardinals, recovered from their disastrous start, challenged for the league lead. The two clubs met at Ebbets Field on August 18 and Robinson again found himself surrounded by controversy. In the opening game of the series Cardinal outfielder Joe Medwick spiked Robinson on the left foot, leaving a bloody gash. Two days later Robinson barely removed his leg in time to avoid Enos Slaughter's spikes on one occasion, but on another, Slaughter slashed Robinson on the left leg, dropping the injured athlete to the ground.

Observers disagreed as to whether the spiking was deliberate. Bill Corum of the *New York Journal-American* called it "as normal a play as anybody, whose imagination wasn't working too fast, ever saw." Robert Burns, in the *St. Louis Gazette Democrat* argued, "If Slaughter had been trying to 'nail' Robinson, you can be sure Jackie wouldn't have been in condition to stay in the game." Slaughter, in a statement that must have surprised most National Leaguers, avowed, "I've never deliberately spiked anyone in my life. Anybody who does, don't belong in baseball." The incident, however, infuriated Robinson's teammates. Noting that the cut on his leg was located eight inches above the ankle on the outside of his leg, one player asserted, "How in the hell could Slaughter hit him way up on the side of the leg like that unless he meant to do it?"[64] Several Dodger players threatened "dire consequences" if the Cardinals continued their attacks on Robinson.

The Dodgers and Cardinals split their four-game series and Rickey, fearing his club might not withstand the St. Louis drive without pitching help, turned to the Negro Leagues for assistance. On August 23 he flew to Memphis to personally inspect right-handed pitcher Dan Bankhead of the Memphis Red Sox. After watching Bankhead strike out eleven men, Rickey purchased his contract from the Red Sox.[65]

One of five baseball-playing brothers (Sam, the oldest was one of the finest shortstops of the age), Bankhead came to the Dodgers touted as the "next Satchel Paige" and the "colored Feller." One report labeled him "the fastest pitcher in baseball, black or white." Bankbead also batted well and boasted a league-leading .385 average in the Negro American League. Despite these superlative notices, Rickey would have preferred to give Bankhead, like

Robinson, some seasoning in the minors. But, explained the Mahatma, "I can't help myself. We need pitchers and we need them badly."[66]

Two days later Bankhead joined the Dodgers in Pittsburgh where he received "a terrific workout from photographers and newshounds." When the Pirates chased Dodger starter Hal Gregg from the mound in the second inning, manager Shotton decided to rush an admittedly nervous Bankhead into the fray. The Pirates, wrote Red Smith, "launched Bankbead by breaking a Louisville Slugger over his prow."[67] They pounded the first black pitcher in the major leagues for eight runs and ten hits in three innings. Bankhead's only solace came at the plate. He slammed a home run in his initial at bat, the first National League pitcher to accomplish that feat.

Bankhead did not prove the savior of the Dodger pitching staff. He appeared in only three more games with indifferent success and the Dodgers dispatched him to the minors for two years before recalling him in 1950.

Even without Bankhead's help the Dodgers continued to stave off the Cardinal pennant bid. When they arrived in St. Louis on September 11 for the final meetings between the two clubs the Dodgers led the second-place Cardinals by four and a half games. The series marked the last opportunity for St. Louis to bring the Brooklyn club within striking distance.

As in the earlier series the first game was marred by a spiking incident. In the second inning Cardinal catcher Joe Garagiola caught Robinson on the heel. "I don't think Garagiola did it intentionally," Robinson said after the game, "but this makes three times in two games with the Cardinals that it's happened. He cut my shoe all to pieces." When Robinson came to the plate in the third inning he made a remark to Garagiola, who responded with a racial slur. For the first time during the long season, Robinson lost his temper. He and Garagiola "engaged in an angry teeth-to-teeth exchange" that brought coach Sukeforth out of the dugout to restrain Robinson, and required intervention by umpire Beans Reardon. *Time* magazine wrote of the episode, "That was the end of it; no fisticuffs on the field, no rioting in the stands. But it was a sign that Jackie had established himself as a big leaguer. He had earned what comes free to every other player; the right to squawk."[68]

Time's celebration of Robinson's acceptance was premature. It would be another year before Robinson could freely retaliate against his tormentors. The outburst against Garagiola merely underscores the pent-up anger and frustration that gathered within Robinson as he submerged his naturally combative instincts and channeled them into his performances. After the spiking Robinson powered a two-run home run to lead the Dodgers to a 4–3 victory. The following night Robinson had two hits and scored two runs in a losing cause and then stroked three hits in the series finale. "In the field," wrote Dan Daniel, "Robinson's tempo was a gradual crescendo which attained the truly spectacular in the eighth inning of the last game," when the rookie first baseman hurled himself into the Brooklyn dugout to make a "brilliant catch" of a foul pop-up.[69] The Dodgers won, 8–7, virtually assuring themselves the pennant.

"This week as the Dodgers raced toward the finish, seven games ahead," attested *Time* magazine in its cover story on Robinson, "it was at least arguable that Robinson had furnished the margin of victory." Dixie Walker agreed. "No other ballplayer on this club, with the possible exception of [catcher] Bruce Edwards, has done more to put the Dodgers up in the race than Robinson has," claimed the once recalcitrant Walker who, despite his own personal ordeal, delivered another .300 plus campaign. Another skeptic also surrendered when Tom Spink and the *Sporting News* awarded Robinson the Rookie of the Year Award.

The judges, wrote Spink, had "sifted only stark baseball values. . . . The sociological experiment that Robinson represented, the trail blazing that he did, the barriers he broke down, did not enter into the decision."[70] Spink personally flew to Brooklyn to present the award to Robinson at the pennant-clinching celebration at Borough Hall.

Throughout most of the season Robinson maintained his batting average over .300, but a late season slump after the Dodgers had clinched the pennant dropped him to .297. He finished second in the league in runs scored and first in stolen bases. Robinson also led the Dodgers in home runs with twelve. Despite his reputation for being injury prone, Robinson appeared in 151 of the 154 contests, more games than anyone else on the club.

Robinson's performance also benefited other National League teams. Throughout the season fans continued to watch him in record numbers. At Pittsburgh in late July spectators overflowed the stands and lined up along the outfield wall. The grounds crew posted ropes to establish the boundaries of the playing field.[71] By the season's end Robinson had established new attendance marks in every city except Cincinnati. Thanks to Robinson, National League attendance in 1947 increased by more than three quarters of a million people above the all-time record set in 1946. Five teams set new season records, including the Dodgers, who attracted over 1.8 million fans for the first, and last, time in the club's Brooklyn history.

In October, the Dodgers met the New York Yankees in the World Series. The 1947 series ranks as one of the most thrilling in baseball history. Fans remember it for Bill Bevens's near no-hitter in the fourth game, Al Gionfriddo's spectacular catch of Joe DiMaggio's line drive in the sixth contest, and the tightly drawn struggles in five of the seven meetings. The Dodgers challenged the Yankees into the last game before succumbing to the effective relief pitching of Joe Page. For Robinson personally, the World Series marked an anticlimax. His presence in the Fall Classic seemed natural, rather than extraordinary. On the field be performed solidly, if not spectacularly. Robinson batted well, hitting .259 despite being robbed of three hits, and he drove in three runs. His baserunning bedeviled Yankee pitchers and catchers and his fielding was flawless. But even Wendell Smith concluded of the Series, "If we must get racial conscious about it in determining the wreath of heroism, we'll have to pass the laurels to the players of Italian extraction," noting the exploits of DiMaggio, Gionfriddo, and Cookie Lavagetto. "In short, it's been a great series," attested Smith, "no matter who your parents were."[72]

The saga of Robinson's first season has become a part of American mythology—sacrosanct in its memory, magnificent in its retelling. It remains a drama that thrills and fascinates, combining the central themes of the illusive Great American Novel: the undertones of Horatio Alger, the interracial camaraderie of nineteenth-century fiction, the sage advisor and his youthful apprentice, and the rugged and righteous individual confronting the angry mob. It is a tale of courage, heroics, and triumph. Epic in its proportions, the Robinson legend has persevered—and will continue to do so—because the myth, which rarely deviates from reality, fits our national perceptions of fair play and social progress. The emotional impact of Robinson's challenge requires no elaboration or enhancement. Few works of fiction could impart its power.

Indeed, so total was Robinson's triumph, so dominant his personality, that few people have questioned the strategies and values that underpinned Branch Rickey's "noble experiment." Rickey based his blueprint for integration both on his assessment of the racial realities of postwar America and his flair for the dramatic. He believed that the United States was ready for integrated baseball, but the balance remained so precarious that the breakthrough had to be carefully planned and cautiously advanced. Americans—both black and white, players and fans—needed time to accommodate themselves to the idea of blacks in baseball. The slightest false step, Rickey concluded, would delay the entry of non-whites into the national pastime indefinitely. Rickey felt that the primary burden of this undertaking had to rest on the shoulders of a lone standard-bearer, upon whose success or failure the fate of the entire venture would be determined. The fact that this gradual process accrued publicity and added to the drama was never central to Rickey's thinking, but rather a natural component of his personality. Rickey conceived of schemes on the grand scale and enacted them accordingly.

Most accounts of the Robinson story unquestionably assimilate Rickey's reasoning, and several conclusions logically evolve from this: had Rickey not shattered the color line in 1945, the barrier would have remained erect for years to come; the success of integration depended upon the Mahatma's elaborate preparations and the selection of one central figure to spearhead the campaign; Robinson himself not only appears indispensable, but in most accounts emerges as the sole black athlete who could have withstood the pressures; and, had Robinson faltered, this setback would have delayed the cause of integration indefinitely. Most contemporary observers of these events shared these conceptions.

The credit for banishing Jim Crow from baseball belongs solely to Branch Rickey and the strategy that he pursued must be judged overwhelmingly effective. Yet the magnitude of his success has eradicated from memory the alternatives that existed. Rickey indeed was the only owner in 1945 with the courage and foresight to sign a black player. But with public pressure mounting, particularly in the New York area, it seems likely that political events would have forced the issue within the next few years. Rickey's action and his presentation of the Robinson case as an "experiment" actually relieved the pressure on other owners and allowed them to delay while awaiting the outcome of Rickey's gamble. It is also likely that if Rickey had not set the precedent, Bill Veeck would have. Veeck purchased the Cleveland Indians in 1946, and, given his background, he most likely would have tapped the Negro Leagues. The color line in baseball faced imminent extinction and probably would have collapsed by 1950, even if Rickey had not courageously engineered that collapse.

Rickey's preparations, in retrospect, also appear overelaborate and unnecessary. The Dodgers might have signed Robinson or another black player and immediately placed him on the Dodger roster with few adverse effects, or they might have launched wholesale signings of black players throughout the farm system and allowed the best to play their way to the major leagues. In subsequent years, the Indians pursued this strategy with great effect. Cleveland, of course, enjoyed the benefit of Robinson's prior success. Nonetheless, their less cautious tactics proved as successful as Rickey's maneuvers in the long run.

The Rickey blueprint placed tremendous pressure upon Robinson, his standard-bearer. Robinson's response to this challenge inspired a legend. His playing skills, intelligence, and competitive flair made Robinson the perfect pathbreaker. Still, did others exist who could have duplicated his feat? Unquestionably, many black athletes possessed major league talent, but could they have performed adequately under the intense pressure and retained their composure amidst insults? Former Negro League players differ on this matter. "I couldn't have done it," says Joe Black. "I might have taken it for a few days, or maybe a week, but then I'd have grabbed one of them in the dugout runway or outside the ballpark and popped him . . . and right there Mr. Rickey's whole program would have gone down the drain."[73] Other black players, however, argue that they could, and did, play in racially charged situations. Baseball was their profession, one that they plied under various conditions throughout the Americas. During the next decade, other blacks re-created Robinson's ordeal in different minor leagues; racial pressures chased few from the game.

Roy Campanella, following in Robinson's immediate wake, blazed an alternate, but nonetheless effective trail. "Roy was a calm man," says Don Newcombe. "He could withstand that kind of pressure. He was just dogged enough to really stick with it."[74] Rickey might have introduced Robinson and Campanella together, thereby relieving the pressures endured by a lone pioneer and increasing the chances of success. It is interesting to speculate on what Rickey would have done had Robinson failed. Would he have given up and cut Campanella, already acknowledged as one of baseball's best catchers, adrift? Or, would Rickey have extended his experiment?

But Jackie Robinson did not fail and Campanella and the others who followed benefited from his example. And in Robinson, Rickey had uncovered not only an outstanding baseball player, but a figure of charisma and leadership. For blacks, Robinson became a symbol of pride and dignity; to whites, he represented a type of black man far removed from prevailing stereotypes, whom they could not help but respect. He would not fade into obscurity after retirement as most athletes do. Robinson remained an active advocate of civil rights causes and African-American interests. Other blacks might have sufficed in his role, concedes Dick Young, who often feuded with him, "But none, I believe, would have done it quite so well as Jackie Robinson."[75]

The true significance of Jackie Robinson and his spectacular triumph in 1947 is reflected in the recollections of Dodger announcer Red Barber. Robinson's arrival had posed a moral dilemma for Barber, but he accepted the black man, "as a man, as a ballplayer. I didn't resent him and I didn't crusade for him. I broadcast the ball." Both Robinson and Rickey expressed their appreciation for Barber's tactful handling of the matter, but, writes Barber in his autobiography, "I know that if I have achieved any understanding and tolerance in my life . . . if I have been able to follow a little better the great second commandment, which is to love thy neighbor, it all stems from this . . . I thank Jackie Robinson. He did far more for me than I did for him."[76]

NOTES

1. Tom Spink in the *Sporting News,* April 16, 1947.

2. Undated clipping, Robinson Scrapbooks.

3. On Ben Chapman's playing career, see Carl T. Rowan, with Jackie Robinson, . . . *Wait Till Next Year: The Life Story of Jackie Robinson* (New York: Random House, 1960), 181; Ben Chapman in the *Pittsburgh Post-Gazette,* May 15, 1947; Harold Parrott, *The Lords of Baseball* (New York: Praeger, 1976), 194.

4. *Sporting News,* May 7, 1947

5. *Sporting News,* May 7, 1947; J. Roy Stockton in the *St. Louis Post Dispatch,* May 11, 1947; *Baltimore Afro-American,* May 10, 1947.

6. Branch Rickey in Rowan, *Next Year,* 181–4.

7. *Pittsburgh Courier,* May 3, 10, 1947; Jackie Robinson and Alfred Duckett, *I Never Had It Made* (New York: Fawcett, Crest, 1974), 64.

8. *New York Daily News,* April 7, 1947.

9. *New York Post,* May 10, 1947; on the Dodgers and Robinson's mail, see Arthur Mann, *The Jackie Robinson Story* (New York: Grosset and Dunlap, 1951), 186–8.

10. Parrott, *Lords of Baseball,* 192.

11. Ibid.; *Baltimore Afro-American,* May 15, 1947.

12. Ben Chapman in the *Sporting News,* March 24, 1973; Jackie Robinson in Rowan, *Next Year,* 184.

13. Robinson, *Had It Made,* 68.

14. *New York Herald Tribune,* May 9, 1947.

15. *St. Louis Post Dispatch,* May 9, 1947; interview with Red Schoendienst; interview with Marty Marion by Bill Marshall, Chandler Papers.

16. Terry Moore in the *St. Louis Post-Dispatch,* May 9, 1947; interview with Dick Sisler.

17. Interview with Marty Marion, Chandler Papers.

18. Ford C. Frick, *Games, Asterisks and People: Memoirs of a Lucky Fan* (New York: Crown Publishers, 1973), 97–9.

19. *Pittsburgh Courier,* May 17, 1947.

20. J. Roy Stockton in the *St. Louis Post-Dispatch,* May 11, 1947; Jimmy Cannon in the *New York Post,* May 10, 1947; John Lardner in the *Chicago Daily News,* May 17, 1947; *Sporting News,* May 21, 1947.

21. *Sporting News,* May 21, 1947.

22. *New York Post,* May 10, 1947; *Sporting News,* May 21, 1947.

23. *Baltimore Afro-American,* May 17, 1947; *Sporting News,* May 21, 1947.

24. Wendell Smith in the *Pittsburgh Courier,* May 31, 1947; Jimmy Cannon in an undated clipping, Robinson Scrapbooks.

25. *Cincinnati Enquirer,* May 13, 14, 1947.

26. Ben Chapman in the *Pittsburgh Courier,* June 28, 1947; Bill Roeder in the *New York World Telegram,* June 25, 1947.

27. Tom Meany in an undated clipping, Baseball Hall of Fame; John Crosby in the *Syracuse Herald,* November 12, 1972; Dink Carroll in the *Montreal Gazette,* April 20, 1946.

28. Interview with Bill Toomey by Bill Marshall, Chandler Papers; Leo Durocher in Roger Kahn, *The Boys of Summer* (New York: Signet Books, 1973), 358.

29. *Sporting News,* September 17, 1947; *St. Louis Post-Dispatch,* August 14, 1947; *Time,* September 22, 1947.

30. Interview with Al Campanis; *Sporting News,* September 17, 1947; a Giant executive in an undated clipping, Baseball Hall of Fame.

31. *Time,* September 22, 1947; Vic Baschi and Gene Conley in Donald Honig, *Baseball: Between the Lines* (New York: Coward, McCann, and Geoghagen, 1976), 173, 197.

32. *New York World Telegram,* June 25, 1947.

33. *Sporting News,* May 21, 1947; on pitcher complaints, see *Sporting News,* August 20, 1947.

34. *Cincinnati Enquirer,* July 15, 1947; Tom Meany in an undated clipping, Baseball Hall of Fame; Jackie Robinson in the *Baltimore Afro-American,* May 10, 1947 and in an undated clipping, Robinson Scrapbooks.

35. *Pittsburgh Courier,* April 26, 1947; Leo Durocber, *The Dodgers and Me* (New York, 1948), 282,

36. On Blackwell and Merullo incidents, see Jackie Robinson and Wendell Smith, *Jackie Robinson: My Own Story* (New York: Greenberg, 1948), 159–60; Jackie Robinson in an undated clipping, Robinson Papers.

37. Branch Rickey in the *Pittsburgh Courier,* April 26, 1947; Vince Johnson in the *Pittsburgh Post-Gazette,* August 25, 1947.

38. *Cleveland Plain Dealer,* September 19, 1947; interview with Bobby Bragan; Jackie Robinson in an undated clipping, Robinson Scrapbooks.

39. Dixie Walker in the *Springfield Republican,* May 7, 1972; Pee Wee Reese in Rowan, *Next Year,* 228; Kirby Higbe, *The High Hard One* (New York: Viking Press, 1967), 106.

40. Clyde Sukeforth in Mann Papers; Kahn, Boys, p. 59; Dixie Walker in Jackie Robinson, *Baseball Has Done It* (New York: Lippincott, 1964), 46; Vincent X. Flaherty in an undated clipping, Robinson Scrapbooks.

41. Arthur Mann, *Branch Rickey: American in Action* (Boston: Houghton Mifflin, 1957), 257–8.

42. *Pittsburgh Courier,* June 28, 1947; Rowan, *Next Year,* 227–28.

43. *New York Times,* July 17, 1977.

44. Don W. Dodson, "The Integration of Negroes in Baseball," *The Journal of Educational Sociology* (October 1954): 81.

45. *Springfield Republican,* May 7, 1972.

46. Wendell Smith in the *Pittsburgh Courier,* May 21, 1947; Gordon Cobbledick in the *Cleveland Plain Dealer,* September 19, 1947.

47. Ernest Gaines, *The Autobiography of Miss Jane Pittman* (New York, 1972), 203–4.

48. *Philadelphia Afro-American,* May 17, 1947; *Sporting News,* August 13, 1947.

49. *Baltimore Afro-American,* September 27, 1947.

50. *Chicago Daily News,* October 26, 1972.

51. *Baltimore Afro-American,* May 3, 1947; *Pittsburgh Courier,* May 10, 1947; *Philadelphia Afro-American,* May 10, 1947.

52. Bernice Franklin to Jackie Robinson, August 20, 1947, Mann Papers.

53. *Pittsburgh Courier,* April 26, 1947; interview with Joe Bostic; Sam Lacy in the *Baltimore Afro-American,* April 19, 1947.

54. On awards to Robinson, see the *Sporting News,* June 12, 1947 and *Pittsburgh Courier,* June 14, 1947; *Time,* September 22, 1947.

55. Unless otherwise noted, all letters quoted on pp. 198–200 may be found in the Arthur Mann Papers, Library of Congress, Washington, D.C.

56. *Pittsburgh Courier,* November 22, 1947.

57. *Philadelphia Tribune,* October 11, 1947; *Cleveland Plain Dealer,* October 6, 1947.

58. Dodson, "Integration of Negroes," 80.

59. Interview with Rachel Robinson.

60. *Sporting News,* September 7, 1947.

61. Interview with Rachel Robinson.

62. *Pittsburgh Courier,* September 27, 1947, and *Sporting News,* October 1, 1947.

63. *Sporting News,* October 1, 22, 1947.

64. Bill Corum in an undated clipping, Robinson Scrapbooks; Robert Burns in the *St. Louis Gazette Democrat,* August 23, 1947; Enos Slaughter in *ibid.;* teammate in the *Baltimore Afro-American,* August 30, 1947.

65. *St. Louis Post-Dispatch,* August 25, 1947.

66. *Cleveland Plain Dealer,* August 26, 1947.

67. *Baltimore Afro-American,* September 7, 1947; Red Smith in the *Baltimore Afro-American,* September 7, 1947.

68. *St. Louis Post-Dispatch,* September 12, 1947; *New York Daily Mirror,* September 12, 1947; *Time,* September 22, 1947.

69. *Sporting News,* September 24, 1947.

70. *Time,* September 22, 1947; *Sporting News,* September 17, 1947.

71. Undated clipping, Robinson Scrapbooks.

72. *Pittsburgh Courier,* October 11, 1947.

73. *Sporting News,* February 3, 1973.

74. Interview with Don Newcombe.

75. *Sporting News,* January 13, 1957.

76. Red Barber with Robert Creamer, *Rhubarb in the Catbird Seat* (Garden City: Doubleday, 1968), 274.

10

MORE THAN A GAME
The Political Meaning of High School Basketball in Indianapolis

Richard B. Pierce

SPORTS TEAMS ARE USUALLY best remembered for their competition record and the idiosyncrasies of team members. But the 1951 Crispus Attucks Tigers basketball team, a state championship semifinalist from a segregated, all-black high school in Indianapolis, Indiana, deserves closer scrutiny. The success of Crispus Attucks basketball teams made the school an institution that blacks and whites warily shared. Attucks's basketball success inspired considerable soul-searching in both the white and black communities, and in the end, Indianapolis residents learned that in addition to sharing common spaces they sometimes shared goals. Investigating Attucks's run to the state championship is more than an opportunity for nostalgic retrieval of past athletic glories.[1] Rather, such an examination allows scholars to integrate sports with the flourishing study of popular culture and examine how that culture shaped racial attitudes.[2] The widespread presumption that success in sports reflected well on a group's potential for citizenship and character shaped the understanding of Attucks's success in 1951 and inspired a range of responses. Black leaders in Indianapolis, in particular, self-consciously worked to parlay athletic achievements into more tangible gains. Their successes, and their failures, reveal the measured pace of racial progress in a midwestern city in the 1950s.[3]

Why basketball means so much to Indiana residents is unclear, but the game has become central to the identity of many of the state's residents. James Naismith, who invented the uniquely American game of basketball while teaching in Massachusetts, claimed shortly before his death in 1939, "Basketball really had its origin in Indiana, which remains today the center of the sport."[4] In the case of Indianapolis and Attucks, however, there is an additional dimension; while the participants in basketball tournaments were playing games, to others, especially elders in the black community, tournaments were political activities. African-American communities throughout the United States had long debated the utility of employing athletic prowess to advance civic and social causes. Most notably, the media organs of the National Association for the Advancement of Colored People (NAACP) and the National Urban League, the *Crisis* and *Opportunity*, respectively, advocated intercollegiate participation in sports as a way to display time-honored qualities of sportsmanship, loyalty, "manly character," and courage. The editors at the *Crisis* and

Opportunity thought such participation would place historically black educational institutions among the "first rank" of colleges and universities.[5]

Crispus Attucks High School represented the African-American community in Indianapolis. Churches and social clubs unquestionably served specific segments of the community, but Attucks appealed to the entire African-American community. In the early 1920s, no doubt prompted by the presence of a sizable black population that constituted nearly 11 percent of the total population, white citizens inundated the Indianapolis Board of School Commissioners with petitions requesting the construction of separate facilities for black and white children.[6] Theretofore, black and white school children had shared the same facilities. Whites clamored for all-Negro schools using the unfounded fear that contagious diseases, particularly tuberculosis, might spread from black to white children. They further justified their "reform" efforts by arguing that black children would benefit from segregated school settings.[7] Separation, however, did not imply autonomy. Whites maintained control over hiring and curriculum through the Indianapolis Board of School Commissioners. For more than twenty years, blacks fought segregated education more ferociously than any other single issue.[8] Their efforts testify to their commitment, their failure to their political weakness. It was in the midst of this struggle that Crispus Attucks High School opened in 1927.

From its inception, the high school reserved for African Americans was controversial. The school board initially intended to christen the school Jefferson High School, but the name Crispus Attucks was adopted after members of the black community objected to the school being named after a former slave owner. They offered the Revolutionary War hero as a more appropriate namesake. In September 1927, a few weeks after Attucks opened, the *Indianapolis Recorder,* the city's black newspaper, offered an editorial arguing that while some blacks had asked for a Negro high school, the great majority of blacks were opposed to the idea.[9] Facilities at white high schools were vastly superior to those at Attucks. Moreover, claims that the new school would provide employment, particularly for African-American teachers, was, according to the *Recorder,* a "small and selfish contribution that means little or nothing to the vast Negro population of this community." The *Recorder* bemoaned the school's creation but wished the school well and hoped that while in existence it would at least try to provide a valuable service to the community. The *Recorder* assisted by enthusiastically publicizing Attucks events to the black community. Through the *Recorder*'s efforts, the African-American community was kept well abreast of the social, athletic, and academic events that took place at Attucks. Rather akin to the principle of hating the sin but loving the sinner, blacks resigned themselves to segregated schools and worked concomitantly toward the seemingly contradictory goals of bringing about the system's demise and establishing an award-winning Negro high school.[10]

Attucks quickly became a vital institution in the African-American community. By 1934, seven years after opening its doors, the sixty-two-member faculty held nineteen master's degrees and two doctorates. The percentage of advanced degrees held by Attucks's faculty far exceeded that of any other high school in the city. Nor did excellence end with the teachers. Students soon filled clubs, a newspaper staff, and athletic teams. Joseph Taylor, who attended an all-black school in Missouri, remembered competing against Crispus Attucks in football and basketball in the 1930s: "Those teams were good. Nothing was worse than traveling all the way to Indiana to play Attucks and then having to ride the bus back to Missouri. They didn't just beat you. They beat you up."[11] Willard Ransom played several sports for Attucks in the 1940s and recalled the feeling of community that existed on the athletic teams. Seven classmates on the football team later enrolled and competed for Talladega College in Alabama after graduating from Attucks. An alumni association actively promoted the school to the community and published a newsletter detailing the exploits of its graduates. Although few African Americans initially supported Attucks's creation, many community members who had no direct association with the high school helped it become a visible symbol of excellence within the community.[12] Student loyalty to Attucks was rarely in question. One student recalled riding the bus directly past Shortridge High School to reach Attucks. "I never felt bad about going to Attucks. I felt sorry for those people having to go to Shortridge."[13] Glenn Howard, of the Attucks class of 1958, recalled, "It was just a friendly atmosphere to have people come from all over the city to attend Crispus Attucks High School."[14] Born out of segregation and discrimination, Attucks established itself firmly as a flourishing African-American institution.

Such institutions were needed in Indianapolis where the city's municipal code called for enforced racial segregation. Despite its deleterious effects, segregation gave African Americans some responsibility for creating their own entertainment, and their own space. It was a circumscribed opportunity to be sure, but one that blacks eagerly grasped. For example, African Americans in Indianapolis were no different from their counterparts around the country in that they, too, defied the utterances of some pastors and traveled to Indiana Avenue, home of numerous clubs and saloons, to while away the evenings and straighten up after a week stooped at labor. Howard Owens fondly remembered Indiana Avenue during the 1930s and 1940s:

> You could walk through the Avenue and get anything you wanted. Friendship . . . entertainment . . . anything. There were people everywhere, all along the sidewalks and even in the street. You could go there at three on a Saturday afternoon, stay there until two Sunday morning, and have a real blast. Even if there had been TV in those days, we wouldn't have watched it . . . we had too much running to do."[15]

It was also along the Avenue, on the hard-packed dirt basketball court at the Lockefield Gardens housing project, that the best pickup basketball games in Indianapolis regularly took place.[16] Drawing black youngsters from around the city, and a few adventurous whites, the court at Lockefield Gardens, still called Dust Bowl long after asphalt covered the dirt, was a proving ground for future Attucks basketball players.[17] In addition to family structure, churches, and fraternal organizations, these recreational activities defined a community culture.[18]

On sporting fields, members of the community, especially young ones, developed self-esteem. Rob Ruck, in his study of sandlot baseball in Pittsburgh, probably best described the role sport played in African-American communities, especially those beset by segregation.[19] Crispus Attucks, as the only high school for blacks in Indianapolis, brought all the members of the African-American community together. The recent migrants and the old-timers, those with limited means and those with greater wealth all sent their children to Attucks. The teams the school fielded represented the economic diversity of the African-American community at large. In a way that was not always found in churches or social clubs, Attucks, and its sports teams, represented a more complete representation of the African-American community than any other public entity.

Nevertheless, it was still a segregated institution, segregated even in interscholastic athletic competition. The Indiana High School Athletic Association (IHSAA) ensured that segregation by refusing to grant Attucks membership. The IHSAA counseled member schools to refrain from playing with schools that were not part of the association.[20] While full membership was supposedly open to all public high schools in Indiana, the IHSAA refused full membership to private, parochial, fraternal, and all-black schools until 1942. Member schools could receive a dispensation to compete against nonmember schools for holiday tournaments, but rarely did teams seek dispensation for a regular season game. Consequently, Attucks competed against the two other all-black schools in Indiana (Gary Roosevelt and Evansville Lincoln), parochial schools around the state, and similar schools as far away as Illinois, Missouri, and Oklahoma.

The IHSAA's actions seemed to contradict its founding constitution, which stated simply that membership was limited to public high schools of the state. Any public high school in Indiana offering and maintaining three or four years of high school work was to be considered a member of the IHSAA if it followed the rules and regulations of the organization and paid annual dues. A special section detailed the fate of "colored schools." Colored schools wanting to join the IHSAA were to be granted limited memberships that allowed them to play member schools under certain circumstances, although this did not include IHSAA-sanctioned tournaments.[21]

By 1940, the IHSAA was under some pressure to change its rules. The organization's objection to blacks playing in the state tournaments seemed indefensible. Integrated schools throughout the state included blacks on their athletic rosters. Ray Crowe, future head coach at Crispus Attucks, was the only black player on Johnson County's Whiteland High School team, where he played during the early 1930s.[22] Evidently, the IHSAA did not exclude black schools in an effort to prohibit African-American participation but rather adopted the segregationist stance of some school systems in the state. Schools denied full membership in the IHSAA continued to badger the organization for full admittance. Parochial and the few remaining all-black schools joined forces to demand a change to the IHSAA exclusionary policies. In 1941, Howard M. Hill, president of the IHSAA Board of Control, alerted member schools that the executive board was studying the possibility of allowing all high schools in the state to become part of the organization.

Finally, in 1942, thirty-eight years after the IHSAA began operation, it opened its doors to every four-year high school in the state. The IHSAA simply revised its official handbook to read,

> Membership in the Association shall be open beginning August 15, 1942, to all public, private, parochial, colored and institutional high schools of the state offering and maintaining three or four years of high school work provided they meet the requirements of the Association and also subscribe to its rules and regulations.[23]

Crispus Attucks no longer had to travel to Louisville or Oklahoma to complete a full basketball schedule. The players were free to compete against any team in Indiana that chose to play them. Yet, despite the IHSAA ruling, Indianapolis schools continued to omit Attucks from their regular season schedules. Attucks was forced to travel to rural Indiana towns to play against teams that viewed it as a visiting novelty act, a high school version of the barnstorming Harlem Globetrotters. Their seemingly freewheeling style of play was foreign to communities whose teams favored numerous passes and set shots.[24]

By 1951, Attucks's position as an institution serving only the African-American population was brought into question because of the success of its basketball team. The team had lost only one game during the regular season and was poised to do well during the state championship. Advancement through the tournament, which included every high school team in the state, irrespective of size, was not assured.[25] Indianapolis, despite its position as the state's capital and largest city, did not usually produce good basketball teams. A city school had advanced to the state finals only three times before 1951. Year after year, teams from the hinterland would journey to Indianapolis to play the championship game, a painful experience for Indianapolis citizens. Despite Attucks's regular season record, Corky Lamm, sportswriter for the *Indianapolis Star,* did not pick Attucks to advance beyond the first round of the tournament. He was not alone. Many skeptics in Indianapolis found that Attucks's relatively weak schedule and recent arrival to the schoolboy tournament portended their quick departure from the field.[26]

The Indianapolis sectional took place at Butler Fieldhouse, the same location as the championship game. High school students from throughout the city considered the Butler sectional, as it was called, the highlight of the school year. One female student from Shortridge High School described the sectional as all consuming: "You lived, breathed, imbibed and just camped out at the Butler Fieldhouse. It was a social experience. It was a total cross-section of Indianapolis." A student from Washington High School recalled simply, "The Sectional was everything. The event of the whole year." Throughout the city, high school administrators allowed students to leave school to attend the sectional.[27]

As Attucks continued to win game after game during the sectional weekend, it became apparent that the team was going to represent the city the following week at the regional. There was an eerie silence at the Butler Fieldhouse, pierced only by the cheers of Attucks followers stuck in the corner of the gym, singing their "crazy song." There was little for opponent fans to do except listen to the crazy song:

Howe thinks they rough;
Howe thinks they tough:
They can beat everybody,
but they can't beat us!
Hi-de-hi-de, hi-de-hi;
Hi-de-hi-de, hi-de-ho;
That's the skip, bob, beat-um;
That's the Crazy Song!

The song, born at a time when Attucks was not allowed to play city schools, took on a new relevance in the waning moments of the game long won. Attucks's fans were telling the rest of Indianapolis that their supposed inferiority had been proven false. They had long known that they could compete evenly with city schools if given the chance. Attucks's team, drawn from the segregated neighborhoods in every part of the city where blacks resided, was now the sectional's representative at the next stage of the tournament.[28]

During the regional tournament, Crispus Attucks was announced as Indianapolis Crispus Attucks, since the custom was to identify first the city and then the school. The team's success in winning the sectional caused many white Indianapolis residents to do considerable soul-searching. Indianapolis was one of the few districts in the state that still relegated

African-American students to one school despite a 1949 law that made segregated schools illegal.[29]

And so here was an all-black team representing the city in the state's most important schoolboy tournament, threatening to do what had never been done—bring a state basketball championship to the city. Some whites were afraid that an Attucks victory would occasion social unrest at the hands of Attucks's black fans. After the sectional victory, Lamm, an Indianapolis *Star* columnist, chided his readers by asking, "Attucks won the sectional and the city's seams didn't come apart, now did they?"[30] Lamm may have mildly scolded his readers for their fears of rioting fans, but he also consoled them by predicting that Attucks would never beat Anderson High School, a perennial power from nearby Madison County in the next round.

While whites in Indianapolis were still a little unsure about whether to adopt the Attucks team wholeheartedly as their own, there was no ambivalence within the city's African-American community. The celebration after the sectional victory was a curious affair. For many, the immediate goal had been won. Attucks had shown Indianapolis that it could compete favorably against every team in the city. In a basketball-crazed state, and in a city starved for a dominant team, a sectional victory was occasion for a celebration. African Americans swarmed to Indiana Avenue. Traffic was nearly at a standstill as cheering fans literally danced in the street. Perhaps some feared that this celebration might be the last, as Anderson was indeed a formidable opponent. The location of the celebration further signified that the team belonged to the African-American community. When the team finally paraded down the street, a throng hardly foreign to them embraced them. These young ambassadors had done for the community what no amount of previous agitation had done. They held the city's focus. No longer relegated to the city's "Bottoms," Attucks's victory moved the African-American community to center stage.[31]

Attucks fever nevertheless failed to infect the larger Indianapolis community. Of the sixteen regional sites, Indianapolis and Lafayette were the only two that did not sell all of their tickets, an unusual occurrence even when no Indianapolis teams were among the regional contenders. Only a week before, the total attendance for all sectionals of the Indiana high school basketball tournament had topped a million for the first time in history. Many of the regional site coordinators had to hold lotteries to equitably allocate tickets to all those who desired entry.[32] The efforts undertaken by the regional site coordinators testified to the tournament's statewide popularity, but the unsold tickets at the Indianapolis regional indicated that Attucks's appeal was limited. Ticket sales lagged in Indianapolis despite widespread media coverage in the *Indianapolis Recorder* and in the white daily press. It seemed that no publicity was needed to stoke the enthusiasm of the African-American fans. Their anticipation was so great that the team had to be sequestered at the Senate Avenue YMCA (the YMCA branch in the city reserved for African Americans), leaving only to attend school during the week leading up to the regional. Coach Crowe wanted his team to get some respite from community well-wishers.

Finally, game day arrived. Two basketball coaches from the northern part of the state sped eighty miles in eighty minutes to make the tip-off, knowing that they would see a "ball game."[33] And they were right. The game was a seesaw affair. Attucks jumped out to a quick lead, but Anderson fought back and trailed by only eight points at halftime. In the second half, Anderson benefited from some "suspicious" calls by the officials, slowed Attucks's attack, and took a seemingly commanding ten-point lead with four minutes to play.

People had segregated after entering Butler Fieldhouse. Whites had the best seats, while blacks sat behind the Attucks bench and in the back bleachers. During the final four minutes, most fans were standing. Some had fainted, and photographs later showed people crying. Although Indianapolis was the site of the game, most of the cheering followed racial lines. On the court, it seemed as if Attucks was playing uphill. Attucks assistant coach, Al Spurlock, later said that the officiating caused him great concern. "I was kind 'a scared because of the bad officiating." Years later, he added, "By the end of the game it seemed as if Anderson had seven players on the court—two with striped uniforms."[34] With twenty-three seconds to go, Anderson led 80–79. Eschewing a time out, Charlie West, an Attucks forward, went down court with the ball. In Indiana, as in most places, scoring the winning basket is the thing of legend. West wanted to be immortal. Unfortunately, his shot went awry, and Attucks was fortunate to get the ball back after an Anderson player tipped it out of bounds.

With seven seconds left, the Fieldhouse was in a near panic as Attucks inbounded the ball. Bailey "Flap" Robertson, a substitute forward on the squad, received the ball and shot.[35] Later reports said the game was "without a doubt, one of the most thrilling high school basketball games ever played in Indiana or the world." Another reporter termed the game "the most dramatic and exciting" in tournament history. There was some controversy as to whether Flap's shot arched beautifully before dipping through the rim or if it had a flat trajectory that lost momentum and simply tumbled into the net. Either scenario provided the same outcome. Flap Robertson became immortal.[36]

After winning the regional championship against Anderson, a school touted as the one to put Attucks in its place, the team paraded down Indiana Avenue again. Somehow, the Attucks fans outdid the previous week's celebration. Traffic was at a standstill. A bonfire blazed outside of Crispus Attucks. People danced until dawn. Responding to the opinion of some city leaders that Attucks's success might lead the African-American community to push for civic and social changes in a city where Jim Crow laws and customs flourished, the police chief sent extra patrolmen to Indiana Avenue, fearing that trouble might erupt. Additional officers were not needed to monitor the crowd. The state championship games were two weeks away, but Attucks had survived its toughest challenge. The two northern coaches who had exceeded the speed limit and had the good fortune to reach the Fieldhouse believed they had already witnessed the state championship game and one of the greatest games they had ever seen. They offered encouraging praise to Attucks fans: "Attucks is a great team. It played the hardest it will ever have to play—and won it. It won't have a game that rough the rest of the way."[37]

The prognostication of the coaches seemed eerily correct a week later when Attucks easily beat Covington and Batesville to escape the semi-state. Their margin over Covington, forty points, was the most lopsided semi-state victory since 1916. Attucks, was now one of four teams remaining in the state tournament. It appeared that Indianapolis might finally have a champion.

It was as if Attucks was the subject of every conversation in the days between the semi-state and finals weekend. One editorial opined, "In the Statehouse, the Courthouse, the marts of business and the homes of rich and poor, the name of Attucks is on every tongue."[38] Finally, the *Indianapolis Star* columnists came around and joined the Attucks bandwagon. Not only did the sports columnist of the paper predict that Attucks would win the championship, but he also claimed the team as the city's representative. The columnists

Figure 10–1
Crispus Attucks High School—Indiana State High School basketball tournament. **The Indianapolis Star.**

saw in Attucks an opportunity for the city to have its own champion—a champion that had not played against city schools during the regular season, a champion that they had wrongly predicted would lose in the first round. When Attucks won the sectional, they predicted a loss during the regional. After Attucks beat Anderson, the columnists finally accepted Attucks as their team and a winning team. All prior events and dim prognostications were forgotten. A column appearing before the semi-state weekend summed up one writer's glee: "For Indianapolis, after 40 years of frustration, to face the rest of Indiana on Saturday and say, [quoting Attucks's "crazy song"] "You can beat everybody, but you can't beat us."[39] Miraculously, Attucks had become Indianapolis's team.

But Attucks was not an orphan up for adoption. The black community, from whom the players emanated, still held them as their own. They had not groomed the team to represent Indianapolis. They had fought to get Attacks into the IHSAA so that their children could compete openly against whites in a manner that many adults were unable to accomplish in their everyday lives. Middle-class black commentators used the team as an example of all that was good in the black community and a visible example of the costs of segregation. The Attucks team was excelling on the most prominent stage in Indiana. With one exception, every city radio station broadcast a tournament game.[40] The team represented the African-American community first and the rest of the city second. The players knew. Willie Gardner recalled, "We were taught from day one that if we did anything stupid, then the whole school and [Negro] community would suffer."[41] For teenage boys to carry the hopes of the community on their shoulders must have been an awesome responsibility. City newspapers commented frequently on the importance of race. The two largest dailies and the *Indianapolis Recorder* agreed that Attucks's standing as a "black school" should not sway city residents' emotions one way or another. Stating the obvious, yet underestimating the attachment African Americans had to the school, the papers affirmed that Attucks was part of Indianapolis.

Yet race could not be ignored. The *Indianapolis Recorder* considered Attucks's success as nothing less than a referendum on race relations in the city. Noting that Attucks's brilliant basketball play had aroused a "veritable tidal wave of interracial democracy," the editor believed he saw the hand of God when he wrote, "Where the appeals of religion, reason and education seem to have fallen on deaf ears, the spectacle of brilliant basketball has turned the trick. In deep humility we observe that God does move in mysterious ways."[42] It was indeed mysterious to see Indianapolis whites cheering Attucks, but the *Recorder* also questioned how widespread had been God's work. It asked whether Hallie Bryant, the team's versatile forward, would be able to get a job as easily as he garnered rebounds and whether Will "Dill" Gardner would be able to move as freely around Indianapolis as he did on the basketball court.[43]

The editors were not trying to mock the team's newest fans. Rather, they sought to extend the significance of the team's success to every facet of African-American life. This team, whose members came from middle-class families as well as from families who could not afford tickets to see the tournament games, stood poised to be an agent of significant change. An advertisement placed by a group of interracial city leaders evinced the broad range of concerns the Tigers addressed:

> For the sake of the school, the improvement of race relations and friendly attitudes among all groups and the boosting of community morale, we heartily cheer for Attucks. And bless this team with our best wishes for a victory that will give us our first state high school basketball championship.[44]

No longer playing at the Dust Bowl for bragging rights over which side of town produced the best basketball players, the team was now supposed to improve race relations and boost the community's morale.

Despite the blessing of city leaders, Coach Ray Crowe understood that winning the championship might harm race relations in Indianapolis.[45] Crowe and some administrators at Attucks feared that Indianapolis was not ready to embrace the Attucks Tigers as its team. Whites needed more time to adjust to this all-black team from the city's west side. Perhaps if Attucks's ascendancy had not been so rapid, Indianapolis might have become accustomed to the basketball power in its midst. But there had been no previous indication that the Tigers were going to steamroller through the 1951 regular season. It was, after all, Crowe's first season as head coach. No other city high school team would have been saddled with the charge to improve race relations. No other team required an official administrative blessing. It is furthermore doubtful whether another team would have required city residents to become accustomed to its title run. Attucks's run to the championship was as direct an assault on racial inequality as had been staged in the city. By the conclusion of the sectionals, city residents knew that they had a new basketball power in their midst; by the time semi-state arrived, that very same team was labeled an ambassador for race relations.[46]

Anointing new ambassadors to fight for increased civic freedoms in Indianapolis was an unusual happenstance. The political culture of the black community had been identified and well entrenched for many years.[47] Few commentators could argue that black leaders, whether Democrat or Republican, secular or ministerial, were radical protesters. Thurgood Marshall, director of the NAACP legal defense fund, had hoped that Indianapolis would be the site for a legal case testing the constitutionality of segregated schools, the issue for which Topeka, Kansas, became famous. African-American leaders from the city and state rejected Marshall's appeal, instead resting their hopes on the legislative process.[48] Such a response was consistent with the manner of change in Indianapolis. Rarely did African Americans forcefully demand change; rather, blacks and whites met frequently within interracial organizations, including political parties, to negotiate change in the Hoosier capital. Negotiating change in such a manner brought agonizingly slow, incremental progress—and sometimes no progress at all. Segregation was the rule in housing, education, church bodies, and most social environments.[49] Frequent and sometimes frank discussions at interracial forums led many whites in Indianapolis to believe that race relations in the city were good. In adopting such a belief, whites were guilty of what William Chafe has labeled the "progressive mystique." They confused dialogue with action.[50] Blacks, too, were accustomed to the process of political negotiation. Their interaction with the city's leadership was marked by its civility. For too long, African Americans believed that repeated appeals to friendly whites would bring desired change.

In offering Attucks as an example of the community's readiness for full participation in civic affairs, blacks were on the cusp of forming a new political strategy. Breaking with their tradition of relying on interracial coalition building, they now offered to go it alone by showing their deservingness. However, they were not cutting all ties to established practices. Attucks players shelved their wide-open and flashy game during the tournament and instead played a more traditional, and slow, basketball style. In so doing, they made themselves recognizable to Indianapolis basketball fans and, by extension, proved that the dismantling of racial restrictions would not dangerously change the city's landscape. Their play and self-reliance spoke to a new front where blacks ascribed political meaning to their public activities and achievements. Moreover, they adhered to the longstanding precept in African-American political protest that rights and freedom would accrue to those who acted respectfully and courteously. In other words, rights would extend to those who showed they deserved them.[51]

Russell Lane, the school's principal, and Coach Crowe emphasized sportsmanship, rather than winning, during the week leading up to the finals. Stressing sportsmanship was not necessary to this team. The players had presented no disciplinary problems and had conducted themselves admirably during the tournament even when referees seemed to favor the other team. They had gone into hostile environments and never violently engaged opposing teams or their fans. Lane was afraid, however, that the team's victory would make players and students too aggressive. He echoed the concern of others that parity on the basketball court might lead to demands for parity in other parts of society.[52] The question, a constant in developing strategy for African-American protest, was what approach would bring advancement. Perhaps author James Baldwin best characterized the dilemma facing African-American protesters, and ironically, he found the dilemma represented in sport. On assignment for the men's magazine *Nugget,* Baldwin covered the championship fight between Floyd Patterson, then heavyweight boxing champion, and the challenger, Sonny Liston, who most people, President John Kennedy and the NAACP leadership among them, considered a dangerous brute. Baldwin admired both men and was torn over whom to support. Baldwin wrote,

> I felt terribly ambivalent, as many Negroes do these days since we are all trying to decide, in one way or another, which attitude, in our terrible American dilemma, is the more effective: the disciplined sweetness of Floyd, or the outspoken intransigence of Liston. . . . Liston is a man aching for respect and responsibility. Sometimes we grow into our responsibilities and sometimes, of course, we fail them.[53]

Lane appeared to represent those who favored the disciplined sweetness of negotiation and compromise. Forceful, incessant demands may have destroyed years of interracial coalition building and white goodwill. Either the team could be a spearhead for change or merely another example leaders could point to when displaying the African-American community's civility. Others, most notably Starling James, president of the Federation of Associated Clubs (FAC), wanted the team to represent a new direction in African-American protest in Indianapolis.[54] James wanted a new style characterized by the same unified, competitive, and winning qualities the team possessed.

While some contemplated the importance and significance of the team's activities, the boys still had games to play. Lane ventured to the team's locker room before the semifinal game against Evansville Reitz. The fans were in a near frenzy as they awaited the team's arrival on the court.[55] The players struggled to hear their principal over the noise coming from the stands above. Lane reminded the boys of their uneasy position as ambassadors. "You are representing much more than your school," Lane said. "You are black Indianapolis. This time the whole state is watching. More important than winning is that you demonstrate good sportsmanship. Be gentlemen."[56] A curious pep talk to be sure, but it reminded the players that they were playing more than a game.

It is difficult to know for sure how many players adhered to Lane's admonition. One player, Bob Jewell, won the Trester Award that goes every year to the tournament player who best exhibits "scholar-athlete-citizen" qualities. The player he was guarding in the semifinal, Jerry Whitesell, led Reitz with nineteen points. Perhaps Jewell, who came from a middle-class family, had heard Lane too well. With most of black Indianapolis at the Butler Fieldhouse for the game, or listening to the proceedings on radio or watching on television, Crispus Attucks lost to Evansville Reitz, 66–59, in the afternoon session of the state final. Crowe realized after the game that talk of sportsmanship, and perhaps the actions of the referees, had reined in his Tigers. Years later, he recalled, "We were not ready, and that was my fault. I made up my mind right then that we would be back, and the next time we would be ready."[57] However, no one accused the Attucks players of acting rudely. In the end, they did not bring disrespect to their community, but they did not provide them with a trophy either.

Many in Indianapolis seemed not to mind that the boys came back without the championship trophy. Henry T. Ice, president of the Indianapolis Chamber of Commerce, stood at a posttournament rally to declare, "Indianapolis proudly claims you as its own." Phillip L. Bayt, a Democratic Party leader and mayor, followed Ice and added, "You're still champions as far as we in Indianapolis are concerned. You displayed honor and sportsmanship.

We would have much better citizens if all were as clean as you Attucks players."[58] The *Indianapolis Recorder* said it all with a headline: "Attucks Tigers Lose; But City's Civic Spirit Rises."[59] Starling James spoke bluntly to the team when he said, "Sportsmanship cost you the game."[60] James, a relative newcomer to the city, having lived in Indianapolis only twenty-one years, had long been frustrated by the black community's unwillingness to fight forcefully for change. Watching Attucks lose at the hands of suspicious referees was one thing, but to add to the complicity by being too mannerly was more than he could take. Their conciliatory posture reminded him too much of the pose adopted by the larger African-American community. The team's conciliation was a lost opportunity to confront directly unequal civic freedoms among Indianapolis residents. The contrasting comments offered by white and black commentators also hinted at the uneasiness with which many whites in Indianapolis came to support Attucks. Whites and blacks supported Attucks's run, but it appeared that whites were more wary in their acceptance, as if supporting the team was part of a civic responsibility.

However, not all was lost. Attucks's run at the championship caused Indianapolis residents to look at themselves in a way that they had not done previously. School desegregation efforts continued, and by 1953, the school board announced that desegregation was complete. This announcement was truthful but not entirely accurate. At the time, about two-thirds of the city's student population attended integrated schools. Whites were minorities in only four schools, and two of the four had only one white student. The *Indianapolis Times* was emboldened to counsel southern states to accept desegregation with little worry. Indianapolis had proven that desegregation could be attained peacefully if done correctly. The *Indianapolis News* reported no "major upheavals" associated with desegregation.[61] The Attucks team had clearly assuaged white anxiety. Herman Shibler, superintendent of Indianapolis public schools and a vocal critic of the school board's foot-dragging on desegregation, assessed the significance of Attucks's run for the championship: "That basketball team accomplished more for race relations in one season than you could accomplish in ten years of forums and discussions. The white people here have a completely new impression of the colored race. It's marvelous."[62]

Angelo Angelopolous, a white reporter for the *Indianapolis News*, placed Attucks's achievement in perspective. He argued that eventually the 1951 team would be best known for its contribution to society and its conscience.

> In its march through the state high school basketball tournament the impact made by Attucks' tremendously talented team took on the aspects of a social revolution in this city of heavy Negro population. The force of Attucks ability alone in the beginning carried along a considerable number of fans here, but the spiritual impetus Attucks provided with its conduct compounded its converts until when 2:30 P.M. came last Saturday there were thousands of sad hearts in Indianapolis belonging to people who wouldn't have felt so a month before. . . . The thing the 1950–51 Attucks team may eventually be known for—its long step toward making Indianapolis one town.[63]

The remaining question is whether these players, and their efforts, really did help to transform Indianapolis. Were Indianapolis residents able, as Angelopolous dreamed, to demolish the walls that divided their community? While efforts to desegregate Indianapolis schools continued, both a state law and the isolated position Indianapolis occupied among other cities in Indiana fueled those efforts. As more and more high schools traveled to the state finals with racially integrated teams, it was harder for Indianapolis to defend its lonely segregationist position.

In the substantive areas of housing and employment, municipal leaders made fewer efforts toward including blacks in the city's prosperity. A World War II–era survey found that a full 60.5 percent of the African-American families surveyed had tried to secure better housing. Faced with a public housing system that was clearly overwhelmed, and blocked from moving into areas where there was housing available, blacks were effectively bottled up.[64] While black leaders urged open housing laws, a housing authority with the ability to censure absentee landlords, and increased public housing, the city offered an inadequate self-help program whereby blacks built homes on land provided by the city.[65]

The labor arena was equally undisturbed by Attacks's tournament run. While striving for more desirable jobs, African Americans, in large measure, were relegated to menial positions. Notwithstanding many initiatives to alter that reality, that situation held through the 1960s. One respondent to a survey conducted by Flanner House in 1938 prophesied accurately when talking of her children's future in the 1950s: "Well, they'll just be laborers, that's about all. They are too young yet, and I've just about given up. It has been so hard."[66] The absence of a National Urban League (NUL) chapter hampered the advancement of Indianapolis's black workers. One of the most important functions of the NUL was the tracking and documenting of black workers and their condition. Those who opposed the establishment of an Urban League chapter pointed to Flanner House and the Association for Merit Employment, a private, nonprofit organization founded by the Quaker's American Friends Service Committee in 1952 immediately after Attacks's fantastic tournament run, as examples of voluntary, cooperative initiatives to increase African-American employment.[67]

In the four years between 1951 and 1955, when Attucks made another run for the state basketball championship, white Indianapolis residents were able to accept the Attucks basketball team as their best chance for victory at the state level. It would have been difficult to judge otherwise, since Attucks dominated city play in the intervening years.[68] Given the limited advancement in pressing social arenas, however, it is clear that white residents were able to compartmentalize their feelings concerning African Americans. Whites saw no hypocrisy in cheering for Attucks as an Indianapolis team while simultaneously denying African Americans full participation in civic affairs. In 1951, African American spokesmen hoped to use Attucks's exploits as a wedge to improve race relations in the city. Four years later, there was little hope that sport would provide the full remedy African Americans sought.

In 1955, led by Oscar Robertson, Flap's younger and immensely talented brother, Crispus Attacks won the first of two consecutive state basketball championships. The players brought neither disrespect nor dishonor to their community, but they did bring a championship trophy. By the time Oscar Robertson led the Tigers, Indianapolis residents no longer wondered whether the team represented them. Instead, they acted as did any other community whose team reached the highest levels of the tournament. The team members were no longer interlopers intruding on a private party; rather, they were fellow Indianapolis citizens. In 1955, Attucks's players were not reined in with concerns about the civility of their play, for they played with seeming abandon. Crowe had vowed that the next time they reached the finals his players would be ready. They were. But so was Indianapolis—more ready than it had been in 1951. Suzanne Mitten-Owen, a white Shortridge student in 1955, recalled that the state championship that Attucks won in 1955 brought a "pride to the whole city which I think helped break down a lot of the color barriers because those kids belonged to Indianapolis."[69] Whites had resolved their ambivalent feelings about Attucks and its black players. They had done so by compartmentalizing their feelings about blacks and their athletic prowess. Robertson noted the changed climate from when his brother played on the 1951 team:

> We became the team. The city team. It wasn't Crispus Attucks at the final game. It was Indianapolis Attucks. . . . Attucks being successful in basketball really gave people a lot better outlook on life. There was not much for blacks to look forward to except going to jobs with a dead end door.[70]

While blacks worked to open the "dead end" door, they took rest from their labor in cheering Attucks's basketball team. The team helped sustain African Americans in their fight to enjoy the fruits of citizenship more fully. The feeling in the African-American community for Attucks's basketball team had never been ambivalent. Attucks continued to be a cultural haven for the black community. African Americans continued to rest their hopes on a group of young men who represented them in open competition with whites. In doing so, they reaffirmed and validated themselves. Blacks from all over Indianapolis, whatever their neighborhood or their length of stay in the city, regardless of class or education, irrespective of occupation or station, rallied around the basketball team. Sport, then, was poised, as Randy Roberts claims, at the "intersection of art and politics, community and finance."[71] At a time when so much about life in Indianapolis was bleak, sports provided a relief. The player representatives sustained a community.

Despite an *Indianapolis Recorder* editorial that noticed that brilliant basketball had succeeded where religion, reason, and education had failed, one can find little immediate improvement in the laboring, housing, and political conditions that blacks endured.[72] However, it may be wrong to look for immediate change in Indianapolis. James H. Madison has argued that Indiana's brand of change was more "evolutionary than revolutionary."[73] What is more evident is that the negotiation between blacks and whites over the construction of their city was not going to be decided on the strength of a high school basketball team. Sport unified them in their athletic opposition to other regions of the state, but the entrenched customs within the city were too strong to be overthrown by sport success.

Nevertheless, a high school sporting event revealed to many city members that there was no danger in lowering some racial barriers throughout the city. Attucks's success made the black community relevant in civic affairs to a political leadership that had long found them irrelevant to the city's political economy. While popular culture found along Indiana Avenue in nightclubs and saloons may have provided an opportunity for escape and rejuvenation, it was on the basketball hardwood that a form of popular culture had a moral connotation that resonated beyond the black community to the city at large. The 1951 Attucks basketball team members were agents of change in a city that altered its course very gradually.

NOTES

1. For insight into the status of race relations in Indianapolis and similarly situated northern cities, see Emma Lou Thornbrough, "Segregation in Indiana during the Klan Era of the 1920's," *Mississippi Valley Historical Review* 47, no. 4 (1961): 594–6; Kenneth Kusmer, "The Black Urban Experience" in Darlene Clark Hine, ed. *The State of Afro-American History: Past, Present, and Future* (Baton Rouge: Louisiana State University Press, 1986), 119; Richard B. Pierce, "Beneath the Surface: African-

American Community Life in Indianapolis, 1945–1970" (Ph. D. diss., Indiana University, 1996); Warren E. Stickle, "Black Political Participation in Indianapolis: 1966–1972," Indiana Academy of the Social Sciences, *Proceedings,* 1974, 3rd series, IX: 114–5. Perhaps Steve Hardy put it best when urging scholars to analyze the negotiations between white and black sports participants and communities. "Most clubs were not heterogeneous communities; rather, they served to sort identities, even within minority cultures." Steven Hardy. "Sport in Urbanizing America: A Historical Review," *Journal of Urban History* 23 (September 1997): 694–5.

2. Robin D. G. Kelley went even further in detailing the significance of leisure among African-American workers in the South. For Kelley, the places that blacks played—clubs and blues halls, parties and dance rooms—were where they recuperated from their labor and found the strength to endure. It was in these "spaces of pleasure" that the solidarity later shown at political mass meetings formed. Ignoring complaints from religious leaders and the black middle class, African Americans packed nightspots on Friday and Saturday night. Robin D. G. Kelley, " 'We Are Not What We Seem': Rethinking Black Working Class Opposition in the Jim Crow South," *Journal of American History* 80, no. 1 (1993): 75–112.

3. Scholars have frequently defined a community by hallmarks such as family, historic preservations, religious beliefs, neighborhoods, and social organizations. Recreational activities are equally important, although less frequently discussed. Within urban environments, where, how, and with whom recreational activities occurred were not always determined by choice. Such was the case in Indianapolis, where a strict legal code created, among other things, segregated public parks, swimming pools, and theater seating. Where the law did not dictate, racial and ethnic groups frequently segregated themselves at churches, nightclubs, and other seemingly public places, such as basketball arenas. See Allan H. Spear, *Black Chicago: The Making of a Negro Ghetto, 1890–1920* (Chicago: University of Chicago Press, 1967); Gilbert Osofsky, *Harlem: The Making of a Ghetto* (New York: Harper & Row, 1963); Arnold R. Hirsch, *Making the Second Ghetto: Race and Housing in Chicago, 1940–1960* (Cambridge, UK: Cambridge University Press, 1983).

4. Quoted in Richard O. Davies, *America's Obsession: Sports and Society Since 1945* (New York: Harcourt Brace, 1994). 103.

5. The positive characteristics of participation in sports lessened as African-American involvement grew. For a fuller discussion of the debate surrounding black college entry into intercollegiate sports, see Patrick B. Miller, "To 'Bring the Race along Rapidly': Sport, Student Culture and Educational Mission at Historically Black Colleges during the Interwar Years," *History of Education Quarterly* 35, no. 2 (1995): 111–33. For a discussion on the varying definitions of manhood, see Gail Bederman, *Manliness and Civilization: A Cultural History of Gender and Race in the United States, 1880–1917* (Chicago: University of Chicago Press, 1995).

6. The perception held by whites that there were a large number of African Americans in their midst was not unfounded. Indianapolis had the highest percentage of blacks in total population among the twelve largest Midwestern cities.

7. When arguing that African-American schoolchildren, in a segregated school, would prosper academically and take more pride in their work, white parents ironically prefigured an argument used by modern-day proponents of separate schools.

8. It was not until 1949 that the Indiana State Legislature passed a law prohibiting segregation based on race. Indianapolis activists were instrumental in getting the law enacted, but they were depressed with the desegregation plan adopted by the Indianapolis Board of School Commissioners. Pierce, "Beneath the Surface," 53–8.

9. The *Indianapolis Recorder* began operation in 1887 and continues weekly service to this day as the third largest African-American–focused newspaper in the United States. Prior to the *Recorder*'s appearance, Indianapolis had three other black-owned newspapers, the *World,* the *Leader,* and the *Freeman.* The *Freeman* ceased publication in 1898 and the *World* closed its doors in 1925. George Stewart created the *Recorder* in part, as a counterweight to George Knox's *Indianapolis Freeman* and to devote more space to Indianapolis events, a perceived weakness of the *Freeman.* Knox was viewed by some as a political opportunist out to curry favor with Republican Party bosses. But once the *Recorder* became the sole black newspaper in the city, it lost some of its partisan flavor and turned its gaze instead on championing increased civil rights and African-American representation on decision-making boards. In the ensuing years, the *Recorder* was an effective vehicle for articulating African-American concerns. It rarely failed to urge controversial actions even when its editorial opinion was unpopular. Pierce, "Beneath the Surface," 68; *Indianapolis Recorder,* August 6, 1927.

10. *Indianapolis Recorder,* August 6, 1927; January 1, 1949.

11. Joseph Taylor, interview by author, tape recording, Indianapolis, Indiana, March 5, 1994.

12. Willard Ransom interview by author, tape recording, Indianapolis, Indiana, March 12, 1994; Emma Lou Thornbrough, *Indianapolis Story* (Indianapolis: Indiana Historical Society, 1995), 43.

13. David Stoelk, director: "Indy in the 50's" (produced by WFYI Television, Indianapolis, Indiana, 1995).

14. *Ibid.*

15. *Indianapolis Magazine,* May 1972, p. 33a. Although many Indianapolis blacks have memories similar to Howard Owens's, an *Indianapolis News* article in 1949 was headlined "Avenue Not Social Hub for Negroes." The lights on Indiana Avenue were beginning to dim. It was still the heart of the community in the 1950s, but it was revered more for its past than its present. In their search for entertainment in a blacks-only environment, African Americans turned to a "myriad of private clubs, social orders, fraternities and sororities." In so doing, they recreated the class-conscious environment the Avenue had promised to alleviate. *Indianapolis News,* November 18, 1949.

16. Lockefield Gardens (LG) was a 784-unit public housing complex solely inhabited by African Americans. Developed in 1937 by the Housing Division of the Federal Emergency Administration of Public Works and the Advisory Committee on Housing of Indianapolis, LG was in the center of Indianapolis's oldest black neighborhood and only a few blocks from Crispus Attucks. In its design and site plan, LG was the model for public housing projects across the United States. Unlike many housing projects that followed, LG was a community of more than simple residential structures; the plan included an elementary school, a play yard, and ample living space between and behind apartment buildings.

17. *Indianapolis Recorder,* March 17, 1951.

18. Scholars have noted recreation's importance in the creation of community—mostly in its impact on working-class popular culture. In his study of Worcester, Massachusetts, Roy Rosenzweig emphasized that knowledge of the leisure activities of the city's working class would enable scholars to understand more fully how workers viewed themselves and society. Workers fought to establish an eight-hour workday in order to leave time for socializing without the censure or permission of an overbearing middle class. Their victory in achieving their goal displayed conflicts in culture and class relationship for when they played, they did so in the fashion in which they lived—racial and ethnic groups separated from each other, men separated from women, workers from people of means. See Gerald R. Gems, *Windy City Wars: Labor, Leisure, and Sport in the Making of Chicago* (Lanham, MD: Scarecrow, 1997); John Hoberman, *Darwin's Athletes: How Sport Has Damaged Black America and Preserved the Myth of Race* (Boston: Houghton Mifflin, 1997); Rob Ruck, *Sandlot Seasons: Sport in Black Pittsburgh* (Urbana: University of Illinois Press, 1987); David Nasaw, *Going Out: The Rise and Fall of Public Amusements* (New York: Basic Books, 1993); Roy Rosenzweig, *Eight Hours for What We Will* (Cambridge, UK: Cambridge University Press, 1983); Kenneth L. Shropshire, *In Black and White: Race and Sports in America* (New York: New York University Press, 1996).

19. Ruck, *Sandlot Seasons,* 14.

20. In the official handbook of the organization, a notice to members read, "Do not compete with Indiana public High Schools that are non-members nor with public High Schools in other states that are not members of their state associations:" *The Indiana High School Athletic Association. Handbook and Report of the Board of Control,* 1928.

21. Constitution of Indiana High School Athletic Association. Article 2 (Membership), sections 1–3, 1904.

22. Ray Crowe interview, "IUPUI: The Evolution of an Urban University" Indiana University, Purdue University at Indianapolis, Special Collections.

23. *The Indiana High School Athletic Association. Handbook and Report of the Board of Control,* 1942, 148.

24. Crowe interview. Perhaps the reception given to Attucks by rural teams is further evidence of the claim made by cultural critic Nelson George, who argues that the Black aesthetic displayed in jazz music, individual virtuosity in an ensemble, was ably represented by basketball players who broke from the regimented, stationary style synonymous with 1950s-era basketball. Nelson George, *Elevating the Game* (New York: HarperCollins, 1992), 60–3.

25. Until very recently, Indiana did not classify its high schools by enrollment. It was typical for the field to include more than 750 schools in the single elimination tournament. Davies, *America's Obsession,* 104–6.

26. *Indianapolis Star,* March 1, 1951; March 5, 1951.

27. Stoelk, "Indy in the 50's."

28. The Indiana tournament proceeded from a sectional that usually included one or two counties to a regional that was held at sixteen locations around the state. The third round, the semi-state, held at four locations, produced the final four

teams that would compete at the state finals. Only the winners of each stage advanced to the next level. In the end, generally speaking, there was a representative from the northern, eastern, western, and southern parts of the state.

29. The peculiar plan for desegregation in Indianapolis called for integration to occur one grade at a time beginning with kindergarten. Students would attend the high school where their elementary school directed them prior to the 1949 law. If the distance of that high school from the student's home was greater than two miles, the school board would entertain appeals for a change.

30. *Indianapolis Star,* March 1, 1951.

31. The area directly north and northwest of downtown Indianapolis is called Pat Ward's Bottom. The Bottoms, so named because it was close to the canals, was also near Indiana Avenue.

32. *Indianapolis News,* March 2, 1951; March 6, 1951.

33. *Indianapolis Star,* March 5, 1951.

34. Randy Roberts, "The Shot," *Traces* 9, no. 3 (1997): 7.

35. Flap Robertson is the older brother of National Basketball Association Hall of Fame player Oscar Robertson.

36. Roberts, "The Shot," 6–8; *Indianapolis Star,* March 5, 6, and 7, 1951; *Indianapolis Recorder* March 10 and 17, 1951; Stoelk, "Indy in the 50's"; Crowe interview.

37. *Indianapolis Star,* March 5, 1951.

38. *Indianapolis Recorder,* March 17, 1951.

39. *Indianapolis Star,* March 12, 1951.

40. *Indianapolis Star,* March 3, 1951. One disgruntled Indianapolis resident complained in a letter to the *Indianapolis News.* "Why, or why can't we get something different on our radios these days? Nothing but 'sectionals' everywhere I turn the dial. For those who like basketball, fine—but everyone simply can't like the same things, and I know of several who are disgusted when they can't get anything else from so many stations. And after the sectionals, then other games are to be forced on us." *Indianapolis News,* March 5, 1951.

41. Roberts, "The Shot," 11.

42. *Indianapolis Recorder,* March 17, 1951.

43. *Ibid.*

44. *Ibid.*

45. Roberts, "The Shot," 11

46. Pierce, "Beneath the Surface," 29.

47. *Ibid.,* 67–73.

48. *Ibid.,* 106–12.

49. To an outsider, it may have appeared that Indianapolis's black residents were complacent in their acceptance of unequal and discriminatory treatment. Beneath the surface, however, a fierce battle was taking place over the structure and culture of the city. The battle was especially difficult for an outsider to notice because it took place in meeting rooms, at the state house, and in the courts. It was not a conflict that transpired on the sheets or was shouted through a bullhorn. African-American resistance was conducted under rules long established by Indianapolis citizens. Both black and white newspapers in the 1950s and 1960s were concerned with the potential violence that social inequities could spawn. Many editorialists agreed that it was communication between the races that prevented violence from erupting in Indianapolis. Pierce, "Beneath the Surface," 29.

50. William H. Chafe, *Civilities and Civil Rights: Greensboro, North Carolina and the Black Struggle for Freedom* (New York: Oxford University Press, 1980), 6–9.

51. Kevin Gaines, *Uplifting the Race: Black Leadership, Politics, and Culture in the Twentieth Century* (Chapel Hill: University of North Carolina Press, 1996), 16.

52. George, *Elevating the Game,* 119–20.

53. Found in David Remnick, *King of the World* (New York: Vintage, 1998), 18–22. Quotation is on page 22.

54. Starling James settled in Indianapolis in 1927, ironically just as the city was about to institute segregated secondary education. He began his organizing efforts soon after settling in by forming the While-Away Bridge Club. Struck by the number of black social clubs in the city, James called together the leaders of nine of these clubs in 1937 and the Federation of Associated Clubs (FAC) was born. James created the FAC in the face of strong opposition from certain segments of the black community. Black social clubs were under attack as being worthless and proponents of class distinctions. James and the members of the FAC did consider themselves promoters of middle-class values. James wanted to educate the black community to uphold similar values, and he subsequently published a series of articles, titled "Guide Right," to help popularize and define his views. James was hardly a cultural radical and in fact admonished blacks for "detrimental behavior that reflected unfavorably on the entire black community." In James's view, blacks were at least partly responsible for their circumstance. "We are not as polite and courteous to others as we should be. Manners are one of the prerequisites of an outstanding personality. Also, some of us are rather crude and loud. We must cultivate softness in our voice." James wanted

to show that clubs could do something for the larger community.

The FAC was one of die most successful organizations in the city. James was able to demonstrate that social clubs did not have to be self-serving. Within ten years of incorporation, the number of groups belonging to the FAC had grown to 125. The FAC's stated purpose was to promote social, civic, and economic benefits for the black community. Throughout his long tenure as president (1937–1969), James kept the FAC intimately involved with some of the more pressing political issues in the post–World War II period. In many ways, the FAC was the most progressive umbrella group in Indianapolis. Pierce, "Beneath the Surface," 50–2.

55. Mrs. Rosa Tolliver, mother of Attucks guard Joe Tolliver, was not among the crowd. Her family would not allow her to watch from the stands because she had almost passed out during the Anderson game. *Indianapolis Recorder,* March 24, 1951.

56. Roberts, "The Shot," 13.

57. Bob Williams, *Hoosier Hysteria! Indiana High School Basketball* (South Bend, IN: Hardwood, 1997), 42.

58. *Indianapolis Recorder,* March 24, 1951.

59. *Ibid.*

60. *Ibid.,* March 31, 1951.

61. Quoted in Thornbrough, *Indianapolis Story,* 136; *Indianapolis Times,* October 10, 1954; *Indianapolis News,* November 30, 1953; Thornbrough, *Indianapolis Story,* 129.

62. *Indianapolis Recorder,* March 31, 1951.

63. *Indianapolis News,* March 20, 1951.

64. Eugenia J. Hollis, "A Critical Analysis of Seventeen Studies of Housing Conducted in Indianapolis from 1935 to 1946" (Ph. D. diss., Indiana University, 1947), 5–22. Flanner House studied 1,501 families out of a total black population of 51,142. The study examined the following areas: physical condition, degree of overcrowding, types of lighting, toilet facilities, heating facilities, and water supply. The study presents a reliable picture of the kind of housing being occupied by blacks. Flanner House, *Flanner House and the Negro Community* (Indianapolis: Flanner House, 1939). The Works Progress Administration (WPA) reported that 23,000 families were living in substandard dwelling units. The study found that out of the total 110,003 residential units on which detailed information was obtained, 15,323, or 14 percent, needed major repair or were unfit for use. Of these, 13,331 units, or 86 percent, were tenant occupied. Fourteen percent of the population was living in physically substandard housing, and a large majority of these families were tenants. *Real Property and Low Income Housing Surveys,* vol. 1 (WPA, 1939), 42. *Population and Housing Statistics for Census Tracts: 1940,* by the U.S. Bureau of the Census, included figures that showed an even greater proportion of substandard housing than in the WPA report. In the 1940 census, 104,928 units of the 116,598 dwelling units in Indianapolis were reported on in detail. Of the reported units, 18,523, or 17.6 percent, were classified as "needing major repair" (p. 3).

65. Pierce, "Beneath the Surface," 154–9.

66. Walter Maddux Collection, Manuscript 510, Box 2, Folder 9, Indiana Historical Society, Indianapolis.

67. The Quaker's American Friends Service Committee founded the Association for Merit Employment (AME) in 1952 as the Job Opportunity Program. Its purpose was the breakdown and eradication of race-specific jobs. AME, Box 1, Folder 4, Indiana Historical Society, Indianapolis.

AME's creation was significant because it was the first group in Indianapolis to focus solely on job opportunities for African Americans. Composed of local retail and industrial executives, AME dedicated itself to working with management, labor, and other affected groups and agencies in spreading the policy and practice of employing and upgrading the "best qualified applicant for each vacancy regardless of applicant's race, religion or national origin." Operating on a purely cooperative basis, AME responded to job discrimination and unemployment by convincing Indianapolis business owners that fair employment was in the city's best interest. AME's method was to invite companies to place personnel directors or other executives involved in hiring and promotion on the committee and have them lead the effort to find employment for black workers in their companies. It was able to attract some of the largest, best known employers in the city. L. S. Ayres and William Block's (both local retail department stores); RCA, producer of electronic products; Lilly Pharmaceuticals; and Allison, manufacturers of engines and transmissions, were represented on the committee. The committee also collected and disseminated information pertaining to jobs in the community open to all races, counseled training agencies on employment opportunities for members of minority groups, and encouraged local businesses to develop and use the special skills and talents of minority members.

AME became so entrenched and central to Indianapolis's labor efforts that it eventually became part of the United Fund of Greater Indianapolis. Indeed, William L. Schloss, vice-president of admissions for the United Fund of Greater Indianapolis, denied funding to establish a National Urban League chapter on the grounds that Flanner House and AME adequately served the African-American community. Although white city officials cited AME's efforts as satisfactory, AME records indicate otherwise. In 1963, AME could find jobs for only seventy-six African Americans who applied to it for assistance. In 1964, even more job hunters filed applications, but in this last year of its operation, AME could place only 64 of the 636 applicants. Despite the visible presence of AME, the organization was ill-equipped for the task. Merely making employers aware of a supply of trained potential employees did not ease unemployment for African-American workers. AME eventually led the fight to bring the Urban League to Indianapolis because even AME found its record unsatisfactory. AME collection, Indiana Historical Society, Indianapolis; Pierce, "Beneath the Surface," 176–80.

68. Between 1951 and 1956, Crispus Attucks, under Ray Crowe and assistant coach Al Spurlock, won 153 games against only 14 losses. They won forty-five consecutive games from the 1954–1955 season until the end of the 1956 season. They won the state championship in 1955, 1956, and again in 1959.

69. Stoelk, "Indy in the 50's."

70. *Ibid.*

71. Roberts, "The Shot," 9.

72. William T. Ray, president of Ray Realty, told a meeting of 175 real estate brokers, lenders, contractors, and civil rights workers from all over Indiana at the governor's conference on discrimination in housing in 1963 that "Negro home seekers have no freedom of choice." Of the "4,500 single family now and used residences offered for sale recently in the Indianapolis area, only 100 were available to Negroes." Rental opportunities were worse. No single major apartment complex housing whites had one black resident. Quoted in Juliet Saltman, *A Fragile Movement: The Struggle for Neighborhood Stabilization* (New York: Greenwood, 1990), 48. Indianapolis advocates had preached voluntary, conciliatory mediation while working to strengthen state laws prohibiting worker discrimination, but they were fighting with worn-out weapons. The piecemeal benefit won were effectively useless in improving the day-to-day job conditions of African Americans or providing access to high-paying union jobs or apprentice programs. But this approach might have been successful in staving off white community unrest—a goal long advocated by employers. Consequently, the one-note song sung by African-American employees in 1941 was still hummed in 1970. African Americans worked, but the jobs they held and the opportunities they encountered were governed by the prevailing racism in Indianapolis. Pierce, "Beneath the Surface," 222.

73. James H. Madison, *The Indiana Way: A State History* (Indianapolis: Indiana University Press, 1990).

GARY PUBLIC LIBRARY

11

"CINDERELLAS" OF SPORT
Black Women in Track and Field

Susan Cahn

AFTER WORLD WAR II forced the cancellation of the 1940 and 1944 Olympic Games, Olympic competition resumed in 1948, hosted by London. Although England remained in a state of grim disrepair, the performance of three female track-and-field athletes shone through the bleakness of the postwar European setting. Francina "Fanny" Blankers-Koen, competing for the Netherlands, won an astounding four gold medals with victories in the one hundred- and two hundred-meter sprints, the eighty-meter hurdles, and four hundred-meter relay. The Dutch athlete was heralded not only for her medals but for achieving her success as an adult married woman—a full-time housewife and the mother of two children. Among Europeans her fame was rivaled only by the French athlete Micheline Ostermeyer, winner of gold medals in the shot put and discus and a bronze in the high jump. Ostermeyer, in addition to her athletic excellence, was a concert pianist whose musical ability and middle-class background marked her as a "respectable" woman in a sport many perceived as unwomanly.[1] The third athlete was Alice Coachman, a high jumper from Albany, Georgia. As a track and basketball star for Tuskegee Institute, Coachman had established a reputation as the premier black woman athlete of the 1940s. Her single gold medal in the high jump could not match the totals of Blankers-Koen or Ostermeyer. Nevertheless, it was historically significant, both as the only individual track-and-field medal won by U.S. women and, more important, as the first medal ever received by a woman of African descent.

The superlative performances of these three Olympic champions earned them only momentary glory in the United States. Their names quickly faded from public view, overshadowed by male Olympians and athletes like Barbara Ann Scott, the Canadian Olympic figure-skating champion, whose sport earned far more attention and approval than women's track and field. Track athletics, like basketball, had excited enormous public interest as a women's sport in the 1920s and early 1930s. But even more so than basketball, track had fallen victim to negative media coverage and organized efforts to eliminate it from school and international competition.

By midcentury the sport had a reputation as a "masculine" endeavor unsuited to feminine athletes. Few American women participated, and those who did endured caricatures as amazons and muscle molls. In this climate, despite the temporary enthusiasm inspired by the female champions of 1948, Olympic governing bodies of the 1950s once again considered eliminating several women's track-and-field events from the games because they were "not truly feminine."[2]

In the discussions that followed, Olympic official Norman Cox sarcastically proposed that rather than ban women's events, the International Olympic Committee (IOC) should create a special category of competition for the unfairly advantaged "hermaphrodites" who regularly defeated "normal" women, those less-skilled "child-bearing" types with "largish breasts, wide hips, [and] knocked knees."[3] This outrageous but prescient recommendation (the IOC instituted anatomical sex checks in 1967, followed by mandatory chromosome testing of women athletes) placed a new spin on a familiar argument. Cox's assertion that victorious women Olympians were most likely *not* biological females rested on the deep conviction that superior athleticism signified masculine capacities that inhered in the male body.

Among the athletes who withstood this kind of ridicule and continued to compete were African-American women, who by midcentury had come to occupy a central position in the sport of track and field. Beginning in the late 1930s, black women stepped into an arena largely abandoned by middle-class white women, who deemed the sport unsuitable, and began to blaze a remarkable trail of national and international excellence. But their preeminent position in the sport had a double edge. On a personal level success meant opportunities for education, travel, upward mobility, and national or even international recognition. The accomplishments of such Olympians as Alice Coachman, Mae Faggs, or Wilma Rudolph also demonstrated to the public that African-American women could excel in a nontraditional yet valued arena of American culture. However, viewed through the lens of commonplace racial prejudices, African-American women's achievements in a "mannish" sport also reinforced disparaging stereotypes of black women as less womanly or feminine than white women.[4]

Footraces have a long and varied history in world cultures. In the United States the immediate precedent for twentieth-century track athletics was the popular nineteenth-century sport of road racing. Race organizers sponsored long-distance running events with cash prizes. Except for rare instances these races were for men only, and almost exclusively white men. In the early twentieth century, elite urban athletic clubs and northern colleges shifted the focus away from road racing to collegiate track meets. Held in stadiums, these meets treated avid fans to a series of shorter distance races and field events. A few black men entered competitions as members of college track teams, but at top levels the sport remained largely white, elite, and exclusively male.[5]

The growth of popular sport in the 1920s expanded opportunities beyond the rarefied atmosphere of amateur collegiate and club athletics. Industrial sport programs occasionally financed workers' track teams, and urban newspapers sponsored citywide track meets as public relations gestures. Immigrant communities, especially Scots, Germans, and Poles, promoted their own ethnic track clubs. The playground movement created additional openings for working-class youngsters through playground meets and municipal track championships. Some of these opportunities extended to girls, typically through school or city park programs. With the growth of women's collegiate sport, middle-class women shared in the enthusiasm, competing in intramural track-and-field meets.

Spurred by the sport's great popularity at the Women's Olympics held in Paris in 1922, American and international sport bodies resolved to begin sponsoring women's track and field.[6] Male athletic officials showed little enthusiasm for women's track but argued that it was better to enter into, and thereby gain control of, the activity than to let a popular sport develop outside their control. In the United States the American Athletic Union (AAU) agreed to offer track-and-field championships for women, beginning in 1924. In a personal letter to Notre Dame football coach Knute Rockne justifying his support for the new policy, AAU president Avery Brundage explained that "regardless of how you and I feel about it," the sheer popularity of women's track and field necessitated AAU sponsorship.[7] After considerable dissension the IOC reached the same conclusion, adding five women's track-and-field events to the 1928 Olympic program.

Organizational support, grudging as it was, helped boost the popularity of women's track and field during the late 1920s and early 1930s, especially among working-class athletes. In 1930, ten thousand spectators crowded the stands to watch fifteen hundred women competing at the Central District AAU meet in Chicago.[8] The sizable number of fans and competitors was not unusual in strongholds like Chicago, where an elaborate system of park district, municipal, and Board of Education playgrounds allowed athletically inclined youth to flourish, even in the absence of extensive press coverage or financial support. Betty Robinson, who in 1928 captured the first Olympic gold medal ever issued in the women's hundred-meter sprint, honed her skills on the playgrounds of Chicago. Following in her footsteps, Tidye Pickett, Annette Rogers, and Ida Meyers ran track in the 1930s on Chicago park district teams. Athletes like these typically made do with a set of loose-fitting running shorts, inexpensive T-shirts, and well-worn spikes, using whatever resources they had at their disposal to pay for transportation to distant meets. Pickett, from a South Side black neighborhood, and Rogers and Meyers, from two of the city's many ethnic white, working-class areas, progressed from neighborhood meets to district meets, city championships, and AAU regional meets. They went on to compete at the national and international levels, Rogers in the 1932 and 1936 Olympics, Pickett in the 1936 games, and Meyers in the 1936 national high-jump finals.[9]

While young athletes like these relished the opportunity to test their skills beyond the schoolyard, the developing network of district, regional, and national competition prompted an altogether different response from physical education leaders of the interwar era. The Women's Division and the Committee on Women's Athletics of the American Physical Education Association (CWA) rallied women's organizations into a solid wall of opposition against AAU and Olympic track. They argued vehemently for the elimination of public track-and-field competitions on the grounds that they subjected women to debilitating physical, emotional, and sexual strains.

In the ensuing debate an assortment of critics attacked women's track by raising the specter of the mannish woman. Where sport in general connoted masculinity, track and field had a particularly masculine image. It featured power and speed unmediated by equipment, teamwork, or complicated rules. Thinly clad running, throwing, and jumping athletes appeared to demonstrate "naked" athletic prowess as they exhibited their strained faces and muscles for an audience entranced by elemental human exertion.[10]

Frederick Rand Rogers voiced common objections in a published critique of Olympic track for women. His 1929 article alleged that the brute strength, endurance, and neuromuscular skill required for track-and-field events were "profoundly unnatural" for female athletes. Asserting that the Olympics "are essentially masculine in nature and develop wholly masculine physiques and behavior traits," Rogers claimed that the masculinizing effects of track would make women unfit for motherhood and would sacrifice their "health, physical beauty, and social attractiveness"—costs he deemed "absolutely prohibitive."[11]

In the eyes of her detractors the "wholly masculine" female track athlete became a freak of nature, an object of horror rather than esteem. John Tunis called the Olympics an "animalistic" ordeal for women.[12] And Rogers concluded his discussion of women's Olympic participation with the ominous suggestion: "Manly women . . . may constitute nature's greatest failures, which should perhaps, be corrected by as drastic means as those by which the most hideous deformities are treated."[13]

Educators and their allies did not succeed in halting either the Women's Games or the International Olympics, but they did promulgate a critical standpoint which shaped public perceptions of women's track. In the 1928 Olympics, at the end of the women's eight hundred-meter race, several runners fell to the ground in emotional and physical exhaustion. Although similar dramatics were known to occur in men's races, a tremendous public outcry followed as enraged critics viewed the "collapse" as irrefutable proof that women were constitutionally unfit for such strenuous competition. The opposition drew strength from the incident and succeeded in getting the Olympic Congress to eliminate all medium- and long-distance races and to consider banning women's events completely.

The phenomenal talent of Babe Didrikson, a young, white, working-class track star from Port Arthur, Texas, temporarily revived American enthusiasm for the sport. In the summer of 1932, the eighteen-year-old Didrikson won the AAU national team championship when competing as the sole member of the Dallas-based Employers' Casualty Company "team." Two weeks later she competed at the Los Angeles Olympics, where she proceeded to capture three medals, golds in the javelin and hurdles and a silver in the high jump.

Her astounding feat, along with her quick wit and disarming honesty, made her an instant celebrity among sport journalists and fans. Standing at five foot four and weighing about 110 pounds, she amazed her followers with the strength and skill of her thin, wiry body. Didrikson's blunt, unpolished manner—both in speech and appearance—was also cause for comment. She dressed in loose-fitting sweatsuits, wore her hair in a short, unstyled cut, and addressed the press with plain talk that pulled no punches. Although these features were at times cause for ridicule, they also intrigued reporters and fans who were fascinated by her unapologetic rejection of conventional femininity.

Hearing that in addition to track and field she also played basketball, football, baseball, and numerous other sports, an astonished journalist asked Didrikson, "Is there anything at all you don't play?" Without missing a beat, she reportedly answered, "Yeah, dolls."[14]

In the long run, however, "the Babe's" success did as much to harm as to help the reputation of her sport. Didrikson's disdain for dresses, men, and middle-class etiquette as well as her later involvement with commercial promotions made her the perfect target for horrified foes of track and field. They saw the young athlete's lean physique, short hair, ever-present sweatsuit, and plain, unadorned appearance as evidence that athletic accomplishment did indeed result from or cause masculinity.

Didrikson's immediate successors, Missouri farm girl Helen Stephens and Polish immigrant Stella Walsh, evoked similar reactions. Depictions of the "bobbed-haired, flat-chested, boyishly built" Stephens, and the deep-voiced Walsh perpetuated an image of mannishness, unmitigated by Didrikson's popular appeal.[15] From the eight hundred-meter debacle of 1928 to the athletic successes of muscular track stars like Didrikson, Walsh, and Stephens, opponents of women's track and field were confirmed in their image of a masculine sport that elevated "mannish" women into stardom and broke down the feminine health of "normal" women.

The combined impact of organized opposition, media criticism, and depression-era financial woes rapidly undermined women's track and field. While working-class sports like softball and bowling thrived during the depression, interest in women's track declined drastically after the 1932 Los Angeles Olympics. Of twenty-nine AAU districts, only eleven reported holding track championships in 1933 and 1934. The national championship meet of 1935 attracted only several hundred spectators and took a mere three hours from start to finish.[16] Waning attendance led to further reductions in AAU support. One survey found that by 1936 AAU women's track and field no longer existed in most regions of the country.[17] After 1937, unable to find a group to host the indoor national meet, AAU officials canceled the event for several years. They revived it in the 1940s, but as few as seven clubs participated in some years. Unable to shake its masculine aura, women's track and field by the late 1940s occupied a marginal, denigrated position within American popular culture.[18]

As white women vacated the sport and amateur athletic organizations withdrew their support, black athletes stepped to the fore of women's track and field. Along with basketball, boxing, football, and baseball, track was one of the most popular sports in black communities during the interwar years. African-American men first gained fame as sprinters in the 1920s. Their reputation grew when Jesse Owens soundly defeated Hitler's vaunted Aryan super athletes in an astonishing quadruple performance at the 1936 Berlin Olympics. The success of Owens and other black Olympians, including Ralph Metcalfe, Archie Williams, and Cornelius Johnson, challenged assumptions of white superiority and further popularized track and field among black sport fans and young athletes, including girls.[19]

Although women's sport clearly played second fiddle to men's in black communities, a significant sector of the population demonstrated interest in women's athletics, whether as fans, recreation leaders, or athletic sponsors.[20] Additional encouragement came from African-American educators and journalists, who expressed an acceptance of women's sport rare for their day. In 1939 prominent black physical educator E. B. Henderson agreed with others in his profession that the first priority of girls athletics should be health, not competition. But he went on to criticize "the narrowed limits prescribed for girls and women," arguing: "There are girls who ought to display their skill and national characteristic sport to a wider extent. These national exponents of women's sport are therefore to be commended for the prominence they have attained . . . The race of man needs the inspiration of strong virile womanhood."[21]

Black women's own conception of womanhood, while it may not actively have encouraged sport, did not preclude it. A heritage of resistance to racial and sexual oppression found African-American women occupying multiple roles as wageworkers, homemakers, mothers, and community leaders. In these capacities women earned respect for domestic talents, physical and emotional strengths, and public activism. Denied access to fulltime homemaking and sexual protection, African-American women did not tie femininity to a specific, limited set of activities and attributes defined as separate and opposite from masculinity. Rather, they created an ideal of womanhood rooted in the positive qualities they cultivated under adverse conditions: struggle, strength, family commitment, community involvement, and moral integrity.[22]

Although these values were most often publicly articulated by women in positions of political and intellectual leadership, they were expressed in more mundane fashion by countless other women who helped build the infrastructure of black churches, community centers, club life, and entertainment—the institutions that sponsored athletic activities for girls and women. The work of earning a living and raising a family, often in near-poverty conditions, prevented the great majority of black women from participating in sport or any other time-consuming leisure activity. Yet by the 1930s and 1940s, as sport became a central component of African-American college life and urban community recreation, women were included as minor but nevertheless significant players.[23]

African-American interest in track and field and permissive attitudes toward women's athletics set the stage for the emergence of black women's track at the precise moment when the majority of white women and the white public rejected the sport as undignified for women. Tuskegee Institute formed the first highly competitive collegiate women's track team in 1929.[24] The school immediately added women's events to its Tuskegee Relays, the first major track meet sponsored by a black college, and soon thereafter began extending athletic scholarships to promising African-American high school girls. Coached by Clive Abbott, Christine Petty, and later Nell Jackson, the Tuskegee team matured into North America's premier women's track club during the 1930s and 1940s, capturing eleven of twelve AAU outdoor championships between 1937 and 1948.[25]

Tuskegee was not alone among black colleges in encouraging women's track and field. Prairie View A&M of Texas added women's events to its annual relays in 1936, followed by Alabama State College. Florida A&M, Alcorn College in Mississippi, and Fort Valley State College of Georgia were among the schools attending early Tuskegee meets. Tennessee A&I (later Tennessee State University, or TSU) first sent participants to the Tuskegee Relays in 1944 and established a permanent program in 1945 under the direction of Jessie Abbott, daughter of Tuskegee athletic director Clive Abbott. Collegiate programs drew primarily from southern high schools. Although travel costs and the scarcity of black high schools prohibited extensive interscholastic competition, high school girls from throughout the South trained hard for annual trips to Tuskegee or other college meets where they competed in special "junior" events organized for high schools from around the region.[26]

In the North independent and municipal track clubs provided initial training and encouragement for black girls interested in the sport. Tidye Pickett and Louise Stokes, a Boston track star, got their start on northern playgrounds and in 1936 became the first African-American women to compete on a U.S. Olympic team.[27] In later years, the CYO Comets of Chicago and Police Athletic League of New York produced sprinters like Barbara Jones and Mae Faggs, who both went on to compete for Tennessee State and the U.S. Olympic team.

African-American track women compiled their record of excellence while suffering the constraints of racial and gender discrimination. In the late 1940s and early 1950s, efforts to end racial segregation in major league sports like baseball and basketball had made little impact on the extensive segregation in school, municipal, semipro, and minor league sport. The white press gave minimal coverage to black sports and seldom printed photographs of African-American athletes. Black women found that sex discrimination, in the form of small athletic budgets, halfhearted backing from black school administrators, and the general absence of support from white-dominated sport organizations, further impeded their development.

The AAU policy of sponsoring white-only meets, where southern state laws permitted, posed another barrier. Southern black women's teams, excluded from regional competitions, were limited to black intercollegiate meets and the AAU national championships. Tuskegee athletes typically competed in only three meets per year—the AAU indoor and outdoor championships and the Tuskegee Relays. Tennessee State University followed a similar pattern until the late 1950s and 1960s, when opportunities increased.[28] En route to these meets, teams faced the additional difficulties of traveling through the segregated South. The shortage of restrooms, restaurants, and motels available to black travelers meant that black athletes had to create makeshift accommodations and endure degrading, exhausting conditions.

Despite these obstacles black women's track survived and even thrived. World War II caused the cancellation of the 1940 and 1944 Olympic Games. In the interlude between 1936 and 1948, African-American women became the dominant force in track, a position they would maintain for decades. Commenting on the fact that white women held only two of the eleven slots on the 1948 U.S. national track team, E. B. Henderson surmised that "American [white] women have been so thoroughly licked over so many years by the Booker T. Washington Girls that they have almost given up track and field competition."[29]

African-American women had found an athletic niche, and when the Olympic Games resumed in 1948, black sport activists sensed a historic turning point. Fay Young of the *Chicago Defender* announced in bold type: "Negro Women Will Dominate 1948 U.S. Olympic Track Team." Young subtitled his commentary "Negro Womanhood on Parade," suggesting that the black public viewed athletics as a terrain of achievement with import beyond the immediate athletic realm.[30]

But what did it mean when "Negro womanhood" was "on parade" in a controversial, "mannish" sport? Throughout the 1950s African Americans made up more than two-thirds of American women chosen to compete in the track-and-field events of the Pan-American Games, international track meets and the Olympics.[31] Among athletes, amateur track leaders, and the broader public, the achievements of African-American women athletes could hold significantly different, even contradictory, meanings. Athletic successes which could, in one context, affirm the dignity and capabilities of African-American womanhood, could also appear to confirm derogatory images of both black and athletic women.

African-American women in their teens and twenties only dimly perceived the historical significance of their athletic achievements. They were far more aware of the personal opportunities and enjoyment they found in track and field. Yet in describing their experiences, athletes commented on the racial and gender barriers they faced, reflecting as well on their knowledge of athletics as a site for personal and social transformation.[32]

Lula Hymes (Glenn) and Leila Perry (Glover) both grew up in Atlanta, Georgia, ran track for Booker T. Washington High School in the 1930s and attended Tuskegee in the late 1930s and early 1940s on college track scholarships. Each won numerous honors in collegiate and AAU competition. Their teammate Alice Coachman (Davis) grew up in Albany, Georgia, and was recruited while still a high school student to attend Tuskegee Institute's secondary school and postsecondary trade school. An extraordinary athlete, Coachman dominated the high jump and sprinting events from 1939 to 1948. Her perseverance paid off in a gold medal for the high jump, the only bright spot for U.S. track women in the 1948 London Olympics.

Shirley Crowder (Meadows), Martha Hudson (Pennyman) and Willye White were part of the next cohort of track women. Crowder and Hudson grew up in Georgia in the 1940s and 1950s, attended Tennessee State University on track scholarships in the late 1950s, and competed in the 1960 Olympics in Rome.[33] Their Olympic teammate White won recognition as a high school sprinter and jumper in her home state of Mississippi. While a member of TSU and Chicago track teams, she competed in five successive Olympic Games from 1956 to 1972.[34]

All six athletes began by running high school track in segregated southern schools. By the 1940s most black high schools offered girls' track and basketball teams, providing at least a modicum of organizational support and coaching for promising young athletes. The women recalled that while it was still unusual for a girl to be heavily involved in sports, they were not lone competitors. Reinforced by teammates and coaches, young athletes also received support from friends and family members.

They were, however, aware that some contemporaries disapproved of female athletes. Willye White learned of these attitudes at an early age, when members of her rural Mississippi community questioned her tomboyish ways. Describing herself as a "tomboy" and an "outcast," she explained, "It was not acceptable in American society." Alice Coachman also met with criticism. Her parents repeatedly tried to prevent her from going to the playground where she played ball and raced with the boys. Coachman recalled that her parents as well as others in the community suspected that athletic girls would suffer injury and poor health: "The general feeling during that time—they just felt that girls were going to break their neck. . . . In my hometown, . . . they were always afraid of them getting hurt. . . . They weren't educated about women's track."

Yet, more often than not, athletes found fellow students and community members to be genuinely supportive, especially if they had an interest in sport or personal contact with the women involved. Shirley Crowder described the atmosphere at Tennessee State:

> If the person was not involved with sports as a participant or a spectator . . . they perhaps thought of it as being too masculine perhaps at that time. Because I've had some people say things like that to me. . . . I just credit it to the fact that some were jealous because we were constantly traveling. I just took it that way. But most of the people who were closer to us appreciated what we were doing.

At Tuskegee athletes rarely encountered criticism. The mannish image of women athletes occupied a remote corner in Leila Perry's mind, since, as she explained: "The people we encountered, you didn't have that kind of a stigma. Like at Tuskegee, everybody was proud of us. Because we were really outstanding. . . . It didn't touch me, because at Tuskegee it wasn't such. They were proud of their athletes."[35]

Insulated from wider cultural criticism by their immediate surroundings, athletes rejected interpretations that conflicted with their own. Lula Hymes reasoned, "They gonna think and talk and say what they want to say anyway, regardless of how you feel about it. I never pay any attention to what people say." Martha Hudson agreed: "I've heard the talk, but it didn't bother me." She explained that her TSU coach and teammates provided a layer of protection: "We were just so prepared for a lot of things—criticism—our coach would talk to us. Things that a lot of people worried about, we didn't. We would discuss it, we would talk about it, but it didn't bother us."

Like Hudson, athletes shielded from public rebuke felt free to participate and enjoy their sport to the fullest. Lula Hymes summarized her experience: "I just wanted to run and win during that time. . . . I was out there just enjoying myself. Because I liked it; [it was] something I wanted to do!" Similarly Shirley Crowder concluded, "I was just always me. . . . I knew what I had to do and I'd do it regardless." Reflecting on the sheer pleasure of her youthful passion, Alice Coachman commented, "When I look back at it now, I just say, 'Lord, I sure was a running thing!' "

Beyond the elemental joy of competing, athletes also placed high value on the educational and travel opportunities that track and field made available. While several had planned to attend local colleges, athletic scholarships gave them the chance to go away to school and expand their horizons. Hymes, Perry, and Coachman especially appreciated the rich cultural and intellectual life of Tuskegee in the 1930s and 1940s: "They had all kinds of activities around the campus for you. And you just kind of grew as a person. You weren't just involved in athletics, you were involved in the happenings of the world. Because they brought the world to Tuskegee."

Athletes described their travels as a combination of painful and wondrous awakenings. Traveling across the South and into northern cities brought young athletes out of the protective fold of black institutions and communities. They encountered the harsh realities of southern segregation and the more confusing, unwritten rules of northern racism. Growing up in Atlanta's black community, Lula Hymes had not experienced segregation as burdensome or painful. "I wasn't aware until we started traveling," she recalled. On the road she found that "if we wanted to go to the bathroom, we had to stop and go in the woods. We couldn't go in the stores to buy anything. We had to go around. It was really hard, segregated." Alice Coachman described a similar contrast between student life at Tuskegee and traveling with the track team. Remarking on the difficulty of obtaining food, gas, and lodging on the road, she explained that travel with the team brought segregation into full view, especially compared to the relative safety of Tuskegee, where "you had your own little world." Although roadside picnics and stops at black colleges, restaurants, or rooming houses might make for pleasant travel, athletes understood the forces of racism that lay behind those "choices."

Young track women found that travel also offered positive experiences. As high school students spending the summer at Tuskegee's or TSU's junior training program, teenagers gained independence, new friends, and sometimes an escape from difficult work or family situations. After spending her first summer at Tuskegee, Alice Coachman begged her parents to let her return during the school year: "I had gotten a taste of traveling with the girls. . . . You know, going to big cities, and I had never been out of Albany, Georgia. And everybody was nice. I wanted to be with the group—I wanted to be there too!" Willye White saw track as a ticket out of Greenwood, Mississippi. "It was my talent, and my ability. And with that I could do a lot of things. I could get away from my grandparents, I could travel throughout the state. . . . It allowed me freedom of movement." Describing escape from grueling work as her "main motivator," White explained: "I left [Mississippi] every May, and that meant I didn't have to go to the cotton fields and I came back in September. As far as what was traditional and nontraditional, I had no idea. All I knew was it was just an escape for me not to have to go to the cotton fields during the summer."

Travel to AAU and Olympic competitions opened even more vistas. Athletes recalled dancing at the Savoy Ballroom and the Cotton Club in New York City, being taken to historical sites like Mount Vernon, and encountering chop suey and chopsticks for the first time. Top black teams occasionally received celebrity treatment, although it might come with a racist twist. Martha Hudson told of being invited as part of the TSU track team to appear on Dick Clark's *American Bandstand* television program, only to find out afterward that they had been kept off camera nearly the entire show. In a similar vein Leila Perry recalled a ceremony honoring the Tuskegee team at the Atlantic City, New Jersey, city hall. Before being presented with the key to the city, the team was asked to sing for the crowd, because "as always, they think that black folks are supposed to be able to sing."

These racial slights were outweighed by profound moments of racial insight and pride. Recalling her first Olympic journey to Melbourne, Australia, Willye White described a life-altering experience: "That's when I found out there were two worlds, Mississippi and the rest of the world. I found that blacks and whites could eat together, sleep together, play together, do all these things together. And it was just eye opening. Had I not been in the Olympic Games, I could have spent the rest of my life thinking that blacks and whites were separate." For White and other African-American athletes, involvement in high-level track and field brought deep satisfactions and worldly knowledge.

Beyond its personal significance to individual athletes, the success of black women in track served as a broader symbol of pride and achievement for black communities. Black colleges and newspapers heralded women's track accomplishments, even when the mainstream press ignored them. When white officials or journalists did occasionally take note of black female athletic accomplishments, their praise represented momentary triumphs in the long struggle against racial oppression. Victorious homecoming ceremonies at which white politicians and reporters showered black Olympians with honors served as a powerful symbolic reversal of racial hierarchy. When the white mayors of Greenwood, Mississippi, and Clarksville, Tennessee, handed Willye White and Wilma Rudolph the keys to their cities, it symbolized a door that could open for all African Americans. It granted due, if temporary, respect and nurtured the hope that racial justice might soon prevail.

Paradoxically, while black communities understood the athletic success of African-American women to be a measure of black cultural achievement, it held a very different meaning when interpreted through the lens of white America's prevailing racial and sexual beliefs. For the most part black women athletes were simply ignored by the white media and athletic establishment. Figures like Alice Coachman, the first black woman in history to win an Olympic medal, or Mildred McDaniel, the only American woman to win an individual gold medal in the 1956 Olympic track-and-field competition, did not become national celebrities, household names, or even the subject of magazine feature stories. The most striking feature of the historical record on black women athletes is neglect. This pattern is not surprising given the invisibility of minority cultures in mainstream discourse. Yet the historical roots of the silence surrounding black women athletes are complex. They lay deep in the traditions of Western thought, in which women of color have long been viewed as distant but definitive repositories of inferior, unfeminine qualities.[36]

For centuries European and Anglo-American art, science, and popular thought had constructed a normative ideal of white womanhood that relied on an opposing image of black women as the inferior "other." Specifically, images of female sexuality, femininity, and beauty were composed along racially polarized axes. North American and British scientists of the nineteenth century described black sexuality as lascivious and apelike, marked by a "voluptuousness" and a "degree of lascivity" unknown in Europe. Citing supposed physical distinctions between African and European women as empirical proof, they contrasted black women's presumed primitive, passionate sexuality to an ideal of asexual purity among highly "civilized" white women. These stereotypes continued to permeate American culture in the early twentieth century. Called "openly licentious" and "morally obtuse," black women posed a negative contrast to the presumed "lily-white" virtue of Anglo-American women.[37]

Theories of sexual inferiority and primitiveness found a corollary in standards of beauty. Early-twentieth-century sexologist Havelock Ellis argued that a scientifically objective chain of beauty ran parallel to the evolutionary chain of being. White European and Anglo-American women occupied the most highly evolved, beautiful end of the scale, while black women were assigned a place at the opposite end.[38] Ellis's "scientific" theory was rooted in popular racial assumptions that found another expression in dominant media standards of beauty. Advertisements, advice columns, and beauty magazines excluded women of color, except for occasional portrayals as dark-skinned exotica from faraway lands.

Racialized notions of sexual virtue and feminine beauty were underpinned by another concept, that of the virile or mannish black female. African-American women's work history as slaves, tenant farmers, domestics, and wageworkers disqualified them from standards of femininity defined around the frail or inactive female body. Their very public presence in the labor force exempted African Americans from ideals of womanhood that rested on the presumed refinement and femininity of a privatized domestic arena. Failing to meet these standards, black women were often represented in the dominant culture as masculine females lacking in feminine grace, delicacy, and refinement.

The silence surrounding black athletes reflects the power of these stereotypes to restrict African-American women to the margins of cultural life, occupying a status as distant "others." In one sense the invisibility was not specific to athletes. With the exception of a few sensational stage performers like Josephine Baker or Lena Horne, African-American women were not generally subjects of white popular interest or adoration. There were, however, more specific causes for the lack of attention to black women's athletic accomplishments, reasons rooted in the striking intersection of racial and gender ideology in sport.

The long exclusion of both African-American women and female athletes from categories of acceptable femininity encouraged the development of analogous mythologies. References to imitative "animalistic" behavior had often been used to describe white female athletes, who by "aping" male athletic behavior were suspected of unleashing animal instincts. Charges of mimicry found an even deeper congruence with racist views of African Americans as simian and imitative. Similarly, the charge that sport masculinized women physically and sexually resonated with scientific and popular portrayals of mannishness and sexual pathology among black women. The assertion that sport made women physically unattractive and sexually unappealing found its corollary in views of black women as less attractive and desirable than white women.[39] The correspondence between stereotyped depictions of black womanhood and athletic females was nearly exact, and thus doubly resonant in the case of African-American women athletes.

The myth of the "natural" black athlete lent further support to the perception that African-American women were biologically suited to masculine sport. Early-twentieth-century education and social science journals, especially in the 1930s, were sprinkled with anthropometric studies of racially determined muscle length, limb size, head shape, and neurological responses. Experts in both science and sport labored to identify genetic factors, including a conditioned "fear-response" and peculiar characteristics of African-American hands, tendons, muscles, joints, nerves, blood, thighs, and eye color, which might explain the fact that black athletes sometimes jumped higher or ran faster than whites.[40] This formulation of the "natural" black athlete represented black athletic accomplishment as a by-product of nature rather than as a cultural attainment based on skill and knowledge. By maintaining the myth that people of European descent were cultured, intellectual and civilized, while those of African heritage were uncivilized beings guided by physical and natural impulses, it also converted black achievements into evidence of racial inferiority.[41]

A legacy of racist thought influenced the reception of black women track athletes. This kind of racism was rarely overt and probably not even intended by many sport enthusiasts. It was signaled primarily as an absence—the lack of popular interest, organizational support, media coverage, and public acclaim. White observers may have tacitly dismissed black women's accomplishments as the inevitable result of "natural," "masculine" prowess. By this logic black women's very success could appear to provide further evidence of track and field's unfeminine character. Advocates of women's track may have ignored black athletes because their existence ran contrary to the image of classic (white) femininity that officials so desperately wanted to convey.[42] While racism was only one factor contributing to the poor reputation of women's track and field, the confluence of powerful racial and athletic stereotypes could only reinforce the stigmatized status of track women in general, and African-American athletes in particular.

The influence of these ideas becomes more obvious when track is compared to swimming, a sport whose development paralleled that of track and field in important ways. The AAU sponsored both activities, opening its doors to swimming in 1916 and to track eight years later. Both sports involved team training and competition but were primarily individual sports that pitted individual athletes against each other in contests over time and distance. Women and men competed in both sports, so neither activity was logically female or male.

However, in stark contrast to track and field's masculine reputation, from its inception observers deemed swimming appropriate and beneficial for women. The media depicted swimmers as the ideal "figures" of American womanhood. *New York Times* columnist Arthur J. Daley praised swimmer Eleanor Holm (Jarrett) as "perfectly proportioned, right in line for the business of 'Glorifying the American Girl.'"[43] Beauty, not ugliness, was the swimmer's hallmark. A 1938 *Amateur Athlete* cover photo likened AAU swim champs to contestants in a Miss America pageant, while headlines repeatedly referred to swimmers as "queens," "beauties," "nymphs," or "pretty plungers" who could put on a dazzling "show of youth and beauty."[44]

Swimmers, like track athletes, relied on strength, speed, and technique. Nevertheless commentators saw the two sports as distinctly different. The core concepts used to impugn the gender of track-and-field athletes—reproductive damage, physical masculinity, and lack of sexual appeal—operated in reverse for swimmers. Motherhood was not an issue in swimming, since as a water sport it did not involve the high impact or jarring effects thought to damage female reproductive organs. Contemporary observers also distinguished between track as an ugly, muscle-bunching sport and swimming as an attractive, muscle-stretching one. In direct contrast to track's masculine effects, swimming purportedly enhanced the feminine physique by keeping it soft and rounded while building up the chest and developing long, supple leg muscles. The aura of beauty and sexual appeal that surrounded women's swimming was reinforced by popular leisure culture, in which speed swimming shaded into recreational bathing and suntanning. The "swimsuit competition" phase of beauty contests further blurred the lines between competitive sport and beauty culture, as did the entertainment careers of swimming stars like Annette Kellermann, Eleanor Holm, and Esther Williams.[45]

Underneath the association of swimming with beauty lay critical distinctions of class and race. The overwhelming majority of competitive swimmers were white and middle class. Most trained in private swim clubs under salaried coaches. Public pools were uncommon in working-class urban neighborhoods and in rural areas. Where they did exist, legal or de facto segregation and the price of admission prevented most African American, Latino, Indian, Asian American, and white working-class youngsters from attaining basic skills, much less a competitive edge.

For years swimming and track existed side by side as the glamorous and ugly sisters of AAU and Olympic sport.[46] The racial, class, and gender prejudices that informed the distinction operated subtly and remained largely unarticulated. However, the situation changed after World War II, when the global conflict between the United States and the Soviet Union suddenly fixed national and international attention on women's track. As a small band of neglected, undertrained female athletes assumed the weight of the "free world" on their backs, sport advocates and journalists were forced to confront the image of women's track and its leading stars.

Like everything from Third World governments to kitchen appliances, sport became part of a Cold War international contest in which the United States and USSR vied not only for athletic laurels but to prove the superiority of capitalism or communism. Under pressure to triumph over Soviet "slave athletics," the national sports establishment focused unprecedented attention on black and female athletes.

American sport officials paid homage to black competitors, sheepishly admitting, "If it weren't for the sensational performances of the great Negro athletes we wouldn't even be in a secondary position in world athletics today."[47] Furthermore, they relied on African-American talent to disprove Soviet charges of pervasive racial discrimination in U.S. society. Claiming that the prominence of black athletes in the United States refuted "Communist ideas about the status of our colored citizens," politicians and sports officials championed black athletic success and the desegregation of major league sports as an answer to communism.[48] This mind-set filtered into U.S. foreign policy of the late 1950s. The State Department worked with athletic organizations to sponsor international tours featuring African-American track and tennis stars. One armchair diplomat boasted that these athletes could do "more to win friends for the United States than formal diplomacy or handouts or economic aid have been able to do."[49]

Though black women were included in the praise for African-American athletes, their tribulations as members of the U.S. women's track team caused serious concern. The lack of adequate training and competition left black as well as white women in poor shape for international events. Overall, U.S. women lagged far behind both Western and Eastern European women who received much greater support from their national sport organizations. The deficiencies of women's track and field had been a minor matter in the past. But with the Soviet Union's first Olympic appearance in 1952, these failings posed an acute problem for U.S. politicians, sport leaders, and a patriotic public. The U.S. men's team ranked even with or above the Soviet men, but the Soviet women so overpowered their American counterparts that the United States was in danger of losing the unofficial but highly publicized competition for Olympic gold.

As early as 1946 track insiders warned that without expanded school and college programs, more opportunities to compete, and more official support, U.S. women would fare badly against superior European and Russian teams.[50] The changes were not forthcoming and predictions of dismal international performances came true. The weakness of women's track and field, a sport that most amateur sport leaders had hoped would quietly fade away, now stood out like a sore thumb and threatened American claims that, whether in politics, economics, or athletics, the United States could do it better.

In this climate of controversy Olympic organizers reopened the question of the suitability of women's track and field. In a summary of the 1953 Olympic Congress in Mexico City, IOC President Avery Brundage described the "well-grounded protest against events which are not truly feminine," including field events and long-distance running. He reported that the IOC favored confining women's track-and-field events "to those appropriate to the feminine sex," and noted that despite the 1953 decision to continue women's competition, about one-third of national Olympic committees "would be happier if there were no events for the opposite sex."[51] IOC member Prince Franz Joseph of Liechtenstein remarked that not only would such a reduction solve the problem of Olympic overexpansion, but "we would be spared the unesthetic spectacle of women trying to look and act like men.[52]

The American media expressed similar sentiments. Before the Cold War many journalists who opposed women's track and field just ignored it. But the Soviet threat to American athletic superiority demanded a response. Sportswriters routinely claimed that track and field, especially the strength events like the javelin and and the shot put, unsexed women. In his 1953 *New York Times* column titled "More Deadly than Male," Arthur Daley described the "grotesque contortions" of track-and-field athletes, noting that "it does something to a guy. And it ain't love, Buster."[53] In a similar vein, in his 1960 article titled "Venus Wasn't a Shot Putter," columnist William Barry Furlong likened patriotic assertions of having the best-muscled girls to claiming the best-looking automobile wreck.[54] According to this view women were a consumer item, "wrecked" for male pleasure by athletic training.

Ironically, the source of the problem—Soviet women's Olympic dominance—provided a partial solution for those officials and journalists who urged support for U.S. women. The American team could shed damning images of unsexed, mannish women by displacing them onto Soviet athletes. Descriptions of "ponderous, peasant-type Russian athletes" and "Amazons from the Russian steppes" created a contrasting "other" whose very presence lent some legitimacy to the less talented U.S. team. These "strong Red ladies" who outshone "frail Red males" shifted the onus away from American athletes onto Soviet women.[55] However, while they could claim to be more feminine than their Russian antagonists, the U.S. team had yet to figure out a way to defeat them.

Concerned observers agreed that to improve women's performance, sport administrators must interest a larger number of girls and women in track and then provide adequate training programs to develop their abilities. The problem was how to popularize a sport deemed by many as unfeminine and undesirable for women. For sport advocates trying to

Figure 11–1
The U.S.A. women's sprint relay team including Olympic Champion Wilma Rudolph, at left. A principal source of this contingent was the Tennessee State Tigerbelles, who dominated intercollegiate and Amateur Athletic Union events for many years. Library of Congress.

revive popular interest in a dying sport, the commanding position of African-American women in track posed an especially vexing problem. To improve the image of track and field, promoters could either incorporate black track women into approved concepts of athletic womanhood, or they could minimize the presence and contributions of black women in order to create a more respectable image of the sport. Black and white athletic officials approached the dilemma with a variety of strategies.

African-American journalists, coaches, and athletic promoters consciously cultivated the feminine image of black women athletes. Tennessee State Coach Edward Temple instituted a dress code and prohibited photographers from taking postrace pictures until after his athletes had retreated to the locker room to touch up their hair and wash their faces. He wanted the visible signs of strain and sweat removed, creating a "public face" of composure. Asked about the masculine image of track athletes, Temple told a reporter, "None of my girls have any trouble getting boyfriends. I tell them that they are young ladies first, track girls second."[56]

Black educator and sports historian E. B. Henderson took pains to establish the femininity of black competitors, asserting in 1948 that "colored girl athletes are as a rule, effeminate. They are normal girls."[57] Contrasting "colored" athletes to those champions who "are more man than woman," one athlete declared that Coach Temple "wanted to show that we were ladies, respectable ladies. . . . They said negative things about athletes, about the way they dress and so on and so forth, so he wanted us to try to set an example that athletes were not what some of them thought we were—that we were ladies."[58]

This carefully composed image of athletic womanhood did double duty, debunking myths of the mannish woman athlete and of the natural black athlete. It also raised a wall of defense against misinformed or malicious representations of black women. By publicly asserting their femininity and sexual respectability, black athletes answered tacit denials of their womanhood and demanded inclusion in the realm of culture.[59]

White track-and-field leaders developed similar strategies to deal with the sport's image problem. The most tenacious defenders of women's track and field were the few women who obtained leadership positions within the AAU. In the 1950s two such advocates—former track champions Roxy Andersen and Frances Kaszubski—spearheaded efforts to revive their sport in the face of widespread public apathy or hostility. Andersen and Kaszubski worked tirelessly to establish feminine credentials for track and field, cajoling sports leaders, issuing press releases to city newspapers, and publishing articles in the *Amateur Athlete.* In one media piece titled "Girls Thrive on Sport," Andersen even conceded that several top athletes "were raw-boned, flat-chested and deep-voiced," but she countered that so were some nonathletic girls, and concluded with a standard defense of athletic femininity.[60] Acknowledging that unsightly sweat and dirt were part of the sport, Andersen reminded readers that "a temporarily strained face doesn't permanently destroy beauty, nor does it reduce a woman's social charm or her ability to bake a pie."[61]

In a similar vein Frances Kaszubski issued a glowing report of an appearance on the *Ed Sullivan Show* by the national women's track-and-field team. Playing on references to track and field as the "cinder sport" (because of cinder tracks), Kaszubski described the women as "Modern Cinderellas," kept in the background by the evil stepmother of public apathy and overshadowed by respectable stepsister sports of swimming and tennis. But finally, at the "big ball" of national television, the women found the magic slipper of public approval. Each member of the team rested happily in the knowledge that "at last she was a member of a sport that was being recognized by Prince Charming, Ed Sullivan." To remove any lingering doubts, Kaszubski informed her readers that such "inner happiness only added to the natural beauty and charm that each of the AAU National Champions already possessed."[62]

Fearing that anecdotal evidence alone would not convince a skeptical public, in 1954 the AAU conducted a statistical survey of former athletes to prove that top-notch women were "photogenic and attractively feminine" and, subsequent to competing, were "establishing families in the good old American tradition." Summarizing the "gratifying" results, Andersen explained that under the public spotlight, athletes became even more image conscious and well mannered. As a result, far from becoming "mannish and hardened, sport helped these women win husbands."[63]

While such statements theoretically included a defense of black athletes as well as white, the language and visual imagery of most AAU publicity indicates an effort to put distance between the sport's image and its African-American stars. The editors of the AAU *Amateur Athlete* rarely printed photos of African-American women, choosing no coverage over black representations. The success of black women forced this magazine and other sports media occasionally to give due praise, but the overwhelming emphasis was on white "hopefuls," women who had not yet earned national honors but nevertheless might appeal to the public as promising stars on the rise. Other journalists followed suit. The media regularly described young Olympic hopefuls as cute, blond, little, and fair. Or in a slightly altered version, articles like *Parade* magazine's "Watch this Housewife jump!" complimented older athletes for their domesticity.[64]

These appeals were implicitly biased against black women. Few had ever had the economic security to combine athletics with full-time housewifery, and none were blond and "fair" skinned. Athletes of all ages and races received the most praise when they met popular ideals of beauty, but mass media beauty standards included black women only insofar as they approached white ideals. The *Amateur Athlete*'s references to fair-skinned blond beauties made the exclusion explicit.

The continued prominence of black women in the sport and the impact of the civil rights movement forced some change in media policy of the early 1960s. African-American women were more often featured and photographed. However, the few athletes who attained a visible presence were often treated as exceptional cases. In reporting on Wilma Rudolph's triple-gold-medal performance at the 1960 Rome Olympics, where she won the one hundred- and two hundred-meter sprints and anchored the four hundred-meter relay, *Time* magazine declared: "In a field of female endeavor in which the greatest stars have often been characterized by overdeveloped muscles and underdeveloped glands, Wilma (Skeeter) Rudolph has long, lissome legs and a pert charm."[65] In this view top women track athletes, who in the United States happened to be black, were masculine freaks of nature, and Rudolph was the exception. Even as they applauded her charm and speed, the press resorted to stereotypical images of jungle animals. They nicknamed Rudolph the "black gazelle."[66] Like other black athletes, she was represented as a wild beast, albeit a gentle, attractive creature who could be adopted as a pet of the American public.[67]

With the exception of Rudolph's short-lived popularity, stereotypes of athletic amazons and muscle molls continued to plague track-and-field athletes. In 1962, Frances Kaszubski seemed to accept defeat when she openly admitted that masculine women had an advantage in track and field. She began her article "In Defense of Women Athletes" with the disclaimer, "There is no doubt that certain women reach the summit of the great competitions at the Olympic Games whose morphology, or functional characteristics, are akin to those of men." She insisted, however, that sport did not create aberrant females. Rather, "women who are apparently 'virilized' by sport are, in reality, women with android tendencies who succeed in sportive competitions simply by reason of their genetic constitution."[68] Given the admission that the most natural women athletes were in fact the most aberrant females, how were sport advocates to make any headway in popularizing track and field?

A clue lay in the photograph positioned right above Kaszubski's remarks. A young, blond, white gymnast lay with her pelvis delicately balanced on a horizontal bar, arms outstretched and chest thrust forward above the caption, "Doris Fuchs . . . lightness, suppleness, virtuosity and grace."[69] More and more, track-and-field leaders followed a strategy of virtue by association. Rather than credit the achievements of African-American athletes who had overcome sexual and racial barriers to excel in their sport, athletic leaders legitimized track and field by treating it as a sister sport to "feminine" and overwhelmingly white sports like gymnastics, swimming, and diving, and the recently adopted sport of synchronized swimming.

Why did the stigma of mannishness prove so intractable? One answer lies in the deeply rooted understanding of track and field as inherently masculine. Given the stifling conservatism of the postwar era, especially with regard to gender norms, this perception was unlikely to be dislodged in the late 1940s and 1950s. But racial issues also played a critical role in reproducing the sport's masculine definition.

Figure 11–2
Wilma Rudolph, Olympic heroine. Rudolph was the soft-spoken diva of black women's sport—and a compelling example of what female athletes contributed to the broader sporting culture, nationally and internationally. National Archives.

Grafted onto the existing image of the mannish female athlete, the figure of the black woman track athlete fused gender and racial stereotypes. When, after decades of media and organizational neglect, American track women suddenly found themselves under the international glare of Cold War athletic rivalries, a complicated matrix of racial and gender issues came to a head. A reservoir of racist beliefs about black women as deficient in femininity buttressed the masculine connotation of track and field. Throughout the Cold War era, the sport was dominated by African American and Soviet women. Thus two symbols of mannishness—black women and Russian "amazons"—stood in the foreground, impeding efforts to overhaul the sport's reputation.

AAU officials and their allies rallied around a feminine ideal rooted in white, middle-class culture. Leaders like Roxy Andersen and Frances Kaszubski did not invent this ideal, nor did they necessarily intend racism. Black athletes along with white benefited from their efforts to advance women's track and field. Nevertheless widespread contempt for women athletes as ugly, unsexed amazons set the terms of public debate. Locked into these terms, defenders of track and field tried to answer criticism with proof that women athletes were indeed pretty, feminine, and sexually normal. To do so they called on historically racist constructions of womanhood that failed to include black athletes within the bounds of athletic femininity.

Constrained by segregation laws, inferior resources, limited competitive opportunities, discriminatory sport agencies, and media "blackouts," African-American women athletes faced tremendous barriers to participation. Sadly, when they surmounted these odds, their commanding presence in the "mannish" sport of track and field could appear to verify their absence from "true" (white) womanhood and athletic respectability.

The subtle interplay of racial and gender stereotypes surely did the greatest damage to African-American athletes, but it also indirectly constricted the athletic possibilities of other women. Sport advocates who stressed white norms of femininity and attempted to distance the sport from its black stars simply reinforced a definition of femininity that confined women physically, sexually, and athletically. They thereby subverted their own genuine interest in expanding women's athletic freedom. As long as the "mannish amazon" could be represented by the liminal figure of the black female track star, sport would remain an illegitimate activity for all women.

NOTES

1. On Blankers-Koen, see Richard Schaap, *An Illustrated History of the Olympics,* 2nd ed. (New York: Alfred A. Knopf, 1967), 241. On Blankers-Koen and Ostermeyer, see Guttmann, *Women's Sports: A History* (New York: Columbia University Press, 1991), 200.

2. Avery Brundage, Brundage Collection, Box 70 (Folder-Circular Letters to IOC's, NOC's, and IF's, 1952–54), University of Illinois Archives.

3. Brundage Collection, Box 115 (Folder-Athletics-Women), "IOC-Quotations for and against women's competition," no date (mid-fifties), University of Illinois Archives.

4. This stereotype has been discussed in much of the historical literature on African-American women. See, for example, Paula Giddings, *When and Where I Enter* (New York: William Morrow, 1984), chaps. 1, 2, 4; Barbara Hilkert Andolsen, *"Daughters of Jefferson, Daughters of Bootblacks:" Racism and American Feminism* (Macon, GA: Mercer University Press, 1986); Patricia Hill Collins, *Black Feminist Thought* (Boston: Unwin Hyman, 1990), chaps. 4, 8.

5. Benjamin Rader, *American Sport: From the Age of Folk Games to the Age of Televised Sport,* 2nd ed. (Englewood Cliffs, NJ: Prentice Hall, 1990).

6. See Mary Henson Leigh and Therese Bonin, "The Pioneering Role of Madame Alice Milliat and the FSFI in Establishing International Track and Field Competition for Women," *Journal of Sport History* 4 (Spring 1977): 72–83.

7. Brundage to Knute Rockne, Brundage Papers, Box 8 (AAU—Rockne Folder), University of Illinois Archives.

8. *Ibid.*

9. Personal communication, Annette Rogers Kelly; interview by the author, Ida Meyers (Glenwood, IL), May 28, 1991. Rogers won successive gold medals in the 1932 and 1936 four-hundred-meter relay competition. Meyers narrowly missed making the 1936 Olympic squad, but the same year won the national indoor high-jump championship at the age of seventeen. Pickett qualified for the 1932 Los Angeles Olympic team but was removed from competition by American track officials under circumstances that remain clouded. For a more detailed account of the events surrounding Pickett in 1932, see Michael B. Davis, *Black American Women in Olympic Track and Field* (Jefferson, NC: McFarland and Co., 1992), 130–3.

10. Donald J. Mrozek argues that perceptions of women's track and field involved a sexual element as well. Victorian notions of female sexual purity supplanted but did not eliminate older beliefs about uncontrolled female passion. The sensual, physical nature of athletics could signal a loss of self-control and a potential slide into sexual depravity. See "The 'Amazon' and the American 'Lady': Sexual Fears of Women as Athletes," in J. A. Mangan and Roberta J. Park, *From "Fair Sex" to Feminism: Sport and the Socialization of Women in the Industrial and Post-Industrial Eras* (London: Frank Cass, 1987), 282–98.

11. Frederick Rand Rogers, "Olympics for Girls?" *School and Society* 30 (August 10, 1929): 190–9.

12. John R.Tunis, "Women and the Sport Business," *Harper's Monthly Magazine* 159 (July 1929): 213.

13. Frederick Rand Rogers, "Olympics for Girls?" *School and Society* 30 (August 10, 1929): 194.

14. This anecdote is retold in Schaap, *An Illustrated History of the Olympics,* 196.

15. "Modern 'Atalantas' at XI Olympiad," *Literary Digest* 122 (August 15, 1936): 32–4.

16. "Women's Sports Committee Report," AAU Annual Meeting Minutes, 1934, AAU Archives, Indianapolis, IN; *Amateur Athlete* (October 1935): 12.

17. Charlotte Epstein, chairwoman of Women's Sports Committee, "Women's Sports," *Amateur Athlete* (January 1936): 5. The American Olympic Committee (AOC also reduced its support. Ida Meyers recalled that the financially strapped AOC paid for only four members of the women's track team to attend the Berlin Olympics, requiring other qualifiers to raise five hundred dollars for their own transport. (Meyers interview)

18. Mary Henson Leigh, "The Evolution of Women's Participation in the Summer Olympics, 1900–1948" (Ph.D. diss., Ohio State University, 1974), 291–4.

19. On Owens, see William J. Baker, *Jesse Owens: An American Life* (New York: Free Press, 1986). On African Americans in track and field, see Arthur R. Ashe, Jr., *A Hard Road to Glory: A History of the African-American Athlete, 1919–1945* (New York: Warner Books, 1988), 73–91.

20. Linda D. Williams's study found that the black press between 1924 and 1948 gave significant and positive coverage to black women athletes. Williams concludes that there was "a more favorable environment for the sportswomen in the black community" and that black women benefited from a diverse and popular black sports culture during this period. See Linda D. Williams, "An Analysis of American Sportswomen in Two Negro Newspapers: The *Pittsburgh Courier,* 1924–1948 and the *Chicago Defender,* 1932–1948" (Ph. D. diss., Ohio State University, 1987), 22, 114.

21. Henderson, *The Negro in Sports,* rev. ed. (Washington, DC: Associated Publishers, 1939), 218.

22. On black women's construction of womanhood, see Giddings, *When and Where I Enter,* 49, 85–94; Deborah K. King, "Multiple Jeopardy, Multiple Consciousness," *Signs* 14 (Autumn 1988): 43–72; Bonnie Thornton Dill, "The Dialectics of Black Womanhood," *Signs* 4 (Spring 1979): 543–5; Patricia Hill Collins, "Learning from the Outsider Within," *Social Problems* 33 (December 1986) 514–32; and Hazel V. Carby, *Reconstructing Womanhood: The Emergence of the Afro-American Woman Novelist* (New York: Oxford University Press, 1987).

23. There may have been class differences in the degree of support for women's sports. In "Organizing Afro-American Girls' Clubs in Kansas in the 1920s," *Frontiers* 9, 2 (1987): 69–72, Marilyn Dell Brady indicates that the largely middle-class National Association of Colored Women sponsored girls' clubs that included athletics among a variety of other cultural activities. But sport was not a major focus of these clubs. While golf and tennis were popular among black country club members, it is not clear whether wealthier African Americans approved of women's involvement in sports like

basketball, bowling, or track, which had greater working-class constituencies.

24. *New York Age,* February 16, 1929, p. 6.

25. See Ashe, *A Hard Road to Glory,* 75–9, and annual reports of AAU track-and-field championships published in the *Amateur Athlete.*

26. On southern high school and collegiate women's track, see *Atlanta Daily World* sports pages from the 1930s and 1940s. On TSU, see Tennessee State University Tigerbelles Clippings Files, Tennessee State University Archives, Nashville, TN; TSU yearbooks; and Fatino Marie Clemons, "A History of the Women's Varsity Track Team at Tennessee State University," master's thesis (April 1975), Graduate Research Number 1766, TSU Archives.

27. On northern track meets, see the *Chicago Defender* and *Pittsburgh Courier* sports pages. Stokes, as well as Pickett, had been deprived of a place on the 1932 Olympic team despite her apparent qualifications. The American Olympic Committee's requirement that most women pay their own travel expenses nearly prevented their participation in the 1936 Berlin Games, until at the last minute money turned up. I was unable to determine how the money was raised, but for a partial explanation, see *Philadelphia Tribune* (August 13, 1936), p. 14. See also Davis, *Black American Women,* 130–3.

28. Interviews by the author, Lula Hymes Glenn and Alice Coachman Davis (Tuskegee, AL), May 7, 1992, Leila Perry Glover (Atlanta, GA), May 8, 1992, and Edward Temple (Nashville, TN), July 7, 1988; Clemons, "A History of the Women's Varsity," 22; and TSU clippings files at TSU Archives. In its first three years, TSU competed in only one meet per year, and in fifteen years never entered more than seven meets per year.

29. *Atlanta Daily World,* August 6, 1948.

30. *Chicago Defender,* May 22, 1948.

31. Black track athletes flourished throughout the postwar era. In the mid-1950s, 350 women competed at the Tuskegee Relays. Teams from Xavier, Albany State of Georgia, Alabama State, Prairie View A&M, TSU, Philander Smith of Arkansas, Bethune Cookman, and Chicago's Catholic Youth Organization (CYO) entered the senior division, while high schools from throughout the South sent girls to the junior division meet. During these years the Tennessee Tigerbelle team took the mantle from Tuskegee's fading program. TSU won the Tuskegee Relays in 1953 and began a string of AAU national championships. Between 1948 and 1968 Tennessee athletes claimed twenty-five of the forty Olympic track-and-field medals won by American women. See Ashe, *A Hard Road to Glory,* 73–91; Nolan A. Thaxton, "A Documentary Analysis of Competitive Track and Field for Women at Tuskegee Institute and Tennessee State University" (Thesis, Department of Physical Education, Springfield (Mass.) College, 1970); and news clippings from the *Chicago Defender,* Box 401, Claude Barnett Collection, Chicago Historical Society.

32. The following accounts are based on six oral-history interviews with women who competed at Tuskegee or Tennessee State University between the late 1930s and the early 1960s. Glenn interviews; Glover interview; Davis interview; interviews by the author, Shirley Crowder Meadows (Atlanta, GA) December 15, 1991; Martha Hudson Pennyman (Griffin, GA) May 8, 1992; and Willye White (Chicago, IL), February 9, 1988. All the quotes that follow are from these interviews. Individual quotations will be cited only if the speaker is not clearly identifiable from the text.

33. Crowder competed but did not medal in the hurdles. Hudson won a gold medal in the 400-meter relay.

34. White won a silver medal in the long jump in 1956 and a second silver in the 400-meter relay in 1964.

35. Perry interview.

36. Sander L. Gilman, "Black Bodies, White Bodies: Toward an Iconography of Female Sexuality in Late Nineteenth-Century Art, Medicine and Literature," in Henry Louis Gates, Jr., ed., *"Race," Writing and Difference* (Chicago: University of Chicago Press, 1986), 223–61.

37. See John D' Emilio and Estelle Freedman, *Intimate Matters* (New York: Harper & Row, 1988), 87–93. Quote from Herbert G. Gutman, *The Black Family in Slavery and Freedom, 1750–1925,* (New York: Pantheon Books, 1976), 536.

38. Gilman, "Black Bodies, White Bodies," 238.

39. Stereotypes about physical beauty and sexuality could be contradictory. Within the dominant white discourse, black women were represented as both unattractive sexual partners and wildly attractive, irresistible seducers of white and black men alike. Similarly, portrayals of the masculinized black woman might endow her body with a kind of virile sexual passion or with a muscular asexuality.

40. Phillip M. Hoose, *Necessities: Racial Barriers in American Sports* (New York: Random House, 1989), 4.

41. This myth had different implications for images of black men and women. While the notion of "natural," "virile" athleticism supported an

image of the black man as a supermasculine, sexual, brawny, "stud" or "buck" figure, thus affirming the masculinity (if not the humanity) of black men, the ideology had the reverse effect for women. Notions of the "mannish," "primitive" black female athlete pushed African-American women even further outside the parameters of femininity as defined by the dominant culture.

42. Since neither critics nor supporters of women's track and field commented publicly on these omissions, explanations are necessarily based on inference.

43. *New York Times*, April 20, 1931, reprinted in *Amateur Athlete* (June 1931): 8.

44. See *Amateur Athlete* (September 1938), and "A Show of Pretty Plungers," *Life* 46 (May 4, 1959): 65.

45. Kellermann gave popular exhibitions of swimming and diving that were combined fashion, beauty, and skill demonstrations. Holm Jarrett toured with her husband's jazz band and also performed swimming exhibitions. Williams turned her synchronized-swimming skills into a successful movie career.

46. Ironically, the crowning glory of swimming, its supposed femininity, was identified as the problem when, in the mid-1950s, American women lost their number one world position in the sport. Ione Muir, manager of the U.S. women's team, worried that Americans "swim like girls." The challenge for the U.S. team was to find a way that "this femininity in sports may best be overcome." See Muir, "As I See It," *Amateur Athlete* (February 1956): 22.

47. Avery Brundage, speech to National AAU Convention, *Amateur Athlete* (January 1959): 11.

48. George P. Meade, "The Negro in Track Athletics," *Amateur Athlete* (August 1953): 10.

49. Charles Bucher, "Sports Are Color-Blind," *JOHPER* (Journal of Health, Physical Education, and Recreation) 28 (December 1957): 22.

50. "U.S. Girls Wake Up!" *Amateur Athlete* (December 1946): 10.

51. Brundage Collection, Box 70 (Folder-circular letters to IOC's, NOC's, and IF's, 1952–1954), and Box 54 (Folder-Exeter, Marquess David), University of Illinois Archives.

52. Brundage Collection, Box 115 (Folder-Athletics-Women), "IOC quotes for and against women's competition," no date (mid-1950s), University of Illinois Archives.

53. *New York Times*, February 8, 1953, sec. 5, p. 25.

54. *New York Times Magazine*, August 29, 1960, p. 144.

55. *Amateur Athlete* (July 1953): 26, quote from J. Powers of *New York Daily News*; Arthur Daley, *New York Times*, February 8, 1953, sec. 5, p. 25; "The Stronger Soviet Sex," *Life*, 29 (September 18, 1959): 60–62.

56. *Detroit News*, July 31, 1962, sec. B, p. 1, in Claude A. Barnett Collection, Box 402, Chicago Historical Society.

57. Edwin B. Henderson, "Sports Comments," *Atlanta Daily World*, August 4, 1948.

58. *Ebony* 10 (June 1955): 28, 32.

59. A single, inviolable image of respectability held white observers at a distance, creating a kind of buffer zone between public settings and less public African-American environments that may have allowed more personalized, flexible styles of femininity. Darlene Clark Hine makes a similar argument about black women's clubs in the Midwest during the early twentieth century. She argues that African-American women developed a "culture of dissemblance" that presented a public face of unimpeachable propriety and apparent openness to counter negative stereotypes, while they hid their inner pain and pleasures under a "self-imposed invisibility" to gain psychic space and freedom from public scrutiny. "Rape and the Inner Lives of Black Women in the Middle West: Preliminary Thoughts on the Culture of Dissemblance," *Signs* 14 (Summer 1989): 912–20.

60. *Amateur Athlete* (November 1950): 28.

61. *Amateur Athlete* (September 1954): 21.

62. Roxy Andersen, "Girls Thrive on Sport," *Amateur Athlete* (November 1950): 28.

63. Andersen, "Statistical Survey of Former Women Athletes," *Amateur Athlete* (September 1954): 10.

64. *Parade* (March 16, 1952), reprinted in *Amateur Athlete* (April 1952): 22.

65. *Time* 76 (September 19, 1960): 74–5.

66. Guttmann, *Women's Sports*, 204.

67. Patricia Hill Collins has argued that when white culture has accepted African Americans it has often been as "pets" rather than as equals, merely changing the terms of oppression from absolute subordination to subordination with affection. Collins, "Toward a Sexual Politics of Black Womanhood," guest lecture at the University of Minnesota (March 31, 1989). See also Collins, *Black Feminist Thought*, 74.

68. Frances Kaszubski, "In Defense of Women Athletes—Part 2," *Amateur Athlete* 3 (October 1962): 16.

69. *Ibid.*

12

JIM CROW IN THE GYMNASIUM
The Integration of College Basketball in the American South

Charles H. Martin

AT THE START OF the twenty-first century, the game of basketball enjoys unprecedented international stature. Once restricted primarily to the United States, the sport is now played extensively around the world and trails only soccer in popularity as a team sport. The 1992 Olympic Games in Barcelona, Spain, proved to be a watershed in the sport's international development. The participation of previously excluded American professional stars such as Michael Jordan, Larry Bird, and "Magic" Johnson in the men's basketball competition greatly stimulated worldwide interest in the game. The ease with which the Americans captured the team championship inspired other countries to upgrade their development and coaching programs. Ten years later, the results of these efforts could be seen in the growing presence of foreign players in the National Basketball Association (NBA) in the U.S., the embarrassing defeat of the American team (missing its top professional stars) in the 2002 world championships in Indianapolis, Indiana, and the selection by the Houston Rockets of 7′6″ Chinese center Yao Ming as the first choice in the 2002 NBA player draft. Nonetheless, American players still dominate the game today, mostly because of the substantial contributions of African-American athletes, who also are the major force within professional and college basketball inside the United States. But just over five decades ago, the social and racial dimensions of the American sport were dramatically different. At the end of the Second World War, basketball in the U.S. was a white sport, and most blacks were either excluded or marginalized within its ranks. This was especially true in the American South, the traditional center of the African-American population, where racial discrimination and rigid segregation permeated virtually every area of public life, including sports.

Southern universities were very much a part of this racial status quo during the era of Jim Crow. At a typical segregated southern college in 1945, the faculty, staff (except for some custodial and food service employees), student body, and athletic teams were all white. African Americans were restricted to poorly funded black colleges, whose academic and athletic worlds were kept virtually separate from their white counterparts. During the late 1940s and 1950s, other regions of the U.S. gradually abandoned the more blatant forms of racial discrimination, but the white South firmly resisted any racial change, even in sports. The struggle to maintain segregation in college athletics represented just one battle within a larger war being fought to preserve what conservative whites called "our southern way of life." Even after the famous 1954 United States Supreme Court ruling in *Brown v. Board of Education,* which declared segregated public schools to be unconstitutional, many historically white southern colleges delayed admitting black students until the early 1960s. Despite the arrival of African Americans on campus, many "big time" athletic programs continued to exclude them from school teams until the end of the decade or even the early 1970s. A few myopic white sports fans even confidently predicted that the inclusion of black athletes would add little or nothing to a team's strength. Regrettably, the basketball court and the football field remained symbols of white supremacy even after other areas of college life were integrated.[1]

Ideally, of course, sport in a democratic society should offer individuals an opportunity to escape the restrictions of race and class, especially since athletic performance is extremely measurable. An editorial writer for the *New York Times* expressed the classic liberal viewpoint in 1959 when he wrote, "Sport . . . puts no artificial barriers as race or religion in the way of performance. What counts and what matters is what the given individual can do." But an athletic meritocracy did not exist in the South, because white supremacy as expressed through segregation excluded African Americans from the premier college programs and relegated them to smaller programs at all-black colleges. White and black liberals of the 1950s and 1960s urged an end to this apartheid in southern college sports. They hoped that athletic desegregation would not only open up opportunities for individual blacks but also create a highly visible model of interracial cooperation that could hasten integration in other areas of American life.[2] Eventually their hopes were fulfilled, as segregationists failed to halt the process of racial change in sports. The decision by university administrators to abandon segregation and voluntarily to recruit black athletes thus represented an important turning point in southern race relations and reflected a new white attitude, which saw integration as inevitable and potentially beneficial.

This study will address several important questions concerning the lengthy process through which southern college sports were integrated: (1) What were the racial dynamics of potential interracial competition between southern and northern colleges prior to the *Brown* decision? (2) What external and internal pressures were mobilized to prevent sports integration? (3) What social and political forces encouraged the abandonment of segregation? (4) What types of schools were willing to take the lead in breaking the color line and how important were university presidents in these decisions? (5) What were the characteristics of those athletes who served as "racial pioneers"? (6) Were college athletic programs in the vanguard of social change in the South, or did sports serve the conservative function of reinforcing racial values that were under attack? The geographical focus will be on the area covered by the Southeastern Conference (the states of Florida, Georgia, Alabama, Mississippi, Louisiana, Tennessee, and Kentucky) and the Southwest Conference (Texas plus Arkansas). Major colleges with independent sports programs in these same states will also be examined.

College basketball today enjoys enormous popularity in all areas of the United States, but several decades ago its appeal was less widespread, especially in the Deep South. The sport itself dates from the 1890s, when James Naismith, a Canadian-born physical educator at Springfield College in Massachusetts, originated an indoor game played with peach baskets and a ball in order to help pass the winter months between football and baseball.

The sport quickly caught on, and by 1900 many white colleges in the South fielded school teams. The Southwest Conference (SWC) inaugurated organized competition in 1915, and the Southeastern Conference (SEC) did so in 1932. By the 1930s, the college game attracted a wider audience. Responding to this fan interest, the National Collegiate Athletic Association (NCAA) established a postseason playoff tournament in 1939. After the Second World War, basketball continued to gain in popularity, although it still lagged far behind college football in public enthusiasm and media exposure.[3]

In 1945, both professional baseball, the number one national sport, and professional basketball remained segregated. Jackie Robinson broke the color line for major league baseball in 1947 when he joined the Brooklyn Dodgers, demonstrating that organized sports could not escape postwar racial change. However, the National Basketball Association remained segregated until 1950, when three African Americans, Charles "Chuck" Cooper, Earl Lloyd, and Nat "Sweetwater" Clifton, signed NBA contracts.[4] On the collegiate level a handful of black players had appeared in uniform for northern basketball and football teams prior to 1930, and a few more participated during the depression decade. Their numbers increased after the war, and by the mid-1950s most college teams outside the South had achieved a token level of integration. This change created the possibility of interracial play whenever southern white squads ventured north of the Mason-Dixon Line.[5]

The idea of playing against an integrated team was a disturbing thought for white southerners who had grown up in a rigidly segregated world. Traditionally, southern whites had avoided such situations either by not scheduling northern teams or by insisting in advance that their opponents refrain from using their black player(s). Most northern schools quietly acquiesced in these so-called gentlemen's agreements in both basketball and football. In December 1945, for example, basketball coach Clair Bee withheld the two black players on his Long Island University team from a game against the University of Tennessee, in deference to the visitors' racial sensitivities. An argument between football coaches from Georgia Tech and the University of Michigan produced the most bizarre application of this policy in 1934 at Ann Arbor, Michigan. Each team withheld one player from competition in order to prevent Tech's southern whites from having to play against the Wolverines' outstanding end, Willis Ward, who was an African American.[6]

During the Second World War, the racial attitudes of northern whites gradually began to change. After 1945, the small but growing presence of black students on northern campuses and the continuing spread of more liberal racial attitudes among white students created a different atmosphere on campus. By 1950, most northern schools refused to withhold an African-American athlete when playing at home against a southern team. Moreover, these colleges were increasingly reluctant to leave behind their black athletes during southern travel, as had been previously customary. This growing sensitivity had clearly evidenced itself by 1956, when several midwestern schools, including Indiana University, announced that they would no longer schedule games in the South if their black players were barred.[7]

From the start, southern universities reacted cooly to the changing racial patterns in postwar college sports. The first of many recurring incidents took place in December 1946, when the visiting University of Tennessee squad refused to take the floor for a scheduled basketball game against Duquesne University in McKeesport, Pennsylvania. The Tennessee

Volunteers demanded assurances that Charles Cooper, an African American and the top scorer for the home team, would not play. Although the Duquesne coach offered to withhold his black star unless the game were close at the end, this gesture was not sufficient to appease the visitors, and the game was cancelled even though 2,600 fans had already assembled. A week earlier, Cooper had been permitted to play in an away game against Morehead State Teachers College at Louisville, Kentucky, possibly becoming the first black cager to play against an all-white college team inside the South. Appropriately enough, he scored the winning basket.[8]

Once southern colleges adjusted to the fact that northern teams might include African Americans, they sought to dodge such encounters through careful scheduling. This technique usually proved successful, but at the cost of avoiding intersectional play. Since basketball was not the premier campus sport, except at the University of Kentucky, a perennial national power, southern administrators received few complaints over these adjustments to regular season schedules.

NCAA basketball playoffs presented a more difficult problem, however, because a southern school could not select its opponents in the postseason championship tournament. Teams representing the Southwest Conference were not overly disturbed about the possibility of such interracial play, reflecting a cultural break with the Deep South on selected racial issues. But for SEC members from the Lower South, interracial tournament play remained highly controversial. The University of Kentucky helped prevent other southern teams from having to face that dilemma, however, for the highly successful Wildcats of coach Adolph Rupp regularly won the SEC title and represented the conference in the NCAA playoffs. In fact, during the ten-year period from 1948 to 1958, Kentucky won the national championship four times. Although the conservative Rupp was at best a paternalist in race relations, he and the university viewed the scheduling of an occasional interracial game as the price of success. In the late 1940s, the University of Kentucky began playing integrated teams on northern trips, and in December 1951 the university even staged a home game in Lexington against a St. John's team from New York City that included one black player.[9]

Federal court rulings further undermined segregation at southern colleges and placed new pressures on their athletic programs. Through a series of rulings in the 1940s and early 1950s, the courts had already established that segregation in graduate and professional education was unconstitutional. When the United States Supreme Court issued its famous *Brown v. Board of Education* ruling in May 1954, segregated undergraduate education also became illegal. Although a few southern schools had already desegregated their graduate programs, the potential integration of undergraduate studies would be far more significant to college athletics, since it created the possibility that black students might attempt to participate in their colleges' athletic programs (restricted to undergraduates only). Even in the relatively liberal atmosphere of the University of Texas at Austin, such a thought was heretical. Although UT admitted five black undergraduates shortly after the *Brown* ruling, it quickly reversed course and expelled them when "one of them expressed interest in playing college football."[10]

In subsequent years, southern white colleges, once legally desegregated, faced a major decision over whether to integrate their athletic programs. Their response followed a pattern demonstrated by the Big Six Conference (later the Big Eight) and the Missouri Valley Conference in the late 1940s. The last major nonsouthern conferences to desegregate, the two midwestern leagues were heavily influenced by members from the southernmost state in the region, Oklahoma, where a transplanted southern heritage delayed integration of public universities. As a result of strong pressure from the Oklahoma schools (Tulsa and Oklahoma A&M in the Missouri Valley, the University of Oklahoma in the Big Six), both conferences established informal gentlemen's agreements whereby member schools promised not to recruit black athletes. Finally, in December 1947, the Missouri Valley Conference voted to end such racial discrimination by September 1950.[11]

The Big Six moved more slowly. In April 1946, student councils at the University of Nebraska and the University of Kansas launched a campaign against the gentlemen's agreement. In May, conference representatives replaced the unwritten policy with a written guideline, which now explicitly authorized a member institution playing at home to bar the use of black athletes by opponents. This evasive action did not fool critics, who continued to crusade for the rule's repeal. Eventually the conference relented and dropped the policy in 1950. Another racial barrier in the Midwest fell in 1948, when the National Association of Intercollegiate Basketball (NAIB, later known as the NAIA) dropped its ban against the participation of black players in its postseason tournament for smaller colleges held annually in Kansas City. The NAIB acted in response to a threatened boycott by several eastern Catholic schools.[12]

During the 1950s, with most formal barriers outside the South removed, black athletes began to make their presence felt in football and especially basketball. Highly skilled players, such as Bill Russell and K. C. Jones of the University of San Francisco, Walter Dukes of Seton Hall, Si Green of Duquesne, and Wilt Chamberlain of Kansas, won considerable acclaim. The growing black presence was dramatically symbolized by the All-America selections of 1958. In the spring of that year four African-American college stars—Wilt Chamberlain, Oscar Robertson, Elgin Baylor, and Guy Rodgers—were named to both the Associated Press and United Press honorary teams. This was particularly startling since only once in any previous major poll had even three black players been selected in the same year. More significantly yet, the National Basketball Coaches Association chose the same four plus Kansas State's Bob Boozer for its honorary squad, thereby creating the first all-black All-America team.[13]

The continuing recruitment of African Americans by northern colleges and the Supreme Court's *Brown v. Board of Education* ruling put pressure on Deep South colleges to modify their policies. Yet at the same time, political demagogues and public opinion inside their states vehemently demanded that they maintain athletic segregation. In the wake of the *Brown* decision, "massive resistance" to federally mandated desegregation spread across the Deep South, as recalcitrant state and local officials solemnly promised to block all racial change. "The South stands at Armageddon," Governor Marvin Griffin of Georgia dramatically proclaimed in 1956. "The battle is joined. There is no more difference in compromising the integrity of race on the playing field than in doing so in the classroom." Constructing a domino theory of integration, Griffin ominously warned, "One break in the dike and the relentless seas will rush in and destroy us." Because of the strength of such segregationist pressure, university officials concluded that they had no alternative but to maintain the existing color line in college sports. In fact, several states and municipalities, such as Birmingham, Alabama, even adopted laws (if they did not already have them) prohibiting interracial sporting events, as part of a larger effort to maintain segregation in such recreational facilities as parks, swimming pools, and athletic fields.[14]

In the early summer of 1956, the Louisiana legislature took the lead in the sports world's "massive resistance" when it passed a bill making it illegal for black and white players to compete against each other in the same "athletic training, games, sports, or contests." The bill's passage upset civic leaders in New Orleans, where the Mid-Winter Sports Association sponsored the Sugar Bowl football game on New Year's Day and the Sugar Bowl basketball tournament. Business leaders and New Orleans legislators attempted to gain an exemption from the law for the city, but their efforts were soundly rejected. They next appealed to Governor Earl K. Long to veto the bill. But Long eventually signed the act, commenting that his mail had been running four to one in favor of the legislation. As a result of the new law, three northern teams promptly withdrew from the Sugar Bowl Basketball Tournament.[15]

The state law also interfered with scheduling by those white Louisiana colleges who were willing to play integrated teams. Loyola University of New Orleans, a Jesuit institute, had dropped its opposition to playing against black athletes after the *Brown* decision and hosted the first integrated collegiate basketball game in the state in December 1954. The new law forced Loyola and also Centenary College to cancel games with northern squads that had already been scheduled for the upcoming season because their opponents refused to withhold their black players. Harvard University even got into the controversy during the fall of 1956 by announcing that it had cancelled a four-game southern tour in order to protest such athletic segregation laws, even though the Massachusetts college did not have an African American on its 1956–1957 basketball squad.[16]

Universities in the state of Mississippi had an even heavier burden to bear. White sentiment there was intensely and sometimes violently anti-integration, and most state officials were extreme segregationists. On December 29, 1956, administrators at Mississippi State University withdrew their basketball team from the championship game of the Evansville, Indiana, Invitational Tournament after Mississippi newspapers revealed that MSU had played against an unexpectedly integrated University of Denver squad in the opening round and that its opponent in the finals, the host Evansville College team, also included black players. The following day, the University of Mississippi (commonly known as Ole Miss) Rebels forfeited the consolation match in the All American Basketball Tournament in Owensboro, Kentucky, rather than play Iona College of New York, which had one black player, Stanley Hill. Ironically, Kentucky Wesleyan, the local, church-related small college that hosted the tournament, played Iona in the opening round without any interference from Kentucky officials.[17]

These political pressures even affected one black Mississippi university. In the spring of 1957, Jackson State College was forced to withdraw its basketball team from the NCAA small college tournament because it would have competed against racially mixed or all-white teams. The state's college board instructed Jackson State President Jacob L. Reddix that it was official policy "that state institutions of higher learning shall not participate in national athletic tournaments under the present conditions." As additional intimidation, one Mississippi legislator introduced a bill in the state legislature which would suspend state funds to any institution that sanctioned an integrated game.[18]

In Georgia, the state assembly began debating in early 1957 a series of measures that would have tightened the state's segregation system, including a proposal to prohibit integrated athletic contests. The bill's main sponsor, Senator Leon Butts, emphasized that interracial sporting events would set a dangerous example, because "when Negroes and whites meet on the athletic fields on a basis of complete equality, it is only natural that this sense of equality carries into the daily living of these people." The bill passed the senate by a unanimous vote, but in the house a small band of legislators, worried that such a law would destroy minor league baseball in Georgia, blocked its passage. Despite the bill's defeat, the Georgia Board of Regents subsequently reaffirmed its institutional prohibition against state colleges scheduling home games against integrated teams.[19]

The federal courts eventually halted these attempts to ban interracial athletic events through state law. Louisiana's Jim Crow system had included a longstanding ban on boxing matches between black and white fighters, as well as the new 1956 law. On May 25, 1959, the Supreme Court upheld a lower court ruling and declared the Louisiana boxing ban to be unconstitutional, thereby also nullifying the 1956 law restricting mixed competition in other sports. Loyola University then announced that it would resume playing northern basketball teams, and Sugar Bowl officials regained flexibility in team selection.[20]

Members of the Southwest Conference in Texas (but not in Arkansas) escaped the kinds of scheduling pressures that influenced Southeastern Conference schools in the states of Mississippi, Georgia, Louisiana, and Alabama. Although Texas historically had been identified as part of the Deep South, the state was culturally diverse enough to be considered part of the Border South by 1955. Texas Governor Allan Shivers did launch a modest effort at "massive resistance" against the integration of elementary and secondary schools, but he and segregationists from East Texas (where most black Texans lived) achieved only limited success before his term of office expired in early 1957. "Race ceased being a statewide factor" in Texas politics thereafter, historian George N. Green observed, "and by failing to embrace the South's tactics of massive resistance, Texas drifted further away from southern moorings." In Arkansas, however, Governor Orval Faubus's active role in the massive resistance movement forced the University of Arkansas to be more cautious than its Texas counterparts in implementing academic and athletic integration.[21]

The most persistent resistance to accepting integrated competition on the basketball court in the late 1950s and early 1960s came in the state of Mississippi. There the continuing integration crisis adversely affected the Mississippi State University basketball team and its hopes of competing in the NCAA Tournament. Under Coach Babe McCarthy, the Bulldogs regularly battled the Kentucky Wildcats for league supremacy during these years. In 1959, Mississippi State captured the SEC crown with an outstanding 24–1 season record, but school officials honored the state's political stand and declined an invitation to the NCAA Tournament. Two years later, Mississippi State captured the SEC title once more but continued its policy of refusing to compete in the NCAA Tournament. In 1962, during the height of the state's school integration crisis, MSU again compiled a remarkable 24–1 record and shared the conference championship with Kentucky. Once more school officials reluctantly bowed to political pressure from segregationist and skipped the NCAA playoffs.[22]

Despite Mississippi State's continuing difficulties, most SEC universities had escaped administrative restrictions on interracial play, at least outside their home states—by the early 1960s, southern resistance to integration had eased somewhat. But politically conscious administrators at Ole Miss and Mississippi State still refused to schedule athletic contests against integrated teams at home or away. In the 1962–1963 season, the MSU basketball team enjoyed yet another highly successful year, going 21–5, winning the SEC title, and finishing sixth in the final Associated Press national poll. Determined to give Coach

Babe McCarthy's squad a chance to display their talent, university officials finally decided to challenge the state's die-hard segregationists and Governor Ross Barnett. In early March 1963, President Dean W. Colvard, a North Carolina native, courageously announced that he would permit the team to participate in the NCAA tournament unless "vetoed by competent authority." Colvard's action came just one semester after the admission to Ole Miss of its first black student, James Meredith, had touched off a violent riot on campus that caused two deaths and required the intervention of national guard troops. His bold decision was politically risky, and he understandably feared that he might lose his job.[23]

Governor Ross Barnett promptly denounced Colvard's decision, and several segregationists in the state legislature threatened to cut off the school's appropriations. The *Jackson Clarion Ledger,* a leading champion of white supremacy, warned that the MSU action was a dangerous one, explaining that playing against a black athlete in the North was just as bad as doing so at home. And if a school would stoop that low, then "why not recruit a Negro of special basketball ability to play on the Mississippi State team? This is the road we seem to be traveling." Another Mississippi newspaper cautioned that although athletic prestige was important, "our southern way of life is infinitely more precious." Encouraged by petitions from MSU alumni and students, however, the State Board of Institutions of Higher Learning voted 8–3 to abandon its unwritten policy of prohibiting interracial athletic competition.[24]

Despite the vote, die-hard segregationists did not give up quite yet. A local judge granted a temporary injunction barring the squad from leaving the state, but Justice Robert Gillespie of the state supreme court dissolved it. Yet on Thursday morning, March 14, MSU players still feared that state or county officials might prevent their departure. As a precaution, only the reserve players initially showed up at the Starkville airport for their flight to East Lansing, Michigan. Then at departure time, when everything seemed safe, the starters suddenly appeared and hastily boarded the chartered plane. The flight made an intermediate stop in Nashville, Tennessee, where Coach McCarthy joined them, having sneaked out of the state during the previous evening as an additional precaution.

Ironically, MSU's opponent in Michigan was Loyola University of Chicago, which started four black players. Tournament officials took extensive security precautions for the contest, and the ceremonial "pre-game handshake was as much a media event as the game itself." The game was a hard-played, clean contest with no incidents. State took the early lead, but Loyola finally broke the game open in the closing minutes and rolled to a 61–51 win. The Ramblers eventually advanced to the NCAA finals, where they upset the University of Cincinnati for the national championship. The *New York Times* heralded Mississippi State's participation in the tournament as an important breakthrough in southern race relations. Noting the existence of excellent black athletes in the South and the potential benefits both in winning and in racial adjustment that might follow their utilization, the newspaper pondered "what tremendous champions might come out of the Southeast, with such recruits to build upon, and what quiet miracles might be worked in better race relations?"[25]

Mississippi State's participation in the 1963 NCAA Tournament closed one phase in race relations for southern college sports and opened another. Now that interracial games were politically acceptable, presidents from several universities in the Border South began to consider the next logical step—the actual integration of a southern white team. In the Southeastern Conference, the University of Kentucky initially took the lead. Campus opinion strongly supported the recruitment of black athletes, and the student newspaper called for the integration of the school's athletic programs just after the Mississippi State incident. In May 1963, the university's athletic board unexpectedly announced that its programs would immediately "be open to any student, regardless of race." President Frank G. Dickey apparently pushed for the change, and his successor, John Oswald, continued the process. The impact of the Kentucky announcement was tempered by the fact that the school had already given out its scholarships for the following year. Moreover, the athletic board stressed that the new policy would be carried out within the context of the college's SEC obligations.[26]

Similar forces were developing in the western portion of the South. Texas colleges had desegregated their undergraduate studies several years earlier than schools in the Deep South and had been less opposed to playing integrated northern teams. Still, in 1960, six years after the *Brown* decision, Southwest Conference basketball and football teams remained segregated, and no immediate change was planned. At the University of Texas in Austin, students began campaigning in the spring of 1961 for the recruitment of black athletes. During the fall, student government presidents of seven Southwest Conference schools jointly issued a resolution urging that "capable athletes of all races" be admitted to members' athletic programs. But university officials ignored the demands and remained silent on the issue.[27]

The inaction of administrators at Southwest Conference schools was understandable. Coaches at these colleges presided over athletic programs with high public prestige and therefore saw little need for change. On the other hand, coaches at major independent and small colleges, both of which suffered from lower status, opportunistically realized that integrating their teams would attract better athletes and help win more games. In the South, a university's public standing was often influenced more by its athletic accomplishments than its academic reputation, so a successful sports program was crucial to improving a school's status. Thus it is not surprising that the first major success in breaking the color line in major college sports in Dixie took place at an ambitious but relatively unknown university located in the Border South.

In 1956, Texas Western College took that giant step. TWC was located in the city of El Paso, in the far western end of the state on the border with Mexico and New Mexico. Now known as the University of Texas at El Paso, Texas Western was at that time an institution with a lackluster athletic tradition but ambitious dreams for the future. In El Paso, African Americans made up only about 3 percent of the total population, which was split almost evenly between Anglo Americans and Mexican Americans. Although racism and segregation existed in El Paso, the city's mixed population and its western orientation diluted traditional southern white attitudes. Acknowledging the city's unique location, the UT board of regents in 1950 gave Texas Western a special dispensation from its policy banning interracial athletic contests, so that TWC could host integrated teams from the states of Arizona, New Mexico, and California. In September 1955, the college officially admitted twelve black undergraduates, becoming the first four-year Texas school to publicly do so.[28]

In September 1956, the first two black basketball players to play for a historically white southern university quietly enrolled at TWC. Charles Brown and his nephew Cecil Brown, transfers from Amarillo Junior College, were politely received by students but were forced to live off-campus during their first year at TWC because campus dormitories remained segregated. Charles Brown, the more successful of the two, attracted considerable attention in the Southwest. During his three-year career, the "Amarillo whiz" led the Miners to two Border Conference titles and three times earned all-conference honors. The hiring of new head coach Don Haskins in 1961 guaranteed that more black players would be recruited, for Haskins ignored political considerations and aggressively recruited the best available athletes, regardless of race. Since almost no other major basketball power inside the state accepted African-American players before the mid-1960s, Texas Western enjoyed a competitive edge in recruiting for nearly a decade.[29]

During the late 1950s and early 1960s, a few additional southern schools also became bolder. In particular, small colleges saw the recruitment of black prep stars as one means of upgrading their programs and winning championships, since they would not have to recruit against the "big name" universities for such athletes. In 1957, St. Mary's College in San Antonio, Texas, recruited its first black player, center Maurice Harris of College Station, where SWC member Texas A&M College was located. In his first varsity game, Harris led St. Mary's to a shocking 69–56 upset of the A&M team. Pan American College in Edin-

Figure 12–1
In November, 1956, Charles Brown of Texas Western College in El Paso, Texas, became the first African American to play Division I basketball for an historically white university in the ex-Confederate South. The 6′1″ forward earned all-Border Conference honors during each of his three seasons at Texas Western. Courtesy of University of Texas-El Paso Archives.

burg, located in far South Texas near the U.S.-Mexican border, began recruiting black basketball players in 1959. In the spring of 1963, the Broncs captured the NAIA championship in Kansas City behind towering center Lucious Jackson. Ironically, no predominantly white major university in the state had bothered to offer Jackson a scholarship when he finished high school three years earlier.[30]

Three additional major colleges abandoned athletic segregation during this period. North Texas State College in Denton, forty miles north of Fort Worth, belonged to the Missouri Valley Conference, in which it competed against integrated teams from the Midwest. North Texas integrated its varsity football team in the fall of 1958 and its varsity basketball team during the 1960–1961 season. The University of Louisville, an independent about to join the Missouri Valley Conference, broke the color line in the Upper South. In November 1964, three black sophomores—Wade Houston, Stan Smith, and Eddie Whitehead—made their varsity basketball debuts for the Cardinals. Western Kentucky University also featured an integrated team that same month.[31]

The Atlantic Coast Conference likewise abandoned segregation in its athletic programs in the mid-1960s. Composed of major colleges in Maryland, Virginia, North Carolina, and South Carolina, the ACC had traditionally been somewhat more flexible on race than the SEC. During the 1930s and 1940s, for example, several members had played against integrated northern teams. Moreover, the state of Maryland had not been part of the Confederacy during the Civil War, and the geographical proximity and cultural interaction of the Mid-Atlantic region with the Northeast made change appear less frightening. Still, it was not until 1962 that the University of Maryland, the northernmost school in the conference, broke the ACC color line by granting an athletic scholarship to an African-American football player. Two years later the university successfully recruited the league's first black basketball player, Billy Jones, of Towson, Maryland. Wake Forest College, a North Carolina Baptist school, also integrated its athletic program in 1964.[32]

Against the background of such change, the growing success of the Texas Western College basketball program called further attention to the potential benefits of recruiting black athletes. Coach Don Haskins's 1965–1966 squad enjoyed the school's most successful season ever, losing only one regular season game and finishing third in both wire service polls. Ahead of Texas Western in the final rankings were traditional southern powerhouses Kentucky (number one) and Duke (number two). Both the Wildcats and the Blue Devils fielded all-white teams, but the racial composition of the Miners was quite different. The Texas Western squad consisted of seven African Americans, four Anglo Americans, and one Mexican American. Although Haskins utilized all of his players during the regular season, the seven African Americans, all starters or top reserves, attracted the most attention. Surviving several close games in the NCAA Tournament, the Miners advanced to the title contest in College Park, Maryland, against the University of Kentucky Wildcats, the SEC champion.

Viewers who turned on their television sets on March 19, 1966, witnessed a game literally played in black and white—both on the TV screen and on the actual floor of Cole Field House. For the first time ever in an NCAA final, five black starters played against five white starters. With guard Bobby Joe Hill harassing the Wildcat ball handlers and intimidating center David Lattin controlling the backboards, the Miners took control of the game midway through the first half and never relinquished the lead, winning 72–65. Texas Western's stunning win shocked many white coaches and infuriated white segregationists. Haskins received an avalanche of "hate mail" denouncing him for using black players. But to black sports fans the game was a major milestone, as the pride of southern white basketball went down to an embarrassing defeat before an all-black lineup. Although one should not exaggerate the influence of one game, it was quite clear after March 1966 that southern basketball teams would have to change or become increasingly noncompetitive nationally. For the African-American athlete, then, the Texas Western victory was the "emancipation proclamation" of southern college basketball.[33]

The first breakthrough in Southeastern Conference basketball took place just two months after the Miners' victory. At Vanderbilt University in Nashville, Chancellor Alexander Heard had been quietly working to liberalize race relations on campus. In May 1966, with Heard's support, basketball coach Roy Skinner signed Perry Wallace, a widely recruited local prep star and high school valedictorian, to an athletic scholarship. Despite speculation by the press that further change was just around the corner, no other SEC school initially followed Vanderbilt's example. Wallace officially broke the SEC's color line for varsity play in November 1967, but not until two years later did Henry Harris of

Figure 12–2
In March, 1966, the Texas Western College Miners upset the University of Kentucky Wildcats, the Southeastern Conference champions, to capture the NCAA basketball title. Texas Western shocked many white fans by starting five African Americans in the game, while Kentucky's team, like every other SEC squad, was all-white. Courtesy of University of Texas-El Paso Archives.

Auburn join him. The only 2 African Americans among 120 SEC basketball players during that 1969–1970 season, Wallace and Harris were often subjected to vicious racial epithets from rival fans and rough play by opposing teams.[34]

The black press and several white sportswriters regularly criticized this slow pace of integration, embarrassing the conference. In 1969, three additional SEC members finally awarded basketball scholarships to African Americans. One of these athletes, Wendell Hudson, was the first black player ever to receive an athletic scholarship at the University of Alabama. In the late fall of 1970, Hudson began his SEC varsity career, as did Ronnie Hogue at the University of Georgia and seven-foot center Tom Payne at the University of Kentucky. These players' appearance in their school's uniforms indicated that recruiting habits in the conference had changed at last. In 1972, Mississippi State, the league's last hold-out, fielded its first integrated varsity squad, as segregation in the SEC finally ended. Over the ensuing years, the number of African Americans awarded basketball scholarships grew rapidly. By the 1975–1976 season, black athletes comprised 45 per cent of all SEC varsity players. During the 1980s, two-thirds or more of conference basketball players were African Americans, a remarkable change from Perry Wallace's first lonely season back in 1966–1967.[35]

Despite a less conservative racial climate in Texas, actual integration of Southwest Conference basketball teams proceeded at a snail's pace. Although two black runners joined the University of Texas freshman track team in 1963, UT did not integrate its basketball or football programs at that time. Other SWC schools cited this inaction by the UT athletic program, the most prestigious in the state, as an excuse for their own inaction. In late 1963, UT, Texas A&M, and Texas Tech did announce that their athletic programs would henceforth be open to student athletes of any color. Other SWC colleges soon issued the same statement, but none of them actually recruited a black player during the remainder of the school year, leaving the seriousness of their commitment in doubt.[36]

At this time, another major independent college in Texas broke ranks and began recruiting African Americans. The University of Houston, which launched an aggressive drive for athletic respectability in the early 1960s, soon upstaged its more prestigious SWC rivals. In 1964, Houston basketball coach Guy V. Lewis successfully recruited black stars Elvin Hayes and Don Chaney, whose three varsity seasons from 1965 to 1968 built Houston into a national power. Lewis's extensive recruitment of African Americans and the Cougars' continued success rankled SWC coaches and put additional pressure on them to follow suit.[37]

The first Southwest Conference member to abandon the color line in basketball was Texas Christian University in Fort Worth, which was affiliated with the Disciples of Christ Church. At the urging of President M. E. Sadler, coach Buster Brannon signed local star James Cash to an athletic scholarship in the spring of 1965. A few months earlier, Southern Methodist University of Dallas had awarded the first SWC football scholarship to an African American—Jerry Levias of Beaumont. The signing of these two prep stars, each of which made his varsity debut in the fall of 1966, "broke the ice" and encouraged others to follow suit. Unlike their counterparts in the SEC, SWC coaches quickly imitated TCU's example. During the 1967–1968 season, Tommy Bowman of Baylor University, a Baptist institution, and Thomas Johnson of the University of Arkansas joined Cash in SWC varsity play. The remaining schools then intensified their efforts, and integration in the conference was almost complete before more than two SEC schools had put any black basketball players in uniform.[38]

Figure 12–3
Perry Wallace of Vanderbilt University was the first African American to play varsity basketball in the Southeastern Conference. Not until his senior season in 1969–1970 did a second African American, Henry Harris of Auburn University, join him in SEC varsity competition. Courtesy of Vanderbilt University Archives.

While the Southwest Conferences eventually moved more rapidly on integration than did the more conservative SEC, major southern independents acted even faster. Loyola University of New Orleans, a Catholic university, signed Charles Powell of Baton Rouge to a basketball scholarship in 1965. In December 1966, in one of his first varsity games, Powell led Loyola to an 87–86 upset win over the all-white team from Louisiana State University, an SEC member. Florida State University in Tallahassee and Memphis State University in Tennessee, also fielded integrated varsity squads in the fall of 1966. In 1967, Miami University of Florida followed suit. Tulane University (an ex-SEC member) and the University of Southern Mississippi integrated their varsity teams in the fall of 1969. Thus it seems clear that the absence of a conference affiliation was an asset which permitted ambitious independents to pursue athletic success without excessive concern for traditional racial politics.[39]

But what of the pioneering athletes themselves? The individuals selected to break the color line were usually young men possessing exceptional athletic talent and often considerable academic ability as well. Coaches also looked for evidence of good character and mental toughness. Such characteristics were essential, because, in addition to the academic and social adjustments these players faced on campus, rival fans often subjected them to racial taunts, opposing players to rough play, and referees to quick whistles.

Most of these pioneers performed quite well on the basketball court, especially considering the pressures they had to face, and several went on to establish successful careers after their playing days were over. James Cash of Texas Christian University was named to the all-conference second team his senior year. A diligent student, he later earned a doctorate from Purdue University, taught in the Harvard Business School, and served on the board of trustees for TCU. Vanderbilt's Perry Wallace, also an all-conference second team selection, earned a law degree at Columbia University and became a law school professor. Charles Brown of Texas Western moved to California after graduation and worked for many years as a senior administrator in the San Francisco Unified School District. Wade Houston of the University of Louisville later served from 1989 through 1994 as the head basketball coach at the University of Tennessee in Knoxville, where he could not play upon graduation from a nearby high school in 1962 because of his race. On the other hand, Henry Harris of Auburn was frustrated by injuries and never achieved his potential on the court. Suffering from severe personal problems after failing to gain a spot in the NBA, he committed suicide in 1974. Most of the other pioneers went on to lead relatively normal and productive lives. Regardless of later developments, each of them was a talented athlete recruited to help his team win, not to further a social experiment. Nonetheless, their presence in the college gymnasium further undermined the white South's defense of segregation and helped hasten its demise.[40]

College sports in the twentieth-century American South did not exist in a social and cultural vacuum. The region's pervasive system of white supremacy and racial segregation controlled athletic policy just as tightly as it did university admissions. During the 1950s and 1960s, conservative southern whites adamantly and sometimes violently resisted federal efforts to eliminate discrimination in such areas as voting rights, employment, and public accommodations. Higher education, including college athletics, served as one of the major battlefields in this protracted conflict. The struggle to integrate southern college sports lasted for nearly three decades, from 1945 until 1972. At the start of this period, most historically white universities simply refused to play against integrated teams, even in the North, and none permitted black students to enroll. The *Brown v. Board of Education* ruling in 1954 led to the eventual desegregation of undergraduate education, but most southern universities initially continued to maintain lily-white athletic programs. Changing student and faculty attitudes, complaints from the small but growing numbers of African-American students on campus, pressure from nonsouthern colleges, the passage of the Civil Rights Act of 1964, and especially the desire to win more games ultimately combined to convince university administrators to abandon the color line in college sports.

Those schools that were the first to integrate their basketball programs tended to be relatively unknown but ambitious independent colleges whose current athletic programs generally lacked the status that went with membership in the prestigious Southwest or Southeastern Conferences. The University of Houston, once derisively known as "Cougar High" to local residents, built up a powerful athletic program and eventually won a prized admission to the Southwest Conference, in large part because of its successful recruitment of black athletes from the Texas-Louisiana region. A Border South location usually made desegregation easier. Two of the leaders in basketball integration—Texas Western College and the University of Louisville—were located literally at the edge of Dixie and played extensively against nonsouthern teams. Church-related schools also seemed to move more quickly than their secular brethren. For example, Texas Christian University first broke the Southwest Conference color line in basketball. The experiences of TCU and Vanderbilt University in the Southeastern Conference also illustrate the key leadership role that a university president could play in accelerating racial change.

It is no great surprise that those colleges that doggedly resisted integration were located in areas of the Deep South where the African-American population was relatively large and where conservative whites remained fanatically committed to racial segregation. Also, schools with the most prestigious athletic programs generally displayed limited interest in altering the color of their recruits. For example, highly successful coach Adolph Rupp of the University of Kentucky disdained any significant changes in his recruiting habits and prevented UK from becoming a trendsetter.

The black pioneers who broke the color line in southern college basketball were exceptional individuals selected because of their special talents on and off the court. Their success fulfilled the *New York Times*' prophecy of the "tremendous champions" that might appear after the inclusion of southern black athletes. And there were a few "quiet miracles" as well. The presence of African Americans on successful biracial teams eventually helped legitimize integration within southern communities. To most college students, many sports fans, and racial liberals, integrated squads ultimately became symbols of a "New South" and a source of regional pride. Although athletic programs did not initially march in the vanguard of racial change in the region, they eventually came to play a significant role in the racial reconciliation of the 1970s. Integrated teams helped to partially heal the painful scars incurred during the racial crises of the 1950s and 1960s by providing badly needed unifying symbols around which both black and white southerners could attempt to forge a new regional identity free from the racism of the past.

NOTES

1. Black colleges in the South began offering limited athletic programs around the turn of the century but were restricted to competition against each other. For information on their programs, see Arthur R. Ashe, Jr., *A Hard Road to Glory: A History of the African-American Athlete,* 3 vols. (New York: Warner Books, 1988); Patrick B. Miller, "To 'Bring the Race Along Rapidly': Sport, Student Culture, and Educational Mission at Historically Black Colleges during the Interwar Years," in Miller, ed., *The Sporting World of the Modern South* (Urbana, IL: University of Illinois Press, 2002), 129–52. Most historically white southern colleges did not sponsor advanced, competitive athletic programs for women until the mid-1970s.

2. *New York Times,* May 31, 1959, p. 8; *Saturday Review,* January 21, 1967, p. 32.

3. Neil D. Isaacs, *All the Moves: A History of College Basketball,* revised ed. (New York: Harper & Row, 1984), 19–22.

4. Nelson George, *Elevating the Game: Black Men and Basketball* (New York: Harper Collins,

1992), 95–102; Jules Tygiel, *Baseball's Great Experiment: Jackie Robinson and His Legacy* (New York: Oxford University Press, 1983).

5. Ironically, the first interracial contest between southern and northern basketball teams took place in January 1938, when Hampton Institute, a historically black college from Virginia, played Brooklyn College in New York City. *Daily Worker,* January 22, 25, 1938; Donald Spivey, "The Black Athlete in Big-Time Intercollegiate Sports, 1941–1968," *Phylon,* 44 (1983): 116–25; Richard Pennington, *Breaking the Ice: The Racial Integration of Southwest Conference Football* (Jefferson, NC: McFarland, 1987), 1–4; Ashe, *A Hard Road to Glory,* vol. 2, 55–58, 423, 470–71; Isaacs, *All the Moves,* 208–10; Charles H. Martin, "The Color Line in Midwestern College Sports, 1890–1960," *Indiana Magazine of History* 98 (2002): 85–112.

6. *Lexington (Kentucky) Herald,* December 24, 1946; *Atlanta Constitution,* "Run for Respect," September 7–14, 1986, reprint, 1; Pennington, *Breaking the Ice,* 8; David K. Wiggins, "Prized Performers, but Frequently Overlooked Students," *Research Quarterly for Exercise and Sport,* 62 (1991): 168–9.

7. *New York Times,* January 24, 1953, p. 20; March 24, 1956, sec. 1, p. 15.

8. Technically Kentucky was a Border State, since it did not join the Confederacy in 1861. However, its universities and professional teams traditionally had followed "southern rules" concerning interracial athletic competition. *Lexington Herald,* December 24, 1946; *Knoxville News Sentinel,* December 24, 1946; *New York Times,* January 10, 1947, p. 26.

9. Bert Nelli, *The Winning Tradition* (Lexington: University of Kentucky Press, 1984), 76, 147–55.

10. *Alcalde* (May/June 1987): 18–20; *University of Texas (Austin) Daily Texan,* September 15, 1954.

11. *New York Times,* December 14, 1947, p. 4; October 24, 1948, sec. 5, p. 6.

12. *New York Times,* April 18, 1946, p. 32; May 19, 1946, sec. 5, p. 2; November 30, 1947, sec. 5, p. 2; December 11, 1947, p. 50; December 14, 1947, sec. 5, p. 3; June 9, 1955, p. 31; *Christian Science Monitor,* March 8, 1948.

13. *Life,* March 10, 1958, pp. 99–102; *New York Times,* March 6, 1958, p. 34; March 13, 1958, p. 36; *Southwest Conference Basketball 1989–1990* (Dallas, TX: Southwest Conference, 1989), 175, 180.

14. Charles R. Wilson and William Ferris, eds., *The Encyclopedia of Southern Culture* (Chapel Hill, NC: University of North Carolina Press, 1989), 196. For extended treatments of "massive resistance," see Francis M. Wilhoit, *The Politics of Massive Resistance* (New York: Braziller, 1973), and Numan V. Bartley, *The Rise of Massive Resistance* (Baton Rouge: Louisiana State University Press, 1969).

15. *Newsweek,* July 30, 1956, p. 79; *New York Times,* July 15, 1956, sec. 1, p. 51; July 17, 1956, p. 13; July 29, 1956, sec. 5, p. 4; September 1, 1956, p. 6; September 14, 1956, p. 12; October 16, 1956, p. 14; February 22, 1959, p. 2. For a fuller description of massive resistance in college athletics in Louisiana and Georgia, see Charles H. Martin, "Racial Change and 'Big-Time' College Football in Georgia: The Age of Segregation, 1892–1957," *Georgia Historical Quarterly* 80 (1996): 551–62.

16. *New York Times,* November 26, 1954, p. 18; July 31, 1956, p. 11; October 5, 1956, p. 1; October 6, 1956, p. 20; October 16, 1956, p. 14; December 13, 1957, p. 31.

17. In March 2001, the Ole Miss and Iona teams met for the first time since the 1956 incident, in the first round of the NCAA Tournament. As an act of reconciliation, the University of Mississippi invited Stanley Hill to attend the game as its special guest and presented him with a basketball signed by the entire Rebel squad, most of whom were African Americans. *Jackson Daily News,* December 29, 31, 1956; *Memphis Commercial Appeal,* February 1, 1956; *New York Times,* December 31, 1956, p. 13; *Jet,* April 2, 2001, p. 51; *New York Post,* March 13, 2001.

18. *New York Times,* January 19, 1957, p. 22; March 6, 1957, p. 25.

19. *Memphis Commercial Appeal,* February 1, 1956; *New York Times,* October 5, 1956, p. 1; *Atlanta Constitution,* February 15, 21–23, 1957.

20. Jeffrey T. Sammons, *Beyond the Ring: The Role of Boxing in American Society* (Urbana, IL: University of Illinois Press, 1988), 190; *New York Times,* May 26, 1959, p. 1.

21. George N. Green, *The Establishment in Texas Politics* (Westport, CT: Greenwood Press, 1979), 186–92.

22. In 1956, the University of Alabama's SEC championship team turned down the automatic NCAA Tournament invitation when all five starters were ruled ineligible for postseason play because of a conflict between conference and NCAA regulations. Auburn University won the league title in 1960 but was ineligible for the national tournament because of NCAA sanctions. Whether Alabama's segregationist political leaders would have permitted either college to compete against integrated teams in the NCAA Tournament is unclear. Nelli, *The Winning Tradition,* 82–3, 154; *SEC Basketball Data Book 1988* (Birmingham, AL: Southeastern Conference, 1987), 130; Dean W. Colvard, *Mixed*

Emotions: As Racial Barriers Fell A University President Remembers (Danville, IL: Interstate Publishers, 1985), 18–9.

23. *New York Times,* September 30, 1962, p. 66; March 11, 1963, p. 5; Colvard, *Mixed Emotions,* 60–70.

24. *New York Times,* March 11, 1963, p. 5; Bill Finger, "Just Another Ball Game," *Southern Exposure,* 7 (1979): 78–9; Colvard, *Mixed Emotions,* 71–85; *Jackson Clarion Ledger,* March 6, 1963; *Grenville, NC The Reflector,* February 28, March 7, 1963; *University of Kentucky (Lexington) Kentucky Kernel,* March 7, 1963. For other accounts of the 1963 incident, see Russell J. Henderson, " 'Something More Than the Game Will Be Lost': The 1963 Mississippi State University Basketball Controversy and the Repeal of the Unwritten Law," *Journal of Southern History* 63 (1997): 827–54, and Paul Attner, "The Defiant Ones," *The Sporting News 1995–96 College Basketball Yearbook* (St. Louis: Sporting News, 1995), 30–35.

25. New York Times, March 15, 1963, 15; April 21, 1963, p. 8; Finger, "Just Another Ball Game," 78–80; *Sports Illustrated,* November 18, 1987, pp. 107–108, 113; Robert Stern, *They Were Number One: A History of the NCAA Basketball Tournament* (New York: Leisure Press, 1983), 190–8; Colvard, *Mixed Emotions,* 87–91.

26. *Kentucky Kernel,* March 22, April 30, 1963; *New York Times,* April 13, 1963, p. 14; April 21, 1963, p. 8; May 30, 1963, p. 13.

27. Pennington, *Breaking The Ice,* 118; Ashe, *A Hard Road to Glory,* 3, 61; *New York Times,* March 12, 1960, p. 10; October 27, 1961, p. 65; December 31, 1961, p. 51; *Daily Texan,* April 11, 1961.

28. Charlotte Ivy, "Foundation of Change," unpublished seminar paper, University of Texas at El Paso, 1987, 20–6; Charles H. Martin, "Integration Turns 35 at UTEP," *Nova* 26 (1991): 4–6.

29. *UTEP (El Paso) The Prospector,* October 6, November 28, 1956; March 13, 1957; Charles H. Martin, "Charlie Brown," *Nova,* 25 (1990): 7–9. Cecil Brown was a reserve player for the TWC squad and saw only limited playing time during his two years, but he provided important emotional support for his better-known cousin.

30. *San Antonio Express,* December 8, 1957; *El Bronco,* 1963 (Pan American College); *Edinburg Daily Record,* February 17, 1963.

31. *1961 Yucca* (North Texas State College); Ronald Marcello, "The Integration of Intercollegiate Athletics in Texas: North Texas State College as a Test Case, 1956," *Journal of Sport History* 14 (1987): 286–88; Gary Tuell, *Above the Rim* (n.p., n.d.), 127–30; author's survey.

32. Patrick B. Miller, "Harvard and the Color Line: The Case of Lucien Alexis," in Ronald Story (ed.), *Sports in Massachusetts* (Westfield, Mass: Institute for Massachusetts Studies, 1992), 143–5; *New York Times,* April 3, 1964, p. 38; April 9, 1964, p. 37. On the ACC, see Charles H. Martin, "The Rise and Fall of Jim Crow in Southern College Sports: The Case of the Atlantic Coast Conference," *North Carolina Historical Review,* 76 (1999): 253–84.

33. Don Haskins, as told to Ray Sanchez, *Haskins: The Bear Facts* (El Paso, TX: Mangan Books, 1987), 53–70; Ray Sanchez, *Basketball's Biggest Upset* (El Paso, TX: Mesa Publishing, 1992); Stern, *They Were Number One,* 223–5, 231–3; Curry Kirkpatrick, "The Night They Drove Old Dixie Down," *Sports Illustrated,* April 1, 1991, pp. 70–81. See also Frank Fitzpatrick, *And the Walls Came Tumbling Down: Kentucky, Texas Western, and the Game that Changed American Sports* (New York: Simon & Schuster, 1999), and "Glory in Black and White: The Story of the 1966 NCAA Basketball Championship," CBS documentary, March 31, 2002.

34. *New Orleans Louisiana Weekly,* May 14, 1966; *Sports Illustrated,* June 14, 1966, pp. 26–7; *Anniston Star,* December 25, 1991; author's interview with Alexander Heard, October 5, 1990. Another African American, Godfrey Dillard from Detroit, joined Wallace on the Vanderbilt freshman team, but he never played on the varsity level.

35. *SPORT* Magazine, quoted in *Dallas Express,* June 17, 1967; Joan Paul, Richard V. McGhee, and Helen Fant, "The Arrival and Ascendance of Black Athletes in the Southeastern Conference, 1966–1980," *Phylon,* 45 (1984): 284–97; author's interview with C. M. Newton, August 7, 1989; author's survey.

36. Pennington, *Breaking the Ice,* 120; *Dallas Express,* April 22, 1967; *New York Times,* November 19, 1963, p. 24; November 20, 1963, p. 6; November 29, 1963, p. 52; December 4, 1963, p. 67; December 8, 1963, p. 14.

37. Pennington, *Breaking the Ice,* 28–30.

38. *This is T. C. U.* 19 (1976): 24; Pennington, *Breaking the Ice,* 137–8.

39. *New Orleans Louisiana Weekly,* December 24, 1966; author's survey.

40. "Business Is His Business," *Ebony* (October 1987): 31–37; *Fort Worth Star-Telegram,* n.d.; *Anniston Star,* December 25, 1991.

13

CIVIL RIGHTS ON THE GRIDIRON

The Kennedy Administration and the Desegregation of the Washington Redskins

Thomas G. Smith

"WE'LL START SIGNING NEGROES," Washington Redskins owner George Preston Marshall once quipped, "when the Harlem Globetrotters start signing whites." In 1961, the Redskins were the only team in professional football without a black player. In fact, in the twenty-five year history of the franchise no black had ever played for George Marshall. Sam Lacy, the gifted black sportswriter for the *Baltimore Afro-American* called Redskins football's the "lone wolf in lily-whiteism." Their owner was "the one operator in the whole structure of major league sports who has openly flouted his distaste for tan athletes."[1]

Elected to office on a pro–civil rights platform and eager to display its commitment to the campaign promise of equal job opportunity, the Kennedy Administration moved to desegregate the Redskins. That action, in the highly visible sports arena, signaled to the nation a more aggressive civil rights policy. On March 24, 1961 Secretary of the Interior Stewart L. Udall warned Marshall to hire black players or face federal retribution. For the first time in history, the federal government had attempted to desegregate a professional sports team. An examination of that effort shows the deep divisions in American society over the struggle for black equality and provides insights into the New Frontier's civil rights program.[2]

Along with George Halas of the Chicago Bears and Art Rooney of the Pittsburgh Steelers, George P. Marshall was one of the founding fathers of the National Football League (NFL). Opinionated, flamboyant and contentious, Marshall was also imaginative, shrewd and persuasive. His contributions to the game have earned him election to the Pro Football Hall of Fame. Born in Grafton, West Virginia, in 1896, Marshall was raised in Washington, D.C. and always considered that city home. He dropped out of high school to pursue acting, but that career was interrupted by two years of service in World War I. Upon his father's death in 1919, he took over the family business: the Palace Laundry. As a businessman, Marshall displayed a knack for promotion through clever advertising. He developed the slogan "Long Live Linen," and once ran a newspaper advertisement which consisted of a blank page except for a few words at the bottom which read: "This space was cleaned by Palace Laundry." By 1946, when he sold-out, he had transformed a small family business into a multi-million-dollar chain with fifty-seven stores.

Marshall first became a sports owner in 1926 when he financed a professional basketball team, the Washington Palace Five. Six years later, he invested in a National Football

League team, the Boston Braves. Renamed the Redskins to eliminate confusion with the baseball team, the franchise enjoyed only modest success. In 1936 the team won the division title, but the fans and press showed little enthusiasm. Angered by the lack of support, Marshall moved the team from Boston to Washington in 1937.[3]

In the late 1930s and early 1940s the Redskins were successful on the field and at the gate. Led by quarterback Sammy Baugh, the team won six division titles between 1937 and 1945. In 1940, the Redskins suffered the worst defeat in championship playoff history, losing to the Chicago Bears 73–0. When the gun sounded ending the massacre one reporter cracked: "That's George Marshall shooting himself." After World War II, the Redskins failed to win another title under Marshall. The owner's stubborn refusal to employ black athletes no doubt contributed to the team's poor record. "Thanks to the Marshall Plan," lamented one sportswriter, the Redskins were "the whitest and worst" team in professional football.[4]

Despite his rigid resistance to integration, Marshall was an active owner who brought many innovations. "He took a dull game," wrote one columnist, "and made it irresistible." He proposed splitting the league into two divisions with a season-ending championship game. He suggested the player draft and roster limitations. He also helped bring several rule changes. One moved the goal posts from the end zone to the goal line to encourage field goal attempts. Another permitted passing from any spot behind the line of scrimmage. Another tapered the ball to facilitate passing. Still another allowed unlimited substitutions. He also proposed an annual all-star game called the Pro-Bowl.[5]

Marshall was a grand showman who promoted football as family entertainment. He introduced the half-time extravaganza because he believed that football was a pageant similar to the "gladiator shows" of ancient Rome. Despite the Great Depression, Marshall organized a 110 piece band and outfitted it with $25,000 worth of burgundy and gold uniforms. His wife, Corinne Griffith Marshall, coauthored a popular fight song, "Hail to the Redskins." And before games, the band played "Dixie." Besides the marching band, half-time shows sometimes featured animal acts, clowns, celebrities from stage and screen, symphony orchestras, and, at Christmastime, Santa Claus.[6]

Although he was an innovator, Marshall found some changes in the game distasteful. Besides integration, he opposed a players' union and pension system. He was extremely frugal in terms of travel expenses and salaries. He once berated fellow owner Art Rooney of the Steelers for driving up salaries by signing University of Colorado star Byron "Whizzer" White for $15,800, the highest contract in football in 1938. One sportswriter referred to Marshall as "the last of the small-time spenders."[7]

His coaches found him a difficult boss. In one seventeen-year span he had nine head coaches. During games he roamed the sidelines, argued with officials and suggested plays. He once recommended reversing the roles of the offensive and defensive linemen. When coach John Whelchel refused, Marshall told quarterback Sammy Baugh: "Hell, I hired him for a disciplinarian. I didn't hire him for a goddamn coach!" Baugh recalled: "Oh that George was wonderful, goddamn him." Even when the volatile owner watched from his box, he communicated his views to players and coaches. When Vice-President Richard Nixon left the White House in early 1961, he told a friend that he would miss watching games with Marshall. That experience, he said, "was just like going to a double feature movie. His priceless comments made the afternoon fun even when we lost."[8]

Marshall enjoyed the limelight and controversy. At NFL meetings, Halas remembered, Marshall would "rave and rant" in order to win a point. He had long-running feuds with

Harry Wismer, a Redskins stockholder who favored integration, and Shirley Povich, a *Washington Post* sportswriter whom he called a "fifth columnist." The Redskins' owner caused a stir among sports-minded Americans when he wrote an article for the *Saturday Evening Post* proclaiming football the national pastime because baseball was dead. And once on a television show, Oscar Levant asked Marshall if he was anti-Semitic. He responded: "Oh no, I love Jews, especially when they're customers." He went on to say that "No one of intelligence has ever questioned my theories on race or religion."[9]

During the 1920s, the formative years of the National Football League, blacks participated on several teams. Paul Robeson and Frederick Douglass "Fritz" Pollard played for Akron, Fred "Duke" Slater with the Chicago Cardinals, and Jay Mayo "Inky" Williams with the Hammond Pros. During the depression decade and war years, however, blacks were excluded. With the departure of Joe Lillard from the Chicago Cardinals and Ray Kemp from the Pittsburgh Pirates in 1933, another black did not play in the NFL until after World War II.[10]

The racial ban is not easily explained. Certainly there were qualified black athletes. Oze Simmons, Homer Davis, Fritz Pollard, Jr., Jerome Holland, Kenny Washington, Marion Motley, and others had all "proved their ability to stand the gaff and grind of the gridiron game." One writer speculated that NFL owners excluded all blacks because one, Joe Lillard, was alleged to have been "a bad actor." It is possible, though not probable, that George Marshall may have persuaded other magnates to follow his discriminatory hiring policies. Marshall was new to the league in 1932, but he had enough influence to initiate several rule changes by mid-decade. But perhaps the best explanation is that football owners decided informally to emulate the policy of racial exclusion that prevailed in major league baseball. By falling into line with the baseball brethren, football titans could avoid the repercussions of hiring blacks while so many Depression–era whites were unemployed.[11]

After World War II, many Americans began to reassess their racial attitudes. Thousands of blacks had joined the armed services to fight totalitarianism abroad. Nearly one million others had moved to northern and western cities to take jobs in war industries. The Cold War, too, helped break down segregation. How could the United States condemn the Soviet Union for civil rights violations when blacks in America were treated as second-class citizens? In 1946, President Harry S. Truman established a committee on civil rights. The next year, that presidential committee issued a report recommending the creation of a permanent federal bureau to insure equal job opportunities and the withholding of federal funds from those states that practiced segregation in public facilities. Those recommendations went unfulfilled due to southern congressional opposition. In 1948, Truman issued an executive order desegregating the armed services and the Democrats inserted a civil rights plank in their party platform.[12]

In the 1950s, African Americans made important strides toward racial equality. In 1954, the United States Supreme Court ruled unanimously against school segregation in the *Brown* decision. The following year the court mandated the integration of public schools with "all deliberate speed." In 1955, a Montgomery, Alabama woman, Rosa Parks, lashed out against segregation in public transportation by refusing to yield her bus seat to a white man. And in 1960, four black students took seats in a segregated Greensboro, North Carolina lunch counter and refused to leave until they were served. Their action sparked sit-in movements against segregation throughout the South.[13]

Jim Crow also started to give way in professional sports. Baseball, basketball, and football all hired black athletes. Although it was done without fanfare, professional football broke the color line in 1946, the year after the Brooklyn Dodgers signed Jackie Robinson to a minor league baseball contract. The "Jackie Robinsons" of postwar professional football were Kenny Washington and Woody Strode of the Los Angeles Rams and Bill Willis and Marion Motley of the Cleveland Browns.[14]

As in major league baseball, full acceptance of blacks on the gridiron came about slowly. Influenced by the success of the desegregated Cleveland Browns, club owners gradually added black players to their rosters. By 1952 only the Redskins and Detroit Lions had failed to desegregate. By mid-decade, the Redskins stood alone. During the 1950s a total of 143 blacks played in the NFL. At the close of the 1960 season there were sixty-one blacks on NFL teams. The following year that figure climbed to eighty-three, an average of six per team. Blacks constituted 16.5 percent of the players in the NFL while only 10 percent of the nation's population was black. Scores of African Americans also played in the rival American Football League. Civil rights activists protested against Marshall's discriminatory hiring policies at NFL meetings and at Redskins' home games at Griffith Stadium. Marshall, however, steadfastly resisted desegregation. For the Redskins' owner, NAACP stood for "Never at Anytime Any Colored Players."[15]

Marshall never fully explained his intransigence. Little is known about his formative years, but his southern origins no doubt contributed to his racism. He once claimed that he did not sign black athletes because white southerners on the team would have balked. That reasoning, however, did not dissuade other owners. Nor did any white players refuse to play with blacks. His desire for profits may have helped shape his position. As the owner of several radio and, later, television stations, he maintained that using black players would drive away advertisers and his white southern audience. Then, too, Washington was a southern city that adhered rigidly to segregation during the 1930s and 1940s. During the 1950s, however, Washington gradually desegregated its schools, movie houses, theaters, churches, playgrounds, swimming pools, bowling alleys, restaurants, hotels, public transportation system, and Constitution Hall. Blacks joined the police and fire departments, the bar association, medical society, and nurses association. Increasingly, blacks were hired by the federal government. And, blacks played for the Washington Senators baseball team.[16]

Despite those strides, racial intolerance and discrimination persisted in the nation's capital. Whites fled to segregated suburbs in Maryland and Virginia. In 1950, whites constituted about 65 percent of the city's population. Ten years later, whites were a minority of 45 percent. In 1960, six years after school desegregation, 76 percent of the public school population was black. Although blacks comprised a majority of the population, the city was governed by an all-white council appointed by the president. The police and fire departments had been integrated, but there were few black officers. Similarly, blacks were generally excluded from responsible positions in city government and business. Private clubs, such as the Cosmos, excluded blacks. Washington, then, was not an integrated city in 1960.[17]

Influenced by the civil rights movement and by a woeful 1960 season consisting of one victory, sportswriters and fans assailed the ban on blacks. Sam Lacy in the *Baltimore Afro-American* repeatedly blasted Marshall's "lily-white stubbornness." "This column has never advocated suicide," he wrote in frustration, "but in GPM's case, it would be readily forgivable." Pulitzer-winning sports columnist Shirley Povich also took the owner to task. The Redskins' colors, he wrote, were "burgundy, gold and Caucasian." "In modern pro-football," he continued, "Marshall is an anachronism, as out of date as the drop kick." His white supremacist policies, designed to please a predominantly white southern radio and television audience, were a disservice to the players, coaches and fans. Even Dixie rooters, he argued, should realize that "what is important is how the man plays the game not the notation on his birth certificate." Finally, Gordon Cobbledick, a respected sports columnist for the *Cleveland Plain Dealer,* observed that the Redskins' Jim Crow policy was "spotting their rivals the tremendous advantage of exclusive rights to a whole race containing excellent football players." In the past, the Redskins had bypassed black athletes such as Jimmy Brown, Lenny Moore, Jim Parker, Roosevelt Grier, Roger Brown, and Big Daddy Lipscomb. Drafting blacks, he cautioned, "is not an argument for social equality. It's a matter of practical football policy."[18]

The criticism was fruitless. Marshall sought to improve the team by replacing coach Mike Nixon with Bill McPeak. At the NFL player draft in late December 1960, the Redskins pursued "state rights football" by shunning blacks. They selected Wake Forest quarterback Norm Snead and nineteen other whites.[19]

Blacks had high expectations when John Kennedy took over the White House in January 1961. As a presidential candidate, he had called for an end to racial discrimination through congressional legislation and strong executive leadership. Blacks supported the Democratic candidate, the *Baltimore Afro-American* editorialized, because "we confidently believe that under Mr. Kennedy America will at last come of age, making a reality the long withheld promise of the democratic ideal." Martin Luther King, Jr., addressing an Emancipation Day rally in Chattanooga, Tennessee, pointed out that blacks had helped to elect the president and "we are expecting him to use the whole weight of his office to remove the heavy weight of segregation from our shoulders." Lincoln's Emancipation Proclamation, he continued, was an executive order. "We must remind Kennedy that when he gets the pen in his hand we expect him to write a little with it."[20]

For some blacks, the field of sports was "still leading the way" toward equality. Sam Lacy and Wendell Smith, a prominent black columnist for the *Pittsburgh Courier,* denounced segregated housing at baseball spring training camps in Florida. Charlie Sifford became the first black to play in a Professional Golfers' Association (PGA) tournament. The PGA also removed a whites-only membership clause from its bylaws. Willie O'Ree signed with the Boston Bruins of the National Hockey League. Heavyweight champion Floyd Patterson insisted upon integrated seating in Miami when he signed a contract to fight Ingemar Johansson. And one pioneer, Nathan Boya, dramatically demonstrated his desire for sports integration by becoming the first black to go over Niagara Falls in a barrel.[21]

As president, Kennedy moved cautiously on civil rights. Instead of pushing legislation, he preferred to combat racial injustice with symbolic gestures and limited executive action. Marian Anderson, the famous black contralto, was invited to perform at his Inauguration. Attorney General Robert Kennedy and Assistant Attorney General Burke Marshall resigned their membership in exclusive, white-only clubs such as the Metropolitan. JFK urged unions to avoid hiring bias and advised schools to end segregation. He asked Cabinet members to avoid speaking engagements at segregated functions. He denounced the decision to hold the Civil War Centennial at a segregated hotel in Charleston, South Carolina. And he belatedly authorized the Justice Department to send U.S. marshals to the Deep South to protect freedom riders protesting segregation in interstate travel.[22]

In his first few months in office JFK appointed more than fifty blacks to important positions. To the dismay of blacks, he also named some white supremacists to the federal bench and failed to deliver promptly on a promise to abolish discrimination in federally subsidized housing. In early March 1961, he issued an executive order creating the President's Committee on Equal Employment Opportunity. At approximately the same time, Secretary of the Interior Stewart L. Udall decided to move against the discriminatory hiring policies of the Washington Redskins.[23]

Born in northern Arizona in 1920, Udall was raised by a Mormon family dedicated to public service. After serving in World War II, he obtained a law degree from the University of Arizona. In 1954, he was elected to the United States House of Representatives. Serving three terms, he won respect as a hardworking, able legislator who supported liberal causes—aid to education, conservation of natural resources, environmental protection, labor reform, and civil rights. Udall's commitment to racial equality came during World War II when he noted the irony of fighting to preserve democracy in segregated military units. In 1960, President-elect Kennedy, who had befriended Udall in Congress, named the forty-one-year-old Democrat Secretary of the Interior.[24]

The impetus for the Redskins' desegregation order came from Interior Department lawyers. Early in March 1961, they informed Udall that the administration might be able "to force Marshall's hand" on the color ban. They pointed out that he had recently signed a thirty-year lease to play all home games, beginning October 1961, at D.C. Stadium, then under construction. Financed with public funds, the new twenty-four million dollar stadium was located at Anacosta Flats, part of the National Capital Parks system. As the "residential landlord" of the parks area, the Interior Department could deny use of the stadium to any party practicing discriminatory hiring policies.[25]

Udall seized the opportunity to act. He moved against the Washington "Paleskins," he later wrote, because he "had personal convictions about civil rights and considered it outrageous that the Redskins were the last team in the NFL to have a lily-white policy." He did not discuss his proposed action with JFK beforehand because he "instinctively felt that JFK and RFK would applaud. To me it was the kind of stance that was all on the plus side."[26]

On March 24, 1961, Udall notified Marshall that the Interior Department had approved regulations prohibiting job discrimination by any party contracting to use "any public facility in a park area." Udall went on to say that "there have been persistent allegations that your company practices discrimination in the hiring of its players." Without prejudging the owner, he nonetheless warned him "of the implications of this new regulation—and our view of its import."[27]

At a news conference that same day, Udall explained that the new guidelines were designed to conform with the administration's antidiscrimination policy. "It is certainly our feeling that here in the Nation's Capital, with the marvelous new facility being built on property owned by all the people of the country, that we ought to set the very highest of standards in terms of adhering to the policies of this Administration with regard to treating everyone in this country equally." If Marshall continued his ban on blacks he would be denied the use of D.C. stadium. "I think it is quite plain that if he wants an argument . . . he is going to have a moral argument with the President and with the Administration." He advised the headstrong owner to "adjust himself to the situation."[28] Udall's ultimatum gained nationwide attention. The *New York Times* and *Washington Post* featured the story on the front page. Not surprisingly, the black press also gave the story prominent coverage. The *Chicago Defender* headlined: "Redskins Told: Integrate or Else."[29]

"I don't know what the hell it's all about," Marshall told reporters. He also attempted to laugh off the incident. "We almost knocked Laos off the front pages," he quipped. "I never

Figure 13–1
Cartoon by Thomas Stockett in the *Baltimore Afro-American*, August 26, 1961, titled "Isn't It About Time to Call a Penalty for Unsportsmanlike Conduct?" Courtesy of the *Baltimore Afro-American*.

realized so many fans were interested in a football team that won only one game." In a brief, defiant letter to Udall, Marshall claimed that he broke no laws and that his "lease was made on that basis." Implying that he would pursue legal action, he informed Udall that he had turned the matter over to his attorneys.[30]

At his office, the pugnacious owner sounded off to reporters. First, he wondered why the government would get involved in such a trifling matter. "I am surprised that with the world on the brink of another war they are worried about whether or not a Negro is going to play for the Redskins." Second, he doubted that "the government had the right to tell the showman how to cast the play." Then he expressed a desire to discuss the issue with the President. "I could handle him with words. I used to be able to handle his old man."[31]

Marshall also raised some pointed questions. Would a black have to appear in every contest and event scheduled at D.C. stadium? Would George Washington University's football team be forced to carry blacks? What about southern colleges that played there? Did Udall also plan to integrate the Army, Navy, and Air Force football squads? What about the national theater, national symphony orchestra, the White House press and photographers corps? Where would the government draw the line?

He also tried to downplay the charge of discrimination against the Redskins. "All the other teams we play have Negroes; does it matter which team has the Negroes?" The Redskins lacked blacks because they recruited players from segregated southern colleges. Recruiting southern white players was not a matter of prejudice, he declared, but a business decision. As the owner of several radio and television stations, he did not want to offend his southern white audience by playing blacks. Although he had never signed a black, he had in the past hired athletes who were Samoan, Hawaiian, American Indian, and Cuban. He was color-blind when it came to selling tickets and he frequently hired blacks to do custodial and other menial tasks. As for Udall's ultimatum, Marshall said that the NFL draft was over and his player roster was frozen. Leaving room to maneuver, however, he claimed that he was always open to the possibility of adding "players of recognized ability."[32]

The next day Redskins' attorneys attempted to soften some of Marshall's statements. The Redskins, they asserted, had no intention of defying the federal government or breaking any laws. The team would cooperate in seeking a workable compromise.[33]

Udall kept up the pressure. At a press conference on March 28, he gave the Redskins a deadline for compliance. To avoid cancellation of the lease and possible criminal prosecution, the owner must comply with the administration's antidiscrimination policy by October 1, the date of the Redskins' first home game. Marshall could best show compliance by hiring a black player. Udall suggested the possibility of a trade. In a final dig, he said that with a black player, Marshall's team "might win a few games."[34]

In July, Udall again warned Marshall to lift the ban on blacks or else lose the right to play at D.C. Stadium. "This guy's making a big mistake if he thinks our department merely is trying to get some publicity out of this thing. We're quite serious." Marshall considered Udall's statement "rather vague." Disillusioned with the administration, he told a reporter that "you can't tell what will happen under the guise of liberalism." Still, he planned to obey the law even it if meant hiring "Eskimoes or Chinese or Mongolians."[35]

Public reaction to forced desegregation reflected the deep divisions over civil rights in the 1960s. Outright racists, such as the American Nazi Party, paraded outside D.C. Stadium with swastika-emblazoned signs reading "America Awake" and "Keep Redskins White!" A man from Tennessee believed America was headed for dictatorship "when a football owner is forced to put a nigger on his team." Another disgruntled correspondent told Udall that if race, instead of ability, was used as a criterion for team membership then the game and society would be doomed "to mediocrity and eclipse!"[36]

Other Americans downplayed the existence of discrimination. After all, they argued, blacks had plenty of opportunity to play for teams other than the Redskins. Some citizens wondered why blacks would want to play for a team that did not want them. Other opponents feared a snowball effect. Once the administration forced the Redskins to employ a black, would it then require the team to hire other nationalities? One critic observed that the Redskins had "no Puerto Ricans, no Christian Scientists, no members of the Raritan Club, and no Pythians. Heavens, Mr. Udall, these people are being discriminated against." Marshall himself took this approach. "Why Negroes particularly?" he asked. "Why not make us hire a player from any other race?" In fact, Marshall continued, why not a woman? "Of course we have had players who played like girls, but never an actual girl player."[37]

Some Americans interpreted the desegregation order as an unwarranted intrusion by big government that threatened democracy and free enterprise. An "aggrieved Redskin fan" asked Attorney General Robert Kennedy to halt "the harassment of private businessmen" by the "cowboy in the New Frontier rodeo." Republican Congressman H. R. Gross of Iowa accused Udall of trying to manage a football team. "If Mr. Marshall doesn't want Negro players on his team that's his business," declared the *Tulsa World.* For some conservatives federal interference in professional sports smacked of communism. "It's done in Russia, and as the Olympic Games' results attest, with some success," noted sports columnist Doc Greene. Another critic believed that in the near future "the authoritarian official will be telling the American worker where he must work." And a Cold War–conscious citizen feared that it would somehow make the nation susceptible to a takeover by Premier Khrushchev. "Once government sticks its icky fingers into free business, there is a hole in the line big enough for Mr. K to smash through and rack up a winning score for his team."[38]

Despite some intense criticism, Udall refused to back down. The President supported his position as did Attorney General Kennedy and Secretary of Labor Arthur Goldberg. A longtime fan, Goldberg announced that he would boycott all Redskins games because their hiring policies were "an outrage and a disgrace." Democratic Congressman Denis Chavez of New Mexico also applauded Udall's order. To those who feared that he would become a "Commissar of Sports," Udall pointed out that he was concerned only with Marshall's hiring policies. Indeed, his focus on Marshall gave credence to the charge that he was following a double standard. Georgetown University's segregated team was allowed to use the stadium on the specious grounds that it used amateur not professional athletes. Udall did put his own house in order. Learning that only 1 of 474 National Park Rangers was black, he moved promptly to improve that "disgraceful record" by recruiting 50 minority candidates.[39]

Perhaps fearful of jeopardizing gains already achieved, black players generally withheld comment. On one occasion, however, Chicago Cardinal running back Ollie Matson admitted that blacks "try a little harder when we play the Washington team." The much-admired Jackie Robinson, who had toppled baseball's color ban, called Udall's position "inspirational and encouraging." Marshall's racial policy, he insisted in contrast, "has no place in sports or in our American way of life."[40]

In the spring and summer of 1961 members of the NAACP and CORE (Congress of Racial Equality) picketed Marshall's home, D.C. Stadium, and the Redskins' exhibition games in the West and South. Many sports owners also supported the government's position. Bill Veeck, maverick owner of the Chicago White Sox baseball team, recommended threatening Marshall with the possibility of having an integrated AFL team play in Washington. William Shea and Jack Kent Cooke, members of the Redskins' Board of Directors, urged Marshall to yield. Edward B. Williams, who would become a stockholder in 1962, recalled Marshall saying "that under no circumstances would he change" his racial policy.

Football owners, who had recently signed a lucrative television contract and dreaded the bad publicity of Marshall's intransigence, asked Commissioner Pete Rozelle to mediate the conflict.[41]

Initially, Rozelle labeled the controversy "strictly a club problem" and refused to intervene. Udall informed him that the government would not back down. And other owners were embarrassed by the bad publicity. In August, Rozelle met with Marshall and persuaded him to relent. Following that meeting, Marshall announced that his team had "no policy against the hiring of football players because of their race." In fact, he had prepared a list of five black players whom he planned to select, if they were available, at the annual NFL draft in December. Running backs Ernie Davis of Syracuse University and Larry Ferguson of Iowa headed the list.[42]

Marshall's conciliatory statement prompted a concession by Udall. He would permit the Redskins to field an all-white team at D.C. stadium in 1961 if they agreed to place a black player on their roster the following year. Udall made it clear, however, that he was not backing down on his commitment to civil rights. "The Kennedy administration," he asserted, "is determined that every American should have a full and equal opportunity to utilize his or her talents in the classroom, in industry, on the playing field and in all areas of our national life." Still, some blacks suspected "a clever diversionary tactic" by Marshall and believed that "the Administration should have held to its requirement of compliance" for 1961.[43]

Others, embittered by Marshall's quarter-century color ban, advised drafted black athletes to shun the Redskins. Sam Lacy ridiculed that position, arguing that civil rights activists had "dramatized under threat of the clenched fist and the Dixie jail, the importance of sacrifice for the sake of justice." If drafted, a black player would have a "moral obligation" to sign with the Redskins. "The principle here is bigger than the individual," Lacy continued. "Suppose Jackie Robinson had taken the position that, since it was a known fact that baseball didn't want him or his kind, back in 1946, he could do without it. Where would we be?"[44]

For the Redskins, the 1961 season was a nightmare. Blacks boycotted games and picketed the stadium with signs reading: "People Who Can't Play Together, Can't Live Together." Udall and other Cabinet officials honored the pickets. President Kennedy refused an invitation to attend the opening game at the new stadium. The new facility was attractive, but ticket prices were the highest in the NFL and attendance was modest. Worst of all, the Redskins' record was "unsullied by victory" until the final game of the year. Counting the previous season, the team of "Nordic supremacy" went seventeen straight games without a win.[45]

Fans and writers heaped abuse upon Marshall and his coaches. "The Redskins end zone has frequently been integrated by Negro players," Povich wrote, "but never their lineup." Although some fans continued to defend Marshall's right to exclude blacks, others believed that African-American players, especially a fleet running back, would improve the team. As the NFL draft approached, Udall gave Marshall a final warning. The draft, he declared, "is the showdown on this" and he expected Marshall to keep his promises made earlier in the year.[46]

With its abysmal record, the Redskins had the first pick on December 4. They selected Ernie Davis, the first black to win the Heisman Trophy. Two days before, the Buffalo Bills of the AFL had also drafted Davis and there was some doubt as to whether Marshall would offer enough money to sign him. For their second pick, the Redskins chose another black halfback, Joe Hernandez from the University of Arizona, Udall's alma mater. They also took Ron Hatcher, a black fullback from Michigan State, in the eighth round.[47]

In an enviable position, Davis awaited offers. He had little desire to be a Jackie Robinson, but he did not rule out playing for the Redskins. In early December, he met President Kennedy in New York, but when JFK asked about his plans he would not commit himself. Meanwhile in Washington, Ron Hatcher became the first black football player to sign a contract with the Redskins. When photographers at the signing asked Marshall to pose with the athlete he refused, saying he did not wish to "exploit" the situation.[48]

In mid-December, Marshall divulged that on the day of the NFL draft he had secretly traded the rights to Davis to the Cleveland Browns. The Browns, who wanted Davis to join the league's leading rusher, Jimmy Brown, in their backfield, gave the Redskins two black players, Bobby Mitchell, an established running back, and Leroy Jackson, a number one draft choice. Several weeks later, the Redskins added another experienced African-American athlete when they acquired offensive guard John Nisby from the Pittsburgh Steelers. Stricken with leukemia in the summer of 1962, Ernie Davis would never play an NFL game. As for the Redskins' players, Hernandez never signed a contract, Hatcher and Jackson rarely played, but Nisby and Mitchell became stars.[49]

Redskins' fans generally cheered the acquisition of Mitchell as the speedy offensive weapon so badly needed. He had performed especially well against the Redskins. In the past season he had scored three long touchdowns against the Redskins in Cleveland. In one game in 1959 he gained 232 yards rushing on only fourteen carries. Redskins' players were also pleased to obtain the experienced veterans. Quarterback Norm Snead recalled that the players, virtually to a man, considered the color barrier "ridiculous." Mitchell and Nisby, he remembered, were talented players and "great human beings" who were "received enthusiastically and with open arms." Nisby recalled that on one occasion a group went to a Virginia nightclub. When the black players were refused admittance, their white teammates left.[50]

Aware of the Redskins' discriminatory policy, both Mitchell and Nisby approached their new team with some apprehension. "I honestly feel good about coming to the Redskins," Mitchell told reporters at the time. Later he described the move as being "traumatic" because he had to endure "verbal abuse" and "a great deal of racial discrimination from the fans and the Washington community."[51]

Although he was a pioneer of sorts, Mitchell downplayed comparisons with Jackie Robinson. "I wasn't quite as tough as Jackie," he declared. The racial slurs "affected me greatly—and I haven't forgotten them." Less sensitive, Nisby found "little difference playing with the Redskins and playing with the Steelers."[52]

Both men differed in their views of George Marshall. Mitchell recalled being treated well by the owner. Marshall was "a nice man" who "never came across to me as a bigot or showed any behavior in that manner." Nisby was less charitable. "I never appreciated the man at all, because of the stand that he took on blacks prior to my arrival here. My relationship with the front office wasn't really that great."[53]

With the addition of Mitchell and Nisby, the Redskins approached the 1962 season with cautious optimism. Both players distinguished themselves. In the first game at Dallas,

Figure 13–2
Bobby Mitchell, Washington Redskins standout halfback during the early 1960s. Courtesy of *The Sporting News*.

which ended in a tie, Mitchell ran back a kick off for a ninety-two yard touchdown and scored on two passes from Snead. In the second game at Cleveland, he caught a fifty yard pass in the final minutes to upset the Browns, 17–16.

The Redskins' first home game was against the St. Louis Cardinals. Udall accepted Marshall's invitation to be a special guest. Once again, Snead and Mitchell, the city's "greatest battery since Walter Johnson and Gabby Street," brought the team victory. Mitchell caught touchdown passes of forty and twenty-three yards. After Mitchell's first score, Udall recalled the remarks of a foghorn-voiced black man seated behind him: "Thank God for Mr. Udall."[54]

The Redskins ended the season with their best record in years, five victories, seven losses, and two ties. Mitchell led the league with eleven touchdowns, and caught seventy-two passes to earn selection to the Pro-Bowl. He had several distinguished seasons and later was elected to the Pro Football Hall of Fame. Today he is the Assistant General Manager of the Redskins. Nisby had three successful seasons with the Redskins and then was released. In 1963, George Marshall suffered a debilitating stroke and turned over control of the team to Edward B. Williams and Jack Kent Cooke. Marshall died in 1969. In his will, he left a sizable bequest to establish a foundation, named in his honor, to help improve the lives of disadvantaged youngsters of all races who resided in the Washington D.C. area.[55]

Successful desegregation of the Redskins won praise for the Kennedy administration. Sportswriters dubbed Udall "coach of the year" and the "most valuable player" in the NFL. Herblock congratulated him for the Redskins' scalp and commemorated the event in a cartoon. Other writers, losing their perspective, called the desegregation of the Redskins an achievement comparable to James Meredith's successful efforts to enroll at the University of Mississippi. "The integration success story of the Kennedy administration," wrote *Boston Globe* columnist Wilfrid Rodgers, "didn't take place in Mississippi but here in the back yard of the nation's capital."[56]

Equating the desegregation of a professional football team with the integration of southern schools and universities is extravagant. Indeed, many critics have assailed the New Frontier for its lack of vigor in the pursuit of civil rights. "When it comes to civil rights," wrote the *Baltimore Afro-American* in January 1962, "the bold profile of courage displayed as a candidate has been concealed by the shameful shadow of appeasement embraced as President." Political cartoonist Thomas Stockett displayed space progress outdistancing race progress. Assessing JFK's civil rights record, black leader F. L. Shuttlesworth wrote that "where so little has been done for so long, any little may appear to be large." And Kenneth Keating, a Republican Senator from New York, called the action against the Redskins a clever subterfuge to distinguish the administration's feeble civil rights record. "I cannot help but feel that Governor Faubus and his cohorts need a little more attention than George Preston Marshall and Company," declaring Keating. "The Redskins may be tough on a football field, but the administration apparently has decided that they are easy targets in the political arena."[57]

The administration's move against the Redskins, however, was more than a political ploy and civil rights tokenism. During the early months of 1961, blacks hailed the desegregation of the Redskins as part of the administration's overall commitment to fight racial discrimination through strong executive action. *Ebony* magazine listed the desegregation of the Redskins as one of many civil rights achievements of 1961. More progress toward racial equality was made in 1961, the magazine declared, "than any other year in the last decade." The *Chicago Defender* praised Kennedy for "opening a New Frontier of human dignity." And the *Baltimore Afro-American* gave special thanks to Udall. "Of all the New Frontiersman, none has been more forthright and determined to change the racial status quo." Kennedy, to be sure, was not fully committed to civil rights. He reneged on campaign promises for fear of alienating white southern congressmen. Foreign policy also took precedence over civil rights. Yet, unlike the Eisenhower administration, the New Frontier took positive steps to combat racial injustice. One of those modest successes was the desegregation of a professional football team in the nation's capital.[58]

NOTES

The author wishes to thank Roger Clark, Jim Conrad, Tom Paterson, and Alan Reinhardt for their suggestions and support.

1. Marshall quoted in Newsweek 60 (October 15, 1962): 99; Sam Lacy in the *Baltimore Afro-American*, October 8, 1960, November 26, 1960.

2. On the Kennedy Administration and civil rights see Carl M. Brauer, *John F. Kennedy and the Second Reconstruction* (New York: Columbia University Press, 1977); William H. Chafe, *The Unfinished Journey: America Since World War II* (New York: Oxford University Press, 1986), 205–214, 217–220; Jim F. Heath, *Decade of Disillusionment: The Kennedy-Johnson Years* (Bloomington, IN: Indiana University Press, 1975), 69–73; Bruce Miroff, *Pragmatic Illusions: The Presidential Politics of John F. Kennedy* (New York: McKay, 1976), 223–270; Victor S. Navasky, *Kennedy Justice* (New York: Scribner, 1971), 96–155; Herbert S. Parmet, *JFK: The Presidency of John F. Kennedy* (New York: Viking, 1983), 249–276; Harvard Sitkoff, *The Struggle for Black Equality, 1954–1980* (New York: Noonday, 1981), 105–8, 111–5, 156–61.

3. George P. Marshall, "Pro Football Is Better Football," *Saturday Evening Post* 211 (November 19, 1938): 20–1, 52; Robert H. Boyle, "All Alone By the Telephone," *Sports Illustrated* 15 (October 16, 1961): 37–43; George Sullivan, *Pro Football's All-Time Greats: The Immortals In Pro-Football's Hall of Fame* (New York: Putnam, 1968), 75–81; Mickey Herskowitz, *The Golden Age of Pro Football* (New York: Taylor, 1974), 182; see also Marshall obituaries in *Newsweek* 74 (August 18, 1969), p. 78; and *Time* 94 (August 15, 1969): 58.

4. Sullivan, *All-Time Greats*, 79; Boyle, "All Alone," 43.

5. Bob Addie in the *Sporting News* 168 (August 23, 1969): 2; George Halas, "My Forty Years in Pro Football," *Saturday Evening Post* 230 (November 30, 1957): 110 *and passim*. Tom Bennett, et al., *The NFL's Official Encyclopedia History of Professional Football* (New York: Macmillan, 1977), 391; George Marshall obituary in *Sporting News* 168 (August 23, 1969): 40; Boyle, "All Alone," 40; *Newsweek* 60 (October 15, 1962): 99.

6. On Marshall's showmanship see Marshall, "Pro Football," 52–3; Corinne Griffith (Marshall), *My Life With The Redskins* (New York: A.S. Barnes, 1947), 39–46, 93, 217; Thomas Sugrue, "Soapsuds and Showmanship," *American Magazine* 124 (December 1937): 32–3, 131–6; "Powwow," *Time* 32 (December 12, 1938): 56–57; "Promoter," *Newsweek* 9 (June 12, 1937): 29.

7. *New York Times*, December 25, 1956; Myron Cope, *The Game That Was: The Early Days of Pro Football* (New York: Bookthrift, 1970), 129; Marshall obituary in *Newsweek* 74 (August 18, 1969): 78.

8. *New York Times* obituary, August 10, 1969; Cope, *The Game That Was*, 116, 169–70; Nixon quoted in the *Washington Post*, June 13, 1961.

9. Cope, *The Game That Was*, 282; Herskowitz, *Golden Age*, 182; Boyle, "All Alone," 43; George P. Marshall, "Speaking Out: Baseball Isn't Our National Sport," *Saturday Evening Post* 234 (December 9, 1961): 10–1.

10. On blacks in professional football see Jack Orr, *The Black Athlete: His Story in American History* (New York: Lion Books, 1969), 89–91; Cope, *The Game That Was*, 238–239; Benjamin G. Rader, *American Sports: From the Age of Folk Games to the Age of Spectators* (Englewood Cliffs, NJ: Prentice-Hall, 1983), 329; William A. Brower, "Has Professional Football Closed the Door?" *Opportunity* 18 (December 1940): 375–7; "Top Negro Stars In Pro Football," *Sepia* 12 (November, 1963): 75–82. Fritz Pollard was not only a player, but he was the only black head coach in the history of professional football. Al Harvin, "Pollard, At 84, Reflects On His Days of Glory," *New York Times*, February 7, 1978.

On the absence of black head coaches in the NFL see Rich Telander, "Shamefully Lily-White," *Sports Illustrated* 66 (February 23, 1987): 80.

11. On black college football players in the 1930s and 1940s see William A. Brower, "Negro Players On White Gridirons," *Opportunity* 19 (October 1941): 307–8; P. W. L. Jones, "All-Time Negro Football Team," *Crisis* 44 (January 1937): 16–21; Ed Nace, "Negro Grid Stars, Past and Present," *Opportunity* 17 (September 1939): 272–4; Roy Wilkins, "Negro Stars On Big Grid Teams," *Crisis* 43 (December 1936): 362–3: "Top Negro Stars," 76. Fritz Pollard, Jr., was also a college track star and won a bronze medal in the 1936 Berlin Olympics.

12. John Hope Franklin, *From Slavery to Freedom: A History of Negro Americans,* 5th ed. (New York: Alfred A. Knupf, 1980), 437–55; Chafe, *Unfinished Journey,* 20–2, 86–91, 107–8.

13. Chafe, *Unfinished Journey,* 152–73; Sitkoff, *The Struggle For Black Equality,* 3–96; William H. Chafe, *Civilities and Civil Rights: Greensboro, North Carolina, and the Black Struggle for Freedom* (New York: Oxford University Press, 1980).

14. Rader, *American Sports,* 242, 324–5, 329; Jules Tygiel, *Baseball's Great Experiment: Jackie Robinson And His Legacy* (New York: Oxford University Press, 1984), 285–344, 355; Orr, *The Black Athlete,* 89–91; Cope, *The Game That Was,* 238–9.

15. "Football's Most Democratic Team," *Ebony* 11 (December 1955): 104–8; Al White, "Can Negroes Save Pro-Football?" *Our World* 5 (December 1950): 60–5; "New Faces in Pro Football," *Our World* 7 (December 1952): 63. In 1960, the AFL had twenty-nine black players, professional basketball twenty-seven, and major league baseball eighty. Figures taken from *Baltimore Afro-American,* January 9, 1960; October 29, 1960; April 22, 1961; *Washington Post,* November 30, 1961. Not until 1959 did all major league baseball teams desegregate their rosters. Tygiel, *Baseball's Great Experiment,* 290–1, 299, 328–31. On the NAACP and Marshall see the *New York Times,* February 1, 1957; October 14, 1957; Joseph Nocera, "The Screwing of the Average Fan: Edward Bennett Williams and the Washington Redskins," *Washington Monthly* 10 (June 1978): 38.

16. On race relations in Washington D.C. see "Segregation in Washington D.C.," *Negro History Bulletin* 16 (January 1953): 79–86: Isaac Franck, "Integration in Washington," *Commonweal* 68 (August 15, 1958): 493–6.

17. Chuck Stone, "Are D.C. Colored People Making Any Progress?" *Baltimore Afro-American,* May 20, 1961; "Race Problems in Nation's Capital," *U.S. News and World Report* 43 (September 27, 1957): 34–38; David Lawrence, "Washington's Worry," *U.S. News and World Report* 46 (April 6, 1959): 120; "The Nation's Capital: A Troubled City," *U.S. News and World Report* 48 (April 4, 1960): 84–5. In 1961, President Kennedy appointed the first black, John B. Duncan, to the Washington D.C. Commission. See Haynes Johnson, *Dusk at the Mountain* (Garden City, NY: Doubleday, 1963), 234.

18. Sam Lacy in the *Baltimore Afro-American,* October 8, 22, 1960; November 26, 1960; December 3, 1960; January 14, 1961; Shirley Povich in the *Washington Post,* December 20, 29, 1960; Bob Addie in the *Washington Post,* December 17, 1960: Gordon Cobbledick column reprinted in the *Washington Post,* December 24, 1960.

19. *New York Times,* December 29, 1960; *Washington Post,* December 18, 19, 25, 28, 1960; Shirley Povich in the *Washington Post,* December 29, 1960.

20. Simeon Booker, "What Negroes Can Expect From Kennedy," *Ebony* 16 (January 1961): 33ff, *Baltimore Afro-American,* editorial, November 26, 1960; Parmet, *JFK,* 50–56; Brauer, *Second Reconstruction,* 30–60. Martin Luther King quoted in the *Pittsburgh Courier,* January 14, 1961.

21. Lee D. Jenkins in the *Chicago Defender,* March 4–10, 1961; Wendell Smith in the *Pittsburgh Courier,* January 7, 28; February 4, 18, 25, 1961; Sam Lacy in the *Baltimore Afro-American,* March 18, 25, 1961; *Washington Post,* June 20, July 16, 1961. On sports and integration see Albert N. D. Brooks, "Democracy Through Sports," *Negro History Bulletin* 14 (December 1951): 56ff.; "Round Table Discussion: The Negro in American Sport," *Negro History Bulletin* 24 (November 1960): 27–31, 47; "Sports as an Integrator," *Saturday Review* 50 (January 21, 1967): 32.

22. *Chicago Defender,* January 28, February 3, March 4–10, 18–24, May 6–12, August 12–18, 1961; *Baltimore Afro-American,* March 18, 25, April 8, 1961; *Washington Post,* March 6, 7, 13, 21, 24, 26, April 12, September 21, 22, October 12, 1961.

23. Brauer, *Second Reconstruction,* 69, 78–9; Sitkoff, *Struggle for Black Equality,* 97–108; Parmet, *JFK,* 256–7.

24. Stewart L. Udall, interview by the author, August 21, 1986, Phoenix, Arizona.

25. Letter, Stewart L. Udall to author, May 28, 1985.

26. *Ibid.;* Frank J. Barry, Solicitor, memorandum for Stewart L. Udall, April 7, 1961. Stewart L. Udall Papers, box 90, University of Arizona Manuscripts Library (hereafter cited as UP with appropriate box number immediately following).

27. Stewart L. Udall to George P. Marshall, March 24, 1961, UP 90,

28. Stewart L. Udall, press conference, March 24, 1961, UP 90.

29. David Halberstam in the *New York Times,* March 25, 1961; *Washington Post,* March 25, 1961; *Washington Evening Star* and numerous other news clippings dated March 25, 1961 in UP 91; *Chicago Defender,* April 1–6, 1961; *Pittsburgh Courier,* April 1, 1961; *Baltimore Afro-American,* April 1, 1961.

30. Tom Yorke in the *Washington Daily News,* March 25, 1961; George P. Marshall to Stewart L. Udall, March 24, 1961, UP W. Morris Siegel in the *Washington Daily News,* April 4, 1961.

31. *Washington Daily News,* March 25, 1961.

32. *Ibid.; Danbury News-Times,* March 27, 1961, UP 91; Wendell Smith, interview with George P. Marshall in *Pittsburgh Courier,* April 22, 1961.

33. *Washington Post,* March 26, 1961.

34. Stewart L. Udall, press conference, March 28, 1961, UP 91; *Washington Post,* March 29, 30, 1961.

35. Jack Walsh in the *Washington Post,* July 13, 1961; Robert J. Donovan in the *New York Herald Tribune,* July 14, 1961.

36. Boyle, "All Alone," 37–40; Curtis Williams to Stewart L. Udall, April 10, Henry M. Cathles to Udall, May 4, 1961, UP 90.

37. Morris Siegel in the *Washington Daily News,* April 4, 1961; Frank Hyde, undated columns from the *Jamestown (New York) Post-Journal,* UP 91 and in the *Congressional Record,* 87 Cong., I Sess., p. A 6668; *Augusta (Georgia) Chronicle,* March 29, 1961, UP 91.

38. Carl B. White to Robert F Kennedy, June 29, 1961, UP 90; *Tulsa World,* editorial, March 31, 1961 and Doc Greene, "Press Box," unidentified, undated newsclip in UP 90; Ernest Gross in the *Congressional Record,* 87th Cong., Sess. 1, 6132, 8558; Dick Darling, "Play Ball or Else," in *Riverside (California) Press,* April 9, 1961, UP 90.

39. Letter, Stewart L. Udall to author, May 28, 1985; Udall, press conferences, April 20, May 31, 1961, UP 91; *Washington Post,* April 12, 21, 1961; *Washington Daily News,* June 27, 1961; Denis Chavez to Udall, June 27, 1961, UP 90; Edward W. Knappman to Congressman Charles Joelson, July 25, Joelson to Udall, July 30, Udall to Joelson, October 22, 1962, Department of Interior Papers, Washington D.C., Freedom of Information Act Request; Udall to JFK and "List of Topics Discussed at Staff Meeting," both April 3, 1962, UP 98.

40. Matson quoted by Shirley Povich in the *Washington Post,* April 27, 1961; Jackie Robinson quoted by Jack Walsh in the *Washington Post,* April 12, 1961; "Negro Athletes and Civil Rights," *Sepia* 13 (June, 1964): 35–9.

41. For the pickets see *Washington Post,* August 3, 10; September 17, 29, 30, 1961. For Veeck's suggestions see Robert M. Paul, memorandum for Orren Beaty, April 5, 1961, UP 90; Shea and Cooke's recollections for their role in the *Washington Post,* September 12, 1962; Williams quoted in David Harris, *The League: The Rise and Decline of the NFL* (New York: Bantam Books, 1986), 145. On Rozelle and the television contract see *ibid.,* 15–16.

42. *Washington Daily News,* April 25, 1961; letter, Udall to author, May 28, 1985; letter, Pete Rozelle to author, June 19, 1985; Jack Walsh in the *Washington Post,* August 15, 1961; George P. Marshall to Pete Rozelle, August 9, 1961, UP 90.

43. *New York Times,* August 15, 1961; *Albuquerque Journal,* August 15, 1961; Udall to Edward J. Collins, October 6, 1961, Department of Interior Papers, Washington, D.C., Freedom of Information Act Request.

44. Sam Lacy in the *Baltimore Afro-American,* November 11; December 2, 16, 23, 1961.

45. *Washington Post,* September 27, 28; October 2, 1961; *New York Times,* October 6, 1961.

46. Shirley Povich in the *Washington Post,* October 17, 20, November 7, 1961; Jack Walsh in the *Washington Post,* October 9, 16, 23, 30, November 6, 13, 20, 27, 1961; letters to the editor, *Washington Post,* October 5, November 9, 1961. Udall's final warning to Marshall in the *Washington Post,* December 1, 1961.

47. *Ibid.,* December 2, 3, 5, 1961; Povich in *ibid.,* December 8, 1961.

48. *Washington Post,* December 7, 10, 1961; Sam Lacy in the *Baltimore Afro-American* December 2, 16, 23, 1961.

49. *Sporting News,* December 13, 27, 1961; *Washington Post,* December 15, 1961, September 12, 1962; *Pittsburgh Courier,* December 30, 1961, April 7, 1962; Sam Lacy in the *Baltimore Afro-American,* December 30, 1961, August 12, 18, September 8, 1962.

50. Letter, Norm Snead to author, undated [June, 1985]; Bill Nunn, Jr., in the *Pittsburgh Courier,* October 8, 1962.

51. *Washington Post,* December 15, 1961; "Historically Speaking," *Black Sports* 7 (January 1978): 57–61; letter, Bobby Mitchell to author, June 14, 1985.

52. "Historically Speaking," 57–61.

53. *Ibid.;* letter, Bobby Mitchell to author, June 14, 1985.

54. *Washington Post,* September 17, 24; October 1, 8, 1962; Tex Maule, "The Redskins Find a

New Kick—Winning," *Sports Illustrated* 17 (October 15, 1962): 61–3; George Dunsmore in the *Pittsburgh Courier,* October 6, 1962; letter, Stewart L. Udall to author, May 28, 1985.

55. "Historically Speaking," 57–61; *Pittsburgh Courier,* December 19, 1962; *Washington Post,* December 11, 20, 1962; Harris, *The League,* 141–6.

56. *Cleveland Plain-Dealer,* October 13, 1962 and unidentified newsclips in UP 90; Wilfrid C. Rodgers in the *Boston Globe,* undated in UP 90; Herbert Block to Stewart L. Udall, undated in UP 90.

57. *Baltimore Afro-American,* editorial, January13, 1962; F. L. Shuttlesworth in the *Pittsburgh Courier,* April 15, 1961; Keating quoted by Sam Lacy in the *Baltimore Afro-American,* May 13, 1961. For a critical assessment of the New Frontier's civil rights record see Chafe, *Unfinished Journey,* 206–20; Miroff, *Pragmatic Illusions,* 223–70.

58. "Negro Progress in 1961," *Ebony* 17 (January 1962): 21–8; *Chicago Defender,* editorials, February 4–10, April 15–21, 1961; *Baltimore Afro-American,* editorial, April 28, 1962.

III

IMAGES OF THE BLACK ATHLETE AND THE RACIAL POLITICS OF SPORT

"THE CIVIL RIGHTS STRUGGLE is not over," the Reverend Joseph Lowery proclaimed early in 2003 during one prominent commemoration of Martin Luther King, Jr.'s birthday. "Some of us are living the dream," said the cofounder (with King) of the Southern Christian Leadership Conference, "but most people, including whites are not. Today's generation does not have to worry about lunch counters and sitting at the back of the bus. But they do have to deal with police brutality and getting unjustly fired and abused at the workplace. Everything has changed, and nothing has changed." (*Chicago Tribune,* January 20, 2003). Just so: more prisons than schools have been built in recent years, and a hugely disproportionate number of their inmates are African Americans; meanwhile the executive branch of the government has registered its unmistakable opposition to even the most modest affirmative action programs in the nation's colleges and universities. Du Bois's fret and forecast about the color line still resonates one hundred years later—as sociologists, cultural commentators, and public policy analysts grapple both with the legacies of segregation and discrimination and the persistence of racism in contemporary America.

At the same time, historians and public intellectuals have added to the doctrine of rights the discourse of "representation." While political battles are still being fought, much of the debate over the meaning of black culture and race relations in America occurs when scholars and commentators such as Henry Louis Gates, Jr., bell hooks, Michael Eric Dyson, Jesse Jackson, and John Edgar Wideman fashion innovative frames of reference for the meanings of civil rights, full citizenship, and black identity in twenty-first century America—even as their principal point of departure is often "the dream" that King enunciated in Washington, D.C, in the late summer of 1963.

These shifting contexts—beyond desegregation—can be assessed in different ways. Today a huge percentage of the competitors in the NFL and NBA are African Americans;

likewise the number of Olympic medalists in track and field. This phenomenon attracts constant commentary, while the overwhelming numbers of European-Americans in major symphony orchestras or corporate boardrooms, or the U.S. Congress receives scant recognition. As a result, sport has become one of the most visible reflections of racial progress and constraint in the new millennium.

Such observations have a long history, which speaks not only to African-American accomplishment in sport, but also to the contests over the meanings affixed to the championships won and world records established by black athletes, their breakthroughs on the playing fields, and now in their attempts to make progress in front offices and the whole world that lies beyond physical skill, speed, strength, and stamina. It was Edwin Bancroft Henderson, among a host of other black sports commentators, who first enlisted athletic achievement in the larger crusade for equal opportunity. What those racial reformers hoped to define was an arc of achievement extending from the sporting realm to far broader fields of endeavor. The qualities of character acquired or revealed through athletic competition *translated* to other tasks and responsibilities and thus demonstrated the readiness of African Americans for full participation in the social, economic, and political life of the nation. Converting white America to this ideal was one of the challenges of the century. For the sociologist Gunnar Myrdal, this translation played a significant role in addressing the "American Dilemma"; for many blacks, it has long represented a means of keeping their eyes on the prize of full equality and opportunity.

The strategy of "muscular assimilationism" was clear in its representation of black athletes as both "race men" and national heroes, though in fact Joe Louis and Jackie Robinson labored under the burden of their role as paragons. For their part, African-American athletes of a later era would publicly present themselves in more complex and various ways, Muhammad Ali as a trickster at times, but also as a conscientious objector to participation in what he regarded as an unjust war, Michael Jordan as a more emphatic spokesperson for Nike corporation than for racial reform. Still, by the end of the century—when Ali and Jordan had been dubbed (along with Tiger Woods and the Williams Sisters) as "trans-racial" as well as "transnational" icons—it would have seemed that the congruence of sporting achievement and civil rights ideology had triumphed over old prejudices. Yet as frequently as scholars and intellectuals declare that "race" is socially constructed, the mass of Americans are just as regularly reminded that *racism* is not vestigial, but rather asserts itself vigorously both within and beyond the ivory tower. The resilience—there may be no better word for it—of pseudoscientific racism in sport remains a significant issue for those who strive to move beyond the hierarchies of privilege and subordination that characterized much of twentieth-century American history.

For the future, the paradoxical nature of the relationship between sport and race relations may best be illustrated by the fact that Harry Edwards, in the last essay in this volume, echoes many of the considerations that animated black activists and commentators one hundred years ago: in the face of vast inequalities of wealth and poverty in the United States and continuing segregation at many levels of society, the creation of sporting institutions for black youth, rooted in the community, could serve to reinforce a sense of pride and hope. "The hook and handle," that is the appeal of athletic competition may still provide a platform for accomplishment beyond the sporting arena.

14

EDWIN BANCROFT HENDERSON, AFRICAN-AMERICAN ATHLETES, AND THE WRITING OF SPORT HISTORY

David K. Wiggins

CHARLES DREW, WHO ATTENDED the prestigious Dunbar High School in Washington, D.C., later starred in several sports at Amherst College, and eventually became a famous surgeon and blood bank pioneer, noted in a 1940 letter that he was very grateful to Edwin Bancroft Henderson. "I owe you and a few other men like you," Drew noted, "for setting most of the standards that I have felt were worthwhile, the things I have lived by and for and whenever possible have attempted to pass on."[1] Drew's comments, which came nearly ten years before his death in a tragic automobile accident, stemmed from an obviously deep admiration for Henderson, who had been both his teacher and mentor during his days as a student in Washington's segregated school system.[2]

The Edwin Bancroft Henderson that Charles Drew so much admired was born on November 24, 1883, in Washington, D.C., to William and Louisa Henderson. He graduated in 1902 from the famous M Street School, attended Dudley Allen Sargent's celebrated Harvard Summer School of Physical Education (HSSPE), and headed the Department of Physical Education in Washington's segregated school system from 1925 until his appointment some twenty-six years later as Director of Physical Education, Safety, and Athletics. Henderson's career was marked by extraordinary accomplishments and many successes, both within and outside the physical education profession. He introduced basketball to black children in Washington, D.C., and organized the district's Public School Athletic League. He cofounded the Washington, D.C. Pigskin Club and helped establish such important organizations as the Inter-Scholastic Athletic Association of Middle Atlantic States; the Eastern Board of Officials; the Washington, D.C., chapter of the American Alliance for Health, Physical Education, Recreation, and Dance (AAPHERD); the Colored Citizens Protection League of Falls Church, Virginia; and the Falls Church, Virginia, branch of the National Association for the Advancement of Colored People (NAACP). Through his numerous organizational initiatives, Henderson fought against various forms of racial discrimination. He waged war against Jim Crow transportation facilities in Virginia, led campaigns to eliminate segregated recreational and organized sports programs on both the local and regional levels, and fought to prohibit southern states from excluding blacks from membership in local AAHPERD chapters.[3]

Henderson was, moreover, a prolific writer. He penned literally hundreds of "Letters to the Editor" to newspapers across the country, wrote numerous unpublished documents as part of his civil rights struggles, contributed important articles to professional journals, and wrote the first books on the history of African Americans in sport. Henderson's achievements did not go unrecognized. He was given the YMCA Distinguished Service Award, selected as a Howard University Alumnus of the Year, appointed Honorary President of the North American Society for Sport History, and elected as a charter member of the Black Athletes Hall of Fame.[4]

Of all these accomplishments and honors, it is Henderson's writings on African-American athletes that have proved most far-reaching and had the greatest influence on subsequent generations. Popular writers, academicians from various disciplines, and scholars of both races and different philosophies have all depended on Henderson's work for source material, analysis, and clues in the designing of their own publications dealing with African-American athletes. If number of citations is any indication of the importance of one's scholarship, Henderson's work merits great respect, and he rightfully deserves to be called the Father of Black Sport History.[5] Nearly every article, book chapter, and survey text written over the last half-century that includes information on the history of African-American athletes has seemingly been influenced by Henderson's work in one way or another. Andrew S. "Doc" Young, in the acknowledgments to his *Negro Firsts In Sports* (1963), was absolutely correct when he noted: "Mr. Henderson was the first person of any race to dig deeply into the total history of Negroes in American sports. A great deal of knowledge which is now shared in common by sports authorities was originally ferreted out, with painstaking effort and no little difficulty, by Mr. Henderson."[6]

Henderson's writings were intended to foster pride among African Americans and alter white racial beliefs. With the commitment and deep emotional involvement that characterized some of the earliest scholarly work of black academicians, Henderson's writings were instrumental in proving that African Americans were just as capable as whites on the playing field and, by extension, in other areas of American life. Possessing boundless optimism in the power of sport to break down racial prejudice and contribute to a more integrated society, Henderson focused much of his attention on the individual accomplishments of black athletes in an effort to provide much-needed evidence of African-American progress. Even when faced with unremitting racial discrimination, Henderson's writings reflected an undying faith in the integrative functions of sport. In large measure, Henderson was, to utilize the terminology of the historian Patrick B. Miller, a "muscular assimilationist" in that he viewed society as an established system of interrelated parts in which sport transmitted shared values and norms and contributed to communal feelings between whites and African Americans.[7]

Henderson's first significant publication occurred in 1910 when he began editing, along with William A. Joiner, an instructor from Wilberforce University and a longtime promoter of sport, the first of a series of four books entitled *Official Handbook: Inter-Scholastic Athletic Association of Middle Atlantic States.* Published as part of the Spalding Athletic Library collection, the books provide a wealth of information, many photographs, rules, and records concerning the involvement of African-American athletes at various levels of amateur sport in the Middle Atlantic states. The series is especially significant because it reflects both the immense pride that African Americans took in their own sporting organizations during the early decades of the twentieth century and their simultaneous concern

Figure 14–1
Edwin Bancroft Henderson, pictured here in his office, was a tireless worker who fought his entire life on behalf of African Americans in their struggle for racial justice and equal opportunity. Courtesy of the Moorland-Spingarn Research Center, Howard University.

that these organizations be as pristine as possible, devoid of much of the corruption that characterized white amateur sport during this period. No one can read Ernest Marshall's "The Negro Athlete" in the 1910 edition or George William Lattimore's "Some Facts Concerning Athletic Clubs in Brooklyn and New Jersey" and Conrad V. Norman's "Athletics in New York City" in the 1911 edition without realizing that African-American sport organizations were crucial examples of black enterprise and symbols of the possibility of reconciliation in racially torn America. At the same time, no one can read the series without recognizing its emphasis on such issues as appropriate athletic behavior, eligibility requirements, protests and sanctions, and definitions of amateurism. The emphasis on these issues in the *Official Handbook* was part of the broader national discussion among African-American educators and social reformers about the proper management of their segregated sporting organizations. In short, educators and social reformers realized that these organizations had to be above reproach if they were not to subvert the cultural achievements and other accomplishments of blacks living in a society that had always allowed them far less room than whites to deviate from standard modes of behavior.[8]

Henderson's coeditorship of the *Official Handbook* set the stage for a number of articles he would publish on African-American athletes in prestigious black publications over the next three decades. His first article, "The Colored College Athlete," was published in the *Crisis*, the NAACP's new monthly journal edited by the great intellectual and civil rights activist W. E. B. Du Bois.[9] The article, which followed closely on the heels of some other noteworthy essays on black athletes in such black periodicals as *The Voice of the Negro* (1904–1907) and *The Colored American Magazine* (1900–1909)[10] primarily recounts the success of African Americans in intercollegiate sport at predominantly white institutions in the North. Adopting an approach that would become a trademark of his many writings, Henderson attempted to chart both the progress and prove the equality of African-American athletes by pointing out the exploits of such former and current college stars as Dartmouth's Matthew Bullock, Amherst's and Harvard's William H. Lewis, Williams' Ernest Marshall, Western Reserve's Edward Williams, Michigan's Leonard Lapsley, Oberlin's Merton Robinson, Pennsylvania's John B. Taylor, Harvard's Ted Cable, and Amherst's John Punkett, Ed Gray, and William Tecumseh Sherman Jackson.

While "The Colored College Athlete" undoubtedly brought him some notoriety and national attention from blacks, Henderson secured his reputation as the foremost authority on African-American athletes with a series of articles in the *Messenger* between March 1925 and January 1928. Henderson's articles in the *Messenger,* the more militant journal edited by A. Philip Randolph and Chandler Owen, are particularly interesting from a journalistic point of view because they were written during the last three years of the magazine's existence and at a time when it had shifted from an emphasis on black workers to the Talented Tenth and the Black Bourgeoisie.[11] Henderson's articles, appearing most often in a column usually titled simply "Sports," were published alongside others devoted to society news, literary accomplishments, successful entrepreneurs and businessmen, and issues related to women and children. He clearly understood that his articles on sports would be attractive to many readers, a fact certainly not lost on the editors of a magazine that had always struggled to remain financially solvent. "Sport writings are proving a tonic to dead print matter," Henderson wrote in the June 1925 issue of the magazine. "Many men and boys to whom our newspapers were unknown now read the sport sheets, and take interest in various local, national and international affairs. The athletic page is a good advertising method for news of more serious import."[12]

True to the new orientation of the magazine, Henderson focused primarily on elite African-American athletes and college sport. Although he wrote frequently of the proposed boxing match between Harry Wills and Jack Dempsey and occasionally about the performances of other black professional athletes and teams, Henderson spent most of his time charting the progress of black college athletes in celebratory terms, stressing the value of amateur sport, and emphasizing the importance of organizational structure and administrative oversight in intercollegiate sport at historically black colleges.

This latter topic was obviously of great importance to Henderson, just as it was to W. E. B. Du Bois, George Streator, and a host of other African-American intellectuals during the early part of the twentieth century.[13] As in his writings in the *Official Handbook,* Henderson devoted much space in the *Messenger* to a discussion about the need for improved management of black college sport because of inappropriate recruiting practices, lack of eligibility requirements, and a number of other rules violations. Always the reformer and forever conscious of what was taking place at all levels of sport, Henderson pointed out some of the problems, publicized new policies being implemented, and made his own recommendations to eliminate the corruption that characterized athletic programs in black colleges. Henderson considered the most serious problems plaguing sport in black colleges to be the limited opportunities, lack of respect, and inequitable pay afforded African-American officials. Henderson, who had the distinction in 1906 of becoming the first African American to officiate at the Howard and Lincoln, Pennsylvania

Thanksgiving Day Football Classic and in 1915 established the all-black Eastern Board of Officials, was especially disturbed by the fact that members of his own racial group frequently chose white rather than black officials because of their perceived competence, trustworthiness, and ability to handle the stressful situations in athletic contests.[14] "How it happens that our pigmy-minded victory-at-any-cost-blinded race people imagine the work of white officials superior to that done by Savoy, Gibson, Westmoreland, Washington, Abbott, Robinson, Pinderhughes, Wright, Morrison, Trigg, Coppage and Douglass and many others is a puzzle to me," wrote Henderson in the January 1927 issue of the *Messenger*. "The only advantage arriving from the use of white officials is from the fact of the peculiar psychology that presents itself when white officials work which causes the poor driven cattle to become blinded to the same errors of commission and omission that would not have escaped had the officials been of the colored race."[15]

In addition to his discussion about black college sport, Henderson devoted much of his *Messenger* coverage to outlining forms of racial discrimination and attempting to burst racial stereotypes associated with black athletes and organized sport. Very attuned to white fears of black bodies and the various forms of racial discrimination in this country, Henderson was especially fond of pointing out how these factors influenced the sport participation patterns of African-American athletes and how this participation was perceived by members of both races. He was cognizant of the complex racial ideology that was used to rationalize the performances of African-American athletes based on skin color, intelligence, moral character, and physical skills. In the June 1925 issue, Henderson encouraged African Americans to compete in track and field because "any man who can clip a second from a race consistently or leap an inch farther or higher is sought out by the coach whether he be Negro, Chinaman, or Indian Chief." It was much more difficult, however, for African Americans to transcend racial barriers in those sports that either required close personal contact between the participants or were identified with white America's upper crust. "In the team games," Henderson noted, "especially the personal contact games like football or basketball it takes a very good Negro athlete to make prejudiced frats and college directors see him. For baseball, crew, tennis, golf and a host of minor sports traditions are in most places yet against him."[16] In the April 1927 issue, Henderson continued this theme by arguing that African Americans found limited opportunities in wrestling because of the close contact the sport required. "Colored boys got their biggest opportunities in non-contact sports, where time and distance records are to be overcome," wrote Henderson. "Wrestling affords the closest contact. Like forms of social contact, it stirs much racial prejudice. Seldom do colored boys get a full chance in such games."[17]

In the May 1927 issue, Henderson refuted the popularly held belief that blacks did not excel in distance running because they lacked discipline and other positive character traits possessed by white Americans. He hypothesized that the small number of African-American distance runners resulted from the unwillingness of coaches to spend the requisite time with them in training to ensure their success. "A colored boy who could start with a bunch from a century dash scratch," Henderson said, "and lead them to the tape, at once got the eye of the coach, but not so the purveyor of distance wares. The coach has to try him out with time and patience. This is one reason why many of our boys have not been distance champions."[18] Finally, in both the March 1926 issue and the June 1927 one, Henderson took exception to those sportswriters who claimed that John B. Taylor, the great black quarter-miler from the University of Pennsylvania, was actually a member of the white race.[19] Henderson was incensed by their refusal to accept the fact that the great performances of Taylor could have been executed by a black man. In the March 1926 issue, he wrote

> Years back when John Taylor of the U. of Pa. was the 440 yards champion, some enterprising Nordic claimed the swarthy son of America for the Nordic race on account of his bulging calves. Our galaxy of champions in sprint events, distance runs, field events, all-around athletic competition, and athletic games have made way with the fallacy. They said the wide-nostrilled, deep-chested colored man of African extraction was physically unsuited to Northern climes, but Matthew Henson, who was a member of Robert Perry's 1909 expedition that erected the American Flag at the North Pole, stepped out on to the North Pole and is yet with us. When the bars are more generally down, it will be found that colored athletes with centuries of dormant potential energies will more than match many inbreeding white race opponents.[20]

Henderson's pieces in the *Messenger* were also important because they were among the plethora of articles that were published on African-American athletes in both black specialty magazines and more comprehensive and nationally recognized journals between the two world wars. The development of separate black sporting organizations at both the amateur and professional levels of competition, increased involvement of African Americans in sport at predominantly white institutions and in the Olympic Games, and the renewed sense of racial pride in the black community as well as the parallel emergence of what Theodore Kornweibel termed the "new journalism" for the "new crowd Negro," all combined to produce a number of important articles on the black athletic experience.[21] For instance, Binga Dismond, the former track star from the University of Chicago, edited a special section on sports titled, "In the Sun," in a short-lived journal, the *Champion Magazine: A Monthly Survey of Negro Achievement,* just before America's entrance into World War I.[22] *The Crusader,* the radical magazine edited and published in New York City between 1918 and 1922 by Cyril Valentine Briggs, ran several pieces on basketball during its four-year existence. Briggs, who loved basketball and apparently was good friends with Robert L. Douglas, the founder and manager of the famous Renaissance Five basketball team, wrote a number of pieces on the sport.[23] Romeo L. Dougherty, well-known sporting editor of the *New York News* and later of the *New York Amsterdam News,* was a contributor to the magazine, including an insightful article in the January 1921 issue, entitled "Behind the Scenes in Basketball."[24] Providing even more expanded coverage of African-American athletes was the *Competitor,* a sports periodical published by Robert L. Vann, the longtime editor of the *Pittsburgh Courier-Journal.* Although in existence only from January 1920 to June 1921, the magazine published articles on everything from the importance of black referees and the future of black basketball to sport in historically black colleges and the founding of the National Negro Baseball League.[25] *The Southern Workman,* initiated and first edited by Samuel Armstrong of Hampton Institute, included coverage of sport, such as Elizabeth Dunham's 1924 essay on "Physical Education of Women at Hampton Institute" and Charles H. Williams's articles on the formative years of the Colored Intercollegiate Athletic Association and black participation in both the 1932 and 1936 Olympic Games.[26] The *Crisis,* with a number of talented and well-known contributors, such as Rollo Wilson, George Streator, Roy Wilkins, William A. Brower, and Dan Burley, published many cogent and nicely written articles on black participation in sport.[27] Finally, the National Urban League's official journal, *Opportunity: A Journal of Negro Life,* published several outstanding articles on the black athlete. With insightful and intelligent analysis, the articles described both the accomplishments of African-American athletes and the forms of racial discrimination evident in sport.[28]

Among the writings in *Opportunity* was Henderson's 1936 article "The Negro Athlete and Race Prejudice," one of his most important and enduring works.[29] There he provided an important analysis of the status of African-American athletes in contemporary sport, his fullest argument yet for the power of sports to break down racial prejudice and serve as the optimal agent for assimilation, and made public the increasing debate over alleged black athletic superiority. Henderson explained, with astuteness and a sociologist's eye for human behavior and social relations, that black college athletes had to be athletically superior to their white counterparts to find success in team sports. They were forced to "make adjustments" when dealing with racial teammates, had to "learn to take plenty from opponents," and suffered the humiliations of "separate lodgement when on tour," and being denied the opportunity to participate in games against the "service schools or the gentlemen of the south." The black "professional or money-seeking athletes in the profit making game," Henderson noted, encountered different problems and situations.[30] While denied the opportunity to take part in major league baseball and many other white organized sport programs, black professional athletes were sometimes allowed to participate in integrated sport by white promoters and entrepreneurs who were willing to suspend their own racist beliefs if it was financially profitable to do so. Henderson explained, without elaborating, that a multitude of factors other than financial ones helped determine the process of desegregation in sport: that "barnstorming 'big leaguers' do not disdain playing against good colored-pros when the gate pays," that "Professional All-Colored basketball teams also find it possible, with an occasional paying venture playing white teams as far south as Washington, D.C.," and that "football professionals are finding expression and compensation by playing on or with white Pro-teams."[31]

In addition to discussing the status of African-American athletes at both the amateur and professional levels of sport, Henderson provided the interesting and detailed argument that these same athletes had done as much as any group to spread tolerance and improve race relations in American society. Although black intellectuals, noted Henderson, had "risen to high planes of social relationships with individuals of other races that transcend the physical," it was African-American athletes who made the greatest contribution to racial understanding and sensitivity. The reasons were clear to Henderson. It was African-American athletes, rather than black musicians, artists, and writers, who were able to instill pride among members of their own community and bring the race greater respect because "the main springs of action are still located in the glands" and the "keenest pleasures and most poignant pains" for human beings "are born of feelings rather than of intellect."[32] To Henderson, then, white supremacist ideology, which was carefully maintained by convincing blacks that they had ugly bodies, were intellectually inferior, and were culturally less civilized, was best confronted by African-American athletes, whose great sport performances were unparalleled in producing the visceral responses necessary to alter racial stereotypes and attitudes. The transformational power of sport helped explain why Joe Louis "captivated the fancy of millions"; why Jesse Owens, Ralph Metcalfe, Eddie Tolan, and a host of others have likewise provided a feeling of pride and joyful relationship for many; why African-American athletes "are emulated by thousands of growing youth of all races"; and why "above all they gain for themselves and the Negro the respect of millions whose superiority feelings have sprung solely from identity with the white race." It is also the reason, Henderson claimed, why every educational institution and agency involved in racial uplift should place more emphasis on the "social use of athletics."[33]

His last major issue was the debate over alleged black athletic superiority. He noted that during the 1930s people from all walks of life had advanced various theories as to why such a seemingly large number of African Americans had put together so many outstanding track-and-field performances. These theories, "many of them honest," Henderson was quick to point out, were intended to prove that African-American athletes "were endowed with some peculiar anatomical structure of foot, leg or thigh that enables them to run or jump better than white athletes."[34]

To combat these theories of innate racial characteristics and sport performances, Henderson cited the work of W. Montague Cobb, a well known professor of anatomy at Howard University, future president of the NAACP, and one of Henderson's former students from the segregated public schools of Washington, D.C., who had taken extensive anthropological measurements of Jesse Owens to help determine the physical dimensions of white and black track athletes.[35] Utilizing the data that had appeared just two months earlier in Cobb's article "Race and Runners" in the *Journal of Health and Physical Education*,[36] Henderson noted that Cobb, through "painstaking research, tests, and X-rays of the body of Jesse Owens," had "scientifically disproved the one and twenty theories that Negro athletes have peculiar anatomical structures."[37] Henderson, never one to avoid debate and always willing to provide an opinion on controversial matters, then entered the fray by stating: "When one recalls that it is estimated that only one Negro slave in five was able to live through the rigors of the 'Middle Passage,' and that the horrible conditions of slavery took a toll of many slaves who could not make biological adjustments in a hostile environment, one finds the Darwinism theory of the survival of the fit operating among Negroes as rigorously as any selective process ever operated among human beings. There is just a likelihood that some very vital elements persist in the histological tissues of the glands or muscles of Negro athletes."[38]

Taken as a whole, Henderson's article is not only thought-provoking but also full of more than just a bit of irony. Although he made cogent observations on the status of African Americans in sport, he helped contribute at the same time to the mythologizing of black athletic performance and to the erroneous belief that sport serves as the great leveler in American society. There is no evidence to support his contention that African-American athletes have helped foster greater respect for their race or contributed "to the spread of tolerance and improved race relations." If anything, the passage of time has shown that the entry of a disproportionate number of African-American athletes into certain sports has served to limit the range of black possibilities in a society still divided by race and characterized by unequal distribution of power and economic resources. Perhaps most important, Henderson's suggestion that the outstanding performances of African Americans in sport resulted from the elimination of physically weaker slaves during the Middle Passage, a suggestion he would continue to proffer throughout his life, lent credence to the belief in innate physiological gifts of black athletes espoused by the very same people he had previously condemned. By offering this theory, Henderson inadvertently provided corroboration for the racialists whose arguments for innate physiological differences have served to maintain the stereotypical notion that African Americans could not excel in the life of the mind and that their outstanding sport performances came naturally and not through hard work, dedication, and other character traits so admired in American society.[39]

In 1939, Henderson published *The Negro in Sports,* the work he is most closely identified with and the one that perhaps has had more influence than any other on subsequent research dealing with the history of the black athlete in American sport.[40] Appearing one decade after the publication of John A. Krout's groundbreaking study *Annals of American Sport* (1929) and in the same year as Robert B. Weaver's *Amusements and Sports in American Life* (1939), Henderson's book, the first survey ever completed on African-American participation in sport, was commissioned by Carter G. Woodson, the Harvard-trained Ph. D. known as the "Father of Negro History."[41] Henderson's book, which includes seventeen chapters, a rather lengthy appendix, and many photographs, fits nicely into the Woodson genre in that it chronicles the individual success of African-American athletes to inspire others and serve as examples of black achievement in a hostile environment. Although the exact number of copies sold is not known, Henderson claimed that "it was the best seller of his [Woodson's] publications for a while" and was "distributed to libraries all over the world. State departments of education, schools and colleges demanded it."[42]

Like his other works, Henderson's book is very readable and intended for a popular audience rather than academics. Because he insisted that the writing be free of undue complexity and easily accessible to as wide an audience as possible, he had confrontations with Woodson over grammar and writing style. "We had many arguments as to style," noted Henderson. "He wanted to use only precise English in describing a football game or a boxing event. I insisted this would prove dull reading to those who loved or knew sports."[43]

The Negro in Sports is based partly on experiential knowledge. Henderson's own involvement in the sporting life of the black community was so extensive that his data often emanated from organizations he had been involved with and his subjects were frequently people he knew personally, either athletes he had coached or students he had mentored or individuals who had befriended him. Henderson also depended on published sources for his information. Although he never cited his sources, Henderson obviously depended a great deal on black sportswriters for much of his information and analysis. He recognized early on that black sportswriters such as Wendell Smith of the *Pittsburgh Courier-Journal,* Romeo Dougherty of the *New York News,* Rollo Wilson of the *Pittsburgh Courier-Journal,* "Fay" Young of the *Chicago Defender,* St. Clair Bourne of the *New York Amsterdam News,* and Sam Lacy and Art Carter of the *Baltimore Afro-American,* were a great source of information on both African American and predominantly white organized sport. He realized, perhaps better than anyone before or since, that black sportswriters often had direct access to African-American athletes, were intimately involved in campaigns to break down the racial barriers in sport, and sometimes established close working relationships with black as well as white entrepreneurs of sport.[44]

Henderson put his sources to good use. He charted the contributions of African-American athletes behind segregated walls and in the larger society at both the amateur and professional levels of sport. His most compelling topics concerned African-American women athletes and what he termed "The Meaning of Athletics." While holding on to stereotypical notions concerning the emotional and physiological differences between the sexes, Henderson provided the first extended analysis of African-American women and their involvement in sport and physical activity. He wrote about such outstanding organizations as the *Philadelphia Tribune*

Basketball team and New York Mercury track club as well as great black women athletes like Ora Washington, Lucy Slowe, Isadore Channels, and Lula Ballard. Henderson's expanded coverage of African-American women athletes perhaps stemmed from their relatively greater involvement in sport, his commitment to providing as many examples of black achievement as possible, and the fact that the black community was seemingly more receptive and encouraging to women athletes. As academicians have recently suggested, women athletes in the African-American community competed in a more favorable environment than their white counterparts. Not considered "real" women by the dominant white culture and never encumbered by the Victorian definition of the innately fragile woman, African-American female athletes participated in more "masculine" sports like basketball and track and field without experiencing the social stigma and role conflict so prevalent among white female athletes.[45]

In the concluding chapter of *The Negro in Sports,* "The Meaning of Athletics," Henderson summed up much of his philosophy concerning sport and its purpose. He began with a brief yet telling discussion of "play in antiquity." Sounding much like a combination of Charles Darwin and Herbert Spencer, Henderson wrote that "primitive man learned early that fleetness of foot or strength of limb and body were means by which to escape from danger or to live in health. As civilized man found substitutes for labor in slaves—human, chemical or physical—he found in games a method to insure growth and normal physiological functioning of the body. More recently organized play served to combat the individual and social deteriorating forces of urban life."[46] After discussing "play in antiquity," he described the role of games and sport in ancient Greek and Roman societies. As is the case in many of his publications, Henderson wrote admiringly of Greek athletics, contrasting the differing roles of sport in ancient Greece and Rome, and drawing parallels between sport in those two cultures with sport in modern American society. Henderson glorified ancient Greek culture, particularly Athens, for its devotion to competitive sport, emphasis on the harmonious development of mind and body, and belief that physical education should be an integral part of the educational process. Henderson then turned to a familiar theme: the role that sport plays in developing character, fostering sportsmanship, and contributing to individual and national health in the increasingly urbanized environment of modern society. Utilizing such phrases as "health engineers," "physical machine," and "animal bodies," all terms suggesting both evolutionary theory and the objectified, reified view of reality so prevalent in the physical education profession, Henderson wrote of the decline in delinquency, development of emotional balance, and other educational outcomes resulting from participation in sport. Henderson then finally discussed sport and African-American athletes. After suggesting that the performances of Jesse Owens and other outstanding African-American athletes obliterated the belief in Aryan racial superiority, he reviewed the debate over alleged black athletic superiority and reiterated the importance of physical activity for the development of optimal health among African Americans.[47]

Henderson's decision to draw a link between Ancient Greek society and African-American athletes helps explain his attitudes toward race, civil rights issues, and the use of sport as an assimilatory tool. Henderson faced a dilemma experienced by other African Americans: he always felt a need to promote a sense of racial pride and solidarity through a celebration of individual black achievements, but at the same time he was reluctant to express any notion of racial separateness or distinctiveness for fear it would jeopardize his integrationist goals.[48] In "The Meaning of Athletics," he dealt with these two seemingly incongruent objectives by chronicling the exploits of African-American athletes within the context of Western civilization. This approach allowed Henderson an opportunity, in what was the last chapter of the book, to illuminate the parallels between ancient and modern sport as well as to hold up African-American athletes as symbols of black possibility while continuing to promote sport for its ability to "develop a real Christian brotherhood among men of the minority and majority groups in our cosmopolitan American life, and in the greater field of international relationships."[49] At the same time, Henderson celebrated the outstanding accomplishments of African-American athletes while emphasizing white racism and avoiding any mention that these accomplishments somehow reflected a distinctive black culture. Unlike early black scholars such as George Washington Williams, William T. Alexander, and Leila Amos Pendleton, Henderson avoided tracing any connection between the achievements of African-American athletes and a distinct black culture in order to prevent imposing yet another barrier to African-American assimilation into American society.

Most of Henderson's writings in the following decade were in the form of "Letters to the Editor," position statements, and committee reports dealing with his civil rights struggles against Uline Arena, the local AAU, and other segregated institutions in and around Washington, D.C. In 1949, however, Henderson came out with a revised edition of *The Negro in Sports,* which included an expanded appendix and two new chapters reflecting the changes that had taken place in American sport since 1939. The revised edition of the book brought Henderson special satisfaction, allowing him to recount the recent elimination of the color line in several sports, a change that reaffirmed his belief in the conciliatory power of sport and its ability to bring the African American greater respect. The level of optimism in the book, not apparent in the previous edition, was an obvious result of Henderson's conviction that the desegregation of sport, particularly the reintegration of professional football and baseball, was clear evidence that America was close to fulfilling its principles of fair play and equal opportunity. He wrote in the preface that "we doubt that the future will necessitate another edition since integration and the growth of true democracy seem nearer."[50] Henderson proved to be right about another edition, but perhaps overly confident about this country being closer to true integration and democracy.

The optimism Henderson displayed in his revised book was also evident in the December 1951 issue of the *Negro History Bulletin,* a special issue on "The Negro in Sports," which he had edited. This special issue seemed perfectly suited for the *Negro History Bulletin,* the journal founded by Carter Woodson in 1937 and intended, unlike his *Journal of Negro History,* for an audience consisting primarily of public school teachers and their students.[51] It had, in addition to a photograph of Jackie Robinson gracing the cover, a foreword by Henderson and a concluding essay on "Democracy Through Sports" written by Albert N. D. Brooks. The issue included ten articles, three by Henderson,[52] written on everything from African-American involvement in the Olympic Games and intercollegiate football to the part they played in tennis and golf. All the authors, many of them close friends of Henderson's, either worked or lived in the Washington, D.C., and Baltimore area. For instance, Brooks was Woodson's former junior high school principal in Washington, D.C.; Arthur Carter, who wrote "New Day in Intercollegiate Football," was a sportswriter and future managing editor of the *Washington Afro-American;* and David Brown, author of "The Negro in Baseball," was a coach at Washington's Phelps Vocational Senior High School.[53] The issue is also noteworthy in that all the authors depended a great deal on Henderson's revised edition of *The Negro in Sports* (1949) for much of their information and analysis. In fact, the similarities in organization, writing style, and content are so great between the two publications, it seems that Henderson should probably be credited with writing more than a forward and three essays.[54]

The special issue of the *Negro History Bulletin*, which came out just three years before his retirement as Director of Health, Physical Education, and Safety in the segregated public schools of Washington, D.C., was Henderson's last major publishing effort until the latter part of the 1960s. The increased involvement of black athletes at all levels of sport, the civil rights movement, and growing fascination in the life and history of African Americans by scholars of both races all combined during this period to create a renewed interest in Henderson's work.[55] The result was that Henderson published four major works on the African-American athlete between 1968 and 1976. These publications, while intended for different audiences and varying in historical significance, were very similar in that they all included much of the same material from Henderson's previous work intermixed with the latest information on African-American athletes and their various accomplishments. It was customary, even formulaic in some ways, for Henderson to blend new information with recycled material. Writing, as he almost always did, in a topical rather than chronological fashion, Henderson raised once again the question of alleged black athletic superiority, traced the accomplishments of African-American athletes, and chronicled key events and individuals involved in the struggle to eliminate racial discrimination in sport.

In 1968, Henderson published *The Black Athlete: Emergence and Arrival,* written with the assistance of the editors of *Sport* magazine, which had always shown a keen interest in African-American athletes. Written at the request of Charles H. Wesley, the successor to Carter Woodson as president of the Association for the Study of Afro-American Life and History, the book is one of Henderson's most frequently cited works. One reason the book has garnered so much attention is that Henderson provided a voluminous amount of details about African-American athletes from the early nineteenth century through the 1960s. Up to that time, no scholar (and few since) had been so expansive in covering the topic, particularly in regard to an analysis of the outstanding African-American athletes who integrated various other sports after Jackie Robinson's debut with the Brooklyn Dodgers. Equally significant is the book's extensive bibliography. Henderson furnished an invaluable list of secondary and primary materials subdivided under the topical headings of general sources, baseball, football, basketball, tennis, boxing, track and field, Olympics, other sports, integration in sports, and education, recreation, and school sports.[56]

In 1970, Henderson published "The Negro As Athlete" in *Crisis,* his last article in the journal. Recapitulating much of his earlier work, Henderson did briefly mention such new topics as television and sport and the great performances of women track-and-field stars from Tennessee State. Two years later he published "Physical Education and Athletics Among Negroes" in *The History of Physical Education and Sport,* edited by Bruce L. Bennett. Originally given as a presentation at the Big Ten Symposium on the History of Physical Education and Sport, the chapter is included alongside others written by such well-known sport historians as John R. Betts, Guy Lewis, Ellen Gerber, and Clarence Forbes. Finally, in 1976, Henderson published "The Black American in Sports," a chapter in Mabel M. Smythe's *The Black American Reference Book.* The chapter, which was Henderson's last publication, had the distinction of appearing in a book sponsored by the Phelps-Stokes Fund, always one of the major financial supporters of scholarship dealing with African-American life and history.[57]

In all four of these publications, Henderson continued to laud sport for the way it brought people together and created the unity and integration necessary to maintain order in American society. It is easy to understand why he did so. Since his early years in Washington, D.C., when segregation was the norm and blatant racial discrimination the rule, Henderson had witnessed the desegregation of sport and enormous success experienced by individual African-American athletes at various levels of competition. He now found himself, however, living in a society where various individuals and groups, including academicians, social commentators, and some athletes, were criticizing sport as a capitalistic tool in which athletes became alienated from their bodies, those in power maintained their privilege through coercion and control, and harmful feelings of nationalistic pride and militarism were encouraged.[58] Even more significant, at least for Henderson, was that some African Americans of the period were highly critical of white organized sport, arguing that it was characterized by various forms of discrimination, perpetuated racial stereotypes and inequities, and helped divert attention from the real source of the problems afflicting the race. From the time Henderson wrote *The Black Athlete: Emergence and Arrival* in 1968 to the 1976 publication of his essay, "The Black American in Sports," America had witnessed the Harry Edwards–led protests of the Mexico City Olympic Games, a plethora of black athletic disturbances on predominantly white university campuses, and numerous racial uprisings in professional sport.[59]

Henderson's attitude toward the black athletic revolt is difficult to discern because he provided such limited information and even less analysis of the topic in his professional publications. He mentioned nothing about the various protests lodged by African-American athletes in either his 1970 article in *Crisis* or his chapter "Physical Education and Athletics Among Negroes" in Bruce Bennett's 1972 symposium proceedings. No information was provided on Tommie Smith, John Carlos, Vince Matthews, or any number of other African-American athletes who staged protests, lodged complaints against their white coaches, and disrupted sport at all levels of competition and by almost any means possible. In both *The Black Athlete: Emergence and Arrival* and his chapter in Mabel M. Smythe's *The Black American Reference Book,* Henderson mentioned the protests staged by African-American athletes without condemning their actions,[60] despite his exaggerated belief about the positive effects of sport and philosophical opposition to the Black Power movement. Why he chose not to pass judgment on protesting black athletes is open to speculation. Perhaps it was the result of restrictions placed on Henderson by publishers insisting on a more encyclopedic approach with limited personal assessments in their reference works.

It is more likely, however, that Henderson chose not to write anything that would diminish the accomplishments or reflect negatively on African-American athletes, not just because it might somehow affect their continued involvement in sport, but out of respect for them personally and in recognition of their efforts, however misplaced and illogical, on behalf of other members of their race. While disapproving of the tactics employed by Black Power advocates, Henderson was always a gentleman and showed the same tolerance toward protesting African-American athletes that he had toward other people who made sacrifices and fought for racial justice and freedom of opportunity. Perhaps he also recognized that however different his methods were from those of militant African-American athletes, they both used sport as a tool to help eliminate racial inequities and discrimination. Whereas protesting African-American athletes used sport to call attention to economic exploitation and oppression, Henderson promoted sport for its power to bring diverse people together and create the unity and integration necessary to maintain order in American society. "We read and hear much irrationality in the oratory and philosophy of black power," wrote Henderson in the *Birmingham News* of April 2, 1967, "but to this writer the courage, stamina and sportsmanship of our Negro athletes evidences real power. Sociologists might well heed the news found on the sport pages. Is it not possible that in the playing together of white and colored boys on the courts and fields more of understanding and good will is thereby developed than in most other social settings?"

In the final analysis, Henderson's writings have proven to be enormously significant and influential. His numerous publications on the African-American athletes' past, particularly *The Negro in Sports* (1939, 1949), and *The Black Athlete: Emergence and Arrival* (1968), served as the framework and historical foundation for the works of other writers and academicians who have examined the topic. Journalists, sport studies specialists, historians, and other scholars from both races have employed Henderson's basic typology, utilized his source material, and researched topics he had originally broached.

Evidence of Henderson's influence can perhaps best be gleaned from the monographs completed on African-American athletes by black authors. Although limited in number and often falling into the category of popular rather than scholarly treatises, there are a number of important works of this genre that rely heavily on Henderson's pioneering research efforts and writings. Henderson's influence is evident in Andrew S. "Doc" Young's frequently cited *Negro Firsts in Sports.* Young used much of the information originally mined by Henderson in his nicely written and more interpretive analysis of black participation in sport.[61] Wally Jones and Jim Washington, former professional basketball players turned authors, utilized Henderson's works for *Black Champions Challenge American Sports.*[62] Arthur Ashe, in his well-known three-volume work, *A Hard Road to Glory: A History of the African-American Athlete,* relied heavily on Henderson for information, source material, and organizational structure. Ashe, who referred in his introduction to Henderson's *The Negro in Sports* as the "first definitive historical review of black sports," patterned his own book along the same lines as some of Henderson's major works, taking a narrative approach to his subjects, focusing on the triumphs of African-American athletes in both segregated and white-organized sports, and including an extensive "reference section" that lists the awards and various other accomplishments garnered by blacks in sports.[63]

Just as indebted to Henderson was Harry Edwards, the well-known sport sociologist from the University of California-Berkeley, who led the proposed boycott of the 1968 Olympic Games in Mexico City and for years has warned African Americans of the dangers of focusing exclusively on sport as the way to realize full equality in America. Edwards, who helped establish the framework for much of the work completed on the black athlete in the sport sociology literature, utilizes Henderson's writings for both *The Revolt of the Black Athlete* and *Sociology of Sport.*[64] In the former book, which is a recounting of the various black athletic disturbances on predominantly white university campuses and events surrounding the proposed boycott of the 1968 Olympic Games, Edwards employs data originally mined by Henderson to discuss the emergence of both black boxers and college athletes in American society. Perhaps most important, Edwards patterned his work after Henderson's books by including a ten-page appendix devoted to "black record-holders."[65] Although troubled by the overemphasis on sport in the black community and skeptical of sport's power to bring the races closer together, Edwards was seemingly no different from Henderson in recognizing the symbolic importance of black athletic triumphs for both the African-American community and society at large. To Edwards and many other blacks as well, Henderson's emphasis on the individual success of African-American athletes to help foster racial pride always struck a responsive chord and was considered one of the important factors in the struggle for equal rights and opportunity.

In sum, Edwin Henderson's writings were indeed an instrument, a tool that even someone as critical of sport as Harry Edwards could not easily ignore because African-American athletes had always served as much-needed examples of possibility for the black community. As chronicler of these athletes, Henderson became an exemplar himself, someone who helped preserve the collective memory of his race and prove that African Americans were capable of great performances both on and off the playing field. The central theme of all his publications was that sport was an enormously influential institution capable of bringing people of diverse backgrounds together in ways that created feelings of unity and togetherness. He never lost faith, even during the most racially oppressive periods in American history, in the power of sport to strengthen social relationships and contribute to the integration of African Americans into the larger society. He continued to believe throughout his life that sport served as a source of inspiration and benefited all members of society, regardless of skin color, religious affiliation, and personal value scheme. He simply refused to acknowledge, unlike many contemporary thinkers, that sport often serves to maintain the interests of the power elite and can be an alienating rather than integrative force in American society.

NOTES

1. Charles Drew to Edwin B. Henderson, May 31, 1940, Edwin B. Henderson Papers, Moorland-Spingarn Research Center (hereafter referred to as EBH Papers, MSRC). This letter is also quoted in Charles E. Wynes, *Charles Richard Drew: The Man and the Myth* (Urbana: University of Illinois Press, 1988), 56; and Spencie Love, *One Blood: The Death and Resurrection of Charles R. Drew* (Chapel Hill: University of North Carolina Press, 1996), 125.

2. The esteem in which Henderson was held by his students is evidenced by the letters of appreciation they sent to him over the years. See, for example, the letter from Montague Cobb March 9, 1971, and from James O. Williams, November 1, 1965, EBH Papers, MSRC.

3. For further details about Henderson's life, see James H. M. Henderson and Betty F. Henderson, *Molder of Men: Portrait of a "Grand Old Man"—Edwin Bancroft Henderson* (Washington, DC: Vantage, 1985); "Biography—Edwin Bancroft Henderson," September 1971; EBH Papers, MSRC; Edwin Bancroft Henderson, "Looking Back On: Fifty Years," *Washington Afro-American*, July 24, 31, August. 7, 10, 28, 31, September 11, 1954; Greg Stuart, "The Beginning of Tomorrow," *Black Sports* (February 1972): 62–7.

4. See Stuart, "Beginning of Tomorrow," 67; Henderson and Henderson, *Molder of Men*, 29–30; "Honors or Awards," *Journal of Health, Physical Education, and Recreation* 25 (October 1954): 34–5; Marvin H. Eyler to Edwin B. Henderson, May 2, 1973, Bruce L. Bennett Papers (hereafter BLB Papers), AAHPERD Archives. Program, The first Annual Black Athletes Hall of Fame Banquet, March 14, 1974, EBH Papers, MSRC; Florence S. Savoy, "News Release," March 15, 1954, EBH Papers, MSRC.

5. This is my own choice of title for Henderson, not someone else's designation.

6. Andrew S. "Doc" Young, *Negro Firsts In Sports* (Chicago: Johnson Publishing, 1963), xi.

7. See Patrick B. Miller, "To 'Bring the Race Along Rapidly: Sport, Student Culture, and Educational Mission at Historically Black Colleges During the Interwar Years," *History of Education Quarterly* 35 (summer 1995): 111–33. For insights into the style, strategy, and method of the earliest writings in African-American history, see August Meier and Elliott Rudwick, *Black History and the Historical Profession, 1915–1980* (Urbana: University of Illinois Press, 1986); and Dickson D. Bruce, Jr., "Ancient Africa and the Early Black American Historians, 1883–1915," *American Quarterly* 36 (Winter 1984): 684–99.

8. Henderson and Joiner, eds., *Official Handbook: Inter-Scholastic Athletic Association of Middle Atlantic States*, 4 vols., Spalding Athletic Library (New York: American Sports Publishing, 1910–1913).

9. Edwin B. Henderson, "The Colored College Athlete," *Crisis* (July 1911): 115–8.

10. Among such essays in the *Colored American Magazine* were the following: G. Grant Williams, "Marshall Walter Taylor [Major Taylor] The World-Famous Bicycle Rider," vol. 5 (September 1902): 336–445; William Clarence Matthews, "Negro Foot-ball Players on New England Teams," 9 (March 1905): 130–2; Phil Waters, "Football: Its Defenders and Champions," 10 (April 1906): 231–35; Thomas J. Clement, "Athletics in the American Army," 8 (January 1905): 21–9; Old Sport, "Zenith of Negro Sport," 16 (May 1909): 295–300. For information on the magazine, see August Meier, "Booker T. Washington and the Negro Press: With Special Reference to *The Colored American Magazine*," *Journal of Negro History* 38 (January 1953): 67–90.

11. See Theodore Kornweibel, Jr., *No Crystal Stair: Black Life and the "Messenger," 1917–1928* (Westport, Conn.: Greenwood, 1975), especially chap. 2.

12. Edwin B. Henderson, *The Messenger* (June 1925): 234.

13. See Patrick B. Miller, "To 'Bring the Race Along Rapidly.'"

14. Edwin B. Henderson, "Athletics," *Messenger*, (April 1925): 170; *ibid.*, (October, November 1925): 365; *ibid.*, (January 1926): 15; *ibid.*, (January 1927): 20.

15. Edwin B. Henderson, *The Messenger* (January 1927): 20.

16. Edwin B. Henderson, *The Messenger* (June 1925): 234.

17. Edwin B. Henderson, *The Messenger* (April 1927): 112.

18. Edwin B. Henderson, *The Messenger* (May 1927): 148.

19. Edwin B. Henderson, *The Messenger* (March 1926): 91; *ibid.* (June 1927): 189.

20. Edwin B. Henderson, *The Messenger* (March 1926): 91.

21. Kornweibel, *No Crystal Stair*, 42.

22. See the *Champion Magazine: A Monthly Survey of Negro Achievement* 1 (October 1916): 47–8; *ibid.* (January 1917): 275–6; *ibid.*, (February 1917): 316–7.

23. "Basketball," *Crusader* 1 (January 1919): 17; "Basketball," *Crusader* 1 (March 1919): 12; "Valentine's All-Negro All-Star Five," *Crusader* 1 (April 1919): 14; C.V.B. "The Sporting Periscope," *Crusader* 2 (December 1919): 17. For information about Briggs and the magazine, see Robert V. Briggs, "*The Crusader Magazine*, and the African Blood Brotherhood, 1918–1922," in Robert A. Hill, ed., *The Crusader*, 6 vols. (New York: Garland, 1987), 1, lxvi.

24. Romeo L. Dougherty, "Behind the Scenes in Basketball," *The Crusader* 3 (January 1921): 13–4.

25. See the following articles in the designated volume of the *Competitor*. Ira F. Lewis, "Our Colleges and Athletics," 2 (December 1920): 290–92; "Who'll Be the Next?" 2 (October–November 1920): 221–4; and "National Baseball League Formed," 1 (March 1920): 66–7; Will Anthony Madden, "The Future of Basketball," 1 (January 1920): 67–8; George M. Bell, "Tennis Stars in the East," 2 (August–September 1920): 158–60; Dave Wyatt, "National League of Colored Clubs Prepare for Season's Opening," 1 (April 1920): 73–4; C. I. Taylor, "The Future of Colored Baseball," 1 (February 1920): 76–9; "Colored Athletes in the Famous Penn Relays," 1 (June 1920): 73–5; "The Colored Basketball Referee Finally Arrives," 1 (March 1920); 69–70.

26. Among the essays on sport in the *Southern Workman* were Elizabeth D. Dunham, "Physical Education of Women at Hampton Institute," 53 (April 1924): 161–8; and Charles H. Williams, "Twenty Years' Work of the C.I.A.A.," 61 (February 1932): 65–76; "Negro Athletes in the Tenth Olympiad," 61 (November 1932): 330–4; and "Negro Athletes in the Eleventh Olympiad," 66 (February 1937): 55–60.

27. The essays in *Crisis* included George Streator, "Football in Negro Colleges," 41 (April 1932): 129–30, 139, 141; W. Rollo Wilson, "They Could Make the Big Leagues," 41 (October 1934): 305–6; Roy Wilkins, "Negro Athletes at the Olympic Games," 39 (August 1932): 252–3; and "Negro Stars on Big Grid Teams," 43 (December 1936): 362–4; William A. Brower, "Our Stars: In Track and Field," 48 (October 1941): 320–1, 324; Dan Burley, "What's Ahead for Robinson?" 52 (December 1945): 346–7, 364.

28. See these articles in *Opportunity:* Elmer A. Carter, "Prelude to the Olympics," 10 (August 1932): 246–52; and "The Negro in College Athletics," 11 (July 1933): 208–10, 219; James D. Parks, "Negro Athletes in the 1936 Olympiad," 14 (May 1936): 144–6; Edward Lawson, "Who Will Be All-American?" 16 (October 1938): 300–1; Ed Nace, "Negro Grid Stars, Past and Present," 17 (September 1941): 272–3; William A. Brower, "Prejudice In Sports," 19 (September 1941): 260–3; and "Time for Baseball to Erase the Blackball," 20 (June 1942): 164–7.

29. Edwin B. Henderson, "The Negro Athlete and Race Prejudice," *Opportunity*, 14: (March 1936) 77–79.

30. *Ibid.*, 77.

31. *Ibid.*, 78.

32. *Ibid.*, 79.

33. *Ibid.*

34. *Ibid.,* 78.

35. Cobb was also an outstanding track-and-field performer at Amherst College and a close follower of sport throughout his life. See Harold Wade, Jr., *Black Men of Amherst* (Amherst, MA: Amherst College Press, 1976), 41–77.

36. See Montague W. Cobb, "Race and Runners," *Journal of Health and Physical Education* 7 (January 1936): 3–6. Cobb wrote yet another article on the subject several years later, "Does Science Favor Negro Athletes?" *Negro Digest* 5 (May 1947): 74–7.

37. Henderson, "Negro Athlete and Race Prejudice," 78.

38. *Ibid.,* 79.

39. For details on the debate over racial differences and sport performance, see Laurel R. Davis, "The Articulation of Difference: White Preoccupation with the Question of Racially Linked Genetic Differences Among Athletes," *Sociology of Sport Journal* 7 (June 1990): 179–87; David K. Wiggins, " 'Great Speed but Little Stamina': The Historical Debate over Black Athletic Superiority," *Journal of Sport History* 16 (Summer 1989): 158–85. A critique of my article, much information on the writings dealing with race and sport, and an overall assessment of the historical literature on African-American athletes are included in Jeffrey T. Sammons's important review essay, " 'Race' and Sport: A Critical, Historical Examination," *Journal of Sport History* 21 (Fall 1994): 203–78.

40. Edwin B. Henderson, *The Negro in Sports* (Washington, DC: Associated Publishers, 1939).

41. Information on Woodson can be found in Meier and Rudwick, Black History and the Historical Profession, esp. 1–71; Jacqueline Goggin, *Carter G. Woodson: A Life in Black History* (Baton Rouge: Louisiana State University Press, 1993); Patricia W. Romero, "Carter G. Woodson: A Biography" (Ph. D. diss., Ohio State University, 1971).

42. Edwin Bancroft Henderson, "Looking Back On: Fifty Years," *Washington Afro-American,* August 28, 1954.

43. *Ibid.*

44. Scholars need to examine more closely the role of black sportswriters in the integration of sport at all levels of competition. For studies that provide information on black sportswriters, see David K. Wiggins, "Wendell Smith, the *Pittsburgh Courier-Journal* and the Campaign to Include Blacks in Organized Baseball, 1933–1945," *Journal of Sport History* 10 (Summer 1984): 5–29 and "The 1936 Olympic Games in Berlin: The Response of America's Black Press," *Research Quarterly For Exercise and Sport* 54 (September 1983): 278–92; Thomas G. Smith, "Outside the Pale: The Exclusion of Blacks From the National Football League, 1934–1946," *Journal of Sport History* 15 (Winter 1988): 255–81; William Simons, "Jackie Robinson and the American Mind: Journalistic Perceptions of the Reintegration of Baseball," *Journal of Sport History* 12 (Spring 1985): 39–64; Jack E. Davis, "Baseball's Reluctant Challenge: Desegregating Major League Spring Training Sites, 1961–1964," *Journal of Sport History* 19 (Summer 1992): 144–62.

45. See Susan Cahn, *Coming on Strong: Gender and Sexuality in Twentieth-Century Sport* (New York: Free Press, 1994); Linda D. Williams, "An Analysis of American Sportswomen in Two Negro Newspapers" (Ph. D. diss., Ohio State University, 1988).

46. Edwin B. Henderson, *The Negro in Sports,* 287–316, 297.

47. *Ibid.,* 298–316.

48. For the basis of this interpretation, see Bruce, "Ancient Africa and the Early Black American Historians."

49. Edwin B. Henderson, *The Negro in Sports,* 310.

50. Edwin B. Henderson, *The Negro in Sports,* rev. ed. (Washington, DC: Associated Publishers, 1949), x.

51. For information on the *Negro History Bulletin,* see Meier and Rudwick, *Black History and the Historical Profession,* 61, 189, 280.

52. "The Negro in Sports," *Negro History Bulletin* 15 (December 1951): 42–56.

53. For information on Brooks, see Meier and Rudwick, *Black History and the Historical Profession,* 189; on Carter, see the Arthur Carter Papers, MSRC.

54. The same thing may be true for the *Official Handbook: Inter-Scholastic Athletic Association of Middle Atlantic States.*

55. The amount of literature on various aspects of African-American life increased dramatically during the latter half of the 1960s and the early part of the 1970s. For some of the literature dealing specifically with sport and the African-American athlete, see Jeffrey T. Sammons, " 'Race' and Sport," 203–78; David K. Wiggins, "From Plantation to Playing Field: Historical Writings on the Black Athlete in American Sport," *Research Quarterly for Exercise and Sport* 57 (June 1986): 101–16.

56. Edwin B. Henderson, with the editors of *Sport Magazine, The Black Athlete: Emergence and Arrival* (Cornwall Heights, PA: Pennsylvania Publishers, 1968).

57. Edwin B. Henderson, "The Negro As Athlete," *Crisis* 77 (February 1970): 51–56; "Physical

Education and Athletics Among Negroes," in Bruce L. Bennett, ed., *Proceedings of the Big Ten Symposium on the History of Physical Education and Sport* (Chicago: Athletic Institute, 1972), 67–83; "The Black American in Sports," in Mabel M. Smythe, ed., *The Black American Reference Book* (Englewood Cliffs, NJ: Prentice-Hall, 1976): 927–63.

58. There is a voluminous amount of literature in the discipline of sport sociology that is highly critical of contemporary sport. See, for example: George Sage, *Power and Ideology in American Sport: A Critical Perspective* (Champaign, IL: Human Kinetics, 1990); Richard Gruneau, *Class, Sports, and Social Development* (Amherst, MA: University of Massachusetts Press, 1983).

59. See Harry Edwards, *The Revolt of the Black Athlete* (New York: Free Press, 1969); David K. Wiggins, "The Year of Awakening: Black Athletes, Racial Unrest and the Civil Rights Movement of 1968," *International Journal of the History of Sport* 9 (August 1992): 188–208 and "The Future of College Athletics Is at Stake: Black Athletes and Racial Turmoil on Three Predominantly White University Campuses, 1968–1972," *Journal of Sport History* 15 (Winter 1988): 304–33.

60. *Black Athlete: Emergence and Arrival,* 260; "The Black American in Sports," in Smythe, ed., *Black American Reference Book,* 953–54.

61. Andrew S. "Doc" Young, *Negro Firsts in Sports* (Chicago: Johnson Publishing, 1963).

62. Wally Jones and Jim Washington, *Black Champions Challenge American Sports* (New York: David McKay, 1972).

63. Arthur R. Ashe, Jr. *A Hard Road To Glory: A History of the African-American Athlete,* 3 vols. (New York: Warner Books, 1988).

64. Harry Edwards, *Sociology of Sport* (Homewood, IL: Dorsey, 1973).

65. Harry Edwards, *Revolt of the Black Athlete,* 167–77.

15

THE GREATEST
Muhammad Ali's Confounding Character

David W. Zang

He is fascinating—attraction and repulsion must be in the same package.
—Norman Mailer, *Life*, 1971

FOR MANY AMERICANS, their first glimpse of the Vietnam era came on February 18, 1964. On that day a group of young men in a Miami Beach fight gym previewed the future of the world. The Beatles, recently landed in the United States for a knockout appearance on the Ed Sullivan Show, had come to meet heavyweight fighter Cassius Clay, who failed to show on time. "Where the fuck's Clay?" groused Ringo Starr. "Let's get the fuck out of here," said John Lennon. When Clay finally strode in, he dispelled the gloom. "Hello there, Beatles," he called. "We oughta do some road shows together, we'll get rich." When he tried out one of his running gags, however, the testiness resurfaced. "You guys aren't as stupid as you look," he said. "No," Lennon responded, "but you are."[1]

The edginess finally passed when the five men ran through a series of comical poses for photographers: Clay dusting all four Beatles with a single punch; the singers forming a pyramid in an attempt to get at the boxer's jaw; Clay thumping his chest above the prostrate quartet as they prayed for mercy. As the group departed, Clay turned to *New York Times* writer Robert Lipsyte and wondered out loud, "Who were those little faggots?"

As their influence built week by week, the importance and connection between the five men dawned on some observers in a way they themselves had not understood. Not all thought the alliance was positive. New York columnist Jimmy Cannon wrote famously and contemptuously that

> Clay is part of the Beatle movement. He fits in with the famous singers no one can hear and the punks riding motorcycles with iron crosses pinned to their leather jackets and Batman and the boys with their long dirty hair and the girls with the unwashed look and the college kids dancing naked at secret proms held in apartments and the revolt of students who get a check from dad every first of the month and the painters who copy the labels off soup cans and the surf bums who refuse to work and the whole pampered style-making cult of the bored young.[2]

Cannon's jumbled rant may have been paranoid, but he was not wrong in recognizing Muhammad Ali as an apocalyptic figure. Throughout the Vietnam era, the boxer upset entrenched notions of sport and character. In most cases, however, he did not merely challenge tradition. Rather, he embodied the tension between new and old by presenting himself as a series of paradoxes, provoking difficult questions to which he offered answers that pleased everyone and no one. Did his popularity, for example, owe to his winning or to his combination of wins and losses? Was his draft resistance cowardice or conviction? Did America want a heavyweight champ who delivered a heavier wallop with his mouth or his fists? One whose face reflected the peril of the ring or the ability to evade its dangers?

Overarching all of the answers—indeed, framing the questions themselves—was the issue of race. This is understandable because from the late nineteenth century forward the idea of sport as a character builder was intended to elevate and prepare white men as leaders of society. Blacks and women, to the minds of white males, were not going to lead American society in the twentieth century; whatever these lesser beings made of sport—exercise, escape, entertainment—would be for their own lesser reasons.

The color lines that existed in sport into the 1950s had grown from an impeachable but nonetheless widely believed foundation of "scientific" race theory that had, for a century, pinched data on bodies and brains into a shape supporting white assertions of intellectual and moral weakness in blacks. Many whites believed character to be an elusive and unreliable quality among blacks, contending that African heritage imparted even to the economically and socially advantaged a genetic predisposition to bad behavior that might reveal itself at an unfortunate moment. Thus, despite Jesse Owens's rebuke of Hitler, Joe Louis's service in the army, Jackie Robinson's willingness to turn the other cheek, or Wilma Rudolph's defeat of childhood polio, white attitudes toward black athletic success remained reserved.

Young Cassius Clay had overcome some of those reservations, endearing himself to Americans as he returned triumphant and irrepressible from the Rome Olympics of 1960. As Lipsyte has remarked, "He was kind of the perfect American ambassador to the world. He was totally lovable."[3] Fighting shortly after his meeting with the Beatles in 1964 Clay "shook up the world" by beating Sonny Liston, the prohibitive favorite, to become the world's heavyweight boxing champion. He shook it harder the next day when he forsook his name (his "slave name," according to him) to become Muhammad Ali. To many whites, claimed onetime Black Panther Eldridge Cleaver, Ali's decision to join the Nation of Islam was a "betrayal." One of the sect's leaders, Malcolm X, explained the fear underlining the betrayal: "They [whites] knew that if people began to identify with Cassius and the type of image he was creating, they were going to have trouble out of these Negroes because they'd have Negroes walking around the street saying, 'I'm the greatest,' and also Negroes who were proud of being black." Black author Wallace Terry later made clear to an interviewer, however, that the change was disturbing to some blacks as well: "You just wanted to say, tell me it ain't true, Muhammad. Tell me you're really Cassius Clay, aren't you?"[4]

Ali's conversion from Christian to Muslim seemed to some whites much like going from Stepin Fetchit to Nat Turner. The change broke a compact that Americans had forged with their black athletes—"be good Negroes and enjoy the fruits of athletic success"—and assured that race would be an explicit issue in all that Ali would touch in the next decade.

Nothing was more explicit—or explosive—than the issue of manliness. Tied as it was to matters of prowess and courage, it was at the heart of racial divisions. By the late nineteenth century many white middle-class men believed that a shift from labor of the body to labor of the mind had left Victorian culture "effeminate."[5] Believing that behavior and

Figure 15–1
A young Muhammad Ali (at the time Cassius Clay) in a press conference prior to his joining the Nation of Islam. Courtesy of the Amateur Athletic Foundation of Los Angeles.

bonding that reinforce male dominance grew "from a more primitive type of manhood," Thorstein Veblen in 1899 wrote that entering a competitive struggle without ferocity and cunning was "like being a hornless steer."[6] Soon thereafter, Sigmund Freud tied dominance, aggression, and bonding directly to man's primitive sexual drives and suppression of them, and thereby made the relationship between sexuality and behavior explicit.

Rising attention to the rapidly organizing and expanding structure of sports served two ends. Sports provided an antidote to effeminacy, allowing an outlet for dominance and aggression while at the same time promising to dissipate sexual urgency and turn it toward constructive ends. Still, as whites remade manhood, "finding new ways to celebrate men's bodies as healthy, muscular, and powerful," they were required to give attention to both gender and race, two things that, according to historian Gail Bederman, "linked bodies, identities, and power." As Bederman has written, civilization at the turn of the century had become, in the minds of white men, an "explicitly racial concept."[7]

It was a conceit that reinforced ideas of white superiority but simultaneously made the physical prowess of blacks a constant threat. It could be turned on white men and summon the ghosts of Nat Turner, or it could be turned on white women and summon the myth of black sexuality. In the case of black athletes, trouble could come in both ways. So it was that first black heavyweight champion Jack Johnson, as conqueror of white men in the ring and white women in the bedroom, touched off race riots in the wake of his many affronts to white society in the early 1900s.

Owens, Louis, Robinson, and other black athletes at midcentury appeared safer, following the unspoken but central rules of being a "good Negro," which entailed a repression of sexual appetite and public deference to whites. Still, the myth of black sexuality in America was an old—even if often an underground—problem for white males. The image of blacks as promiscuous animals of wanton sexual appetites has been a part of American consciousness for centuries. Eugene Genovese, in his account of American slavery, *Roll, Jordan, Roll,* revealed that the idea of black moral laxity had existed in seventeenth- and eighteenth-century Europe. Before long, he wrote, "Europeans and Americans were hearing lurid tales of giant penises, intercourse with apes, and assorted unspeakable (but much spoken of) transgressions against God and nature."[8] In the 1950s, Lillian Smith, in *Killers of the Dream,* proposed that modern white fears of blacks stemmed from the idea that black men, if not dominated, would go after white women as vengeance for the white humiliation of black female slaves in previous centuries.[9]

As steps were taken at the time of Smith's book to desegregate American society, fear of black sexuality presented itself in several ways. In the South, there was militant resistance to the repeal of Jim Crow laws that broke down the physical separation of the races.[10] One of the stumbling blocks to integrating Baltimore's golf courses and swimming pools in the 1940s was the fear of some parks' board members that those settings would allow black men too near to white women.[11] More subtly, the first serious attempts at rock music censorship came when rhythm and blues, the code name for black music, began to cross over into the white marketplace.

Even in the loftiest of social settings palpable distrust and sexual suspicions were present. University of Pennsylvania's black Rhodes Scholar and basketball star John Wideman told *Look* magazine in 1963: "At college, I've found that there's no cleavage (between the races) beyond the physical fact, although in a way—socially, I suppose—I've often wondered if things would have gone along the same way if I'd had a white girl friend on campus. There's a fine line there, a line that is a kind of threat, something that even in the most liberal circles isn't talked about, and that's the idea of . . . well, probably sex. The actual fact of a Negro-white relationship . . . (means) then there is complete equality, and there's nothing that would actually separate the races anymore. Anything that goes toward that direction creates a tension. And that's a psychological situation that can't be remedied by any amount of constitutional reforms."[12]

As the specter of black militancy loomed in the late 1960s, it highlighted the second of white fears—that of black revolt. During a 1968 Columbia University controversy about where to build a new gymnasium, Harlem blacks instilled fear among whites by threatening to make the situation a violent one. In June of 1966, *Life* magazine investigated the real possibility of black violence in an article titled "Plotting a War on 'Whitey.' " In San Francisco's hippie haven, Haight-Ashbury, an oft-heard belief among whites was "Spades are programmed for hate."[13]

The possibility that the hate would erupt into confrontation was what made the menacing Sonny Liston—posed in a Santa Claus hat and a scowl for the cover of the December 1963 *Esquire*—"America's worst nightmare." Ali's embrace of his blackness blended both threats: the sexual and the vengeful. Los Angeles sportswriter Jim Murray once said about

Ali: "I'd like to borrow his body for just forty-eight hours, there are three guys I'd like to beat up, and four women I'd like to make love to."[14] Murray was often simultaneously funny and astute, so what was the nation to think when he managed with that quip to expose every white man's fears—black physical retribution coupled with the myth of black sexual potency? At best, white America could laugh uneasily.

It might have been easier to know what to think had Ali been more like Liston. Instead, he presented a complex puzzle. He boasted constantly of being "pretty," an assertion counter to traditional manliness, yet one that some blacks saw as the anchor for their claim that "black is beautiful."[15] He often laughed with white reporters, yet he was fully aware of white fear. Before his mid-70s bout with George Foreman he told the press: "What you white reporters got to remember is, black folks ain't afraid of black folks that way white folks are afraid of black folks."[16] As for sex, those who followed Ali closely in the 1960s report that he had a healthy libido that was often gratified. If any of his dalliances included white women, they never came to public light.

Of all the factors that constituted manliness, none were more instrumental in defining Ali and confusing white America than his position as a conscientious objector against the draft. For many young men doubts about the value of military service in Vietnam blossomed in two ways: in a preoccupation with the draft that indicated reluctance to serve in Vietnam and in the consequential guilt over not having served. Males either went to Vietnam and fought or they stayed behind with the knowledge that others less fortunate were fighting.

For most draft-age men the most pressing reason for their dilemma was President Lyndon Johnson's commitment to the war as evidenced in draft numbers. In February 1965, only 3,000 men were called to service. In the next six months the total was 87,300, and the estimate for September through November of that year was 97,050.[17]

In claiming exemption on religious grounds in early 1966 Ali absolved himself of the guilt. Conscientious objection was a stand that insinuated reflection, not cowardice. When he was stripped of his title shortly after refusing induction in May of 1967, thereby forfeiting what would become three years of income, Ali's refusal to serve appeared to be one of indisputable moral conviction. For the millions of Americans who supported the Vietnam War, however, Ali's stance looked more like hustle than moral fortitude. But for all those who perceived the war to be unjust, Ali's RSVP to Uncle Sam's invitation became a shining example, though not one without problems.

For one, not fighting in Vietnam seemed to be turning off the very path that Joe Louis and Jackie Robinson had taken while earning the respect of all Americans. Both had served in the military and, despite Robinson's court-martial, it served their images well. Though a number of black athletes—including Jim Brown, Kareem Abdul-Jabbar, and Bill Russell—supported Ali's decision not to report for induction, Louis and Robinson did not. "I think it's very bad," said Louis. Robinson was more specific: "He's hurting, I think, the morale of a lot of young Negro soldiers over in Vietnam." Wallace Terry, author of *Bloods: An Oral History of the Vietnam War by Black Veterans,* has met many of those black soldiers. He recalled for an interviewer, "Many of them told me that Muhammad Ali had given up being a man when he decided not to be inducted into the armed forces . . . They were absolutely stunned; they were shocked, they were upset, they were angry, they were frustrated, they were bitter. They hated him for it."[18] Ali's refusal also reinforced the bitter feelings that many Americans felt for athletes who managed to evade combat. The indifferent stance of elite and professional athletes toward military service was certainly not unique, but it was, to many Americans, galling.

A greater puzzle was the irony, apparently unnoticed, that Ali's resistance carried for blacks generally. His membership in the Nation of Islam marked him as a figure whose life was indivisible from his color, and his use of his Islamic ministry as the basis for avoiding war marked him as someone who could not fight on grounds of pacifism. How strange, then, in 1966 when, in a fit of pique at yammering reporters, Ali declared, "Man, I ain't got no quarrel with them Vietcong." As Lipsyte, who spent several years covering Ali for the *New York Times,* has written, the famed comment came from exasperation and may not have accurately (certainly not fully) reflected Ali's draft stance.[19] Nonetheless, antiwar Americans seized upon it as an expression of common sense rather than religious opposition. This meant that Ali essentially agreed with those whites who claimed generally that the nation had no legitimate quarrel with North Vietnam. It was also precisely what any black draftee, those fighting the war in disproportionate numbers, could have claimed as well. Oddly enough, many blacks who opposed the war did not lean on this practical argument but stood instead on moral grounds, claiming the draft to be institutional genocide. Even then, however, they did not adopt the same antimilitary attitudes that characterized white student opposition, and they did not, by and large, follow Ali's example.

Ali's draft position was further confounded by this question: why did Ali have no remorse about quarreling with unknowns in the ring—the killing game? It was a paradox that did not escape Congressman Robert Michel of Illinois, who noted on the floor of the House: "Apparently Cassius will fight anyone but the Vietcong." Ali himself openly declared, "There's one hell of a lot of difference in fighting in the ring and going to the War in Vietnam," but the anger in his voice, not any philosophical thinking, lent the claim its sound of conviction.[20]

In an era given to inquiry about the application of might, a pacifist as heavyweight champion of a brutal sport made some sense. In his 1969 work on male bonding, Lionel Tiger proclaimed that "the amalgamation of size, power, dramaturgical savoir faire and dominance" were central to sport's appeal to males.[21] The heavyweight champion was the supreme symbol of dominance. How significant was it, then, that the physical aura of Muhammad Ali was one that stung like a bee and floated like a butterfly, particularly when contrasted to the brutish and violent style of the man he dethroned, Liston?

Before losing to Ali, Liston had dismissed the young boxer's style. "As a fighter," he told newsmen, "I think he should be locked up for impersonating a fighter."[22] But Ali's promotion of a style that featured lightning speed, grace, and an unhittable defense that protected his beauty went over big with the public. Boxing, after all, was not at the height of popular appeal. The deaths of fighters Benny Paret (in the ring in March 1962) and Davey Moore (in March 1963, four days after sustaining injuries in the ring) drew criticism that depicted boxing as an archaic contest in a civilized world. Bob Dylan's scathing indictment, "Who Killed Davey Moore?" badgered the public conscience with an accusatory chorus, "Why, and what's the reason for?" There were, then, public relations payoffs to be reaped from a heavyweight champ for whom boxing seemed a softer exercise. The portrayal of Ali as a dancer ("Fred Astaire," one observer remarked of him regarding his 1966 fight against Cleveland Williams— "just like he was in a jitterbug contest.")[23] masked the brutality that is the essence of the fight game and, once in place, obscured the cruel side of Ali's nature.

But cruelty and brutality were integral parts of Ali's ring persona, and obscuring them only contributed to his paradoxical stance.

In the ring he was both Brer Rabbit and John Henry. The sledgehammer aspect of his fighting showed only intermittently, but when it did Ali was revealed as a warrior willing to club and be clubbed. When he fought Joe Frazier for the third time, in 1975, both men stood toe to toe, drawing on power and resources that tested more than their will to win. It also tested their willingness to punish another man, their will to live, and, thus, their willingness to kill. Ali's cousin Coretta Bavers recalled, "He told me the next morning that he was closer to death than he'd ever been."[24] It was a confession he often repeated.

If that contest seemed to smack of valor and nobility, the flip side of the champ's brutality was evident in two earlier fights. In the 1960s, at the top of the boxing world, Ali had a range of tools at his disposal. Norman Mailer noted that, at times, Ali "played with punches, was tender with them, laid them on as delicately as you put a postage stamp on an envelope." It was not a style that most heavyweights would have valued.

But, as Mailer observed, Ali's attack also included, "a cruel jab like a baseball bat held head on into your Mouth."[25] In his November 1965 bout with former champion Floyd Patterson, and then a year and a half later against Ernie Terrell, Ali used mostly the latter, his game turning pitiless and sadistic. Angered because both opponents had dismissed his religious conversion (Terrell insisting on calling him "Clay"), Ali laid on punches and words with venom. Against Patterson, a proud black man well past his prime, Ali was relentless. Lipsyte, who recalled the bout as "the ugliest prizefight I've ever seen," asserted, "You really had the sense that he was just this little boy picking the wings off a butterfly. Floyd was so small; he was bent over with a back spasm; he could barely defend himself, and Ali was taunting him and hitting him. I personally was disgusted." *Life* magazine agreed, calling the fight "a sickening spectacle."[26]

The fight with Terrell was similar, Ali hitting him at will while demanding that Terrell call him by his Muslim name. Ali biographer Thomas Hauser told film documentarians, "Ali went out there to make this a horribly vicious, humiliating experience for Ernie Terrell, and he carried it on long past the time when Terrell was competitive in any way. And it's ugly. It's fifteen rounds of 'What's my name?' "[27]

Perhaps it was just coincidence, but, with the exception of the third Frazier fight, Ali's dark side was most apparent when he was on top. The 1960s were full of dynasties—Vince Lombardi's Green Bay Packers, the UCLA basketball Bruins, the Boston Celtics. They were popular antidotes in a society forced to witness the impotent American war effort nightly on the network news. But Ali was never more lovable or popular than when he was the underdog, a phenomenon that brought out his Brer Rabbit cunning and again connected him to powerful currents of the Vietnam era. He had risen to prominence after defeating Sonny Liston, the boxer that Ali's trainer, Angelo Dundee, called the "Monster Man." Clay had, many writers agreed, outfoxed Liston, disarming and unnerving him with his loudmouthed bravado, appearing manic nearly to the point of insanity. The mythic significance of the win was not lost on Clay or his admirers. Malcolm X's widow, Betty Shabazz, claimed: "My husband said all he had to do was to put his mind to it—surely if God had seen fit for David to be successful over Goliath, he could be successful over Sonny Liston."[28]

Strangely enough, though the United States was at an impasse against North Vietnam, antiwar protestors and Ali, through his rhetoric ("I ain't got no quarrel with them Vietcong"), both portrayed America's enemy as an underdog, a tiny force trying to hold on against an overwhelming power. It is ironic, then, that as Ali became ensconced as champion, fought as the favorite with power and a lack of mercy, he increasingly annoyed the establishment but appealed to the counterculture. After he lost his title for refusing induction, his martyrdom appealed to those who opposed the war, but he regained his more widespread popularity only after a loss in the ring reduced him once more to underdog. Following Ali's loss to Ken Norton in 1973, the acerbic Jimmy Cannon had crowed: "He is the guy the hungry kids want to get their hands on. No one appreciated being a winner more than Muhammad Ali. He is a loser now."[29]

He was not one for long. In 1974, when he upset George Foreman to regain the crown, the victory seemed moral vindication and proof positive to his many sympathizers in the draft case that the Vietnam War had been immoral. The war, by then, was more widely held to have been wrongfully fought by the United States, so it is no surprise that Americans generally applauded Ali's reemergence. Strangely, what was most praised was his cunning—the very type of deceit employed by the Vietcong. During the war, American spokesmen went to great pains to point out that the North Vietnamese's guerilla fighting was an immoral way of fighting—comparable to terrorism—and one at odds with American tactics, in which there was "a vested interest in abstaining from such acts."[30] West Point football star and Vietnam combatant Pete Dawkins tried to explain tactfully what he felt was a basic difference between Americans and the North Vietnamese, but he could not disguise a sense of righteousness. "They're not devious people," he told *Life* in 1966, "they're Oriental. Part of their culture is that they attack a problem indirectly—they sneak up on an issue."[31] In planning his strategy for facing Foreman, Ali decided on an indirect attack. Of course, most Americans missed this irony as they missed, as well, the shabbiness that the cunning camouflaged.

The triumph over George Foreman not only saw many Americans cheering for the reluctant draftee to defeat a man who had proudly waved the American flag in the Olympic ring at Mexico City in 1968; it also delivered a jolt to the concept of worthy opposition. Falling back on an old tendency to demean opponents, Ali had decided on a new tactic for his fight with the huge slugger. Threatening Foreman with a "ghetto whopper" (because "it's thrown in the ghetto at three o'clock in the morning, which is when me and George are gonna fight"),[32] Ali decided instead that the way to beat Foreman was to slump against the ropes and let Foreman hit him until exhausted. The tactic was brilliant, but smacked of the duplicity that many whites believed characterized both blacks and the Vietnamese. It was clearly reminiscent of Brer Rabbit's Tar Baby tactic, and Ali's label for it, "Rope-a-Dope," and his nickname for Foreman, "The Mummy," were best appreciated by a culture now fixated on victory and fast losing touch with the idea of worthy opposition.

Maybe the least noted but most significant aspect of the Foreman fight was that Ali made victory appear easy. Unlike his fatiguing earlier bouts with Frazier, the "rope-a-dope" seemed to deny the tenet of character-building that demanded hard work. The tactic was, on the one hand, intelligent and clever, in the same way that Paul Newman as Butch Cassidy had been in the immensely popular 1969 film of a Western outlaw fueled by wit and optimism. However, it was also akin to playing possum and, in Ali's case, thus tied to the trickster of black folklore and white suspicions of blacks as naturally gifted but not hardworking athletes. The idea that whites were hard workers while blacks were shirkers was one that had been necessarily absent from much of the discourse on sport during the decades prior to integration. The breakdown of segregation following 1954's *Brown v.*

Board of Education (the Supreme Court's rescinding of its 1896 approval of the doctrine of "separate but equal" in *Plessy v. Ferguson*) released blacks into many fields theretofore closed off, a flood that some southern white gentlemen still refer to despairingly as "The Deluge." Perhaps nowhere did the before-and-after numbers climb more steeply than they did in sports. By the early 1960s blacks already constituted percentages of professional teams in numbers disproportionate to their representation in the larger population. More revealing were their inroads in intercollegiate circles, where all manner of ruses had been used for decades to deny opportunities to blacks. The Southeastern Conference (SEC) was the last major conference to integrate, but when its schools did, the result was explosive. Just seven blacks played sports at four schools in 1966, the initial year of SEC integration. But by 1980, nearly 70 percent of the conference's basketball players were black, as were nearly one-third of its football players and track athletes.[33]

The new prominence of black athletes—and their refusal to acknowledge sport as a confirmation of "good" American values dramatically undercut the idea of character-building by calling into question the depth and genuineness of American goodness. Besides Ali, important athletes like Henry Aaron, Arthur Ashe, Jim Brown, John Carlos, Curt Flood, Kareem Abdul-Jabbar, Bob Gibson, Oscar Robertson, Bill Russell, and Tommie Smith pointed out the disparities between sport's claim to being a meritocracy and their own experiences as second-class citizens. Any hope that some whites may have been harboring for a return to old ways was dashed for good in 1966.

The NCAA basketball championship that year was expected to go to the University of Kentucky. Adolph Rupp, Kentucky's curmudgeonly coach, had become college basketball's leader in games won without playing a single black player in his thirty-six years at the helm. As he took his all-white team into the title game in College Park, Maryland, he was opposed for the first time by a starting five that was all black. The underdogs from Texas Western (now the University of Texas at El Paso) stunned Rupp and the nationwide television audience with a 72–65 victory. Afterward, it was impossible to evade the question of black athletic competency, and Kentucky—which had been slow to integrate—accelerated its use of black players.

The sudden rise of the black athlete—refutation of a century of the myth of white superiority—demanded explanation. The most convenient for whites was to acknowledge it as the necessary outcome of a biological physical advantage. As blacks became increasingly visible on Vietnam era playing fields, the nineteenth-century notion of a primitive, physically superior race was recycled and picked up new adherents, even among blacks. Peter Andrews, a basketball player at Penn in the mid-60s, said that if you took the blacks off of the school's great basketball teams of the late 60s and early 70s, "you got another Dartmouth and Brown."[34]

The most controversial and visible declaration of this possibility came early in January of 1971 when *Sports Illustrated* published Martin Kane's article, "An Assessment of Black Is Best." While granting that "not all the successes of the black man . . . have been entirely due to physical characteristics," Kane nonetheless leaned heavily in that direction, concluding: "Every male black child, however he might be discouraged from a career with a Wall Street brokerage firm, knows he has a sporting chance in baseball, football, boxing, basketball, or track."[35]

If blacks were scientifically certified as natural athletic talents, it was one more reason for some whites to deem them unfit for the character-building club. Character meant hard work, and who could be sure of effort in the face of such God-given talent? The notion that blacks had developed a racially distinct style of play, especially in basketball, that touted individual flamboyance at the expense of teamwork,[36] heightened the portrayal of whites as hard workers—and intelligent—while demeaning blacks as something less.

In the matter of effort, the stereotype of the lazy black lingered in the background of many situations and turned others into hostile confrontations. When Peter Andrews, though the captain, quit the Penn team in the middle of his final season, he felt that coach Dick Harter did not really believe that he had had an earlier injury that affected his play. According to Andrews, Harter merely "thought I had a cavalier attitude."[37] The possibility that white coaches would view black athletes as fakers and laggards may have unwittingly pushed some black athletes toward even greater effort. An unidentified black athlete at Penn told the *Daily Pennsylvanian,* "everything I do is representative of my race. I don't care if I'm the only black athlete playing—I'm pushing just a bit harder than the whites."[38]

Muhammad Ali was supremely gifted with physical skill. No doubt, when it came to character, it was easier for his detractors to see him that way than to acknowledge his intelligence or work ethic. In fact, the press made a good deal of Ali's initial failure to pass the armed services intelligence test, printing samples of the types of simple questions—fractions and the like—that Ali had wrestled with unsuccessfully. "Rope-a-Dope," though widely applauded as shrewd and masterly for an old fighter, nonetheless served to distance Ali from the tenets of character-building. It not only raised entertainment above fair play but also implied an otherworldly sense of self that tapped into another aspect of Vietnam era lore.

It was as a poet—in making predictions and then carrying them out—that Ali was at his most perplexing and pleasing. Only Ali the verse maker seemed to know ahead of time what disaster, like "Rope-a-Dope," might befall his opponents. His poetry in and out of the ring put him at odds with sport's alliance with science. Scientifically grounded theories of athletic achievement, begun in the nineteenth century, produced a performance principle that encouraged people to see athletes as mere representations of their conditioning regimens, nutritional supplements, and illicit drugs—that is, athletes as scientifically created performers. Though the performance principle was necessarily at odds with character-building from the outset—character being a subjective, unscientific measure of a person—one of the reasons that character-building had become so firmly entrenched in public consciousness was that it was effectively disguised as a scientific quest—a submission of the will in step with the demands of a progressive, modern, scientific, and secular world.

The Vietnam era neither quickened nor slowed interest in the scientific quest for enhanced performance. The increasing use of steroids, weight training, and ergogenic aids were merely new steps in the progression. The sixties were, however, the time that brought science and character into noticeable collision. Ironically, the counterculture, which strove for a more human, less technocratic society, ridiculed what appeared to be human strengths—effort, ethics, discipline—when critiquing sport; likewise, many coaches and administrators who believed wholeheartedly in character-building—and who, like Vince Lombardi, could be highly emotional and volatile—tried to lessen the effects of emotion on performance. Justifying the new use of computers as evaluation tools in 1968, Dallas Cowboy executive Tex Schramm explained, "I thought we had to find a way to judge players without emotion."[39]

Though Martin Kane, the same *Sports Illustrated* writer who would later offer explanation for black athletic superiority, tried to discover the scientific Ali, photographing and timing his punches in 1969 with an Omegascope, and though Ali was tied explicitly to the politics of his time—both of race and war—his charisma and success seemed to come from a mystic place that stood outside of convention and was rooted in emotion. In fact, the ten-page spread of Ali's technique as dissected by the Omegascope was ironically titled "The Art of Ali."[40] In his crowing, soaring, playful ascendancy to pop culture icon, Ali seemed to be, like the Beatles, the rollicking incarnation of another baby boom icon, Peter Pan, whose popularity took wing with the 1960 television airing of a stage production starring actress Mary Martin.

The characteristics of Pan—disdain for the adult world, for the specter of aging, for gender distinction, and for rules—were those of the "Eternal Child." According to one observer of popular culture, the myth of this *puer aeternus* ran through sixties counterculture as a symbol or metaphor for favored beliefs and behaviors.[41]

A boxer—subject to so many manly ravages—was unlikely to serve as an Eternal Child, but Clay/Ali fit the bill. He was undeniably playful. Even sitting atop a pile of cash for a *Sports Illustrated* cover, he seemed unfettered by material—or adult—concerns. In his early years his skin was smooth and pretty, his verses elementary and comical. Even after his body had begun to go slack, his demeanor remained boyishly mercurial. As trickster supreme he was impossible to pin down. He wore at one time or another each of the masks that various historians have identified as those that blacks donned to survive slavery: the deferential "Jack," the submissive "Sambo," the ferocious and threatening "Nat." In scheduling his fights from Manila in the Philippines to the African jungles of Zaire, his restless globetrotting made the world his home.

The myth of the Eternal Child also holds that the trickster in that child represents a "Powerfully anarchic, anti-authoritarian impulse, a drive to revolt, to disrupt or overturn the existing order."[42] In an age that featured a rejection of old authority and a search for new, Ali was most vivid as a figure who recognized little authority other than his own.

As a fighter Ali supported an entourage of trainers, friends, promoters, advisers, and newsmen. He was, however, beholden to few. His ring decisions became his own, from his need to punish Patterson and Terrell to his slugfest with Frazier to the adoption of "Rope-a-Dope." As trainer Angelo Dundee notes, "I won't kid you. When he went to the ropes, I felt sick."[43]

Outside the ring Ali's self-reliance was the archetype of an entire generation's affair with individualism and independence. When Hollywood filmed his biography, *The Greatest,* in 1977, the song that became the film's centerpiece explained that Ali had rejected heroes early in life, settling on self-dependence and self-love as "The Greatest Love of All." In defending his draft resistance he eschewed complexity. It was simple. "All I did," he said, "was stand up for what I believed." Continuing, he noted that "everything I did was according to my conscience. I wasn't trying to be a leader. I just wanted to be free."[44] Freedom, of course, is the flag-bearer for American claims to greatness, but it is also the spark that ignites debate about the relative merits of anarchy and conformity.

Ali had no qualms about whom he upset. His rejection of authority was both broad and significant. In spurning the army he thumbed his nose at America's most important civil institutions—the government, the military, and the capitalist economy that supported them both. In converting to Islam, he rejected the Christian God. Indeed, in conversation with sportswriter Jerry Izenberg, Ali intimated that Christianity rested on an unforgiving foundation. Asked how he thought his draft problems would be resolved, Ali told the writer, "Who knows; look what they done to sweet baby Jesus."[45]

As it turned out, Ali's self-comparison with Jesus accentuated a final aspect of the Eternal Child, that of "gods who die or are slain and then are resurrected in the spring—so that they become, in effect, undying, immortal, eternally youthful."[46] When boxing's officials stripped Ali of his crown in 1967 they made him that rarest of treasures—the living martyr—and prepared the way for his resurrection and ascension three years later. Ali reveled in his martyrdom. In April of 1968, he posed for the cover of *Esquire,* his beautiful body riddled with arrows.

All of the ways by which Ali became a symbol—unconsciously or not—were instrumental in his largest rejection, that of the entrenched racial hierarchy. His early fight promoters, draft officials, money men, even Christianity's most important figures were white. Ali chafed at this. His public declamations on politics, wars, and religion were evidence that his actions were undertaken deliberately in the spotlight. His separatist yearnings for a black homeland ("We want a country. Why can't we have our own land?"), black pride ("When are we going to wake up as a people and end the lie that white is better than black?"), and black sovereignty ("I will die before I sell out my people for the white man's money")[47] may have derived from his dealings with the Muslim leaders Malcolm X and Elijah Muhammad, but his fame made his stances on civil rights crucial to all of America, particularly to black athletes.

But it was as black athlete that Ali became embroiled in some of his strangest contradictions. When it comes down to it, whatever there was of an actual "athletic revolution" owed more to the actions of black athletes than it did to the indignities expressed by white athletes and sportswriters. It was black players who boycotted the AFL's 1965 All-Star game over an issue of pay; the raised fists of John Carlos and Tommie Smith at the 1968 Olympics forced the nation to acknowledge that the sports world was not one big happy place; and Curt Flood's decision to challenge the reserve clause would have lost some of its symbolic power had Flood been white. Still, when sociologist Harry Edwards proposed a black boycott of the 1968 Olympics, one of the unconditional demands for shelving the boycott was the restoration of Ali's title. Edwards often repeated his dictum that whites universally exploited black athletes as modern-day gladiators. How strange, then, that Edwards never hesitated to bring all of his influence to bear on restoring Ali to the top of that gladiatorial world. No doubt Edwards saw Ali as a figure who could help transform the arena into something less exploitative, but historically who has created more capital for entrenched sporting interests than the heavyweight champion of the world?

Even stranger was Ali's own paradoxical contribution to the meaning of race and color: that he, light-skinned and pretty, the popular suspicion of his white ancestry tainting his claims to racial exclusivity, had come to embody the hopes, anger, and venom of so many blacks; that he had risen to become king of the world not only by beating other blacks but also by humiliating them publicly in the demeaning language used for centuries by whites by addressing them as "nigger" in the most casual of utterances, by pronouncing them dumb and unworthy,[48] and by pointing out their similarity to apes. If Joe Frazier was, as Ali constantly maintained, a "gorilla" in contrast to his own café au lait look—it was a stern refutation of more than Frazier's countenance. If black was truly beautiful, then how could Frazier be an "ugly gorilla"?

In noting the "intense chords of ambiguity" that Ali struck as a black public figure, writer Gerald Early recently asked if Ali was "a star boxer, or through his genius, the utter undermining of boxing? Was he a militant or the complex unmasking of militancy?"[49] Paradox invites these questions and others. How could the nation countenance such ambiguity in either its heroes or its villains? How could someone so instrumental in undermining traditional notions of character end up idolized decades later as a man of unassailable character? The answer may be that it was the ambiguity itself that made Ali such an enduring and fitting symbol of the Vietnam era. In a competitive, capitalist society Americans find dichotomy and opposition so inescapable that we fall in naturally with those who seem to reconcile them for us. The Vietnam era, so fraught with polar tensions, demanded no less than a contradictory figure of Ali's stature and style.

We were never quite sure what to do with Ali during the time that he strode the world stage, alternately clowning, stinging, mocking, laughing, scorning, and humiliating. As Ali once pointed out:

> All kinds of people came to see me. Women came because I was saying, 'I'm so pretty,' and they wanted to look at me. Some white people, they got tired of my bragging. They thought I was arrogant and talked too much, so they came to see someone give the nigger a whuppin'. Long-haired hippies came to my fights because I wouldn't go to Vietnam. And black people, the ones with sense, they were saying, 'Right on, brother; show them honkies.' Everyone in the whole country was talking about me.[50]

By the time Atlanta hosted the 1996 Olympic Games, we were sure what to do with him. His reputation now softened by time, his many controversial stances left largely unchallenged, his swagger undone by Parkinson's syndrome, we handed him the torch that lit the stadium flame. It was a mighty moment of symbolic reconciliation—of black and white, old and young, amateur and pro. Ali had indeed become the seeming essence of an America more whole than it had been a quarter century earlier.

His magic, once performed solely in the ring, is now a handful of tricks—a disappearing handkerchief, a levitation illusion—that he uses to entertain the people that still trail in his wake. He is generous with his time and his person. He signs Muslim tracts by the thousands for free. Still, Ali retains an edge, an unknowableness that can be unsettling. By turns he is the comic, his lips pulled back tight against his teeth in a parody of anger, and the militant. Looking over a group of four white men waiting to be immortalized by posing with the champ for a photo, Ali calls them "four vanillas" to his "chocolate." Giving the up and down to another middle-aged white man who has waited two decades to be introduced to the "greatest of all time," Ali labels him the "Great White Dope." In both cases, Ali smiles. It is charming, but not convincingly warm.

Did history shape the man or the man history? Anytime you have to ask the question, you can be sure that it is neither, but rather both. If the biggest issues of his times were the Vietnam War and civil rights, no figure who meant more to each survived to the new millennium. Of the countless athletes who came through the era, none were more representative of the issues related to sport's character-building capacities.

It is probably no coincidence that character-building as the paradigm for sport was eclipsed at the same time that blacks took over the highest levels of play. The idea that blacks and whites were distinct races owed much to Ali. In selecting an identity as "black" rather than "Negro," by adopting separatist leanings after converting to Islam, and by making color matter on his very large stage, Ali reinforced the polarity of the times. What could be further apart, after all, than black and white? Everything in between mattered little. In 1972, Three Dog Night topped the charts with "Black and White," a song that claimed dichotomy and featured it in lyrics open to the possibility of both segregation and integration: "a child is black, a child is white/Together we learn to read and write." By the time that Paul McCartney and Stevie Wonder's 1982 duet, "Ebony and Ivory," similarly conveyed the idea that the races could produce harmony but were nonetheless as different as night and day, it was clear that desegregation and integration meant quite different things.

The idea of racial exclusivity has resurfaced often in the ensuing decades. When Hall of Fame running back O. J. Simpson stood trial for murder in 1995, many whites recirculated the possibility that Simpson was evidence of the atavistic violence still lurking in angry black men, ready to be directed at white women. The questionnaire for his prospective jurors included the queries: "If you are not currently a fan, have you in the past ever been a fan of the USC Trojans football team?" and "Does playing sports build an individual's character?" What became clear in the divisive debate over his trial and its meaning was that most Americans had come to believe that color, money, and celebrity were the decisive factors—not lessons from the gridiron. In December of 1997 *Sports Illustrated* asked "What Ever Happened to the White Athlete?" The question came twenty-nine years after the magazine's series on the plight of the black athlete, three decades during which the idea of race had become more pronounced.

Much of American sport at the turn of the century owes at least something to Ali's legacy. His collaboration with Howard Cosell embodied the transition from black-and-white to color television. His insistence on being seen prepared the public for the image-hungry likes of Andre Agassi, Dennis Rodman, and Hollywood's *Rudy.* The poetry and the monologues delivered to Terrell and Patterson legitimized and accelerated trash talking. And, against all odds, his most enduring legacy—that of conviction—means that we still take seriously the idea of sports and character.

NOTES

1. Robert Lipsyte, *SportsWorld: An American Dreamland* (New York: Quadrangle, 1975), 81; Thomas Hauser, *Muhammad Ali: His Life and Times* (New York: Simon and Schuster, 1991), 63; David Remnick, *King of the World: Muhammad Ali and the Rise of an American Hero* (New York: Vintage Books, 1998), 158. In Remnick's version, Ali checks to make sure that Lennon is smiling. The fact that he was, given Lennon's nettlesome ways, doesn't mean he wasn't serious.

2. *New York Journal American,* February 22, 1996, cited in Thomas Hauser, *Muhammad Ali,* 145–6.

3. *Muhammad Ali—The Greatest,* directed and produced by Martin Davidson, Arts and Entertainment, 1996.

4. *Ibid.*

5. *Ibid.*

6. Thorstein Veblen, excerpt from *The Theory of the Leisure Class* (1899), in *Sport and Society: An Anthology,* ed. John T. Talamini and Charles H. Page (Boston: Little, Brown and Co., 1973), 52.

7. Gail Bederman, *Manliness and Civilization: A Cultural History of Gender and Race in the United States, 1880–1917* (Chicago: University of Chicago Press, 1995), 15, 20, 25.

8. Eugene D. Genovese, *Roll, Jordan, Roll: The World the Slaves Made* (New York: Random House, 1976), 458.

9. Lillian Smith, *Killers of the Dream*, rev. ed. (New York: W. W. Norton and Co., 1961). Evidence of the ongoing existence of the fear was seen in the 1992 rape trial of black heavyweight boxer Mike Tyson. His white counsel settled upon a defense strategy that portrayed Tyson as a sexual animal of such renown and obvious intent that his accuser should have known to avoid him. Tyson was convicted.

10. See C. Vann Woodward, *The Strange Career of Jim Crow*, 3d rev. ed. (New York: Oxford University Press, 1974), 149–88.

11. Barry Kessler and David Zang, *The Play Life of a City: Baltimore: Recreation and Parks, 1900–1955* (Baltimore: Baltimore City Life Museums, 1989), 33.

12. "The Astonishing John Wideman," *Look* 27 (May 21, 1963): 36.

13. Jerry L. Avorn et al., *Up Against the Ivy Wall: A History of the Columbia Crisis* (New York: Atheneum, 1968), 60–1; Russell Sackett, "Plotting a War on 'Whitey,' " *Life* 60 (June 10, 1966): 100; Nicholas von Hoffman, *We Are the People Our Parents Warned Us Against* (Greenwich, Conn.: Fawcett Publications, 1968), 102.

14. Lipsyte, *SportsWorld*, 252.

15. *MuhammadAli—The Whole Story*, produced by Joseph Consentino, directed by Sandra and Joseph Consentino, Turner Network Television, 1997.

16. Hauser, *Muhammad Ali*, 266.

17. [University of Pennsylvania] *Daily Pennsylvanian*, October 4, 1965, 2.

18. *Muhammad Ali—The Greatest*, 1996.

19. Hauser, *Muhammad Ali*, 145.

20. *Ibid.*, 166; *Fields of Fire: Sports in the 60s*, produced by George Roy, directed and written by Steven Stern, Home Box Office in association with Black Canyon Productions, 1995.

21. Lionel Tiger, *Men in Groups* (New York: Random House, 1969), 115–25.

22. *MuhammadAli—The Whole Story*, 1997.

23. *Ibid.*

24. *MuhammadAli—The Greatest*, 1996.

25. Norman Mailer, "Ego," *Life* 70 (March 19, 1971): 22.

26. *Muhammad Ali—The Whole Story*, 1997; *Muhammad Ali—The Greatest*, 1996; *Life* 59 (December 1965): 42A.

27. *Muhammad Ali—The Greatest*, 1996.

28. *Ibid.*

29. *New York Post*, April 7, 1973, cited in Hauser, *Muhammad Ali*, 253.

30. Douglas Pike, "The Viet Cong Strategy of Terror," monograph, U.S. Mission, Saigon, February 1970, 9, cited by Frances Fitzgerald, *Fire in the Lake: The Vietnamese and the Americans in Vietnam* (New York: Random House, 1972), 505. See also Fitzgerald's chapter, "Guerillas," 507–17.

31. Sam Angeloff, "Tough, Punishing Work—But Dawkins Asked for It," *Life* 60 (April 8, 1966): 96.

32. Hauser, *Muhammad Ali*, 267.

33. Joan Paul, Richard V. McGhee, and Helen Fant, "The Arrival and Ascendance of Black Athletes in the Southeastern Conference, 1966–1980," *Phylon* 45 (December 1984): 284–97.

34. Peter Andrews, personal interview by the author, December 17, 1985.

35. Martin Kane, "An Assessment of Black Is Best," *Sports Illustrated* 34 (January 18, 1971): 83.

36. See Peter Axthelm, *The City Game—Basketball in New York* (New York: Harper's Magazine Press, 1970), and David Halberstam, *The Breaks of the Game* (New York: Alfred A. Knopf, 1981), for journalistic impressions of this idea.

37. Andrews, personal interview.

38. Mark Lieberman, "Pride and Awareness," *Daily Pennsylvanian*, March 4, 1968, 5.

39. Tex Maule, "Make No Mistakes About It," *Sports Illustrated* 28 (January 29, 1968): 25.

40. Martin Kane, "The Art of Ali," *Sports Illustrated* 30 (May 5, 1969): 48–57.

41. Harold Schecter, "The Myth of the Eternal Child in Sixties America," in *The Popular Culture Reader* ed. Jack Nachbar, Deborah Weiser, John L. Wright (Bowling Green, Ohio: Bowling Green University Press, 1978): 69–70.

42. Schecter, "The Myth," 70.

43. Hauser, *Muhammad Ali*, 276.

44. *Ibid.*, 171.

45. *Ibid.*, 168.

46. Schecter, "The Myth," 69.

47. Hauser, *Muhammad Ali*, 188–9.

48. Mark Kram, "Lawdy, Lawdy, He's Great," *Sports Illustrated* (October 13, 1975): 26.

49. Gerald Early, *The Muhammad Ali Reader*, ed. Gerald Early (New York: Rob Weisbach Books, 1998), xiii–xiv.

50. Hauser, *Muhammad Ali*, 158.

16

THE SPORTS SPECTACLE, MICHAEL JORDAN, AND NIKE

Douglas Kellner

MICHAEL JORDAN IS WIDELY acclaimed as the greatest athlete who ever lived, named "Athlete of the Century" by the ESPN television network. Yet he is also a major media spectacle on a global scale, combining his athletic prowess with skill as an endorser of global commodities. In Michael Jordan, globalization, commodification, sport, entertainment, and media come together to produce a figure who serves as a totem of athletic achievement, business success, and celebrity. Yet Jordan's participation in a series of scandals and periods of bad press, mixed with his usually laudatory media presentation, captures the contradictions of spectacle culture, illustrating that those who live by media spectacle can also be brought down by its cruel omnipresent power and surveillance.

As the millennium came to a close, Jordan reigned as one of the most popular and widely known sports icons throughout the world. The announcement of his retirement from basketball in January 1999, after leading the Chicago Bulls to six NBA championships, unleashed an unparalleled hyperbole of adjectives describing his superlative athletic accomplishments. In China, the *Beijing Morning Post* ran a front-page story titled "Flying Man Jordan is Coming Back to Earth," and in Bosnia, Jordan's statement declaring his retirement was the lead story on the evening television news, pushing aside the war in Kosovo.[1] An icon of the global popular culture, Jordan is "a kind of new world prince," in the words of Pulitzer-prize–winning author David Halberstam: "You hear time and again about people being in Borneo or somewhere and coming across a kid in a tattered Michael Jordan T-shirt. He's the most famous American in the world."[2]

Not only has Jordan been acclaimed as a global superstar, but he is also frequently characterized in terms of deity. Boston Celtics great Larry Bird marveled that he had encountered "God disguised as Michael Jordan" after Jordan scored sixty-three points against the Celtics in a 1986 playoff game. Jason Williams of the New Jersey Nets sanctified him as "Jesus in tennis shoes" while many referred to him as a "Black Jesus." At a 1992 Olympic press conference, Jordan was embarrassed to be asked if he were a "god" and *France Soir* headlined: "Michael Jordan in France. That's better than the Pope. It's God in person."[3]

In addition to being perhaps the greatest basketball player of all time, Jordan is one of the most successfully managed idols and icons of media culture. Parlaying his athletic triumphs into commercial product endorsements, Jordan became the highest-paid celebrity-advertising figure ever, endorsing a multitude of products for multimillion dollar fees, promoting his own line of athletic shoes, cologne, and clothing. Jordan also participated in film spectacle, starring with Bugs Bunny in a popular movie *Space Jam* (1996) and serving as the subject of a popular I-Max film, *Michael Jordan to the Max* (2000), as well as a series of documentaries in a 2002 DVD *Ultimate Jordan*.

Michael Jordan is thus an icon of media spectacle, combining extraordinary athletic prowess, an unrivalled record of winning, high entertainment value, and an ability to exploit his image for business success. In a commercial culture that blends celebrity, product, and image, it is only natural that sports shoe transnational Nike—as well as many other corporations—would purchase Jordan's star power to promote its products. The Jordan/Nike nexus calls attention to the sports-entertainment colossus that has become a major feature of media culture in the new millennium. The Nike/Jordan alliance discloses the extent to which contemporary global culture is constituted by image and spectacle and mediated by the institutions of the media, advertising, public relations, and image-management.

THE SPORTS SPECTACLE

Sports are today a major part of the consumer society whereby individuals learn the values and behavior of a competitive and success-driven society. Sports heroes are among the best-paid and wealthiest denizens of the consumer society and thus serve as embodiments of fantasy aspirations for the good life. Whereas participation in sports involves an active engagement in creative practice, spectator sports involves passive consumption of images of the sports spectacle, which mobilizes spectator energies into deification of players and teams and the celebration of values of competition and winning. Yet there is also an active dimension in fandom, in which sports consumers learn tremendous amounts of folklore, become experts and critics, and thoroughly participate in sports communities.

While sports have been an important mode of participation and assimilation into modern societies during the postindustrial era, spectator sports emerged as the correlative to a society that is replacing manual labor with automation and machines, and requires consumption and passive appropriation of spectacles to reproduce consumer society. The present-day era also sees the expansion of a service sector and highly differentiated entertainment industry, of which sports is a key part. Thus, significant resources are currently devoted to the expansion and promotion of the sports spectacle. Athletes like Michael Jordan are accordingly recipients of the potential to amass high salaries from the profits being generated by the sports-entertainment colossus, while spectators are taught to idolize stars like Jordan, making them the deities of everyday life.

Recent years have exhibited a dramatic implosion of the sports spectacle, commerce, and entertainment with massive salaries and marketing contracts for the superstar players/celebrities. The major media conglomerates are becoming increasingly interested in sports channels and franchises and the most marketable athletes earn enormous multimillion dollar salaries. Moreover, sports stars are able to secure even more lucrative marketing deals to endorse products, star in film or TV programs, and even, in the case of Michael Jordan, to promote their own product lines.

NBA basketball has increasingly featured superstar feats of individual brilliance, especially during the heyday of the Michael Jordan spectacle. Professional basketball is the ideal television sport, fast-paced, full of action, and resplendent with spectacle. Hard-charging full-court action, balletic shots, and ubiquitous instant replays make basketball the right sport for the era of MTV and ESPN. NBA commissioner David Stern remarked in a 2000 Museum of Broadcasting lecture that sports is "the most important programming on television" because it is original, exciting, dramatic, entertaining, and highly compelling. It is a primal form of live TV with immediacy, action, and drama built-in to the event. Sports, Stern argued, drove cable penetration, creating demand for the new technology that allowed it to brilliantly succeed, and in time sports became the U.S.'s major export, the cultural ambassador of choice for American games, heroes, values, and products.

In 1989, the ESPN network began broadcasting sports full-time on cable and soon became a powerhouse. ESPN originally signified Entertainment Sports Programming Network, an instructive anagram that called attention to the nexus between sports and entertainment in the Age of Television. "ESPN" also signaled the way that the sports-entertainment colossus was programming the nation to become sports addicts and to idolize its celebrities, values, and dramas, so as to be networked into a sport/entertainment/consumer society.[4] By the 1980s, ESPN began applying MTV-esque techniques to sports events and broadcasting celebrity sports shows that helped elevate athletic stars like Jordan to super icon status. Initially aimed at a male audience, the network went after female viewers by adding more entertainment features and women commentators. They also cultivated audiences of color, adding black sportscasters like Stuart Scott who combined ethnic street talk and attitude with cutting-edge flashy suits and idiosyncratic style, as with his signature "Boo-ya!" salutation, which itself became part of the contemporary sports idiom, signaling especially spectacular moves and plays.

Basketball is a speed game that moves rapidly down the court, and television made a spectacle of velocity, totally appropriate for an ever faster-paced society, intensifying motion and action with quick cuts, close-ups, and zooms. Helping to speed up the game for television, the NBA instituted a twenty-four-second "shot clock," forcing teams to accelerate the pace of the game. In addition, playbacks highlighted the mechanics of brilliant plays, while the intimacy of TV caught the sweat and concentration, anger and exultation, and other moments of physical and emotional intensity. Furthermore, basketball is sexy, showing glistening and well-honed male bodies in a state of semi-undress, clad in skimpy jerseys and shorts. Compared to the male gladiator body armor of football players and the nineteenth-century full body attire of baseball, basketball presented a mode of male beefcake, especially with TV close-ups capturing the hard and agile bodies of NBA hunks.

Thus, NBA basketball became a powerful media spectacle, and television helped the sport gain popularity and importance in the 1980s by broadcasting more games and heavily promoting basketball as it became ever more fashionable and followed. Completely embodying the fragmentary postmodern aesthetics, razzle-dazzle technical effects, and accelerating pace of today's television, basketball has emerged as a major arena of the spectacle, the ultimate game for the sports/entertainment society. Once a primarily American game, by the 1990s it has become globally popular.

Consequently, while the NBA was once the ne'er-do-well stepchild of the more successful professional baseball and football franchises, in recent years it has become one of the most popular of the U.S. sports industries on the global scale.[5] While the NBA only fed 35 weekly telecasts to foreign companies in the mid-1980s during the beginning of Jordan's basketball career, by 1996 the roster had swelled to 175 foreign broadcasts in forty languages to 600 million households. By 2000, the NBA was broadcasting to 205 countries in forty-two languages with a total worldwide audience of over 750 million fans.

Many credit Michael Jordan as one of the chief figures in promoting NBA basketball to global popularity. David Halberstam described him as "the first great athlete of the wired world"[6] and "arguably the most famous American in the world, more famous in many distant parts of the globe than the President of the United States or any movie or rock star"[7] In his book *Michael Jordan and the New Global Capitalism,* Walter La Feber describes the process whereby Jordan, NBA basketball, and U.S. global corporations like Nike all attained a global reach, transnationalizing American sports, products, and idols. The globalization of Michael Jordan and Nike was made possible by an international network of cable and satellite television that broadcasts U.S. media, sports, and advertising throughout the world, and a global economy that distributes its products, services, sports, and images. The Internet, too, contributed to the globalization of sports and culture and, as we will see later, played an ambiguous role in Michael Jordan's own personal saga.[8]

The dramatic evolution of the sports spectacle thus has a global dimension with the major players now becoming international figures, marketed in global sports extravaganzas, advertising campaigns, product promotions, films, websites, and other venues of media culture. As Michael Jordan's highly successful and respected agent David Falk puts it: "Michael has transcended sport. He's an international icon."[9] Indeed, in 1996–1997, Falk put together deals that netted Jordan a record-breaking thirty million dollar contract for the next season. Moreover, Falk's deals continued the lucrative connections with Nike and other corporations to promote their products to the estimated tune of forty million dollars. Jordan was also able to inaugurate his own cologne line, Eau de Michael Jordan, and negotiated a contract to star in a high tech film pairing Jordan with other NBA superstars, Bugs Bunny, and various cartoon characters.[10] Cumulatively, with accompanying product lines, estimates circulated that Jordan could conceivably earn twenty million dollars from his commercial projects, pointing to a growing convergence between the sports spectacle, entertainment, and business.

THE SPECTACLE OF MICHAEL JORDAN

Among the spectacles of media culture, Michael Jordan is a preeminent figure. As a NBA superstar, Jordan is the very picture of grace, coordination, virtuosity, and all-around skill—adeptly marketed to earn a record salary and endorsements. Jordan received thirty million dollars to play for the Chicago Bulls in 1997 and thirty-three million in 1998; he earned over forty million dollars in endorsements and promotions in 1995, making him the highest paid athlete in the world, then reaped over forty-five million in endorsements in 1996, continuing his position as the world's highest paid athlete. In June 1998, *Fortune* magazine estimated that Jordan had generated over ten billion dollars during his spectacular professional career in terms of an increase in tickets sold, television advertising revenue, increased profits of products Jordan endorsed, basketball merchandising exploiting his figure, and his own films, businesses, and product lines.[11] Jordan *is* big business and has accelerated the trends toward the implosion of business, entertainment, and sports.

Jordan first appeared as a rookie with the Chicago Bulls in 1984 and although he was not yet a full-fledged superstar, his agent signed him to what turned out to be an incredibly influential and lucrative contract with Nike. With Jordan and a new marketing agency, Wieden and Kennedy, the Air Jordan product line and Nike's Swoosh symbol became icons of American and then global culture. At the same time, Michael Jordan became an authentic American hero, generally acknowledged as one of the greatest basketball players of all time, one of the most popular and well-known celebrities of media culture, and since 1988, the sports celebrity most desired to market corporate products. Nike/Jordan's ascendancy, cable and satellite television, and the aggressive promotion of the NBA by its commissioner David Stern increased tremendously the visibility and popularity of professional basketball. The Jordan/Nike era had arrived.

There seemed to be nothing that Jordan could not do on the basketball court. His slam-dunk is legendary and he seems to defy gravity as he flies through the air toward the Holy Grail of the basket. His "hang-time" is fabled and as Cheryl Cole points out, designations like "Rare Air" "render him extraordinary . . . and even godlike," a figure of transcendence.[12] Nike developed a product line of "Air Jordan" sports shoes around the flying mythology and a 1989 NBA Entertainment documentary titled "Michael Jordan: Come Fly With Me" describes the player as "the man who was truly destined to fly," and celebrates him as the very embodiment of professional excellence, morality, and American values. The collection of photographs of Michael Jordan as sports icon, media celebrity, and down-home good guy is titled *Rare Air,* highlighting the efficacy of the Michael Jordan publicity machine in fine-tuning his image as a transcendent figure, a god of media culture.

There have been, to be sure, some glitches in the Michael Jordan success story. After dropping out of professional basketball to pursue a professional baseball career,[13] Jordan returned to the Chicago Bulls in 1995 and led the team to three straight NBA championships. In the process, he reinvented himself as a superstar player, moving from his patented flying air shots to become one of the great distance and jump shot scorers of all time. In the words of one analyst: "At 33, Jordan is a half-step slower than he once was. He is more beholden to gravity, less nuclear in his liftoff. He can still take wing and be *Air* when he needs to, still shift into turbo and batter the rim, but he chooses his spots now, waits for clear paths. He no longer hurls himself into walls of elbows and forearms, giving the other side's behemoths free shots at his kidneys. He has traded risk for feel, nerve for guile, spectacle for efficiency . . . and because he is Jordan, even his efficiency can seem spectacular."[14]

During the 1996–1998 seasons, the Bulls emerged as a media culture spectacle of the highest order, setting records for attendance, winning many regular season games and three straight NBA championships. With Jordan, bad-guy extraordinary Dennis Rodman, all-around star Scottie Pippen, and Zen-inspired coach Phil Jackson, the Bulls earned unparalleled media attention and adulation. The Jordan spectacle helped make NBA basketball globally popular and Michael Jordan a superstar of extraordinary resonance.[15] Jordan henceforth was identified with ardent competition and winning, embodying the values of drive, success, and coming out on top; his shots repeatedly won key games and he became fabled for the magnitude of his competitiveness and drive to win.

In the sports/entertainment colossus, a vast marketing apparatus of television, radio, magazines, and other publications help to promote and manufacture the stars of sports and entertainment, attesting to an implosion of media and sports cultures, and thus sports and commerce. Indeed, Jordan himself is an entire sports franchise with special pitches geared toward kids (i.e. an 800 number to order Nikes that Jordan gives them "permission" to call), toward urban teens, and targeting young adults with his fragrance products. And as Cole has documented, Jordan was part of a Nike P.L.A.Y. program ("Participate in the Lives of American's Youth") designed to present a positive corporate image and promote its products to a youth audience. Then, in 1999, he began his own Jordan Fundamentals Grant Program, to provide funds to schools with outstanding youth programs.[16]

Michael Jordan is thus a dazzling sports spectacle who promotes both commercial sports and the products of the corporations that sell their goods to sports audiences. His distinctive image is often noted and Jordan's look and style are truly striking. His shaved head, extremely long shorts, and short socks are often-cited defining features that are highlighted in a Spike Lee Nike ad that in a brilliant effort to get the Nike message across repeatedly insists, *"It's gotta be the shoes!"* (i.e. which make Jordan the greatest). In addition, his wristband, jersey number 23, and tongue wagging and hanging while he concentrates on a play are distinctive signs of Jordan's trademark image. In fact, Jordan is so handsome that he has often been employed as a model, and his good looks and superstar status have won him countless advertising endorsements for products like Nike, McDonald's, Gatorade, Coca Cola, Wheaties, Hanes shorts, and numerous other products. A Gatorade ad tells the audience to "be like Mike," establishing Jordan as a role model, as the very icon of excellence and aspiration. In antidrug ads, Jordan tells the nation to just say no, to avoid drugs, to do the right thing, and to be all you can be, mobilizing the various stereotypes of conservative postindustrial America in one figure. Michael Jordan is the paradigmatic figure of the "hard body" that was the ideal male image of the Reaganite 1980s, a model of the powerful bodies needed to resurrect American power after the flabbiness of the 1960s and 1970s.[17]

MICHAEL JORDAN AND THE SPORTS/RACE SPECTACLE

Initially, Jordan was perceived as both black and not black, as a superior athlete and all-American clean-cut young man who transcended race and yet was obviously an African American. Throughout his career, there were attempts by image-managers and commentators to present Jordan as a quasi-deity who transcended racial markers, and yet at other times his color and race were part of the spectacle. It is generally acknowledged that he was one of the first African-American athletes to break advertising's color barrier, paving the way for lucrative contracts for the next generation of black athletes.[18] During the difficult transitional year of 1993, when Jordan was under intense critical scrutiny by the media and NBA because of his alleged gambling problems and the unsolved murder of his father—whose death many speculated was related to gambling debts—he became for the first time the recipient of the sort of negative press visited upon such African-American sports luminaries as Muhammad Ali, Mike Tyson, and his onetime Chicago Bulls teammate Dennis Rodman.

The Jordan publicity machine has consistently taken the line that Jordan "transcends race" and commentators have claimed that Jordan is "trans-racial."[19] Jordan himself usually plays it both ways in interviews, admitting that he recognizes he is black, while calling upon people to see him as a human being. Yet, as a cultural signifier, as the "universal singular" who represents more general social significance, Jordan is a polysemic signifier who encodes conflicting meanings and values. Michael Jordan is an example of what Lauren

Berlant calls the "national symbolic" as well as the "global popular." Jordan embodies national values of hard work, competitiveness, ambition, and success. As a black superstar, he presents the fantasy that anyone can make it in the society of competition and status, that one can climb the class ladder and overcome the limitations of race and class. As a national and global superstar, he also represents many different things to different people in different countries. Indeed, as Wilson and Sparks remind us, different individuals and audiences are going to receive and appropriate the text of Michael Jordan in different ways according to their own race, gender, class, region, and other subject positions.[20]

As a polysemic signifier, Jordan thus presents a figure that mobilizes many fantasies (i.e. athletic greatness, wealth, success, and upward mobility) for the national and global imaginary, providing a spectacle that embodies many desirable national and global features and aspirations. Yet Jordan is extremely black and his race is a definite signifier of his spectacle, though his blackness too has conflicting connotations. On one hand, he is a privileged role model for black youth ("Be like Mike"), he reportedly helps mentor young athletes, and he is a symbol of the African American who has transcended race and who is integrated into American society, representing the dream of assimilation, wealth, and success. But as David Andrews has demonstrated, Jordan's blackness is overdetermined and has also served to signify black transgressions, as when his gambling behavior became a subject of negative media presentation and his father's murder led to speculation on connections to organized crime. In these images, Jordan is presented as the threatening black figure, as the negative fantasy figure of black deviance from white norms. Jordan's physique, power, and dominance might also feed into the fear of black bodies, as Henry Giroux suggests in his analysis of how contemporary media culture is characterized by a simultaneous fascination with the accomplishments of the black male body while also fearing the threat it poses.[21]

Yet Jordan also lends his personality to antidrug ads and campaigns, represents constructive ideals of hard work and discipline, and is regularly presented as a positive role model. However, Jordan's "Just say No!" conflicts with his "Just do It!," creating an ambiguous figure who at once represents restraint and control and misbehavior and excess. "Just say no" implies morality and constraint, whereas "Just do it!" signifies indulgence and immoderation, as well as determination and grit. Indeed, Nike's self-proclaimed corporate philosophy of "Just do It!" is itself self-contradictory, connoting both the indulgence and thrust toward gratification that makes a consumer society work (i.e. just go out and buy the shoes!), with evocation of the commitment and hard work needed to succeed in sports or business. Jordan combines both of these impulses, but linking the "Just do It!" philosophy with his well-known interest in gambling and self-gratification, could condone behavior coded as immoral by a traditional morality.

The Jordan mythology wants it all ways at once, to combine individualism and morality, but these ideologies can come into conflict, as would Jordan himself occasionally come into conflict with conventional morality in his own life. On the whole, however, Jordan is positioned in media culture as the "good black," especially against the aggressiveness and visual transgressions of his one-time Chicago Bulls teammate Dennis Rodman. Rodman seemed to cultivate and revel in the bad-boy image of his bleached and undisciplined hair, ear and nose-rings, fancy clothes, and frequent rebellious behavior, coming to represent the "bad" black figure, as opposed to Jordan's "good" one. Jordan is also a privileged figure of the corporate black, held in renown for his business acumen, as well as his athletic skill.

He is the role model who incarnates basic American values and who fashioned his image into a highly beloved celebrity. Indeed, Jordan was deemed the most popular person alive between 1987–1993, tying with God in an *Associated Press* survey as the person who black children most admired, and in a poll of Chinese students, he ran neck and neck with Zhou Enlai.[22]

Thus, for the most part, the Michael Jordan spectacle serves as an icon of positive representations of African Americans. Jordan's concentration is often remarked and his awesome skills are obviously mediated by intelligence. His "airdriven bullets" seem to be guided by a highly effective mental radar system and his trademarked "aerial ballets" represent grace and spiritual transcendence as well as brute force. Todd Boyd sees Jordan's talents as exemplary of a black aesthetic and compares him to great black musical performers, writing: "You can't watch Michael Jordan and not be moved in the way one has been moved, at an earlier time, listening to a John Coltrane solo."[23]

Jordan combined grace and cool, style and skill, drive and polish, energy and aptitude. Like the great American jazz musicians, he merged formal mastery of the instrument and its rules with great improvisational panache. Moreover, Jordan seems to embody key American values and to serve as a role model for American youth and as the white fantasy of the good African American. Thus, while it appears wrong to claim, as is often done, that Michael Jordan transcends race, the Jordan spectacle projects unusually positive representations of African Americans, undercutting racist stereotypes and denigration.

The extent to which the spectacles of sports have promoted the interests of African Americans and people of color has not yet been adequately understood. As recently as the 1940s, professional sports were segregated and athletes of color were forced to toil in "colored" leagues, condemned in effect to the minor leagues. With the breaking of the color line in professional baseball in the 1940s by Jackie Robinson, African-American athletes could be part of professional sports and eventually icons of the sports spectacle. Indeed, during the 1950s and 1960s prominent African-American baseball players like Willie Mays, Larry Doby, and Hank Aaron were acknowledged as superstars of the spectacle.

Black and brown athletes succeeded in equally spectacular ways in professional football, boxing, and basketball. Sports thus became an important route for people of color to grab their share of the American dream and their cut of the great spectacle of "professional" (read commercial) sports. On the positive side, the American fascination with sports promoted racial equality, acceptance of racial difference, and multiculturalism. With the incorporation of black athletes into professional sports they entered mainstream media culture as entertainment icons, as role models for youth, and as promoters (often unaware) of racial equality and integration.

Sports has aided the cause of women's rights as well. Women played basketball shortly after its invention in 1891 and in the early 1970s the U.S. government passed Title IX, which required equal facilities for men's and women's sports at institutions that received federal funding. Over the past decade, the WNBA has become increasingly popular and powerful with televised games, devoted fans who often sell out the stadiums, media attention, and an active official website. Women's basketball is now one of the most popular high school and college games and more and more women are participating in sports and getting recognized for their achievements. Indeed, women's sports are now popular in several fields and both the September 11, 2000 *Time* and *Newsweek* covers featured superstar

African-American track icon Marion Jones. Consequently, sports, once a white male preserve, is becoming open to women and players of color, thus spearheading development of a multicultural society. In fact, I would argue that the prowess of black sports heroes and the rhythms of rock music have done much to promote racial equality and the rights of African Americans and people of color.[24] Postindustrial America became more and more of a media culture and professional sports and entertainment became key features of media spectacle. Once African Americans were allowed to sparkle and shine in media culture they were able to enter the mainstream—or at least major figures of the spectacle such as O. J. Simpson, Hank Aaron, and Michael Jordan were so empowered.

Nike has often presented African-American athletes as "different" in their ads, as well as part and parcel of the American dream, thus helping promote them to superstar celebrity status. Nike also helped promote the NBA and professional basketball to global iconic status, it enabled black athletes like Michael Jordan to attain world-class superstar status, and addressed the situation of black America. Yet one could argue that these appropriations of the black sports spectacle were geared to sell shoes and other commercial products. Thus, the commodity transformation offered the consumer by the Nike shoe is arguably a false transcendence. Such commodity transformation does not produce a new super-self, but simply exploits its customer's pocketbook, forcing the unwary purchaser to buy a product much more expensive than many competing products, simply because of its sign value and prestige. And while one can affirm Nike's emphasis on activity and exercise over passivity and boredom, it is not clear that the sort of activity that Nike is promoting is really going to promote the interests of minority youth. Gangs versus sports is not the only dichotomy of contemporary urban life, and one might argue that education, technical skills, and career choice and motivation are more important for contemporary youth than running down to a basketball court and shooting hoops.

Moreover, the elevation to cultural icons of black athletes like Michael Jordan itself is a double-edged sword. On one hand, Jordan is a spectacle of color who elevates difference to sublimity and who raises blackness to dignity and respect. An icon of the sports spectacle, Michael Jordan is *the* black superstar and his prominence in sports has made him a figure that corporate America can use to sell its products and its values. Yet such are the negative representations and connotations of blackness in American culture and such is the power of the media to define and redefine images that even the greatest black icons and spectacles can be denigrated to embody negative connotations. As Michael Jackson, O. J. Simpson, and Mike Tyson have discovered, those who live by the media can die by the media—overnight their positive representations and signification can become negative.

Media culture is only too happy to use black figures to represent transgressive behavior and to project society's sins onto African Americans. Indeed, despite an endemic national and global problem of sexual harassment, Clarence Thomas became the representative figure for this transgression in the 1990s. Despite the troubling problem of child molestation cutting across every race and class, Michael Jackson was the media figure who came to represent this iniquity (until 2002 when Catholic priests became the poster people for child abuse). Furthermore, despite an epidemic of violence against woman, O. J. Simpson became the ultimate wife abuser, and although date rape is a deplorable frequent and well-documented phenomenon across races, classes, and regions, it was Mike Tyson who emerged as "poster boy" for this offense. Indeed, Tyson was denigrated in 1997–1998 for all

Figure 16–1
Michael Jordan. Courtesy of **The Sporting News.**

of the ills of professional boxing after his behavior in a title fight, his violence against seniors in a driving accident, for which he was sentenced to a year in jail, and his generally aberrant behavior.[25]

Such is the racism of American culture that African Americans are the figures of choice to represent social transgressions and tabooed behavior. Michael Jordan has had his bouts with negative media representations, though on the whole his representations have been largely positive and his figure has been used to represent an ideal of blackness that American society as a whole can live with. Indeed, for many, Jordan presents an image of the transcendence of race that many celebrate as a positive ideal. Yet despite his adulation, it would be a mistake to make Michael Jordan *the* role model for African Americans or the youth of the world. Comparing Jordan with baseball star Jackie Robinson who broke the major league color barrier in 1947, Jack White describes Robinson's speaking out against racial injustice, his actions with Martin Luther King, and his constantly standing by his political principles:

> You can hardly imagine contemporary black sports superstars taking an equally brave stand on a divisive moral issue. Most are far too concerned with raking in endorsement dollars to risk any controversy. In 1990 Michael Jordan, who occupies the psychological spot that Robinson pioneered as the dominant black athlete of his time, declined to endorse his fellow black North Carolinian Harvey Gantt over troglodyte racist Jesse Helms in a close contest for the U.S. Senate on the grounds that "Republicans buy shoes too." More recently, Jordan brushed off questions about whether Nike, which pays him $20 million a year in endorsement fees, was violating standards of decency by paying Indonesian workers only 30 cents per day. His curt comment: "My job with Nike is to endorse the product. Their job is to be up on that." On the baseball field or off it, when Robinson came up to the plate, he took his best shot and knocked it out of the park. The superstar athletes who have taken his place, sadly, often strike out.[26]

When asked what he thought about the L.A. uprisings after the police who beat Rodney King were declared not guilty in May 1992, Jordan replied, in Todd Boyd's paraphrase: "I'm more concerned with my jump shot." Boyd comments: "Nobody's asking you to be Malcolm X, but when an opportunity arises, don't run from it."[27] But Michael Jordan, like many athletes corrupted by the sports spectacle and commercial culture, has abrogated his basic political and social responsibilities in favor of expensive clothes, commodities, and a megastock portfolio. Nike has played a key role in promoting these values and is thus a major cultural force, a powerful instrument of socialization, and arbitrator of cultural and social values, as well as a shoe company. Thus, the Nike/Jordan nexus is worthy of critical reflection as the contradictions of Michael Jordan's persona come to the fore in a striking way with regards to his intimate connection with the Nike Corporation.

MICHAEL JORDAN, NIKE, AND THE COMMODITY SPECTACLE

Media culture is notorious for destroying precisely the icons it has built up, especially if they are black. Jordan eventually received his share of bad, as well as adulatory, press. During the 1990s, Jordan was regularly criticized when Nike was sharply attacked in the media for its labor policies. Put on the defensive, Jordan was frequently asked to comment on Nike's labor practices. As first he refused to answer questions about Nike's corporate practices, and then in a carefully prepared public relations response, Jordan countered that it's up to Nike "to do what they can to make sure everything is correctly done. I don't know the complete situation. Why should I? I'm trying to do my job. Hopefully, Nike will do the right thing."[28] Yet the media continued to pester him and he was often portrayed in images during the summer of 1996 turning away from interviewers with a curt "No comment," when asked what he thought of Nike's exploitation of Third World workers, especially women, at extremely low wages.

Nike and Michael Jordan are thus intricately connected. As noted, Nike signed the relatively untested young basketball player to a contract in 1984 and evolved one of the most successful marketing campaigns in history. There have been seventeen annual editions of Nike's Air Jordan shoes as of 2002, and Jordan has helped make Nike's corporate logo and Swoosh design one of the most familiar icons of corporate culture, as well known as McDonald's Golden Arches and the Coca Cola bottle. From the beginning, Nike deployed the image of Michael Jordan and produced ads that celebrated its products in a commodity spectacle that connected Jordan's prowess and image with their product.

Behind the Nike spectacle, there is, of course, the unedifying reality of underpaid workers, toiling at subsubsistence wages and under terrible working conditions to produce highly overpriced shoes for youth, many of whom cannot afford and do not need such luxury items. Nike was one of the first major corporations to shift to a mode of production labeled "post-Fordism" and "flexible accumulation."[29] Shifting production of its shoes from the U.S. to Asia in the early 1980s, Nike first set up factories in Taiwan and South Korea. Both countries had at the time military dictatorships, low wages, and disciplined work forces. They frequently subcontracted work to local companies, which would then be responsible for such things as wages, working conditions, and safety. While there were no established unions, the largely women workers in South Korea began organizing in response to poor working conditions, humiliating treatment by bosses, and low wages. At the same time, a democracy movement began in South Korea and when mounting labor unrest was apparent:

> Factory managers called in government riot police to break up employees' meetings. Troops sexually assaulted women workers, stripping them, and raped them "as a control mechanism for suppressing women's engagement in the labor movement," reported Jeong-Lim Nam of Hyosung Women's University in Taegu. It didn't work. It didn't work because the feminist activists in groups like the Korean Women Workers Association (KWWA) helped women understand and deal with the assaults. The KWWA held consciousness-raising sessions in which notions of feminine duty and respectability were tackled along with wages and benefits. They organized independently of the male-led labor unions to ensure that their issues would be taken seriously, in labor negotiations and in the pro-democracy movement as a whole.[30]

Conditions and wages improved for Korean women workers, but Nike was in the process of moving production to countries with lower wages and more control of labor, such as China and Indonesia. From the 1980s to the present, Nike's shoes have been produced mostly in Asia where the average wage paid to their workers is often below the subsistence level. There was much publicity over Nike's Indonesian sweatshops where women would be paid approximately $1.20 per day to produce shoes in the early 1990s. In 1992, 6,500 workers in the Sung Hwa Dunia factory in Serang, Indonesia went on strike and wages were raised to $1.80 a day and eventually to $2.20 a day. Under intense pressure from the

Clinton administration to improve working conditions and labor rights in order not to lose privileged trading status, the Indonesian government raised the minimum wage to (a still pitiful) $1.80 an hour and promised that the military would no longer harass and brutalize workers. But, as William Greider reports, the concessions were largely a charade because "despite the official decrees, the military kept on intervening in labor disputes, showing up at the plant gates and arresting strike activists, herding the women back into the factories. This occurred 22 times within the first month following the supposed reform."[31]

In addition, companies often refused to pay the workers even the legal minimum wage. The response of the Indonesian workers were a series of wildcat strikes, international campaigns to publicize their plight, and continued efforts to organize workers. Accordingly, Nike sought other sites of production, increasing the number of their factories in China and then moving to Vietnam where the minimum wage is thirty dollars per month and they can return to the one dollar plus change a day wages of an earlier era. Basing his figures on an analysis by Thuyen Nguyen, an American businessman who studied the conditions of Nike workers in Vietnam, Bob Herbert wrote in a *New York Times* op-ed piece on "Nike's Boot Camps" that Nike workers in Vietnam are paid $1.60 a day while three meager meals cost $2.10 a day and renting a room costs $6 a month. Nike's workers are paid subsistence wages and work in conditions described as "military boot camps" with widespread corporal punishment, molestation of women workers, and deteriorating health of the workers.[32]

There was so much negative publicity concerning working conditions in sweatshops producing Nike gear that the corporation hired Andrew Young to review its labor practices and working conditions. When Young returned some weeks later with a report that whitewashed Nike, they took out full-page ads to trumpet the results, though generally there was skepticism concerning Young's account and his inadequate inspection of the Asian worker's plight.[33]

Thus, Nike shifts production from country to country to gain ever lower labor costs. NAFTA and GATT treaties have made it even easier for Nike and other global corporations to move production across the U.S. border. Nike is able to shift around its manufacturing at will, searching for the lowest labor costs and most easily exploitable working conditions. Meanwhile, its CEO Phil Knight earns millions per year and his stock is worth an incredible $4.5 *billion,* and Jordan, Andre Agassi, and Spike Lee are paid staggering sums for their endorsements and advertisements. Nike's profit margins have been enormous: Cynthia Enloe estimated that for a $70 pair of Nike Pegasus shoes, $1.66 goes for labor; $1.19 to the subcontractor; $9.18 goes for materials; $2.82 for administration and overhead; and Nike ultimately pockets $22.95 while their retailer takes in $32.20.[34]

With the late 1990s Asian financial crisis, the situation of Nike workers became even more dire. The *Village Voice* reported that Jeff Ballinger, director of the workers' rights group Press for Change, "would like to see Jordan make good on his pledge to visit factories in Southeast Asia where Michael-endorsed products are manufactured. In a cover story for *ESPN: The Magazine* last April, Jordan said, "I want to go to Southeast Asia to see the Nike plants for myself . . . when basketball is done." Ballinger says that a Jordan visit would highlight the plight of Nike workers in countries like Vietnam and Indonesia that have been hit by the Asian financial crisis. He estimates that: "Nike factory wages in Indonesia have dropped to the equivalent of about $1 a day since the currency crash—while the plummeting value of the rupiah has translated into about $40 million in labor-cost savings for Nike."[35]

While Michael Jordan tries to present himself as the embodiment of all good and wholesome values, he is clearly tainted by his corporate involvements with Nike in the unholy alliance of commerce, sports spectacle, and celebrity. His symbiosis with Nike is so tight, they are so intertwined with each other, that if Nike is tarnished so too is Jordan (and vice versa—which is one of the reasons that Hertz moved so quickly to sever its ties with O. J. Simpson after the discovery of the murder of his former wife Nicole and her friend Ron Goldman). The fate of Nike and Michael Jordan is inextricably intertwined with Nike taking on Jordan to endorse their products early in his career, helping make him a superstar known to everyone, while the Air Jordan product line helped reverse declining sales and helped make Nike an icon of corporate America with a global reach that made Nike products part of the global popular. Thus, whereas Jordan was no doubt embarrassed by all the bad publicity that Nike received in the 1990s, his involvement with the corporation was obviously too deep to "just say no" and sever himself from this symbol of a greedy and exploitative corporation.[36]

THIRD COMING, SEX SCANDALS, AND THE CONTRADICTIONS OF THE SPECTACLE

About a year after his announced retirement in January 1999, Michael Jordan declared on January 12, 2000 that he was returning to basketball as president of operations and part owner of the Washington Wizards, at the time one of the least successful basketball teams in the NBA. The Baltimore Bullets franchise had moved to Washington in 1973 and in 1997 the name was changed to Wizards, allegedly to send out a nonviolent and anti-gangs message to the community, and this semantic shift helped create an image that Michael Jordan could ally himself with.

It appeared that Jordan had new aspirations, to become a successful CEO and major player in the corporate world that he had long admired. Before his retirement, Nike had opened a new high-end shoes and clothing line called "Brand Jordan" and appointed Jordan as CEO. But Jordan had even higher corporate ambitions and, as Sam Walker tells the story, a meeting in October 1999 with former AOL marketing genius Ted Leonsis pointed to the direction of Jordan's aspirations. Leonsis had purchased part ownership of the Washington Wizards and majority ownership of the Washington Capitals NHL hockey team, and obviously had ambitions of a sports empire and wanted Jordan aboard. Jordan in turn dreamed Internet dot.com fantasies and craved connection with the Internet mogul Ted Leonsis of AOL fame.

Indeed, Jordan had already begun efforts to build his own Internet empire and in January 2000 announced the formation of an Internet sporting good site, MVP.com, along with partners retired athletic stars John Elway and Wayne Gretzky. In February, Jordan added Sports.com to his Internet portfolio, a joint venture with Tiger Woods, Shaquille O'Neil, and various venture capitalists. Jordan was also approached to associate himself with an Internet company run by a Chicago software entrepreneur called Divine Interventures that would help organize, run, and produce stock offerings for Internet companies. Jordan announced that when his current string of endorsements expired he would not renew them, and thus it appeared he was on the way to a new career and success as a corporate player and rising Internet business star.

Unfortunately for Jordan, the dot.com boom was coming to a close and although his Internet ventures raised money and got publicity, they failed to yield the golden goose of capital accumulation and Jordan's CEO dreams appeared to be going bust. Jordan broke his promise not to sign any more endorsement contracts when he decided to promote a new Palm Pilot, but this venture also was not a big success. On top of this, the Washington Wizards performed poorly during Jordan's first year as president, and he was criticized for not being hands-on and on the site in Washington with his team.

Hence, around the time of the September 11, 2001 terror attacks, rumors were flying that Jordan was planning to return to the court, making his second major comeback and what could be called a "third coming." On September 25, Jordan formally announced his return, claiming that he would again play because of "his love of the game," a repackaging of a slogan used to promote a book he had done earlier on basketball. Not everyone was pleased that Jordan had chosen to make another comeback. Some, like his good friend Charles Barkley, feared that he might fail, disappointing his fans and letting himself down. Others felt that the NBA needed to cultivate new stars and heroes, and that Jordan should allow them the spotlight and opportunity to fill his shoes. Promoters and advertisers worried about the consequences of a Michael Jordan failure on adversely affecting NBA profits and advertising revenues.[37]

Speculation raged concerning why Jordan had chosen to return to the game. Some believed it was ego and a need to continually challenge himself and succeed. Others thought he needed the adrenaline rush and fix of the game and adulation of the fans. Yet others speculated that it was business that motivated Jordan who believed he could help build up a profitable franchise with his participation and position himself as a key force once again in NBA basketball and the attendant media spectacle. As is often the case, it was probably all these motivations and more that led the by-then thirty-eight year old Jordan to get his aging body back in shape and become once again a professional basketball player.

In the Fall 2001 season, Jordan did return and performed reasonably well. Although he was sluggish in his initial highly publicized game with the fabled New York Knicks, missing crucial last-minute shots and the possibility of hitting the "money" in a close 93–91 loss, Jordan's playing picked up and he turned a losing team into a winning one. Jordan indeed provided a big boost to the sagging fortunes of the NBA, as he sold out almost every game he played in, generated increased television interest, and thus generally helped NBA revenues and image.

In 2002, however, Michael Jordan faced the greatest image crisis and most potentially destructive media spectacle of his career, when his wife Juanita filed for divorce on January 4 citing "irreconcilable differences." There had long been rumors of Jordan's womanizing and tabloids had published stories of women claiming to have had sex with Jordan, but on the whole he had maintained a positive family image. Jordan's initial media figure was that of a squeaky-clean good kid from Carolina who refused to party with the more rowdy Chicago Bulls and who was a devoted son who had appropriated strict family values. In fact, Jordan's closeness to his parents was legendary and his handlers continued to project the image of Jordan as ideal father and husband after he married and had three children. Jordan had continually projected the image of a wholesome family man, an image necessary to secure his lucrative promotions, and to serve as black role model and man of good American values.

Jordan had, in fact, long carried contradictory connotations in the dominant representations of his body and physical activity. Representations of male athletes like Jordan, especially basketball players, present a sexual dimension via images of their physical bodies in a state of undress and as potent and powerful. Jordan also emphasized sensuality in his fragrance ads as an essential part of his being, and his bald head and glistening hard body easily led to appropriation as a sex symbol. Yet Jordan's potentially potent and transgressive sexuality was always contained in the framework of family values and apparent morality.[38]

At the time of the February All-Star game, Jordan was appearing a bit worn, had begun to limp, and was facing injuries that were forcing him to have fluid drained from his right knee. On February 27, Jordan underwent arthroscopic surgery to repair torn knee cartilage. Although the surgery was deemed a success, there was a wealth of speculation concerning whether Jordan's career was finished and although he returned some weeks later, his future was uncertain, adding a spectacle of mortality and bodily wear, tear, and breakdown to the now copious repertoire of Michael Jordan mythologies. Jordan sat out only twelve games after his surgery, returning to play on March 20. He was obviously in great pain, playing only in reserve, and managing a career-low twelve minutes and a career-low two points in a 113–93 loss to the Los Angeles Lakers on April 2. The comeback saga came to a provisional end on April 3 when Jordan announced that he was packing it in for the season, although he hoped to return the next year, for which he had signed on to play, thereby guaranteeing a media circus of speculation as to whether Jordan would or would not be able to play again.[39]

The Third Coming was thus a mixed experience, with Jordan generating his customary excitement, turning a losing team into one that, before his departure at least, had a shot at the play-offs. Jordan himself averaged 22.9 points, the second lowest scoring average of his career, but certainly respectable (he had averaged 22.7 in his second season with the Chicago Bulls in 1985–1986, when he played only eighteen games because of a broken foot; otherwise he rarely missed a game and had not previously missed a game due to injuries since 1992). Although Jordan had some very good moments, it was clear that he could not defeat the unbeatable Father Time and the finitude of an aging body. Hence, Michael Jordan added the spectacle of mortality and aging to his collection of spectacles.

CONTRADICTIONS OF MICHAEL JORDAN

Over the now wide span of a spectacular career, the media figure of Michael Jordan has accumulated highly contradictory representations and effects. While he was a symbol of success in corporate America, his record has been spotty since his 1999 retirement and he has become tarnished with the scandals and negative portrayals of excessive greed, competitiveness, predatory sexuality, and dishonesty. Earlier, Jordan embodied the contradictions of capitalist globalization as he was tainted with the negative images that corporations to whom he had sold himself were fouled, such as Nike's exploitative labor practices, as well as embodying positive images of corporate power and success.

Now Jordan is fated to live out not only the contradictions of corporate global capitalism, but also his own moral contradictions and conflicts. In a sense, these contradictions, as well as his array of successes and failures, make Jordan more remarkable, more human, and in many ways a more engaging and more compelling media spectacle. Michael Jordan the all-American mythology was always something of a fraud and an ideological gloss over the seamy side of corporate business, the sports-entertainment colossus, and inevitable imperfections of a mortal human being. As a bearer of complexity and contradiction, however, Jordan presents the drama of a human life that could evolve in any number of directions, ranging from yet further unforeseen success and greatness to moral abjection and failure.

Although Jordan's contradictions and tensions were somewhat suppressed by his ideological halo, to some extent Jordan always was his own contradictions. The representations of his magical athletic body and his presentation of the body in advertising combined the well-behaved corporate black athlete and endorser with a sexy, powerful, and potentially threatening masculine image. Michael Jordan's combination of athletic prowess and his association with fashion, cologne, and the good life always made him a potential transgressor of bourgeois middle-class family values and propriety. Although Jordan's family values images articulated well with the conservative ethos of the Reagan-Bush I era (1980–1992), there was always an aura of threatening sexuality and masculinity in Jordan as a potentially transgressive figure.

Moreover, in an era of media spectacle, avaricious and competitive media machines are eager to exploit every scandal and weakness of its stars and celebrities, even those like Michael Jordan who have provided so much to so many. It is an irony of media spectacle, however, that what appears as scandal and transgression can augment the power and wealth of the bearer of such negativity. Dennis Rodman built a career on his bad-boy image, and Bill Clinton's popularity seemed to grow with every new revelation of scandal and transgression, although this dialectic is itself complex, overdetermined, and risky in practice.

READING JORDAN CRITICALLY

Jordan thus seems fated to live out the cultural contradictions of contemporary American capitalism and his own personal conflicts, embodying a multifarious mixture of images and mythologies. Since Jordan's spectacle is open and ongoing, and could yield future surprises, critical interrogation of the Jordan effect and of how the media constructs and publics appropriate and live out the Michael Jordan spectacle emerges as an important challenge for a critical cultural studies.

To begin, it could be argued that Jordan represents an overvaluation of sports in contemporary U.S. and indeed global culture. Although it is positive for members of the underclass to have role models and aspirations to better themselves, it is not clear that sports can provide a means to success for any but a few. A revealing 1991 documentary "Michael Jordan's Playground" features a fantasy about a young African-American boy who, like Michael Jordan, had been cut from his school basketball team. Jordan appears to tell the boy, not to give up, to apply himself, and to struggle to make it. The rest of the story interweaves the young boy's hard work with images of Jordan's heroic basketball accomplishments, providing at once a morality tale for youth and a self-glorification of Michael Jordan as role model and teacher of youth as well as basketball deity.

The 1994 Nike-financed campaign P.L.A.Y. that Jordan participated in provided images of antithesis between gangs and sports, urging youth to choose the latter. But this is arguably a false antithesis and there are surely other choices for inner-city and poor youth, such as education, computer skills, or training for a profession. The 1995 documentary *Hoop Dreams* brilliantly documented the failed hopes and illusory dreams of ghetto youth making it in college basketball and the NBA. For most would-be stars, it is a false hope to dream of fame and athletic glory, thus it is not clear that Jordan's "be like Mike" is going to be of much real use to youth. Moreover, the widespread limitation of figures of the black spectacle to sports and entertainment might also contribute to the stereotype, as Kobena Mercer suggests, that blacks are all brawn and no brain, or mere spectacular bodies and not substantive persons.[40] Yet some criticism of Jordan as a basketball player has also circulated. Amidst the accolades after his announced retirement, some negative evaluations emerged of his style and influence on the game. Stating baldly that "I hate Michael Jordan," Jonathan Chait wrote:

> Whenever I declare this in public, I am met with stammering disbelief, as if I had expressed my desire to rape nuns. But I have my reasons. First, he has helped to change the culture of sports from one emphasizing teamwork to one emphasizing individualism. The NBA has contributed to this by promoting superstars ("Come see Charles Barkley take on Hakeem Olajuwan!"), but Jordan buys into it, too. Once he referred to his teammates as his "supporting cast," and in last year's finals he yelled at a teammate for taking a shot in the clutch moments that he, Jordan, should have taken—after his teammate made the shot. The result is a generation of basketball players who don't know or care how to play as a team.[41]

Thus, it is important to read the spectacle of Michael Jordan critically for its multifarious social and political meanings, as well as the wealth of meanings generated by Jordan as sports and race spectacle, and the complexity of his life. Jordan's obsession with wealth, highlighted in Spike Lee's nickname for Jordan ("Money"), circulates capitalist values and ideals, promoting the commercialization of sports and greed which many claim has despoiled the noble terrain of sports. Jordan is the prototypical overachiever, pushing to win at all costs with his eyes on all the possible prizes of the rewards of competition and winning. Yet, so far, Jordan has not assumed the political responsibilities taken on by other athletic idols of his race such as Paul Robeson, Jessie Owens, Joe Louis, Jackie Robinson, or Muhammad Ali. As Kwame Touré put it:

> Any cause he might have championed—from something as morally simple as supporting the candidacy of fellow North Carolinian Harvey Gantt, who lost two close Senate races against Satan's cousin, Jesse Helms, to any stand against any sort of American injustice—would have been taken seriously because it was endorsed by Jordan. Yet as careful as he has been at vacuuming every possible penny into his pocket . . . he has been equally diligent about leaving every bit of political potential on the table. Couldn't the world's greatest endorser have sold us something besides shoes?[42]

Jordan has generally symbolized the decline of politics and replacement of all social values by monetary ones that has characterized the past couple of decades in which he became a major media spectacle of our era. Such issues are relevant in assessing the Jordan effect because superstar celebrities like Michael Jordan mobilize desire into specific role models, ideals of behavior, and values. They produce an active fantasy life whereby individuals dream that they can "be like Mike," to cite the mantra of the Gatorade commercial, and emulate their idol's behavior and values. Thus, part of the Jordan effect is the creation of role models, cultural ideals, values, and modes of behavior. Consequently, critical scrutiny of what sort of values and behavior the Jordan spectacle promotes is relevant to assessing its cultural significance.

In a more somber and serious cultural milieu that is the U.S. after the 9/11 terror attacks, questions arise whether so much celebrity and adulation should be invested in sports figures, who themselves are ever more subject to commercialization and commodification, of which Michael Jordan serves as the model. Understanding how media culture works and generates social meanings and ideologies requires a critical media literacy which empowers individuals and undermines the mesmerizing and manipulative aspects of the media spectacle.[43] Critical cultural studies is thus necessary to help demystify media culture and produce insights into contemporary society and culture. Reflection on the Jordan/Nike nexus reminds us that media culture is one of the sites of construction of the sports-entertainment colossus and of the icons of contemporary society. Media culture is also the stage in which our social conflicts unfold and our social reality is constructed, so that the ways that the dynamics of gender, race, class, and dominant values are played out is crucial for the construction of individual and society in contemporary culture. Since Michael Jordan embodies crucial dynamics of media culture, it is important to understand how the Jordan spectacle functions, its manifold and contradictory effects, and the ways that the Jordan sports-entertainment spectacle embodies social meanings and circulates multiple Jordan effects. Significantly, the Michael Jordan adventure is not yet over and his figure remains a source of fascination that should evoke evaluative inquiry by critical cultural studies and social theory.

NOTES

1. On the China and Bosnia references, see Dan McGraw and Mike Tharp, "Going out on top," *U.S. News and World Report* (January 25, 1999): 55. Summing up Jordan's achievements, Jerry Crowe writes: "His resume includes five most-valuable-player awards, twelve All-Star appearances, two Olympic gold medals and a worldwide popularity that filled arenas and boosted the stock of the companies with which he was affiliated," *Los Angeles Times,* January 13, 1999, p. D1. In addition, Jordan garnered six NBA championship rings, ten NBA scoring titles (a record); a 31.5 regular-season scoring average (best all-time), a record 63 points in a playoff game, 5,987 career playoff points (best all time), and made the game-winning shot a record twenty-six times during his NBA career.

2. Halberstam, quoted in *People,* January 25, 1999, p. 56. In its front page story on Jordan's retirement, *USA Today* employed three "greats," five "greatests," one "greatness," two "marvelouses," three "extraordinarys," one "unbelievable," one "unmatched," two "awe-inspirings," two "staggerings," one "superstar," and a superhybolic "great superstar," *Sports Illustrated* (January 25, 1999): 32.

3. Walter LaFeber, *Michael Jordan and the New Global Capitalism* (New York: W. W. Norton and Co. 1999), 15; David Halberstam, *Playing for Keeps: Michael Jordan and the World He Made* (New York: Random House, 1999), 4.

4. ABC bought ESPN in 1985 and its official website states that ESPN now "doesn't stand for anything, but the story is this . . . when ESPN started in 1979 we were the Entertainment and Sports Programming Network (thus, ESPN). However, the full name was dropped in February 1985 when the company adopted a new corporate name—ESPN, Inc.—and a new logo. We are a subsidiary of ABC, Inc., which is a wholly owned subsidiary of The Walt Disney Co. The Hearst Corporation has a 20 percent interest in ESPN." The connection with Disney and Hearst signify how sports has become absorbed into the infotainment society and is a crucial part of a globalized entertainment/sports colossus.

5. David Andrews, "The (Trans)National Basketball Association: America's Commodity Sign Culture and Global Localization," in A. Cvetovitch and D. Kellner, eds., *Articulating the Global and the Local: Globalization and Cultural Studies* (Boulder, CO: Westview Press, 1997); LaFeber, *Michael Jordan.* See also, Andrews, "The Fact(s) of Michael Jordan's Blackness: Excavating a Floating Racial

Signifier." *Sociology of Sport Journal,* 13, 2 (1996): 125–158; Andrews, et al. "Jordanscapes: A Preliminary Analysis of the Global Popular," *Sociology of Sport Journal,* 13: 4 (1996), 428–57.

6. Halberstam quoted Jeff Coplon, "The Best. Ever, Anywhere." *The New York Times Magazine.* April 21, 1996, quote on p. 35.

7. Halberstam, *Playing for Keeps,* 7.

8. LaFeber, *Michael Jordan.*

9. Falk quoted in Lynn Hirschberg "The Big Man Can Deal," *The New York Times Magazine,* November 17, 1996, pp. 46–51, 62–5, 77–8, 82, 88 (quote on p. 46). On Falk's role in promoting the Jordan spectacle, see Halberstam, Playing for Keeps, 136ff. With Jordan, basketball players began being promoted as entertainment stars and were becoming top dog icons of the spectacle and major corporate endorsers.

10. *USA Today,* October 14, 1996: p. 6B.

11. *Time* (July 29, 1996): 61; *The Guardian,* June 11, 1996, p. 6.

12. Cheryl L. Cole, "American Jordan: P.L.A.Y., Consensus, and Punishment," *Sociology of Sport Journal,* 13, 4 (1996): 366–97.

13. For the complex events that led Jordan to this seemingly bizarre decision, see Sam Smith, *Second Coming: The Strange Odyssey of Michael Jordan—from Courtside to Home Plate and Back Again.* (New York: HarperCollins 1995); Halberstam, *Playing for Keeps.* During 1993, Jordan's gambling habits were criticized and increasingly the subject of inquiry, and when his father was mysteriously murdered there were speculations that the murder was related to gambling debts. The NBA and media intensified its scrutiny of Jordan, and he abruptly quit basketball to pursue a quixotic and failed minor league baseball career, returning to professional basketball eighteen months later to achieve his greatest athletic triumphs.

14. Coplon, "The Best Ever, Anywhere."

15. Halberstam, *Playing for Keeps.*

16. Cole, "American Jordan."

17. Susan Jeffords, *Hard Bodies: Hollywood Masculinity in the Reagan Era* (New Brunswick, NJ: Rutgers University Press, 1994).

18. Football star O. J. Simpson preceded Jordan as an African-American icon who crossed the color line in the world of celebrity endorsements.

19. The claim that Jordan transcended race frequently appeared in interviews upon Jordan's retirement by Mark Vancil who edited the *Rare Air* Jordan photography books, and it has been regularly repeated by commentators since the mid-1990s. Frank Deford argued in the *Sports Illustrated* collector's issue published after Jordan's retirement that Jordan is not "a creature of color" and transcends the racial divisions that have so sundered U.S. society. Matthew DeBord has written that Jordan is "trans-racial, the first African American cultural hero to massively evade blaxploitation by rising above it, elevating to a zone of rarefied commerce where the only pigment that anyone worries about is green." See his "Children of the Jordan Age," *Feed* (January 1999): www.feedmag.com/essay/esl67.shtml. At times in Jordan's reception, this transcendence of race appears to be taking place, but such claims ignore the negative press of 1993 and the fact that African-Americans celebrities can easily become whipping boys as well as poster boys. For a more nuanced analysis of the stages of Jordan's racial signification, see David Andrews, *Michael Jordan, Inc.: Corporate Sport, Media Culture and Late Modern America* (Albany: State University of New York Press, 2001). For a critique of the oft-cited claim that Jordan transcends race, see the article by Leon E. Wynter, "The Jordan Effect: What's race got to do with it?" *Salon* (January 29, 1999).

20. See Norman K. Denzin, "More Rare Air: Michael Jordan on Michael Jordan," *Sociology of Sport Journal,* 13:4 (1996): 319–324; Lauren Berlant, *The Anatomy of National Fantasy.* (Chicago: University of Chicago Press, 1994); Cole, "American Jordan"; Andrews, "The Fact(s) of Michael Jordan's Blackness," in Kellner and Andrews 1996; Brian Wilson and Robert Sparks, " 'It's Gotta Be the Shoes': Youth, Race, and Sneaker Commercials." *Sociology of Sport Journal,* 13:4 (1996): 428–57.

21. Andrews, "The Fact(s) of Michael Jordan's Blackness"; Henry Giroux, *Disturbing Pleasures* (New York: Routledge, 1994).

22. Coplon, "The Best Ever, Anywhere," 37.

23. For fuller development of this concept of a black aesthetic, see Todd Boyd, "Hoopology 101: Professor Todd Boyd deconstructs the game." *LA Weekly,* May 23–29, 1997, p. 49. See also, Todd Boyd, *Am I Black Enough for You? Popular Culture From the 'Hood and Beyond* (Bloomington, IN: Indiana University Press, 1997).

24. Of course, Malcolm X, Martin Luther King and the civil rights movement did more to dramatize and ameliorate the plight of African Americans, but I would argue that sports and entertainment helped significantly to promote the interests of blacks. Moreover, I believe that the tremendous achievements of black athletes, music performers, and entertainers were essential in getting mainstream America to accept and respect blacks and to

allow them into the mainstream—in however limited and problematic a fashion.

25. Although the problem of sexual abuse in the church had been festering for years, the issue emerged in media focus for the first time in 2002; abusers were by and large white men. On the demonization of black figures in contemporary media culture, See Michael Dyson, *Reflecting Black* (Minneapolis: University of Minnesota Press, 1993); Earl Ofari Hutchinson, *Beyond O. J.: Race, Sex, and Class Lessons for America* (Los Angeles: Middle Passages Press, 1996).

26. Jack E. White, "Stepping Up to the Plate," *Time*, March 31, 1997, p. 90.

27. Todd Boyd, "Hoopology 101."

28. Jordan quoted in Bob Herbert, "Nike's Pyramid Scheme," *The New York Times*, June 10, 1996, p. A19.

29. David Harvey, *The Condition of Postmodernity* (Oxford: Basil Blackwell, 1989).

30. Cynthia Enloe, "The Globetrotting Sneaker." *Ms.* (March/April, 1995): 12.

31. Gayle Kirshenbaum, "Nike's Nemesis," *Ms.* (November/December 1996): 23; William Greider, "The Global Sweatshop." *Rolling Stone* (June 30, 1994): 43–4.

32. *New York Times*, March 31, 1997, p. A16.

33. *New York Times*, March 25, 1997. For a detailed critique of Young's report, see the study by Stephen Grass, "Blood, Sweat and Shears: The Young and the Feckless," *New Republic* 1997.

34. See Herbert, "Nike's Pyramid Scheme"; Enloe, "The Globetrotting Sneaker," 13.

35. *Jockbeat*, January 20–26, 1999.

36. Andrews, "The Fact(s) of Michael Jordan's Blackness."

37. Doubters included sportswriters Bill Plaschke, "From Air Jordan to Err Jordan" (Los Angeles Times, September, 11, 2001): pp. D1 and 6; Allen Barra, "Air Ball: Michael Jordan's Rumored Return to the Court Sounds like a Great Idea for the NBA. It Isn't" *Salon*, April 18, 2001; and Mark Hyman, "Betting That His Airness Will Soar Again," *Business Week*, October 8, 2001.

38. Mary G. McDonald's study "Safe Sex Symbol? Michael Jordan and the Politics of Representation" in Andrews, ed. *Michael Jordan, Inc*, 153–74, written before the 2002 Jordan sex scandals, adroitly lays out the contradictions between Jordan's sexual and potentially transgressive black male body and the ideology of family values and morality with which he has packaged his product.

39. Michael Jordan's website in April 2002 featured an *Associated Press* story headlined "Pollin Says Jordan Will Return" (April 9, 2002), claiming that the owner of the Washington Wizards said he expects Michael Jordan to return next season "and that his comeback was a 'great success,' even though a knee injury cut short his season." But Washington Wizards Coach Doug Collins stated that he would be "surprised" if Jordan returned; see Steve Wyche, "Collins Wary of Jordan's Return to Wizards Next Year," *Washington Post*, March 28, 2002, p. D1.

40. Kobena Mercer, *Welcome to the Jungle: New Positions in Black Cultural Studies* (London and New York: Routledge, 1994).

41. Jonathan Chait, "I Hate Michael Jordan," *Slate*, January 19, 1999.

42. For a probing comparison of Paul Robeson and Michael Jordan, see C. Keith Harrison, "From Paul Robeson to Althea Gibson to Michael Jordan: Images of Race Relations and Sport" in Andrews, *Michael Jordan, Inc*, vii–xii. See also *Village Voice*, January 27–February 4, 1999.

43. Douglas Kellner, *Media Culture* (London and New York: Routledge, 1995).

17

THE ANATOMY OF SCIENTIFIC RACISM

Racialist Responses to Black Athletic Achievement

Patrick B. Miller

IN THE LATE 1940S, a highly regarded critic for the *New York Times* wrote that the modern dance revolution had opened the way for black Americans to find themselves as "creative artists." The widespread embrace of new choreographic styles had enabled them, John Martin asserted, to "release in communicative essence the uninhibited qualities of the racial heritage, no matter what the immediate subject of any specific dance might be." Martin's survey text (republished in 1963 and in 1970) ranged over a large number of themes. But what stood out, from first version to last, was the chapter "The Negro Dance," with its persistent references to the "intrinsic" and the "innate." One feature of the Negro dancer, Martin insisted, "is his uniquely racial rhythm":

> Far more than just a beat, it includes a characteristic phrase, manifested throughout the entire body and originating sometimes so far from its eventual point of outlet as to have won the description of "lazy. . . . Closely allied to this pervasive rhythm is the wide dynamic range of his movement itself, with, at one extreme, vigor and an apparently inexhaustible energy (though, be it noted, a minimum of tension), and at the other extreme, a rich command of relaxation.[1]

For all their contributions to jazz and modern dance, Martin declared, African Americans had been "wise" not to take up academic ballet, "for its wholly European outlook, history and technical theory are alien to [them] culturally, temperamentally and anatomically." He went on:

> In practice there is a racial constant, so to speak, in the proportions of the limbs and torso and the conformation of the feet, all of which affect body placement; in addition, the deliberately maintained erectness of the European dancer's spine is in marked contrast to the fluidity of the Negro dancer's, and the latter's natural concentration of movement in the pelvic region is similarly at odds with European usage.[2]

If other commentators have advanced less meticulous formulations than Martin's, they have unselfconsciously—but no less emphatically—stacked value judgments upon matters of "scientific" measurement without addressing either the segregation and racial prejudice that largely contributed to the development of distinctive social customs and expressive cultural practices or the hard work, discipline, and creativity that distinguish artistic innovations irrespective of color or culture.

Indeed, by underscoring "a minimum of tension" or "a rich command of relaxation" among black performers, many white intellectuals like Martin have surveyed an enormous distance between what has been studied, which those image makers exalted for a particular conciseness, cleverness, and formality, and what they believed to inhere and thus could disparage as free or flowing or loose. At one level, references to the "pelvic region" derive from an expansive European and U.S. literature that has reduced racial and cultural difference to matters of sexuality. At another, the insistent contrast between mind and body within the Western tradition renders black physicality as a kind of compensation for the absence of cerebral qualities and the traits of a purportedly advanced, or advancing, culture.[3]

Beginning in the early nineteenth century, the distinctions that eventually found their way into Martin's appraisals were becoming central elements of what was considered pioneering scholarship in anthropology as well as the "scientific" study of history, helping to define Western notions of civilization. Critically, an observation concerning the "natural concentration of movement" of African Americans, when contrasted to the ideal of "European usage," was meant to reinforce a longstanding hierarchy of values and standards, with the cultural achievements of the Continent at its head. Long before Martin measured the "uniquely racial rhythm" of jazz dancers against the accomplishments of ballerinas, to differentiate was for many European-American commentators to denigrate. When African-American artists and athletes pursued excellence within the boundaries of Western aesthetic and agonistic traditions, they encountered more than customary biases and myriad discriminatory acts. They confronted a discourse of difference, which, inscribed as a set of "racial constants," effectively discounted the efforts of black Americans or denied the cultural significance of their achievements.

Ultimately, this particular dimension of the politics of culture has engaged a vast scholarship that ranges far beyond the history of racial relations in the United States. Within one frame of analysis, the origins and development of the discourse of difference have been examined specifically with regard to the Nazi eugenic theories that finally marked Jews and gypsies, as well as homosexuals, for extermination. Such cultural boundary marking has also been assessed with consideration of the linkages between gender and race in the construction of hierarchies of privilege and subordination over time. As scholars of postcolonial ideology and experience have demonstrated, furthermore, the ranking of racial traits—especially as it has elaborated the dichotomy between mind and body—continues to serve as a means of suppressing the claims of people of color around the world. What remains is the relationship between the pseudoscience of racial difference and the pernicious social policies it both inspires and informs.[4]

It is significant, then, that even those who endeavor to expose and thus dispose of the cultural hierarchies predicated on the tired old versions of ethnicity and race have lately become involved in earnest and extensive debates over Charles Murray and Richard Herrnstein's *The Bell Curve,* an elaborate ranking of so-called racial and ethnic groups in terms of IQ—with African Americans at the bottom of the list. Scholars have also felt compelled to address the claims made by Dinesh D'Souza, who in *The End of Racism,* has gone so far as to describe the civilizing and Christianizing effects of slavery on the majority of blacks in the United States.[5] In such instances, progressive writers and educators must still regularly engage the persistent stereotypes concerning the "natural" physical abilities of blacks, which are said to explain the "dominance" of African Americans in sports such as basketball and football.

To account for achievement in biologically essentialist terms effectively discounts the traits identified with "character": discipline, courage, sacrifice. And therein lies the significance of inquiries into racial science when they have been applied to athletics.[6] Ultimately, the questions of who can run faster or jump higher are simplistic, but they are pernicious as well as foolish if conceived as measures of innate racial difference. In light of this ongoing cultural dynamic, John Martin's observations not only help us understand the anatomy of racialist thinking in historical terms. Their similarity to more recent comments reminds us of the persistence of "academic" racism in contemporary American society.

Since "race matters," as the title of one of Cornel West's recent books avows, we need to discuss not only why it should but when it should not—in judgments of individual abilities and accomplishments. With regard to the historical construction of racial categories, we ought to consider that the *body* continues to loom large in many people's thinking about difference. TV sports reports often provide the most obvious marker of distinctions associated with race and ethnicity. In basketball, the trope of the white point guard—court savvy, disciplined, and controlled—has stood in striking contrast to prevailing images of black male athletes, able and all too willing to shatter backboards with their slam dunks. And if that juxtaposition appears too stark and simple—in light of the widespread recognition of what was Michael Jordan's mastery, not just of the mechanics of his game, but also of modern media techniques—we can turn to the lecture hall. "I don't know whether or not most white men can jump," the historian of science Stephen Jay Gould wrote during *The Bell Curve* controversy:

> And I don't much care, although I suppose that the subject bears some interest and marginal legitimacy in an alternate framing that avoids such biologically meaningless categories as white and black. Yet I can never give a speech on the subject of human diversity without attracting some variant of this inquiry in the subsequent question period. I hear the 'sports version,' I suppose, as an acceptable surrogate for what really troubles people of good will (and bad, although for other reasons).[7]

The "sports version" of human diversity, still placing population groups up and down a vertical axis of accomplishment, suggests another significant topic. Without discussing the economic and educational practices that mark "racial" distinctions in the United States, without examining the concepts of whiteness and blackness in cultural terms, and without recognizing the facts of mixed heritage, most racialist formulations have had as their objective the demonstration of African-American inferiority, for example, on intelligence tests. But judgments about culture or ideologies of success also come in response to *black achievement*. Frequently, in reaction to triumphs by African Americans, we hear explanations that qualify excellence fashioned out of the notion of "natural ability."

When African Americans began to register an increasing number of victories on the playing fields during the first decades of the twentieth century, mainstream commentators abandoned the athletic creed that linked physical prowess, manly character, and the best features of American civilization. Although many African Americans had subscribed to the ideal that achievement in sport constituted a proof of equality, a mechanism of assimilation, and a platform for social mobility, the recognition successful black athletes actually received from many educators and journalists explained away their prowess by stressing black anatomical and physiological advantages or legacies from a primitive African past.[8]

Many academicians, beginning in the mid-nineteenth century, thus turned away from the discourse of culture when interpreting the physical talents of blacks—and other Others. As they became engrossed in the "scientific" analysis of racial difference, various anthropologists and anthropometrists reached for their calipers and tape measures in search of a gastrocnemius muscle with a certain diameter or of an elongated heel bone in order to explain the success of certain sprinters or jumpers. In the dominant discourse, an individual's performance was bound to attributes ascribed to the group of his or her origin. Such a racialized view of excellence defined the physical accomplishments of Europeans in terms of diligence and forethought, the application of the mind to the movements of the body, while it framed the achievements of people of color with words such as "natural" and "innate." Ultimately, then, racialized responses to the athletic as well as the artistic accomplishments of blacks have served both to shape and reinforce prevailing stereotypes. In so doing, they have also served to rationalize exclusionary social practices and discriminatory public policies.

THE HISTORY OF RACIAL RANKING

The construction of racial typologies can be traced in general terms to Aristotle's attempt to justify slavery. Pictorial representations of Africans dating back to Greek antiquity, as well as the patterns of thought that shaped the characterization of Caliban and Othello, for instance, undergird modern European racism. Such images speak to a lengthy history of racial boundary marking and the color coding of culture. Yet it is in the mid nineteenth-century writings of Joseph Arthur, Comte de Gobineau, that many scholars perceive the racist ideologies that first alluded to measurable distinctions and pretended to scientific objectivity. In *The Inequality of Human Races* (1853–1855), Gobineau asked: "Is there an inequality in physical strength?" His answer, according to the intellectual historian Elazar Barkan "mixed aristocratic pessimism, romanticism, theology together with biology, all of which became part of a shared European value system based on racial differentiation."[9] "The American savages, like the Hindus, are certainly our inferiors in this respect, as are also the Australians. The Negroes, too, have less muscle power; and all these people are infinitely less able to bear fatigue."[10]

Gobineau's observations, which extended to three printed volumes, leapt from individual display to the characteristics defining a group, thus exposing powerful exceptions to exceedingly flimsy generalizations. The anthropology devoted to the ranking of peoples nevertheless had enormous influence, not despite but because of the inconsistencies in the criteria it used to render innate and immutable distinctions between population groups. What Gobineau implicitly promulgated was a bipartite notion of culture: the Western tradition involved social developments and creativity; the accomplishments of non-Western peoples derived from natural selection and genetics. If, for those who succeeded Gobineau as taxonomists of culture, Shakespeare and Beethoven illustrated European civilization, then Darwin and Galton explained all the rest. Ultimately, the African or the African American could not win within such a framework, not even on the playing fields.[11]

Such assertions about European superiority, as strained as they were, also constituted arguments for white supremacy. The ideology of empire thus incorporated the so-called feeble races into elaborate systems of hard labor: the institution of slavery in the United States and colonial workforces elsewhere around the world. Stamina, therefore—as a kind of brutish endurance, the ability to "bear fatigue"—would ultimately be conceived as a trait characterizing subject peoples who would work on the plantations and in the mines that fed, clothed, and enriched imperialism. Yet, at the same time, persistence—the exaltation of hard work and steady accumulation—also stood as a key feature of nineteenth-century interpretations of the rise of modern civilization; bourgeois values and the doctrine of possessive individualism extolled toil over time above the heroic acts conventionally associated with generals and kings. To render this cruel paradox in somewhat different terms: the supposed hardihood characterizing people of color was used to justify the exploitation of their labor. Simultaneously, the cultivation of hardihood, as suggested by exhortations to the strenuous life from Theodore Roosevelt in the United States and his counterparts across the North Atlantic, was intended to (re)invigorate various imperial elites. Neither the ideologues like Gobineau nor the imperialists they informed ever addressed the illogic of these patterns of thought, which only begins to suggest the contingency and opportunism of such putatively "scientific" formulations.[12]

At the turn of the century, standard reference books continued to include broad generalizations about racial difference based on observations and measurements. Under the subject heading "Negro," the canonical *Encyclopaedia Britannica* of 1895 distinguished between cranial capacities (an average European, 45 ounces; Negro, 35; highest gorilla, 20) and underscored a differential development of the cranial sutures wherein the "premature ossification of the skull" was said to account for the intellectual limitations of blacks. Significantly, such prematurity was said to result in "the inherent mental inferiority of the blacks, an inferiority which is even more marked than their physical differences."[13] Later versions of these notations would accentuate the so-called primitive features of the Negro physiognomy in order to explain the relative failure of African Americans—in the aggregate—on intelligence tests. Such references would also inform the doctrine of racial eugenics as it was elaborated on both sides of the Atlantic.[14]

By 1900, however, another dimension of scientific racism could be discerned. Rather than simply reinforce prevailing notions of Negro inferiority, experts felt compelled to account for the extraordinary achievements of some black athletes. In the face of an increasing number of victories posted by African Americans, the mainstream culture began to *qualify* the meanings of excellence in sport. The *Encyclopaedia Britannica* had described "the abnormal length of the arm, which in the erect position sometimes reaches the knee-pan, and which on an average exceeds that of the Caucasian by about two inches," and "the low instep, divergent and somewhat prehensile great toe, and heel projection backwards ('lark heel')." Increasingly, these specifications would be advanced as reasons for black success in sports. Thus, in 1901 the champion sprint cyclist Marshall "Major" Taylor was X-rayed, as well as measured up and down by a number of French medical anthropologists, in an effort to reveal the source of his triumphs in the velodrome. In similar terms, comment on the speed of the black Olympian John Taylor, and on the prepossessing strength of the heavyweight champion boxer Jack Johnson a few years later, included "scientific" speculation.

Throughout the twentieth century, it would often be the accomplishments of people of color in the realm of sport that particularly vexed and intimidated those who endeavored to defend a long-standing racial hierarchy. The response would not be subtle. Indeed, the Western discourse of racial difference carefully juxtaposed black athletic achievement—assessed in terms of compensation—to the supposed intellectual disabilities or cultural shortcomings of African Americans.

Critically, the initial forays into the anthropometry of athletic difference were expounded against the backdrop of increasing segregation in the United States, which involved—beyond the enforcement of Jim Crow in housing, transportation, and education—the exclusion of the vast majority of African-American ballplayers, jockeys, and boxers from mainstream sporting competitions. The cyclist Major Taylor, for instance, competed when he could in Europe and Australia because of the hostility he encountered at home. Hypocrisy was piled upon paradox when those who spoke for the dominant culture began to contrast the alarming vitality of African Americans (as well as immigrant newcomers to the United States) to the alleged degeneration of Anglo-America. Such works as Madison Grant's *The Passing of the Great Race* and Lothrop Stoddard's *The Rising Tide of Color against White World Supremacy* reflected nearly hysterical feelings about the links between demography and democracy. Vaguely informed by statistical data, such discussions of the relative birthrates among the Mayflower descendants, the sons and daughters of the shtetl, and those who were moving from southern farms to northern cities revealed a deep fear about the claims black Americans and "hyphenated" Americans might well make against hallowed ideals such as equality and opportunity.[15]

Black leaders like W. E. B. Du Bois—alongside the guiding lights of the new immigrant groups—did indeed seek full participation in the social, economic, and political mainstream, though they demanded fairness not merely as a measure of their numbers but on the basis of their contributions to American culture. And according to the "muscular assimilationists" among them, there was no better argument for inclusion than success in the "national" pastimes. Major Taylor and Jack Johnson were not the first African Americans to make their mark in sports, and it was clear to racial reformers that they would not be the last to tread "the hard road to glory." Well before the appearance of Joe Louis and Jesse Owens in the 1930s, and a decade later, of Jackie Robinson, black leaders saw in athletics a platform for social change.[16]

Resistance to such assertions was formidable, however. Those who would maintain Jim Crow guarded the portals of the stadium just as they stood at the schoolhouse door. Others reinforced racial hierarchy by constructing elaborate frameworks to distinguish between the laurels won by whites and blacks in sport. During the interwar period, anatomy and physiology were frequently invoked to explain the athletic success of African Americans, circumscribing declarations that prowess in contests of speed, strength, and stamina bespoke fitness for other realms of endeavor. In the idiom of sports, to deny the correspondence between athletics and other accomplishments (more profound and long-standing), numerous mainstream commentators "moved the goal posts."

By the 1930s, generalizations from individual performances to group characteristics dominated many descriptions of black prizefighters, such as the heavyweight champion

Joe Louis. Likewise, to account for the medals won by the sprinters Eddie Tolan and Ralph Metcalfe during the 1932 Olympics and by Jesse Owens, Metcalfe, and many other African-American champions at the Berlin Games of 1936, white commentators insisted that black success derived from innate biological advantages. Early in the decade, E. Albert Kinley—whose claim to expertise was that he was an X-ray specialist—repeated the canard about the elongated heel bone, then predicted more world records for African Americans in events that depended on a certain kind of anatomical leverage. Working from a similar premise, Eleanor Metheny, a well-known physical educator, conducted a number of studies on body proportions. Though somewhat guarded in her conclusions, she asserted that kinesiological differences—in the movements generated by individuals with longer legs and narrower hips, for instance—could account for black dominance in sport. Significantly, and ultimately ironically, Metheny would declare that a different, somehow deficient chest construction, as well as lower breathing capacity among blacks, handicapped them in endurance events such as distance running. In David Wiggins's apt phrase, "great speed but little stamina" became the watchword for many white commentators on black athletics. In formulations repeated both in scholarly journals and the popular press, the science of sport further insinuated itself into the broader history of racism in the United States.[17]

If experiments like those conducted by Metheny were as flawed in their conception as in their conclusions, other writers appeared just as intent on defending myths of Anglo-Saxon or Aryan superiority. "It was not long ago," wrote the track-and-field coach Dean Cromwell in 1941, "that his [the black athlete's] ability to sprint and jump was a life-and-death matter to him in the jungle. His muscles are pliable, and his easygoing disposition is a valuable aid to the mental and physical relaxation that a runner and jumper must have." The attempt thus to "historicize" racial difference in sport revealed a significant strand of popular thought. To invoke an African past, the primitive Other, a state-of-being predicated solely on physical prowess, was literally to denigrate what flowed from it. By extension, it was also to exalt its presumed obverse—civilization and the attributes of the dominant order.[18]

Cromwell's interpretation was a curious notion of nature and culture at odds. It imagined that when blacks in Africa had been off running and hunting, the ancestors of white athletes were composing symphonies and building cathedrals, which placed their descendants at a substantial disadvantage at the modern-day Olympics. If the black athlete's "easy-going disposition" lay at or near the center of his success, then again by contrast, white competitors may have been thwarted from starting blocks to finish line by their particular worries about the fate of Western civilization.

Such luridly imagined observations as Cromwell's never stood alone or without amplification. In the ensuing years, black athleticism fell prey to the Harvard anthropologist Carleton S. Coon, who began his commentary on the inherited advantages of African Americans in sport with a depiction of their slender calves and loose jointedness. But what started with anatomy ended with a striking analogy, as was so often the case with racial scientists. The biological features that suited African Americans for certain sports, Coon declared, were characteristic of "living things (cheetahs, for instance) known for their speed and leaping ability." Two later chroniclers of the history of college football continued to rely on gross stereotype, though they had relocated their analogies from the African jungle to the American palladium. "Because of their tap-dancer sense of rhythm and distinctive leg conformation, blacks excel as sprinters," John McCallum and Charles Pearson averred. "It follows naturally that on the football field they stand out as broken field runners."[19] The links between these comments and the discriminations advanced by the dance critic John Martin are unmistakable.

After midcentury, racial science often focused on the triumph of black athletes in the track-and-field events of the Olympic Games. The stopwatch and the tape measure seemed to offer a certain validation to the claims of the hereditarians that significant and fixed anatomical and physiological differences accounted for the medals won by black Americans in the sprints and jumps. But then, rather suddenly, racial commentators were confronted by the stellar efforts and world records of African distance runners. On the heels of successive gold medal performances in the marathon, steeplechase, and 10,000-meter race by competitors from Ethiopia and Kenya during the 1960s, the notion of fast-twitch and slow-twitch muscle fibers—which had for a time been used to distinguish between the speed of blacks and the stamina of whites—was displaced as a frame of analysis. Substituted for it were assertions that strove to mark differences between East-African and West-African physiques, long and lithe versus compact and muscular. From the vantage not so much of a later era but of a different ideological stance, this swift shift in explanations suggests that the persistence of scientific racism lay not so much in the consistency of the science but in the constancy of its racism.

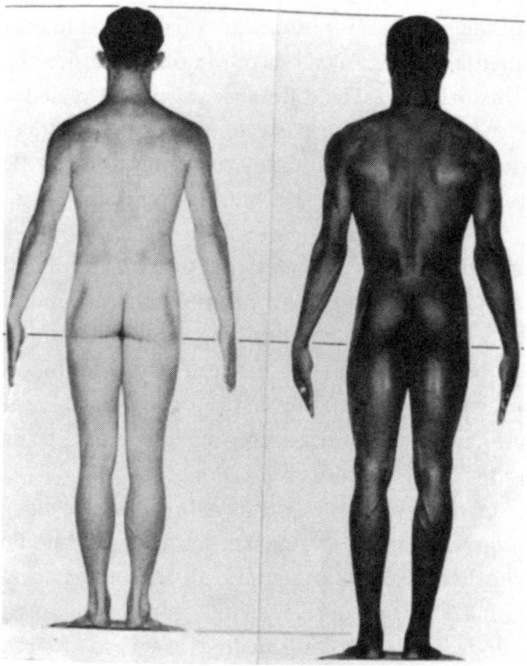

Figure 17–1

"Comparison of White and Negro competitors in the same event [400-meters], with the photographs enlarged so both have the same sitting height (actually head-to-buttock distance)." J. M. Tanner, *The Physique of the Olympic Athlete*. This study of 137 track and field athletes at the 1960 Rome Olympics did not formally assert a correlation between physique and performance, but it dwelled on racial differences in limb structure, proportion, and size.

At odds with such racially essentialist notions, an increasing emphasis on cultural interpretations of African-American success in sports characterized the social science of sport as well as mainstream journalism. A five-part series by Charles Maher in the *Los Angeles Times,* March 24–29, 1968, that surveyed current biological studies of black athletic performance concluded that hard training and motivational factors accounted for the increasing success of African-American athletes. Mainstream sociological opinion had begun to yield the same conclusions.[20] These were noteworthy developments whose stress on black struggle and triumph within the boundaries marked by the athletic establishment reflected the growing influence of the civil rights movement and its integrationist appeal.

Still, the (bio)logic of athletic taxonomy remained largely in place. Indeed, it received its most thorough exposition in 1971 when *Sports Illustrated* published Martin Kane's "An Assessment of 'Black is Best,' " a survey of expert commentary on racial difference and athletic achievement intended to be impressive in its range. In fact, the findings of assorted anatomists and the observations of a number of successful athletes overwhelmed other perspectives. The article ignored historical and sociological considerations of discrimination on the playing fields and beyond. Conversely, it failed to discuss the notion that athletics offered a platform for social mobility or a move from margins to mainstream for many who were acutely aware of their outsider or minority status. Despite a slight qualification here and there, Kane's main point was ultimately that "physical differences in the races might well have enhanced the athletic potential of the Negro in certain events."[21]

RESPONSES TO THE RACIAL "SCIENTISTS"

References to innate athletic differences between population groups persisted well beyond the era of desegregation in sport. But such ways of thinking have also provoked a variety of reactions, often passionate and profound, from black Americans. From Du Bois at the turn of the century to educators and athletes such as Harry Edwards and Arthur Ashe in our own time, most African-American commentators have objected to the use of stereotype and the misuse of science to distinguish the accomplishments of black and white athletes. Urgently and insistently, many intellectuals and activists in the civil rights movement have asserted that the claims made by excellent black athletes against the mainstream rhetoric of equality and opportunity have stood for the larger aspirations of Afro-America. They have also drawn upon the findings of numerous physical scientists and social scientists, who have disproved the allegations of biodeterminism and dismissed the idea of legacies from a primitive past.

During the early years of the century Du Bois enlisted a new generation of anthropologists led by Franz Boas to refute the tenets of scientific racism. In 1906, at the invitation of Du Bois, Boas delivered a paper titled "The Health and Physique of the Negro American" at the eleventh annual Atlanta University Conference. Emphasizing the significance of culture in perceived racial differences, he was instrumental in prompting young African-American scholars, such as Zora Neale Hurston, to undertake research in black folklore and culture. Through the first half of the century, Boasians were popular speakers on the campuses of historically black colleges. The environmentalism embraced by an increasing number of social scientists in the ensuing years seemed to remove black athletic accomplishment from the shaky anthropometrical foundations first advanced by ideologues like

Gobineau and to place excellence in sport, for instance, within the sturdier frames of analysis that address social circumstance and cultural innovation.[22]

At the same time, biological scientists also challenged the generalizations based on anthropometry. Few if any offered findings more emphatic or timely than the African-American scholar W. Montague Cobb. Drawing on his experiments in physiology and anatomy, particularly his biopsies of the muscle tissue of Jesse Owens during the late 1930s, Cobb assailed the proposition that specific biological determinants could account for black athletic success. With reference to the prevailing classification systems, the Howard University professor declared without equivocation that the "Negroid type of calf, foot, and heel bone" could not be found in the Olympic champion; if anything, Cobb asserted, the diameter of Owens's gastrocnemius conformed to "the caucasoid type rather than the negroid."[23]

In professional as well as popular journals, Cobb extended his analysis in important ways. He was neither the first scientist, nor the last, to underscore the salience of physical variations *within* population groups as well as between them. Nevertheless, he discussed that notion within the context of sporting accomplishment and thus engaged, at an early date, the athletic typologies then in place. What is more, Cobb indicated his clear sense that racial mixing subverted any assertion about fixed and isolated genetic determinants of muscular or mental prowess. Howard Drew had been a co-record holder in the 100-yard-dash and the first black sprinter to be acclaimed "the world's fastest human," Cobb noted

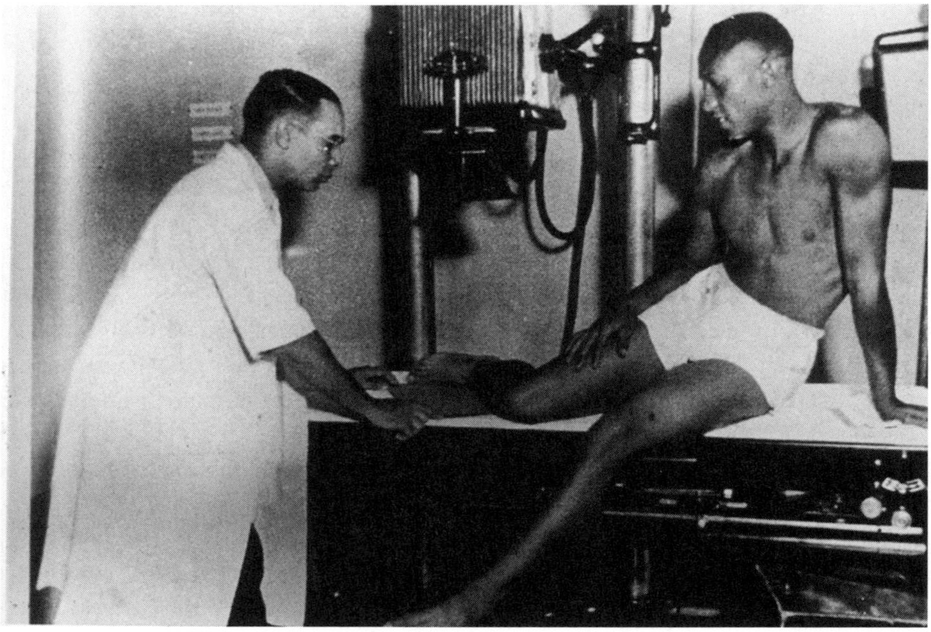

Figure 17–2
Responding to myriad assertions about racial differences in calf size and the formation of the heel bone, W. Montague Cobb—noted Howard University anatomist and physical anthropologist—undertook anthropometric measurements of the great black sprinter Jesse Owens. In the words of historian David Wiggins, Cobb sought to determine "if racially linked physical characteristics accounted for differences in sport performance." Cobb, shown here in his lab with Owens, "ultimately concluded that proper training and [the] motivation to succeed were the most important factors in determining athletic success." Courtesy of the *Chicago Defender*.

in 1936. But Drew was also light-skinned and "usually taken for a white man by those not in the know." Edward Gourdin, the Harvard sprinter and former world-record holder in the broad jump, was similarly light skinned. "There is not one single physical feature, including skin color, which all our Negro champions have in common which would identify them as Negroes," Cobb asserted. A mixed heritage, he concluded, obviously removed such stellar athletes from consideration when rigid racial dichotomies were being cast, thus exposing as arbitrary and contrived the very principles of racial taxonomy.[24]

Cobb's scientific investigations stood among a host of scholarly articles and books that debunked biodeterminist assertions regarding athletic performance. Yet they have ultimately not been sufficient to counter prevailing speculation on black success in sport. Neither, for the most part, have been the arguments of the sociologist Harry Edwards, whose stinging responses to the Kane article, in addition to his other writings and position statements, have both inspired and informed numerous critics of racism in sport and society. Nor have the appeals of such popular figures as Arthur Ashe, Jr., whose three-volume text, *A Hard Road to Glory,* documented a history of white hostility to black effort and accomplishment in the realm of athletics. These commentaries might well have sent the innatists to the sidelines for good. Sadly, however, the muscular assimilationists—whether they positioned themselves as moderate or militant in the civil rights movement—have been largely unsuccessful in altering the terms of discourse from the natural to the cultural and social.[25]

The massive resistance to the efforts of the integrationists might begin to explain why other African-American commentators have come to subscribe to essentialist considerations of physical hardihood and athletic prowess. The attempt to strategically appropriate the notion of racial difference—to turn it on its head, as it were—may have been born of frustration. It was clearly sustained by considerations of cultural nationalism and Black Power during the late 1960s and 1970s. But today such racialism is not only manifest in African-centered assertions regarding distinctive patterns of cultural development; it also makes its appeal through the notions of melanin theory, no less weird or pernicious than the pronouncements of coach Cromwell or the journalist Kane. Although the various tenets of Afrocentrism certainly speak to racial pride, it is important not to confuse such a sociological phenomenon with a solidly grounded school of critical analysis; while Afrocentrism may be good therapy, as one prominent scholar has noted, it is not good history.[26]

Like cultural nationalism, black racial essentialism serves many purposes, though its separatist assertions and implications do much more than reinforce the notion of a fixed social identity and a consolidated political stance. They also divide persistent racial reformers from those who have attenuated their commitment to the civil rights crusade. The distinctions between integrationist appeals and essentialist formulations have not always been sharply drawn, however, just as the hazards of perpetuating athletic taxonomies have not always been apparent to some black athletes and African-American commentators. Edwin Bancroft Henderson, for example, for more than fifty years one of the leading chroniclers of black sport and perhaps the foremost promoter of the ideal of "muscular assimilationism," devoted his career to civil rights activism. Yet in what seems a striking departure from his campaign to establish a level playing field of athletic competition, he embraced, at least in some measure, the prevailing discourse of difference. Specifically, in a 1936 article in *Opportunity,* the journal of the National Urban League, he alleged that it might have been the rigors of the Middle Passage that had winnowed the slave population, allowing only the fittest to survive. It was from this group, he suggested, that the great athletes descended.

> When one recalls that it is estimated that only one Negro slave in five was able to live through the rigors of the Middle Passage, and that the horrible conditions of slavery took a toll of many slaves who could not make biological adjustments in a hostile environment, one finds the Darwinian theory of survival of the fit operating among Negroes as rigorously as any selective process ever operated among human beings. There is just a likelihood that some very vital elements persist in the histological tissues of the glands or muscles of Negro athletes.[27]

Thirty-five years later, the Yale graduate and NFL star Calvin Hill echoed Henderson's peculiar notion. Black athletes were "the offspring of those who [were] physically and mentally tough enough to survive," Hill asserted. "We were simply bred for physical qualities." This explanation resonated for a number of African-American commentators and athletes who had embraced certain elements of the Black Power movement.[28] Recast in a more positive way, such thinking drew attention to an African past and pride in physical accomplishment, which would eventually be manifest in many achievements by black athletes. In telling counterpoint, the basketball player Isiah Thomas argued in 1987 against "the perpetuation of stereotypes about blacks": "When [Larry] Bird makes a great play, it's due to his thinking and his work habits. It's all planned out by him. It's not the case for blacks. All we do is run and jump. We never practice or give a thought to how we play. It's like I came dribbling out of my mother's womb."[29]

The most solid reaction to notions of white supremacy at the time, the construction of an idealized black superhero in sports, has also played into a cultural taxonomy that ranks athletes as performers (with the line between the symbolic and substantive importance of their accomplishments still firmly drawn). Paradoxically, such assertions of a "strategic essentialism" have served to tighten the boundaries around the athletic ghetto. As the cultural historian and social critic John Hoberman argues passionately, when the foremost black cultural heroes are the celebrities of the football field and basketball arena, and when they are held in esteem mainly for their innate abilities, the effect is to diminish the significance of other African-American leaders as well as the years of dedication that lie behind their accomplishments.

RECENT DEVELOPMENTS

If racial essentialism was ever in retreat during the era of civil rights and national liberation, as some scholars maintain, its resurgence has been dramatically illustrated in recent years. Indeed, the emergence of melanism seems but a sidelight to other renderings of difference and dominance that reflect traditional patterns of thought within the mainstream culture. One of the most notorious episodes of "typing" occurred in the late 1980s when a major-league baseball official, Al Campanis, stated that blacks performed well on the field but lacked "the necessities" to occupy managerial positions or places of responsibility and authority in the front offices of sports organizations. Another involved Jimmy "the Greek" Snyder, a bookmaker turned loose on television, who linked the heritage of slavery to the modern playing field. "The slave owner would breed his big black with his big woman so that he could have a big black kid," Snyder maintained. The consternation evinced by their respective interviewers and the summary firing of both men indicated a shift of values and standards toward such public declarations and their racist underpinnings. Yet many Americans continue to mark racial differences in the athletic arena in terms both calculated and crude. Toward the end of the 1996–1997 basketball season, a sportscaster was fined by the

NBA for his retrograde appraisal of black athletic ability. Commenting on a stellar play by one athlete, David Halberstam, who announced the games for the Miami Heat, remarked that "Thomas Jefferson would have been proud of that pass. When Thomas Jefferson was around basketball was not invented yet, but those slaves working at Thomas Jefferson's farm, I'm sure they would have made good basketball players."[30]

Clearly, such instances draw attention to the prevalence of racialist thinking about athletic accomplishment. Other commentary has been less forthright in addressing the meaning of the success of blacks in sport. In the aftermath of the firing of Jimmy the Greek, the syndicated columnist Richard Cohen vaguely suggested that civil rights activists would want to steer clear of any assessment of the racial dimension of physical attributes for fear of having to engage intellectual and psychological distinctions. Raising the issue of "political correctness," Cohen then shied away from further speculation about racial difference in sport or other endeavors.[31]

Cohen's comments nevertheless made their way into the much more purposive arguments of Dinesh D'Souza in *The End of Racism,* a book that deals with scientific racism principally by repeating its most atrocious pronouncements and ignoring its critics. Thus in a short section concerning athletics, intended to set up his selective digest of IQ statistics, D'Souza not only recapitulated the "categorical imperative" that has long prevailed among racial scientists, he also reiterated the notion of compensation. "It stands to reason that groups that are unlike each other in some respects may also differ in other respects," D'Souza contends offhandedly. "Why should groups with different skin color, head shape, and other visible characteristics prove identical in reasoning ability or the ability to construct an advanced civilization? If blacks have certain inherited abilities, such as improvisational decision making, that could explain why they predominate in certain fields such as jazz, rap, and basketball, and not in other fields, such as classical music, chess, and astronomy." The end of racism indeed.[32]

The racial essentialism that continues to shadow much of the commentary on sport is confined neither to American culture nor to considerations of the achievements of African Americans. A 1993 article from a popular New Zealand magazine, for example, titled "White Men Can't Jump"—how ironically it is hard to tell—documented the increasing prominence of native peoples in rugby, a sport long identified with British colonialism as a means of toughening those who administered the Empire. Amid a wide-ranging discussion of changing demographics in New Zealand as well as an analysis otherwise sensitive to Maori and Samoan cultural patterns, several white sports figures speculate, first, on the innate abilities vis-a-vis the acquired skills of Polynesian squads. "Polynesian players were naturally superior to us in talent," one former player declared, "but a lot of them aren't there now because they didn't have the discipline for physical conditioning. They lacked the right kind of mental attitude. They'd just turn up and play." Said another, it was once the case that "your typical Polynesian rugby team would have just lost their head in a pressure situation. It was almost as if it was the Polynesian way to do something really stupid that gave the game away." Another passage indicates the malleability of such typologies, however. Polynesians have come to excel at the sport because they are bigger now and play a "more physical and confrontational" brand of the game. Inevitably size will win out in such appraisals: "The Polynesian is basically mesomorphic, tending to be big-boned, muscular, of average height, wide shoulders, thin waist," one trainer asserts. "They have a higher proportion of fast twitch muscle fibre which is the source of their explosive style and the reason they are fast over short distances." Contrasting feats of character to mere physicality, the article offers yet another instance where innatist constructs can be placed in comparative perspective, encouraging us to generalize somewhat about the phenomenon of racial essentialism. In New Zealand as in the United States, athletic competition has offered a way for people of color to fashion significant emblems of identity and pride as well as to challenge the discriminatory practices of old. It is a critical commentary on both social systems that those initiatives are still contested, that racialist thinking continues to qualify such hallowed notions as sportsmanship and fair play, equality and opportunity.[33]

Significantly, taxonomic conventions in the representation of population groups have long stood as the predicate of social authority. That the dominant culture can employ them—and modify them when necessary—to maintain hierarchies of privilege and subordination means that minority cultures cannot use such typologies in the same ways. If the strategy of "muscular assimilationism"—a prominent element of the civil rights campaigns of the twentieth century—has not been entirely successful in creating a level playing field, it is more certain still that the separatism manifest in Afrocentrism and melanin theory is patently self-defeating in the long run. Moreover, to the extent that many African-American youth exalt athletic heroes over other role models—spending their formative years in "hoop dreams"—the emphasis on athletic striving has been overplayed. What remains is yet another troubling fact. Even as sociological surveys and a new generation of biographies and

Figure 17–3
The 40-yard dash, timed as a part of the NFL draft process each spring. The image depicts the black athletic as performer, while an array of coaches determines the standard of measurement and judges the skill and fitness of the athlete. Although in this photograph, taken in 1995, two of the coaches are African American, the percentage of black players in the NFL still greatly exceeds the percentage of black coaches and officials. Courtesy of the *Arizona Daily Star*.

memoirs tell us about the increasingly *multiracial* character of U.S. society, the discourse of innate and immutable racial difference still looms large in the popular consciousness. A recent addition to the long shelf of pseudoscientific racism, Jon Entine's *Taboo: Why Black Athletes Dominate Sports and Why We're Afraid to Talk About It* promises that future genetic research will provide the evidence he begs for—mainly concerning the success of Kenyan runners in the marathon and Steeplechase. Though historians, anthropologists, and sociologists shredded the book, it received a mild reception by most sports columnists, which may reveal the deep-rootedness of racial lore in America.[34]

Ultimately, for intellectual historians, cultural theorists, social scientists, as well as journalists who hope to engage entrenched modes of racialist thought and to create a more expansive conception of culture, it may be well as a first step to adopt a new perspective regarding the texts devoted to innatist thinking. Central to this undertaking would be the compilation of a roster of phrases and pronouncements that clearly links academic racism, past and present. To be sure, as we strive to move beyond category, the idea of an index of racialist literature involves a troubling dimension. Yet it is nevertheless crucial that progressive, or expansive, thinkers on the subject—rather than institute- and foundation-based conservative ideologues—become the cartographers of the contemporary discussion of race. Better still, though from a different interpretive position, we might start erasing racial boundaries altogether.

With notions of history and collective memory in mind, perhaps it would be wise to evaluate such books as *The Bell Curve, The End of Racism,* and *Taboo,* deftly written as they might seem to some reviewers,[35] through the same lens that we would use to assess the essentialist observations of the dance critic John Martin, as contrived as they were and remain. From there we could examine the arguments still insisting on a broad-based anatomy of racial difference with an eye toward the ideological stance they share with those who spoke before, with the sportswriter Martin Kane, for instance, with the anthropologist Carleton Coon, and with Coach Cromwell. We could allude, then, to the polemics on white supremacy by Madison Grant and Lothrop Stoddard as well as to the pronouncements on European superiority by the Count de Gobineau. For, "essentially," de Gobineau and D'Souza are of a kind. To read such works together, indeed to draw the significant connections between nineteenth-century social theories and the most recent versions, would ultimately reveal the shared racism of their premises as well as of their prescriptions.

NOTES

1. *John Martin's Book of the Dance* (*The Dance,* 1947; reprint, New York: Tudor, 1963), 177–89.

2. *Ibid.,* 178–9.

3. See, for example, Joyce Aschenbrenner, *Katherine Dunham: Reflections on the Social and Political Contexts of Afro-American Dance* (New York: Congress on Research in Dance, 1981), which quotes Martin on pp. 35–36.

4. See, for example, Stephen Jay Gould, *The Mismeasure of Man* (New York: Norton, 1981); Nancy Stepan, *The Idea of Race in Science: Great Britain, 1800–1860* (London: MacMillan, 1982); Nancy Leys Stepan and Sander Gilman, "Appropriating the Idioms of Science: The Rejection of Scientific Racism," in Dominick LaCapra, ed., *The Bounds of Race: Perspectives on Hegemony and Resistance* (Ithaca: Cornell University Press, 1991), 72–103; Gilman, *Difference and Pathology: Stereotypes of Sexuality, Race, and Madness* (Ithaca: Cornell University Press, 1985); *idem., The Jew's Body* (New York: Routledge, 1991); *idem., Picturing Health and Illness: Images of Identity and Difference* (Baltimore: Johns Hopkins University Press, 1995);

idem., Smart Jews: The Construction of the Image of Jewish Superior Intelligence (Lincoln: University of Nebraska Press, 1996); William H. Tucker, *The Science and Politics of Racial Research* (Urbana: University of Illinois Press, 1994). See also George Mosse, *Toward the Final Solution: A History of European Racism* (New York: Harper, 1980) and Michael Adas, *Machines as the Measure of Men: Science, Technology, and Ideologies of Western Dominance* (Ithaca: Cornell University Press, 1989); Laura Nader, ed., *Naked Science: Anthropological Inquiries into Boundaries, Power, and Knowledge* (New York: Routledge, 1996); Ivan Hannaford, *Race: The History of an Idea in the West* (Baltimore: Johns Hopkins University Press, 1996). See also William R. Stanton, *The Leopard's Spots: Scientific Attitudes Toward Race in America, 1815–1859* (Chicago: University of Chicago Press, 1960); Thomas Gossett, *Race: The History of an Idea in America* (New York: Schocken, 1965); John S. Haller, *Outcasts from Evolution: Scientific Attitudes of Racial Inferiority, 1859–1900* (Urbana: University of Illinois Press, 1971); and George Fredrickson, *The Black Image in the White Mind: The Debate on Afro-American Character and Destiny, 1817–1914* (New York: Harper & Row, 1971).

5. See Charles Murray and Richard J. Herrnstein, *The Bell Curve: Intelligence and Class Structure in American Life* (New York: Free Press, 1994); *idem.*, "Race and I.Q.," *The New Republic* (October 31, 1994): 10–37; Russell Jacoby and Naomi Glauberman, eds., *The Bell Curve Debate: History, Documents, Opinions* (New York: Times Books, 1995); Steven Fraser, *The Bell Curve Wars: Race, Intelligence, and the Future of America* (New York: Basic Books, 1995); Ashley Montagu, *Race and IQ* (New York: Oxford University Press, 1995); Robert Newby, ed., *The Bell Curve: Laying Bare the Resurgence of Scientific Racism,* special issue of *American Behavioral Scientist* 39 (October 1995); John L. Rury, "IQ Redux," *History of Education Quarterly* 35 (Winter 1995): 423–38; Leon J. Kamen, "Behind the Curve," *Scientific American* 272 (February 1, 1995): 99–103; Claude S. Fischer, Michael Hour, Martin S. Anchez Jankowski, Samuel R. Lucas, Ann Swidler, and Kim Voss, *Inequality by Design: Cracking the Bell Curve Myth* (Princeton, NJ: Princeton University Press, 1996). See also Marek Kohn, *The Race Gallery: The Return of Racial Science* (London: Jonathan Cope, 1995) and Dinesh D'Souza, *The End of Racism: Principles for a Multiracial Society* (New York: Free Press, 1995).

6. See, for example, "The Black Athlete Revisited," *Sports Illustrated* August 5, 12–19, 1991, pp. 38–77, 26–73, 40–51. The prevailing representation of black and white athletes had not changed significantly, the authors discovered, since 1968, when the magazine published its first exposé of racism in the realm of U.S. sport.

7. Gould, "Ghosts of Bell Curves Past," *Natural History* (February 1995): 12.

8. See, for example, Patrick B. Miller, " 'To Bring the Race along Rapidly': Sport, Student Culture, and Educational Mission at Historically Black Colleges during the Interwar Years," *History of Education Quarterly* 35 (Summer 1995): 111–33.

9. Elazar Barkan, *The Retreat of Scientific Racism: Changing Concepts of Race in Britain and the United States between the World Wars* (Cambridge, UK: Cambridge University Press, 1992), 16. See Michael D. Biddiss, *Father of Racist Ideology: The Social and Political Thought of Count Gobineau* (London: Weidenfeld and Nicolson, 1970).

10. Gobineau, *The Inequality of Human Races* (London: William Heinemann, 1915), 151–3. I am indebted to Scott Haine for bringing this passage to my attention.

11. Gobineau also addressed racial mixing, referring to "tertiary" and "quaternary" races. In the paintbox formulation he advanced, Polynesians had "sprung from the mixture of black and yellow." *Ibid.*, 148–9

12. See, for example, Ronald Takaki, *Iron Cages: Race and Culture in Nineteenth-Century America* (New York: Alfred A. Knopf, 1979); Amy Kaplan and Donald Pease, eds., *Cultures of United States Imperialism* (Durham, NC: Duke University Press, 1993).

13. *Encyclopaedia Britannica,* American edition, vol. 17 (New York, 1895): 316–20.

14. See, for instance, Thurman B. Rice, *Racial Hygiene: A Practical Discussion of Eugenics and Race Culture* (New York: MacMillan, 1929). For historical assessments of eugenics, see Mark H. Haller, *Eugenics: Hereditarian Attitudes in American Thought* (New Brunswick, NJ: Rutgers University Press, 1963); Gould, *The Mismeasure of Man*; Daniel J. Kevles, *In the Name of Eugenics: Genetics and the Uses of Human Heredity* (New York: Alfred A. Knopf, 1985); Troy Duster, *Backdoor to Eugenics* (New York: Routledge, 1990); Tucker, *The Science and Politics of Racial Research,* 54–137; Joseph Graves, Jr., *The Emperor's New Clothes: Biological Theories of Race at the Millenium* (New Brunswick, NJ: Rutgers University Press, 2001).

15. Madison Grant, *The Passing of the Great Race; or The Racial Basis of European History* (New York: Scribner, 1916); Lothrop Stoddard, *The Ris-*

ing Tide of Color against White World Supremacy (New York: Scribner, 1920).

16. The "contributionist" writings of George Washington Williams and Carter G. Woodson, for example, closely parallel those of immigrant American authors. With respect to sport, see Edwin Bancroft Henderson, the foremost chronicler of black achievements: *The Negro in Sports* (Washington: Associated Publishers, 1939) and *The Black Athlete: Emergence and Arrival* (New York: Publishers Co., 1968).

17. On Kinley, see the *New York World,* March 14, 1931. Eleanor Metheny, "Some Differences in Bodily Proportions between American Negro and White Male College Students as Related to Athletic Performance," *Research Quarterly* 10 (December 1939): 41–53; David K. Wiggins, " 'Great Speed but Little Stamina': The Historical Debate over Black Athletic Superiority," *Journal of Sport History* 16 (Summer 1989): 162–4.

18. Dean Cromwell and Al Wesson, *Championship Technique in Track and Field* (New York, London: McGraw-Hill, 1941), 6; Wiggins, "Great Speed But Little Stamina," 161.

19. Coon quoted in Marshall Smith, "Giving the Olympics an Anthropological Once-Over," *Life,* October 23, 1964, p. 83; John McCallum and Charles H. Pearson, *College Football, USA, 1869—1973* (New York: Hall of Fame Publishers, 1973), 231.

20. See D. Stanley Eitzen and George Sage, *Sociology of American Sport* (Dubuque, IA: W. C. Brown, 1978), 300; Jay Coakley, *Sport in Society: Issues and Controversies* (St. Louis: Times Mirror/Mosby College, 1986), 146–50.

21. Kane, "An Assessment of 'Black is Best,' " *Sports Illustrated,* January 18, 1971, 74.

22. See David Levering Lewis, *W. E. B. Du Bois: Biography of a Race, 1868–1919* (New York: Holt, 1993), 351–52. See Boas, *The Real Race Problem from the Point of View of Anthropology* (New York: National Association for the Advancement of Colored People, 1912) and *Race and Nationality* (New York: American Association for International Conciliation, 1915).

23. W. Montague Cobb, "Race and Runners," *Journal of Health and Physical Education* 7 (January 1936): 3–7, 52–56.

24. *Ibid.* See also W, Montague Cobb, "The Physical Constitution of the American Negro," *Journal of Negro Education* 3 (1934): 340–88, and "Does Science Favor Negro Athletes?" *Negro Digest* 5 (May 1947): 74–7.

25. On his responses to the Kane article, see Harry Edwards, "The Sources of Black Athletic Superiority," *Black Scholar* 3 (November 1971): 32–41, "The Myth of the Racially Superior Athlete" *Intellectual Digest* 2 (March 1972), 58–60, and "20th Century Gladiators for White America," *Psychology Today,* November 1973, 43–52. Edwards's survey works include *The Revolt of the Black Athlete* (New York: Free Press, 1969) and *Sociology of Sport* (Homewood, IL: Dorsey, 1973). in the mode of Edwards's cultural critique, see Gary Sailes, "The Myth of Black Sports Supremacy," *Journal of Black Studies* 21 (June 1991): 480–7. See also Arthur Ashe, Jr., *A Hard Road to Glory: A History of the African-American Athlete* (New York: Warner Books, 1988).

26. On African-centered social commentary, see Molefi Kete Asante, *Afrocentricity: The Theory of Social Change* (Buffalo, NY: Amulefi, 1980) and *The Afrocentric Idea* (Philadelphia: Temple University Press, 1987; rev. ed., 1997). See also Cheikh Anta Diop, *Civilization or Barbarism: An Authentic Anthropology* (Brooklyn, NY: Lawrence Hill Books, 1991); Bernal, *Black Athena.* An impressive introduction to the mode of thought can be found in Carl Pedersen, "Between Racial Fundamentalism and Ultimate Reality: The Debate over Afrocentrism," *Odense American Studies International Series,* Working, Paper no. 4 (1993). And, concerning its appeal, see Gerald Early, "Understanding Afrocentrism: Why Blacks Dream of a World Without Whites," *Civilization* (July/August 1995): 31–39. See also Clarence E. Walker, "You Can't Go Home Again: The Problem with Afrocentrism," *Prospects* 18 (1993), 535–43; on "therapy" and "history," see Leon Litwack, "The Two-Edged Suspicion," *American Historical Association Perspectives* 31 (September 1993), 13–14. For a somewhat different view of this strand of black nationalism, see bell hooks, *Black Looks: Race and Representation* (Boston: South End Press, 1992), 30.

27. Edwin B. Henderson, "The Negro Athlete and Race Prejudice," *Opportunity* 14 (March 1936): 77–79. To read the large body of Henderson's works (as well as those of W. Montague Cobb) would be to understand their primary concerns as assimilationist or integrationist; the stray passages that speak to essentialist notions of black excellence need to be read within this broader context. See David K. Wiggins, "Edwin Bancroft Henderson, African American Athletes, and the Writing of Sport History," in *Glory Bound: Black Athletes in White America* (Syracuse, NY: Syracuse University Press, 1997).

28. Hill quoted in Kane, "An Assessment of 'Black is Best'", 76, 79. See also David W. Zang,

"Calvin Hill Interview," *Journal of Sport History* 15 (Winter 1988): 334–55. In a *Time* article, "Black Dominance," O. J. Simpson argued that blacks "were built a little differently . . . built for speed—skinny calves, long legs, high asses are all characteristics of blacks," (May 9, 1977): 57–60; Wiggins, "Great Speed But Little Stamina," 172–4.

29. Thomas quoted in David K. Wiggins, "The Notion of Double-Consciousness and the Involvement of Black Athletes in American Sport," in *Ethnicity and Sport in North American History and Culture,* ed. Wiggins and George Eisen (Westport, CT: Greenwood, 1994), 151.

30. On these episodes, see Wiggins, "Great Speed but Little Stamina," 179–81; Phillip M. Hoose, *Necessities: Racial Barriers in American Sports* (New York: Random House, 1989); *New York Times,* March 27, 1997.

31. See Richard Cohen, "The Greek's Defense," *Washington Post,* January 19, 1988.

32. D'Souza, *The End of Racism,* 440–1.

33. Tom Hyde, "White Men Can't Jump," *Metro: Essentially Auckland,* September 1993, 63–9. I am indebted to Charles Martin for pointing this work out to me. More recently still, the New Zealand anthropologist Phillip Houghton has spoken of the ways Polynesians, such as the great rugby player Jonah Lomu, have finally reached their "genetic potential." Houghton, *People of the Ocean: Aspects of Human Biology of the Early Pacific* (Cambridge, UK: Cambridge University Press, 1996). See also Julia Leilua, "Lomu and the Polynesian Powerpacks," *New Zealand Fitness* (February/March 1996), 24–7. I am grateful to Douglas Booth for sharing this article with me. In broader terms, Marek Kohn discusses the "race science system" directed at the control of the Romani (gypsy) population that has in recent years been established in parts of Southern and Eastern Europe; see Kohn, *The Race Gallery,* 178–252. On issues of classification and discrimination, see also Saul Dubow, *Scientific Racism in Modern South Africa* (Cambridge, UK: Cambridge University Press, 1995).

34. Entine, *Taboo* (New York: Public Affairs, 2000); Paul Spickard (review), *Journal of Sport History* 27 (Summer 2000), 338–400; Mark Dyreson, "American Ideas About Race and Olympic Races from the 1890s to the 1950s: Shattering Myths or Reinforcing Scientific Racism?" *Journal of Sport History* 28 (Summer 2001), 173–215. The historians of science who have made the most telling rebuttals to the new scientific racists include Jonathan Marks, *Human Biodiversity: Genes, Race, and History* (New York: Aldine De Gruyter, 1995); idem, *What It Means To be 98% Chimpanzee: Apes, People, and Their Genes* (Berkeley: University of California Press, 2002), esp. ch. 6. See also Graves, *The Emperor's New Clothes.*

35. See, for example, Malcolm Browne, "What Is Intelligence, and Who Has It?" *New York Times Book Review,* October 16, 1994; George M. Fredrickson on D'Souza, "Demonizing the American Dilemma," *The New York Review of Books* 42 (October 19, 1995), 10–16.

18

CRISIS OF BLACK ATHLETES ON THE EVE OF THE TWENTY-FIRST CENTURY

Harry Edwards

FOR MORE THAN TWO decades I have been adamant in my contention that the dynamics of black sports involvement, and the blind faith of black youths and their families in sport as a prime vehicle of self-realization and social-economic advancement, have combined to generate a complex of critical problems for black society. At the root of these problems is the fact that black families have been inclined to push their children toward sports career aspirations, often to the neglect and detriment of other critically important areas of personal and cultural development.

Those circumstances have developed largely because of: (1) a long-standing, widely held, racist, and ill-informed presumption of innate, race-linked black athletic superiority and intellectual deficiency; (2) media propaganda portraying sports as a broadly accessible route to black social and economic mobility; and (3) a lack of comparably visible, high-prestige black role models beyond the sports arena. The result is a single-minded pursuit of sports fame and fortune that has spawned an institutionalized triple tragedy in black society: the tragedy of thousands upon thousands of black youths in obsessive pursuit of sports goals that the overwhelming majority of them will never attain; the tragedy of the personal and cultural underdevelopment that afflicts so many successful and unsuccessful black sports aspirants; and the tragedy of cultural and institutional underdevelopment throughout black society at least in some part as a consequence of the drain in talent potential toward sports and away from other vital areas of occupational and career emphasis, such as medicine, law, economics, politics, education, and technical fields. Sandlots, parks, and even backyard recreational sites in many instances have been taken over by drug dealers, or they have become battlegrounds in gang disputes, or they have simply become too dangerously exposed to eruptions of violence to be safely used. Cutbacks in educational budgets and shifts in funds from school athletic, physical education, and recreation programs to concerns deemed more vital in these fiscally strapped, troubled communities (including campus and classroom security) have further narrowed sports participation opportunities. Even where interscholastic sports participation opportunities have survived, security problems and fears of violence and other disruptions in an increasing number of cases have restricted both the scheduling of events and spectator attendance.

Figure 18–1
Harry Edwards. Courtesy of Rick Rockamora.

In the face of such discouraging circumstances, many black youths have opted to go with the flow, exchanging team colors for gang colors or simply dropping out of everything and chillin'. They move utterly beyond the reach and scope of established institutional involvements and contacts—save the criminal justice system, hospital emergency services, and the mortuary services industry.

The social circumstances facing young black males are particularly germane here. Nationally at least a quarter of all black males aged sixteen to twenty-nine are under the control of the courts; in some states (such as California) this figure is approaching one-third of the black males in this age range. One-third of all the deaths in this group nationally are homicides (usually perpetrated by other black males), and suicide ranks only behind homicides and accidents as a cause of death. Moreover, since the age range sixteen to twenty-nine represents the prime years of self-development and career establishment, it should be no surprise that black males are declining as a proportion of the population in virtually every institutional setting (e.g. higher education, the workforce, the church) save the prison system.

Predictably, black sports involvement is threatened as well. As alluded to earlier, developments at the intersection of race, sports, and education have over the years generated a situation wherein increasing numbers of black youths have focused their efforts on athletic achievement only to find themselves underdeveloped academically and unable to compete in the classroom.

Nonetheless, their talents were so critical to the success of revenue producing sports programs—most notably basketball and football—at major colleges and universities competing at the Division I level that those athletes were typically recruited out of high school or junior college notwithstanding their educational deficiencies, with the predictable result of widespread black athlete academic underachievement and outright failure. It was this tragedy and the attention it generated from sports activists and the media from the late 1960s into the 1980s that ultimately prompted the most far-reaching reform efforts in modern collegiate sports history.

But because black athletes' academic problems are in large part rooted in and intertwined with black youths' societal circumstances more generally, there can be no effective resolution of the educational circumstances of black athletes at any academic level except in coordination with commensurate efforts in society. In fact, to the extent that remedial efforts neglect such a coordinated dual approach, they are virtually guaranteed to exacerbate rather than better the situation of the black athletes that they impact.

Indeed, that has been the impact of much recent activity aimed at academic reform in athletics. At the high school level, the institution of more demanding academic requirements for athletic participation prompted many black athletes who subsequently have been declared academically ineligible to drop out of high school altogether.

At the collegiate level the establishment of Proposition 48, officially National Collegiate Athletic Association (NCAA) Bylaw 14.3, has had even more negative consequences. Proposition 48 required that before he or she could participate in Division I college varsity sports, a student had to have a minimum grade point average (GPA) of 2.0 in at least eleven courses in core subjects in high school and a minimum SAT score of 700 (ACT score of 17). The rule was instituted to counteract academically lenient recruitment practices, and though the specific requirements mandated under the regulation have been adjusted to accommodate various sliding scales of eligibility over the last decade, the essential thrust and intent of regulatory efforts remains the same today as does their disparate impact on black athletes.

In the first two years of Proposition 48 enforcement (1984–1986), 92 percent of all academically ineligible basketball players and 84 percent of academically ineligible football players were black athletes. As late as 1996, the overwhelming majority of Proposition 48 casualties were still black student-athlete prospects. Despite attempts to the contrary, such horrifically disproportionate numbers cannot be justified on grounds that ineligible athletes would not have graduated anyway. Richard Lapchick, director of the Center for the Study of Sports in Society, reports that if Proposition 48 had been in use in 1981, 69 percent of black male scholarship athletes would have been ineligible to participate in sports as freshmen, but 54 percent of those athletes eventually graduated.

Complicating the effects of Proposition 48 is Proposition 42, which was passed by the NCAA in 1989 and was designed to strengthen Proposition 48 by denying athletes who failed to meet Proposition 48 eligibility requirements all financial aid during the freshman year. Proposition 42 effectively prevented prospective scholarship athletes who did not qualify under Proposition 48 and who could not pay their own college expenses from attending college at all. Of course, this regulation disproportionately affected black athletes, since they numbered disproportionately among Proposition 48 casualties.

In 1990, following widespread objections to the draconian nature of Proposition 42 (most notably the protest efforts of Georgetown basketball coach John Thompson), Proposition 42 was modified to allow student-athletes who were "partially qualified" (i.e., who met either minimum grade point average or test score requirements) to receive nonathletic, need-based financial aid during the freshman year. Those who did not qualify under either test score or grade point average requirements still could not receive any type of financial aid. Still, black athlete prospects, always among the poorest and neediest of athlete recruits, continued to bear the brunt of the measure's negative impact.

It is now clear that the greatest consequence of Proposition 42, and similar regulations, has been to limit the opportunities—both educational and athletic—that would otherwise be available to black youths. Those measures were neither conceived nor instituted with due consideration of black youths' circumstances beyond the academy and the sports arena. In consequence, while there has been some minor improvement in such concerns as black athlete college graduation rates (an increase estimated to be about 8 percent and possibly due as much to improved academic support services for black student-athletes after they arrive on college campuses as to any prerecruitment screening function of propositions 48 or 42), those results must be weighed against the profoundly negative cost of lost opportunities and more subtle consequences such as the stigmatizing of black youths as Proposition 48 cases or casualties.

The diminution of opportunities for black youths to succeed at the high school and collegiate levels must inevitably register and be manifest in all sports and at all levels traditionally accessible to black athletes in numbers. Already many high schools are unable to field teams or schedule dependable competition. Beyond the high school ranks, in recent years there has been disturbing evidence of a downward trend in the statistics of virtually every skill category in Division I collegiate basketball: team and individual points per game averages; individual and team field goals percentages; individual and team free throw percentages; and assists.

Both college coaches and officials, and the media, tend to assume that such declining performance figures are due mostly to early entry into the professional ranks by star collegiate players. Many star players leave college after only one or two years of collegiate competition, and, in some instances, talented high school players skip college altogether and go directly into the National Basketball Association (NBA). But the NBA itself appears to be slumping statistically and, in any event, the league shows no evidence of having benefited from any would-be talent windfall.

In 1997, the average NBA team scored only 96.7 points, the lowest regular season league average since the 24-second shot clock was instituted. Moreover, in the 1996–1997 season the average age of players in the NBA was the highest in league history—older players are apparently able to hold on to their jobs and stay around longer because younger players are not able to displace them. Thus, regardless of how many collegiate basketball players are leaving or skipping college for the professional ranks, they are having no discernible impact as basketball talents at the professional level.

Other trends that individually would seem of little significance appear more troubling when considered within the context of emerging trends in black sports involvement. For example, black attendance at sporting events other than basketball and football games is virtually nonexistent. As ticket prices continue to increase and more leagues and teams choose "pay per view" and cable television broadcast options, ever fewer numbers of blacks will be watching even basketball and football either in person or on television. Those trends are likely to affect most severely people abiding in the lower- and working-class strata of black society that have traditionally produced the greater proportion of black athlete talent. With school and community sports and recreation programs and opportunities on the decline, declining personal access and exposure to elite athletic performances virtually guarantees that both the interest and the involvement of that population in sport are likely to wane.

In this regard, the character of black involvement in baseball may be a harbinger of the future of black involvement in sports overall. Though major league baseball teams claim not to keep track of the race of their players and other personnel, it is estimated that approximately 18 percent of major league players are black. (In 1996, in a team by team count, I arrived at figures of 14 to 17 percent, depending on how some players of Caribbean or black Latino heritage counted themselves). Eighteen percent is approximately the same black player representation in the major leagues as ten years ago.

Relatively speaking, this stagnation in the proportion of black players in the major leagues may be the good news. It has been fairly well-established that, for the most part, in urban areas (where over 80 percent of the black population lives) black adolescents and teenagers no longer either follow baseball or play it. Few black adults take their children to baseball games; in fact only about one percent of all major league baseball tickets sold are bought by blacks. Indeed, on opening day of the 1997 baseball season—a day which marked the fiftieth anniversary of Jackie Robinson breaking the color barrier against black participation in the major leagues—Jackie Robinson's former team had the same number of black players on its roster as it did the day that he fast stepped on the field in a Dodger uniform—ONE!

All considered, unless steps are taken to reverse present trends in both sport and society, we could be witnessing the end of what in retrospect might well come to be regarded as the golden age of black sports participation. We are, quite simply disqualifying, jailing, and burying an increasing number of our potential black football players, basketball players, baseball players, and other prospective athletes right along with our potential black lawyers, doctors, and teachers.

In the past I have resoundingly rejected the priority of playbooks over textbooks because of the triple tragedy scenario outlined above. So long as the traditional black community and the larger society—particularly in the wake of hard-won civil rights advances and opportunities—effectively created and sustained some realistic broad spectrum access to legitimate means of personal and career development for the black youths in question (that is, access beyond the dream of sports stardom), criticisms and admonitions warning of a black overemphasis on sports participation and achievement not only were justified but necessary and even obligatory correctives to misguided attitudes and dispositions toward sports in black society. But today there is no option but to recognize that for increasing legions of black youths, the issue is neither textbooks nor playbooks—the issue is survival, finding a source of hope, encouragement, and support in developing lives and building legitimate careers and futures.

Without question, the ultimate resolution to this situation must be the overall institutional development of black communities and the creation of greater opportunity for black youths in the broader society. In the meantime, however, if community and school sports programs can provide a means of reconnecting with at least some of those black youths who we have already lost and strengthening our ties with those who, by whatever miracle of faith and tenacity, have managed to hold on to hope and to stay the course, then those programs and the youths involved deserve our strongest support and endorsement.

Therefore, I now say that we must reconstitute and broaden access to school sports programs. We must create secure and supervised playgrounds, park recreation areas, and community sports facilities; open school sports facilities for supervised weekend community use and midnight basketball, volleyball, tennis, bowling, badminton, swimming, and other sports opportunities; recruit counselors, teachers, people trained in the trades, health care professionals, and religious leaders to advise, mentor, and tutor young people at those sports sites; network with corporate and government agencies to establish apprenticeship and job opportunities; and bring in students of sport and society who understand and can articulate the applicability of the great lessons and dynamics of black youths' sports success and achievement to their life circumstances and goals more generally.

Far from deemphasizing or abandoning sport, or simply allowing our involvement to wane, black people must now more than ever intelligently, constructively, and proactively pursue sports involvement. We cannot afford to wait passively for better times or allow ourselves to be swept and herded along in the flow of events and developments at the interface of race, sports, and society. We must understand the forces threatening black sports participation while also recognizing that black sports participation need not become an obsession or preoccupation.

Today it is desirable, even necessary that black youths and black society as a whole continue to harbor dreams of achieving excellence in sports—there is much to be learned and gained from both the challenges of sports competition and the experiences of meeting those challenges. But all involved must learn to dream with their eyes open, always remaining fully cognizant of participation's pitfalls no less than its positive possibilities, of its potential as a dead end trap no less than its promise as a vehicle for outreach and advancement. As in the past, the responsibility for perpetually mapping the sports terrain and for the ongoing acculturation and education of black youths as they seek to productively navigate the possibilities of athletic achievement fall most heavily upon black people themselves.

In the final analysis, exploiting black youths' overemphasis on sports participation and achievement may be our only remaining avenue for guiding increasing numbers of them out of circumstances that today lead to even more devastating destructiveness and a greater waste of human potential than that which I, and others, have long decried in connection with unrealistic black sports aspirations. Not at all coincidentally it could also salvage the golden age of black sports participation.

FURTHER READING

Aaron, Hank with Lonnie Wheeler. *I Had a Hammer: The Hank Aaron Story.* New York: Harper Collins, 1991.

Abdul-Jabbar, Kareem and Peter Knobler. *Giant Steps: The Autobiography of Kareem Abdul-Jabbar.* New York: Bantam, 1983.

Abrahams, Roger D. *Singing the Master: The Emergence of African American Culture in the Plantation South.* New York: Pantheon Books, 1992.

Ali, Muhammad with Richard Durham. *The Greatest: My Own Story.* New York: Random House, 1975.

Allen, Maury. *Jackie Robinson: A Life Remembered.* New York: Franklin Watts, 1987.

Andrews, David. "The Fact(s) of Michael Jordan's Blackness: Excavating a Floating Racial Signifier." *Sociology of Sport Journal* 13 (1996): 125–158.

———, ed. "Deconstructing Michael Jordan: Reconstructing Postindustrial America." *Sociology of Sport Journal* 13 (1996).

Armstrong, Henry. *Gloves, Glory and God: An Autobiography.* Westwood, NJ: Fleming H. Revell Company, 1956.

Ashe, Arthur, Jr. *A Hard Road to Glory: A History of the African American Athlete.* 3 vols. New York: Ballantine, 1976.

Ashe, Arthur and Arnold Rampersad. *Days of Grace: A Memoir.* New York: Knopf, 1993.

Astor, Gerald. *And a Credit to His Race: The Hard Life and Times of Joseph Louis Barrow.* New York: Saturday Review Press, 1974.

Axthelm, Pete. *The City Game.* New York: Harper & Row, 1970.

Azevedo, Mario, and Jeffrey T. Sammons. "Contributions in Science, Business Film, and Sports." In Mario Azevedo, ed., *Africana Studies: A Survey of Africa and the African Diaspora.* Durham, NC: Carolina Academic Press, 1993, 353–60.

Bacote, Clarence A. *The Story of Atlanta University: A Century of Service, 1865–1965.* Atlanta: Atlanta University Press, 1969.

Bak, Richard. *Joe Louis: The Great Black Hope.* New York: Taylor, 1996.

Baker, William J. *Jesse Owens: An American Life.* New York: Free Press, 1986.

———. *Sports in the Western World.* Urbana: University of Illinois Press, 1988.

Baker, William. "Kings and Diamonds: Negro League Baseball in Film," *Journal of Sport History* 25 (Summer 1998), 303–8.

Ball, Donald. "Ascription and Position: A Comparative Analysis of 'Stacking' in Professional Football." *Canadian Review of Sociology and Anthropology* 10 (May 1973): 97–113.

Banker, Stephen. *Black Diamonds: An Oral History of Negro League Baseball.* Princeton, NJ: Visual Education Corporation, 1989.

Bankes, James. *The Pittsburgh Crawfords: The Lives and Times of Black Baseball's Most Exciting Team!* Dubuque, IA: Win. C. Brown Publishers, 1991.

Barrow, Joe Louis, Jr., and Barbara Munder. *Joe Louis: 50 Years an American Hero.* New York: McGraw-Hill, 1988.

Bass, Amy. *Not the Triumph but the Struggle: The 1968 Olympics and the Making of the Black Athlete.* Minneapolis: University of Minnesota Press, 2002.

Bederman, Gail. *Manliness and Civilization: A Cultural History of Gender and Race in the United States, 1880–1917.* Chicago: The University of Chicago Press, 1995.

Behee, John. *Hail to the Victors! Black Athletes at the University of Michigan.* Ann Arbor, MI: Swink-Tuttle Press, 1974.

Bennett, Bruce L. "Supplemental Selected Annotated Bibliography on the Negro in Sports." *Journal of Health, Physical Education, and Recreation* 41 (September 1970): 71.

———. "Bibliography on the Negro in Sports." *Journal of Health, Physical Education, and Recreation* 41 (September 1970): 77–8.

Bennett, Jr., Lerone. *Before the Mayflower: A History of Black America.* Chicago: Johnson Publishing Company, 1982.

Berkow, Ira. *The Du Sable Panthers: The Greatest, Blackest, Saddest Team from the Meanest Street in Chicago.* New York: Atheneum, 1978.

Berry, Bonnie and Earl Smith. "Race, Sport, and Crime: The Misrepresentation of African Americans in Team Sports and Crime." *Sociology of Sport Journal* 17 (2000): 171–97.

Berryman, Jack W. "Early Black Leadership in Collegiate Football: Massachusetts as a Pioneer." *Historical Journal of Massachusetts* 9 (June 1981): 17–28.

Billet, Bret L. and Lance J. Formwalt. *America's National Pastime: A Study of Race and Merit in Professional Baseball.* Westport, CT: Praeger, 1995.

Birrell, Susan. "Women of Color, Critical Autobiography, and Sport." In Michael A. Messner and Donald F. Sabo, eds., *Sport, Men, and the Gender Order: Critical Feminist Perspectives.* Champaign, IL: Human Kinetics, 1990, 185–99.

Birrell, Susan, and Cheryl Cole, eds. *Women, Sport, and Culture.* Champaign, IL: Human Kinetics, 1993.

Bontemps, Arna. *Famous Negro Athletes.* New York: Dodd, Mead, 1964.

Boyd, Todd. *Am I Black Enough For You? Popular Culture From the 'Hood and Beyond.* Bloomington, IN: Indiana University Press, 1997.

Brailsford, Dennis. *Bareknuckles: A Social History of Prizefighting.* Cambridge, MA: Lutterworth Press, 1988.

Brashler, William. *Josh Gibson: A Life in the Negro Leagues.* New York: Harper & Row, 1978.

Brawley, Benjamin. *History of Morehouse College.* Atlanta: Morehouse College, 1917.

Brooks, Dana D. "African American Head Coaches and Administrators: Progress But . . . ?" In Dana D. Brooks and Ronald C. Althouse, eds., *Racism in College Athletics: The African American Athlete's Experience.* Morgantown, WV: Fitness Information Technology, 2000, 101–42.

Brooks, Dana M. and Ronald C. Althouse. *The African American Athlete Resource Directory.* Morgantown, WV: Fitness Information Technology, 1996.

———, eds. *Racism in College Athletics: The African American Athlete's Experience.* Morgantown, WV: Fitness Information Technology, 2000.

Broome, Richard. "The Australian Reaction to Jack Johnson, Black Pugilist, 1907–09." In Richard Cashman and Michael McKerman, eds., *Sports in History: The Making of Modern Sporting History.* St. Lucia, Australia: University of Queensland Press, 1979, 343–63.

Brown, Jim. *Off My Chest.* New York: Doubleday and Company, 1964.

Brown, Jim with Steve Delsohn. *Out of Bounds.* New York: Kensington Publishing, 1989.

Brown, Roscoe C., Jr. "A Commentary on Racial Myths and the Black Athlete." In Daniel M. Landers, ed., *Social Problems in Athletics.* Urbana: University of Illinois Press, 1976, 168–73.

Bruce, Janet. *The Kansas City Monarchs: Champions of Black Baseball.* Lawrence: University Press of Kansas, 1985.

Bryant, Howard, *Shut Out: A Story of Race and Baseball in Boston.* New York: Routledge, 2002.

Cahn, Susan. *Coming on Strong: Gender and Sexuality in Twentieth-Century Women's Sport.* New York: Free Press, 1994.

Capeci, Dominic J., Jr., and Martha Wilkerson, "Multifarious Hero: Joe Louis, American Society, and Race Relations during World Crisis, 1935–1945." *Journal of Sport History* 10 (Winter 1983): 5–25.

Captain, Gwendolyn. "Enter Ladies and Gentlemen of Color: Gender, Sport, and the Ideal of African American Manhood and Womanhood during the Late Nineteenth and Early Twentieth Centuries." *Journal of Sport History* 18 (Spring 1991): 81–102.

Carroll, John M. *Fritz Pollard: Pioneer in Racial Advancement.* Urbana: University of Illinois Press, 1992.

Cashmore, Ernest. *Black Sportsmen.* London: Routledge and Kegan Paul, 1982.

Chadwick, Bruce. *When the Game Was Black and White: The Illustrated History of Baseball's Negro Leagues.* New York: Abberville Press, 1992.

Chalberg, John C. *Rickey and Robinson: the Preacher, the Player, and America's Game.* Wheeling, IL: Harlan Davidson, 2000.

Chalk, Ocania. *Pioneers of Black Sport: The Early Days of the Black Professional Athlete in Baseball, Basketball, Boxing, and Football.* New York: Dodd, Mead, 1975.

———. *Black College Sport.* New York: Dodd, Mead & Company, 1976.

Chambers, Ted. *The History of Athletics and Physical Education at Howard University.* Washington, DC: Vantage, 1986.

Coakley, Jay J. *Sport in Society: Issues and Controversies.* 5th ed. St. Louis: Times Mirror/Mosby, 1994.

Cone, Carl B. "The Molineaux-Cribb Fight, 1810: Wuz Tom Molineaux Robbed?" *Journal of Sport History* 9 (Winter 1982): 83–91.

Cottrell, Robert Charles. *The Best Pitcher in Baseball: The Life of Rube Foster, Negro League Giant.* (New York: New York University Press, 2001).

Creeden, Pamela J., ed. *Women, Media and Sport: Challenging Gender Values.* Thousand Oaks, CA: Sage, 1994.

Davies, Richard O. *America's Obsession: Sports and Society Since 1945.* New York: Harcourt Brace & Company, 1994.

Davis, Jack E. "Baseball's Reluctant Challenge: Desegregating Major League Spring Training Sites, 1961–1964." *Journal of Sport History* 19 (Summer 1992): 144–62.

Davis, John P. "The Negro in American Sports." In John P. Davis, ed., *The American Negro Reference Book.* Englewood Cliffs, NJ: Prentice-Hall, 1966, 775–825.

Davis, Laurel R. "The Articulation of Difference: White Preoccupation with the Question of Racially Linked Genetic Differences among Athletes." *Sociology of Sport Journal* 7 (1990): 179–87.

Davis, Laurel R. and Othello Harris. "Race and Ethnicity in U. S. Sports Media." In Lawrence R. Wenner, ed., *Media Sport.* New York: Routledge, 1998, 154–169.

Davis, Lenwood G. *Joe Louis: A Bibliography of Articles, Books, Pamphlets, Records, and Archival Material.* Westport, CT: Greenwood Press, 1983.

Davis, Lenwood G., and Belinda Daniels, comps. *Black Athletes in the United States: A Bibliography of Books, Articles, Autobiographies, and Biographies on Professional Black Athletes, 1800–1981.* Westport, CT: Greenwood Press, 1983.

Davis, Michael D. *Black American Women in Olympic Track and Field: A Complete Illustrated Reference.* Jefferson, NC: McFarland, 1992.

Davis, O. K. *Grambling's Gridiron Glory: Eddie Robinson and the Tigers Success Story.* Rustin, LA: M&M Printing, 1983.

Davis, Timothy. "The Myth of the Superspade: The Persistence of Racism in College Athletics." *Fordham Urban Law Journal* 22 (November 3, 1995): 615–98.

———. "African American Student-Athletes: Marginalizing the NCAA Regulatory Structure." *Marquette Sports Law Journal* 6 (Spring 1996): 199–227.

Dawkins, Marvin P. and Graham C. Kinloch. *African American Golfers During the Jim Crow Era.* Westport, CT: Greenwood Publishing Group, 2000.

Dixon, Phil, and Patrick J. Hannigan. *The Negro Baseball Leagues: A Photographic Essay.* Matotuck, NY: Ameon, 1992.

Dorinson, Joseph and Joram Warmund, eds. *Jackie Robinson: Race, Sports, and the American Dream.* Armonk, NY: M.E. Sharpe, 1998.

Duval, Earl H., Jr. "An Historical Analysis of the Central Intercollegiate Athletic Association and its Influence on the Development of Black Intercollegiate Athletics: 1912–1984," Ph. D. dissertation, Kent State University, 1985.

Dyreson, Mark. "American Ideas About Race and Olympic Races from the 1890s to the 1950s: Shattering Myths or Reinforcing Scientific Racism?" *Journal of Sport History* 28 (Summer 2001), 173–215.

Dyson, Michael Eric. "Be like Mike? Michael Jordan and the Pedagogy of Desire." In Michael Eric Dyson, *Reflecting Black: African American Cultural Criticism.* Minneapolis: University of Minnesota Press, 1993, 64–75.

Early, Gerald. *Tuxedo Junction: Essays on American Culture.* New York: Ecco Press, 1989.

———. *The Culture of Bruising: Essays on Prizefighting, Literature, and Modern American Culture.* New York: Ecco Press, 1994.

———. *The Muhammad Ali Reader.* New York: Ecco Press, 1998.

Edmonds, Anthony O. "Second Louis-Schmeling Fight: Sport, Symbol, and Culture." *Journal of Popular Culture* 7 (Summer 1973): 42–50.

———. *Joe Louis.* Grand Rapids, MI: William B. Eerdmans, 1973.

Edwards, Harry. *The Revolt of the Black Athlete.* New York: Free Press, 1970.

———. *Sociology of Sport.* Homewood, IL: Dorsey Press, 1973.

Eisen, George, and David K. Wiggins, eds. *Ethnicity and Sport in North American History and Culture.* Westport, CT: Praeger, 1995.

Eitzen, D. Stanley, and George H. Sage. *Sociology of North American Sport.* Dubuque, IA: Brown and Benchmark, 1993.

Elias, Robert, ed. *Baseball and the American Dream: Race, Class, Gender and the National Pastime.* Armonk, NY: M. E. Sharpe, 2001.

Entine, Jon. *Taboo: Why Black Athletes Dominate Sports and Why We Are Afraid to Talk About It.* New York: Public Affairs Press, 2000.

Falkner, David. *Great Time Coming: The Life of Jackie Robinson from Baseball to Birmingham.* New York: Simon and Schuster, 1995.

Farr, Finis. *Black Champion: The Life and Times of Jack Johnson.* London: Macmillan and Company, 1964.

Fetter, Henry D. "The Party Line and the Color Line: The American Communist Party, the *Daily Worker,* and Jackie Robinson." *Journal of Sport History* 28 (Fall 2001), 375–402.

Fitzpatrick, Frank. *And the Walls Came Tumbling Down: Kentucky, Texas Western, and the Game That Changed American Sports.* New York: Simon & Schuster, 1999.

Fleischer, Nat. *Black Dynamite: The Story of the Negro in the Prize Ring from 1782 to 1938.* New York: Ring Magazine, 1947.

Fletcher, Marvin E. "The Black Soldier Athlete in the United States Army, 1890–1916." *Canadian Journal of History of Sport and Physical Education* 3 (December 1971): 16–26.

Fox, Stephen. *Big Leagues: Professional Baseball, Football, and Basketball in National Memory.* New York: William Morrow and Company, 1994.

Franklin, John Hope and Alfred A. Moss, Jr. *From Slavery to Freedom: A History of African Americans.* 8th ed. New York: Alfred A. Knopf, 2000.

Gaddy, Charles. *An Olympic Journey: The Saga of an American Hero: Leroy T. Walker.* California: Griffin Publishing Group, 1998.

Gardner, Robert and Dennis Shortelle. *The Forgotten Players: The Story of Black Baseball in America.* New York: Walker, 1993.

Gems, Gerald R. "Shooting Stars: The Rise and Fall of Blacks in Professional Football." *Professional Football Research Association Annual Bulletin* (1988): 1–16.

———. "Blocked Shot: The Development of Basketball in the African American Community of Chicago." *Journal of Sport History* 22 (Summer 1995): 135–48.

George, Nelson. *Elevating the Game: Black Men and Basketball.* New York: HarperCollins, 1992.

Gerber, Ellen, et al. *The American Woman in Sport.* Reading, MA: Addison-Wesley, 1974.

Gerlach, Larry R. "Baseball's Other 'Great Experiment': Eddie Klep and the Integration of the Negro Leagues." *Journal of Sport History* 25 (Fall 1998): 453–81.

Gibson, Althea. *I Always Wanted to Be Somebody.* New York: Harper and Brothers, 1958.

Gilmore, Al-Tony. *Bad Nigger: The National Impact of Jack Johnson.* New York: Kennikat, 1975.

———. "The Myth, Legend and Folklore of Joe Louis: The Impressions of Sport on Society." *South Atlantic Quarterly* 82 (Summer 1983): 256–68.

Gissendanner, Cindy Himes. "African American Women and Competitive Sport, 1920–1960." In Susan Birrell and Cheryl Cole, eds., *Women, Sport and Culture.* Champaign, IL: Human Kinetics, 1993, 81–92.

———. "African American Women Olympians: The Impact of Race, Gender, and Class Ideologies, 1932–1968." *Research Quarterly for Exercise and Sport* 67 (June 1996): 172–82.

Goodman, Michael H. "The Moor vs. Black Diamond." *Virginia Cavalcade* 29 (Spring 1980): 164–73.

Gorn, Elliott J. *The Manly Art: Bare-Knuckle Prize Fighting in America.* Ithaca, NY: Cornell University Press, 1994.

———, ed. *Muhammad Ali: The People's Champ.* Urbana: University of Illinois Press, 1995.

Gorn, Elliott J., and Warren Goldstein. *A Brief History of American Sports.* New York: Hill and Wang, 1993.

Grundman, Adolph. "Image of Intercollegiate Sports and the Civil Rights Movement: A Historian's View." *Arena Review* 3 (October 1979): 17–24.

Grundy, Pamela. "From Amazons to Glamazons: The Rise and Fall of North Carolina Women's Basketball, 1920–1960." *The Journal of American History* 87 (June 2000): 112–46.

———. *Learning to Win: Sports, Education, and Social Change in Twentieth-Century North Carolina.* Chapel Hill: University of North Carolina Press, 2001.

Guttmann, Allen. *A Whole New Ball Game: An Interpretation of American Sports.* Chapel Hill: University of North Carolina Press, 1988.

Harris, Francis C. "Paul Robeson: An Athlete's Legacy." In Jeffrey C. Stewart, ed. *Paul Robeson: Artist and Citizen.* New Brunswick, NJ: Rutgers University Press, and the Paul Robeson Cultural Center, 1998, 35–48.

Harrison, C. Keith. "Black Athletes at the Millenium," *Society* 37 (March/April 2000), 35–39.

Harrison, C. Keith and Lampman, Brian, "The Image of Paul Robeson: Role Model for the Student and Athlete," *Rethinking History* 5 (2001), 117–30.

Hartmann, Douglas. "Rethinking the Relationships Between Sport and Race in American Culture: Golden Ghettos and Contested Terrain." *Sociology of Sport Journal* 17 (2000): 229–53.

Hartmann, Douglas. "The Politics of Race and Sport: Resistance and Domination in the 1968 African American Olympic Protest Movement," in Jodi O'Brien and Judith A Howard, eds. *Everyday Inequalities: Critical Inquiries* (Cambridge, UK: Blackwell, 1998), 337–54.

Hartmann, Douglas. *Golden Ghettos: Race, Culture and The Politics of the 1968 African American Olympic Protest Movement,* forthcoming, University of Chicago Press.

Hauser, Thomas. *The Black Lights: Inside the World of Professional Boxing.* New York: McGrawHill, 1986.

———. *Muhammad Ali: His Life and Times.* New York: Simon and Schuster, 1991.

Hawkins, Billy, *The New Plantation: The Internal Colonization of Black Student Athletes.* Winterville, GA: Sakiki Pub. 2000.

Henderson, Edwin B. *The Negro in Sports.* Washington, DC: Associated Publishers, 1939, 1949.

———. *The Black Athlete: Emergence and Arrival.* Cornwall Heights, PA: Pennsylvania Publishers, 1968.

———. "Physical Education and Athletics among Negroes." In Bruce L. Bennett, ed., *Proceedings of the Big Ten Symposium on the History of Physical Education and Sport.* Chicago: Athletic Institute, 1972, 67–83.

Henry, Grant. "A Bibliography Concerning Negroes in Physical Education, Athletics, and Related Fields." *Journal of Health Physical Education, and Recreation* 44 (May 1973): 65–70.

Hietala, Thomas R. *The Fight of the Century: Jack Johnson, Joe Louis and the Struggle for Racial Equality.* New York: M.E. Sharpe, 2002.

Hine, Darlene Clark, William C. Hine, and Stanley Harrold. *The African American Odyssey,* 2 vols. New Jersey: Prentice Hall, 2000.

Hoberman, John. *Darwin's Athletes: How Sport Has Damaged Black America and Preserved the Myth of Race.* Boston: Houghton Mifflin, 1997.

Holt, Thomas. *The Problem of Race in the 21st* Century. Cambridge, MA: Harvard University Press, 2001.

Holway, John. *Voices from the Great Negro Baseball Leagues.* New York: Dodd, Mead, 1975.

———. *Blackball Stars: Negro League Pioneers.* Westport, CT: Meckler, 1988.

Hoose, Philip M. *Necessities: Racial Barriers in American Sports.* New York: Random House, 1989.

Horton, James Oliver and Lois E. Horton. *Hard Road to Freedom: The Story of African America.* New Brunswick, NJ: Rutgers University Press, 2001.

Hotaling, Edward. *The Great Black Jockeys: The Lives and Times of the Men Who Dominated America's First National Sport.* Rocklin, CA: Primo Publishing, 1999.

Hurd, Michael. *Black College Football, 1892–1992: One Hundred Years of History, Education, and Pride.* Virginia Beach, VA: Donnin and Co. Pub., 1998.

Jable, J. Thomas. "Sport in Philadelphia's African American Community, 1865–1900." In George Eisen and David K. Wiggins, eds., *Ethnicity and Sport in North American History and Culture.* Westport, CT: Greenwood Press, 1994, 157–76.

Janis, Laura. "Annotated Bibliography on Minority Women in Athletics." *Sociology of Sport Journal* 2 (September 1985): 266–74.

Jarvie, Grant, ed. *Sport, Racism and Ethnicity.* London: Falmer Press, 1991.

Jiobu, Robert. "Racial Inequality in a Public Arena: The Case of Professional Baseball." *Social Forces* 67 (1988): 524–34.

Johnson, Jack A. *Jack Johnson Is a Dandy: An Autobiography.* New York: Chelsea House, 1969.

Johnson, Rafer with Philip Goldberg. *The Best That I Can Be: An Autobiography.* New York: Random House, 1998.

Jones, Greg, et al. "A Log-linear Analysis of Stacking in College Football." *Social Science Quarterly* (March 1987): 70–83.

Jones, Wally, and Jim Washington. *Black Champions Challenge American Sports.* New York: David McKay, 1972.

Jones, William H. *Recreation and Amusement Among Negroes in Washington.* Westport, CT: Negro Universities Press, 1970.

Jordan, Larry E. "Black Markets and Future Superstars: An Instrumental Approach to Opportunity in Sport Forms." *Journal of Black Studies* 11 (March 1981): 289–306.

Jordan, Pat. *Black Coach.* New York: Dodd, Mead and Company, 1971.

Kahn, Lawrence M. "Discrimination in Professional Sports: A Survey of the Literature." *Industrial and Labor Relations Review* 44 (April 1991): 395–418.

Kaye, Andrew M. "The Canonization of Tiger Flowers: A Black Hero for the 1920s." *Borderlines: Studies in American Culture* 5 (1998): 142–59.

Kaye, Andrew M. " 'Battle Blind': Atlanta's Taste for Black Boxing in the Early Twentieth Century." *Journal of Sport History* 28 (Summer 2001), 217–32.

Kelley, Robin D.G. and Earl Lewis, eds. *To Make Our World Anew: A History of African Americans.* New York: Oxford University Press, 2000.

Kennedy, John H. *A Course of Their Own: A History of African American Golfers.* Kansas City, MO: Andrews McMeel Publishing, 2000.

Keown, Tim. *Skyline: One Season, One Team, One City.* New York: McMillan Publishing Company, 1994.

Kimball, Richard Ian. "Beyond the Great Experiment: Integrated Baseball Comes to Indianapolis." *Journal of Sport History* 26 (Spring 1999): 142–62.

King, C. Richard and Charles Fruehling Springwood. *Beyond the Cheers: Race as Spectacle in College Sport.* Albany: State University of New York Press, 2001.

King, Wilma. *Stolen Childhood: Slave Youth in Nineteenth-Century America.* Bloomington: Indiana University Press, 1995.

Lacy, Sam with Moses J. Newsom. *Fighting for Fairness: The Life Story of Hall of Fame Sportswriter Sam Lacy.* Centreville, MD: Tidewater Publishers, 1998.

LaFeber, Walter. *Michael Jordan and the New Global Capitalism.* New York: W. W. Norton, 1999.

Lamb, Chris. "I Never Want to Take Another Trip like This One: Jackie Robinson's Journey to Integrate Baseball." *Journal of Sport History* 24 (Summer 1997): 177–91.

Lanctot, Neil. *Fair Dealing and Clean Playing: The Hilldale Club and the Development of Black Professional Baseball, 1910–1932.* Jefferson, NC: McFarland, 1994.

Lansbury, Jennifer H. " 'The Tuskegee Flash' and 'The Slender Harlem Stroker': Black Women Athletes on the Margin" *Journal of Sport History* 28 (Summer 2001), 233–52.

Lapchick, Richard. *The Politics of Race and International Sport: The Case of South Africa.* Westport, CT: Greenwood Press, 1975.

———. *Broken Promises: Racism in American Sports.* New York: St. Martin's Press, 1984.

———. *Five Minutes to Midnight: Race and Sport in the 1990's.* Lanham, MD: Madison Books, 1991.

Lavoie, Mark. "The Economic Hypothesis of Positional Segregation: Some Further Comments." *Sociology of Sport Journal* 6 (1989): 163–66.

Lawson, Hal A. "Physical Education and Sport in the Black Community: The Hidden Perspective." *Journal of Negro Education* 48 (Spring 1979): 187–95.

Lee, George L. *Interesting Athletes: Black American Sports Heroes.* New York: Ballantine, 1976.

LeFlore, James. "Athleticism among American Blacks." In Robert M. Pankin, ed., *Social Approaches to Sport.* Toronto: Associated University Presses, 1982, 104–21.

Leonard, Wilbert M., II. "Stacking in College Basketball: A Neglected Analysis." *Sociology of Sport Journal* 4(1987): 403–9.

———. "Salaries and Race/Ethnicity in Major League Baseball: The Pitching Component." *Sociology of Sport Journal* 6 (1989): 152–62.

———. *A Sociological Perspective of Sport.* New York: MacMillan, 1993.

Levine, Lawrence W. *Black Culture and Black Consciousness: Afro-American Folk Thought From Slavery to Freedom.* New York: Oxford University Press, 1977.

Liberti, Rita. " 'We Were Ladies, We Just Played Basketball Like Boys': African American Womanhood and Competitive Basketball at Bennett College, 1928–1942." *Journal of Sport History* 26 (Fall 1999): 567–84.

Lipsyte, Robert and Peter Levine. *Idols of the Game: A Sporting History of the American Century.* Atlanta: Turning Publishing, Inc., 1995.

Logan, Rayford. *Howard University: The First Hundred Years, 1867–1967.* New York: New York University Press, 1969.

Lomax, Michael E. "Black Baseball's First Rivalry: The Cuban Giants Versus the Gorhams of New York and the Birth of the Colored Championship." *Sport History Review* 28 (November 1997): 134–45.

———. "Black Entrepreneurship in the National Pastime: The Rise of Semiprofessional Baseball in Black Chicago, 1890–1915." *Journal of Sport History* 25 (Spring 1998): 43–64.

———. *Black Baseball Entrepreneurs, 1860–1901: Operating By Any Means Necessary* (Syracuse, NY: Syracuse University Press, 2003).

Louis, Joe with Edna and Art Rust, Jr. *Joe Louis: My Life.* New York: Harcourt Brace Jovanovich, 1978.

Lowenfish, Lee. "Sport, Race, and the Baseball Business: The Jackie Robinson Story Revisited." *Arena Review* 2 (Spring 1978): 2–16.

Loy, John, and Joseph McElvoque. "Racial Segregation in American Sport." *International Review of Sport Sociology* 5 (1970): 5–23.

Lucas, John A., and Ronald A. Smith. *Saga of American Sport.* Philadelphia: Lea and Febiger, 1978.

MacDonald, William W. "The Black Athlete in American Sports." In William J. Baker and John M. Carroll, eds., *Sports in Modern America.* St. Louis: River City Publishers, 1981, 88–98.

Magriel, Paul. "Tom Molineaux." *Phylon* 12 (December 1951): 329–36.

Majors, Richard. "Cool Pose: Black Masculinity and Sports." In Michael A. Messner and Donald F. Sabo, eds., *Sport, Men, and the Gender Order: Critical Feminist Perspectives.* Champaign, IL: Human Kinetics, 1990, 109–14.

Marable, Manning. "Black Athletes in White Men's Games, 1880–1920." *Maryland Historian* 4 (Fall 1973): 143–9.

Marcello, Ronald E. "The Integration of Intercollegiate Athletics in Texas: North Texas State College as a Test Case, 1956." *Journal of Sport History* 14 (Winter 1987): 286–316.

Martin, Charles H. "Jim Crow in the Gymnasium: The Integration of College Basketball in the American South." *International Journal of the History of Sport* 10 (April 1993): 68–86.

———. "Racial Change and Big-Time College Football in Georgia: The Age of Segregation, 1892–1957." *Georgia Historical Quarterly* 80 (1996): 532–62.

———. "Integrating New Year's Day: The Racial Politics of College Bowl Games in the American South." *Journal of Sport History* 24 (Fall 1997): 358–77.

———. "The Rise and Fall of Jim Crow in Southern College Sports: The Case of the Atlantic Coast Conference." *North Carolina Historical Review* 76 (July 1999): 253–84.

———. "The Color Line in Midwestern College Sports, 1890–1960." *Indiana Magazine of History* 98 (2002): 85–112.

Mathewson, Alfred Dennis. "Black Women, Gender Equity and the Function at the Junction." *Marquette Sports Law Journal* 6 (Spring 1996): 239–66.

Matthews, Vincent with Neil Amdur. *My Race Be Won.* New York: Charterhouse, 1974.

Mazuri, Ali A. "Boxer Muhammad Ali and Soldier Idi Amin as International Political Symbols: The Bioeconomics of Sports and War." *Comparative Studies in Society and History* 19 (April 1977): 189–215.

McDaniel, Pete. *Uneven Lies: The Heroic Story of African-Americans in Golf.* Greenwich, CT: The American Golfer, 2000.

McKinney, G. B. "Negro Professional Baseball Players in the Upper South in the Gilded Age." *Journal of Sport History* 3 (Winter 1976): 273–80.

McMahon, David R. "Remembering the Black and Gold: African-Americans, Sport, Memory, and the University of Iowa," *Culture, Sport, Society* 4 (Summer 2001): 63–98.

———. "Pride to All: African-Americans and Sports in Iowa." In Bill Silag, ed. *Outside-In: African American History in Iowa, 1838–2000.* Des Moines, IA: State Historical Society of Iowa, 2001.

McPherson, Barry D. "Minority Group Involvement in Sport: The Black Athlete." *Exercise and Sport Science Reviews* 2 (1974): 71–101.

Mead, Chris. *Champion: Joe Louis, Black Hero in White America.* New York: Scribner's, 1985.

Mergen, Bernard. *Play and Playthings: A Reference Guide.* Westport, CT: Greenwood Press, 1982.

Messner, Michael A., and Donald F. Sabo, eds. *Sport, Men, and the Gender Order., Critical Feminist Perspectives.* Champaign, IL: Human Kinetics, 1990.

Miller, Patrick B. "Harvard and the Color Line: The Case of Lucien Alexis." In Ronald Story, ed., *Sports in Massachusetts: Historical Essays.* Westfield, MA: Institute for Massachusetts Studies, 1991, 137–58.

———. " 'To Bring the Race Along Rapidly': Sport, Student Culture, and Educational Mission at Historically Black Colleges during the Interwar Years." *History of Education Quarterly* 35 (Summer 1995): 111–33.

———. "The Anatomy of Scientific Racism: Racialist Responses to Black Athletic Achievement." *Journal of Sport History* 25 (Spring 1998): 119–51.

———. "Slouching Toward A New Expediency: College Football and the Color Line During the Depression Decade." *American Studies* 40 (Fall 1999): 5–30.

———. "Sport as 'Interracial Education': Popular Culture and Civil Rights Strategies during the 1930s and Beyond," in Patrick B. Miller, Therese Frey Steffen, and Elisabeth Schäfer-Wünsche, eds., *The Civil Rights Movement Revisited: Critical Perspectives on the Struggle for Racial Equality in the United States* (Hamburg: LIT Verlag, 2001), 21–38.

———, ed. *The Sporting World of the Modern South.* Urbana: University of Illinois Press, 2002.

Moore, Joseph T. *Pride against Prejudice: The Biography of Larry Doby.* Westport, CT: Greenwood Press, 1988.

Morris, Willie. *The Courting of Marcus Dupree.* Garden City, NY: Doubleday and Company, 1983.

Nathan, Daniel A. "Sugar Ray Robinson, the Sweet Science, and the Politics of Meaning." *Journal of Sport History* 26 (Spring 1999): 163–74.

Norwood, Stephen H. "The Making of an Athlete: An Interview with Joe Washington." *Journal of Sport History* 27 (Spring 2000): 91–145.

Norwood, Stephen H. and Harold Brackman. "Going to Bat for Jackie Robinson: The Jewish Role in Breaking Baseball's Color Line," *Journal of Sport History* 26 (1999), 115–54.

Noverr, Douglas A. and Lawrence E. Ziewacz. *The Games They Played: Sports in American History, 1865–1980.* Chicago: Nelson-Hall, 1988.

Olsen, Jack. *The Black Athlete: A Shameful Story.* New York: Time-Life Books, 1968.

O'Neil, Buck, with Steve Wulf and David Conrads. *I Was Right on Time.* New York: Simon & Schuster, 1996.

Oriard, Michael. *King Football: Sport and Spectacle in the Golden Age of Radio and Newsreel, Movie and Magazines, the Weekly and Daily Press.* Chapel Hill: University of North Carolina Press, 2001.

Orr, Jack. *The Black Athlete: His Story in American History.* New York: Lion Books, 1969.

Owens, Jesse with Paul Neimark. *Blackthink: My Life as Black Man and White Man.* New York: William Morrow and Company, 1970.

Paino, Troy D. "Hoosiers in a Different Light: Forces of Change vs. the Power of Nostalgia." *Journal of Sport History* 28 (Spring 2001), 63–80.

Paul, Joan, et al. "The Arrival and Ascendence of Black Athletes in the Southeastern Conference, 1966–1980." *Phylon* 45 (December 1984): 284–97.

Pennington, Richard. *Breaking the Ice: The Racial Integration of Southwest Conference Football.* Jefferson, NC: McFarland, 1987.

Peterson, Robert W. *Only the Ball Was White.* Englewood Cliffs, NJ: Prentice-Hall, 1970.

———. *Cages to Jump Shots: Pro Basketball's Early Years.* New York: Oxford University Press, 1990.

Pierce, Richard B. "More Than a Game: The Political Meaning of High School Basketball in Indianapolis." *Journal of Urban History* 27 (November 2000): 3–23.

Porter, David L., ed. *African American Sports Greats: A Biographical Dictionary.* Westport, CT: Greenwood Press, 1995.

Rader, Benjamin G. *American Sports: From the Age of Folk Games to the Age of Spectators.* Englewood Cliffs, NJ: Prentice-Hall, 1983.

Rampersad, Arnold. *Jackie Robinson: A Biography.* New York: Alfred A. Knopf, 1997.

Rayl, Susan J. "The New York Renaissance Professional Black Basketball Team, 1923–1950." Ph.D. Dissertation, Pennsylvania State University, 1996.

Reed, Harry A. "Not by Protest Alone: Afro-American Activists and the Pythian Baseball Club of Philadelphia, 1867–1869." *The Western Journal of Black Studies* 9 (1985): 144–50.

Reisler, Jim. *Black Writers/Black Baseball: An Anthology of Articles from Black Sportswriters Who Covered the Negro Leagues.* Jefferson, NC: McFarland, 1994.

Remnick, David. *King of the World: Muhammad Ali and the Rise of a Hero.* New York: Random House, 1998.

Ribowsky, Mark. *Don't Look Back: Satchel Paige in the Shadows of Baseball.* New York: Simon and Schuster, 1994.

———. *The Power and the Darkness: The Life of Josh Gibson in the Shadows of the Game.* New York: Simon and Schuster, 1996.

———. *A Complete History of the Negro Leagues, 1884 to 1955.* New York: Birch Lane Press, 1995.

Richardson, Joe. *A History of Fisk University, 1865–1946.* University: University of Alabama Press, 1980.

Riess, Steven A. *Major Problems in American Sport History.* New York: Houghton Mifflin Company, 1997.

Ritchie, Andrew. *Major Taylor: The Extraordinary Career of a Champion Bicycle Racer.* San Francisco: Bicycle Books, 1988.

Roberts, Randy. "Heavyweight Champion Jack Johnson: His Omaha Image, a Public Reaction Study." *Nebraska History* 57 (Summer 1976): 226–41.

———. "Galveston's Jack Johnson: Flourishing in the Dark." *Southwestern Historical Quarterly* 82 (July 1983): 37–56.

———. *Papa Jack: Jack Johnson and the Era of White Hopes.* New York: Free Press, 1983.

———. *But They Can't Beat Us! Oscar Robertson's Crispus Attucks Tigers.* Champaign, IL: Sports Publishing, Inc., 1999.

Roberts, Randy, and James Olson. *Winning Is the Only Thing: Sports in America since 1945.* Baltimore: Johns Hopkins University Press, 1989.

Robinson, Frazier, with Paul Bauer. *Catching Dreams: My Life in the Negro Baseball Leagues.* Syracuse: Syracuse University Press, 2000.

Robinson, Jackie with Alfred Duckett. *I Never Had It Made.* New York: Putnam, 1972.

Rogosin, Donn. *Invisible Men: Life in Baseball's Negro Leagues.* New York: Athenaeum, 1987.

Ross, Charles K. *Outside the Lines: African Americans and the Integration of the National Football League.* New York: New York University Press, 1999.

Ruck, Rob. "Soaring above the Sandlots: The Garfield Eagles." *Pennsylvania Heritage* 8 (Summer 1982): 13–18.

———. *Sandlot Seasons: Sport in Black Pittsburgh.* Urbana: University of Illinois Press, 1987.

Rudman, William S. "The Sport Mystique in Black Culture." *Sociology of Sport Journal* 3 (1986): 305–19.

Russell, Bill as told to William McSweeney. *Go Up for Glory.* New York: Conrad-McCann, 1966.

Russell, Bill and Taylor Branch. *Second Wind: The Memoirs of an Opinionated Man.* New York: Random House, 1974.

Rust, Art, and Edna Rust. *Art Rust's Illustrated History of the Black Athlete.* Garden City, NY: Doubleday, 1985.

Rutkoff, Peter M., ed. *The Cooperstown Symposium on Baseball and American Culture, 1997 (Jackie Robinson).* Jefferson, N.C.: McFarland & Company, Inc, 1997: 25–41.

Sage, George H. *Power and Ideology in American Sport: A Critical Perspective.* Champaign, IL: Human Kinetics, 1988.

Sailes, Gary. *African Americans in Sport.* New Brunswick, NJ: Transaction, 1998.

Salzberg, Charles. *From Set Shot to Slam Dunk: The Glory Days of Basketball in the Words of Those Who Played It.* New York: E. P. Dutton, 1987.

Sammons, Jeffrey T. "Boxing as a Reflection of Society: The Southern Reaction to Joe Louis." *Journal of Popular Culture* 16 (Spring 1983): 23–33.

———. *Beyond the Ring: The Role of Boxing in American Society.* Urbana: University of Illinois Press, 1988.

———. " 'Race' and Sport: A Critical Historical Examination." *Journal of Sport History* 21 (Fall 1994): 203–98.

Sellers, Robert. "African American Student-Athletes: Opportunity or Exploitation?" In Dana D. Brooks and Ronald C. Althouse, eds., *Racism in College Athletics: The African American Athlete's Experience.* Morgantown, WV: Fitness Information Technology, 2000, 143–74.

Scully, Gerald. "Economic Discrimination in Professional Sports." *Law and Contemporary Problems* 39 (Winter-Spring 1973): 67–84.

Shropshire, Kenneth L. *In Black and White: Race and Sports in America.* New York: New York University Press, 1996.

Sifford, Charlie with James Gallo. *Just Let Me Play: The Story of Charlie Sifford, the First Black PGA Golfer.* Latham, NY: British American Publishing, 1992.

Simons, William. "Jackie Robinson and the American Mind: Journalistic Perceptions of the Reintegration of Baseball." *Journal of Sport History* 12 (Spring 1985): 39–64.

Sinnette, Calvin H. *Forbidden Fairways: African Americans and the Game of Golf.* Chelsea, MI: Sleeping Bear Press, 1998.

Sloan-Green, Tina, et al. *Black Women in Sport.* Reston, VA: AAHPERD, 1981.

Smith, Maureen M. "Identity and Citizenship: African American Athletes, Sport, and the Freedom Struggles of the 1960s" (Ph. D. dissertation, The Ohio State University, 1999).

Smith, Ronald A. "The Paul Robeson-Jackie Robinson Saga and a Political Collision." *Journal of Sport History* 6 (Summer 1979): 5–27.

Smith, Thomas G. "Civil Rights on the Gridiron: The Kennedy Administration and the Desegregation of the Washington Redskins." *Journal of Sport History* 14 (Summer 1987): 189–208.

———. "Outside the Pale: The Exclusion of Blacks from the National Football League, 1934–1946." *Journal of Sport History* 15 (Winter 1988): 255–81.
Smith, Yvonne. "Women of Color in Society and Sport." *Quest* 44 (Summer 1992): 228–50.
Spivey, Donald. "Sport, Protest, and Consciousness: The Black Athlete in Big-Time Intercollegiate Sports, 1941–1968." *Phylon* 44 (June 1983): 116–25.
———. "Black Consciousness and Olympic Protest Movements, 1964–1980." In Donald Spivey, ed., *Sport in America: New Historical Perspectives*. Westport, CT: Greenwood Press, 1985, 239–59.
———. "End Jim Crow in Sports: The Protest at New York University, 1940–1941." *Journal of Sport History* 15 (Winter 1988): 282–303.
Spivey, Donald, and Tom Jones. "Intercollegiate Athletic Servitude: A Case Study of the Black Illinois Student Athletes, 1931–1967." *Social Science Quarterly* 55 (March 1975): 939–47.
Strode, Woody and Sam Young. *Goal Dust: The Warm and Candid Memoirs of a Pioneer Black Athlete and Actor*. New York: Madison Books, 1990.
Taylor, Marshall Major. *The Fastest Bicycle Rider in the World*. Battleboro, VT: Green-Stephen Press, 1971.
Telander, Rick. *Heaven is a Playground*. Lincoln: University of Nebraska Press, 1995.
Thomas, Damion. " 'The Good Negroes': African-American Athletes and the Cultural Cold War, 1945–1968" (Ph. D. Dissertation University of California, Los Angeles, 2002).
Thompson, Richard. *Race and Sport*. London: Oxford University Press, 1964.
Torres, Jose. *Sting like a Bee: The Muhammad Ali Story*. New York: Abelard-Schuman, 1971.
Tygiel, Jules. *Baseball's Great Experiment: Jackie Robinson and His Legacy*. New York: Oxford University Press, 1983.
———, *Extra Bases: Reflections on Jackie Robinson, Race, and Baseball History*. Lincoln: University of Nebraska Press, 2002.
———, ed. *The Jackie Robinson Reader: Perspectives on an American Hero*. New York: Penguin Dutton, 1997.
Van Deburg, William. *A New Day in Babylon: The Black Power Movement and American Culture, 1965–1975*. Chicago: University of Chicago Press, 1992.
Vertinsky, Patricia, and Gwendolyn Captain. "More Myth than History: American Culture and Representations of the Black Female's Athletic Ability." *Journal of Sport History* 25 (Fall 1998): 532–61.
Wacquant, Loic. "The Social Logic of Boxing in Black Chicago: Toward a Sociology of Pugilism." *Sociology of Sport Journal* 9 (1992): 221–54.
Walker, Chet with Chris Messenger. *Long Time Coming: A Black Athlete's Coming-of-Age in America*. New York: Grove Press, 1995.
Watkins, Ralph. "Recreation, Leisure and Charity in the Afro-American Community of Buffalo, New York: 1920–1925." *Afro-Americans in New York Life and History* 6 (July 1982): 7–15.
Watterson, John Sayle. *College Football: History, Spectacle, Controversy*. Baltimore, MD: The Johns Hopkins University Press, 2000.
Weaver, Bill L. "The Black Press and the Assault on Professional Baseball's Color Line, October 1945–April 1947." *Phylon* 40 (Winter 1979): 303–17.
Welch, Paula. "Tuskegee Institute: Pioneer in Women's Olympic Track and Field." *The Foil* (Spring 1988): 10–13.
Wenn, Stephen R. and Jeffrey P. Wenn. "Muhammad Ali and The Convergence of Olympic Sport and U.S. Diplomacy in 1980: A Reassessment from Behind the Scenes of the U.S. State Department" *Olympika: The International Journal of Olympic Studies* 2 (1993), 45–66.
West, Cornel and Henry Louis Gates Jr. *The African-American Century: How Blacks Shaped Our Country*. New York: Free Press, 2000.
White, G. Edward. *Creating the National Pastime: Baseball Transforms Itself, 1903–1953*. Princeton, NJ: Princeton University Press, 1996.
Wideman, John Edgar. *Hoop Roots: Basketball, Race, and Love*. New York: Houghton Mifflin, 2001.
Wiggins, David K. "Issac Murphy: Black Hero in Nineteenth-Century American Sport, 1861–1896." *Canadian Journal of History of Sport and Physical Education* 10 (May 1979): 15–32.
———. "Sport and Popular Pastimes: The Shadow of the Slavequarter." *Canadian Journal of History of Sport and Physical Education* 11 (May 1980): 61–88.
———. "The Play of Slave Children in the Plantation Communities of the Old South, 1820–1860." *Journal of Sport History* 7 (Summer 1980): 21–39.
———. "Wendell Smith, the *Pittsburgh Courier-Journal* and the Campaign to Include Blacks in Organized Baseball, 1933–1945." *Journal of Sport History* 10 (Summer 1983): 5–29.

———. "From Plantation to Playing Field: Historical Writings on the Black Athlete in American Sport." *Research Quarterly for Exercise and Sport* 57 (June 1986): 101–16.

———. "The Future of College Athletics Is at Stake: Black Athletes and Racial Turmoil on Three Predominantly White University Campuses, 1968–1972." *Journal of Sport History* 15 (Winter 1988): 304–33.

———. "Great Speed but Little Stamina: The Historical Debate over Black Athletic Superiority." *Journal of Sport History* 16 (Summer 1989): 158–85.

———. "Prized Performers, but Frequently Overlooked Students: The Involvement of Black Athletes in Intercollegiate Sports on Predominantly White University Campuses, 1890–1972." *Research Quarterly for Exercise and Sport* 62 (June 1991): 164–77.

———. "The Year of Awakening: Black Athletes, Racial Unrest, and the Civil Rights Movement of 1968." *International Journal of the History of Sport* 9 (August 1992): 188–208.

———. "Critical Events Affecting Racism in Athletics." In Dana D. Brooks and Ronald C. Althouse, eds., *Racism in College Athletics: The African American Athlete's Experience.* Morgantown, WV: Fitness Information Technology, 1993, 23–49.

———. *Glory Bound: Black Athletes in a White America.* Syracuse, NY: Syracuse University Press, 1997.

Wiggins, David K. and Patrick B. Miller, *The Unlevel Playing Field: A Documentary History of the African Amerian Experience in Sport.* Urbana: University of Illinois Press, 2003.

Wiggins, William H. "Jack Johnson as Bad Nigger: The Folklore of His Life." *Black Scholar* 2 (January 1971): 4–19.

———. "Boxing's Sambo Twins: Racial Stereotypes in Jack Johnson and Joe Louis Newspaper Cartoons, 1908 to 1938." *Journal of Sport History* 15 (Winter 1988): 242–54.

Williams, Linda. "Sportswomen in Black and White: Sports History from an AfroAmerican Perspective." In Pamela J. Creeden, ed., *Women, Media and Sport: Challenging Gender Values.* Thousand Oaks, CA: Sage, 1994, 45–66.

Winters, Manque. *Professional Sports: The Community College Connection.* Inglewood, CA: Winnor Press, 1982.

Woolfolk, George. *Prairie View: A Study in Public Conscience, 1878–1946.* New York: Pageant Press, 1962.

Young, Alexander, Jr. "Joe Louis, Symbol." Ph. D. dissertation, University of Maryland, 1968.

———. "The Boston Tarbaby." *Nova Scotia Historical Quarterly* 4 (September 1974): 277–93.

Young, Andrew S. "Doc." *Great Negro Baseball Stars and How They Made the Major Leagues.* New York: A. S. Barnes, 1953.

———. *Negro Firsts in Sports.* Chicago: Johnson Publishing, 1963.

Zang, David W. "Calvin Hill Interview." *Journal of Sport History* 15 (Winter 1988): 334–55.

———. *Fleet Walker's Divided Heart: The Life of Baseball's First Black Major Leaguer.* Lincoln: University of Nebraska Press, 1995.

———. *Sportswars: Athletes in the Age of Aquarius.* Fayetteville: The University of Arkansas Press, 2001.

Zuckerman, Jerome, et al. "The Black Athlete in Post-bellum 19th Century." *Physical Educator* 29 (October 1972): 142–6.

CONTRIBUTORS

Susan Cahn is Associate Professor of History at the University of Buffalo, State University of New York. She is the author of *Coming on Strong: Gender and Sexuality in Twentieth Century Women's Sport* (1994), which won the 1995 Book Prize from the North American Society for Sport History. Cahn has also commented frequently online and in other public forums about gender issues in sport; she has written a two-part article in the *Journal of Women's History* on "Women's History in the New Millenium," and is currently completing a book titled *Sexual Reckonings: Adolescent Girlhood in the Modern South, 1920–1960* (forthcoming).

Harry Edwards is Professor of Sociology at the University of California, Berkeley and the author of *The Revolt of the Black Athlete* (1969), *Sociology of Sport* (1973), *The Struggle that Must Be* (1980) and numerous articles on race and sport. A principal organizer of the Olympic Project for Human Rights, which sought a black boycott of the 1968 Olympic Games, he has been an activist as well as a scholar for more than three decades. He continues to comment frequently about minority participation in school, college, and professional sport.

Pamela Grundy is an independent historian who lives in Charlotte, North Carolina, where she pursues a variety of writing, teaching, and museum projects. She is the author of *Learning to Win: Sports, Education, and Social Change in Twentieth-Century North Carolina* (2001), which won the 2002 Book Prize from the North American Society for Sport History and the Herbert Feis Award of the American Historical Association. Grundy has also written several award-winning articles on southern folk culture appearing in the *Journal of American History.* She is currently working on a history of American women's basketball and a study of the desegregation of historically black West Charlotte High School.

Douglas Kellner is George Kneller Chair in the Philosophy of Education at UCLA and is the author of many books on social theory, politics, history, and culture, including *Herbert Marcuse and the Crisis of Marxism* (1984); *Critical Theory, Marxism and Modernity* (1989); *Jean Baudrillard: From Marxism to Postmodernism and Beyond* (1989); *Television and the Crisis of Democracy* (1990); *Postmodern Theory: Critical Interrogations* (with Steven Best) (1991); and *Media Culture* (1995).

Neil Lanctot is an Adjunct Assistant Professor of History at the University of Delaware. The author of *Fair Dealing and Clean Playing: The Hilldale Club and the Development of Black Professional Baseball, 1910–1932,* (1994) he has written extensively about the institutional workings of the Negro Leagues. His forthcoming study is tentatively titled *Helping the Race Morally and Financially: Black Professional Baseball and the Negro National Leagues, 1933–1952.*

Rita Liberti is Assistant Professor in the Department of Kinesiology and Physical Education at California State University, Hayward. Her dissertation is entitled " 'We Were Ladies, We Just Played Basketball Like Boys': A Study of Women's Basketball at Historically Black Colleges and Universities in North Carolina, 1925–1945" (1998). She is currently conducting research on women's competitive basketball at Black Colleges in the South prior to integration.

Michael E. Lomax is Associate Professor in the Sport Management Program at the University of Georgia. He has contributed a number of articles and presentations related to black business development in sport and is a member of the editorial boards of both the *Journal of Sport History* and the *Journal of African American Men.* His most recent work is a two-volume study, *Black Baseball Entrepreneurs, 1860–1901: Operating By Any Means Necessary* (2003).

Charles H. Martin is Associate Professor of History at the University of Texas at El Paso. His articles on sports history, race relations, and labor history have appeared in the *Journal of Southern History, Journal of Sport History, Journal of Negro History, Georgia Historical Quarterly,* and other historical reviews. Martin has just completed a book manuscript on the color line in intercollegiate sports between 1890 and 1980, which is tentatively titled *More Than a Game was at Stake.* He is also the author of *The Angelo Herndon Case and Southern Justice* (1976).

Patrick B. Miller is Associate Professor of History at Northeastern Illinois University in Chicago. He is the author of *The Playing Fields of American Culture: Athletics and Higher Education, 1850–1945* (forthcoming) and, with David K. Wiggins, *The Unlevel Playing Field: A Documentary History of the African American Experience in Sport* (2003). Editor of *The Sporting World of the Modern South* (2002) and coeditor of *The Civil Rights Movement Revisited: Critical Perspectives on the Struggle for Equality in the United States* (2001), he has also contributed articles to *The Journal of Sport History, Olympika, American Studies,* and the *History of Education Quarterly,* among other journals.

Richard B. Pierce is Carl E. Koch Assistant Professor of History at the University of Notre Dame. He teaches political economy as well as race and sport in urban America. He has contributed articles to a number of journals, including the *Journal of Urban History.* His forthcoming book, *Polite Protest: The Political Economy of Race in Indianapolis,* focuses on the history of African Americans with special attention to the demographic shifts and political negotiation during the interwar years and the era of the civil rights movement.

Randy Roberts is Professor in the History and American Studies Departments at Purdue University, with a concentration in popular culture and sport history. He is the author of numerous books, including textbooks, with a wide range of subjects. Among them are *Jack Dempsey: The Manassa Mauler* (1979); *Papa Jack: Jack Johnson and the Era of White Hopes* (1983); *Winning is the Only Thing: Sports in America Since 1945* (with James Olson) (1989); *John Wayne: American* (1995); and *A Line in the Sand: The Alamo in Blood and Memory* (with James Olson) (2000).

Rob Ruck is a Senior Lecturer in the Department of History at the University of Pittsburgh, where he is also on the Faculty of the Center for Latin American Studies. He coauthored *Steve Nelson, American Radical* (1981) with Steve Nelson and James R. Barrett and wrote *Sandlot Seasons: Sport in Black Pittsburgh* (1987) and *The Tropic of Baseball: Baseball* *in the Dominican Republic (1991).* Ruck was the project director for "Kings on the Hill: Baseball's Forgotten Men," which aired on NBC and PBS. He is currently writing a history of Pittsburgh with Ted Muller and a biography of Art Rooney with Mike Weber and Maggie Patterson.

Thomas G. Smith is Professor of History and department chair at Nichols College in Dudley, Massachusetts. Besides "Civil Rights on the Gridiron" and other articles on sport, he has written about U.S. foreign policy and environmental history in articles appearing in a variety of historical journals. He has coauthored *Independent: A Biography of Lewis Douglas* (1986) and is presently completing a biography of Pennsylvania congressman John P. Saylor.

Donald Spivey is Professor of History at the University of Miami. His publications include *The Politics of Mis-education: The Booker Washington Institute of Liberia, 1929–1984* (1986), *Sport in America: New Historical Perspectives* (1985), *Union and the Black Musician* (1984), and *Schooling for the New Slavery: Black Industrial Education, 1868–1915* (1978), *Fire From the Soul: The African Journey in America* (forthcoming), and *Playing with Jim Crow: A Story of Protest to End the Gentlemen's Agreement in College Sports* (forthcoming).

Jules Tygiel is Professor of History at San Francisco State University. He is the author of *Baseball's Great Experiment: Jackie Robinson and His Legacy* (1983); *Past Time: Baseball as History* (2000); edited *The Jackie Robinson Reader* (1997); *The Great Los Angeles Swindle: Oil Stocks and Scandal in the Roaring Twenties* (1994).

David K. Wiggins is Professor and Chair of the Department of Health, Fitness, and Recreation Resources at George Mason University. He is the author of *Glory Bound: Black Athletes in a White America* (1997), Coauthor (with Patrick B. Miller) of *The Unlevel Playing Field: A Documentary History of the African American Experience in Sport* (2003), Editor of *Sport in America: From Wicked Amusement to National Obsession* (1995), *African Americans in Sport* (forthcoming) and Co-Editor (with George Eisen) of *Ethnicity and Sport in North American History and Culture* (1994).

William H. Wiggins, Jr. is professor of Folklore and Afro-American Studies at Indiana University. He has published widely in the field of racial representation and is the author of "Boxing's Sambo Twins: Racial Stereotypes in Jack Johnson and Joe Louis Newspaper Cartoons, 1908–1938," in the *Journal of Sport History,* as well as *Joe Louis: American Folk Hero* (1991).

David W. Zang is Associate Professor in the Kinesiology Department and head of the Sports Studies Program at Towson University. His most recent book is *SportsWars: Athletes in the Age of Aquarius* (2001). He is also the author of *Fleet Walker's Divided Heart: The Life of Baseball's First Black Major Leaguer* (1995) and numerous articles, including "Rowing on Troubled Waters," a study of the Harvard 1968 crew team, which will be published in a forthcoming anthology on Boston sports.

PERMISSION ACKNOWLEDGMENTS

The following essays were previously published. Permission to reprint in whole or in part is gratefully acknowledged here.

Cahn, Susan, "'Cinderellas' of Sport: Black Women in Track and Field" is reprinted with the permission of The Free Press, a Division of Simon & Schuster Adult Publishing Group, from *Coming on Strong: Gender and Sexuality in Twentieth-Century Women's Sport* by Susan K. Cahn. Copyright © 1994 by Susan K. Cahn. All rights reserved.

Edwards, Harry, "Crisis of Black Athletes on the Eve of the Twenty-first Century" first appeared in *Society* Vol. 37 (March/April 2000): 9–13. Reprinted with permission by Harry Edwards.

Grundy, Pamela, "A Special Type of Discipline: Manhood and Community in African-American Institutions, 1923–1957" first appeared in Pamela Grundy, *Learning to Win: Sports, Education, and Social Change in Twentieth-Century North Carolina.* Chapel Hill: The University of North Carolina Press, 2001. © 2001 by Pamela Grundy. Use by permission of the University of North Carolina Press.

Kellner, Douglas, "The Sports Spectacle, Michael Jordan, and Nike" first appeared as "The Sports Spectacle, Michael Jordan and Nike: Unholy Alliance?" in *Michael Jordan, Inc. Corporate Sport, Media Culture, and Late Modern America,* edited by David Andrews," SUNY Press, 2001: 37–64.

Lanctot, Neil, "'A General Understanding': Organized Baseball and Black Professional Baseball, 1900–1930" is reprinted from *Fair Dealing and Clean Playing: The Hilldale Club and the Development of Black Professional Baseball, 1910–1932* by Neil Lanctot by permission of the University of Nebraska Press. © 1994 Neil Lanctot.

Lomax, Michael E., "Black Entrepreneurship in the National Pastime: The Rise of Semiprofessional Baseball in Black Chicago. 1890–1915" first appeared in the *Journal of Sport History* 25 (Spring 1998); 43–64. Reprinted with permission by Michael E. Lomax.

Liberti, Rita, "'We Were Ladies, We Just Played Basketball Like Boys': African American Womanhood and Competitive Basketball at Bennett College, 1928–1942" first appeared in the *Journal of Sport History* 26, (Fall 1999): 567–584. Reprinted with permission by Rita Liberti.

Martin, Charles H., "Jim Crow in the Gymnasium: The Integration of College Basketball in the American South" first appeared in *The International Journal of the History of Sport* 10 (April 1993): 68–86. Reprinted with permission by Frank Cass Publishers.

Miller, Patrick B., "The Anatomy of Scientific Racism: Racialist Responses to Black Athletic Achievement" first appeared in the *Journal of Sport History* 25 (Spring 1998); 119–151. Reprinted with permission by Patrick B. Miller.

Pierce, Richard B., "More Than a Game: The Political Meaning of High School Basketball in Indianapolis" first appeared in the *Journal of Urban History,* 27 November 2000, pp. 3–23. Reprinted by permission of Sage Publications.

Roberts, Randy "Year of the Comet: Jack Johnson versus Jim Jeffries, July 4, 1910" is reprinted with the permission of The Free Press, a Division of Simon & Schuster Adult Publishing Group, from *Papa Jack: Jack Johnson and the Era of White Hopes* by Randy Roberts. © 1983 The Free Press.

Ruck, Rob, "Sport and Black Pittsburgh, 1900–1930," first appeared in Rob Ruck, *Sandlot Seasons: Sport in Black Pittsburgh.* University of Illionois Press, 1987. Reprinted with permission by University of Illinois Press.

Smith, Thomas G., "Civil Rights on the Gridiron: The Kennedy Administration and the Desegregation of the Washington Redskins" first appeared in the *Journal of Sport History* 14 (Summer 1987); 189–208. Reprinted with permission by Thomas G. Smith.

Spivey, Donald, "'End Jim Crow in Sports': The Leonard Bates Controversy and Protest at New York University, 1940–1941" first appeared in the *Journal of Sport History* 15 (Winter 1988) 282–303. Reprinted with permission by Donald Spivey.

Tygiel, Jules, "Jackie Robinson: 'A Lone Negro' in Major League Baseball" first appeared as "A Lone Negro in the Game" in *Baseball's Great Experiment: Jackie Robinson and His Legacy,* 2nd Edition by Jules Tygiel. © 1997 by Jules Tygiel. Used by permission of Oxford University Press, Inc.

Wiggins, David K., "Edwin Bancroft Henderson, African-American Athletes, and the Writing of Sport History" first appeared in David K. Wiggins, *Glory Bound: Black Athletes in a White America.* Syracuse, NY: Syracuse University Press, 1997. Reprinted with permission by Syracuse University Press.

Wiggins, William H., "Joe Louis: American Folk Hero" first appeared in *Joe Louis: American Folk Hero,* Bloomington, IN: Phi Delta Kappa, 1991. Reprinted with permission by William H. Wiggins.

Zang, David W., "The Greatest: Muhammad Ali's Confounding Character" first appeared in David K. Zang, *Sportswars: Athletes in the Age of Aquarius,* Fayetteville, AR: University of Arkanas Press, 2001. Reprinted by permission of the University of Arkansas Press. © 2001 David W. Zang.

INDEX

GARY PUBLIC LIBRARY

Bl stud 796.08996 S 2004

Sport and the color line

FEB 26 2004

GARY PUBLIC LIBRARY

3 9222 02526983 3